A BOX OF SAND

'Tripoli is nothing more than an immense and valueless box of sand.'
GAETANO SALVEMINI, AUGUST 1911.

TATTERED
FLAG
Tattered Flag Press · East Sussex

A BOX OF SAND

The Italo-Ottoman War 1911-1912

 THE FIRST LAND, SEA AND AIR WAR

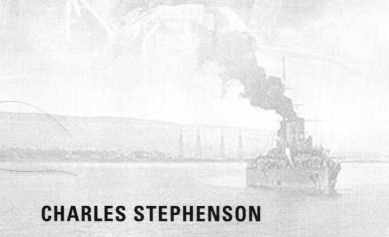

CHARLES STEPHENSON

This book is dedicated to the
Axons: David, Tracey, Isabel
and William.

The Author

Charles Stephenson is a naval and military historian and is the author of several books including *The Admiral's Secret Weapon: Lord Dundonald and the Origins of Chemical Warfare* (2006), *Germany's Asia-Pacific Empire: Colonialism and Naval Policy, 1885-1914* (2009), and (as Consultant Editor) *Castles: A Global History of Fortified Structures: Ancient, Medieval & Modern* (2011). He is also responsible for the two works that (thus far) comprise 'The Samson Plews Collection'; *The Face of OO* (2013) and *The Niagara Device* (2015). He lives in Flintshire, North Wales.

Published in Great Britain in 2014 by
Tattered Flag Press
11 Church Street
Ticehurst
East Sussex TN5 7AH
England

office@thetatteredflag.com
www.thetatteredflag.com

Tattered Flag Press is an imprint of Chevron Publishing Ltd.

A Box of Sand
© Charles Stephenson

Jacket Design and Typeset: Mark Nelson, NSW

British Library Cataloguing in Publication Data

A Catalogue Record for this book is available from the British Library

ISBN 978–0-9576892-2-0

Printed and bound in the United Kingdom
Copyright

For more information on books published by Tattered Flag Press visit
www.thetatteredflag.com

CONTENTS

INTRODUCTION

ON 29 September 1911 Italy declared war on the Ottoman Empire and proceeded to attempt the conquest of that Empire's North African *vilayet*, or province, of Tripoli (now Libya). The resultant conflict, dubbed variously, by English writers, as the Italo-Turkish, the Turco-Italian or the Tripolitan War, was to Italians the *Guerra di Libia* (The Libyan War) and has come to be called in Turkish *Trablusgarp Sava ı* (The War of Tripoli) or *Osmanlı- talyan Harbi* (Ottoman-Italian War).

The recently unified (1861) Kingdom of Italy sought, on the fiftieth anniversary of its founding, to conquer this largely barren territory for purely jingoistic purposes. Italy was a state on the rise with pretensions to Great Power status, and already the possessor of a small empire in East Africa. Conversely, the Ottoman Empire was a state in decline that had been losing territories to other powers, not all of them deemed Great, for a long period of time. This steady loss of Ottoman territory led to the advent of the 'Eastern Question,' which concerned itself mainly with the matter of what might, or should, happen to the Ottoman Balkan territories if and when the Empire disintegrated? Should this occur then the potential for conflict between, in particular, the Great Powers of Austria-Hungary and Russia was extremely high. The 'Question,' at bottom, revolved around managing Ottoman decline in such a way as to obviate that potential.[1]

The Great Powers were, by 1911, divided, both formally and informally and with much equivocation, into two blocs; the Triple Alliance of Austria-Hungary, Germany and Italy, and the Triple Entente consisting of Britain, France and Russia. Italy though was, as Richard Bosworth phrased it in the title of one of his books, the 'Least of the Great Powers' and was also regarded, by allies and potential enemies alike, as somewhat lukewarm in its adherence to the Triple Alliance.

Because none of the Great Powers desired any great upset in the equilibrium that their alliance system precariously maintained, the Italian decision to go to war against the Ottoman Empire created a situation of great diplomatic delicacy. They had to try to find a middle way that neither encouraged nor discouraged Italian ambitions for fear of driving them into the arms of the opposing bloc. On the other hand, and with the Eastern Question very much in mind, a somewhat similar policy towards the Ottomans was also necessary. Thus one of the most important effects of the Italo-Ottoman War was upon European Great Power politics.

It was an unusual war in other respects too, inasmuch as in order to conduct it at all Italy had to confine its military and naval activities to areas where they would neither cause a widening of the conflict, nor conflict with the interests of the Great Powers. This led to most of the fighting being restricted to North Africa, though it did widen as time went on to much international concern. This occurred because the fighting in the Tripoli *vilayet* became, as it would be today termed, asymmetrical in character when the Ottoman military were forced to resort to a guerrilla strategy. Due to the nature of the terrain, and the training and capabilities of the Italian military, this led to tactical and operational deadlock and the subsequent paralysis of Italian strategy. Basically put, the invaders were largely compelled to remain within their coastal enclaves, protected by extensive field works and covered by the guns of their fleet.

The defenders, Ottoman regulars and their Arab and Berber co-fighters, were not equipped to assault such works, and the strategy of the Ottoman commanders was, by default, mainly based around attempting to lure the Italians out so that they could be attacked in the desert.

Consequently, the Italians were forced into attempts to bring the Ottoman Empire to terms by applying pressure in other areas, thus bringing them into potential conflict with the Great Powers. It was then no easy war for either the Italian military, or the Italian Government, to wage with any seeming degree of success, and what was foreseen as a short and victorious war of easy conquest turned into a protracted and bitter conflict that endured for just over a year.

This book is the story of that conflict, which has been almost forgotten given the events that followed it in short order, particularly the First World, or Great, War. Indeed, though there are several works in Italian and Turkish in print that cover the subject, there is nothing in English that deals with it either holistically or in any great depth. This work is an effort to remedy this deficiency, and indeed the conflict has many interesting facets, not least the introduction of aircraft into combat situations for the first time and the deployment of armoured vehicles similarly. It was a war where one side, Italy, held and maintained naval supremacy, though the existence of an Ottoman 'fleet in being' exercised the *Regia Marina* to the extent that attempts were made to penetrate the Dardanelles and sink it. The difficulties encountered in so doing were lessons that other navies might have studied with profit.

It was also a campaign that was generally considered to have done nothing to bolster Italian military prestige. This judgement is however rather unfair, inasmuch as the Italian Army did what the politicians asked of it, and no army could have done much more given the state of technology at the time. It was, as has been stated, a war fought for jingoistic or social-imperialistic purposes and was in any event totally unnecessary. The Italian government, or more precisely Prime Minister Giovanni Giolitti and Foreign Minister Marquis Antonio di San Giuliano, could have had virtually all they wanted without going to war, but needed a smashing victory in order to placate the ascendant nationalist right-wing politicians and newspapers whose prisoners they had become. The conflict turned out very differently however, and whilst retrospectively it seems incredible that any sensible government would embark on a military venture with so much wishful thinking as to the likely reaction and outcome, it is perhaps the case that they were not so uncommon after all. Recent history teaches us that at least.

This book then attempts to set out the background to the Italo-Ottoman War of 1911-1912, and then follows its course until peace came about with the Treaty of Ouchy (or First Treaty of Lausanne) on 18 October 1912. Those with knowledge of the history of the period will note that the month of the signing coincided with the outbreak of the First Balkan War between the Ottoman Empire and the Balkan Federation. The question of cause and effect between this war and the conflict with Italy will be considered, but also reflected on are the implications of the Italian invasion for the peoples of what was to become, as an Italian colony, officially entitled Libya in 1934. These paid the highest price of all, until freed from Italian rule during the Second World War. The text proceeds more or less chronologically, though those who are interested only in following the military and intertwined diplomatic course of the Italo-Ottoman conflict, and who are not interested for whatever reason in the historical and political contexts within which it took place, should probably skip the first two or three chapters.

Though I have been careful in correctly attributing the sources upon which the work is based, I have attempted to aim it at the general, rather than the academic, reader. There are no 'theories' of history to be found within, nor any startling conclusions. It is, or attempts to be, a narrative history which encompasses several perspectives with all the hazards inherent in such an approach. A large proportion of the sources are Italian, particularly for the operational history of the military and naval forces involved, but whilst these are generally accurate in terms of dates and units involved, they are extremely partial in interpreting, or admitting, successes and failures. I have also used a great deal of eyewitness account as there were many war-correspondents present on both sides. These tended in the main however to be extremely partisan in their reporting, dependent upon which side they were with. Nonetheless, they have been extremely valuable, if not exactly neutral, in providing some much needed colour to the tale. Accounts from those participating directly on the Ottoman side are much rarer, though I have used generous excerpts from Enver Pasa's diary, *Um Tripolis,* published in 1918. This is, I believe, the first English language work that has used this source to any extent, or at least since Askew in 1942. For the Arab and Berber side of the war I have used Angelo Del Boca's translations of the writings of Mohamed Fekini and others. A full bibliography is provided and, in any event, all translations into English from whatever language are my work, and any errors thus mine alone. The same applies to the work in general, though I would like to acknowledge the generous help given me by Charles Blackwood, who very kindly drew the maps that accompany the text, and Michael Perratt, who provided the ultimate test for a work of this kind; is it intelligible and accessible to the intelligent lay-reader. Happily he thought so. I am also most grateful to Shaun Barrington for his generous efforts on my behalf, for commenting on the text, and for coming up with the title.

A word or two needs to be said about the rendering of names into English. Although, strictly speaking, the state of Turkey did not come into being until after the First World War many writers used, and still use, the word synonymously with the Ottoman Empire, as well as dubbing most Ottoman citizens as Turks. I have tried to stick with the correct form, but have not altered any quotations to that effect. The same applies to Libya, which only officially came into being in Italian usage in the 1930s. The whole territory invaded by Italy in 1911 was properly called Tripoli, as was the main city there. I have tried to keep to the proper usage, whilst simultaneously attempting to avoid confusing the province and the city. Hopefully I have succeeded. The names of many of the places within the Tripoli theatre, and indeed elsewhere, are also a source of difficulty and potential confusion. I have generally stuck with what seemed to me the most sensible version; though mention some of the other possibilities in brackets on the first occasion I do so. This seemed to me to be the optimum solution, though of course it risks offending some. If you are one of them, then please accept my apologies.

Charles Stephenson
August 2014

[1.] For an examination of the 'question' see: Matthew Smith Anderson, *The Eastern question, 1774-1923: A Study in International Relations* (London; Macmillan, 1966).

CHAPTER ONE

The Sick Man

'Nous avons sur les bras un homme malade – un homme gravement malade…'
[We have on our hands a sick man – a very sick man]
Czar Nicholas I referring to the Ottoman Empire during conversations (the 'Seymour Conversations')
with Sir George Hamilton Seymour, the British Ambassador to St Petersburg
on 9, 14 and 20 January 1853.[1]

'We have cured the sick man.'
Enver Pasa, commenting on the CUP-driven overthrow of the Ottoman government,
from Koprulu (Veles) in the Kosovo *vilayet* (now Macedonia) on 23 July 1908.[2]

I N 1911 Europe was divided, formally and informally and with some wriggle room as it would be termed today, into two Great Power blocs; the Triple Alliance of Austria-Hungary, Germany and Italy, and the Triple Entente consisting of Britain, France and Russia. Three of these Great Powers, Austria-Hungary, Germany and Russia, were basically intra-European Empires – though Germany had extensive territories in Africa and the Pacific - whilst the others had extra-European Empires. The largest of these was the British, closely followed by the French. Italy, the least of the Great Powers, had very little empire at all.

There was one other power that, if not included amongst those deemed Great, was nevertheless of vital importance in terms of the relationships between the two blocs; the Ottoman Empire, often, if strictly incorrectly, referred to as Turkey. This importance may perhaps be expressed in the term the 'Eastern Question,' which mainly concerned itself with the matter of what might, or should, happen to the Ottoman's Balkan territories if and when the Empire disintegrated?[3] That the Ottoman Empire was in a state of decay, and had been characterized from before the Crimean War as being akin to a 'sick man' in danger of imminent death, was a proposition accepted by the Great Powers.[4] This decline had been gradual and had taken place against a high point probably reached during the 16th century. It has been argued that, between 1526 and 1596, there was no question of international politics with which it was not involved. In other words it was a world power at a period when those territories that bound the Mediterranean formed a significant portion of the world. During the early period of the reign of Sultan Suleiman I, who ruled from 1520-1566 and whose appellations included the 'Magnificent' and the 'Lawgiver', great advances in Ottoman power had been made. These included the conquest of Rhodes, the capture of Buda in 1529 (though the same year also saw defeat at Vienna) and the annexation of Hungary in 1541. These successes however were the high points of Ottoman expansion and despite the conquest of Cyprus in 1570-71 – the last great military success – the years 1565 and 1566 marked the beginning of a halt in Ottoman advances, and thus the start of a decline, albeit a very slow one, in the fortunes of the Empire.

Ottoman expansion and conquest into the Balkan region had resulted in a complex mosaic of ethnic, national, and religious rivalries in that region. The dynamics of this might be exemplified by considering the history of the city of Belgrade, which is situated at the confluence of the Sava and Danube rivers and therefore in a position of immense strategic importance. Following the conquest of Constantinople in 1453, Sultan Mehmed II advanced northward, unsuccessfully besieging Belgrade in 1456. Some 65 years later, in 1521, an Ottoman force reckoned to be some 250,000 strong under Sultan Suleiman I marched on the city and this time succeeded in taking it before moving on into Central Europe. It was not until the aftermath of the Ottoman defeat at Vienna in 1688 that Belgrade again became a focus of battle, being conquered by the forces of the Holy League towards the end of that year. The Ottomans returned two years later, taking the city again on 14 October 1690 after a six-day siege. Prince Eugene of Savoy though, in a brilliant military action, retook it in 1717. However, by the Treaty (sometimes called the Peace) of Belgrade in 1739, Austria returned the fortress to the Ottomans and accepted the Danube-Sava River as delineating the common frontier. During the Austro-Turkish War of 1787–1791, Belgrade changed hands yet again, in 1789, but under the 1791 Treaty of Sistova which ended the conflict the Ottoman Empire once again took possession. Serbia won a degree of autonomy from the Ottoman Empire following the two uprisings comprising the Serbian Revolution (1804-1817) and Belgrade became its capital.

The slow Ottoman retreat from areas they once held had led to encroachments and competition from the empires of Austria-Hungary and Russia, and the rise of independent states. Of the latter, Greece fought its war of independence between 1821 and 1829, whilst Montenegro achieved *de facto* independence in 1858 after Great Power intervention to demarcate its borders with the Ottoman Empire.

Bulgaria declared itself an independent state in 1908 following the 'Young Turk' revolution, of which more later. As previously noted, the Great Powers were keenly interested in maintaining stability in the region and they attempted to set limits on the extent of the independent states. However the annexation of Bosnia, or more properly Bosnia-Herzegovina, by Austria-Hungary precipitating the Bosnian, or Annexation, Crisis,[5] caused a strong reaction from Russia, which saw its influence in the region as being seriously weakened.

Bosnia was deemed legally, if not factually, to be a part of the Ottoman Empire. Ottoman suzerainty had been affirmed in 1856 when Austria, Britain, France, Germany, the Ottoman Empire, the Italian state of Piedmont-Sardinia and Russia, which was forced to terms by the outcome of the Crimean War, had signed the Treaty of Paris. Modifications to this treaty were however made in 1878 at the Berlin Conference. This had been convened following the uproar caused by the aftermath of the April Uprising of 1876, when a revolt took place in what is now the Pazardzhik Province of Bulgaria against the Ottomans. Perhaps because the insurrectionists were Christians, who reportedly indulged in massacres of Muslims, the insurrection was savagely repressed. Subsequent reports of horrendous retaliatory massacres of Christians by Muslim forces, including the much-feared irregular 'bashibazouks,' caused a furore in Western Europe. Though the Uprising was a failure – indeed a tragic failure for the Christian victims, of whom somewhere between 3,700[6] and 15,000[7] were barbarously murdered – publicity concerning the reprisals led to general European demands for reform of the Ottoman Empire. In perhaps more concrete terms, it also led to the Russo-Turkish War of 1877-78, which ended in Turkish defeat.

This upset of the 'balance of power' – Russia was thought to have gained unduly by the other Great Powers – caused the convening of the Congress of Berlin, which in turn resulted in the 1878 Treaty of Berlin. Under the terms of the treaty Romania, which had been formed from the regions of Moldavia and Wallachia in 1861, became independent, as did Serbia and Montenegro. Bulgaria became an autonomous region, and Austria-Hungary took over the administration of Bosnia-Herzegovina, the latter portion of which had also risen in the Herzegovinian Rebellion of 1875, whilst much the same arrangement was imposed in terms of Cyprus and Britain. There were other complexities that need not detain us overmuch, but that the Ottoman Empire was greatly injured in several contexts is generally accepted by scholars.[8]

Neither was Balkan stability ensured. Indeed, despite agreeing to the transfer beforehand, the way the 1908 Bosnian Annexation was handled gave rise to Russian anxieties concerning Austro-Hungarian expansionism, and, because it was felt to have been humiliating to Russian diplomacy, hardened attitudes for the future. Despite then the matter being not much more than a legal or constitutional nicety, merely overturning as it did the rather ephemeral notion of Ottoman suzerainty, it nevertheless had the potential to lead to conflict between Austria-Hungary on the one hand and Russia on the other. It was also a serious blow to Serbia, being perceived as a major impediment to territorial aspirations.[9] This was a factor, but only one of several, that pushed Russia and Serbia together in opposition to Austria-Hungary. A further potential source of conflict came the same year with Bulgaria declaring independence. Though, again, the difference between autonomy and outright independence was perhaps more apparent than real, it again had the effect of increasing the likelihood of tension between Austria-Hungary and Russia. This in turn, because of the system of alliances and blocs, had the potential to instigate a general conflagration. Indeed, the great Otto von Bismarck had supposedly predicted such a scenario at the end of the previous century; 'If there is ever another war in Europe, it will come out of some damned silly thing in the Balkans.'[10] On this occasion however diplomacy succeeded in resolving the effects of the Bosnian Crisis, though relations between Austria-Hungary and Russia were, and remained, somewhat damaged.

The nominal loss of Bulgaria and Bosnia-Herzegovina greatly diminished the European territory remaining in Ottoman possession. Indeed, following the actions of Bulgaria and Austria-Hungary in 1908, the only Ottoman possessions left in mainland Europe were Eastern Thrace, a territory corresponding more or less to today's Trakya, and the *vilayet* (province) of Salonika. There were also the *vilayet*s of Manastir, skodra, Shkoder and Yanya (roughly corresponding to modern day Albania), as well as the *vilayet*s of Kosovo (approximately corresponding to the modern-day entity) and Selanik. Portions of these territories were also known as Macedonia, though not by the Ottomans who strictly forbade use of the term.[11] To the Ottomans the European portions of their empire were dubbed *Rumelia*; 'the land of the Romans'.

The Ottomans also retained provinces in North Africa, the pertinent one in the current context being the *vilayet* of Tripoli (*Trablusgarp* (*Trablus-i Garb*); *Tripoli in the West* to differentiate it from the *vilayet* of the same name (*Trablus-ı am* or *Trablus- am; Tripoli near Damascus*) in what is now Lebanon and Syria). Tripoli was not a single geographical unit, but was made up of several parts or regions, which differed in many important respects. Tripolitania, also often known as Tripoli, consisted of the coastal territory from the Tunisian frontier to the Gulf of Sidra. To the east of this was Cyrenaica, also known as Ben Ghazi or Barca, which is bounded to the south by the Libyan Desert. To the south of Tripolitania was Fezzan (Fazzan, Fezan), 'the southern province of Tripoli – a collection of oases separated from the coast region by the stony desert, or Hamada-el-Homra.'[12] Politically, Tripolitania and Fezzan on the one hand, and Cyrenaica on the other, had been divided into separate provinces and then reunited on a number of occasions since the 1830s. Between 1836 and 1863, Cyrenaica was a subcounty, or *qaimmaqamiyya,* linked to the province, or the *iyala,* of Tripoli, but in the period between 1863 and 1872, it became an independent county, or *mutasarrifiyya,* directly tied to the imperial capitol, Istanbul. Later, between 1872 and 1888, Cyrenaica became a fully independent province, or *vilayat,* like Tripoli. Finally, by 1888 and until 1911, it was reduced again to a county linked to Tripoli.[13] Taking all areas together, the whole was estimated to form an area of some 42000 sq km in 1876.[14] This is a good deal less than the area covered by modern Libya (1,759,540 sq km[15]); which may be accounted for by the fact that the borders, the greater extent of which exist only as lines on a map, had yet to be agreed internationally, or at least between the European colonial powers.[16]

Tripoli, and the other Ottoman territories in the region, had become semi-detached following the Ottoman defeat at the 1571 Battle of Lepanto. This was fought between a combined 'Christian' fleet, consisting of Spanish, Venetian, and Papal ships, augmented by the galleys of the Knights of St. John from Malta. Commanded by John of Austria, the fleet of the 'Holy League' numbered about 200 galleys, whilst the Ottoman fleet under Uluc Ali Pasa had some 208; they were thus evenly matched in terms of numbers. Despite this the battle ended with the virtual destruction of the Ottoman navy, a mere 40 galleys escaping destruction or capture. According to accounts of the conflict, approximately 15,000 Turks were slain or captured, some 10,000 Christian galley slaves were liberated, and much booty was taken. Lepanto was the first major maritime Ottoman defeat by the Christian powers, and it ended the myth of Ottoman naval invincibility. The battle was decisive in the sense that victory for the Ottomans would have made them supreme, whilst their defeat meant increasing difficulty in maintaining communications with territories in the west. This meant that naval forces in Tunis, Algiers, and Tripoli no longer formed a regular part of the Ottoman fleet. Politically too, these territories were forced into de facto autonomy. This autonomy was exemplified and reinforced in 1711 when Ahmad Qaramanli, variously described as a Turkish-Arab cavalry officer or a local janissary officer, seized power in Tripoli. He and his descendants were to rule Tripoli, one of the three Barbary states that became notorious for their piracy, until the last of them, Yusuf Pasa Qaramanli was deposed in 1835. Yusuf Pasa was, according to the explorer Major Alexander Gordon Laing, who was at Tripoli between February and July 1825:

A cruel and unprincipled tyrant who never honoured his engagements unless it suited him [. . .] he had soaring ambitions for his country which he pursued ruthlessly. He used his army to such effect against the ever lawless tribes of the hinterland that his influence was felt, and his name feared, nearly as far as Bornu.[17]

However, the age of the Barbary Corsairs was effectively over by the second decade of the nineteenth century; two wars conducted in 1801-5 and 1815 had largely destroyed their power.[18] The end of organised piracy meant however the destruction of the main source of Tripoli's income, and to compensate for this lost revenue attempts were made to bolster the trans-Saharan slave trade. This strategy failed, and economic hardship led to a diminution of Yusuf Pasa's prestige and power. His abdication in 1832 in favour of one of his sons failed to guarantee the security of the Qaramanli dynasty; it merely caused his other sons to rebel and a multi-polar civil war began. The Ottoman Sultan Mahmud II feared that this anarchic situation would cause foreign intervention – France had moved into Algeria on 1830 – and, at the same time, saw a chance to re-establish imperial authority. Consequently, a fleet and military force ostensibly sent to restore order in May 1835 went on to exile the Qaramanli family and re-establish direct rule.[19] Halim Pasa, a cavalry officer of distinction, became C-in-C at Tripoli with the task of bringing the Bedouin under control and extending Ottoman rule into the interior of the province. By 1842 he had subdued most of the coastal areas, but the Fezzan however remained outside any form of central control, with the lawlessness having a harmful effect on the trans-Saharan trade routes.[20] Peace returned only following an accommodation with the Senussi, with which the Ottoman local government was forced to treat since they controlled the trade upon which the prosperity of Tripoli largely depended. The Senussi however refused to end their slaving activities even after the Ottoman Empire abolished the practice in 1857.[21]

This story however also concerns another of the Ottoman *vilayets*; that of the White Sea Islands (or Islands of the White Sea *Djeza'ir-i bahr-I Sefid*), also known as the Ottoman, or Turkish, Archipelago. The White Sea was the Ottoman name for what most Europeans termed the Aegean, and the islands in it that were Ottoman territory were often collectively known as the Sporades. The Sporades were, generally, the islands between Crete and the west coast of Asia Minor, though the terminology varied greatly and had done since ancient times.[22] Following the Law of the Provinces promulgated in 1864, these territories were mostly organised as a single administrative unit, the *vilayet*, and sub divided into *sanjaks* as follows:

Sanjak of Bigha: Bozcaada (Tenedos), Limni (Lemnos), Semadirek (Samothrace), and Imroz (Imbros)

Sanjak of Midilli: Midilli (Mytilene, Lesbos)

Sanjak of Sakız: Sakız (Khios), Ipsaria (Psara)

Sanjak of Istankoi (Kos): Istankoi (Kos), Kelemez (Kalymnos), Patino (Patmos), Incirli (Nisyros), Nicaria (Icaria), leriye (Leros).

Sanjak of Rhodes: Rodos (Rhodes), Karpathos (Kerpe), Kharki (Calki), Kasos (Kasot).

There were, as with most things Ottoman, anomalies in the region. Beyond the above units the island of Tasoz (Thasos) had been gifted as a personal fiefdom to Muhammad Ali of Egypt following his intervention during the Greek War of Independence between 1821 and 1830, whilst the same struggle saw the island of Samos established as a semi-autonomous entity under Ottoman suzerainty. The status of Thasos changed in 1908 when it became a part of the *vilayet* of Salonika.[23]

The most important of the Ottoman islands in the early years of the 20th century was undoubtedly Rhodes, which had fallen to the Ottoman Empire in the 16th century. It had been under the rule of the Knights of St John of Jerusalem, also known as the Knights Hospitaller, since 5 September 1307, when Pope Clement V confirmed that Rhodes was to become their home. Situated only some 17 kilometres from the southern coast of Anatolia (Asia Minor), the island inevitably became vulnerable to the expansionist tendencies of the Ottoman Empire, particularly after their conquest of Constantinople in 1453. The main base of the Knights was Rhodes City, which they heavily fortified, making great efforts to update the Byzantine defences they had inherited. The expected Ottoman attack occurred in 1480, and the city endured a siege lasting from 23 May-17 August before the attackers gave up – temporarily. They were to return in June 1522 led by Suleiman the Magnificent, who employed a large corps of miners. These, utilising the long forgotten Hellenic culverts, tunnels, and cisterns over which the fortifications had been built, severely damaged the defences with mines and outflanked them from below. The Knights eventually capitulated in December, but were allowed to leave with their possessions. They occupied a new home in Malta in 1830, and were to successfully resist the Ottoman attempt to dislodge them from there in 1565.

Rhodes having fallen, the other main islands that came to constitute the Dodecanese, Agathonisi, Astipalea, Halki, Kalimnos, Karpathos, Kasos, Kastelorizo, Kos, Leros, Nisyros, Patmos, Symi, and Tilos, were to swiftly follow into Ottoman rule. However, according to Ottoman customs and precepts only those that had resisted, principally Rhodes and Kos, were treated as conquered territory and governed directly. The others, because they had submitted voluntarily to the Sultan, were allowed privileges in return for paying an annual tax (*maktou*). In return they enjoyed administrative and judicial autonomy and they were permitted to practice their own religion, and retained their own language and culture.

Because of these factors the majority of the inhabitants maintained a sense of being Greek, and during the Greek War of Independence (1821-1830) against the Ottoman Empire many sided with the insurgents. However, when an independent Greek state came into being following the London Protocol of 30 August 1832 the Dodecanese were excluded. The decline in Ottoman power during the 19th century meant however that Greece was able to satisfy some of its territorial ambitions, based roughly on the philosophy that Greece included any territory that had Greek history or where those that considered themselves Greek were present.[24] The Ionian Islands, which had never been under Ottoman rule but had come under British control in 1815, became a part of Greece in 1864 and portions of modern Thessaly and Epirus were also incorporated in 1883; both being acquired diplomatically. Other than military weakness vis-à-vis the Ottoman Empire, the main obstacle to Greek territorial claims originated with the Great Powers, particularly the UK. British foreign policy was generally unsympathetic towards Greek expansionism, considering that it would hasten the collapse of the Ottoman Empire. The Greek government though remained less concerned with what might happen to the Ottoman Empire than it was with acquiring further unredeemed territory from it. In furtherance of this, principally to attain more of Thessaly and the island of Crete, Greece determined to move into Crete in 1897. Ottoman authority had broken down on the island and Greek troops were landed to support militias demanding union with their motherland. The situation threatened civil war and, the matter that concerned the Great Powers, an extension of the conflict to the Balkans. Though the Ottoman Empire declared war on 17 April 1897, a resolution to the conflict was largely enforced by the naval forces of the Great Powers, who despatched powerful fleets to the area and threatened a blockade of Greece unless they withdrew both their forces and their claims. This move was successful, a peace treaty was signed on 4 December 1897, and Greece was forced to back down and admit defeat, which led to diplomatic isolation and the stalling of Greek irredentism.

Greece had a small, but generally effective navy based around three small (4,885 tonnes) French constructed battleships of the Hydra Class – *Hydra*, *Spetsai*, and *Psara* – all laid down in 1885. That the Greek navy was to contribute virtually nothing to the conflict was however not due to the opposition of its Ottoman counterpart, but rather to the fact that the conflict broke out precipitately and it was caught totally unprepared.[25] However unprepared the Greek navy was it was still greatly superior to its opposite number inasmuch as the Ottoman navy had, to all intents and purposes, ceased to exist in any meaningful form. This was a fairly recent occurrence; until the accession of Abdülhamid II as Sultan, following the deposition of his brother Murad on 31 August 1876, the Ottoman navy is generally credited with being powerful and efficient. Certainly in terms of size it was reckoned to be the third in Europe, and compared favourably with the second; that of France.[26] The Ottoman fleet was maintained at the *Tersane-i Amire*, the huge Imperial dockyard and arsenal sited on the Golden Horn. This scimitar-shaped estuary is a 1.8 kilometre wide natural inlet of the Bosphorus Strait, situated where it joins the Sea of Marmara, forming the natural harbour of Istanbul. The complex, which had been originally constructed by the Genoese, was greatly expanded under the reign of Selim I, who reigned 1512-20, and became the principal centre of Ottoman shipbuilding and repair. Indeed, in the late 15th and early 16th centuries this naval works, together with other military complexes, gave Istanbul what was probably the largest military-industrial concentration in early modern Europe, rivalled only by the Venetian Arsenal.[27] By 1876 the base was able to maintain a modern fleet partly thanks to over 200 British engineers, mainly from Clydeside and Tyneside, who worked there superintending shipbuilding and ship repair. British input also extended to the officer corps of the fleet, many of whom had been trained by the Royal Navy, and exercises were carried out regularly.

Abdülhamid did not however trust the navy. A number of explanations have been offered for this, including the part played by naval officers in deposing Murad, that these officers threatened mutiny if arrears of pay where not made good, and that he feared a coup instigated by them. Whatever the truth, it was certainly the case that from 1876 the navy was neglected and allowed to run down. The new Sultan would not sanction the fleet leaving the Golden Horn whilst, by 1880, the vast majority of the British engineers had been discharged and sent back to the UK. The officer corps was also dispersed, and by 1890 it no longer existed as a coherent force. Indeed, so anxious was Abdülhamid that he decreed that essential parts of the machinery and armament were removed from the vessels and stored onshore, whilst the ships themselves were allowed to disintegrate.

It naturally followed that when the threat of conflict with Greece broke out in 1897, the Ottoman navy was in no shape to intervene. The most it could manage was to send the central battery ship *Mesudiye* (1875) together with four other vintage vessels escorted by three torpedo boats to the Dardanelles. This flotilla left the Golden Horn on 19 March 1897, with the larger vessels having to tow the smaller, and berthed at Canakkale in the strait. Two Ottoman naval advisers, officers from Germany and Britain, arrived at Çanakkale to inspect the vessels on 15 April 1897. The report from Vice-Admirals Kalau von Hofe and Sir Henry F Woods is devastating; many of the guns had been rendered useless by corrosion and damage, whilst some vessels had weapons, or vital parts of weapons, missing.[28]

Even Abdülhamid was forced to concede that the Ottoman fleet had degenerated to a state that was both an embarrassment and a source of great weakness for the Empire. Accordingly he had a naval commission set up to examine ways of restoring some degree of Ottoman naval power. There were however a growing group of influential figures within the Empire who had become dissatisfied in the extreme with the ramshackle and corrupt nature of the governing and administrative institutions. This eventually led to the formation of a movement that called itself the Committee of Union and Progress (İttihat ve Terakki Cemiyeti) or CUP, also colloquially known as the 'Young Turks.' The origins of the CUP can be traced back to 1889, and it was basically an alliance of several discontented and otherwise fissiparous factions within the Empire. Most importantly was the joining, in 1907, of officers of the Ottoman 3rd Army Corps based in the European vilayets. One of these, the comparatively junior Major Ahmed Niyazi inaugurated what became a revolution on 23 July 1908[29] when he led a revolt against the authorities at the town of Resna (Resen), now in the Republic of Macedonia. This rebellion rapidly spread throughout the empire, and the next day the reigning Ottoman Sultan Abdülhamid II conceded to its demands; the restoration of the 1876 constitution and the recall of parliament.

The CUP had then succeeded in establishing a government ostensibly committed to liberal and constitutional rule of the Ottoman Empire as part of their reform programme. Under the terms of the 1876 constitution elections were held throughout the Empire in November 1908, and on December 17 the Ottoman parliament was reopened. The deputies were elected according to a somewhat complex two-tier system. The first stage saw taxpaying male citizens over the age of 25 voting for a member on the basis of 500 voters per member. Those members so chosen then took part in a second stage, voting in turn for a deputy to represent them in Istanbul on the basis of one deputy per fifty-thousand voters.[30] Eight deputies were sent to the Ottoman capitol from Tripolitania and Cyrenaica, including Sulyman al-Baruni and Farhat al-Zawi, who will appear later.[31]

The CUP programme was ambitious, even revolutionary, and dedicated to, as part of their name suggests, union of all the peoples of the empire on an equal footing. Though there is a great deal of scholarly debate about whether or not the Ottoman Empire was an Islamic State it had certainly discriminated against non-Muslims. Whilst Islam was the state religion, the population of the Empire comprised peoples of many different religious and national groupings, and most of these had a degree of communal autonomy. Within limits, these communities were allowed to order their own social and religious lives and apply their own laws to civil matters, such as marriage and inheritance. Only in respect of penal laws were they subject to Islamic regulation. These minority communities, or millets, elected or otherwise chose a high-ranking religious figure as their leader, who became their representative responsible to the Sultan. These leaders, who were accorded the status of state officials, had the authority to settle civil legal matters between members of their community and collected taxes. In other words, and put simplistically, the Ottoman Empire was not a strongly centralised polity.

The CUP sought to change this, and the government after 1908 introduced initiatives intended to promote the unity and modernisation of the Empire. These involved the removal of foreign influence in the internal affairs of the state, the construction of a strong central government, a process of industrialisation, and administrative reforms; the latter included secularisation of the legal system, subsidies for the education of women, and the modernisation of state-operated schools. The notion of a common Ottoman citizenship, and thus identity, had been introduced in the 19th century but met with resistance, not only from the Islamic majority but also from the leaders of the various communities who would see their status disappear. However the CUP proved ineffective at controlling the new government and was subjected to a reactionary counter-revolution the following April. This was in turn defeated by the raising of an 'Action Army' in the European *vilayets* commanded by Mahmud Sevket, with one Mustafa Kemal as chief-of-staff, which moved by train to occupy Istanbul. There was little or no fighting upon its arrival and the Sultan was forced to abdicate in favour of his brother, who became Sultan Mehmed V. Though the counter-revolution was unsuccessful, its defeat came at the price of elevating the army to the position of guarantor of political stability via martial law.[32]

Improvements in the naval position of the Empire were also sought as the complete lack of battleships was perceived as a great source of weakness. Accordingly, following the deposition of Abdülhamid the government initiated attempts to acquire one or two capital ships as well as modern armoured cruisers. Incredibly, the Germans initially appeared to be willing to sell the hybrid *Blucher*, a large armoured cruiser that was nearly a battlecruiser, or even Germany's first pure battlecruiser *Von der Tann* or the newer *Moltke*. Such discussions as took place over the matter were seemingly conducted without the knowledge of Admiral Alfred von Tirpitz, State Secretary at the Imperial Naval Office. Tirpitz, who was famously attempting to construct a battle-fleet to rival the British Royal Navy, stopped any further discussions over the matter in July 1910, but did indicate that some older ships were available. Eventually, two Brandenburg Class vessels, *Kurfürst Friedrich Wilhelm* and *Weißenburg,* were purchased and transferred to the Ottoman Navy on 1 September 1910 along with some smaller ships.[33] Renamed *Barbaros Hayreddin* and *Turgut Reis* respectively, this accretion of naval strength was of an order that may have been useful against the Hellenic Navy, the most likely main enemy, but it was to prove of no utility against the much more powerful Italian fleet.

However, despite corruption, bureaucratic bungling, and personal rivalries creating huge difficulties, some modernisation of the existing larger naval vessels was completed and new purchases of small warships made. Things did not however improve greatly. In 1904 the future British admiral, Captain Mark Kerr, had visited the Ottoman capital and opined that 'it is no longer possible to talk about the Turkish Navy, as it is practically non-existent.'[34] That he had not exaggerated was made evident some four years later when Rear-Admiral Sir Douglas Gamble inspected the fleet in December 1908. Gamble found 'vegetable gardens growing on the decks of the ageing warships (for Abdülhamid had considered that men-of-war in fighting trim might turn their guns on his palace).'[35] Gamble was not inspecting the remains of the Ottoman Navy out of idle curiosity. He had been appointed as head of the British Naval Mission to the Empire, which had the brief of supervising the reorganization of the fleet for the new government. During his tenure, between February 1909 and January 1910, he re-organized the fleet, reduced the number of officers and sent some young naval officers to Britain for training.

Clearly he, and the British Naval Mission in general, had a formidable task, but a rationalization of the available resources was undertaken and a certain amount of progress was reported:

> The obsolete vessels which had been lying at the Dardanelles and elsewhere have been collected at the Golden Horn and offered for sale by treaty. The latest ships, which possess a certain amount of fighting value, have had their crews completed and have undergone training, a certain amount of target practice having been carried out, and the ships sent on cruises.[36]

These cruises, the first of which took place in the Sea of Marmara on 27 May 1909 with another held in the Mediterranean in September, demonstrated that the Ottoman Navy needed a lot of work. As a 1910 British report put it: 'At present the Turks have neither the officers to navigate and fight, nor the crews to man the ships which they have bought from the Germans, nor are they likely to for some time to come.'[37] They had also lost their leader early that year following the resignation of Gamble. The British admiral had clashed with the Ottoman Government over the organisation and finances of the fleet, considering that such decisions should be left in his hands. He was replaced in April 1910 by Vice-Admiral Hugh Pigot Williams, who also found himself at loggerheads with the government and resented his local 'demotion' to the rank of Rear-Admiral. Williams was to be at sea with the main body of the fleet, which was built around the two ex-German battleships, when war broke out with Italy.

The authority of the Empire was threatened by insurrections in the Kosovo *vilayet* in 1910 and Shkoder *vilayet*, near the border with Montenegro, the following year.[38] Clearly the stability of the Ottoman Empire had not been greatly enhanced by the accession of the 'Young Turks.' Indeed, despite Enver's claim to have cured the 'sick man,' the CUP attempts to bring union and progress to the Ottoman Empire arguably resulted in less union and only marginal progress. Therefore the 'Eastern Question,' which at bottom revolved around managing Ottoman decline in such a way as to obviate potential conflicts between the Great Powers, was very much a live issue in 1911. It was a question that Italy was about to become deeply involved in, despite the possibility, or even probability, of shattering the status quo. Indeed, the administration of Prime Minister Giovanni Giolitti decided to undertake the conquest of the *vilayet* of Tripoli despite Italy's rather gloomy history in terms of war and colonial adventures.

CHAPTER TWO

Making Italy and making Italians

The history of Italy between [...] 1861 and [...] 1922
is the history of a state in search of a nation.
Suzanne Stewart-Steinberg, *The Pinocchio Effect: On Making Italians, 1860-1920*[1]

'Unfortunately we have made Italy, but we have not created Italians.'
Massimo d'Azeglio.[2]

THE unified Kingdom of Italy was a state born out of conflict, of which Victor Emmanuel II of Piedmont-Sardinia was crowned King in 1861. Curiously, he did not retitle himself to become Victor Emmanuel I, and so appeared to be the second King of Italy. The Kingdom of Piedmont-Sardinia itself was one of eight Italian states that had been recreated after the defeat of Napoleon at the Congress of Vienna in 1815. Autocratic governments ruled all those states, and, though nominally independent, many of them depended on Austrian protection and were effectively satellites of the Austrian Empire. Patriotic sentiments had begun to spread among Italian elites during Napoleonic rule (1805–14), under which large parts of Italy had been politically unified. The post-Napoleonic restoration led to growing demands for the granting of constitutional charters and independence from foreign rule. These, in 1820-21, led to a series of insurrections in the Kingdom of the Two Sicilies and Piedmont-Sardinia. They achieved very little and were brutally crushed. In the case of the Two Sicilies, an Austrian army was despatched under the auspices of the Holy Alliance who feared that the notion of constitutional government might spread to other Italian states and perhaps even further.[3]

Attempts to shrug off Austrian dominance resulted in what became known as the First Italian War of Independence. This was fought in 1848 between Piedmont-Sardinia and the Austrian Empire. The conflict arose from the local manifestation of the widespread revolts of 1848, a pan-European phenomenon. The population of Lombardy-Venetia, under Austrian rule, rose as did the people of Sicily. With similar trouble occurring in Vienna the Austrian forces evacuated the island. Perceiving a time of apparent Austrian weakness, several Italian states, including Piedmont-Sardinia, the Kingdom of the Two Sicilies, Tuscany and the Papal States, sent their military forces into Lombardy-Venetia. After some initial success, the Italian alliance fractured; the Pope

The Kingdom of Italy in 1911, showing the pre-unification states and the dates of their accession.
Having created an Italian state in 1861, with King Victor Emanuel II of Piedmont-Sardinia becoming Victor
Emanuel II of Italy, the problem then was, as Massimo d'Azeglio put it, creating Italians. The capital city,
after previously being located at Turin (1861-64) and Florence (1864-71), was moved to Rome in 1871
following the surrender of Pope Pius IX to military force. (© Charles Blackwood).

recalled his troops and the Kingdom of the Two Sicilies also withdrew. The Grand Duke
of Tuscany, Leopold II, greatly alarmed at the course of events in his native state where
'revolutionaries' had taken control, decided to follow the Papal example.[4] Piedmont-
Sardinia was left to face Austria alone, and was too weak to prevail, being forced to
acquiesce in a short-lived armistice before having to come to terms on 9 August 1849
and pay an indemnity of 65 million francs. The outcome of the conflict brought home

to Piedmont-Sardinia the unlikelihood of being able to defeat Austria single-handedly, and left insurrectionist regimes in Venice (the Republic of San Marco), Florence, the capital of Tuscany, and Rome as the sole representatives of defiance to Austrian domination.[5] This was fairly short lived; the Austrians retook the Republic of San Marco in August 1849 after a long siege, and Leopold II was restored to his capital the same year with the assistance of Austrian troops, who occupied Tuscany until 1855.[6] One insurrectionary government that was defeated by other than Austrian assistance was that which had risen in the Papal States during March 1849. A constituent assembly had been formed, which abolished the temporal power of the Pope and proclaimed a Roman Republic. A new constitution was proclaimed, which guaranteed a government subject to legal constraints, a free press, freedom of conscience, the abolition of capital punishment and universal male suffrage amongst others. One of the leaders of the Republic was Giuseppe Mazzini, a politician, journalist and activist, known popularly as 'The Beating Heart of Italy'. He is usually ranked alongside Cavour and Garibaldi as one of the leading figures of the Italian Risorgimento.

The reactionary forces that sought to 'restore the Pope' came this time from France. France was then under the presidency of Louis Napoleon. His motives in intervening were largely domestic-political; French ultramontane Catholics formed a large part of his core constituency.[7] A French expeditionary corps, with some Spanish assistance, was duly despatched and one of the French commanders, General Charles Oudinot, when told that he would meet resistance uttered the quip 'Italians don't fight' (*les Italiens ne se battent pas*). He was wrong, and as he found to his cost the Italians did fight and bloodily repulsed his advance.[8] Indeed, it was only after fierce resistance that the short-lived Roman Republic surrendered in June 1849.[9]

The fact that Piedmont-Sardinia alone, or with unreliable allies, could not prevail against Austrian military strength, even when this was diluted by domestic discontent, seemed to pose an insoluble problem. A solution however came from the former French President, Louis Napoleon, who had, since 2 December 1852, reinvented himself as Emperor Napoleon III. Since that time the two states had been allied during the Crimean War against Russia, fighting alongside the forces of the United Kingdom and The Ottoman Empire. Napoleon III had chosen to pick a quarrel, indeed a fight, with Austria in a bid to extend French influence in Italy; 'a new Bonapartist hegemony' in A J P Taylor's phrase.[10] He did not expect that his strategy would lead to the creation of a unified Italian state. Rather, in the south, he expected the Kingdom of the Two Sicilies to remain as it was, whilst in central Italy the Papal States would endure and the smaller territories would combine to form a kingdom that France might control. Northern Italy would be dominated by Piedmont-Sardinia, which would receive Lombardy and Venetia; the whole confederation would be presided over by the Pope.[11]

The Emperor invited the Piedmontese Prime Minister, Camillo Benso, Count Cavour, to a secret meeting at Plombieres, in eastern France on 20-21 July 1858. The outcome of this meeting was an agreement, the main strands of which were that France would help Piedmont-Sardinia to fight against Austria, and Piedmont-Sardinia would then give Nice and Savoy to France in return.[12] There were caveats, inasmuch as Austria had to be seen as the aggressor, and that 'the war should have no revolutionary taint to alarm the reactionary governments of Europe.'[13]

In order to provoke Austria, Cavour arranged for military manoeuvres to be held close to the Austrian border and did nothing to discourage the Austrian belief that Piedmont-Sardinia had been supplying armaments to separatists in Lombardy. The desired effect was realised when Austria issued an ultimatum on 23 April 1859 demanding the disarming of the army of Piedmont-Sardinia. This of course went unheeded, and Austria accordingly, on 29 April, declared war. Napoleon, declaring he had come to 'liberate Italy from the Alps to the Adriatic,' decided to lead his army in person, and on 13 May he met the Piedmontese king, Victor Emanuel II, at Genoa. The combined, though overwhelmingly French, armies fought and won two significant battles over the next four weeks; the Battle of Magenta on 4 June and the much larger Battle of Solferino, or Solferino and San Martino as it is also known, on 24 June. The latter was a particularly vicious struggle lasting some nine hours; the casualties on the French and Piedmontese side have been computed as around 17,000 whilst Austria suffered some 22,000 losses.[14] These figures are probably underestimates; an anonymous correspondent of the *New York Times*, who had been at the scene on the day and was in the area for two week afterwards, calculated that the Franco-Piedmontese army alone had suffered 45,000 killed and wounded.[15]

These victories, though they were hardly decisive in the military sense, nevertheless meant that Austria was weakened and in danger of being pushed from northern Italy completely. But then, it appears, Napoleon got cold feet. Far from proceeding with the project to liberate Italy as far as the Adriatic, he resolved that the action would go no further than Lombardy.[16] His motives for this have provoked much debate, but were probably manifold. The threat of Prussian mobilisation and revulsion at the butcher's bill occasioned during the June battles are often cited, but in any event, he sent a French general under a flag of truce to the Austrian HQ on 10 July, with a request that the Austrian Emperor, Franz Joseph, meet him at Villafranca di Verona the next morning. This was acceded to, and over the heads of the Piedmontese, the two emperors met and concluded an armistice. Cavour resigned when he learned of it.[17]

The agreements reached, (basically that Lombardy was to be united with Piedmont while Venice was left to Austria), were formalised in the Treaty of Zurich. This was signed by Austria, France and, in some disgust, Piedmont-Sardinia on 10 November 1859. There were three parts, or, more correctly, three treaties; one between France and Austria which ceded Lombardy to France and re-established peace between the two emperors. The second treaty, between France and Piedmont-Sardinia, passed Lombardy along to the latter power, whilst the third re-established a state of peace between Austria and Sardinia.[18]

Even whilst it was being signed, the treaty was, in reality, a dead letter. Provisional governments had usurped power in the Austrian guaranteed statelets of Tuscany, Parma, Modena and the northern portions of the Papal States (also known as Romagna).[19] They had gone on to elect representative assemblies, which, being dominated by Italian patriots, were vociferous about becoming Italian under the auspices of Piedmont-Sardinia. Certainly they were not about to put themselves back under the authority of Grand Duke Ferdinand IV, Duke Robert, Duke Francis V, and Pope Pius IX respectively.[20] They formed a federation, generally known as the United Provinces of Central Italy, which was a short-lived affair. Plebiscites were held on 11-12 March 1860 on the question of independence or annexation to Piedmont-Sardinia.

The outcome of these referenda was, in all cases, a massive vote in favour of annexation to Piedmont-Sardinia. The electorate consisted of males over the age of 21, and around seventy-five per cent of those eligible to vote did so. There were accusations that the votes had been rigged,[21] and the one-sidedness of the result is of a magnitude that invites suspicion: Parma: For 53,782 - Against 165. Modena: For 52,499 - Against 56. The Papal Legations (Romagna): For 200,659 - Against 244. Tuscany: For 371,000 - Against 15,000.[22] However, whilst there is evidence of irregularity in respect of the elections of the provisional governments, with, for example, the more conservative rural voters prevented from casting ballots, there seems little doubt that the results of the plebiscites reflected popular opinion.[23] Despite having effectively reneged on his promise in respect of the amount of Italian territory he would liberate, Napoleon still wanted his share of the spoils as agreed at Colombiers in 1858. On 25 March 1860 a general election was held throughout the recently enlarged state, including Nice and Savoy, and on 2 April the deal regarding the territorial transfer, formalised by the Treaty of Turin signed on 24 March 1860, was revealed to the assembly.[24] One of the newly elected members was Giuseppe Garibaldi, voted in as deputy for his birthplace – Nice.[25]

Garibaldi was a unique figure. He was renowned internationally for his exploits in pursuit of liberation in South America, whilst similar feats in pursuit of a united Italy, particularly during the 1848 revolutions, had raised him to almost legendary status domestically.[26] On 12 April he made his first address to Parliament. He read to the assembly the fifth article of the Constitution, which stipulated that no part of the state could be transferred without the consent of parliament.[27] He referred to the pressure being exerted on the citizens of Nice, where no public meetings to discuss the matter were allowed, and no canvassing or leafleting arguing against the annexation was permitted. A new governor, Louis Lubonis, had been appointed, and he bent his whole efforts to securing a vote in favour. Garibaldi asked that the referendum in Nice be postponed from 15 April to 22 April.

Cavour, who had returned as Prime Minister on 20 January 1860, dismissed Garibaldi's arguments by pointing out that to have refused to honour the Colombiers agreement would have destroyed all hope of advancing the cause of Italian nationalism. He advised Garibaldi to 'turn your eyes beyond the Mincio and beyond the confines of Tuscany.'[28] Garibaldi is supposed to have described Cavour as being a 'low intriguer' for his dealings,[29] but whatever the status assigned to his secret diplomacy it was undoubtedly effective; large amounts of territory had been added to what was soon to become Italy.

Garibaldi was, in the interim, to famously add even more. However, on the evening of his plea to the assembly he decided on a more parochial course of action; at the head of two hundred men he would sail for Nice and enter the town immediately after the referendum had taken place. His men would then appropriate the ballot boxes and scatter their contents, thus forcing a rerun prior to which Garibaldi and his followers would actively campaign against annexation.[30] This project was abandoned the same evening however; as the Englishman Laurence Oliphant recorded it following his visit to Garibaldi, who was ensconced with a number of others:

> I am very sorry, but we must abandon all idea of carrying out our Nice Programme. Behold these gentlemen from Sicily. All from Sicily! All come here to meet me, to say that the moment is ripe, that delay would be fatal to their hopes; that if we are to relieve their country from the oppression of Bomba, we must act at once. I had hoped to be able to carry out this little Nice affair first, for it is only a matter of a few days; but much as I regret it, the general opinion is,

that we shall lose all if we try too much; and fond as I am of my native province, I cannot sacrifice these greater hopes of Italy to it.[31]

Nice and Savoy voted undisturbed on the given dates, with the result being, as expected, hugely in favour of union with France.[32] Garibaldi's quoted comment about the moment being 'ripe' as regards Sicily was prompted by unrest that had broken out there. It was also provoked, it has been argued, by his annoyance at Cavour and the Piedmontese government regarding the cession of Nice.[33] In any event, it was the case that an insurrection had begun in Palermo on 4 May. This quickly spread, leading to it becoming known as the 'April revolution'.[34] In order to support this revolution Garibaldi assembled a force of around 1,000 nationalists (*i Mille*), and this contingent of redshirts (*camicie rosse*) embarked in two 'requisitioned' paddle-steamers, which they renamed *Piemonte* and *Lombardo,* from Quarto near Genoa on 5 May.[35] Pursued by vessels of the Neapolitan Navy,[36] the Thousand nevertheless landed safely at Marsala, Sicily, on 11 May where they were joined by local insurrectionist forces.[37] The armed forces of Francis II, ruler of the Kingdom of the Two Sicilies, had been weakened somewhat shortly following that monarch's accession on 22 May 1859. On 7 June some detachments of the Swiss Guard, considered to be the best troops available to the regime, had mutinied. The mutineers had then been massacred by order of General Alessandro Nunziante, Duke of Majano and an intimate of the king, and the rest of the guard then disbanded.[38]

This perhaps goes some way to accounting for the victory of around 800 of the redshirts over the Neapolitan forces during the course of an apparently minor engagement near the village of Calatafimi on 15 May. Led by Garibaldi in person, some 1500 of the enemy were beaten, but the battle was decisive inasmuch as without this initial success the whole campaign might have failed. It also fed the Garibaldi legend; it was before this battle that he is supposed to have uttered the immortal phrase 'here we make Italy or die' (*qui si fa l'Italia o si muore*). Garibaldi survived the battle, declared himself dictator of Sicily in the name of King Victor Emmanuel, and went on with the quest to 'make Italy.' On 4 June he renamed his force the Southern Army (*Esercito Meridionale*); it was enlarged by volunteers from northern Italy, deserters from the Neapolitan forces, local volunteers, and foreigners (mainly Hungarian). Though there was a good deal of fighting Garibaldi's progress seemed inexorable. Having successfully crossed the Straits of Messina he travelled to Naples on 7 September and, almost alone and seemingly without any resistance, took control of the capital. His arrival was greeted with popular approval:

> At the railway National Guards were stationed at all the entrances, and flags were coming down in rapid succession, for the arrival of the Dictator was sudden, like everything he does, and people were unprepared. [. . .] At last 12 o'clock strikes, and a bell sounds, and from a distance a signal is made that Garibaldi is approaching. 'Viva Garibaldi' rises from a thousand voices, and the train stops; a few [redshirts] get out, and they are seized, hugged, and kissed with that most unmerciful violence which characterises Italian ardour. [. . .] There was one poor elderly man who, by virtue of his white beard, was taken for Garibaldi, and was slobbered so that I thought he must have sunk under the operation; but the great man had gone round by another door, and so there was a rush in all directions to intercept him.[39]

The accomplishments of the Southern Army led to concerns in the camp of Garibaldi's ostensible allies, the Piedmontese regime. Indeed, Victor Emanuel and Cavour, despite having winked at his exploits whilst officially disapproving of them, had become troubled by the rapidity and extent of his success. Garibaldi, though he was well known for his republican views, had of course, in the middle of May, announced that his assumption of the role of dictator was in the name of Victor Emanuel. His subsequent achievements, and there is no denying that they had been remarkable, had propelled him not only to the forefront of the struggle for Italian unity, but also to international fame, or indeed notoriety dependant upon point of view. The Piedmontese regime had, in short, rather lost the initiative, but yet it was they that had to contend with the foreign policy implications that Garibaldi's advance raised. These devolved essentially upon the position of the Pope and the extent of the territory he ruled. Garibaldi had made little secret of his intention to lead the Southern Army into the Papal States and indeed Rome itself, a course of action that would have caused French intervention.

Accordingly, and in order to forestall such an eventuality, Cavour played off Napoleon III and Garibaldi against each other, by, in the words of Mack Smith, threatening, 'with exquisite tact [...] Napoleon with Garibaldi, and Garibaldi with Napoleon.'[40] This diplomatic strategy was backed by direct action, and on the pretext of using force to quell unrest and disturbances in the Marches and Umbria, which he had arranged for, and to protect Papal authority, Cavour sent a Piedmontese army into those territories on 10 September 1860 of some 50,000 men under the command of General Enrico Cialdini. Pius IX had forces of his own, a cosmopolitan army of some 8,000 men formed in April 1860 under the command of the anti-Napoleonic French general Christophe Leon Louis Juchault de Lamoricière. This heterogeneous force fought with the invaders at the Battle of Castelfidardo on 18 September, and was heavily defeated. Forced to retreat, Lamoriciére concentrated his remaining troops at the fortress of Ancona, but was forced to capitulate on 29 September 1860. Meanwhile other Piedmontese troops had advanced to the south, fighting and winning battles at Perugia and Spoleto. The latter was defended by a contingent of Irishmen, the Brigade of Saint Patrick, under the command of Major Myles O'Reilly. This force held out for two days against a more numerous and better-armed detachment commanded by General Filippo Brignone, but was forced to terms on 18 September.[41] Napoleon III had done nothing to prevent the conquest of most of the Papal States.

Upon Garibaldi's entry into their capital, the Neapolitan regime had decamped to the city fortress of Gaeta, some 80 kilometres north of Naples. Here the now effectively deposed Francis II attempted to reform his army and seek, a hope looking increasingly forlorn, assistance from another power that would intervene on behalf of those who opposed Italian unification under Piedmont Sardinia. The Neapolitan army was put under the command of 66-year-old War Minister, Field Marshal Giosuè Ritucci, who regrouped and reorganised it at Capua, some 25 kilometres north of Naples. His strategy involved purging his command of unreliable elements, and then utilising this reinvigorated force to fight a battle based on the line of the Volturno river, whereby they hoped to defeat and scatter the Southern Army.

There were initial signs that the Neapolitan military strategy at least was sound when elements of the Southern Army, advancing from Naples under the leadership of the Hungarian Stefano Türr (Türr István), suffered a repulse at Caiazzo (Cajazzo) on 19 September. Ritucci's force, numbering over 40,000 men in total according to some sources, also had some success in the recapture of the difficult position of Castel Morrone on 1 October during its advance to the south. This exploit, part of the larger action of the Battle of Volturno, was however to be the last of its kind. Over two days, 1–2 October, Garibaldi, who had returned to lead his forces in person, fought to prevent around 30,000 Neapolitan troops from moving to retake Naples. Despite his 20,000 strong force being outnumbered, they were successful in stopping the enemy advance and driving them back to Capua. In fact the game was almost up for Francis II and his government, who were now being assailed from both north and south as the Piedmontese army, under the personal command of Victor Emanuel II, advanced across the Neapolitan frontier on 13 October. Ritucci was thus forced to leave Capua garrisoned against an attack by the Southern Army, whilst redeploying the majority of his force northwards to the line of the Garigliano some 60 kilometres miles to the north-west. Garibaldi followed, leaving a detachment to contain Capua, which eventually surrendered on 2 November, and on the 26 October 1860 he and Victor Emanuel met at Teano. This meeting later became immortalised in Italian culture because of the supposed 'Handshake of Teano,' whereby Garibaldi is depicted shaking the hand with Victor Emanuel and acknowledging him as the (future) King of Italy.

The same day, Ritucci was relieved of his command and replaced by Giovanni Salzano, but no amount of tinkering could now alter the facts on the ground. A series of fairly minor battles were fought and won by the Piedmontese between 29 October and 4 November, including that of Mola di Gaeta on 2 November, which cut off the Neapolitan regime at Gaeta along with some 10-16,000 troops. These were supported by the, thus far, passive presence of a French squadron of warships, and all that was left for them to hope for was the military intervention of Austria. That this was not to be forthcoming has been attributed to the actions of Prussia under Bismarck, which refused to back Austria and thus left her isolated. Whether this was part of Bismarck's plan for the unification of Germany is the subject of scholarly disputation, but the effect was to support Italian unification under the auspices of Piedmont-Sardinia.

Unification was however very much incomplete when Victor Emmanuel II was crowned King of Italy on 17 March 1861. Indeed, Italian society as a whole had immense problems. These included the alienation of the Catholic Church, always likely to be a problem in an overwhelmingly observant population, which believed that a unified nation was against its own interests and argued that Italy, as a state, was illegitimate. Such was Pius IX's detestation of the concept of an Italian State, or perhaps the removal of the temporal powers of the Papacy that such a polity not only implied but was instrumental in causing, that he:

> [...] had recourse to the most formidable weapon at his command: the greater Excommunication, which, with all mediaeval pomp, was pronounced on April 23, 1860 [...] No particular individuals were named, but all, beginning with the King of Sardinia, who had taken part or should take part [...] or in any way, even outside of Italy, should assist by work or will in the accomplishment of the new order of things, or in any way profit by it, were included.[42]

Indeed, the future capital of Italy remained outside the control of that state for nearly a decade following reunification. The Pope, as King, ruled Rome and its environs including Civita Veccchia, Velletri, Frosinoni and Viterbo. These formed the final remnant of the Papal States most of the rest of which had joined the Kingdom of Italy in 1861.

Bismarck certainly played a part in the next acquisition of territory considered to be 'unredeemed' (*Italia irredenta*) or incorporated into the Italian state. The Austro-Prussian War, also known as the Third War of Independence to Italians, began with Prussia declaring war on Austria on 16 June 1866 followed by Italy three days later. Italy had agreed to assist Prussia on the condition that Venetia was ceded to it after the conflict, which it obviously expected Prussia to win. Italy hoped to conquer the territory single-handedly and moved two armies against Austria for that purpose. One of them, under General Alfonso Ferrero la Marmora, met with disaster at the Battle of Custoza on 24 June 1866 when it was soundly beaten by an inferior Austrian force under Field Marshal Archduke Albrecht and driven out of Venetia. The defeat was caused by a badly defective supreme command, which divided its forces and had no clear conception of what it wanted to do. Accordingly a series of uncoordinated attacks were made and the Austrians, who kept their forces concentrated, were able to defeat the attackers in a series of isolated encounters. It was hardly a hard-fought battle, (according to Whittam the Austrian casualties far outweighed the Italian), but it destroyed Italian self belief in the military value of their army.[43] As a future Chief of Staff put it in his study of the battle published in 1903; 'the defeat of Custoza still weighs down our army like a cloak of lead (*cappa di piombo*) 36 years later' [44] However, if the Battle of Custoza was perceived as a huge, if indecisive, defeat for the army, the outcome of the Battle of Lissa (Vis) on 20 July was as bad, if not worse, for the navy.[45]

The National Italian Navy had been created on 17 November 1860, when the regional navies – Sardinian, Bourbon, Sicilian, Tuscan and Papal – combined. Four months later, on 17 March 1861, it became the *Regia Marina Italiana*, following the proclamation of the Kingdom of Italy. The outcome of Lissa largely revolved around the irresolution and poor strategic and tactical judgement of the Italian Commander in Chief, Admiral Carlo Pellion di Persano. Urged by the government to take some Austrian territory before the war ended, particularly after Custoza, he conceived a plan to sortie with virtually the entire Italian fleet in order to effect a bombardment of, and landing on, the Austrian island of Lissa (now Vis in Croatia) in the Adriatic.[46] Persano deployed twelve ironclad warships and twenty-two unarmoured vessels (including transports for some 3000 troops) against which the Austrian fleet, under vice admiral Wilhelm von Tegethoff, could pit only seven armoured frigates (built of wood and plated with thin armour), seven steam-driven wooden ships without armour, and an assortment of thirteen screw-driven and paddle-wheel gunboats.

Persano left from the port of Ancona on 16 July, and was off the island by 18 July whereupon he commenced firing on the defences. No attempt was made to land as the Italian commander, despite his materiel superiority, feared the Austrians might arrive whilst the procedure was underway. The bombardment continued the next day and some of the troops were landed. Persano however failed to provide a covering force for these landings and was unaware that Tegethoff, who had been informed of the attack by cable, was hurrying to the scene from the Austrian base at Fasana, near Pola (Pula), on the southern tip of the Istrian peninsula. Tegethoff arrived off Lissa on the morning of 20 July, and approached the position with his command organised in three divisions, arranged in succession; armoured ships first, then unarmoured large ships. Each division was in a chevron formation, the flagship of the division in the centre with the rest of the ships echeloned sternwards to port and starboard. The Italians were disorganised and Persano

attempted to form a line of battle whilst, for reasons unknown, simultaneously deciding
to switch his flagship and thus interrupt command and communication. The end result
was that the Austrians were able to charge through and sunder the Italian battle line and
defeat them in detail. Persano, who compounded all his earlier errors by initially reporting
that he had won the engagement, was dismissed from the navy, which was itself left under
a cloud. It was perhaps then unsurprising that one of the government's first moves after
the disaster was to reduce the Navy's budget, ushering in what the historian Aldo
Fraccaroli called 'dark, sad years for the Navy, [it being] relegated to a position of minor
importance'.[47]

However, despite the defeats of Custoza and Lissa, Italy got what it wanted from the
war. Following the Prussian victory at Königgrätz (Sadowa) on 3 July 1866 Austria sought
to make peace, and Bismarck was keen to oblige. He did not seek any Austrian territory,
but rather wanted to exclude Austria from Prussian and wider German affairs and to
bind the small German states that had been allied to Austria to Prussia, mostly by
annexation. Bismarck kept his word to Italy however, and Austria was forced to cede
Venetia under the terms of the 'Peace of Prague,' the treaty that ended the war on
23 August 1866. However, Austria refused to hand the territory directly to Italy, preserving
national *amour-propre* by handing it to Napoleon III, who, in turn ceded it to Italy. The
province ceded equates roughly with the modern Italian regions of Veneto, including the
capital Venice, and Friuli-Venezia Giulia, though minus its capital, Trieste, which remained
in Austrian hands. Austria also retained the Trentino territory (the modern semi-
autonomous province of Trento), which remained a major bone of contention.

Otto von Bismarck was again to play an important, albeit indirect, part in the next
major redemption of Italian territory; that of Rome and the Lazio. That Rome and the
surrounding area had remained beyond the control of the Italian state was mainly due to
the presence there of French troops, tasked with preserving the remnant of Papal temporal
power by Napoleon III. However, the outbreak of the Franco-Prussian War in 1870
resulted in the withdrawal of this force, and more importantly the backing of the Second
Empire for Papal temporal power, leaving the way clear for the Italian state to take control.
Without the support of Napoleon III, who was captured at the Battle of Sedan on
2 September and whose rule was ended by the effective declaration of a Third Republic
on 4 September 1870, the Papal regime was doomed. The Italian State quickly formed
a force of some 50,000 men under general Raffaele Cadorna (the father of the First
World War general) which moved on Rome on the 11 September. On the Italian side
the hope was for a peaceful solution, and the King of Italy wrote to the Pope on
8 September guaranteeing his person and position:

> The Government of the King will protect the interest which the whole Catholic world
> possesses in the entire independence of the Sovereign Pontiff [...] The Government of the King
> is firm in assuring the guarantees necessary to the spiritual independence of the Holy See, and
> that the head of the Catholic Church shall preserve on the banks of the Tiber a seat honourable
> and independent of all human sovereignty.[48]

Pius IX was however determined upon offering at least token resistance, and he had
sufficient force to do so; defending the Papal territory was a force of some 11,000[49] troops
under a German general, Hermann Kanzler.[50] These consisted of members of the Palatine
Guard (*guardia palatina*), Noble Guard (*guardia nobile*), and the famous Swiss Guard (*guardia*

svizzera), together with the colourful Papal Zouaves (*zuavi pontifici*) under the command of Roger de Beauffort.[51]

The Italian army reached the ancient Aurelian Wall on 19 September and took up position. The rituals of siege-craft, formulated over the centuries, stipulated that the defenders of a position could honourably surrender once a 'practicable breach' had been made in the wall.[52] The Aurelian Wall, built between 270 and 282 AD,[53] had been designed, to utilise Gibbon's picturesque prose, 'only to resist the less potent engines of antiquity' and it was no match for the 'thundering artillery' that was now pointed at it.[54] Nevertheless there was some fighting:

> Six battalions of the reserve *Bersaglieri* had been assigned to advance against Porta Pia. The artillery was still targeting the wall to open the breach [. . .] [and] it was announced that a large hole had been opened near Porta Pia, and that the Pontifical guns, which had been very ineffectual in rate of fire, had been dismounted and silenced. Papal Zouaves were stationed on the thick walls of the *Castrum Praetorium* and their fire was causing much suffering to one of our regiments. A few hundred metres from the wall two of our large artillery pieces were firing at the wall and with every shot more pieces of the wall fell away. When the Porta Pia was clear [of enemy troops] and the breach nearby open almost to the ground, the infantry launched the attack and the six battalions of *Bersaglieri* rushed by and entered the city.[55]

The news of the breach and its successful storming was brought to Pius IX around 09:00 hrs, who was at the time conferring with the diplomatic corps in the throne room of the Vatican. He is said to have murmured '*fiat voluntas tua in coelo et in terra*' [thy will be done on earth as in heaven] before turning to the diplomats and announcing that he intended to surrender to save the unnecessary shedding of blood, but asked them to witness that he did so only under the threat of violence. The Zouaves, who were manning that particular portion of the defences, and had asked to be allowed to fight to the end, were ordered to surrender after showing sufficient resistance to prove the Pope's point.[56] Casualties were low; the Italians lost 56 dead and some 140 wounded whilst on the Papal side 20 died and 49 were wounded.[57] As had occurred in all previous annexations, the people of the areas under question voted in a plebiscite that was held on 2 October 1870. The issue was worded as follows: 'We wish to be united with the the Kingdom of Italy under the constitutional government of King Victor Emmanuel II and his successors'. The result was promulgated on 9 October. In the City of Rome, 40,785 voted for incorporation in the Italian State, as against 46 for remaining under the Pope. In the region as a whole out of 167,548 registered voters, 133,681 voted for incorporation with 1,507 against.[58] The Pope, refusing all entreaties from, and guarantees offered, by the Italian government retreated into the Vatican and became a self-imposed prisoner. Thus began a long period of stand-off, and the state and the church did not reach agreement on their relationship until 1929.[59]

The incorporation of Rome into Italy seems like a victory for democracy, however it has been convincingly argued that the plebiscites, which were used to legitimise the formation of Italy from its component parts from 1860 onwards, were rigged.[60] Certainly, it is difficult to visualise what would have happened had the vote gone against. The vast majority of the population was in any case excluded from any form of political participation. Suffrage, linked to property and literary qualifications, was extremely limited, and the parliamentary system was such that governments were formed from 'the variable and casual fluctuations of groups and personalities' over the members of which the Prime Minister, and the monarch, deployed a powerful patronage system. This system was used to ensure that Members of Parliament who toed the line were rewarded. This process was known as *transformismo*, whereby opposition was 'transformed' into support.[61]

Further, by the Papal decree *non expedit* of 29 February 1868, Roman Catholics were forbidden to take any part in the political life of the new state. Enough observed this prohibition so as to ensure that prominent politicians were 'commonly secular or anticlerical, and often Freemasons.'[62] Internationally, the Roman Catholic hierarchy were fiercely critical of Italy as a constituted state. The English Cardinal Henry Edward Manning wrote in 1877 that:

> The present Chamber, elected by less than a hundredth part of the Catholic Italian people, represents the Revolution, and nothing but the Revolution. The Catholic electors refuse to vote: less than two hundred and fifty thousand elect the Parliament, which Englishmen believe to represent the 26,000,000 of Italy.[63]

Despite his obvious bias, it has to be conceded that Manning had a point.

Political power at the provincial level was vested in a government appointed prefect, a system borrowed from France, who was responsible for implementing centrally derived policy. The prefect was a powerful figure, being also the head of the police in his province. Prefects could, and did, utilise these powers to neutralise political opposition to the government, dissolve councils and proscribe political associations which posed a threat to what they perceived as 'public security.' These measures were applied during election periods when the prefect was able to use these powers so as to disadvantage anti-government candidates.[64] This centralisation process, known as *Piedmontisation*, ensured that Italy was, ostensibly at least, a highly centralized state, albeit with a number of very disparate regions. Division was also evident along class lines; the nobility was in decline but, as late as 1909, 'over most of the south the old-established oligarchies still retained control.'[65] Here the prefect assumed the status of a 'diplomatic agent' accredited by a 'foreign' government to the local potentates, and the southern peasant – really landless day labourers (*braccianti*) – remained, in fact, an 'oppressed serf.'[66] Perhaps unsurprisingly, emigration from southern Italy was on a large scale. Between 1876 and 1914 a total of 13,882,000 Italians are calculated to have left Italy. By 1913 sixty-three percent of these had left the northern and central regions, whilst despite only having thirty-eight per cent of the population, forty-seven per cent departed from the south. Most of the latter migrated to the US, Latin America and Australia, whilst the majority of emigration from northern and central Italy was to European destinations.[67] However, by far the largest single recipient of Italian immigrants was the US.[68]

Physical hardship accounted for a large degree of this flight. The standard of living became worse in the whole of Italy between 1870 and 1900, especially in the countryside, where the majority of the population resided. For example, in the 'pellagra triangle' of Veneto, Lombardy and Emilia-Romagna the eponymous condition, causing dermatitis, diarrhoea and, in many cases, dementia, was endemic and considered unavoidable. In fact it was easily avoidable; whilst the causes (a deficiency of niacin, which was not present in maize, the staple diet of the rural poor) were not properly identified until early in the twentieth century, that it could be alleviated, if not eradicated, by a slight dietary improvement was well known. It has been calculated that, merely to stay alive, the rural poor were forced to spend up to seventy-five percent of their income on food, which despite its relative cost, did not contain enough nutrition.[69] The trouble was, as Zamagni has pointed out, 'in order to rid the countryside of pellagra the social relations that existed in these areas would have to be revolutionised, and this was something that only started to happen towards the end of the nineteenth century.'[70] There is undoubtedly truth in Ashley's statement that 'The fact that Italian politicians came from the propertied class made them singularly sanguine about alleviating poverty by stimulating capitalism.'[71]

The Italian state also suffered from endemic malaria – widely regarded as the 'Italian national disease' during the second half of the nineteenth century and the first half of the twentieth – throughout nearly the entire peninsula and the islands of Sicily and Sardinia. Southern Italy, including Rome, was however afflicted with the *falciparum* strain, the most dangerous and acute type, whilst the north suffered from the less deadly, but still debilitating, *vivax* malaria. This disease was a part, and probably an important part, of the reason for the large-scale emigration, particularly from the south, causing a cycle of economic backwardness. Perhaps unsurprisingly, in 1900 the average life expectancy for both sexes in Italy has been computed to be about 43 years, which compares rather unfavourably with England and Wales at just over 48 years, France at 47.7, and Germany at a little over 45. It was however better than Austria-Hungary, whose combined figures average out at around 38 years, and much better than Spain at 35 years.[72]

Perhaps also having an effect on emigration was the widespread social unrest that manifested itself through violence and uprising. One prime example of this was the insurrection that took place in Sicily in 1893; instigated by the *fasci* movement in protest at an increase in food prices and onerous working terms, it led to the government initiating a state of siege, under which those participating were brutally suppressed. The rural police force, the *Carabinieri*, was unable to cope and 40,000 troops were sent to Sicily, martial law was declared and military tribunals were established.[73] A form of internal exile (*domicilio coatto*) to penal colonies, usually on islands off the coast such as Pantelleria, was resorted to, and over 1000 were deported without trial.[74] Most alarmingly, in January 1894 this unrest spread to the north, leading to an uprising in what is now the province of Massa Carrara in the Tuscany region. Luigi Molinari, an anarchist, syndicalist, and lawyer, and in 1901 the founder of the newspaper *L'Università popolare*, was held to have been the instigator. At least this was the verdict of the military tribunal that tried him following the extension of the state of siege to the area. Molinari was sentenced to 23 years in prison. This, however, provoked a huge protest movement, and he received an amnesty the following year.[75]

Anarchism was a powerful force to be reckoned with on the Italian left, and in July 1894 the government of Crispi put in place a series of laws that greatly restricted the exercise of free association. These measures, basically curtailing the ability of workers to collectivise in the name of eliminating 'incitement to class hatred,' were defined as 'anti-anarchic.'[76] Furthermore, the electoral registers were 'amended', the Socialist Party of Italian Workers was barred, its deputies arrested, and parliament prorogued in October 1894.[77] Crispi justified such measures, which made prosecution possible on mere suspicion, on the grounds that they guaranteed the punishment of those criminals who would otherwise have been acquitted for lack of evidence.[78] Automatic sentencing for belonging to organisations deemed subversive was also introduced.[79] There were many more internal and social problems as helpfully if briefly itemised in 1913 by the historian and politician Pasquale Villari when he noted the continuing prevalence of 'illiteracy, crime, the camorra, the mafia' and the North-South divide of the country.[80]

In its relations with other European states the cornerstone of Italian foreign policy was membership of the Triple Alliance, or Triplice, with its old enemy Austria-Hungary, as Austria had become following the 'Compromise of 1867,' and its past ally Germany. One of the primary reasons for Italy joining with the members of what had been the Dual Alliance on 20 May 1882 was rivalry with France. Italy and France had been at something approaching loggerheads over North African territory since 1881. In that year France had established a protectorate over the nominally Ottoman territory of Tunis, which Italy had coveted since reunification. The Italian claim was based on it having the largest European population, some 97,000, in residence, and, somewhat more ephemerally, on Roman occupation in antiquity. Whatever merits the Italian claim might have had, it was as nothing when confronted with the realities of French and British power. These states had, as one scholar has put it, 'abandoned their former policy of working to uphold [Ottoman] territorial integrity and were now helping themselves to its real estate.'[81] Perhaps this is overstating the matter, but certainly Britain had also taken charge of Ottoman territory when it gained administrative responsibility, though not sovereignty, over the Ottoman island of Cyprus in 1878. Having been thwarted in her colonial ambitions, Italy was fearful that the resultant discord with France might mean that she was, as Francesco Crispi told Herbert Bismarck, in danger of being placed 'between two enemies, one on our right and the other on our left.'[82] Avoidance of this situation was the leading factor behind Italy joining what then became the Triple-Alliance.[83]

The failure to prevail against French expansionism in Tunisia did not however blunt Italy's wish to acquire a colonial empire. There had been an Italian presence in what became Eritrea since the mid-1880s when an Italian shipping company purchased a harbour at Assab from the Sultan of Obock. The Italian government took over the harbour in 1882 and developed it whilst spreading its presence along the coast and inland. In 1885 the Italians occupied Massawa but this expansion caused them to come into conflict with the Abyssinians, ruled by Yohannes IV, particularly when they occupied the town of Sahati. This confrontation resulted in the Dogale Massacre, when the Abyssinian forces encircled an Italian contingent at the town of that name some 18 kilometres from Massawa and defeated and killed them all. However, rather than finding this incident discouraging it only spurred the Italian government on, and they determined to increase their military presence with a view to colonising more of the area. This process, encouraged by Britain, continued until the Treaty of Ucciale (Wichale) (*Trattato di Uccialli*) formalised the matter. Agreed between Italy and King Menelik II of the autonomous Abyssinian Kingdom of Shewa (who later became Emperor of Abyssinia), and signed on 2 May 1889, it ceded what became Eritrea to the Italians. They named it as such, *Colonia Eritrea,* and declared it their *Colonia Primigenia* on New Years Day 1890.[84]

Under the terms of the treaty Italy recognised Menelik as Abyssinian Emperor and agreed to provide financial assistance and military aid. However, the two parties swiftly came into dispute over the wording and meaning of it. The Amharic version and the Italian version differed it appears, and whilst Menelik thought he had agreed only to consult with Italy over foreign policy if he so desired, the Italian version stipulated that he would do so as a matter of course. In other words, Menelik considered he had been duped into conceding an Italian protectorate over Abyssinia and formally repudiated the treaty on 22 February 1893.[85]

Bordering Abyssinia to the east was another Italian territory, Italian Somaliland or *Somalia Italiana*. Italy had acquired this area piecemeal, reaching agreements with Sultan Ali Yusuf regarding a protectorate over Hobyo Sultanate in December 1888, and similarly with Sultan Osman Mohamoud and the Alula Sultanate in April 1889. Negotiations with the Sultan of Zanzibar, Sayid Barqash, yielded a fifty-year lease on the ports of Mogadishu, Merka, Warsheikh (Warshiikh) and Brava (Barawa) in 1892, which were purchased outright in 1905.[86] Administratively, Italian Somaliland was divided into six administrative subdivisions; Brava, Merca, Lugh, Itala, Bardera, and Jumbo.[87]

The difference of opinion regarding the Treaty of Ucciale led to Italy mounting an invasion. The governor of Eritrea, General Oreste Baratieri, led a force into Abyssinia in December 1894, but was unable to force the opposion to a decisive battle. In January 1895 he fell back to a defensible position close to the border and hoped to induce the enemy to attack him there, knowing that such a tactic would allow his superiority in rifles and artillery to tell. Bariateri commanded some 20,000 men in four brigades with fifty-six artillery pieces whilst Menelik, who commanded in person, had around 100,000 though not all possessed firearms. Wisely refusing to fight on Italian terms, Menelik's army advanced as far as Adwa (Adowa) and remained there throughout February. However, as Bartieri was aware, his enemy could not keep large forces in the field for long periods because they lacked any effective logistical organisation, and so by waiting he would compel the enemy to either attack or disperse. Political considerations then intervened when the government in Rome, led by Francesco Crispi, became frustrated at the apparent lack of success. Bartieri received a telegraph message from the Prime Minister on 28 February in which he likened the campaign to a progressive wasting disease. The admonition continued:

> I have no advice to give you because I am not on the spot, but it is clear to me that there is no fundamental plan in the campaign, and I should like one to be formulated. We are ready for any sacrifice in order to save the honour of the army and the prestige of the monarchy.[88]

Although worded diplomatically there could be little doubt what was expected, and following consultation with his subordinate commanders on 28 February Bartieri determined to advance to the attack the next day. Accordingly, on the evening of the 29 February the four brigades advanced towards Adwa; three brigades abreast under Matteo Albertone on the left, Giuseppe Arimondi in the centre and Vittorio Dabormida on the right. One brigade, under Giuseppe Ellena, followed as the reserve.

The fighting began soon after 05:30 hrs on the morning of 1 March. By noon the battle was effectively over. It had ended in utter disaster for the Italians, and the Battle of Adowa has been accurately dubbed 'the bloodiest defeat ever suffered by a colonial power in Africa.'[89] It was certainly bloody; out of some 17,700 engaged on the Italian side only about 9,000 – about half Italian and half locally recruited – survived the retreat to Eritrea. Amongst the senior officers Dabormida and Arimondi were killed, Albertone was taken prisoner and Ellena was wounded. Only Bartieri, who had boasted he would bring Menelik home in a cage, escaped unscathed. When the news reached Italy the next day it caused civil unrest on a considerable scale, particularly in urban areas, which the army was called out to control. Bartieri was swiftly recalled to Rome to face a court martial (he was acquitted). Crispi was forced to resign whilst Menelik, who might have attempted a pursuit into Eritrea, retired into Ethiopia to await negotiations. On 26 October 1896, he signed the Treaty of Addis Ababa, which abrogated the Treaty of Ucciale. Adowa was considered a national disaster.

The army, disgraced though it had been by Adowa, continued to be used against the Italian people, particularly those who were perceived as threatening the stability of the state such as the socialists. The Italian Socialist Party (PSI), which changed its name from the Socialist Party of Italian Workers at Parma on 13 January 1895, was composed of several strands, including anarchists, advocates of revolution, and evolutionary socialists. The latter strand became the dominant one in the 1890's and though ultimately committed to the socialisation of production and exchange the party opted for an evolutionary, rather than revolutionary, approach under the leadership of Filippo Turati.[90] Despite opting for a constitutional approach, Turati and the PSI were viewed with extreme suspicion by the Italian government. Indeed Turati was sentenced to twelve years in jail for 'instigating civil war' following the Bava-Beccaris massacre on 6 May 1898.[91]

Named after General Fiorenzo Bava-Beccaris, the massacre took place as part of the bloody repression of widespread strikes and riots in Milan in early May 1898. On 5 May 1898 a large-scale strike was organised to protest against the increase of food prices amidst the near famine that was affecting the country. The police were unable to control the crowds and resorted to shooting, which led to one demonstrator in the town of Pavia, Muzio Mussi, the twenty-three year old son of a prominent radical, being shot and killed.[92] On the morning of 6 May the workers at the Pirelli factory went on strike and leaflets denouncing the killing the previous day, were distributed. Rioting broke out, and 'owing to the imbecility of the authorities, sufficient force was deployed to provoke, not to overawe, and they allowed the riots to make head.'[93] Two rioters were shot dead and several wounded. In response the government proclaimed a state of siege in Lombardy and ordered Bava-Beccaris, the commander of VIII Corps, to the area. Reserves were also mobilised, raising the total manpower available to the general to around 45,000, including infantry, cavalry, artillery and, because the railway men were on strike, railway troops. The forces were comprised particularly of men from rural districts and the alpine regions as these were considered to be more reliable than those recruited from the urban working class.

On 7 May 60,000 Milanese went out on strike and large numbers of them began to move towards the city centre from the outlying working class districts. Bava-Beccaris was determined to stop them and force them back into their districts. Accordingly he deployed forces in the Piazza del Duomo, the central square overlooked by Milan Cathedral. From this position they began to move outwards, clearing the demonstrators' barricades and pushing them back into the districts of Ticinese to the south, Romana, Vittoria and Venezia in the east and Garibaldi to the north. He also wanted to regain control of the central station and the railway in general.[94] This however proved more difficult than was envisaged. Some of the insurrectionists had armed themselves with rifles, removed from the workshops of arms manufacturers, whilst many had installed themselves on the roofs of the houses and pelted the troops with stones and roof tiles. The state of the streets, encumbered with rubble and barricades, limited the use of the cavalry and blocked the movement of artillery. Bava-Beccaris however had authorised the use of both rifle and cannon fire against the insurgents, and the streets were thus cleared.

Reinforcements arrived outside the city on 8 May and began moving in with the aim of trapping the insurrectionists between two fires. The whole affair was over by the evening of the following day, with order definitely restored by 10 May. Casualty figures are much disputed; the contemporary official accounts reckoned a cost of 80 dead and 450 wounded on the civilian side, whilst two policemen and soldiers had been killed and twenty-two wounded. By way of comparison, it might be noted that the massacre at the Winter Palace in St Petersburg in 1905, which sparked off a full-blooded revolution, left 130 dead and around 300 seriously wounded according to official figures.[95]

It is possible that Bava-Beccaris thought he had been facing a revolutionary situation. He had military tribunals set up, over some of which at least he personally presided. Around 1,500 Milanese were sentenced to prison terms, and 'the whole conduct of the authorities was a travesty of justice and a mockery of legal procedure.'[96]

The repression went further; any press organ deemed to be in opposition to the government was muzzled, and Catholic and socialist associations were dissolved. As already related, amongst those jailed was Turati, who, far from instigating the disturbances, had attempted to calm the situation issuing a leaflet arguing that the 'days for street fighting are past' and calling on the populace to be 'calm and patient.'[97]

In an astonishingly crass move, Umberto I, who had succeeded Victor Emanuel II on 9 January 1878, awarded Bava-Beccaris a medal for 'great services to the State in the suppression of the revolution,' the *Gran Croce dell'Ordine Militare di Savoia*,[98] and promoted him to the Senate. There was a massive and popular backlash against the monarch, the soldier, and the repression in general. One of the results of this was that Turati was released in 1899. He drew certain lessons from his experiences. Battles with the power of the state were to be avoided and the disavowal of anarchist methods was confirmed; both in Sicily in 1893-4 and again in 1898 the Italian army had demonstrated it had the capacity, and the willingness, to maintain order. The way ahead was via the parliamentary route, and when necessary, alliances with Liberals and others would be enacted in order to preserve a constitutional system within which a socialist party could exist at all.

Indeed, it was via the parliamentary route that the political left won a significant victory. General Luigi Pelloux, who had filled the same role as Bava-Beccaris in Bari in May but without resorting to martial law and overt aggression, had become Prime Minister in June 1898. This was following the fall of the previous ministry, largely because of the results of the policies that had led to the massacres and repression. In February 1899 Pelloux presented to parliament a comprehensive Public Safety Bill, also known as the coercion bill, which would have severely curtailed civil liberties. The opposition parties – socialist, radicals and republicans – combined to thwart attempts to get the bill passed, and when Pelloux had parliament prorogued, and the bill passed by royal decree, he caused uproar. This episode was known as the 'Obstructionist Crisis' and even members of his own side accused him of acting unconstitutionally. With little support outside the normal bastions of extreme conservatism and reaction, Pelloux dissolved the chamber in May 1900 and elections were held the next month. Despite the highly restrictive franchise,[99] which meant that only eight per cent of the Italian population could vote, he was defeated, inasmuch as he could no longer count on a parliamentary majority.[100] The President of the Senate, Giuseppe Saracco, was able to muster such a grouping, including of course the socialists, and thus form a 'Cabinet of Pacification.'[101]

This peace was to be relatively short lived, for in a reversal of the ususal direction of travel, a silkworker domiciled in Paterson, New Jersey, Gaetano Bresci, travelled to Monza, Italy and, on the evening of 29 July 1900, fired three revolver shots into Umberto I. The King perished, and Bresci, a self-proclaimed anarchist justified the regicide on the grounds of avenging those people killed during the Bava-Beccaris massacre. Bresci had been a skilled textile worker in Tuscany before becoming a victim of state repression; he was placed in internal exile on the island of Lampedusa in 1895. In early 1898 he emigrated to the US where he acquired a wife of Irish extraction. He had been horrified to discover that Umberto had decorated Bava-Beccaris for the Milan massacres, rather than hanging him, and determined to take revenge.[102] Umberto could not, even if he had so desired, hanged Bava-Beccaris.[103] The Kingdom of Italy's first penal code, the Zanardelli Code of 1889, abolished capital punishment. Justice minister Giuseppe Zanardelli had argued that it was 'absurd that the law should avenge homicide by itself perpetrating homicide' and that capital punishment was 'calculated to blunt the best sensibilities of mankind.'[104] This of course meant that Bresci could not be executed for murdering the king and he was accordingly sentenced to life imprisonment on 29 August. 'I shall appeal after the coming revolution' he is supposed to have said, but whilst serving his sentence at the Santo Stefano *Ergastolo* (a place of confinement for those serving life sentences) he committed suicide, or was murdered, on 22 May 1901.[105]

Saracco, who was seventy-nine when he assumed the premiership, did not remain long in office. His administration was brought to an end in February 1901 by a vote in the chamber condemning his perceived weakness in relation to a large-scale strike on the docks at Genoa. The inability of the government, any government, to achieve industrial peace, (it has been calculated that in the period 1890-1901 there were some 1,700 major strikes),[106] was to become manifest over the next decade or so. Although the Socialist PSI had remained united while there was something tangible to unite against, it remained a grouping of strands, and indeed strands within strands. The members of these factions, when released from the common threat, seemed more concerned with their differences rather than unity as a whole. Accordingly, by 1902 the PSI had fractured into three parts, each antagonistic to the others and all, naturally enough, claiming to be the only real socialists. Whilst Turati continued to head the revolutionary wing, the leader of those professing revolution was Enrico Ferri.[107] Ferri said of Turati: 'He hates me because he thinks there is not enough room for two cocks in the same chicken house.'[108]

The labour unrest of the period culminated in the general strike of 16-20 September 1904 – Italy's first. Encouraged by revolutionary elements in the PSI, the strike resulted from the use of the military in shooting workers engaged in lesser industrial action. Whilst the strike was effective inasmuch as 'for three whole days the city of Genoa was left without light and bread and meat; all economic life was paralysed,'[109] it swiftly collapsed thereafter. One side effect of the militancy was the relaxation of the Papal *non expedit*; in 1904 Pius X urged Catholics to vote to halt the spread of socialism.

There is no doubt that up to that time the PSI exerted a powerful influence upon the workers. To the intellectuals at the head of the party however, general strikes were akin to forms of revolutionary experimentation.[110] After the general strike that influence began to wane very rapidly. The workers began to suspect the motives of those who led the party. In the opinion of Agostino Lanzillo, who moved from revolutionary syndicalism to Fascism, the primary aim of the intellectuals, who included parliamentarians, lawyers, physicians, and teachers, was financial success through 'a socialist career.'[111] The PSI had made progress in terms of parliamentary success; despite the restricted franchise there were fifteen PSI deputies in 1897 and thirty by 1904.[112] Had it managed to remain united, and had there been even a semblance of party discipline, it is possible that it might have made great strides, as did the SPD in Germany. It was however not to be, and internecine strife between the reformists and revolutionaries wracked the movement up until 1906, when the reformists themselves started to fragment.[113]

Despite the various stresses, and indeed fractures, and general instability in Italian political and social life over the period, and despite even the disaster of Adowa, there was one foreign policy and colonial aim that remained more or less constant. It became, following the French acquisition of Tunis, an axiom of Italian foreign policy that Tripoli, with its long Mediterranean littoral, must some day be Italian territory.[114] Indeed, those who had a hope of seeing Italy as an independent state had foreseen that colonies, including Tripoli, would figure in the national life. Italian interest in the acquisition of colonial territory was undoubtedly related to what is now termed social-imperialism; an attempt to focus the population on foreign policy rather than domestic issues and to arouse patriotic feelings. This policy was undoubtedly encapsulated by the maxim attributed to Massimo d'Azeglio after his death in 1864 - 'we have made Italy, now we must make Italians.'[115] This dictum was generally adopted by the Italian political elite following the debacle of Adowa, and its use, or resurrection, has been attributed to the former minister, and Governor of Eritrea from 1897 to 1907, Fernando Martini.[116] Martini blamed the failure of the army on a lack of patriotism amongst the soldiery.[117] There had always been a bellicose side to Italian nationalism,[118] but rather than being quelled somewhat by the disaster that had attended the attempts to realise this facet, it became, if anything, enhanced by them. Indeed, to the political elite, foreign adventurism of some sort seemed to be the only answer to many of Italy's problems, which did not lessen as the fiftieth anniversary of unification approached.

The Donkey and the Minaret

Francesco Crispi's 'youthful passion for freeing Italians from the empire of Austria matured as a passion for saving Africans from the empire of France and subjecting them to that of Italy.'
Leonard Woolf, *Empire & Commerce in Africa: A Study In Economic Imperialism*[1]

'I think that the constant study of maps is apt to disturb men's reasoning powers.'
The Marquess of Salisbury, House of Lords, 10 July 1890.
Lady Gwendolen Cecil, *Life of Robert Marquis of Salisbury, Volume IV 1887-1892*[2]

'Italy appears to have gone to war with Turkey and to have occupied Tripoli and Benghazi.
Extraordinary piratical business.'
C E Callwell, *Field-Marshall Sir Henry Wilson: His Life and Diaries,* Volume I[3]

CESARE Balbo, who anticipated the future of Italy as a confederation of separate states led by Piedmont-Sardinia, had written in 1844:

Italy, as soon as she is independent [...] will have in turn to think of that need of expansion, of expansion eastwards and southwards [...] Then, Naples [...] will be called upon to play the first part in this work of external expansion. Whether it be to Tunis, or to Tripoli, or to an island [...] matters not.[4]

Giuseppe Mazzini had also continued this theme in his 1871 essay 'Principles of International Politics' arguing that 'Italy was once the most powerful coloniser in the world.'[5]

Tunis, Tripoli, and the Cyrenaica belong to that part of Africa up to the Atlas Mountains that truly fits into the European system. [...] Already in the past, the flag of Rome was unfurled on top of the Atlas Mountains, after Carthage had been vanquished, and the Mediterranean became known as *Mare nostrum.* We were the masters of that entire region until the fifth century. Today the French covet it and they will soon have it if we don't get there first.[6]

Italy failed to get to Tunis first, leaving only Tripolitania and Cyrenaica as potential Italian territory. To Italian nationalists these areas had much to commend them, being close to Italy with a geographic position that promised strategic value. One Cyrenaican port, Tobruk, possessed one of the finest natural harbours along the entire coast.

The Tripoli *vilayet* had also, as Mazzini stated, been a part of the Roman Empire from the first century BC until its loss in the fifth century AD, and this counted for much amongst those who thought of fulfilling the long standing patriotic dream of building a Third Roman Empire.[7]

Indeed, though there was no 'master plan' as such for taking possession of Tripoli, it is unarguable that the ground, as it were, was well prepared for such an undertaking. The other members of the Triple Alliance were the first to be squared, at least formally, with the renewal of that Alliance in 1891. At that time a separate treaty was negotiated with Germany under the auspices of that renewal, Article IX of which stated:

> Germany and Italy engage to exert themselves for the maintenance of the territorial status quo in the North African regions on the Mediterranean, to wit, Cyrenaica, Tripolitania, and Tunisia. The Representatives of the two powers in these regions shall be instructed to put themselves into the closest intimacy of mutual communication and assistance. If unfortunately, as a result of a mature examination of the situation, Germany and Italy should both recognize that the maintenance of the status quo had become impossible, Germany engages, after a formal and previous agreement, to support Italy in any action in the form of occupation or other taking of guaranty which the latter should undertake in these same regions with a view to an interest of equilibrium and of legitimate compensation. It is understood that in such an eventuality the two Powers would seek to place themselves likewise in agreement with England.[8]

During the negotiations for the fourth renewal of the Alliance, in 1902, Italy managed to gain Austro-Hungarian approval of its position vis-à-vis Tripoli. This was not expressed via the text of the treaty, which remained the same as that of 1891. However, on 30 June 1902 the Austro-Hungarian Ambassador to Rome, Baron Marias Pasetti, wrote an official declaration to the Italian Government, setting out his government's position. This document was to be 'secret' and would be 'produced only in virtue of a previous agreement between the two Governments.'

> I the undersigned, Ambassador of His Imperial and Royal Apostolic Majesty, have been authorized to declare to the Government of His Majesty the King of Italy, that, while desiring the maintenance of the territorial status quo in the Orient, the Austro-Hungarian government, having no special interest to safeguard in Tripolitania and Cyrenaica, has decided to undertake nothing which might interfere with the action of Italy, in case, as a result of fortuitous circumstances, the state of things now prevailing in those regions should undergo any change whatsoever and should oblige the [Italian] Government to have recourse to measures, which would be dictated to it by its own interests.[9]

Having asked for and gained these gestures of highly qualified approval from formal allies, approaches were made to Britain and France in search of something similar. In 1900 an exchange of letters between the Italian Foreign Minister and the French ambassador was initiated. The thrust of this correspondence was that Italy would, diplomatically, give France a free hand in Morocco in exchange for a reciprocal arrangement vis-à-vis Italy and Tripoli. This exchange was symptomatic of a more general rapprochement between the two states. Indeed, it was obvious from this point on that Italy's involvement in the Triple Alliance was somewhat tenuous. As Andre Tardieu, who later served as Prime Minister of France on three occasions, put it in his 1908 book: 'Since the rapprochement, the Triple Alliance has lost its edge.'[10]

The new friendship between France and Italy was notable in several contexts. On 8 April 1901 an Italian squadron under the command of Prince Tommaso, the Duke of Genoa and uncle of Victor Emmanuel III, arrived at Toulon on an official five-day visit. The Duke met with Emile Loubet, the French president, and invested him with Italy's highest decoration, the Collar of the Annunciation.[11] The relationship between the two states deepened. Victor Emmanuel III was feted at Paris during a state visit on 14 October 1903, and at the conclusion of a banquet at held at the Elysée Palace, Loubet commented on the significance of the visit as demonstrating:

> […] the close agreement which, responding equally to the sentiments and interests of the Italian and French peoples, has been established between their Governments. It is assured that the two countries can pursue their national tasks with reciprocal confidence and goodwill.[12]

The following March the visit was reciprocated, an event that greatly upset the Pope, Pius X, who, because he was ignored, saw it as a provocation.[13] The Pope was not alone in feeling discomfited by the Franco-Italian rapprochement. Italy's allies were also troubled. Count Karl von Wedel, Ambassador at Rome for the German Empire enunciated some of these worries in a letter written to Friedrich von Holstein, the 'grey eminence' who headed the political department of the Foreign Office, on the final day of the Toulon naval visit:

> The festivities in Toulon are today happily reaching their end, after having finally after all exceeded the limits of a simple exchange of courtesies. This was to be expected. What causes me most concern in all this is the undoubtedly increasing megalomania in certain Italian circles. France's wooing strengthens the Italians' consciousness of their own importance and of the great value of Italian friendship.[14]

Despite the obvious, and continually improving, diplomatic relationship with France, the Italian foreign office nevertheless continued to insist to Germany and Austria-Hungary of the centrality of the Triple Alliance in Italian Foreign policy.[15]

The symbolic manifestations of Franco-Italian cooperation and friendship were underpinned however by rather more concrete results, such as the mutual abandonment of the concentration of military forces on the Franco-Italian frontier.[16] In the colonial context, the rapprochement culminated in an exchange of notes during July 1902 whereby it was agreed:

> […] that each of the two powers can freely develop its sphere of influence in the above mentioned regions [Tripoli and Morocco] at the moment it deems opportune, and without the action of one of them being necessarily subordinated to that of the other […][17]

Italy also recognized at this time a settlement over the borders of Tripoli and Chad (later, from 1910, French Equatorial Africa) that had been agreed under an Anglo-French convention of 14 June 1898, which delineated British and French spheres of influence east of the Niger River. Further to this, a joint declaration of 21 March 1899 stated that the French zone started from the point of intersection of the Tropic of Cancer with the 16th degree of longitude and then ran south east until it met the 24th degree of longitude (the latter not determined until 1919).[18]

This proprietorial interest in the international border of a territory that, formally and legally, had nothing to do with Italy was not a novel phenomenon. In December 1887

Africa in 1911, showing the colonial possessions of the various powers. Many of the territories bordering the Mediterranean and Red Sea were nominally Ottoman, but only Tripoli (roughly modern-day Libya) was not under European domination of one kind or another. In the entire continent, only Liberia and Abyssinia (Ethiopia) were independent. (© Charles Blackwood).

Italy had reacted with indignation to a report in that month's *Bulletin de la Société de Géographie* announcing that an agreement had been reached between the Ottoman Empire and France regarding the border between Tunis and Tripoli. What particularly aroused the ire of the Italian foreign office and government was the supposed shift of the border, as it touched the Mediterranean coastline, eastwards by some thirty-two kilometres. The Italian Ambassador to the Ottoman Empire, Baron Alberto de Blanc, was ordered as a matter of urgency to seek an audience with the Ottoman government, in order to clarify, and if necessary to protest regarding, the matter. He was assured, both by the Grand Vizier (Prime Minister) and the Sultan, that there was no such agreement.[19] Indeed, real or imagined disputes with France regarding the Tunis–Tripoli border were to be a recurring theme in Franco-Italian relations right up to the time of the relaxation of tensions.

It can be reasonably argued then that, by the early years of the twentieth century if not before, it had become an article of faith, perhaps even an *idée-fixe* in foreign policy terms, amongst important sections of the Italian political class at least, that Tripoli was destined to become Italian territory. The Italians hoped that under their management the country, which had had a reputation for great productivity in ancient times, might become once more a garden. Perhaps most importantly of all, it was the only area on the southern Mediterranean littoral to which Italy could aspire without coming into conflict with the interests of England or France. Indeed, it is hardly an exaggeration to say that it became axiomatic to any Italian government, no matter what its political complexion, that Tripoli was a 'promised land' that would some day belong to Italy.

This was a matter that was not just confined to the political right. On 13 April 1902, the journalist Andrea Torre published in *Giornale d'Italia* an interview he had conducted with Antonio Labriola, the 'father of Italian Marxism.'[20] Labriola was a theoretician whose 1896 *Essays on the Materialist Conception of History* have been described as soon becoming 'a classic in European Marxist literature,' whilst their author is considered as being a forerunner of Gramsci in formulating the concept of neo-Marxism.[21] Trotsky also described Labriola's writings, which he had read in their French translation, as having influenced him.[22]

During the course of the interview Torre asked Labriola about the usefulness of Italian expansionism into Tripoli, and if he, and socialism generally, would be opposed to it. Labriola replied that socialist interests couldn't be opposed to national interests; indeed they must promote it in all its forms.[23] This coincidence of interests came about because Labriola visualised Tripoli under Italian occupation or control as an outlet, a destination, for Italian workers, who might otherwise emigrate to foreign countries and be lost to Italy thereafter.[24] The latter opinion was optimistic; as an experienced reporter was later to put when the opportunity arose for Italians to actually live in Tripoli: 'No Italian emigrant will go [to Tripoli], so long as there is such a place as Chicago.'[25] Labriola the theoretician was to be proven rather too cerebral in his general thesis also; most Italian socialists were to prove violently opposed to Tripolitanian colonialism.

Internationally, the UK, the power with the longest standing modern commitment to, and interest in, stability vis-à-vis the Mediterranean, would also have to be squared. British sea power in the area was centred on Malta, a strategically vital point so situated as to be able, especially with a powerful fleet based there, to control communication between the eastern and western Mediterranean. The sea route through the Mediterranean was, even before the advent of the Suez Canal exponentially increased its importance, a vital imperial artery to India and Britain's far eastern possessions and territories. Prior to the construction of the canal, the journey to India via the Mediterranean had involved disembarking on the Syrian coast and travelling overland through Mesopotamia to the Persian Gulf before boarding ship again. The land portion of the journey was then one through Ottoman-controlled territory and was thus dependant upon Ottoman goodwill and stability, neither of which could be considered reliable or eternal. The more secure sea route involved an immense voyage via the Cape of Good Hope. Accordingly, following the opening of the Suez Canal in 1869, albeit that Egypt was nominally Ottoman territory, the Mediterranean sea-route, and thus the island of Malta, became of vital importance to the British Empire.[26] It naturally followed that Malta then became the base for the largest and most powerful Royal Navy fleet, comprised of the most modern ships.[27]

This was to change however; as Admiral Sir John Fisher, who had become First Sea Lord in 1904 and remained in the post until the beginning of 1910, put it in 1906:

> Our only probable enemy is Germany. Germany keeps her *whole* Fleet always concentrated within a few hours of England. We must therefore keep a Fleet twice as powerful concentrated within a few hours of Germany.[28]

This strategic realignment was, as is well known, brought about by the contemporaneous Anglo-German naval race. Despite the downgrading of the Mediterranean, the British Admiralty still retained powerful forces there; the core of the fleet in 1907 comprised six (pre-Dreadnought) battleships.[29] These forces were gradually withdrawn, the French Navy concentrating its fleet there whilst the British concentrated in the North Sea. However, the Royal Navy, which held that dependence upon the French fleet was 'unpalatable', still possessed the ability to send heavy units there if required.[30] The 1912-13 deployment of battle-cruisers is evidence of this.[31]

Since Malta and the Royal Navy also sat athwart the north-south sea-lanes between Italy and Tripoli, it followed that any Italian intervention in the latter area would have to take place with at least the tacit agreement of the British government. This had been, at least to some extent, obtained in 1902 when Britain's Lord Lansdowne, 'the Foreign Secretary who abandoned isolation,'[32] authored a note to his opposite number Guilio Prinetti:

> His Britannic Majesty's Government have no aggressive or ambitious designs in regard to Tripoli as above described; that they continue to be sincerely desirous of the status quo there, as in other parts of the coast of the Mediterranean and that if at any time an alteration of the status quo should take place it would be their object that, so far as is compatible with the obligations resulting from the Treaties which at present form part of the public law of Europe, such alteration should be in conformity with Italian interests. This assurance is given on the understanding and in full confidence that Italy on her part has not entered and will not enter into arrangements with other Powers in regard to this or other portions of the Mediterranean of a nature inimical to British interests.[33]

This and the other somewhat hazy and heavily qualified statements of support for Italian designs on Tripoli have been dismissed as agreements which, 'the other Great Powers had simply signed to pacify Italy's apparently insatiable appetite for verbal [sic] agreements which would never be acted on.'[34] While this is a statement that is difficult to controvert, there seems little doubt that they were taken seriously by Italian politicians. For example, Prinetti's successor but one, Tommaso Tittoni, was called upon to elucidate Italian foreign policy in respect of Tripoli in the Senate on 10 May 1905. He began by pointing out that he could not detail all the various understandings reached with other states regarding the matter:

> If the necessary reserve incumbent upon the Government forbids me from speaking of the single acts by which all the interested Powers have recognized Italy's prior rights on Tripoli as before those of any other nation, nothing prevents my saying that these rights have been assured in the most explicit and efficient manner.[35]

He went on to make clear that, at least at the present time, these 'rights' so assured did not translate into the physical occupation of the territory. He did however leave open the question as to whether this might occur in the future:

> [...] To my mind Italy should not occupy Tripoli except when circumstances will make such a course absolutely indispensable. In Tripolitania Italy finds the element which determines the balance of influence in the Mediterranean, and we could never allow this balance to be disturbed to our damage.[36]

Though couched in diplomatic terms, Tittoni was telling the senate that as long as no other power gained any territory in the Mediterranean, then he saw no reason for Italy to take formal control of Tripoli. He went on to point out that this did not mean that Italian influence there should be neglected:

> But, if we do not wish to occupy Tripoli at present, that does not mean that our action there should be nil. It is evident that the rights we have upon Tripoli for the future must give us, even at present, a preference in the economic field, in directing our capitals to that region and in promoting commercial currents and agrarian and industrial enterprises. We count upon doing this with the full consent of the Sublime Porte,[37] with which we are in the best relations, and which should have the greatest interest in facilitating Italy's peaceful and civilizing action.[38]

Tittoni listed some aspects of this peaceful and civilizing action:

> Italian importation in Tripolitania, which in 1899 amounted to 1,626,000 lire, today amounts to 2,618,000 lire. It is not much, but some progress has been made. In the same way the exportation from Tripoli to Italy has risen to 979,418 lire. The postal service has been better developed by us, also the Royal Schools, which have at present about eleven hundred pupils, and the subsidized ones two hundred. That these schools have had a useful effect is shown by the fact that in Tripolitania, after Arabic, Italian is the language which is most spoken, and it has become so necessary that also other nations have had to adopt it in their schools, because it is an indispensable instrument for whoever in that country wishes to employ his abilities under any form.[39]

The implication in the above statements was that if Italy's economic interests in Tripoli were small, they were in any event secondary to political interests. Tittoni made this explicit in a debate in the Chamber of Deputies that took place over two days on 12-13 May 1905.

> [I]f Tripolitania may be for us of small economic value, it must not be forgotten that economic penetration in that region comes second to our political interest, and the latter, as every one recognizes, is of the very first importance.[40]

Nevertheless, as he had assured the Senate on 10 May, the 'care of the Government' was, at least for the moment, directed towards 'our work of economic penetration in Tripolitania.'[41]

The most visible agent for economic penetration, also known as peaceful penetration (*penetrazione pacifica*), was the Bank of Rome (*Banco di Roma*). The bank was founded on 9 March 1880 by three aristocrats with close ties to the papacy, and remained rather parochial inasmuch as it largely confined its activities to Rome and the immediate area. In 1892 Ernesto Pacelli, members of whose family had been officials in the Papal States and who had refused to serve under the auspices of the Italian state, joined the bank, becoming president in 1903. Pacelli was the uncle of Eugenio Pacelli, who became the controversial Pope Pius XII in 1939, and was a close confidant of Pope Leo XIII. The latter entrusted him to a large degree with the papal finances and this injection of capital allowed the bank to expand its activities. However its close ties with the papacy, (it became known as 'the bank of the Vatican'), made it an object of some suspicion vis-à-vis the Italian government.[42] This estrangement, it has been claimed, was overcome by the expedient of co-opting Romolo Tittoni, the brother of the Foreign Minister, onto the board in 1904. This appointment also instigated a new policy, initiated by Tittoni, whereby, during a period of 'frenetic expansion' lasting around six years, the bank sought to expand and increase its presence 'in the areas that international diplomacy had set aside for Italian control, in particular Libya.'[43]

By 1907 the bank had begun making investments in Tripoli, recruiting Enrico Bresciani, an Italian financier and businessman who had worked for several years in Somalia, as its local agent.[44] Difficulties were encountered, inasmuch as Ottoman laws placed restrictions on foreign ownership of land and businesses. These were partially overcome by way of diplomatic pressure in the long term and, in the short, by purchasing an existing mercantile venture, complete with land, from the Arbib family of Tripoli; Jewish merchants with joint British-Italian nationality.[45] This transaction was attended with some difficulty,[46] but expansion was nevertheless rapid thereafter and the total value of the capital put into Tripoli by the Bank of Rome up to 1911 was about four to five million dollars. These involved 'a whole series of the most diverse undertakings:' a coastal shipping line, which linked various ports on the Tripolitanian coast, and businesses such as olive oil processing, flour milling, and alfa, or esparto, grass pressing – 'largely exported to Great Britain for paper making.'[47] Indeed, at the onset of the Banco di Roma's interest in the area, processed esparto grass was Tripoli's leading export commodity.[48] By 1911 it owned 'an enormous Esparto Grass mill, the most colossal building in all Tripolitania.'[49]

Expansion indeed seemed rapid; during its first year of operation the bank opened branches at Benghazi (Bengasi, Bingazi), Homs (Khoms), Zlitan (Zletin), Misurata (Misratah), Zawara (Zwara) and Derna.[50] Despite it being illegal, the bank also began acquiring land, either through foreclosing on mortgages or via an agent. These private measures, as they might be termed, were paralleled; the Italian government established schools and post offices in the province. However, despite official encouragement few Italians were prepared to settle, or start businesses, there. This is perhaps unsurprising given the conditions. The American explorer and writer Charles Wellington Furlong visited the area in 1904-5 and later published his observations.[51] According to him:

> […] the oasis of Tripoli, [is] a five-mile tongue of date-palms along the coast at the edge of the Desert. Under their protecting shade lie gardens and wells by which they are irrigated. In this oasis lies the town of Tripoli. It is beyond this oasis that the Turks object to any stranger passing lest he may be robbed or killed by scattered tribes, which the Turkish garrisons cannot well control.[52]

> Tripoli is a land of contrasts – rains which turn the dry wadis [river beds] into raging torrents and cause the country to blossom over night, then month after month without a shower over the parched land; suffocating days and cool nights; full harvests one year, famine the next; without a breath of air, heat-saturated, yellow sand wastes bank against a sky of violet blue; then

the terrific blast of the gibli, the south-east wind-storm, lifts the fine powdered desert sand in great whoofs of blinding orange, burying caravans and forcing the dwellers in towns to close their houses tightly.[53]

Through lack of rain the Tripolitan can count on only four good harvests out of ten. This also affects the wool production, and in bad years the Arab, fearing starvation, sells his flocks and his seed for anything he can get.[54]

The Scottish geographer and author Arthur Silva White had assessed the area some two decades previously, and his assessment shows that little had changed by the time of Furlong's visit:[55]

[…] in Tripoli, along the remainder of the Mediterranean coast [from Tunisia] up to the Nile Delta, except in the peninsula of Barka [Cyrenaica] and the narrow coastal zone in its neighbourhood, we encounter a soil of almost universal barrenness, favourable for little else but the growth of marketable grasses, vegetables, and Tropical fruits. The steppes and deserts extend in many places right up to the sea, and are backed, at a very short distance inland, by stony plateaus. The terrible Libyan Desert itself advances to the coast-line and encroaches upon the Nile Delta.[56]

[…] the Turkish province of Tripoli is so barren that, beyond esparto grass, fruits and vegetables, its products are not at present of any considerable value. The port of Tripoli is, however, the terminus of the caravan-trade across the Sahara, and the oasis of Murzuk, in Fezzan, is another important trade-centre. Fez and Morocco city are other centres of the caravan-traffic of the Sahara, the principal 'commodity' of which would appear to be slaves.[57]

Furlong was of the opinion however that under a 'Christian European power' the introduction of the 'artesian well' would allow Tripoli to be 'reclaimed from the desert.'[58] Presumably the trade in slaves would have to be abandoned, but in any event the Bank of Rome lost heavily, suggesting, as one scholar has put it, that the ventures were essentially political in aim:

[…] neither well managed not necessarily conceived of as likely to be profitable in their own right; rather, it appears, that the directors hoped to receive subsidies and government financial business in exchange for promoting Italian interests in areas staked out for Italian colonization.'[59]

Indeed, it has been convincingly argued that the Bank of Rome was the Italian government's 'chosen instrument' to carry out its policy of peaceful penetration. The intended aim of this policy being to create an increasing Italian presence in the area such as would eventually absorb Libya without the necessity of resorting to force.[60] If this was indeed the policy of the Italian government, then it was a dismal failure. As Eugene A Staley put it:

The desert sands of Tripoli were not too enticing, however, and most of the 'economic interests' had to be created by the Banco di Roma. The Italian population of the whole region in 1911 was hardly a thousand, and scarcely two hundred of these had come from Italy.[61]

Nevertheless, the quest for diplomatic approval of Italy's 'rights' continued, with the Russians being brought into the arena. Alexander Izvolsky, Russian Foreign Minister from 1906, engineered a royal visit by Nicholas II to Italy in October 1909. The Tsar met

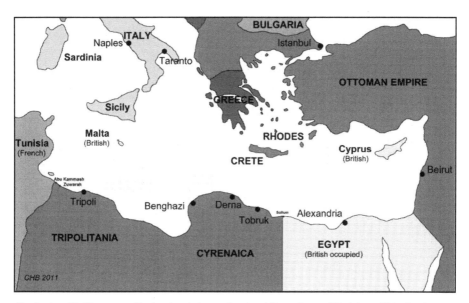

The Eastern Mediterranean. The borders between Egypt and Cyrenaica, and Tunisia and Tripolitania, were not well delineated beyond the coast, and not even there with any great exactitude. This was a matter of little import until the Italians occupied Tobruk and the British feared the creation of a naval base there, whereby Italy would be able to dominate the adjacent coastline and local sea area. This included the only other decent anchorage for several hundred kilometres at the Bay of Sollum. Accordingly, the logic went, if Italy had Tobruk then Britain, via Egypt, would have to have the use of Sollum. This small port was however garrisoned by the Ottomans. To the intense annoyance of Italy, Britain did not move to occupy Sollum until after it had negotiated the matter with the Ottoman government. France also took advantage, occupying the Oasis of Djanet in the far south-west of Fezzan. (© Charles Blackwood).

with King Victor Emmanuel III at the Castle of Racconigi, during which visit their respective foreign ministers Tittoni and Izvolsky concluded a secret agreement. Known in English as *The Racconigi Bargain*, the relevant article of this agreement stated that 'Italy and Russia pledge themselves to regard with benevolence, the one Russia's interests in the matter of the Straits [the Bosphorus and Dardanelles], the other Italian interests in Tripoli and Cyrenaica.'[62] This 'bargain' was kept secret; the Russians failed to inform Britain and France and Italy likewise neglected Germany and Austria-Hungary.

It is of course impossible to judge how the two strands of Italian policy, if it can be called that, towards Tripoli and the Ottoman Empire – the seeking of diplomatic acquiescence in terms of rights on the one hand and peaceful penetration on the other – would have played out had not there been a conjuncture of other factors.

The first of these was the 'Young Turk' revolution of 1908. The CUP proved keener to resist 'peaceful penetration' and this was given effect when a new Governor (*vali*) was appointed in October 1910. He quickly made his presence felt, as was made clear in a statement by Antonino Paternò-Castello, the Marquis of San Giuliano (*marchese di San Giuliano*) who had become Italy's Foreign Minister on 1 April 1910. According to San Giuliano:

Antonino Paternò-Castello, marchese di San Giuliano. The Italian Foreign Minister, Antonino Di San Giuliano, as he was more usually known, had the tricky diplomatic task of steering his and Giolitti's foreign policy in respect of Tripoli and war with the Ottoman Empire between the competing interests and demands of the Great Powers, particularly as these related to the potentially unstable Balkan region and Ottoman rule there. Insisting that Italian policy was based on maintaining the integrity of the Ottoman Empire, whilst simultaneously waging war on it in order to force it to disgorge Tripoli, was a delicate business. (Author's Collection).

[…] the new *Vali*, Ibrahim Pasa, declared quite frankly […] that he would offer unceasing and systematic resistance against all Italian initiative, and he made it clearly understood that these were the instructions of his Government. Hence all Italian proposals and attempts to obtain concessions such as aqueducts, wireless installation, road-making, etc., were simply rejected. In defiance of our treaties the Turks hindered our subjects from acquiring land and from conducting any other similar operations. At Homs, Bengasi, and Derna the natives willing to sell land to the Italians were menaced, and revenge was taken under futile pretexts on those who disobeyed. Contrary to definite agreements, every possible obstacle was put in the way of our archaeological and mineralogical missions. The same opposition was raised against all other Italian enterprises, such as mills, oil-presses, and especially against our shipping. The terrorized natives, fearful of the revenge threatened, dare not avail themselves of any of our benevolent institutions or enterprises.[63]

This was of course provocation, or at least deemed so by Italy, but it did not necessarily constitute a case for war. What furthered that particular case at least to some extent was the more or less contemporaneous rise of a jingoistic movement that quickly gained popularity. This was the Italian Nationalist Association or ANI (*Associazione Nazionale Italiana*). Founded by nationalist writers Enrico Corradini and Luigi Federzoni at Florence in 1910, the organisation organised a vigorous pro-colonial policy, which it saw as only being realisable through war. Indeed, according to Corradini's keynote speech to the three hundred delegates of the First Congress of the ANI in December 1910, war was a prerequisite for what he termed 'national redemption:'

[…] there are proletarian nations as well as proletarian classes; that is to say there are nations whose living conditions are subject to great disadvantage, compared to the way of life of other nations, just as classes are. Once this is realised, nationalism must, above all, insist firmly on the truth: Italy is, materially and morally, a proletarian nation. What is more, she is proletarian at a period before her recovery. That is to say, before she is organised, at a period when she is still groping and weak. And being subjected to other nations, she is weak not in the strength of her people but in her strength as a nation. […] Nationalism […] must become, to use a rather strained comparison, our national socialism. That is to say that just as socialism taught the proletariat the value of the class struggle, we must teach Italy the value of the international class struggle. But international class struggle means war. Well, let it be war! And let nationalism arouse in Italy the will to win a war […] In a word, we propose a means of national redemption which we sum up in the expression 'the need for war.'[64]

No great powers of perception are required to see great similarities between such utterances and those of a later era in Italian politics.[65] Certainly many of the personalities associated with the ANI, including Corradini and Federzoni, were not disadvantaged during Mussolini's regime.[66] As per Corradini's address, and as is now known to be a common tactic of jingoistic political movements, the ANI framed part of their appeal in terms of grievance. According to them Italy had suffered from humiliation in the past that needed to be avenged; events such as the 'loss' of Tunis to France and the defeat at Adowa were examples.[67] Seizure of Tripoli would avenge the political loss of face vis-à-vis Tunis whilst the triumph of Italian arms would do likewise in respect of Adowa. That 1911 was the half-centenary of the founding of the Italian state was a matter also exploited, as was the long standing Italian 'holy mission' to acquire the area.[68] The arguments, if they may be deemed such, of the ANI began to gain traction with the Italian public and, much more importantly, with the political class. A tipping point came when existing liberal and conservative parties agreed to adopt the nationalist position, and, aside from parliamentary pressure, organised grass-roots demonstrations in favour of war.[69]

The Italian government, from 30 March 1911 under Giovanni Giolitti for the fourth time, found itself in a political bind. On the one hand Giolitti was pledged to political reform, one of the main planks of which was a move towards universal manhood suffrage. On the other however, his government found itself on the wrong side of 'public opinion' when warning parliament that invading Tripoli, and thus violating Ottoman sovereignty, could well trigger a European war.[70] It would also involve a complete volte-face in foreign policy. San Giuliano put it thus in June 1911: 'Our policy, like that of the other Great Powers, had for its foundation the integrity of the Ottoman Empire.'[71] There were further, domestic, problems occasioned by a weakening of the Italian economy, which caused problems with both industrialists and trade unions.[72] Victor Emmanuel III signalled his affinity with the nationalist cause when he attended the Colonial Institute's second Congress of Italians Abroad (*Congresso degli Italiani all' Estero*) held in Rome during June 1911. Delegates from 84 cities in 22 countries attended the Congress, which deliberated

Giovanni Giolitti. The period 1901-14 in Italian political life came to be known as the 'Giolittian era' because of Giolitti's domination of parliament and politics. During this period he was to be Prime Minister on three occasions – 1903-05, 1906-09, and 1911-14 having served in that position once before in 1892-93 (he attained the office once more in 1920 and retained it for some eleven months). During the period in question Giolitti's governments sought to democratise Italy by extending the franchise and by introducing other liberal reforms such as old-age pensions. There were many opponents of these, and in order to survive and get them through parliament, Giolitti had to placate the right wing groupings there, the most powerful and certainly most vocal being the Associazione Nazionale Italiana. These were extreme nationalists who wanted a colonial empire, and he determined to give them one in the form of the Ottoman territory of Tripoli (Libya), the possession of which had long been an unredeemed Italian ideal. (Author's Collection).

issues concerned with Italian emigration. The predominant matter they concerned themselves with was however that of Tripoli. Federzoni put forward a resolution for energetic military action to guarantee Italian rights in the province, and this was approved unanimously.[73] Ciro Paoletti has argued that 'Gioletti did not like wars. He considered them useless, especially when it was possible to negotiate.'[74] Indeed, Gioletti is reported as arguing that:

> The integrity of what is left of the Ottoman Empire is one of the principles upon which is founded the equilibrium and peace of Europe [...] And what if, after we attack Turkey, the Balkans move? And what if a Balkan war provokes a clash between the two groups of powers and a European war? Is it wise that we saddle ourselves with the responsibility for setting fire to the powder?[75]

Nevertheless Bosworth posits that the circumstances the Giolitti government found itself in 1911 led it to believe that 'a relatively cheap colonial war' – social-imperialism; an attempt to focus the electorate on foreign policy rather than domestic issues – was a way out.[76] Indeed Childs points out that he is 'persuaded' that it was the ANI and the press that provided the main domestic impetus for war.[77]

Perhaps the final factor in the mosaic of conjunction came with the actions of Italy's ally Germany. The German Chancellor Bethmann-Hollweg had been pursuing a policy of détente with Britain, but this was damaged, by the Second Moroccan, or Agadir, Crisis, which occurred following the dispatch of a French military expedition to Fez, the Moroccan capital, on 11 May 1911 after an appeal for assistance from the ruling Sultan who was facing a rebellion.[78] Though Germany had legitimate grounds for complaining of this action, which was undertaken without consultation, the German Foreign Minister, Alfred von Kiderlen-Wächter, saw it as an opportunity for scoring a foreign policy coup. Determined to back up diplomatic action with a touch of sabre rattling, he had the German warship *Panther* dispatched to Agadir to safeguard German 'interests.' He outlined his rationale in a memorandum of 3 May, before the French had moved:

> The occupation of Fez would pave the way for the absorption of Morocco by France. We should gain nothing by protesting and it would mean a moral defeat hard to bear. We must therefore look for an objective for the ensuing negotiations, which shall induce the French to compensate us. If the French, out of 'anxiety' for their compatriots, settle themselves at Fez, it is our right, too, to protect our compatriots in danger. We have large firms at Mogador and Agadir. German ships could go to those ports to protect the firms. They could remain anchored there quite peacefully – merely with the idea of preventing other Powers from intruding [...] The importance of choosing those ports, the great distance of which from the Mediterranean should make it unlikely that England would raise objections, lies in the fact that they possess a very fertile hinterland, which ought to contain important mineral wealth.[79]

The diplomatic style of Kiderlen has been characterised as being 'to stamp on his neighbour's foot and display aggrieved surprise if he received a kick in return',[80] though he had the approval of the Chancellor in despatching *Panther*.[81] What the German Foreign Minister wanted to extract from France was the territory known as the French Congo or French Equatorial Africa, an immense area about four times the size of France.[82] In gaining this colony he was thinking two steps ahead, inasmuch as he foresaw the advantages the possession of the territory would give Germany should the Belgian

Congo ever be broken up. He clearly stated his position in a letter to Bethmann following upon the outbreak of the crisis:

> The French understand that they must grant us compensation in the colonial realm. They want to keep this to a minimum, and the government will be bolstered in this by its fear of both parliament and the public sentiment generated by the Colonial Party. The French will only agree to an acceptable offer if they are firmly convinced that we are otherwise resolved to take extreme action. If we do not demonstrate this, then we will not receive, in return for our withdrawal from Morocco, the kind of compensation that a statesman could justify to the German people. This, in any case, is my conviction. We must gain all of the French Congo – it is our last opportunity to get a worthwhile piece of land in Africa without a fight. Regions in the Congo that have rubber and ivory, as nice as they may be, are of no use to us. We must go right up to the Belgian Congo so that, if it is divided up, we will take part in the partitioning. If this entity continues to exist, we will have access through it to our territories in East Africa. Any other solution would be a defeat to us, which we must be firmly resolved to avert.[83]

Perhaps thinking ahead two steps led him to neglect to ensure that the first step was achievable. In any event the German actions, in particular the '*Panther's*' leap to Agadir' (*Panthersprung nach Agadir*) as it became popularly known, produced a huge reaction. In Churchill's words: 'All the alarm bells throughout Europe began immediately to quiver. France found herself in the presence of an act which could not be explained, the purpose behind which could not be measured.'[84] Nowhere did the alarm bells quiver more than in the Italian foreign ministry. The British Ambassador to Italy, Sir James Rennell Rodd, reproduced the Italian version of events in his memoirs:

> On the 1st of July 1911, the German Ambassador in Rome went to the Italian Foreign Office to announce to San Giuliano that the cruiser *Panther* had been sent to Agadir. The alleged reason for this step, the protection of German firms in the south of Morocco, was naturally received with considerable scepticism. It was not till nearly two years afterwards on the recurrence of the same date that San Giuliano admitted to me that on Jagow's leaving his room he called in Prince Scalea [Pietro Lanza di Scalea], the Under-Secretary of State, and, taking out his watch, which marked five minutes to midday, observed to him that from that moment the question of Tripoli had entered on an active phase. Thereafter the process of preparing public opinion for what was to take place at the end of September began.[85]

We can probably discount the detail of this incident, particularly the notion that the Italian government was 'preparing' public opinion, but there is little doubt that the episode furnished further reasons for the ANI and their ilk. As one set of apologists for Italy's actions were to put it: 'if the cheque [Italy] had upon Tripoli was not to be rendered valueless in her hand she must cash it at once.'[86] It was believed, or at least the nationalists tried to believe, that if Italy failed to seize Tripoli then Germany would:

> [...] the *Panther* incident showed Germany's heavy-mailed fist in a very ugly light. This fact, coupled with that of Germany's growing influence at the Porte, and the granting of favours to Germans in Cyrenaica, lent colour to the report that an arrangement had been concluded for the *Panther's* successor at Agadir to go to Tobruk. Italy's 'political necessity' was plain.[87]

Such retrospective arguments have been correctly characterised as no more than 'crude propaganda puffery,'[88] but there seems little doubt that similar sentiments expressed at the time inflamed that all-important 'public opinion.' Indeed, whilst American 'yellow journalism' on the part of the Hearst and Pullitzer-owned titles[89] is erroneously supposed to have led directly to the Spanish-American War – 'The yellow press is not to blame for the Spanish-American War. It did not force – it could not have forced – the United States into hostilities with Spain over Cuba in 1898'[90] – there seems little doubt that the Italian yellow press was instrumental in causing war with the Ottoman Empire. As Francesco Malgeri stated it, the press campaign 'helped to create [. . .] a climate of excited expectation, to delude which would have been [. . .] very perilous for the survival of the Giolitti government.'[91]

This pressure is reflected in a memorandum drawn up by San Giuliano and dated 28 July 1911. Sent to the Prime Minister and Monarch, the document outlined the problems of reconciling an invasion of Tripoli with the ostensible policy of maintaining the Ottoman Empire. He considered that 'within a few months' Italy might be 'forced to carry out the military operation to Tripoli,' though should seek to avoid it. The reason for this avoidance being the 'probability (though not certainty) that the blow [. . .] would give to the prestige of the Ottoman Empire, will induce the people of the Balkans to action.' This would then, in all likelihood, cause Austro-Hungarian intervention, which could damage Italian interests there. His solution to these matters was that Italy, once decided on invasion, should act quickly and with such force as to have the matter decided before complications could arise: 'It is necessary that all of Europe should find itself in the presence of a fait accompli almost before examining it, and that the situation which follows in international relations should be rapidly liquidated.' He pointed out that Ottoman military problems, and Italian naval preponderance, would render it difficult for the province to be reinforced. The enterprise was therefore, in the military and naval context, feasible though future Ottoman naval improvements would make this less so in the future. The extent of the operation should go no further than the occupation of the port cities of Tripoli and Benghazi, and:

> This done, we should give to the exercise of our sovereignty over Tripoli the form best suited to reducing to a minimum, at least for a few years, our expenses and the permanent employment of Italian military forces in those regions. It would probably be possible to use the dynasty of the Qaramanli, which has not yet been extinguished, or to come to a solution with Turkey like that adopted for Bosnia in 1878 or with China by Germany and the other European powers.[92]

It was, in the context within which it was constructed, a reasonable summary of the situation, together with a solution to potential problems. Though it was to be proved hopelessly optimistic in several areas, it was only factually wrong in its assessments of Ottoman naval potential. The Ottoman Navy in 1911 was a negligible force. In terms of battleships its most modern units were two ex-German Brandenburg class vessels. Commissioned in 1894 as SMS *Kurfürst Friedrich Wilhelm* and SMS *Weißenburg* they had been purchased in 1910 and renamed *Hayreddin Barbarossa* and *Turgut Reis* respectively. With a displacement of some 10,500 tonnes, and armed with a main battery of six 28 cm guns, these vessels were obsolete stopgaps. The CUP, aware of Ottoman naval incapacity, had sought to remedy it by ordering two new dreadnought battleships from British shipbuilders in June 1911, only one of which was to come to fruition. Vickers laid down this vessel, *Reshadiye*, a slight variation on the Royal Navy's King George V class battleship design, on 1 August 1911. The ship was not to be completed until 1914.[93]

The *Hayreddin Barbarossa* was one of two Brandenburg Class battleships acquired by the Ottoman Empire from Germany in 1910. Originally *SMS Kurfürst Friedrich Wilhelm*, and dating from 1893, the vessel was utterly obsolete when Italy declared war and the Ottoman Fleet wisely refused battle with the more modern and powerful enemy. That this was prudent was confirmed somewhat during the First Balkan War when, during the battles of Elli (3 December 1912) and Lemnos (5 January 1913), an Ottoman contingent centred on the two battleships was unable to prevail against a Greek detachment consisting of lighter ships. They were thus prevented from venturing into the Aegean. The heaviest Greek unit was the armoured-cruiser *Georgios Averof* that had been constructed in Italy and was a member of the Pisa Class, though with a slightly lighter main armament. (Author's Collection).

The Italian Navy was also lacking dreadnoughts in 1911, though had laid four down; one in 1909, *Dante Alighieri*, and three more, *Conte di Cavour, Giulio Cesare* and *Leonardo da Vinci*, in 1910. Nevertheless, against anything other than a dreadnought-armed opponent it was still a powerful force, and against the Ottoman Navy an irresistible one. Its main units comprised the four Regina Elena (sometimes categorised as Vittorio Emanuele) class battleships; *Regina Elena, Vittorio Emanuele, Napoli,* and *Roma*. Commissioned between 1901 and 1903 these were fast vessels, though somewhat lightly armed with a main battery of only two 305 mm guns each in single turrets. There were also two ships of the slightly older, (though with main batteries of four 305 mm more heavily gunned), Regina Margherita class, *Regina Margherita* and *Benedetto Brin*. Completed in 1904 and 1905 respectively, the former was the Mediterranean fleet flagship, though unavailable in 1911 due to explosion damage sustained whilst in dock. Complementing these were two Ammiraglio di Saint Bon class ships, *Ammiraglio di Saint Bon* and *Emanuele Filiberto,* each having four 254 mm guns in their main battery and commissioned in 1901. There were a further three battleships of the Re Umberto class; *Re Umberto, Sicilia* and *Sardegna*. Completed 1893-1895, and each armed with obsolescent main batteries of four British 13.5 inch naval guns (also known as the '67-ton gun'), these ships would have been of little utility against even a moderately armed naval opponent.

If Ottoman naval strength in terms of capital ships was pathetic, its strength in cruisers was equally feeble, basically consisting of two protected cruisers (having a protective deck covering the machinery and other vitals). These were the British built *Hamidiye* (*Hamidieh*) launched in 1903 and the US constructed *Medjidieh* (*Medjidiye*) completed in 1904. Italy though could deploy a number of modern armoured cruisers (fitted with side armour in addition to a protective deck), such as the two vessels of the San Georgio class completed in 1910. *San Giorgio* and *San Marco* were powerful ships heavily armed with four 254 mm and eight 203 mm guns and capable of attaining some 23 knots. Also modern were the Pisa class ships; *Pisa* and *Amalfi* commissioned in 1909. These were also relatively heavily gunned; the main battery consisted of four 254 mm guns mounted in two twin turrets, whilst there were eight 190.5 mm in the four turrets of the secondary battery. The navy also deployed three older armoured cruisers of the Giuseppe Garibaldi class, *Giuseppe Garibaldi* (1902), *Francesco Ferruccio* (1899) and *Varese* (1902), as well as two Vettor Pisani class ships: *Vettor Pisani* (1895) and *Carlo Alberto* (1896). A single, eponymous, member of the Marco Polo class (1892) completed the list.[94]

Ottoman vessels of the lighter types were more modern. They possessed four German constructed destroyers of the S165 class laid down in 1910. Renamed *Jadhigar-I-Millet*, *Numene-I-Hamije, Muavenet-i Milliye* and *Gairet-I-Watanije,* these ships displaced some 620 tonnes and were able to make 33 knots. The Imperial German Navy had originally designated them as large torpedo boats, and accordingly their main armament consisted of three 45 cm torpedo tubes. Slightly older (1908), and rather smaller at 305 tonnes, were four French Durandal class vessels, designated as Basra class in Ottoman service: *Basra, Tasoz, Samsun,* and *Yarhisar.* These might have been roughly comparable with Italian units of the same type, such as the 910 tonne Soldati Artigliere class of 1906-10 or the 924 tonne 1911 Soldati Alpino class. However, to paraphrase Sir Andrew Cunningham's alleged phrase, whilst it may take only a few years to build a ship, it takes a lot longer to build a navy. Put simply, in contradistinction to the Italian, the Ottoman Navy had no real organisation, doctrine or culture in 1911, and it would take time to rectify these deficiencies.

There was thus no way that the Ottoman Navy could catch up with the Italian in any reasonably foreseeable future. Command of the sea was then easily achievable by Italy, and despite the Ottoman territory not being an island it was this command that would dominate the issue; Ottoman military forces in Tripoli could not be easily reinforced or indeed supplied via that route.

If San Giuliano's conversion to the principle of Italian military intervention seems established by his memorandum of 28 July, then his diplomatic moves sought to camouflage this. For example, on 26 July the Italian ambassador to London, Guglielmo Imperiali, had met with the British Foreign Secretary, Sir Edward Grey. The 'problems' Italy was having with the regime in Tripoli were related, and, according to Grey's account of the conversation sent to his representative in Rome two days later, he had told Imperiali:

> [...] I desired to sympathize with Italy, in view of the very good relations between us. If it really was the case that Italians were receiving unfair and adverse economic treatment in Tripoli – a place where such treatment was especially disadvantageous to Italy – and should the hand of Italy be forced, I would, if need be, express to the Turks the opinion that, in face of the unfair treatment meted out to Italians, the Turkish Government could not expect anything else.[95]

It does not seem, however, that Grey expected military action to ensue as a result of the 'unfair and adverse' treatment described. Indeed, on 30 August 1911 he apprised the British ambassador to the Ottoman Empire, Sir Gerard Lowther, of his discussion with Imperiali, and asked him to convey to the Ottoman Foreign Minister the message that 'His Majesty's Government understands the complaint of the Italian Government to be that they receive less favourable treatment in Tripoli than other nations.'[96] Further, San Guiliano's conversations on the subject with the ambassadors of Italy's allies, Austria-Hungary and Germany, held on 29 July 1911, seem to have revolved around telling them that his government might be forced into 'energetic action' by the 'atrocious calumnies' being published in Tripoli regarding the Italian Army.[97]

It was certainly the case that San Giuliano and Giolotti were reluctant to inform any of the other Great Powers over the true nature of their deliberations concerning Tripoli. This was from fear that, as had happened vis-à-vis France and Germany concerning Morocco in the Tangier, or First Moroccan, Crisis of 1905-6, and indeed the more recent Second Moroccan, or Agadir, Crisis that was still in the process of being negotiated away (the Treaty of Fez was signed on 30 March 1912), pressure would be brought to organise a conference where Italy would have had her demands effectively arbitrated. As Giolitti put it in his memoirs (published some eleven years later):

> [...] while European public opinion worried much of the dangers of the Moroccan crisis, our action would have attracted smaller attention [...] waiting for the resolution of the Moroccan issue, meant the issue of Libia [Tripoli] would be itself introduced into the diplomatic field [and] Great Power consent would have been subject to negotiation and conditions that would have much complicated the matter.[98]

At roughly the same time as the British Foreign Secretary was telling his ambassador to the Ottoman Empire to pass on his understanding of the Tripoli situation, his Italian counterpart was sounding opinion from Italy's ambassadors to the various Great Powers. Some discretion was required of these diplomats, as they were required to ascertain the attitudes of the states they were accredited to in the event of Italian action in Tripoli, without giving away the fact that such action was forthcoming. Despite, in particular, Germany's friendly policy towards the Ottoman Empire (*politica turcofila*[99]), but probably because the intent behind the inquiries was kept well concealed, none of the replies were wholly negative; Giolitti specifically remarks on the 'cordial attitude of England, France and Russia.'[100] However during an interview between San Giuliano and Ludwig Ambrozy, the Austro-Hungarian *Charge d'affaires* at Rome, on 28 August the former had disingenuously argued that no immediate occupation was being considered provided legitimate Italian economic interests could be satisfied. Referring to the Italian press campaign, Ambrozy had replied that it was 'a little too much to ask Turkey to promote the Italianisation of the economic life of Tripoli, when daily the press contests her right to the undisturbed possession of these provinces.'[101] Indeed, such was the intensity of the campaign at this time that the British Ambassador was positive that public opinion in Italy, as expressed by the press, would cause the downfall of the government if it failed to do in Tripoli what it was perceived France was likely to do in Morocco.[102] This press agitation intensified during September, when even those influential organs that had previously been neutral as regards Tripoli began pressing for action.[103]

The decision to definitely go to war has been traced by scholars as, according to Malgeri, occurring on the 14th, or, as per Bosworth, the 15th September 1911.[104] This was the occasion when it was agreed between San Giuliano and Giolitti that, despite the potential disapproval of its Allies in the Triple-Alliance, whom they kept especially in the dark, military action would commence in November.[105] However, on 2 September, San Giuliani, after being so informed by the deputy chief of the naval staff, had already warned Giolitti that the vagaries of late autumnal weather made a naval expedition at that time problematical.[106] Having originally forgotten this perhaps he then remembered it the following day; in any event that was when he suggested that the date be brought forward to October.[107]

At more or less the same time, messages from Italy's diplomats stationed in the capitals of the other Great Powers began to show various degrees of comprehension and alarm amongst those powers at what was afoot. Perhaps the most forthright was ventured by Germany, as Giolitti related it in his memoirs:

On the eve of the day on which hostilities were to begin, the Foreign Minister of Germany, Kiderlen-Wàchter, called our ambassador, Pansa, and tried persuading the Italian government not to declare war on Turkey, postulating the danger of perturbations in the Balkans and of the break-up of the Ottoman Empire.[108]

Childs unearthed the original of Pansa's communication, dated 23 September, in the Italian archives, and it is rather more explicit than the version that made it into Giolotti's memoirs:

[…] Italian military action and […] an Italo-Turkish war […] could have the gravest repercussions, provoking the separation of Crete, new risings in Albania, rebellion in the Yemen and perhaps an aggression by Bulgaria with the danger of the destruction of the Ottoman Empire […] in the presence of this eventuality there was room to consider if there were not some way to satisfy Italy's aspirations in the future, who in the first place wanted to guarantee against the peril of Tripoli being occupied by another power.[109]

It may be recalled that the 1891 agreement with Germany, and the similar 1902 arrangement with Austria-Hungary, over Tripoli had stated that consultation would take place before any Italian move on the territory. These conditions, if they may be called that, would be disregarded if Italy suddenly invaded unilaterally. This did not seem to concern Giolitti who had already warned the military, under the Minister of War, General Paolo Spingardi, and the Chief of Staff, General Alberto Pollio, in August 1911 that an invasion was a probability in the near future. He had also told Pollio to calculate the forces necessary to accomplish it.[110] Pollio, who had been appointed to his position in 1908, was a cerebral and scholarly soldier who had penned several works of military history including a work on the Battle of Custoza. He and Spingardi, who had been Minister for War since December 1909, were faced from the start with instituting and carrying through far-reaching army reforms, and these were far from complete when they were informed of the need to organize an expedition to Tripoli.[111]

Nevertheless, it cannot be argued plausibly that such a venture had to be extemporized at short notice. The problem, whilst still theoretical, had been the object of much study, with plans to carry it out dating back as far as 1884. These were updated following the defeat at Adowa in 1896, where deficient planning was deemed to have been a cause of the disaster, and two detailed studies were completed the following year. Further revisions were made in 1899, 1901, 1902, and again when the Tangier, or First Moroccan, Crisis of 1905-6 erupted. All of these plans were essentially variations on the same theme; the military expedition would, after landing, confine itself to occupying the various ports and significant coastal towns. A force of *circa* 35-40,000 men would be required for this operation, and there were no plans beyond taking the coastal areas or for advancing into the interior. That the possibility of having to carry out the mission was in Pollio's mind before the crisis erupted is evidenced by his actions early in 1910. On 22 February he had distributed *Circular 219* to army headquarters throughout Italy. This contained details relating to the mobilisation of an expeditionary force to Tripoli should the necessity arise, and there was a heavy correspondence on the matter throughout the latter part of 1910 and 1911 right up until September.[112]

One document, *Study for the Occupation of Tripolitania*, produced in August 1911, considered 'all the complex problems' and 'studied the eventualities that might arise' following the seizure of the initial coastal objectives. These included defending the Italian held territory from counter-attack from 'the Turkish part of the country' and measures to protect convoys. Further advances were to be limited to consolidating occupation of the coast by occupying secondary objectives. The military occupation of the hinterland was to proceed only by degree, and then only after the appropriate political and administrative action had been completed by the new regime installed in the capital, Tripoli.[113] In other words, pacification, if it were required, of the interior would only take place, and then gradually, after the war with the Ottoman's had been won.

Giolitti was to later claim that, following his August 1911 meeting with Pollio, he had advised the Chief of Staff that his initial estimate of the number of troops required to successfully carry out the operation was insufficient. According to Giolitti, writing in 1922, Pollio's initial estimate was that 22,000 (*ventiduemila*) would suffice, which he advised should be increased to 40,000 (*quarantamila*). He also observed that 'in reality' the number of men required eventually exceeded 80,000 (*ottantamila*).[114] Since Pollio died in 1914 he could not give his version. It is though probably safe to conclude that Giolitti's memory was playing him false when he composed his memoirs. It seems unlikely that Pollio would explain a plan to him that was so at variance, in terms of numbers, with previous, and long standing, versions. Further, it might be thought a curious coincidence that the number of men settled on at Giolitti's alleged insistence was much the same as the number the General Staff had been planning to utilize for over a decade.

It is also the case that Pollio knew what he was facing, at least in terms of topography and enemy numbers, via information collected by the General Staff's intelligence office. The formal establishment of an intelligence section, *Ufficio I*, of the General Staff did not occur until 1900. Its growth was small; it employed only three agents outside Italy in 1906 and had no deciphering or code breaking section until 1915.[115] This was undoubtedly due to the tight financial leash upon which it was kept. A new officer, Silvio Negri, a Colonel in the *Bersaglieri*, was appointed to head *Ufficio I* in July 1905, in which position he was to remain until September 1912.[116] The majority of the intelligence work was directed towards the north-east of the state where lay the border with Austria-Hungary. However, from 1906, Colonel Negri also gathered information on Tripoli, utilising the information gathered by Italian geographers and similar, to produce detailed maps of the territory, particularly the coastal areas where any Italian landings would take place.[117] What seems to have been neglected though is any appraisal of the likely attitude of the local population to a change of colonial masters, which, as will be seen, was to be a matter of no small consequence.

Unaware of the behind-the-scenes machinations of the government, the Italian press campaign had, by 24 September, reached a crescendo. The papers were full of the suffering being occasioned to Italians in Tripoli, claiming that they were in fear of being massacred by armed mobs egged on by militant imams preaching vitriolic hatred of infidels.[118] This was all nonsense, of course, but San Giuliano seems to have used this supposed 'explosion of fanaticism' in Tripoli, fomented as he claimed by Turkish officials, to inform the ambassadors to the Great Powers that the Italian government might be obliged to take action.[119] Others, both in government and otherwise had, of course, deduced that Italian action was imminent. For example, *The New York Times* of 25 September 1911 carried a report, sent by 'special cable' from London the previous day:

> The quarrel between Italy and Turkey over Tripoli has developed with surprising suddenness. The Italian Government has called the reservists of 1908 back to the colours, and warships and troops are ready to sail for Tripoli. […] Italian merchant ships are leaving Turkish ports without waiting for complete cargoes […] The ostensible cause of the trouble between the two powers is the treatment of Italian subjects and Italian trade in Tripoli […] The Turkish Government on its part has for some time been dispatching arms and munitions of war to Tripoli […][120]

Though the press has never been noted for its accuracy, the last point made in the piece had some veracity. Though sources differ, sometimes considerably, the Ottoman garrison in Tripoli and Cyrenaica, which consisted of the regular 42nd Division, had a nominal strength of around 12,000. However, this division had been 'raided' in January 1911 in order to provide manpower for suppressing a rebellion that had broken out in Yemen. Accordingly, there were only about half that many, and possibly only about a quarter, available in September 1911.[121] There were also a number of territorial troops, reservists, and the like, amounting to several thousand. In order to assist this weak force a shipment of 20,000 modern rifles, probably 'Turkish Model 1893' Mausers, plus two million rounds of ammunition, and several light artillery pieces were dispatched aboard the steamer *Derna* on 21 September. The shipment arrived at Tripoli on 25 September and was no doubt swiftly unloaded.[122]

This was the only military action, if it may be called that, taken by the Ottoman government prior to the outbreak of war. Indeed, Ottoman passivity in the face of what was an obvious and building crisis is, in retrospect, astonishing. As one Turkish scholar has stated it: 'the Sublime Porte officially kept repeating that, "Italy had no intentions on Tripoli" until war was actually declared by the latter.'[123] Even in the diplomatic sphere the Ottoman's appeared very slow to realize the threat from Italy. However on the same day as the *Derna* docked, the German ambassador to Istanbul, the former State Secretary for Foreign Affairs Adolf Marschall von Bieberstein, discussed the Tripoli situation with Ibrahim Hakkı Pasa, the Grand Vizier. Germany would be placed in an awkward position if conflict arose; its *politica turcofila* in terms of one state would have to be reconciled with its formal alliance with the other. This was a situation that Marschall, who had been ambassador at Istanbul since 1897 and who had overseen the recent growth of friendly relations with, and German presence in, the Ottoman Empire, sought to avoid. He was it seems pushing at an open door, in the sense that Hakki was prepared to concede almost anything – Italy could construct railways, roads, ports and the like – 'consonant with the character of the country as a Turkish province.'[124] Whilst Marschall passed this information on to his government, Hakki reiterated it to the Italian *chargé d'affaires,* Giacomo De Martino whom he saw next. This information was passed to San Giuliano on 26 September, the same day that Marschall met De Martino to impress upon him that Italy should avoid military action. His reasons being similar to those that his superior in Berlin was attempting to impress on the Italian ambassador there: the danger of perturbations in the Balkans and of the break-up of the Ottoman Empire. Also on 26 September, the Ottoman *chargé d'affaires* in Rome reinforced Hakki's point about concessions to San Giuliano.[125]

Thus, as Childs points out, San Giuliano and Giolitti knew on that date that a peaceful resolution was possible, but rejected such a solution.[126] Or, as Raymond Poincaré, the soon to be Prime Minister (1912) and then President of France (1913), unequivocally stated it: 'To the belated Turkish overtures Italy replied with a blunt ultimatum, in which she announced a military occupation of Tripoli.'[127] Indeed, it was on 26 September that San Giuliano ordered his staff at the Consulta (the Italian Ministry of Foreign Affairs, from its location in the *Palazzo della Consulta* adjoining the *Piazza del Quirinale*) to finalise the ultimatum, which was undeniably bluntly phrased and full of disingenuous humbug (the full text, and that of the Ottoman reply, can be found in Appendix A). The essentials of it though were contained in the penultimate paragraph:

> The Italian Government, therefore, finding itself forced to think of the guardianship of its dignity and its interests, has decided to proceed to the military occupation of Tripoli and Cyrenaica. This solution is the only one Italy can decide upon, and the Royal [Italian] Government expects that the Imperial [Ottoman] Government will in consequence give orders so that it may meet with no opposition from the present Ottoman representatives, and that the measures which will be the necessary consequence may be effected without difficulty. Subsequent agreements would be made between the two governments to settle the definitive situation arising therefrom. The Royal Ambassador in Constantinople has orders to ask for a peremptory reply on this matter from the Ottoman Government within twenty-four hours from the presentation of the present document, in default of which the Italian Government will be obliged to proceed to the immediate execution of the measures destined to ensure the occupation.[128]

This was telegraphed to De Martino on 27 September, and he duly delivered it to an apparently surprised Hakki at 14:30 hrs on 28 September.[129] The 'dignified and concilitary' Ottoman reply, which was in total contradistinction to the hectoring tone of the Italian text, was delivered within the twenty-four hour period. It sought to offer assurances, and argued that differences between the two governments were the results of easily adjusted misunderstandings:

> Reduced to its essential terms the actual disagreement resides in the absence of guarantee likely to reassure the Italian Government regarding the economic expansion of interests in Tripoli and in Cyrenaica. By not resorting to an act so grave as a military occupation, the Royal Government will find the Sublime Porte quite agreeable to the removal of the disagreement.

> Therefore, in an impartial spirit, the Imperial Government requests that the Royal Government be good enough to make known to it the nature of these guarantees, to which it will readily consent if they are not to affect its territorial integrity. To this end it will refrain, during the

parleys from modifying in any manner whatever the present situation of Tripoli and of Cyrenaica in military matters; and it is to be hoped that, yielding to the sincere disposition of the Sublime Porte, the Royal Government will acquiesce in this proposition.[131]

No reply, unless it immediately conceded the unfettered right of Italy to occupy Tripoli, could have satisfied San Giuliano and Giolitti, or indeed Italian 'public opinion.' Indeed, it is doubtful if even that would have sufficed. They wanted a war, not, as Clausewitz had it, as a continuation of politics by other means, but as a matter of policy in order to satisfy 'public opinion.' Accordingly, on the day the reply was received, De Martino handed the following text to the Ottoman government:

[…] the period accorded by the Royal Government to the Porte with a view to the realisation of certain necessary measures has expired without a satisfactory reply […] The lack of this reply only confirms the bad will or want of power of which the Turkish Government and authorities have given such frequent proof […] The Royal Government is consequently obliged to attend itself to the safeguarding of its rights and interests as well as its honour and dignity by all means at its disposal. The events which will follow can only be regarded as the necessary consequence of the conduct followed for so long by the Turkish authorities. The relations of friendship and peace being therefore interrupted between the two countries, Italy considers herself from this moment in a state of war with Turkey.[131]

There is an Arabic saying to the effect that 'he who takes a donkey up a minaret must take it down again.' Giolitti and San Giuliano, with much additional pushing from Italian 'public opinion,' had then quite easily carried their donkey to the very top of the Tripol minaret; they were to discover that getting it down again was a somewhat more complex, and infinitely more arduous, task.

CHAPTER FOUR

Adriatic Veto

'The operations brilliantly begun by the Duke of the Abruzzi against the Turkish torpedo boats encountered at Preveza were stopped by Austria in a sudden and absolute manner.'
Prime Minster Antonio Salandra on Italy's entry into the Great War
on the side of the Entente Powers, 23 May 1915[1]

THE war was scarcely an hour old when a series of incidents fraught with potential danger to the Italian cause in particular, and European peace in general, began. Five destroyers, the *Artigliere* (Flag), *Corazziere, Fuciliere* (Soldati Artigliere class), *Alpino* (Soldati Alpino class), and *Zeffiro* (Nembo class) of Rear-Admiral, the Duke of Abruzzi's' command, the 'Division of the Torpedo Boat Inspector,' were at sea, and approaching the eastern coast of the Ionian Sea. At about 16:00 hrs this force, under Commander (*capitano di fregata*) Guido Biscaretti di Ruffia, sighted two Ottoman torpedo-boats, *Takat* and *Anatalia* (Antalya class) heading north-west just off Preveza. These were part of a six-boat detachment deployed on the Ionian and Adriatic coast and stationed variously at Prevesa, Gomenitza (Igoumenitsa, Hegoumenitsa), and Durazzo (Durres). The Italians moved to the attack whereupon the torpedo-boats split up; the *Takat* (*Tokat* or *Tokad*) fleeing to the north whilst *Anatalia* (*Antalya*) turned and headed back towards Preveza. Three of the destroyers chased northwards whilst the remainder attempted to catch *Anatalia*. The northern chase was successful, with *Takat* being badly hit by 75 mm gunfire and driven onto the beach at Nicopolis with the loss of nine men killed. *Anatalia* successfully regained the safety of Preveza without loss.

Preveza is a port located at the mouth of the Gulf of Arta (the Ambrakian or Amvrakikos Gulf). Dating from an arrangement of 1881, the Greek-Ottoman border ran through the Gulf, the southern shore being Greek. The entrance to the Ionian Sea was protected, on the northern side, by a number of ancient fortifications dating from the fifteenth century, the Venetian period. Some of these had been equipped with modern guns, and there were also a few more modern, though obsolete, works. The principle defences at the time consisted of the ancient St. George's Castle, which covered the port, and Fort Pantokrator, a 'small triangular fort [. . .] built to hinder ships passing through the narrows' dating from circa 1800.[2] This was surrounded by a ditch and covered the

The Adriatic. Austria-Hungary was highly sensitive to any disturbance to the status quo in the Balkans, and effectively vetoed further Italian naval operations, begun precipitously by the Duke of Abruzzi, on the eastern littoral. Only minor Ottoman naval assets were in the theatre in any event. (© Charles Blackwood).

approach to the gulf entrance, supplemented by a coastal artillery battery mounting two 210 mm guns. These weapons fired 76 shells over a period of about 45 minutes at the Italian ships, though without any effect. Other than the coastal battery, the remainder of the artillery, comprising five 150 mm Krupp pieces and twenty field guns, did not engage the Italian vessels.

The Italian ships could not run the gauntlet of these defences without some risk, but it was known that other Ottoman warships were further north at Gomenitza. That night, an Italian officer was put ashore to conduct a reconnaissance of the port. He was able to ascertain the location of the vessels and report this information back to Biscaretti. On the morning of 30 September two of the destroyers, *Artigliere* and *Corazziere* entered the port without being fired on and attacked the *Alpagot* (Akhisar class) and *Hamid-Abad* (*Hamidabad*) (Demirhisar class). The Ottoman ships were swiftly sunk, and whilst this action was proceeding the *Alpino* managed to cut out and tow off the steam yacht *Tetied*

(*Theties*). Meanwhile an operation was undertaken at Valona (Vlore), whereby a destroyer entered the port and seized an Ottoman merchant ship.

Whilst these actions were nothing more than minor skirmishes and, of themselves, inconsequential, they had great significance in political terms. All the European Great Powers, and most particularly Italy's ally Austria-Hungary, were extremely sensitive to any disturbance of the status quo in the Balkans. Might Italy's action prove to be the 'damned silly thing in the Balkans' that would, so Otto von Bismarck is supposed to have predicted, precipitate a wider European war?[3] Count Alois Lexa von Aehrenthal, the Austro-Hungarian Foreign Minister, certainly feared so. He is recorded by Sir Fairfax Cartwright, the British Ambassador to Vienna, as flying into 'a perfect fury' when Italy declared war over Tripoli, precisely because he feared it would increase the danger of war in the Balkans.[4]

Aehrenthal's fears cannot have been soothed by the subsequent naval actions during the last days of September, and on 1 October he had called in the Italian ambassdor, Giuseppe Avarna di Gualtieri. According to Giolitti's memoirs, Avarna had been informed that such operations were in 'flagrant breach of our promises to localize the war in the Mediterranean,' and that 'serious consequences' would ensue if they continued. Albania had been engulfed in insurrection against the Ottoman Empire since late 1910, which the government had difficulty suppressing. Attempts were still being made to pacify the area during the summer of 1911 with little success; the Albanian nationalists wanted the consolidation of four *vilayets*, those of Iskadora, Kosovo, Manastir, and Yanya, into a unified, self-governing, Albanian state.[5] As Austria-Hungary perceived it, Italian interference in this unstable and troublesome region could only be in pursuit of national advantage.

Giolitti claimed that, because he feared that Italian actions at Prevesa might give Austria-Hungary the excuse to occupy Durazzo, he ordered Abruzzi to abstain from any operations near to, landing on, or bombardment of, the Ottoman coast.[6] Giolitti's successor as Prime Minister, Antonio Salandra, who assumed office in 1914, further stated that on 2 October 1911:

> [...] the German Ambassador at Vienna, in a still more threatening manner, confidentially informed our Ambassador that Count Aehrenthal had requested him to telegraph to his Government to give the Italian Government to understand that if it continued its naval operations in the Adriatic and in the Ionian Seas it would have to deal directly with Austria-Hungary.[7]

The order to desist did not apparently get through to Abruzzi until 3-4 October. This can be deduced by noting that on the former date the vice-admiral was to be found, aboard the *Vettor Pisani* with the *Ammiraglio di Saint Bon* in support, off Preveza. From this position he sought permission from his superiors to issue an ultimatum to the effect that unless the Ottoman vessels surrendered to him within twenty-four hours he would bombard the place. He was promptly ordered to desist and no bombardment took place as Abruzzi withdrew.

Commander Biscaretti though was on detached duty, and he must not have received the order by 5 October. On the morning of that day *Artigliere* in company with *Corazziere* and the armoured cruiser *Marco Polo* stopped an Austro-Hungarian vessel in the bay at San Giovanni di Medua (Shengjin or Shen Gjin); a primitive harbour with 'an open roadstead [...], almost unprotected from the sea winds.'[8] A boat party was sent to board the vessel, but this came under fire from artillery batteries on the shore. The Italian vessels replied and after some 45 minutes, and the expenditure of almost all the ship's ammunition, the batteries were silenced and the Italians withdrew. During this exchange the *Artigliere* was slightly damaged and Biscaretti wounded in the foot by a shell burst, requiring his evacuation to the port of Brindisi.

The Austro-Hungarian protest was 'quick and lively' (*subito e vivacemente*) to quote Giolitti.[9] The subsequent events are perhaps best conveyed by a press dispatch from Vienna dated 7 October 1911, that appeared in several English language newspapers around the world:

Italy apologized to Austria today for the naval activity it has been displaying on the coast of European Turkey since the war with the sultan broke out.

The apology followed an open threat from Vienna of an Austrian demonstration in Italian waters unless there was prompt explanation of the bombardment of San Giovanni de Medua. From the first Austria has been displeased with Italy's disposition to carry its campaign from Africa into Europe. The San Giovanni de Medua affair was the last straw.

Italy is probably not much afraid of the Austrian navy, but it was realized that the threatened naval demonstration might be accompanied by an invasion of land from the north. Italy is not prepared to face such a development. It was, accordingly, prompt with its explanation that the naval commander who bombarded San Giovanni de Medua had exceeded his instructions, would be severely reprimanded, and that King Victor [Emmanuel III] had decided to withdraw all ships from the waters of European Turkey as an assurance that the incident would not be repeated.[10]

There is no doubt that the Italian actions seriously worried the Austro-Hungarian government, particularly the unfounded reports of troops landing. Admiral Rudolf Montecuccoli, the head of the Austro-Hungarian fleet, sent reinforcements in the shape of a division of battleships from Pula (Pola), the main naval base, to the south at Cattaro (Kotor). Even if the newspaper report quoted was correct in asserting that 'Italy is probably not much afraid of the Austrian navy' an outbreak of hostilities in the Adriatic, albeit limited, would have been a most unwelcome diversion. Much more serious, would have been the invasion from the north mentioned. This, though unrelated to Italy's Adriatic adventures, was actually canvassed by the Chief of the Austro-Hungarian General Staff, Conrad von Hötzendorf. Conrad was intensely anti-Italian, regarding Italy as an uncertain and untrustworthy ally who would likely ignore treaties and prove hostile to Austria-Hungary in the event of a European war. He had translated these thoughts into, literally, concrete form by ensuring that modern fortifications, which could also provide a base for offensive operations, were constructed on the Folgaria and Lavarone plateau in the Dolomites. Built along the line of the border as it then was, these works were completed by 1910 and were intended to facilitate an Austro-Hungarian advance into Venetia and Northern Italy. With the Italian Army otherwise engaged in Tripoli, Conrad pressed for war, arguing that 'Austria's opportunity has come and it would be suicidal not to use it.' This attitude was in direct contradiction to the foreign policy of Aerenthal, and the foreign minister was backed by the Emperor who slapped down the field marshal. On 15 November Franz Joseph summoned Conrad and informed him that his, and Austria-Hungary's, policy was peace and the military had to conform. A fortnight later Conrad was replaced as Chief of Staff.[11]

Though the fears of Austria-Hungary were assuaged by the political decision to withdraw Italian naval units from the Ottoman coast – thus 'virtually acknowledging Austria-Hungary's hegemony over the Adriatic'[12] – it was not entirely the fault of the politicians that they had been operating there in the way that they had. Or, if Giolitti and San Giuliano and their colleagues had sinned it was by omission rather than commission. Sergio Romano mentions the politicians 'irritation at the navy's initiative' emerging in correspondence between them and the king, as well as with the Minister of Marine, Admiral Pasquale Leonardi-Cattolica.[13] Indeed, Cattolica had to meet with Abruzzi and order him to carry out patrols but not to engage the enemy without precise orders to do so. Prior to this, the instructions from the ministry had been somewhat ambiguous.

The Duke of Abruzzi, Prince Luigi Amedeo Giuseppe Maria Ferdinando Francesco di Savoia Aosta, was a cousin of Victor Emmanuel III and famous as an explorer and mountaineer; Mount Luigi di Savoia in Uganda and the Abruzzi Spur on K2 are named after him.[14] It seems undoubted that this gallant officer, and his subordinates, were anxious to make an impression that, as Romano remarks, would, with 'brilliant success' redeem the ignominy still lingering – the 'grey years' – after the Battle of Lissa.[15] In the absence of clear orders to the contrary it was perfectly natural that they should seek to engage enemy forces; Italy and the Ottoman Empire were at war; there were Ottoman naval forces along the Adriatic coast; ergo, Italy should attack them.

It seems then that what the government of Austria-Hungary, and no doubt that of the Ottoman Empire, saw as a premeditated plan was nothing more than the over enthusiastic reaction of Abruzzi and his subordinates. Of course, the fault, ultimately, lay with Giolitti and the Italian government for not issuing clear and unambiguous orders. When they did so, the navy withdrew, though according to Romano the episode caused much dissatisfaction amongst naval officers who considered that Giolitti and the government had bowed to foreign pressure. Indeed they had, and, as a writer put it in 1913, the Austro-Hungarian veto rankled.[16] It still rankled in 1915, at least enough to have been included in Salandra's declaration justifying Italy's entry into the Great War against Austria-Hungary and Germany:

> We see now [...] how our [former] allies aided us in the Libyan undertaking. The operations brilliantly begun by the Duke of the Abruzzi against the Turkish torpedo boats encountered at Preveza were stopped by Austria in a sudden and absolute manner.[17]

Austria-Hungary, with its common land border with Italy, could then have stopped the 'Libyan undertaking' had the political will been there. The intent might not have been to stop it, but if Conrad's ideas had been put into practice then that would have been the effect. But of course Austria-Hungary, despite Conrad, had no wish to alienate Italy and thus rend the Triple-Alliance over a part of the world where it had no interests.

Britain was the other Great Power that could, quite easily, have stopped Italy's invasion, and although British interests were not directly effected, they were impacted indirectly because of the large Islamic population of the British Empire, particularly that of India. The attack on Tripoli convinced many Indian Muslims that there were anti-Islamic forces bent upon subjugating and crushing the forces of Islam whenever and wherever possible.[18] Thus Muslim loyalty to the Raj 'received jolts' from Italy's invasion, and Britain's perceived acquiescence in it.[19] Sir Charles Hardinge, the Viceroy of India, noted this phenomenon and communicated it to Lord Crewe, the Secretary of State for India in London: 'I hear from the North West Frontier Province where practically the whole population is Mahommedan that the war between Italy and Turkey is sole topic of discussion in the villages and among the tribes, and the bazaar version is that we have conspired with Italy to help her to seize Tripoli.'[20]

Even discounting the bazaar gossip, there seems no doubt that Italy's action caused significant support for the Ottoman cause. The Right Honourable Syed Ameer Ali,[21] the eminent jurist, author, Privy Councillor, and establisher of London's first mosque in 1910, wrote to *The Times* from The Reform Club, Pall Mall. His letter was published on 11 October 1911:

> It cannot be to the advantage of the British Empire or to the cause of peace to draw a veil over what is transpiring in the East as a consequence of the war that Italy is waging against Turkey. In this conviction I ask your permission to draw attention to two facts of peculiar significance.

> The war is causing immense ferment throughout the [Muslim] world, and the resentment it has aroused has so far found expression in admirably restrained language. The news of the mass meetings held in British India, South Africa, and elsewhere to protest against the Italian action has not penetrated the principal organs of public opinion in this country; nevertheless the fact remains that the ferment and resentment are universal and deep.

> The other fact is one of more sinister import – the Italians appear bent on giving a religious turn to this singular war.

> A little while ago it was reported that the Pope had sent a blessed rosary to be hung on the Italian Admiral's flagship as a harbinger of victory over the Turks; and now the Apostolic Delegate speaks in his message to his Holiness of the raising of the Cross of Christendom in Tripoli; whilst only a few days ago an Italian resident in London, lecturing to a fairly large audience, is reported to have urged the expulsion of the Turks from Europe and their 'dispersal over the globe like the Jews.' Similar hopes and wishes have been expressed in other quarters.

> Now I venture to ask all those to whom the interests of the British Empire are sacred beyond temporary opportunities or the demands of expediency, what is the prospect that these two facts open up? England has unquestionably the greatest stake in the maintenance of peace in the Eastern world. She has in her charge the welfare and progress of 400,000,000 of people of whom fully one fourth are [Muslim].[22] As a British subject who has worked for many years past in strengthening the bonds of sympathy between the East and West, I feel that it is of the utmost importance to England, for the sake of her great trusteeship, to do all in her power to bring the one-sided struggle to an early termination on an equitable basis. No one suggests that she should go to war single-handed in defence of the law of nations. But I am not singular in believing that the voice which has often spoken successfully against wrongdoing and injustice can still make itself heard without resort to force.[23]

This 'immense ferment' mainly took the form of collections to aid the Ottoman's and boycotts of Italian goods.[24] For example, at a mass meeting of around forty thousand Muslims in Bengal held on 22 October, one of the leaders of the Aid to Ottoman Red Crescent Society, founded earlier that month,[25] argued that 'according to the Qur'an all Muslims are brethren. Therefore Muslims should unite and help Turkey in every possible way, including the boycott.' Another speaker insisted that the boycott should be universal so that 'not a penny should be allowed to go into the pockets of the enemies' who had attacked Islam.[26] Collections were also made to raise funds to assist the Ottoman war effort.[27] More direct methods were also mooted, as by, for example, when The London

Muslim League, founded by Syed Ameer Ali in 1908 to 'impress on [Muslims in England] the fact that their interests, their well-being and their development were bound up with British rule,' threatened to raise volunteers who would attempt to travel to Tripoli and fight the Italian invasion.[28]

Hardinge, the man with ultimate responsibility for any disturbance or disruption that may have occurred amongst a Muslim population of nearly 66 million, was outraged by the Italian action. In a message of 15 October to Sir Arthur Nicolson, the Permanent Under-Secretary of State for Foreign Affairs he stated that he had 'never heard of a worse case of brigandage' and asked 'Were we squared by Italy? Because I do not otherwise understand how Italy could dare to move in the Mediterranean as her communications are entirely at the mercy of our Fleet.'[29]

British foreign policy was in the hands of Sir Edward Grey. Grey served twice as Foreign Secretary, firstly from 1892-95 in Gladstone's final administration, and then from 1905-16 in the Campbell-Bannerman and Asquith administrations. From 1906 he authorised secret 'discussions' between the General Staffs of France and Britain but kept these hidden from his cabinet colleagues, and the full import of them even from the Prime Minister.[30] As Lloyd George was to put it:

> During the eight years that preceded the war, the Cabinet devoted a ridiculously small percentage of its time to a consideration of foreign affairs. [...] Nothing was said about our military commitments. [...] We were made to feel that, in these matters, we were reaching our hands towards the mysteries, and that we were too young in the priesthood to presume to enter into the sanctuary reserved for the elect.[31]

Grey's policy towards Italy was, in essence, fairly simple; he wished to do nothing that might reinforce her adhesion to the Triple Alliance; Britain and France had need to 'gain Italy against the darkening German menace.'[32] This was, of course, the exact opposite of Austro-Hungarian and German policy. In purely naval terms, if Italy and Austria-Hungary were allied then their combined fleet could be a major factor in the Mediterranean. As previously related, Italy had four dreadnoughts under construction in 1911, whilst Austria-Hungary in reply had decided to build a similar number. Two of these Tegetthoff class vessels, *Viribus Unitis* and *Tegetthoff*, had been laid down in July and September 1910 respectively, whilst two more, *Prinz Eugen* and *Szent István*, were to be begun in January 1912. However, if Italy and Austria-Hungary were opposed, or at least not in active alliance, then their fleets, even with the additions proposed for the former, tended to cancel each other out. Since the British Royal Navy sought to concentrate its main strength in the North Sea, this was a matter of great strategic importance. Politically, Grey saw the danger that any unilateral intervention in the matter had the potential to upset European political equilibrium and thus precipitate a war. On the other hand he saw equal danger in a drawn out conflict causing Balkan problems. Given this, it comes as no surprise to note that Grey's policy in respect of the Italo-Ottoman conflict was one of strict neutrality.[33] He explained it in a message to Sir James Rennell Rodd, outlining his account of a meeting with Guglielmo Imperiali:

> In 1902 we had made an agreement with Italy respecting Tripoli. From this we realized that in Tripoli especially Italy could not tolerate her interests being thrust aside or unfairly treated. Besides that the traditional friendly relations between England and Italy, the friendly feelings of the two peoples were such that steps, which were forced upon Italy in any part of the world

to redress the wrongs of Italian subjects or protect Italian interests from unfair treatment would have our sympathy. But the outright and forcible annexation of Tripoli was an extreme step that might have indirect consequences very embarrassing to other Powers, and amongst others to ourselves, who had so many Mohammedan subjects. I hoped therefore that the Italian Government would conduct affairs so as to limit as far as possible the embarrassment to other Powers.

The Ambassador said that it would be impossible for Italy to retire from Tripoli and asked me what precisely I meant by suggesting that Italy should limit the consequences of her action.

I replied that we could not foresee what developments would follow the action of Italy and I hoped that in any developments which occurred Italy would so conduct affairs that the consequences might be as little far-reaching and embarrassing as possible.

The Ambassador asked whether I meant that we might intervene if there was war between Italy and Turkey. I replied that I was speaking from the point of view of non intervention.[34]

This policy of 'non intervention' was replicated by all the Great Powers and all of them took the position that the 'consequences' would be 'as little far-reaching and embarrassing as possible' provided the conflict was contained in North Africa. Whilst it was much to Italy's advantage, at least initially, it was highly detrimental to Ottoman interests. It meant that when Hakki Pasa sought assistance from them he was in effect advised 'to give way as gracefully as he could.'[35]

CHAPTER FIVE

The Italian's Land

'We advised the Ottoman government to conduct a guerrilla war from the interior of the country.
The Italians may control the coast, which will not be difficult for them with the assistance of the
heavy guns of their fleet. Mounted Arab troops led by young Turkish officers will remain in
constant contact with the Italians, giving them no rest by day or night. Small detachments of the
enemy will be overwhelmed and crushed, whilst larger ones will be avoided. We shall try to lure
the enemy from his coastal bases with night attacks, and destroy those that advance.'
Enver Pasa, diary entry, 4 October 1911[1]

ABRUZZI'S command in the Adriatic and Ionian Seas was not the only independent Italian naval unit. The outbreak of hostilities in Tripoli overlapped with Ottoman troubles in the Yemen *vilayet* and the neighbouring *mutasarrifiyya* (sub-governorate) of Asir (now a province of Saudi Arabia). Ottoman sovereignty was particularly disputed by the Idrisi, under the leadership of Sayyid Muhammad Ibn Ali al-Idrisi, who had been in a state of more or less continual insurrection from 1904.[2] Indeed, part of the reason for Ottoman forces in North Africa being weak related to Yemen and Asir; a goodly proportion of the Tripoli garrison had been redeployed there to restore order.[3] A new *Vali*, Muhammad 'Ali Pasa, had been appointed in 1910 and his policy, aided by Sharif Faysal (Feisal) of later Arab Revolt fame, was one of repression and military occupation. This policy had succeeded, to the extent that by the beginning of October 1911 the Ottoman forces had regained control of the port city of Jizan, Asir.[4]

When the Italo-Ottoman conflict broke out, Idrisi saw it as a case of 'my enemy's enemy is my friend.' The Italians thought along similar lines, and under this temporary and unofficial alliance their naval units in the Red Sea, based in Eritrea, actively aided the insurgents and attacked Ottoman coastal installations. Fear of this policy caused the hurried abandonment of Jizan, with a great loss of stores and equipment, whereupon the Idrisi quickly took repossession. From Italy's point of view this meant it was neutralised, but there were still several major Yemeni ports in Ottoman hands, mainly al Hudaydah (Hodeidah, Hudayda), al Mukha (Mocha, Mocca Mokha) and Cheikh Said (Shaykh Said).

The Italian naval presence in the Red Sea was neither large nor powerful, the main units in October 1911 being the old Umbria class protected cruisers *Elba* (1893), *Liguria* (1893), and *Puglia* (1898), together with the similarly designated Etna class *Etna* (1885) and (later) the Piemonte class *Piemonte* (1888). Other vessels of note included the

Partenope class torpedo-cruiser *Aretusa*, the Curatone class gunboat *Volturno* (1887) and Governolo class *Governolo* (1894). This still greatly outgunned anything the Ottoman navy would be likely to deploy, their available units in the theatre amounting to seven torpedo boats. In any event, and despite the age and weakness of his vessels, a blockade of the coast was maintained without undue difficulty under the dynamic leadership of Captain Giovanni Cerrina-Feroni.

One minor incident occurred on 2 October when *Aretusa* and *Volturno* engaged the torpedo gunboat *Peik-I-Shevket* (*Peyk i evket*) near al Hudaydah and chased it into the harbour there. The Italians then bombarded the quays and forts before withdrawing, having destroyed a small vessel belonging to the customs. As elsewhere, Italian naval preponderance prevented much in the way of Ottoman activity, though there was to be a fight of sorts on 7-8 January 1912 at Al Qunfidhah (Konfida, Kunfuda, Qunfudah, Cunfida).

More immediately though, the Italian C-in-C, Vice-Admiral Augusto Aubry, a former

The Italian armoured cruiser *Pisa* off Derna. The town was approached by the armoured cruisers of the 2nd Division under Rear-Admiral Ernesto Presbitero on 15 October 1911. The division was escorting transports carrying troops from the 22nd Infantry Regiment who were to take possession of the town. However the Ottoman garrison rebuffed attempts at negotiations and *Pisa* opened fire against two observably military installations; a barracks and a fort. There was no reply and after 45 minutes the bombardment ceased and an attempt was made to send in a boat flying a flag of truce. This however this was met with rifle fire from Ottoman forces entrenched around the town. The four armoured cruisers then opened fire on Derna itself, and virtually destroyed it within 30 minutes. Attempts at landing were however thwarted by the sea state combined with the fire of Ottoman troops stationed on the beach. Despite heavy shelling from the fleet, these troops could not be dislodged and only after a stalemate lasting until 18 October did the Ottoman forces abandon their positions, allowing the landing of some 1,500 men. (Author's Collection).

parliamentary deputy and State Secretary of the Navy (December 1903-December 1905), had organized his available units into two Squadrons and a separate Division and made ready to seize objectives on the coast of Tripoli. Aged 62 and a Neapolitan of humble background, Aubry had fought at Lissa and had extensive naval experience.[5] He commanded the 1st Squadron, and its 1st Division, made up of the four battleships of the Vittorio Emanuele class, in person, flying his flag aboard *Vittorio Emanuel III*.[6] The 2nd Division was under Rear-Admiral Ernesto Presbitero and consisted of the armoured cruisers *Pisa* (flag), *Amalfi*, *San Giorgio* and *San Marco*, together with supporting vessels.[7] The 3rd and 4th Divisions were organized as the 2nd Squadron under Vice-Admiral Luigi Faravelli. Faravelli commanded the 3rd Division from *Benedetto Brin*, the other major units being *Regina Margherita* (which was repairing and did not join until 5 October), *Ammiraglio di Saint Bon* and *Emanuele Filiberto*. The 4th Division under Rear-Admiral Paolo Thaon di Revel was constructed around three armoured cruisers: *Giuseppe Garibaldi* (flag), *Francesco Ferruccio* and *Varese*. *Marco Polo*, following the cessation of activity in the Adriatic, was also appointed to the 4th Division. Established outside the two Squadrons was a fifth Division under Rear-Admiral Raffaele Borea Ricci. Entitled the 'Training Division' the heavy units consisted of the older and obsolete battleships *Re Umberto, Sicilia* (flag) and *Sardegna*, plus the armoured cruiser *Carlo Alberto*.

Aubry had concentrated the greater portion of his fleet at Augusta, Sicily, prior to the declaration of war on 29 September. Even before that declaration, on 28 September, the greater part of the 2nd Squadron and the Training Division, under the overall command of Faravelli, had left. This fleet then cruised between Malta and Tripoli, ready, as one enthusiast for Italy's mission put it, 'to bear down on the latter place if the Turkish and Mussulman fanatics of the town should attack our fellow-countrymen or the many other Europeans in residence there.'[8] They arrived off the coast on the evening of 1 October and proceeded to dredge up the Malta-Tripoli cable, which was then cut. Tripoli was thus prevented from communicating with Istanbul in particular and the outside world in general.

Some twenty-four hours later the *Giuseppe Garibaldi*, with Rear-Admiral Revel aboard, entered the harbour. Under a white flag of truce Revel communicated a demand for the capitulation of the town; if no surrender was forthcoming by noon the next day (3 October) it would be subject to naval bombardment. He also offered safe passage to the various foreign consuls, and indeed any Europeans in general, who wished to leave in safety before any action began. Sources differ as to the details of what happened in response to this

Ottoman Commanders in Tripolitania. From left-right: Fethi Bey, Nesat Bey, Taher Bey and Ahmed Choukri Baba. The latter was captain of the artillery.

ultimatum. Some claim that at the instigation of the German Consul Dr Alfred Tilger, who was greatly concerned about the economic harm an Italo-Ottoman conflict would cause, a meeting was convened between the other consuls and the Ottoman authorities.[9] During the course of this meeting the Ottoman authorities, the effective military commander being Nesat Bey under the nominal command of Munir Pasa, passed on the information that it had already been decided to evacuate the town. The upshot was that other than a small force left to man the coastal defences, the garrison had already withdrawn; a manoeuvre proposed by Enver on 4 October.

One of the leading lights in the CUP, Enver had been the Ottoman military attaché in Berlin since 1909. He resigned his post upon hearing of the Italian invasion and travelled back to the Ottoman capitol via Thessalonica (Salonica), where the annual conference of the CUP was being held. According to his diary published in 1918 he was met at Thessalonica railway station on 4 October 1911 by friends who took him directly to the CUP Central Committee.[10]

According to Enver's account the debate lasted more than five hours, but eventually it was agreed that the government would be advised that Ottoman forces withdraw from the coast into the interior of the country and adopt a guerrilla strategy. The coastal area would be left to Italy, who, with the heavy artillery of their naval vessels would not find it difficult to control, whilst the resistance gathered their forces in the interior. These, consisting of 'Mounted Arab troops, commanded by young Turkish officers, will remain in constant touch with the Italians and constantly harass them day and night.' Small detachments of the enemy would be 'overwhelmed and crushed' whilst larger formations would be avoided. Attempts would be made to lure the enemy out of the coastal enclaves by subjecting them to night attack, and any advance that thus ensued would be destroyed.[11] Hakki had resigned upon the commencement of hostilities, but Enver's advice, perforce, was taken by the new cabinet under Said Pasa and announced in the press.[12] Enver was one of those sent to command this effort.[13]

That Enver was entirely correct in his calculation concerning conventional warfare may be adjudged by the state of the defences of Tripoli, which consisted of obsolete coast defence fortifications. To the west, and some way inland, there were a group of three earthen works, designated simply as A, B and C. To the north of these there was a coastal earthwork named Fort Sultanje or Fort Gargaresch. The harbour defences consisted of three masonry works; the Lighthouse Fort and Fort Rosso (Red Fort) built on the harbour wall, and the Spanish Fort constructed on the mole. A larger earthwork, Fort Hamidije or Scharaschat, was constructed to the east of Tripoli at a distance of about 5.5 kilometres.

Despite the decision to not defend Tripoli, there was no formal surrender. Accordingly, Faravelli moved in on 3 October, arranged his fleet into divisions for the attack. The 3rd Division bombarding the harbour forts, whilst the 4th Division took on Fort Hamidieh to the east and the Training Division Fort Sultanje. There were many foreign correspondents present to describe the event; Francis McCullagh of the *Westminster Gazette* for example:

> The central forts were attacked first and the first shot was fired at the red fort on the mole at exactly 3.35 p.m. It was fired by the *Brin* and it hit the exterior surface of the fort, but injured nobody. The second shot was also fired by the *Brin*. When a third shot was fired the lighthouse battery answered for the first time, but the shot did not reach half-way to the ship for which it was intended.

This bombardment – for it cannot be called a duel – was carried on at a distance of only three or four miles and was the tamest affair imaginable. The Italians were so close that they could hardly have missed if they had tried. Consequently they did great damage, knocking down the lighthouse, overturning the guns, and converting the fort into a heap of ruins.[14]

The harbour works ceased firing at 17:00 hrs whilst the outer earthworks, being less susceptible to naval shell, continued firing until sunset at about 18:00 hrs. No fire had been directed into the city; nevertheless several stray rounds had missed their target and caused damage and fires. Much of the population of Tripoli that remained (most of the Europeans had, taking advantage of the offer to evacuate, already left aboard the SS *Hercules*) now found itself in an anarchic situation as the Ottoman forces withdrew. Though many people had fled the urban area out of fear of naval gunfire, those that remained indulged themselves during the absence of the forces of order. One community that found itself under attack from rioters and the like were the Jews. This population was to a degree segregated inasmuch as it was congregated in its own quarters, areas that were well defined and relatively easy to defend. Fortuitously, the CUP Ottoman government had in 1911 begun conscripting non-Muslims in the Tripoli vilayet into the army. It followed that some 59 Jews had received military training and, more importantly, had been mobilised and thus issued with arms.[15] At least some of these remained in the city with their arms, and managed to defend their communities, fighting off the mob that tried to invade the Jewish areas during the interregnum between Ottoman and Italian rule.[16]

The Italian fleet returned at 06:00 hrs the next morning (4 October) and, after being fired on by Fort Hamidije, resumed bombarding the earthwork forts. Within an hour these were silenced, and after having satisfied himself that they would offer no further resistance Faravelli ordered a landing: Aboard the fleet were some 1,700 marines or naval infantry (*fanteria di marina*), and under the guns of the fleet the majority of these made landfall at Gargaresh to the west of the city.[17]

Since these marines were the only troops available to the Italians until such time as army mobilisation was completed, it was fortunate for the Italian cause that the Ottoman military had completed their withdrawal two days earlier. Indeed, Nesat Bey, though still under the nominal command of Munir Pasa, had commandeered all the transport camels within Tripoli and its environs, collected provisions for 5,000 men for three months, and mobilised as many militia troops as he could locate and moved them all away from the coast to the inland oases. The regular forces he had also removed but these were initially kept concentrated around Bumeliana (Bu Meliana, Boumelliana). This was the site of several wells from which Tripoli, via a station equipped with a reciprocating steam pump, drew most of its water.[18] Situated some three kilometres south of the city on the edge of the desert it was, by virtue of the water supply, a strategically important point. It seems likely that if Nesat had known of the weakness of the Italian landing force he would have modified his strategy and attempted some form of resistance or counterattack. Indeed, the landing was only possible because of the Ottoman withdrawal under the threat from the guns of the fleet, which would have been of little utility in terms of supporting any fighting in the urban environment of Tripoli. The marines, under the command of Captain Umberto Cagni (the President of the International Polar Commission, who had been with Abruzzi during several of his explorations), swiftly moved beyond the urban area and formed a thin defensive perimeter on the outskirts of the oasis of Tripoli, the hinterland immediately beyond the city. This included Bumeliana, and since this was well within range of the fleet the majority of the Ottoman force withdrew a distance of around 80 kilometres – or about two days travel – to Gharian, a mountain stronghold some 580 metres above sea level. Nevertheless, the situation was militarily precarious for the Italian cause until such time as army units arrived in sufficient numbers to form a properly manned perimeter and to keep order within Tripoli if necessary.

If the military gaps could not be immediately filled, the same did not apply, or at least not to the same degree, in the civil sphere; Rear-Admiral Borea Ricci was appointed provisional governor. His deputy was Hassuna Qaramanli (Karamanli) who had occupied the position of mayor of Tripoli under the Ottomans. It may be recalled that San Giuliano had, in his memorandum of 28 July 1911, explored the possibility of using 'the dynasty of the Qaramanli' as a fig-leaf for Italian rule. Hassuna was indeed a member of that dynasty, being a descendant of Yusuf Pasa Qaramanli who had been deposed as ruler of Tripoli in 1835. He was in the pay of the Italian government to the tune of 4000 lira per month.[19]

That there was little or no disorder, and that the small force of marines was not overmuch troubled by attacks from the desert (there were several skirmishes) suggests two things. Firstly, that there was at that time little resistance to Italian occupation in the small area occupied, and, secondly, that the Ottoman forces were neither sure of the numbers they would face, nor organised enough, to mount any kind of well planned attack.

Whilst the 2nd Squadron and the Training Division supported the landing at Tripoli City and continued to help defend its occupiers Aubry and the 1st Squadron had sailed eastward, joining some units of his 2nd Division en route. His target was the Ottoman 'fleet'; almost the entire operational Ottoman navy, the battleships *Barbaros Hayreddin* and *Turgut Reis*, together with the cruisers *Hamidiye* and *Medjidieh* and ten escorts, were exercising in the eastern Mediterranean during late September. This division-sized command had sailed from Beirut on 28 September and was headed north-west towards the islands of the Dodecanese (Southern Sporades). Not being equipped with wireless telegraphy equipment the vessels remained unaware of the Italian declaration of war, however whilst off Kos (Istankoy) they were hailed by an Ottoman vessel and informed of the situation. They immediately broke off their exercises and headed northwards at maximum speed, avoiding the central Aegean and keeping close in to the Anatolian coast. As the fleet transited the Gulf of Edremit between Lesbos (Midilli) and the mainland on 30 September it caused alarm at the island's capital Mityleni, being mistaken for an Italian force. However, despite some erroneous reports of fighting a battle en route, the safety of the well-fortified Dardanelles was reached on 1 October and the Ottoman sea-going navy was safe, if rendered impotent. It was perhaps just as well for Anglo-Italian relations that Aubry, despite searching into the northern Aegean, was unable to find his target. It cannot have been unbeknown to him that it contained several British officers on secondment. Headed by Vice-Admiral Hugh Pigot Williams (a Rear Admiral in the Ottoman navy), these constituted the personnel of the 1910-1912 British Naval Mission to the Ottoman Empire. Williams had decided that he and his subordinates would remain onboard after receiving the news of war at Kos, but they went ashore for the duration of hostilities once safety was reached.[20] On 4 October, and under exclusively Ottoman command, the fleet ventured out of the Dardanelles and stayed out for 24 hours whilst cruising in the vicinity of the entrance. Following this brief and ineffectual sortie the vessels remained anchored off Istanbul until 16 October.

His attempt to bring about a naval victory – which would probably have obviated the need to still refer to the 'shame of Lissa' as a reason for going to war in 1915[21] – having failed, Aubry then sailed for Cyrenaica. On 3 October his squadron anchored off Tobruk (Marsa-Tobruk, Tubruq) whilst the destroyer *Agordat* reconnoitred the harbour. Finding the defences minimal, the rest of the squadron entered the anchorage the following morning. The flagship fired a salvo at the 'Turkish Fort', which promptly signalled surrender by hauling down its flag. A landing party of some 500 marines and seamen then went ashore and, virtually unopposed, entered the fortification and raised the Italian flag. It had been a ridiculously easy victory and had gained for Italy the best natural harbour on the Cyrenaican coast, described by the British ethnologist Augustus H Keane in 1895 as 'a spacious natural haven 34 feet [10.3 metres] deep and two miles [3.3 kilometres] long, sheltered from all except the east winds.'[22] The marines were easily able to hold Tobruk, (the Ottoman garrison there had been reckoned to number perhaps 70 men), until elements of the first detachments of the Army Expeditionary Force, a battalion of the 40th Infantry Regiment supported by coastal artillery personnel and engineers, landed there on 10 October.

Meanwhile, the Ottoman regular forces had undertaken a probing attack at Bumeliana on 8 October and dispatches from Tripoli on 10 October carried accounts of two further attacks at the same location during the night. According to a report which appeared in several papers internationally, including the English *Daily Express*:

> The Bumeliana fortification was attacked at 2 this morning with the object of cutting the aqueduct furnishing Tripoli with drinking water. The earthworks were held by 250 Italian marines under the command of Major Cagni. After twenty minutes heavy firing the Ottoman troops were repulsed. […] It had been expected that the Turks would attack the city, and the guards had been doubled at the wells […]

> [A second attack] took place at about 3 o'clock, when sixty two men who had left their horses with the rear guard advanced within forty yards of the Bumeliana earthworks. They were obliged to leave a number of wounded on the field. […] Cagni had ordered his force to allow the Turks to advance to within 200 yards. There was absolute silence. When the Ottoman soldiers had deployed their entire line of skirmishers they dashed forward, but were stopped by heavy fire, direct and admirably regulated, which gave an impression of forces much superior to those which were really engaged.

> The Turks were flung back into the sands. For five or six minutes small blue flames from their Mausers were seen, but immediately afterward they fled in disorder behind the dunes. The guns of the *Carlo Alberto* and *Sicilia*, which could now be used without danger to the Italians, began to thunder, following up with their missiles the flight of the retreating Turks.[23]

The Italians had reconnected the Malta-Tripoli cable, the sole means of communication to the outside world, shortly after taking occupation of Tripoli. They did though enforce a rigorous censorship, so that nothing but information that was approved by them could be despatched. Accordingly, all contemporaneous reports despatched from Tripoli have to be treated with the greatest caution; the very fact that they were sent at all means their contents were officially approved. So whilst some of the details of the skirmish described must be treated with prudence, that there was a fight of some kind is without doubt accurate. Nesat Bey was undoubtedly probing the Italian defences.

Indeed, the marines had held their Tripoli bridgehead for nearly a week unassisted and it could only be expected that Ottoman attacks would increase; reinforcements were urgently required. However, General Pollio had refused to be rushed. In a 'Memorandum on the Occupation of Tripolitania and Cyrenaica' dated 19 September 1911, he stated that 'it is absolutely necessary, not only for the good name of the army but also for the dignity of the Nation, that this expedition to Tripolitania be organised in a perfect manner.'[24] Organising such a venture in a perfect manner took time, particularly as he had to maintain sufficient forces to defend Italy's northern and north-western frontiers with Austria-Hungary and France. He therefore ordered Army mobilisation, calling up the reserves on 27 September, whilst simultaneously drawing units from around the country to form an Expeditionary Force. This consisted of an army corps of 44,408 officers and men under Lieutenant-General Carlo Caneva di Salasco [Table 1 below]. Although the first units had been sent to Tobruk, in response to the potential situation at Tripoli, two regiments were despatched ahead of the main body aboard the fast ocean-going liners, *Verona* and *Europa*. Having sailed from Naples the 11th *Bersaglieri* under the direct command of Caneva, and (less one battalion) the 40th Infantry (forming part of Lieutenant-General *Conte* Pecori Geraldi's 1st Infantry Division) disembarked at Tripoli on 11 October. These two regiments were required to reinforce the line for only one day, as, on the morning of 12 October, a fleet of some 18 transports plus escorts anchored off Tripoli with the rest of the Army Expeditionary Force. With the arrival of Caneva's main body, the Italians were now secure in Tripoli and Tobruk.

Table 1.

Army Expeditionary Force
Order of Battle: October 1911
(Excluding ancillary, such as medical and
veterinary, units)

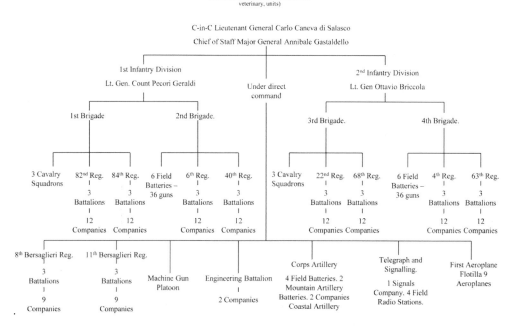

The Armoured Cruiser *Pisa*. An excellent view from the starboard quarter of the stern armament on this armoured cruiser. The stern turret contained twin 254 mm (10 inch) guns whilst the wing turret was armed with a pair of 190.5 mm (7.5 inch) weapons. The two 75mm (3 inch) guns, the lower being casemate mounted, are also visible. The *Pisa* and her sister *Amalfi* were powerful examples of their type, though saw no ship-to-ship combat due to the Ottoman Navy's (sensible) refusal to give battle.
(George Grantham Bain Collection/Library of Congress)

Pollio's instructions from San Giuliano via Spingardi stipulated that the primary aims of the occupation force were twofold; the coastal region was to be occupied and the Ottoman forces were to be neutralised. There was to be no advance into the hinterland and, as the Italians were expecting to be welcomed as liberators, the non-Ottoman population was to be respected.[25] Indeed, the army plan for the operation, as tweaked in August 1911, had called for nothing more than had now been accomplished other than 'a few displays of force at coastal points duly selected as secondary objectives.' Occupation of the rest of the *vilayet* 'by degrees' was perceived to be achievable by non-military means via 'appropriate political and administrative action on the part of the new government installed at Tripoli.'[26] This 'new government' was installed on 13 October when Caneva was named as Governor in succession to Borea Ricci. On the same day the marines were relieved of their military duties and rejoined the fleet.

The navy then began operations against the secondary objectives. Derna (Darnah) was approached by the armoured cruisers of the 2nd Division under Rear-Admiral Presbitero, escorting transports carrying troops from the 22nd Infantry Regiment, on 15 October. The town, some 200 kilometres west of Tobruk, is located at the eastern end of the inland Jebel Akhdar mountain range, which rises to some 500 metres and is one of the few regions that are forested. The area receives an annual rainfall of some 400-600 millimetres, meaning it was one of the few fertile portions of the territory the Italians were attempting to conquer. After the Ottoman garrison rebuffed attempts at negotiations, *Pisa*, Presbitero's flagship, opened fire against two observably military installations; a barracks and a fort. Probably intended as an object lesson in the futility of resistance, fire continued for some 45 minutes but was not answered. Having ceased fire, Presbitero attempted to send in a boat flying a flag of truce, but this was met with rifle fire from Ottoman forces entrenched around the town. The four armoured cruisers then opened fire on Derna itself, and virtually destroyed it within 30 minutes. Attempts at landing via boat were however thwarted by the heavy sea combined with the fire of Ottoman troops stationed on the beach. Despite heavy shelling from the fleet, these troops could not be dislodged and thus undertaking an opposed amphibious landing was hazardous in the extreme. It was perhaps fortunate for the Italian Navy that after a stalemate lasting until 18 October the Ottoman forces abandoned their positions, allowing the landing of some 1,500 men.[27]

Whilst the operations against Derna proceeded, the armoured cruisers of the 4th Division, under Rear-Admiral Thaon di Revel, were despatched to carry out a similar mission against Homs (Al Khums, Khoms, Lebda), about 130 kilometres east of Tripoli. Aboard the transports were the 8th *Bersaglieri* Regiment and a field artillery battery, but a landing was found impossible to carry out on 16 October due, as at Derna, to the heavy sea and entrenched opposition. The defenders were estimated to number some 500 regulars with around 1,000 irregulars. The 4th Division conducted a long bombardment of the Ottoman positions, but it was not until 21 October that, the defenders having withdrawn, a difficult landing, during which two boatloads of soldiers were capsized, was completed.

If Derna and Homs were taken and occupied relatively easily then the overlapping operation at Benghazi contrasted somewhat. There the Italian force had to carry out that most hazardous of manoeuvres; an opposed amphibious landing. The operation was undertaken by marines supported by elements of the 2nd Division of the Army Expeditionary Force. Though Briccola, as divisional chief, was in ultimate command, the force that was designated to undertake the operation was the 4th Brigade under Major-General Giovanni Ameglio, who had with him the 4th Regiment and two battalions from the 63rd Regiment. They were convoyed from Tripoli in eight transports under escort from Aubry's 1st Division, arriving on the morning of 18 October. Although Benghazi was the second largest town in the *vilayet*, its population was estimated to be only around 5,000, it being a small trading post for the trans-Sahara caravan trade and an outpost for the Ottoman military.[28] The permanent defences were minimal, consisting of a 16th century Ottoman fort, but there were a number of troops there, estimated at between 400-1,000 regulars and 2,500-3,000 irregulars equipped with about twelve field artillery pieces.

A Bersaglieri officer, Tullio Irace, was despatched with one companion under a flag of truce to demand the surrender of the place.

> Towards noon the Admiral sent me shorewards with one other officer, to deliver to the Mutessarif, or Governor, his 'ultimatum' to surrender. Stopping our steam launch just off the Custom-house, we send to request the foreign Consuls to be good enough to meet us in conference [...] We present to the Consuls the Admiral's 'ultimatum' already made known to the Mutessarif. Time for decision is granted till 8 o'clock on the following morning: if by that hour the city has not hoisted the white flag or otherwise given proof of its decision to surrender, we should be compelled to have recourse to a forcible landing of troops.[29]

No sign of the surrender having been given, the next morning, with the weather being decidedly unpleasant, the Italians began operations. These opened with naval gunfire being directed on four areas: Juliana (Giuliana) beach ('so called because the

daughter of a foreign consul, of that name, had been buried there after an epidemic'[30])
where it was intended to land the troops, the Berca (Berka) barracks and fortress and
nearby Governor's residence, and a magazine to the north of the town.

The marines, numbering about 800, landed unopposed at about 08:50 hrs and moved
to occupy positions in the dunes behind the beach and, using two 75 mm mountain
artillery pieces, established a battery on high ground at Cape Juliana. It seems likely that
the descent on Juliana Beach surprised the defenders. Had they foreseen it they could
have occupied Cape Juliana and enfiladed the landing ground, even though any such
forward defence would have been rendered problematical by naval gunfire. Indeed, a
large proportion of the Ottoman force had been stationed to the north of Benghazi, and
those south of the town were mainly deployed away from the shore. The latter group's
main position was on the narrow ground between the shallow water and a marsh to the
south of it, with a thin line extended from the marsh to the south-west almost to Buscaiba
Point. Perhaps realising the initial error of failing to occupy Cape Juliana an attempt was
made to capture the Italian battery there and take the high ground. This manoeuvre was
though thwarted by naval gunfire.

The marines managed to secure the beach to the extent that engineers were able to
construct piers onto which troops could disembark from the ships' boats, which, as well
as a number of pontoon-floats and lighters, were used to ferry them from the transports.
At 10:00 hrs Ameglio led the first of the military contingent ashore and took command
of the beachhead. He ordered the marines to advance further inland in order to prevent
any interference with the subsequent waves of troops. As they moved between the shallow
water and the marsh they came up against the Ottoman position and found themselves
unable to advance. However, they were quickly reinforced as more troops landed and
were supported by the mountain battery on Cape Juliana. The divisional commander
landed at 12:20 hrs and according to his retrospective report of the situation:

> A strong detachment of the 4th Regiment and marines were entrenched, facing south and
> east, at the south end of the beach on the high ground near Point Buscaiba. Between the salt
> lake and the beach a mountain battery was in action, with the main body of the 4th Regiment
> forming up close by. Between this battery and the higher ground on Point Giuliana were the
> main body of the marines, detachments of the 4th and 63rd Regiments and the second
> mountain battery. On the high ground at Point Giuliana were two companies of the
> 63rd Regiment.[31]

By this time two battalions of 4th Regiment and one battalion of the 63rd Regiment
were ashore, but the weather was becoming rougher causing problems in the landing of
troops and equipment. It had been found impossible to disembark the mules that carried
the mountain artillery – so the guns could not easily be moved – and ammunition in
particular was running short. Briccola therefore decided to regroup and await
reinforcement and supplies whilst considering the next phase of the operation.
The objective was Berca, and the attack was to be made by advancing on and thus holding
the enemy between the shallow water and the marsh whilst a second formation circled
around the marsh and approached from the south.

The attack resumed at 15:30 hrs and was successful, with the result that by about
18:30 the Italians had dislodged the defenders. They advanced north and then north-
west around the salt-lake, and past Berca, where the Italian flag was hoisted just as the sun
set, to Sidi Ussein and the outskirts of Benghazi. It was now dark, but the defenders in

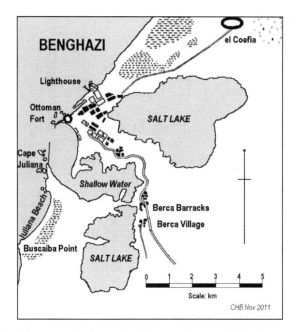

Benghazi. Utilizing their command of the sea the Italians made an amphibious descent at Juliana Beach, Benghazi, on the morning of 19 October 1911. Though the landings were virtually unopposed, strong resistance was encountered on the neck of land between the shallow water and the marshy salt lake. The enemy was fixed there whilst a second formation circled around the marsh and approached from the south. By about 18:30 hrs the Italians had dislodged the defenders and they advanced north and then north-west to Berca, where the Italian flag was hoisted. It was now dark but the defenders in Benghazi continued to fire at the invaders. The Italian fleet then bombarded the town for some twenty minutes, after which the white flag was raised. Amongst the buildings destroyed by the bombardment was the British Consulate. (© Charles Blackwood).

Benghazi continued to fire at the Italians. Briccola therefore signalled to the fleet to bombard the town. The shelling started at 19:00 hrs and lasted some twenty minutes, after which the white flag was raised. However, amongst the buildings destroyed was the British Consulate, though the consul, Francis Jones, was unhurt. However, eight Maltese British subjects were amongst the twelve Europeans killed – nobody bothered to count how many non-Europeans perished – and according to Irace the British Consul was furious; 'The Italians have fired on the British flag. This act will cost Italy dear!'[32] It didn't! In fact the only 'cost' was to Sir Edward Grey, who had to endure some rather irate questioning in the House of Commons.[33]

The Italian forces took possession of Benghazi on the morning of 20 October. They were unopposed within the urban area as, unable to respond to naval gunfire, the Ottoman forces had retreated to the hills inland of the town. Indeed, it had been the fire support from offshore that had made the enterprise possible. As a later exponent of the art, Sir Roger Keyes, was to put it: 'To launch and maintain an amphibious operation, it is necessary to possess Sea Supremacy in the theatre of the enterprise [...].'[34]

The Italian Monument to the Fallen at Benghazi (*Monumento ai caduti della Cirenaica*).
Those who perished during the operations to captures Benghazi on 19-20 October 1911 were
commemorated by an obelisk-like structure erected on Cape Juliana. Designed by Marcello Piacentini it
bore the words 'At dawn on 19 October 1911, the ships of Italy gave Cirenaica Latin civilization.'
It was bombed by the RAF during the Second World War and destroyed. (Author's Collection).

The possession of such superiority does not of itself guarantee success however, and there can be no doubt that the Italian landing forces had performed a hazardous operation with skill. Some 6,000 troops were eventually landed, with losses amounting to 36 killed and 88 wounded, the most senior amongst the former being *guardiamarina* (midshipman) Mario Bianco. The dead in general were commemorated by a *Monumento ai caduti della Cirenaica* erected on Cape Juliana. Designed by Marcello Piacentini it bore the words '*At dawn on 19 October 1911, the ships of Italy gave Cirenaica Latin civilization.*' (The RAF bombed it in 1941, presumably in error). [35] The death of Bianco in particular inspired the poet Gabriele D'Annunzio to write *La canzone di Mario Bianco*, one of his *Canzoni delle gesta d'Oltremare* ('Songs of Overseas Deeds' or 'Songs from the Overseas Action') in 1912. This work was initially suppressed and then censored by the Giuliotto government, mainly because of one song entitled *La canzone dei Dardanelli*, which attacked other European nations, particularly Italy's allies Austria–Hungary and Germany, for their indifference towards Ottoman barbarity and general dislike of Italy. [36]

By 21 October 1911, Italian arms had gained all that the politicians had asked of them. However, the plan for invading Tripoli left several interrelated questions unanswered. One of the most important from the military point of view being what was to be done to the Ottoman forces that had retreated from the beachheads? Caneva had pointed out to the Minister for War on 18 October the difficulties he foresaw in this regard. He stated that operations against the 'main nucleus of regular Turkish troops' were problematical because such a body did not exist. The Ottoman forces had become 'dislocated,' and now formed only 'meagre detachments,' which were at least six hours march from Tripoli. Dealing with them was a political rather than a military matter, achievable via a peace treaty with the Ottoman Empire rather than by force.[37] Indeed, wearing his political hat as Governor, Caneva had, on 12 October, issued a proclamation to the inhabitants of Tripoli, and indeed to the wider population if they got to see it, to the effect that they had been liberated from Ottoman rule. They were assured that their own chiefs, under the patronage of Victor Emmanuel III, would govern them. All their customs and religious laws would be respected, whilst unjust Ottoman taxes would be abolished. The address concluded by reiterating that Italy desired that Tripoli shall remain a land of Islam under the protection of Italy.[38]

It has to be admitted that Caneva had made several good points to his superior. The Italian army in general, and the Expeditionary Force that he commanded in particular, was neither trained nor equipped for desert warfare. This extended to small matters; as Francis McCullagh noted, 'The water bottle of the French soldier in Algiers always holds two litres. The water bottle of the Italian soldier here does not hold half a litre.'[39] This was of no small significance given that the inland oases where the Ottoman forces were located were anything from 10 to 50 kilometres away or, as Caneva had pointed out, a six-hour march at least. In terms of clothing the officers and men wore the low visibility grey-green uniform that had been introduced following the lessons by observers of the Russo-Japanese War of 1904-5.[40] McCullagh, who had also observed the Russo-Japanese War, was unimpressed with its suitability: 'It is a thick, grey, heavy material, quite hot enough for St Petersburg at this time of year, but absurdly, criminally, out of place here. It closely resembles the stuff used in Ulster for making heavy overcoats.' [41]

Given that Caneva considered that military operations against the 'meagre detachments' of Ottoman forces was militarily beyond the capabilities of his force, he had made the best of his situation by ensuring that the Italian position, particularly at Tripoli City, was as secure as possible. There the thin lines of marines had been replaced with entrenched soldiers, some 37,000 in number, backed up with their own artillery and, ultimately, by the guns of the fleet. The Italian trenches formed a rough somewhat flattened semicircle around Tripoli and its oasis, running south-east from the coast at Fort Sultanje, to the outskirts of the oasis encompassing the wells at Bumeliana. From there they arced back north-eastward towards the coast, touching it slightly beyond Fort Hamidije at a place called Shara Shatt (Sharashet, Shara-shett, Shar al-shatt). The total area enclosed was about 10.5 hectares.

The line between Fort Sultanje and Bumeliana was held by four battalions of Gaetano Giardino's 2nd Brigade, two from each of the regiments, whilst from Bumeliana to Fort Sidi Messri the 1st Brigade under Luigi Rainaldi manned the entrenchments. From Fort Sidi Messri to the sea, a front of around six kilometres, about 1,800 men of the 11th Bersaglieri were deployed; the 1st and 3rd Battalions were between Sidi Messri and the plateau of Henni, with the 2nd Battalion between there and the sea, based on Shara Shatt. It was to be their misfortune on 23 October to discover that far from being militarily defeated, the Ottoman forces were not only capable of offensive action, but had managed to recruit significant allies. This, and a similar action two days later, and more particularly the Italian reaction, was to profoundly change the course and nature of the war.

CHAPTER SIX

The Battle of Tripoli

'It is true that soldiers sometimes commit excesses which their officers cannot prevent;
but, in general, a commanding officer is responsible for the acts of those under his orders.
Unless he can control his soldiers, he is unfit to command them.'
H W Halleck, International Law: or, Rules Regulating
the Intercourse of States in Peace and War, 1861[1]

T HE inability of the Army Expeditionary Force to project its power much beyond
the Tripoli oasis prevented any interference with the Ottoman forces outside. Nesat
Bey, who based his command at the oasis of Ain Zara, thus had time to assess the
situation and to organise and arm the Arab and Berber tribesmen that wished to join the
fight against the Italians. Though the numbers of regular army troops available to him vary
widely according to source, there were probably somewhere around 4,000 *nizams*
(Regular Ottoman Troops) under his command. This force possessed a small contingent
of artillery comprised of four field batteries and two mountain batteries.

Italian inactivity also allowed a potentially weak area in the Italian line to be identified.
All the evidence suggests that Caneva, and his political and military masters at home,
were labouring under an illusion concerning the attitude of the Arab and Berber
population to the occupation. They believed, and honestly so it would appear, that this
population was overwhelmingly hostile to Ottoman rule and friendly towards Italy.
As one commentator wryly put it:

[T]he Italians had not the slightest idea of how the administration of an occupied territory
should be carried out. The General Staff evidently believed in grandiloquent proclamations, and
the arrival of the army was signalled by the publication of several proclamations, some of
which, if I mistake not, were plagiarisms from Prussian proclamations found in some history
of the Franco-German War. […] no adequate measures were taken, either to police the town
and its environment, or to picket the outlying villages and hamlets in the palm-groves. […]
A descendant of the house of Karamanli was appointed as vice-governor of the town, and
some Moslem as the mayor. With these measures the entire staff and army reposed a confidence
in the Arab population which, though engaging enough in the simplicity that prompted it, was
a culpable weakness in the stern path of war.[2]

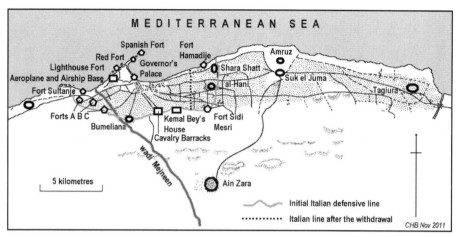

The City and Oasis of Tripoli, and Ain Zara, in October-November 1911. Following their initial landings, and the withdrawal of Ottoman forces to Ain Zara, the Italians dug in around the southern edge of the Oasis of Tripoli, but their eastern line ran north-south within the dense oasis. This was a front of around six kilometres, defended by about 1,800 men of the 11th Bersaglieri Regiment. On 23 October 1911 the Ottoman forces assaulted this line, an attack coordinated with a rising of the people of the oasis. Attacked from front and rear the Italians lost 21 officers and 482 other ranks missing or killed, though the assault did not succeed in totally penetrating their lines and occupying the oasis. The next morning a further assault breached the Italian lines around Kemal Bey's house, though again did not succeed in a complete penetration. The Italian reaction to The Battle of Tripoli was drastic, and out-of-control soldiery massacred thousands of the oasis' inhabitants. That the Italian command believed they had come close to disaster is borne out by their response. In an attempt to bolster the strength of the defensive line it was shortened and withdrawn some two kilometres on the afternoon of 26 October. Huge reinforcements were also ordered from Italy. Any Italian illusions that their conquest would be easy were now dispelled.
(© Charles Blackwood).

It is difficult to ascertain where this belief originated. McCullagh blames Captain Pietro Verri of the General Staff, who had travelled to Tripoli prior to the outbreak of hostilities. Utilising the pseudonym Vincenzo Parisio, and pretending to inspect the Italian post offices, he had gathered information on the disposition of Ottoman forces and defences and passed this information on to the invasion force. Verri arrived only a week or so prior to the declaration of war however, so any inquiries he might have made would inevitably have been somewhat cursory. In any event, if he did advise that the population would be receptive to an Italian takeover he was to be proved mistaken. Angelo del Boca finds Carlo Galli, head of the consulate general in Tripoli, guilty of much the same attitude. He quotes his communication of 19 August 1911:

> Once we have overwhelmed the resistance of the garrison in Tripoli, the small garrisons will fall, nor should we fear in any case that there will be a call for holy war. The coastal population in any case would not answer the call, because it is all too well aware of what a European government can do. And the tribes that might conceivably respond to such an appeal are poor, unarmed, or too distant to present any real threat.[3]

There seems little doubt that there was in any event a great deal of wishful thinking on the part of the Italian government and General Staff.[4] Indeed Senator Maggiorino Ferraris, a former government minister and the proprietor and chief editor of *La Nuova Antologia*, admitted it in the February 1912 edition of the magazine. He 'frankly' acknowledged 'that the Italian nation was deceived as to the probable attitude of the Arabs towards them, and that the resistance of the latter has introduced an entirely new element into the military situation.'[5] In concrete terms though, this deception, this 'confidence in the Arab population,' led to some errors in the defensive arrangements of the territory occupied.

The Italian entrenchments encompassed most, though not all, of the oasis of Tripoli, so that immediately behind the greater part of the line, and stretching backwards to the town itself, were a number of villages and hamlets. These were interspersed amongst a large number of gardens, orchards, olive groves, and the like, intersected by sandy roads and winding paths. Earthen walls or hedges formed of prickly pear cactus delineated the roads and gardens, the whole forming what the journalist William Kidston McClure, who visited the area in November 1911, called 'a bewildering labyrinth.'[6] Dotted amid this maze were the dwellings of the local people, and where a number of these were clustered together, usually around a well, there was a hamlet or village.

The Tripoli Oasis. Following the initial landings the Italian entrenchments roughly encompassed the majority of the periphery of the oasis of Tripoli, so that immediately behind the greater part of the line, and stretching backwards to the city itself, were several villages and hamlets. These were interspersed amongst a large number of gardens, orchards, olive groves, and the like, intersected by sandy roads and winding paths. Earthen walls or hedges formed of prickly pear cactus delineated the roads and gardens, the whole forming 'a bewildering labyrinth.' The eastern portion of the Italian line was within the oasis however, which allowed the enemy to approach unseen. This part of the line was broken during the Battle of Tripoli (23-24 October 1911). (Author's Collection).

To the south and west the Italian trenches generally overlooked scrub and desert, meaning that the opportunities for an enemy to concentrate and launch a surprise attack were limited. This had not prevented several approaches being made by Ottoman forces, particularly in the region of Bumeliana, but these had seemingly achieved little. They had, nevertheless, tended to focus Italian attention on that portion of the line. To the east however the Italian defences were within the oasis itself, so that the ground was much the same in front of the lines as it was behind them. According to an Italian officer who was there, the occupied zone in this area was delineated by 'A wide, sandy track, near which the palm trees thinned out.'[7] What this, of course, meant was that it was possible to approach the defences whilst unobserved.

This was the area chosen by the Ottoman forces to attempt to penetrate the Italian lines, the operation being supported by diversions at several other points of the perimeter. Francis McCullagh told of how he arose early on the morning of 23 October and went up onto the roof of his hotel. Two Italian aeroplanes were aloft, and these flew to the south to conduct a reconnaissance mission over the desert. Returning after some thirty minutes they reported that they had observed four Ottoman encampments between 5 and 8 kilometres south of the Italian lines. Numbers of these forces, consisting of both Ottoman regulars and Arab tribesmen, moved forward until they were within visual distance and artillery range of the southern line of defences, though dispersed so as not to offer a favourable target. These manoeuvres caught the attention of the defenders and the Italian artillery, and at least some of the guns of the fleet, fired upon them.[8]

Meanwhile, concealed by the foliage of the oasis, a large force of regular Ottoman troops, formed of the 8th Infantry Regiment reinforced with Arab irregulars, had approached the eastern flank of the defences and was concentrated facing the line between Fort Sidi Messri to the sea. This was a front of around six kilometres, defended by about 1,800 men of the 11th *Bersaglieri* Regiment; the 1st and 3rd Battalions were between Sidi Messri and al-Hani (Hanni), with the 2nd Battalion between there and the sea and based on Shara Shatt. Al-Hani was a sandy hill some 50 metres tall topped with a plateau, upon which stood a villa, in some sources referred to as the 'white castle,' formerly occupied by an Ottoman official but now used as the HQ of the Regiment. Apart from the position at al-Hani, which was also the location of a machine gun battery, it seems that no great effort had been put into constructing proper defences along the eastern flank. Indeed, several sources state that there were few, if any, entrenchments. This seems doubtful; would the troops have just stood and sat around without any cover? What is beyond doubt, however, is that the eastern flank in general, and the area around Shara Shatt in particular, had been identified by Nesat Bey and his officers as the weakest point of the line.

McCullagh included in his book an account of what happened from a *Bersaglieri* who survived. According to this informant, one Evangelista Salvatore from Ravanusa, Sicily, he and his colleagues were awakened just before dawn by the sound of the native dogs barking, particularly in that portion of the oasis outside the Italian line. At about 07:00 hrs this cacophony was drowned by the sound of coordinated rifle fire; a large number of assailants had surreptitiously approached through the 'bewildering labyrinth,' and opened close-range fire on the Italian positions. Though taken by surprise and outnumbered (estimates of the attackers vary greatly between 1,000 and 6,000), the 4th and 5th companies of *Bersaglieri* around Shara Shatt might well have held their own, had not another blow been planned for them. As they sought to defend themselves from the frontal attack they suddenly found themselves assaulted from the rear as well. As McCullagh's informant put it: 'The Saraceni seemed to rise out of the earth on every side of us.'[9]

Up to the point of the encirclement of the *Bersaglieri* most accounts are in broad agreement, but events afterwards were to become enmeshed in deep controversy and violently partisan disagreement. Basically put, the Italian version, one also propagated by those sympathetic to the Italian cause, was that the Arabs of the oasis had treacherously risen and, literally in some cases, stabbed their liberators in the back. The alternative account, which arose mainly from amongst the foreign correspondents based in Tripoli, was that the Ottoman forces had infiltrated the Italian lines and conducted a successful attack on the Italian rear. Whilst this distinction may appear to be academic, and arguments around it somewhat sterile, it was to become the very crux of the matter due to subsequent events. However, there now seems little doubt that the Italian version is correct and that at least some of the inhabitants of both Tripoli and the Oasis joined in the attack and that this had been carefully coordinated. According to Angelo del Boca:

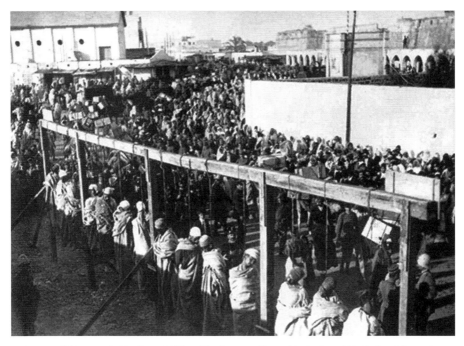

I quattordici strangolati in piazza del Pane (The Fourteen Hanged in the Bread Market) on 5 December 1911. They were: Hussein Ben Mohamed (22); Mohamed Ben Ali (22); Ismail Bahammed el Fituri (20); Mohamed Ben Salemi (50); Ali Ben Sala (50); Ali Ben Hussein (60); Mohamed el-Sium (50); Tahia Ben Tahia (50); Abdul Ben Abdall (45); Allin Ben Gassin (65); Mustafa Ben Glabi (40) and three others whose names are lost. They were seen as the ringleaders of the revolt of 23 October 1911 and were convicted by a court martial on slender evidence obtained from spies and informers. The corpses were left to hang for three days. Paulo Valera, 'Le giornate di Sciarasciat fotografate' in Antonio Schiavulli (Ed.), *La guerra libica: il dibattito dei letterati italiani sull'impresa di Libia* (Ravenna; Giorgio Pozzi, 2009) p. 158. Valera's work was first published in 1912. (Author's Collection).

An aerial view of the Italian lines to the southern edge of the Tripoli Oasis. Overlooking scrub and desert there were clear fields of fire, meaning that the opportunities for an enemy to concentrate and launch a surprise attack were limited. Despite this, the Italian line was effectively breached on 24 October 1911 and a number of the attackers, generally considered to be in the region of around 250-300 strong, were able to penetrate into the oasis. However the Ottoman Commander, Nesat Bey, was unable to get reinforcements through the gap due to their approach being interdicted by artillery and naval gunfire. It took the Italians two days to dislodge those attackers who had penetrated the line, with artillery and explosives freely utilised. (Author's Collection).

The revolt involved men and women, old people and children, and it was as ruthless as any rebellion that mixed not only xenophobia but also religious fanaticism. The triggering event, though, was the blameworthy behavior of the Italian *Bersaglieri* toward Arab women.[10]

There are hints of this 'blameworthy' attitude to be found in McCullagh, who recounts an example of a young lieutenant attempting to assist a young woman who had fallen ill, but who was 'unaware of the fierce jealousy of the Moslems in everything which regards their women.'[11] What can be stated with certainty is that, caught between two fires, the men of the 11th *Bersaglieri* suffered badly and the attackers penetrated the Italian lines and began to fan out. A detachment, mainly of Ottoman regulars, moved to the south to attack the strongpoint at al-Hani, whilst the rest, mainly tribesmen, moved into the oasis. The *Bersaglieri* HQ at al-Hani was one of the few points in the Italian line through the oasis to be well fortified. It also had a battery of machine guns, making it a formidable position for what were, in effect, unsupported light infantry to attack. Indeed, the Ottoman troops were unable to make an impression and the successful defence of the HQ, under the command of Colonel Gustavo Fara, was, from the Italian perspective, one of the few bright spots of the whole episode. Given it was the only 'success' it is unsurprising that Italian propaganda accorded it a level of importance.

Communications between the Italian formations, including GHQ at Tripoli and the advanced HQ at Bumeliana, seem to have failed or been cut, inasmuch as Colonel Fara and his unit were left unsupported for around six to eight hours. In any event there was no general, centrally directed, reserve as all available units were deployed to the defensive perimeter. Two of the three companies of the 2nd Battalion, the 4th and 5th, between al-Hani and the sea were shattered by the attack, whilst the reserve company, the 6th, attempted to fight its way towards Fara's position. They were severely hampered in this, because the fighters that had broken through the lines now interdicted all Italian movement within the oasis. They had spread throughout it up to the edge of Tripoli itself:

> [...] the whole intervening country between the *Bersaglieri* front and the town was alive with armed Arabs, who shot every uniformed Italian on sight. The roads running from the town to the outposts were naturally full of men on various fatigues connected with supply, and these unsuspecting escorts were the first victims.[12]

When it was finally realized that a serious battle was in progress on the eastern flank of the occupied zone, reinforcements were dispatched. The nearest were the reserve companies of the 82nd Infantry Regiment (1st Brigade) manning the defences immediately to the right of the *Bersaglieri*. These had been moved close to the front, lured there by the earlier demonstrations, but eventually one of them, later reinforced by three more, attempted to move to support their comrades. However, they were unable to make fast progress through the labyrinthine terrain and were eventually stopped at the village of Feschlum until evening. By then the attackers had begun to withdraw from the oasis, and it became possible for troops to move around in comparative safety; sniping continued but at a much reduced level. Having held out all day Colonel Fara at al-Hani was then relieved and the gaps in the line were filled.

Several hundred Italians had been killed (later established as 21 officers and 482 other ranks)[13] or gone missing during the attack, but what changed the course of the whole occupation was the psychological jolt: 'It is no exaggeration to say that the events of 23 October shocked the Italian army of occupation from top to bottom.'[14] The battle was the first serious fight of the war, and the first in which Ottoman regular forces fought side by side with irregulars, thus dissipating in no uncertain terms all Italian illusions concerning the local population, both inside and outside the zone of occupation. Believing, seemingly genuinely, that his force had been subject to 'treacherous attacks', Caneva gave orders the next day that the inhabitants of the Oasis were to be disarmed and, where necessary, punished: '[...] ordinary methods of enforcement against the animosity and ferocity of the rebels [being ineffectual] we were obliged to have recourse to severe and energetic measures [...].'[15]

What this translated to in effect was a house-to-house search of the Oasis by detachments of soldiers and sailors. Though the Italians, both officially and unofficially, strenuously denied it, this turned into a wholesale massacre of the Arab inhabitants of the Oasis, which, unfortunately for the deniers, was witnessed by the many correspondents present. The massacre of peoples believed, rightly or wrongly, to be hostile to the ruling power, in whatever context, was hardly a novel facet of modern warfare. All powers had been guilty at some point, and the Italians were certainly not the first, and definitely not the last, to indulge in methods of barbarism in furtherance of, as they perceived it, civilisation. From contemporaneous accounts it is probably the case that Caneva and his subordinates lost control of their soldiers:

Caneva and his Staff, however, had not calculated upon what this order meant to troops that had just seen their mutilated dead, who believed that they were again about to be attacked treacherously in the rear, and who had ever over them the shadow of Adowa. The carrying out of the duty necessitated the breaking up of the troops into small detachments, which loosed the control upon the inflamed passions of the soldiery. Nor did the Staff know how or when to place a period upon the licence they thus gave the troops. The result was a retribution upon the Arabs which will live in the memory of the Tripolitaine for generations, and which will react for many a year upon the perpetrators themselves.[16]

The results were horrific. Thomas E Grant, correspondent of the *Daily Mirror,* rode through the oasis and his description of what he observed appeared in the 2 November edition of his newspaper:

> The two-mile ride to the cavalry barracks was a perfect nightmare of horrors. To begin with, one had to pass a huddled mass of some fifty men and boys, who were yesterday herded into a small space enclosed by three walls and there fired upon until no one was left alive.

> It must have been a veritable carnival of carnage. The heap of cartridge cases in the road is evidence of how the execution was bungled. A fellow correspondent witnessed this, and his description of the ghastly scene is too shocking to write down.[17]

That they did not explicitly order a massacre does not excuse the Italian commanders in general and Caneva in particular. As the American general and lawyer Henry Wager Halleck had stated in 1861: 'Unless [the commander] can control his soldiers, he is unfit to command them.'[18] The principle of Command Responsibility, though the term was not itself used until 1921, had been enshrined in International Law in 1907 under the auspices of the Hague Convention. This entered into force on 26 January 1910 with Italy as a signatory, and thus by not controlling his subordinates properly and allowing the massacres to take place, Caneva had almost certainly violated International Law. This might seem like an academic point inasmuch as there was no authority to prosecute him at that time. In this he was perhaps lucky; Yamashita Tomoyuki, the 'Tiger of Malaya', best known for accepting the surrender of 130,000 British Imperial troops at Singapore in 1942, was held to have violated the principle during his trial in 1945, and was hanged the following year.[19]

Caneva also had other matters on his mind. Fearing further external attacks, he ordered that the defensive perimeter be strengthened. The troops in the oasis were reinforced by marines and sailors, and the personnel from heavy artillery batteries, whose guns had yet to be landed, were pressed into service as infantry. The unloading of field and mountain batteries was expedited and the heavy units of the 'Training Division,' the battleships *Sicilia* and *Sardegna* to the east and the *Re Umberto* with the armoured cruiser *Carlo Alberto* to the west, were anchored close inshore to provide heavy fire support on the flanks. The existing trenches and earthworks were also expanded and reinforced with machine gun positions.

That Caneva's fears were justified was confirmed by the observations of Captain Carlo Piazza and Captain Riccardo Moizo. Piazza was the commander of the 'air fleet' that had become active at Tripoli on 21 October – a 'fleet' that consisted of nine aircraft; two each manufactured by Blériot, Farman and Etrich, together with three Nieuports. Piazza had made aviation history on 23 October when he made the first ever combat flight, reconnoitring Ottoman positions during an hour-long sortie. On 25 October

The first wartime aviators. The airmen that went with the Italian expeditionary force to Tripoli became the first to ever participate in combat operations. Aviation history was thus made on 22 October when Captain Riccardo Moizo performed a reconnaissance flight over enemy positions in a Bleriot. Moizo is second from the right. (Author's Collection).

Piazza and Moizo, in a Bleriot and Nieuport respectively, observed three columns of enemy troops, which they estimated as some 6,000 men in total, approaching Tripoli from the south.[20] Later that day an Ottoman officer approached the Italian lines under a flag of truce and demanded, dependant upon which source one believes, either the surrender of the whole occupied zone, or the eastern area of the oasis. This approach was rebuffed, with the officer allowed to return unharmed.

Shortly after 05:00 hrs the next morning, Francis McCullagh was awoken in his room at the Hotel Minerva (a part of the Bank of Rome-funded hotel business, *Societa Albergo Minerva*) by the 'roar of the naval guns.' Through the pre-sunrise half-light he saw that the whole of the Italian line was in action but discerned that the firing was heaviest at the eastern side of the oasis around Shara Shatt and al-Hani. Accordingly, he set off through the oasis towards the sound of the guns, noting as he went how empty it appeared following the depredations of the last two days:

> I walked along a street of houses which had just been looted and destroyed. I was alone, and the echo of my own footsteps resounded as if I were walking in a tomb. This suburb, so filled with noisy life four days earlier, was now as uninhabited as Pompeii. I did not see a single Arab all the way, nor did I meet with a single Italian.

> The oppressive solitudes of the oasis were heavy with a sense of tragedy. The stillness was hostile, the very air was dense with unutterable menace. The shattered doorways and windows gaped like the mouths of dead men. Black with blood and pitted with bullets, the naked walls exhaled the quintessence of malignity and hate.[21]

A Farman aeroplane at Derna. On 15 October 1911 elements of an aviation battalion, designated the
First Aeroplane Flotilla, arrived in Tripoli under the command of Captain Carlo Piazza. He had command
of eleven officer pilots, 30 ground crew, and nine or ten aeroplanes: two Blériot, three Nieuport, two (some
sources say three) Etrich *Taube*, and two Farman biplanes. With this unit being the first ever deployed in an
active theatre of war, it was inevitable that it recorded several aviation 'firsts' whilst carrying out its
missions. Aviation history was made on 22 October when Captain Riccardo Moizo, an artillery officer,
performed a combat reconnaissance flight over enemy positions. The Second Aeroplane Flotilla was sent
to Cyrenaica with three aircraft. To provide reinforcements recourse was made to civilian resources, and
eight civilians together with eight army pilots, were deployed to Tobruk and Derna along with nine Blériot
and one Farman aircraft. One of the civilians, the sportsman and politician, Carlo Montu, who was given
the rank of captain, made aviation history on 31 January 1912 when he became the first casualty
of anti-aircraft fire. (Author's Collection).

If the Ottoman assault at the eastern end of the oasis seemed to occasion the greatest
amount of fighting, this may well have been a feint on their part, or they might have
been probing for a weak point. If the latter then it was on the south-eastern front that
they found it and where a breakthrough was made. Tullio Irace was with the *Bersaglieri*
around al-Hani and he recounted the switch of emphasis:

> Towards 9 o'clock the enemy on our front had lost all combined action, and was now carrying
> on a desultory fight in various scattered detachments under cover of the palm trees. About this
> time the main body of Turks and Arabs had shifted westward, pressing heavily on the centre of
> our lines between Messri and Bu-Meliana.[22]

The weak point revealed was around a position centred on a large two-storey building,
known to the Italians as Kemal Bey's House, which was complete with an overgrown
garden totalling a little over a hectare. Situated some 1.5 kilometres to the west of Fort Sidi
Mesri (for which the battle is often known, though it is also named Henni-Bu-Meliana in
some accounts), this position was held by the 7th Company of the 84th Regiment under
the command of Captain Hombert. It appears that the defenders were deployed mainly in

the building as a group of attackers, numbering around 250, was able to approach them unseen via the garden. The raiders were able to get into the property seemingly unobserved and, in a near repeat of the events of three days before, take the defenders unawares. There is some evidence that the area had been selected as a potential weak point previously and the defenders subjected to crude, though seemingly effective, attempts at psychological warfare. Amongst the attackers was a British officer, Lieutenant Herbert (sometimes rendered as Harold) Gerald Montagu of the 5th Battalion, Royal Fusiliers. Quite what impelled Montagu, an officer of Jewish extraction, to travel to Tripoli and join the Ottoman effort is obscure.[23] He later furnished an account of the preparations for the assault:

> On the night before [the attack] six Arabs sallied out of the city with a quantity of cord, with which they secretly looped up a dense plantation of prickly pear bushes, joining up the cords to a main rope, which they entrusted to an Arab urchin of 11 years. During the night the urchin, acting on instructions, pulled the rope vigorously for some time, causing the bushes to rustle. This scared the Italian troops in the vicinity, and they fired on the bushes for six hours, literally blowing the jungle away and leaving themselves without ammunition.[24]

There is some corroboration of this from the writer and correspondent Ernest Nathaniel Bennett. A former MP for Woodstock and fellow of Hertford College, Oxford, he travelled to Tripoli via Tunisia in late November 1911. Bennett was an experienced hand and the author of several books detailing his experiences. Working under a commission from the *Manchester Guardian* he joined with the Ottoman forces and the next year published an account of his adventures and observations. During the course of his stay he interviewed several of the participants in the attack, and, according to the stories related to him, the members of the 7th Company were found 'half-dazed' and many were 'roused from sleep merely to die.'[25] McCullagh, who got his story from Italian survivors, corroborates this to an extent, relating that during the night 'there were mysterious and inexplicable tappings and movings in the underwood, and the sentinel's morbid imagination was crowded by phantom shapes from the blood-curdling folk-lore of Sicily.' He reported their accounts of how, later, 'when their ammunition was exhausted, they had been most treacherously set upon.'[26] Even if the personnel of the 84th Regiment were drawn from Florence rather than Sicily, it is still possible to visualise their discomfiture and fear. That many were taken unawares is perhaps evidenced by noting that most of the deaths in 7th Company were caused by the curved knives of the Arabs. According to Bennett, these did 'terrible execution.'[27]

With the taking of Kemal Bey's House the Italian line was effectively breached and a number of the attackers, generally considered to be in the region of around 250-300 strong, were able to penetrate into the oasis. Though relatively few in number they were able to cause a great deal of confusion by attacking from the rear the Italian positions on either side of the breach, which were occupied by the 4th and 6th companies of the 84th Regiment. Despite causing around 100 casualties within these troops, the attackers were unable to exploit their success due to the effectiveness of the Italian artillery, both land- and sea-based. In particular three batteries based at Bumeliana were effective, though, as on the 23 October, Italian movement within the oasis was somewhat circumscribed by riflemen concealed in the labyrinthine interior.

Nesat Bey was unable to get reinforcements through the gap in the lines due to their approach being interdicted by the gunfire, supplemented by the fire of the machine guns. Troops, including the 1st and 2nd (dismounted) Squadrons of the Lodi Cavalry from the nearby barracks and eight companies of infantry from the 4th and 40th Regiments supported by artillery, were sent into the oasis in an attempt to clear out those attackers that had managed to pass through the Italian line. It took the Italians two days to dislodge some of these, with artillery and explosives freely utilised. Ellis Ashmead Bartlett, the distinguished correspondent under commission to Reuters, recounted how some 30 of the invaders resisted all attempts at expulsion from several houses at the edge of the oasis until, on 28 October, these properties were demolished with high explosive.[28]

One enterprising officer, commanding a company of the 82nd Regiment sent to reinforce the front line, evolved a method of ameliorating the difficulties of negotiating the seemingly sniper-infested oasis. Finding that the sniping rendered his movements exceedingly slow, the commander, Captain Robiony, adopted a 'successful stratagem.' He collected together some 30-40 Arab inhabitants from their houses, including women, children, and the elderly, and put them at the head of his column. 'The effect was miraculous. All opposition ceased. The houses, the olives, the palms, the fig-trees ceased to vomit fire.'[29] Robiony's force was thus able to continue unimpeded. Several of the war correspondents present witnessed and recorded this event. Those representing Italian papers, such as Giuseppe Bevione of Turin's *La Stampa,* were approving. Most foreign correspondents, Otto von Gottberg of the *Berliner Lokal-Anzeiger* for example, differed. The former called Robiony's act a 'stratagem that happily succeeded' [*stratagemma riuscito felicemente*] whilst the latter commented that 'neutral witnesses were shocked and outraged' [*Neutrale Augenzeugen waren entsetzt und empört*].

Gottberg was to be shocked and outraged further. On the morning of 27 October he was near the cavalry barracks:

> Out of an Arab hut, I saw a young woman emerge holding in her right hand the fingers of her little son, and in her left a water pitcher. The street was perfectly tranquil, but suddenly three shots rang out and the woman fell dead. The screaming child fled back into the house. I must admit that the horror of this sight made me stagger and almost fall to the ground.[30]

The killing of the inhabitants of the Oasis of Tripoli had not ceased since 23 October, but it intensified following the attack three days later. According to Ashmead Bartlett:

> [From 24 -27] October […], the troops proceeded to make a clean sweep of all that portion of the oasis of which they held possession. There is no certain proof that any Arabs in the west end of it ever took part in the rising; but, even admitting that there were, there were vast numbers of men, women, and boys who were perfectly innocent, and of these nearly all the men, and even the boys above a certain age, were shot, while undoubtedly many women perished in the confusion […] Although there was no fighting on the afternoon of 27 October, there was continual firing in all parts of the oasis. This was entirely produced by small bodies of soldiers, in many instances without officers, roaming throughout and indiscriminately massacring all whom they met. We must have passed the bodies of over one hundred persons on this one high road, and as similar scenes were enacted through the length and breadth of the oasis some estimate of the numbers of innocent men, women, and children who were butchered, doubtless with many who were guilty of attacking the Italian troops in the rear, may be appreciated.[31]

Such scenes were witnessed and later reported by many more of the correspondents. There can be no doubt that whilst the attack of 23 October had struck a profound psychological blow, the second breaking of the line was shattering. As McCullagh phrased it: 'For the Italian army this was near being the end of all things [...] a disaster to which Adowa would be as but a street accident, and which the House of Savoy could hardly hope to survive.'[32] That he believed his command had come close to disaster is borne out by Caneva's response to the second attack in particular. In an attempt to bolster the strength of the defensive line he decided to shorten it, and on the afternoon of 26 October he ordered that the eastern flank be withdrawn some two kilometres. This was achieved on 28 October, abandoning Fort Hamidije, Fort Sidi Messri, Shara Shatt and al-Heni to the enemy. In order to hold what he had, take back what he had lost, and to make even modest gains beyond that, Caneva requested large-scale reinforcement, and a second Army Corps was swiftly mobilised. By 7 November another 30,000 men had been deployed within the Tripoli perimeter.

According to 'Kepi' these 'were about the two worst military measures that could have been undertaken.'

> The first had a still further depressing effect upon the troops, and gave opportunity to the Turkish commander to report sensational victories to Stamboul. The second will only swell the tale of sickness which must be the lot of this great Italian army cooped up in Tripoli.[33]

The latter point was well made. Supplying the occupying army and population of Tripoli with potable water was a major concern, as the available wells were not of sufficient capacity. Consequently, considerable quantities had to be shipped from Sicily. In addition the sewage system of Tripoli, such as it was, was unable to in any way cope with the additional strain, leading to the inevitable outbreaks of cholera and dysentery. The military hospitals were kept at full stretch and the mortality rate amongst the troops from the former over the three-month period from October 1911 to January 1912 was in the order of 4-5 men per day.[34] It was probably much greater amongst the non-military population though no-one bothered to keep accurate figures. In any event this population had been reduced by the actions of the Italians. There is no reliable figure for the number who were killed between 23-27 October, though many of the foreign correspondents estimated it at *circa* 4,000. Another 3,425 are known to have been deported by the military authorities to the various island penal colonies, mainly those on Ustica, Ponza, Favignana and Tremiti, as well as mainland prisons at Caserta and the Neapolitan fortress of Gaeta.[35] These deportations were in many cases little more than a delayed death sentence. Reports in the *L'Ora di Palermo* of 8 and 9 November 1911 stated that

> 'The conditions on Ustica are now extremely alarming. Because of the Arab corpses tossed into the sea from the steamship *S. Giorgio* not far from the beach, the fish market has been suspended. [...] The burial of other Arabs who died of cholera, in shallow graves in the sand on private property, make easy pickings for stray dogs and constitutes a further menace to the public health.'[36]

Due to the inability of the Italian authorities to admit that they had ever suffered any military setback whatsoever, a recurring theme throughout the course of the conflict, the shortening of the line was presented as conforming to a manoeuvre already planned. According to Irace:

> To give our men a rest and also to make the line of defence stronger for the repelling of possible future attacks, the front of our position near Henni, in the oasis, was slightly altered by withdrawing it about one mile. This change in the front had been deemed necessary since the first days of our landing, when it was soon seen that such an extensive defence-line could not

everywhere withstand the enemy's onslaught when he was in considerable force. By restricting the line it not only becomes stronger, but also leaves more men to act in the reserve and keep the oasis clear, and, moreover, to guard us from fresh surprises in the rear.[37]

One other effect of the withdrawal was to allow the Ottomans to reoccupy part of the oasis. There was a military side to this inasmuch as installations such as Fort Hamidije and Fort Sidi Mesri, the useful equipment of which was destroyed before evacuation, were recovered. Some five pieces of artillery were either found in, or taken to, the former as an ineffective bombardment of the city was attempted on 31 October. This was swiftly silenced by naval gunfire. However in the oasis itself the Ottoman forces, and particularly the Arabs, then discovered the bodies of their people left by the events of the previous days; one of the reasons Caneva gave for the withdrawal itself was 'because of the effluvium from the unburied corpses' and McCullagh says that 'the oasis stank with unburied bodies.' The only first-hand account of this initial discovery was by Herbert Montagu; indeed he is credited with being the first to publicise the Italian massacres, as the official correspondents based in Tripoli could not, of course, immediately report what they had seen because of the strict censorship. Montagu's report, dated 2 November, was sent via Dehibat (Dahibat) in Tunisia and appeared in the London papers on 4 November:

> I feel it my duty to send you the following telegram, and I beg you, in the name of Christianity, to publish it throughout England. I am an English officer, and am now voluntarily serving in the Turkish army here. [...]

> Imagine, then, my feelings when, on entering and driving the Italians out of the Arab houses which they had fortified and were holding, we discovered the bodies of some hundred and twenty women and children, with their hands and feet bound, mutilated, pierced, and torn. Later on at (omitted) we found a mosque filled with the bodies of women and children, mutilated almost beyond recognition. I could not count them, but there must have been three or four hundred.

> Sir, is this European war? Are such crimes to be permitted? Cannot England do something to stop such horrors? In our civilisation and times you can hardly believe it, but it is nevertheless true. I myself have seen it, and so I know. Even now we are getting news of further massacres of women and children discovered in different farms lately occupied by the Italians.

> [...] The idea of the Italians when they slaughtered these innocents was obviously one of revenge, from the way the bodies were mutilated – revenge for their heavy losses in battle. [...] Hoping you will do all you can to bring the barbarous atrocities I have mentioned before the British public and authorities.[38]

This was, justifiably, treated with some suspicion. Montagu was self-confessedly contravening the 1870 Foreign Enlistment Act, which made it a crime for any citizen of the United Kingdom to enlist in a foreign force. Furthermore as a serving British officer he was in danger of losing his commission in disgrace. However, shortly after it appeared and been denounced as a total fabrication by the Italian government and press, it was corroborated by the accounts of McCullagh and von Gottberg. The latter two had 'sent back' their credentials as war correspondents to Caneva on 27 October in order 'to leave an army in which such things were done.' W T Stead put it rather more strongly: 'he refused any longer to be associated with an army which had degenerated into a band of assassins.'[39] McCullagh in particular then began a campaign in the UK to alert the British public, and the wider world, to the behaviour of the Italian army in Tripoli. For this he was twice challenged to a duel by Italians, one of them being none other than the founder of the Futurist movement, Filippo Tommaso Marinetti. Marinetti wrote a series of articles for the the French newspaper *L'Intransigeant* about the attacks of 23-26 October 1911, later published as a book, *La battaglia di Tripoli* [The Battle of Tripoli].[40]

The Battle of Tripoli – and the twin battles of Shara Shatt and Sidi Mesri are probably best grouped and understood under one heading – was a major turning point in the conflict and had several far reaching consequences. The Italians were faced with what can only have been the shocking realisation that the Arab people of Tripoli were not, contrary to expectations, waiting for them with open arms. From late October onwards then the enemy, or more particularly the Arab component of that enemy, were considered 'non-belligerent fighters' (unlawful combatants) and either slaughtered or immediately deported according to Angelo del Boca.[41] This demonization did not extend quite as far with respect to those who had proven their allegiance to the Italian cause. This included Hassuna Qaramanli who had been proclaimed Vice-Governor of Tripoli at the time of the Italian landing. However, a certain amount of suspicion extended even to him and his situation seems to have been nebulous. Despite his 'official position' he was often referred to as the Mayor, and according to McCullagh 'it does not seem to be quite certain what sort of a tenth-rate honorary position the unfortunate man held'. His prerogatives, such as they were, were circumscribed following the Battle of Tripoli: 'For the sake of the general tranquillity, the powers accorded to the Mayor of the city have been limited to matters of strict necessity in exclusive connection with local customs.'[42]

The racial-religious animosity stirred up by the Battle of Tripoli was not confined to the Italians. As Herbert Montagu reported it, 'the Arabs were maddened beyond all restraint by the outrages in the oasis.'[43] This clamour was to spread and the correspondent of the London *Times* was to inform the readership of that organ on 27 March 1912:

> From Tunis to Aziziah [Al'Azizah in Lower Egypt] the country rings with tales of wanton destruction committed by the Italians, of the massacre of defenceless men, and the slaying of women and small children, even children at the breast. [...] The longer the struggle lasts, the more men will flock to the Crescent from the interior. The Arab version of the massacre, and of other reported excesses upon the part of the Italians, has now travelled into the desert and the Sudan. Recruits and reinforcements, with promises of more, are daily pouring into camp. El Senussi, the mysterious Sheikh, who wields such power in the interior, has formally declared war against the Italians [...][44]

The situation following the battle indicated that in both military and political terms Italian strategy had proven a failure if not entirely collapsed; Caneva was to report to Rome on 6 November that the situation was quite different from that which we expected to find when we landed on these shores. It would no longer be possible to take possession of the rest of the *vilayet* without resort to military methods. There was no obvious means by which this could be achieved in any event, and that the Ottoman forces were possessed of a considerable capacity was now palpable. In other words, there was no quick military solution to the war once the initial landings had failed to bring about an enemy collapse. The situation on the ground in Tripoli was, militarily, at stalemate. Politically and diplomatically the situation was similar, though there were still moves, with varying degrees of risk attached, which were available.

CHAPTER SEVEN

'The Jaws of the Sahara'
(*Le fauci del Sahara*)

*But around me is a silence of death: a word seems to spring from the horizon: – Back! –
Back to all of you who want to violate my secret, you who were not born in my restless dunes,
you were not burned by my fire, taught not to wait, against the earth, the passage of my rage . . .
Back! – And these words of challenge rose as knights armed with a deadly struggle, only a few
men, naked, implacable as the expanse of sand and the scorching sun . . .
and launched by the jaws of the great desert [...]*

Domenico Tumiati, 'Le fauci del Sahara' in *Tripolitania*, 1911[1]

CANEVA'S request for reinforcements was swiftly met with two more divisions being mobilised and transported to Tripoli. The first to arrive on 4-5 November was the 3rd Division under the command of Lieutenant General *Conte* Felice de Chaurand de Saint Eustache. The 4th Division under Lieutenant General *Conte* Vittorio Trombi, less one regiment, was sent to Cyrenaica where Trombi was appointed as governor of Derna. All in all by around the middle of November 1911, there were some 85,000 Italian troops based in the enclaves along the coast. With the reinforcements came another Lieutenant General, Pietro Frugoni. Frugoni had been the commander of IX Army Corps headquartered in Rome, and it was announced there on 5 November that he had left to take command of the newly formed I Special Army Corps (*i° Corpo d'Armata Speciale*) formed at Tripoli from the 1st and 3rd Divisions. Caneva though remained as Governor and in overall command of the army of occupation. By 20 November the Italian Army in the *vilayet* was around 90,000 strong, the main components being 16 regiments of infantry (48,000), 3 regiments of *Bersaglieri* (9,000), 3 battalions of Grenadiers (3,000), and 4 battalions of *Alpini* (4,000). In addition there were 12 cavalry squadrons (*circa* 2,500 men) and the equivalent of 4 regiments of artillery (around 6,000 men and some 200 guns of various types) as well as 5 battalions of pioneers and engineers (4,000). Support troops, including units of *Carabinieri*, made up the rest.

These, and later additional reinforcements, ensured that the Italian occupation could not be dislodged. However from the Italian politicians' point of view, stalemate appeared to be leading towards a considerable problem and the longer it endured the greater it became. What haunted the government was the possibility of the Great Powers becoming involved and brokering a peace that would leave Italy without total, undisputed and undiluted, sovereignty over Tripoli. That one or more of the Powers would try to become involved seemed highly likely, as none of them would wish to see the Ottoman Empire weakened. The last thing they wanted was for the Eastern Question to violently erupt and shatter the status quo in several areas. For Austria-Hungary this area was the Balkans, for Britain and Russia the Turkish Straits (The Bosphorus and Dardanelles). France had massive Ottoman financial investments and Germany was also cultivating the Empire; the Berlin-Baghdad railway being an example. Indeed, both Italy's partners in the Triple Alliance had begun mediation efforts from the moment Italy had delivered the ultimatum. Moreover, as long as the military situation remained stalemated then the greater the likelihood that diplomatic pressure would be applied to the Italian government to come to reasonable terms, with 'reasonable' meaning allowing the Ottoman Empire some face-saving device. The historic precedents for this were several; Britain administered and ran Egypt and Cyprus under purely nominal Ottoman sovereignty and had done so for a number of years, whilst the same applied to France and Tunisia and, until 1908, Austria-Hungary and Bosnia.

Initially Giolitti and San Giuliano appeared to favour some such measure, as was signalled by the Prime Minister in a speech at the *Teatro Regio*, Turin, on 7 October. Though he described the conflict as a 'crusade,' he also implied that Italy's best interests would be served by coming to compromise resolution with the Ottoman Empire to end it. It is arguable that some arrangement with the Ottoman government was, at that time, at least possible. The Grand Vizier Hakki Pasa and his government had resigned upon the outbreak of hostilities, to be replaced by a cabinet headed by Mehmed Said Pasa. The new Grand Vizier indicated in talks he held with the German Ambassador, Baron Adolf Marschall von Bieberstein, early in October that he foresaw a compromise solution. On 4 October he noted the inevitability of abandoning Tripoli to Italian occupation and administration, though under the maintenance of the Ottoman Sultan's sovereignty. Marschall conveyed these views to his government in a series of telegrams, noting particularly that the new Foreign Minister, Assim Bey, told him on 11 October that the Ottoman government recognised that any residual sovereignty left to the Sultan would be 'fictitious,' but that on such a basis mediation by Germany could proceed.[2]

'Public opinion' put paid to such notions on the Italian side. Compromise was anathema to the jingo right and the full force of their invective was unleashed on Giolitti and his government for even hinting at such a thing. Enrico Corradini's newspaper *L'Idea Nazionale* predictably viewed any such notion as 'treachery' and anything less than Italy dictating peace terms as 'humiliation.' The opposition leader Sidney Sonnino was 'incensed' by such notions, claiming that anything less than full and outright annexation would be detrimental to Italian prestige.[3] Having pandered to 'public opinion' in respect of the invasion of Tripoli, the government now found itself the prisoner of it, and by the end of the month Giolitti changed his opinion to match that of the 'public.' Though the cliché about riding the tiger springs unbidden to mind, he was later to justify this by the effect it would have on the local population:

> Now, even leaving aside the impression on Italian public opinion, the maintenance of the Sultan's nominal authority in Tripolitania and Cyrenaica had several serious consequences. Such a solution would have reduced much of our authority on the Arab population, who would continue to regard the Sultan as their sovereign as well as their religious leader.[4]

What Giolitti's change of mind amounted to in real terms was the issuing of an annexation decree. On 5 November Victor Emmanuel III proclaimed Italian sovereignty over Tripolitania and Cyrenaica:

We have decreed and do decree: Tripolitania and Cyrenaica are placed under the full and complete sovereignty of the kingdom of Italy. An act of parliament will establish the final regulations for the administration of the said regions. Until this act shall have been promulgated, they shall be provided for by royal decrees. The present decree shall be placed on the table of parliament for the purpose of its conversion into a law.[5]

This was the burning of diplomatic bridges taken to extremes, and there were several consequences. Perhaps the least important was the ridicule it brought upon Italy in the foreign press and elsewhere. The British journalist, W T Stead, put it thus: 'From the point of view of international law this annexation was as null and void as from the point of view of the actual facts it was grotesquely absurd.'[6] The point about international law was well made; according to the respected jurist Lassa Oppenheim, annexation of conquered enemy territory, whether of the whole or of part, confers a title only after a *firmly established* conquest, and so long as war continues, conquest is not firmly established.[7] Under this principle it followed that as long as the Ottoman Empire refused to end the war by negotiation then the war could not end, and whilst this was the case Italy's annexation would not be recognised by any other powers. The announcement that Tripolitania and Cyrenaica was Italian sovereign territory also led to the curious situation of Italy seemingly carrying out a blockade of her own coastline. Indeed, because of Italian supremacy in the maritime sphere, this duty devolved upon four armed merchant ships, formerly mail steamers each armed with six 150 mm guns, from 10 November. Italy was in danger of looking foolish. However the international press agencies began, from 7 November, to carry messages to the effect that the Italian government regarded the annexation 'as a second ultimatum.' If the Ottoman Empire refused to concede on Italian terms then the Italian fleet would be ordered 'to attack Turkey at one of her vital points.'

Unfortunately for Italian aspirations, the Ottoman government had also had a change of mind. Following the Battle of Tripoli it suddenly became clear that resistance to the Italian occupation was not a forlorn hope. The local population, or at least the significant proportion of it, would fight under Ottoman leadership. The Ottoman military leadership also recognised that the Italian Army was, as currently organised, incapable of winning an outright military victory. They therefore decided to send as much assistance as possible to the forces resisting the Italians. This was no easy task due to Italian command of the sea and the attitude of the British. Cyrenaica shared a frontier with Egypt, which was nominally Ottoman territory under the 'Khedive of Egypt and the Sudan,' Abbas II (Abbas Hilmi). On 20 September 1911 Lord Kitchener of Khartoum had left England for Cairo to become agent and consul-general to the Khedive, and it was he who effectively ruled during the time of the conflict. Despite a popular clamour from several sections of the Egyptian population, he was able, in accordance with British neutrality, to prevent any overt large-scale assistance being offered to the Ottomans from Egypt.

Kitchener was often credited with having knowledge of the workings of the 'oriental mind' and he seemingly managed the matter diplomatically. When a number of officers in the Egyptian Army asked permission to volunteer to fight against the Italians, he gave the impression that he would not oppose this. However, he warned them that when they returned their positions might not be open and they would have to retire from the army. Similarly, he told the Bedouin chiefs that if they raised levies from their people to fight for the Sultan, then the Khedive would no longer exempt them from conscription into the Egyptian army. Accordingly, neither group went ahead with the idea.[8] Similarly, the Ottoman government was denied the use of Egyptian territory for sending materiel or personnel to the war zone. Given the size and nature of the area concerned, and the lack of communications, the appearance of an Ottoman army on the frontier of Cyrenaica was not a realistic prospect in any circumstances.

What was possible was the covert infiltration of individuals and small groups into Cyrenaica via Egypt. This operation was carried out under the auspices of the *Teskilat-i-Mahsusa* or Special Organisation. The origins of this organisation are, because of the lack of any documentary evidence, obscure. Some accounts trace its origins back to 1903, whilst others argue that it did not come into being until the advent of the First World War. Then it was to become infamous for its role in the Armenian Genocide, as well as being involved in operations in the Caucasus, Egypt, and Mesopotamia. Having sifted all the available evidence, the Turkish historian Taner Akcam has concluded that a group of officers associated with Enver Bey began to describe themselves as the Special Organisation, which was founded in order to organise and supply the guerrilla war that was to be waged in the Tripoli *vilayet*.[9]

A number of Ottoman officers, totalling 107 according to Stoddart, were to travel surreptitiously to Tripoli and Cyrenaica via Tunisia and Egypt. Several of these were to achieve high status, including Enver Bey, later the Ottoman minister of war and member of the triumvirate that took the Empire into the Great War on the side of Germany.[10] Robert Graves was later to memorably, if inaccurately, describe him as 'the son of the late Sultan's chief furniture-maker, and a soldier politician who had worked his way up, it was said, by murdering every superior officer who stood in his way.'[11]

Enver, according to his 1918 account, left the Ottoman capitol in 'absolute secrecy' on a steamer bound for Alexandria in Egypt on 10 October 1911. He was in disguise with 'dark glasses, clean shaven, [and] wearing a black fez down to the eyebrows.' Nevertheless he feared that he would draw attention to himself and be recognised. This fear was unfounded, but he records that he was feeling depressed about the magnitude of the task of getting to the war zone and fighting the Italians.

The ship arrived off Alexandria at noon on 14 October, but the docks were in quarantine and so the vessel had to moor offshore and await clearance until the next day. After disembarking and passing through an 'unpleasant half hour' clearing immigration and baggage inspection, Enver was taken to a hotel by his guide. This guide is identified as one Arif Pasa about whom nothing further is known, though Salvatore Bono has speculated that he might have been the former Governor of Adrianople (1907) and Navy Secretary (1909).[12] If so he was of very high rank and perhaps not the best person to meet someone travelling incognito. In any event, Enver seems to have maintained his guise as an academic until 22 October, when he records that he has changed identity and moved to 'a dirty little room, where a stifling air prevails,' the gloom of which is only partially relieved by a candle. Feeling depressed by his surroundings Enver went out but records that he had an encounter with the police, who 'seemed to suspect that I was not the innocent merchant from Syria who I now pretend to be.'

Two days later however he was en route to Cyrenaica by train, travelling third class to avoid being recognised and with 'an Arab woman with two young children, a German and a Frenchman as travelling companions.' The journey was not a comfortable one:

> Through the sea of sand our little train rolled slowly forward. Heavens, what a train! I feel every part of my body. I've just had breakfast: raw dates, that was all. I now need to get used to this diet. [...] The desert wind covers us in very fine sand, which penetrates even though the windows are all closed. Our faces and hair are covered with it and it is very unpleasant! It fills the mouth, and one has to swallow it.[13]

At some point in the journey to the terminus of the railway at Ed-Daba Enver records that he had to change trains for an even more uncomfortable berth in a freight wagon; 'it was terrible being in there, and it stank such that I could hardly breathe.' The ordeal was not overly prolonged and after sleeping a night on the train he started the rest of the journey on horseback with five companions and seven horses; 'Five Arabian horses for me and my comrades [...] and two horses for our luggage.'

By 7 November Enver and his small caravan had reached a point some 15 kilometres west of Tobruk. He records that he had ridden 60 kilometres the previous day on a *Hegin*, the largest and strongest type of camel, which covered the distance in ten hours. During the course of this journey he had carried out a reconnaissance of Tobruk, concluding that there were only two battalions of Italian troops stationed there, and heard of an action five days previously in which an attempt to cut the Ottoman telegraph lines had been repulsed. This arduous journey could not of course have been undertaken without the active assistance of the Arab inhabitants. For example, on the night of 16 November Enver and his companions were at the *zavia*[14] at Unirn er-Rezm, some 10 kilometres northwest of Bomba. He records that they were given a room to stay the night, though there were no beds; 'the carpets on the floor are the beds.' Of much more importance though was the allegiance sworn to him as commander of the Ottoman forces by the leaders of the various tribes in the area. This meant, according to his calculations that in two days around 10,000 irregular fighters could be mobilised if necessary.

By 19 November Enver had reached the *zavia* of Martuba, situated some 20 kilometres south east of Derna on the strategically important caravan route. This was close to his final destination and around 800 kilometres from the starting point at Alexandria. It was the day after he had reconnoitred the defences at Derna:

> Yesterday I was very close at Derna. The hostile pioneer trenches [earthworks] lay at my feet, and outside the city was an armored cruiser. The Arabs are happy when they see me. Initially they had been terrified of the shells from the warship but have now realised that the thousands of shots fired have caused no damage or injuries. The Italian advanced positions have been driven back and they do not try further advances. They are afraid of the Arab forces, in bands from 10 to 100 strong, who swarm around them and attack, especially at night.[15]

The first Ottoman regular officers had arrived by the middle of October 1911 and their influence began to be felt on the character of the war almost immediately as they took over the coordination of military resistance to the Italians. One example of this was the harassment referred to at Derna, with a particularly worrying (from the Italian point of view) probing attack on 17 November. Most notable in retrospect was the presence of Mustafa Kemal, who arrived after travelling through Egypt disguised as a carpet

Mustafa Kemal (left) and Enver Bey in the hinterland south of Derna in 1912. Enver Bey (Ismael Enver) was one of the leaders of the Committee of Union and Progress (CUP) or 'Young Turks' as they were known colloquially. He was serving in Berlin as Ottoman Military Attaché when Italy declared war and hurried back home. According to his own account, he persuaded the government to adopt a guerrilla strategy in the Tripoli vilayet and journeyed clandestinely to the theatre to put it into practice as commander in Cyrenaica with the rank of Lieutenant-Colonel. Headquartered near to the Italian occupied port of Derna, the Ottoman led forces were able to prevent the invaders from venturing beyond their coastal enclaves where they were covered by the guns of their fleet. Major Mustafa Kemal, who joined Enver's command on 18 December 1911 after travelling incognito via Egypt, initially commanded the Ottoman-led forces around Tobruk. He stressed discipline and order to the men under his command, and divided them into small units. As soon as he arrived he personally reconnoitred the Italian positions and recommended a small-scale attack. This, his first engagement with the enemy, took place outside Tobruk on 22 December, and was deemed a victory. It was though, as elsewhere, impossible to do more than attempt to hold the Italians within their defences. On 30 December Kemal was reassigned to Ayn al-Mansur (Ain Mansur), where he was to command the forces before Derna and Tobruk while Enver commanded the whole Cyrenaican theatre from the same place. (Author's Collection).

salesman according to some sources, and crossed the Egyptian–Cyrenaican border on 8 December. Some ten days later he reported to Enver, who had been promoted to Lieutenant Colonel on 12 November 1911 and appointed as commander of the forces in Benghazi.[16] Enver accordingly informed the Ottoman War Ministry that 'Staff Major Mustafa Kemal joined the army at his own request on 18 December 1911.'[17]

Enver had written on 20 October that the morale of the Arabs was improving and that their understanding that he was related to the Caliph had affected them enormously.[18] As early as 4 October Enver had foreseen that countering Italian aggression would be impossible by conventional measures, and argued that a fallback on guerrilla warfare should be made.[19] The Ottoman Army had significant experience in counter-insurgency warfare and they used this knowledge, albeit in reverse as it were, to organise the resistance movement, the manpower for which had of necessity to come from the inhabitants of the *vilayet*.

There was at the time little in the way of a national identity amongst these peoples, though a nascent version was to be forged during the period of resistance to Italian rule. Indeed, one of the local leaders who came to the fore during this episode, Farhat al-Zawi (Farhat Bey), is reported to have told a French journalist who reported from the Ottoman side during the conflict that the population were 'patriots in bare feet and rags,

like your soldiers of the revolution, and not religious fanatics [. . .] if the Turkish
government abandons us we will proclaim that it has forfeited its right over our country.
We will form the Republic of Tripolitania.'[20] Despite this, and his admonition to the
same journalist not to write of 'Holy war' as it would make the resistance suspect in
French eyes, there is no doubt that the backbone of the struggle was indeed religious and
based on the Senussi Movement.

The Senussi (also transliterated into English as Sanusiya, Sanusiyyah, Sanusi and
Sanussi) was founded by Muhammad bin Ali al-Senusi (1787-1859) in 1837 as a
missionary effort among the Bedouin people of Cyrenaica. Initially its rationale was to
restore the original purity of Islam and to guide adherents towards a better understanding
of it, and to combating alien beliefs and practices. Grounded in the Maliki school of
religious law (one of the four schools of religious law within Sunni Islam) it soon
advanced towards being a political movement, though it would be a misrepresentation to
consider it fanatical or reactionary. According to Muhammad Khalil the movement did
not advocate violence or aggression unless provoked and 'professedly and openly declared
that its foremost weapons were 'guidance and persuasion.'[21] This began to change at the
turn of the century when Senussi influence reached the southern edge of the Sahara and
began to clash with French colonial expansionism. A new leader also arose in 1902 when
the grandson of Muhammad bin Ali al-Senusi inherited the title. Under Sayyid Ahmad
al-Sharif al-Sanusi the Senussi became more politically engaged and started to organise
military resistance, principally amongst the Bedouin peoples, against French
encroachment from the south.

The ideas and practices of the Senussi, who founded centres of both educational and
economic importance, gained traction with the inhabitants of the Ottoman *vilayet* to such
an extent that by the time of the Italian invasion the territories they effectively administered,
spiritually and materially, were almost independent of Ottoman governance. The leaders of
the Senussi were regarded not just as religious teachers but as leaders who were able to
exert both political and religious influence over the various tribes and, crucially, command
their respect and allegiance. Knut S Vikør argues that the movement could be considered
a brotherhood, which welded the ethnic identity of the Saharan Bedouin and neighbouring
peoples into something resembling a proto-nationalist movement.[22]

One of the few Europeans to come into contact with them was Hanns Vischer, the
Swiss-born British colonial administrator and explorer. He became famous for crossing
the Sahara from north to south, from Tripoli to Lake Chad, on horseback in 1906. Vischer
published an account of his journey in 1910 and made several references to the hospitality
he had received from the Senussi, and how they had protected his caravan from brigands.
His experiences led him to entertain respect for them and their ways:

> I have seen the hungry fed and the stranger entertained, and have myself enjoyed the hospitality
> and assistance enjoined by the laws of the Koran. My own experiences among the Senussi lead
> me to respect them as men, and to like them as true friends, whose good faith helped me more
> than anything else to accomplish my journey in spite of all difficulties.[23]

Rather presciently he did note: 'Should, however, the Senussi decide to fight the
Christians whose advance into the countries once ruled wholly by Islam they
naturally deplore, their number, organisation, and armament would make them a
formidable enemy.'[24]

They remained willing to acknowledge the Ottoman Sultan as their ruler, and Caliph, provided that his government did not in any way encroach upon their autonomy. This nominal allegiance was acknowledged by the Ottoman authorities, who accorded recognition to the Senussi and maintained cordial relations with them. Indeed, as has been pointed out, Ottoman representation in the *vilayet* was weak and enfeebled and, in reality, largely ineffectual, or, as Rosita Forbes put it: 'When the Italians landed in Libya in 1911, there existed a kingdom within a kingdom and the Turks were only masters in name.'[25]

The population that the Senussi sought, and were able, to unite at least to some degree, was around 1.5 million strong and composed mainly of Arab tribes, with a smaller proportion of Arab-Berber and non-Arab tribes.[26] Among the non-Arab grouping were the Berber tribes, many of whom had migrated from Algeria and Morocco, and the nomadic Tuareg, the latter being of Berber origin and living mainly in the south-west of Fezzan. There were also sub-Saharan Africans who had in many cases intermarried with both Arabs and Berbers. Those Arab tribes that lived mainly in the desert, and were usually nomadic or semi-nomadic, were collectively categorised as Bedouin.[27] There were also a number of Ottoman citizens of different backgrounds numbering around 50,000 mainly from Anatolia, Armenia and Albania. These were for the most part concentrated in urban, or semi-urban, areas and some at least were Christians. Also in the towns were other Christians from Spain and Malta totalling about 17,000, as well as around 20,000 Jews. These latter groups were, in the main, in areas occupied by Italy and in any event would have been immune to calls for resistance based on religious solidarity.

When Italy invaded Sayyid Ahmad al-Sharif al-Sanusi (Sidi Ahmed) was at Kufra (Kufara) in Cyrenaica. Kufra is a group of large oases located some 1500 kilometres south of Benghazi and spread over a roughly 200 kilometre long, vaguely crescent shaped, area. Situated in an extremely remote area it had only been described by one European, the German explorer Friedrich Gerhard Rohlfs who had visited it in 1878-9.[28] It was however a waypoint on an important trade and travelling route and, since the late nineteenth century, had been the main centre of the Senussi movement, hence the presence of the leader. Lisa Anderson points out that it may have been Enver Bey who personally convinced Ahmad al-Sharif to declare a *jihad* against the Italians.[29] However he was not a dictator and was obliged to call a meeting of the tribal chiefs and adherents and attempt to convince them to join in such a struggle. Given the remoteness of Kufra and the vastness of the area concerned, this council of war, as it may perhaps be called, did not convene until January 1912. According to Abdul-mola al-Horeir, when al-Sharif addressed it he encountered some reluctance as regards fighting, with many at the meeting arguing that the Italians were too powerful an enemy.[30] However, he rallied them by sheer force of personality it seems, and reinforcing his argument with apposite Quaranic quotations reiterated that *jihad* was a duty that had to be carried out against the invaders despite their superior power. He concluded his argument by stating that he would, if necessary, fight the Italians alone, armed only with his staff. This swung the attendees behind him, and on 23 January 1912 *jihad* was declared and al-Sharif effectively became the leader of the resistance movement. The call was swiftly answered:

> In Cyrenaica [...] a large number of tribal chiefs and tribesmen, roused by the call, hastened to rally around the Sanusi flag. In the Fezzan, the call to *jihad* [...] met a similarly favourable response. And in Tripolitania, steps were taken for the co-ordination of Arab resistance [...][31]

Even before any potential manpower deficiency was solved by the religious mobilisation of the population against the invaders, the Ottoman officers were putting into practice what Uyar and Erickson call their 'de facto strategic plan; they sought to wage a campaign of attritional unconventional warfare.'[32] To this end the *vilayet* was divided into operational areas, with Tripoli and Benghazi being the main ones. In these areas mission oriented units under the command and control of regular officers were formed from the tribesmen, de facto if not yet de jure *mujahedin,* leavened with regular soldiers and members of the gendarmerie.

Ottoman strategy was then dictated by a mix of Italian predominance at sea, the neutrality of the Great Powers, and Italian conventional military strength in the enclaves it held. On the other hand Italian strategy was, militarily, constrained by its inability to come to grips with the main body of the enemy, and, politically, by the need to maintain the neutrality of the Great Powers. Not offending one or other of these whilst bringing Italian strength to bear at some vital point, and thus forcing the Ottoman government to come to terms, was a conundrum that Giolitti and San Giuliano pondered. Their military and naval advisers had applied their minds to it even before the Battle of Tripoli. Pollio had raised the issue in a letter to his naval opposite number, Admiral Carlo Rocca Rey, on 19 October 1911.

> [...] I think it might be useful for us in the current war to occupy some part of the Ottoman Empire that will compel them to accept peace. Unfortunately we do not have a free hand and so we cannot act, for example, on the west-coast of the Balkan peninsula, or, by forcing the Dardanelles, go to Constantinople [...] But we can [...] take some island, as a bargaining counter at least. Strategically the island of Rhodes would be most valuable, and by taking it we would avoid the pitfalls of acting in the Cyclades Islands or Sporades.[33]

There would certainly have been pitfalls in acting in the Cyclades; they had been part of the Kingdom of Greece since 1832. Similar considerations applied to the Sporades, or at least the Northern Sporades as they were often called at that time. The Southern Sporades, or Dodecanese as they are now known, included Rhodes and had been Ottoman territory since 1522. Attention was though to turn to them again in 1912.

That the politicians were highly sensitive to the dangers of, even inadvertently, causing an international incident whilst conducting operations outside the main theatre had been exemplified in the Red Sea. The light cruiser *Puglia,* under *Capitano di Fregata* Pio Lobetti Bodoni, had been deployed there on 2 August 1911, and on the 5 November (some sources say 3 November) she discovered the Ottoman gunboat *Alish* hiding at the (now Jordanian) port of Aqaba (Akaba) and sank her by gunfire. This was hardly a major engagement; the Ottoman vessel was a wooden steamer armed with two 37 mm guns. The *Puglia* returned on 19 November and, in company with the older *Calabria,* bombarded the port and ancient castle. Despite the paucity and weakness of any potential targets, the navy was ordered to suspend all operations in the Red Sea from 20 November. This was because on 11 November the British vessel RMS Medina had left Portsmouth for Calcutta. Though the vessel had initially been escorted from the harbour by eleven Dreadnought battleships, the majority of the journey was completed under the protection of four armoured cruisers; *Argyll, Natal, Cochrane* and *Defence.* The route of these five ships was via Port Said, Suez, and Aden, which took them through the war zone. Aboard *Medina* were King George V and Queen Mary, whilst the whole was under the command of

Rear Admiral Sir Colin Keppel. The King Emperor and his consort were en-route to the 1911 Delhi Durbar, held in December to commemorate their coronation as Emperor and Empress of India. Not until the division had cleared any potential scenes of action, it arrived at Aden on 27 November, did Italian activity resume. On 30 November the Yemeni port of Shaykh Sa'id (Sheikh Said, Cheikh Saïd) the defensive guns of which controlled the southern exit of the Red Sea, was bombarded as was Mocha. On 1 December Khawkah was destroyed and twenty people killed, whilst Mocha, Dhubab, and Yakhtul were again bombarded on 3 December.

In any event, whilst grand strategy was the province of the politicians and military and naval leadership, the men on the ground in the main theatre, Tripoli, had designs of their own to accomplish. These included the recovery of the ground lost after the Battle of Tripoli, and expansion beyond. Frugoni lost no time in utilising the I Special Army Corps attempting the former, and on 6 November an assault, directed by Lieutenant General *Conte* Felice De Chaurand de Saint Eustache, was made by the 5th Brigade from the eastern trenches with the aim of retaking Fort Hamidije. According to Italian sources, both official and unofficial, this was accomplished without effort and resulted in great losses. As Irace related it: 'The resistance of the Turks and Arabs stationed there in considerable force was completely futile; and equally futile were their desperate attempts to make a counter-attack with both infantry and artillery, in the endeavour to drive back the Italian brigade. They were repulsed and routed with heavy loss.'[34]

However, those who were with the Ottoman forces told a slightly different tale. According to the journalist Sir Ernest Nathaniel Bennett, a 'disaster' overtook the 93rd Infantry Regiment, elements of which attempted a flanking movement from the sea.[35] This amphibious approach, covered by the guns of the ships, saw the troops landed on a beach in the vicinity of Shara Shatt. This move had been foreseen and a large number of Arab fighters deployed to counter it. Some 200 Italians managed to disembark, but they were immediately attacked and very few escaped alive. Five were, however, taken prisoner, and it was from these and Ottoman reports that Bennett got the story. Nevertheless, no matter how many setbacks the Ottoman forces were able to inflict upon the Italian army, they could not resist their attacks backed as they were by superior artillery and naval gunfire.

Fort Hamidije was accordingly retaken by 7 November, and the next day more ground was recovered around the Tombs of the Qaramanli. This high ground, which included a large Arab graveyard, an ancient tomb containing the remains of a holy man, and two domed buildings accommodating the Sarcophagi of the Qaramanli, lies on the flank of any advance towards Fort Hamidije. Heavy rain, 'which converted the trenches and rifle-pits into pools, and made the movement of guns or ammunition-carts almost impossible,' then forced a suspension of offensive operations for over a fortnight. According to one eyewitness, *The Times* correspondent, William McClure:

> Lakes formed in the desert and remained all through the winter, while the main torrents burst through the trenches at Bumeliana, drowning one soldier, seriously damaging the waterworks, and pouring down the Bumeliana road till the streets of Tripoli were a foot deep in swift-running water.[36]

It was only on 26 November that conditions had moderated enough for operations to be resumed. The main direction of this attack was to be easterly within the oasis.

The assault was to be made by de Chaurand's 3rd Division and the objectives were Fort Sidi Messri in the south, al-Hani in the centre, and Shara Shatt next to the coast. Fort Sidi Messri was to be assaulted by the 6th Brigade (23rd and 52nd Regiments) under Major General *Conte* Saverio Nasalli Rocca, reinforced with the 50th Regiment from the 4th Division, which had been held back from Cyrenaica. Supported by four batteries of artillery this force was to advance along the southern limits of the oasis, with its right flank protected by cavalry. The thrust on Shara Shatt was to be made by the 5th Brigade (18th and 93rd Regiments), whilst the centre was to be assaulted by an ad hoc force consisting of the *Fenestrelle* battalion of *Alpini*, the 11th *Bersaglieri* Regiment, and two Grenadier battalions. The whole operation was supported by artillery and the naval guns of the 'Training Division.'

In order to shield the attack the 1st Division kept a defensive watch on the southern side of the oasis in case any substantial attempt at reinforcement was made by the Ottomans. As an extra precaution a demonstration was made to the south, with a force estimated to be in the region of 5,000 strong. Moving in two columns the Italians advanced only about a kilometre and their behaviour puzzled observers. George Frederick Abbott later reported what had transpired: '[…] the Italians crept on, digging trenches at every one hundred metres - admirable tactics for defence, but for an advance purely imbecile. Finally, as the sun was setting, they began to beat a retreat.'[37] Their tactics, however apparently imbecilic, had succeeded inasmuch as they had fully engaged the attention of the Ottoman forces in the desert and at Ain Zara. This prevented any reinforcement of the forces in the oasis where, despite their overwhelming superiority, it was slow going for the Italians. The difficulties of the terrain made the combat akin to fighting in a built up area, and many of the Ottoman strongpoints had to be demolished with explosives. However by about 16:00 hours most of the ground that had been vacated following the Battle of Tripoli had been retaken and the troops were consolidating their positions. Their casualties had been comparatively light, somewhere around 120-160 officers and men killed and wounded dependent upon source, but the operation gave rise to another controversy.

Whilst searching the ground that they had retreated from on 23 October the Italian troops made a grisly find. The journalist William Kidston McClure, who was on the Italian side of the lines, related what he heard and what he saw.

Three bodies were discovered first, in a garden a little to the north-west of El Hani, three crucified and mutilated bodies. […] On the evening of [27 November], about fifty more bodies were discovered, indescribably mutilated, and some of them bearing obvious traces of torture. Early on the morning of 28 November, I visited an Arab house and garden, which had been used as a *posto di medicazione* (advance field hospital) by the 2nd battalion of the 11th Bersagheri, up to and during the fight of October 23. In the house there were five bodies, in the garden nine, and in a hollow at the back of the house, beside a well, there was a ghastly heap of twenty-seven bodies. […] No object would be served by detailing the record of human savagery displayed by those dreadful remains, the crucifixion, torture, and mutilation that had been practised upon living and dead. One case will suffice as an illustration, the case of a body which was identified by means of a pouch as that of a stretcher-bearer attached to the 6th Company of the *Bersaglieri*. His feet were crossed and his arms extended: he had clearly been crucified. There were holes in his feet, but his hands had been chopped off. His eyeballs appeared to have been threaded laterally by thick, rough palm-twine, and his eyelids were stitched in such a way as to keep his eyes open. In addition he had been shamefully mutilated.[38]

There were other foreign correspondents that were brought to witness these terrible scenes and who subsequently reported them to the wider world. One of these was Gaston Chérau (Leroux), author of *Le Fantôme de l'Opéra* (translated into English as *The Phantom of the Opera* in 1911), correspondent for *Le Matin*. His report appeared in the 30 November edition of the paper under the sub-heading *Horribles tortures infligées par les Arabes aux bersaglieri prisonniers ou blesses* (Horrible tortures inflicted by the Arabs on the *Bersaglieri* prisoners and wounded), and was extremely graphic:

> I was present at the interment of the mortal remains of many Italian soldiers who had fallen prisoners into the hands of the Turks and Arabs, and been by them barbarously massacred. These *Bersaglieri* who fell on October 23 died not merely as heroes, but also as martyrs. I cannot find words to express the horror which I felt to-day, when we discovered these luckless remains in an abandoned graveyard [...]
>
> In the village of Heni, inside the Arab burial ground, had been perpetrated an absolute butchery. Of the eighty ill-starred men whose bodies we discovered there, there is no doubt that quite half had fallen alive into the enemy's hands, and that all had been carried to this place, surrounded by walls, where the Arabs knew they were safe from Italian bullets. There took place here the most vile and loathsome carnage that can possibly be imagined.
>
> The victims' feet were cut off and their hands torn from their bodies. Some of them were crucified. The mouth of one was split from ear to ear; a second had his nose sawn off; others had ears cut away and nails torn out by some sharp instrument. Finally, there is one who has been crucified and whose eyelids have been sewn up with pack-thread.[39]

The unfortunate stretcher bearer also featured in the account of Bennet Gordon Burleigh, the *circa* 71-year old veteran correspondent for *The Daily Telegraph* in the 26 November edition of the paper:

> It was near the mosque by the Henni I had my attention called to the bodies of those who had fallen into the hands of the fiends of the desert. Five soldiers, *Bersaglieri*, had been tied to a wall, crucified as on a cross, and afterwards riddled with bullets. It is needless to dwell upon the nature of the further atrocities which savage Muslims invariably practise on the bodies of Christians. A sergeant had also been crucified, but with the head down, and in the hands and feet were still left enormous nails.
>
> A little farther away from this mosque a field hospital had been rushed, and every one put to torture and to death – doctors, hospital attendants, and wounded Italian soldiers. Bodies had been torn asunder, faces hacked, and limbs struck off as well as heads. [...] But worst of all was this. A hospital attendant under the Red Cross, named Libello, of the sorely tried 11th Regiment *Bersaglieri*, who also had been crucified, had first had his upper and lower eyelids perforated and laced with tightly tied coarse string. Each eyelid was then pulled, and the cord being tied behind his head, the eyes were held wide open, and could neither be blinked nor closed in life or merciful death. Flies and insects abounded. The look of unutterable horror on the strained face of Libello will remain fixed for ever before me.[40]

In many ways the discovery of the unfortunate Libello and his comrades was a blessing for the Italians and their supporters; they now had a counter to the accusations of massacre and uncivilised behaviour levelled at them. Accordingly, and as with the massacres, the atrocities committed on the *Bersaglieri* were either played up or pooh-poohed according to the disposition of the commentator. Those who were pro-Italian used the incident as evidence of the barbarity of their opponents in general. McClure, for example, noted that one of the bodies had been 'treated in a manner which is more familiar to those who have seen Turkish handiwork in Armenia and Bulgaria than to those whose experience has been confined to Arab practices.'[41] Similarly, the Italophile Richard Bagot, who had never visited Tripoli, delivered his judgement in 1912: 'these unnamable atrocities were committed, at the direct instigation and approval of Turkish officers, and in some cases actually perpetrated by Turks [...].'[42]

In the 1880s Manfredo Camperio, the president of the Milanese *Società di esplorazioni commerciali in Africa,* had asked 'How dignified, good, and interesting is the Libyan race! Who would have the courage to disturb these primitive people in their tranquil, pastoral life?'[43] Some thirty years later, and whatever the precise identity of the perpetrators, 'these primitive people' had, from the Italian soldiers' perspective been transformed into beasts (*belve*); the enemy had become inhuman (*disumano*).[44] This perspective translated into popular culture also. The Italian poet Gabriele d'Annunzio produced ten poems, *Canzoni per le gesta d'Oltremare* [Songs of Overseas Deeds], published in the *Corriere della Sera* from 8 October 1911 to 14 January 1912. These celebrated the war while it was happening and depicted it as a racial and religious crusade. Indeed, according to Lucia Re:

> The Christian rhetoric of the crusades is evoked in the description of the fight against 'the infidels,' who are depicted not only as vicious and inhuman beasts, but as ethnically and biologically unchangeable, animals destined to be locked in the inhumanity of an everlasting, unsurpassable barbarism. Eternally treacherous, bloody, and barbaric, they are doomed to replicate their sacrilegious and cruel acts over and over whenever their race is again confronted with the Christian world.[45]

If d'Annunzio be thought somewhat highbrow, then Carolina Invernizio, one of the most popular Italian writers of the early twentieth century might be considered. Her 1912 novel *Odio di araba* [*The Hatred of Arabs*] was set in Tripoli and contains a prologue which outlines her perspective:

> 'We are in the trenches of the eastern oasis of Tripoli at Sciara-Sciat on the morning of 23 October 1911, a fatal date which will remain a shining moment of glory in the history of Italian bravery, and will also mark the vile Arab attack, their ambush, their inhuman betrayal, while our sons were still trusting their acts of submission, and were convinced that they intended to surrender. How little did they know the true character of the Arabs, who [...] are the most despicable, deceitful, treacherous, ungrateful beings in the world! Their cruelty has no limits, their pride is boundless. [...] The hate that the Arabs feel for us and everything European is in their blood and depends not only on the horror which the Christian religion provokes in them, but also on the instinct which keeps them from any modification in their customs, in their clothing, in their life-style.'[46]

With this irrevocable breach the last strand of Italian pre-war strategy was broken, and all hopes for a short victorious war shattered. They could not, without extending the war into other theatres, force the Ottoman Empire to sue for peace. On the other hand, arriving at a compromise peace that would allow the Ottomans to cede the *vilayet* with some saving grace had, because it was domestically unacceptable, been rendered impossible by the decree of annexation. Italy was thus forced to remain in a seemingly open-ended conventional war, with all the consequences this entailed, whilst simultaneously conducting another, unlimited and hugely expensive, asymmetric colonial campaign against a population that was now viewed as irrevocably alien and hostile. Wishful thinking still prevailed to a certain extent; the French and British authorities in Tunisia and Egypt were blamed for not preventing 'the trade in contraband of war' across the frontiers. If this ceased, and the encouragement and interference of Ottoman officers was prevented, then the 'tribes from the interior will come and submit to their new masters when they realise that famine is at the door, as they are sure to be overtaken by that formidable scourge.'[47]

In the meantime however the 'tribes from the interior' – 'implacable as the expanse of sand and the scorching sun' in Tumiati's words – remained a defiant and potent force. It was in an attempt to curb their potency and drive them further back into 'the jaws of the Sahara' that Frugoni, having completed the recovery of the territory lost during the Battle of Tripoli, intended to take the fight beyond.

Table 2.

Reorganisation and
Reinforcement

November 1911

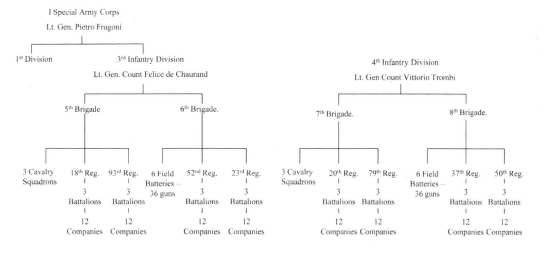

CHAPTER EIGHT

The Italians Advance

Tripoli, topographically and climatically, is an impossible country to invade.
Charles Wellington Furlong in *The New York Times*, 4 May 1912.[1]

O N 5 November the Italian authorities released a statement, the contents of which were, intrinsically, of little moment. Nevertheless the document is of historic importance, containing as it does the first official communication ever made pertaining to an operation by aeroplanes in warfare.

> Yesterday Captains Moizo, Piazza, and De Rada carried out an aeroplane reconnaissance, De Rada successfully trying a new Farman military biplane. Moizo, after having located the position of the enemy's battery, flew over Ain Zara, and dropped two bombs into the Arab encampment. He found that the enemy were much diminished in numbers since he saw them last time. Piazza dropped two bombs on the enemy with effect. The object of the reconnaissance was to discover the headquarters of the Arabs and Turkish troops, which is at Sok-el-Djama [Suk el Juma].[2]

Italian military aviation, as in all states that pursued the matter, had begun with lighter-than-air craft – balloons. Pre-unification Italy could boast at least one pioneer in this regard in Vicenzo Lunardi, who had first flown in London on 15 September 1784 whilst stationed there as secretary to the Neapolitan Ambassador. Following his return to Naples Lunardi made several ascents, including one from Sicily in July 1790 that lasted two hours.[3] Pre-unification Italy also had the distinction, if that is the correct term, of being the first target to be subjected to aerial bombardment. During the Austrian campaign to reduce the Republic of San Marco in 1849, the city of Venice was invested by Austrian forces. During the final stages of the conflict a novel expedient was attempted by the besiegers. According to Lieutenant General Gugliemo Pepe, the Commander-in-Chief of the forces of the Venetian Republic, they developed a scheme to utilise 'balloons and other aerostatic devices.'

After talking of these for two or three months, and after numerous experiments made in the Austrian camp near the Adriatic, and in that of Isonzo, they at last carried them into execution. They sent up some fire-balloons from their war-vessels stationed in the Adriatic, and opposite the Island of Lido. These went high enough to pass over that island, and the enemy flattered themselves that they would arrive and burst in the city of Venice; but not one ever reached so far. Under these balloons was a large grenade full of combustible matter, and fastened by a sort of cord, also filled with a composition, which, after a certain given time, was to consume itself. As soon as this happened, the grenade fell, and in its fall burst against the first obstacle which it struck. Of all these balloons that were sent up, one only left its grenade in the fort of St. Andrea del Lido. The others were all extinguished in the waters of the Lagoon, and sometimes sufficiently near the capital to amuse the population more than any other spectacle.[4]

The Italian Army gained a balloon detachment in the 1880s, with the 3rd Engineer Regiment, based at Rome, forming a company-sized aeronautical section on 6 November 1884. This 'Aerostatic Section' (*Sezione Aerostatica*), under Lieutenant Alessandro Pecori Giraldi, was equipped with two balloons purchased from France. The first manned flight of one of these took place on 7 November when Pecori Giraldi ascended to several hundred metres. The capability of the Aerostatic Section was demonstrated in the field in Eritrea in 1887-8, when three balloons were successfully utilised. Italian military aviation took further steps forward in 1894 with the inclusion of the section into a specialist brigade (*Brigati Specialista*) and the construction in 1908 of a dirigible, semi-rigid, airship which first flew on 3 October that year.[5] Designed and flown by two engineering officers of the specialist brigade, lieutenants Gaetano Arturo Crocco and Ottavio Ricaldoni, this craft was designated N1. Constructed at a base at Vigna di Valle on the southern shore of Lake Bracciano (*Lago di Bracciano*), its maiden flight saw it journey from Vigna di Valle to Rome and back. It covered the distance, some 70 kilometres in total, at an average speed of about 60 kph flying at an altitude of around 500 metres, and was the first aircraft ever to fly over Rome.

In terms of heavier-than-air craft, the first aeroplane flights in Italy were undertaken by the French aviator Léon Delagrange, who established several duration records there in 1908. On 23 June he flew continuously for 18 minutes 30 seconds at Milan, and on 8 July at Turin he took Thérèse Peltier aloft as a passenger, making her the first, though some sources argue second, woman to fly in an heavier than air machine. On 13 January 1909 a triplane, the first aircraft of wholly Italian construction, rose from the grounds of the Royal Palace at Venaria Reale near Turin. Designed and built by the automobile engineer Aristide Faccioli the flight was only partially successful inasmuch as the machine crashed and was severely damaged. This did not discourage Faccioli however, who went on to reconstruct the craft and design several more.

More reliable types were introduced to Italy in 1909 by the Wright brothers, who were invited to Rome by the head of aeronautics of the Special Brigade, Major Massimo Mario Moris. Moris had travelled to France to meet the brothers and invite them to bring an aircraft to Italy, which would be bought, as well as to train Italian officers to fly. The Wrights arrived at Centocelle near Rome (now *Aeroporto di Roma-Centocelle*) on 1 April 1909 and began assembling their 'Wright Model A Flyer' aircraft. Several notable persons, including King Victor Emmanuel, attended the demonstrations, which began on 15 April, and on one flight a cameraman was taken aboard producing the first motion picture taken from an aircraft. Between 15 and 26 April 1909 the Wright aeroplane performed 67 flights and carried 19 passengers aloft. Two officers, Lieutenant Mario Calderara of the navy and Lieutenant Umberto Savoia of the army, were trained by Wilbur Wright to operate the aeroplane; the former, having more experience, completing the training of the latter. The following year, on 17 July 1910, army aviation was reorganised as a separate battalion of the Special Brigade under the command of Lieutenant Colonel Vittorio Cordero di Montezemolo. New equipment and facilities were ordered; six new Crocco-Ricaldoni dirigible airships, ten foreign-built aeroplanes (2 Bleriot, 2 Nieuport, 3 Farman, and 3 Voisin) and two new airfields, at Somma Lombardo (at Varese in Lombardy) and Mirafiori (at Turin in Piedmont).[6]

On 15 October 1911 elements of the aviation battalion, designated the First Aeroplane Flotilla, arrived in Tripoli under the command of Captain Carlo Piazza. Under him were eleven officer pilots, 30 ground crew, and nine or ten aeroplanes: 2 Blériot, 3 Nieuport, 2 (some sources say 3) Etrich *Taube*, and two Farman biplanes. A further three aeroplanes were sent to Cyrenaica. The Tripoli unit became active on 21 October at a site, a narrow field, near the Jewish Cemetery (*Il cimitero degli Ebrei*) just to the west of the city on the coast. The construction of hangars to hold dirigibles was also begun. The force had been extemporised at somewhat short notice; the decision to furnish the expeditionary force with an aviation component had only been made on 28 September.[7]

With this unit being the first ever deployed in an active theatre of war, it was inevitable that it recorded several aviation 'firsts' whilst carrying out missions. As has been related, aviation history was made on 22 October when Captain Riccardo Moizo, an artillery officer, performed a combat reconnaissance flight, albeit apparently on his own initiative,

A *Taube* monoplane at Tripoli City, or at least the fuselage and tail section. Presumably the wings have yet to be attached or have been removed for some reason. Designed and built in Austria-Hungary in 1909 the *Taube* (Dove) was heavily utilised in the aviation forces of the Triple-Alliance as well as, to a lesser extent, further afield. It has two significant aviation 'firsts' to its credit; the first bombing mission (1 November 1911) and the first air to air combat (28 September 1914). (George Grantham Bain Collection/Library of Congress)

Captain Moizo's aeroplane. Having made aviation history by being the first person to perform an aerial reconnaissance mission in a combat situation and then, less fortunately, becoming the first aviator to have his craft hit by ground fire, Riccardo Moizo was to chalk up yet another first. On the morning of 10 September 1912 he took off from Tripoli in a Nieuport monoplane which, whilst over enemy territory, suffered an engine failure. He was forced to land near Azizia and was swiftly taken prisoner by Arab forces. This photograph, which appeared in the French newspaper *L'Illustration* on 5 October 1912, shows his craft together with some formally attired Ottoman officers posing alongside. (Author's Collection).

over enemy positions in a Bleriot. The first official flight was though made the next day, with Piazza flying west along the coast to Zanzur before returning – a mission lasting over an hour. The same day Moizo flew a mission double that length, with an observer, in a two-seater Nieuport. Moizo recorded another first on 25 October when he became the first pilot in history to have his aircraft hit by anti-aircraft fire. The dangers of enemy fire, whilst not to be discounted, were however comparatively slight compared with the perils of flying over the desert. Treacherous and unpredictable air currents, combined with the possibility of sand storms, made such an enterprise innately hazardous, whilst the inherent unreliability and fragility of the first aeroplanes and their engines only served to multiply the danger.

Another 'first' came on 1 November 1911 when 2nd Lieutenant Giulio Gavotti dropped four 'bombs' on enemy positions at Ain Zara (Ainzarra) and Tagiura (Tajura) from a height of 600 metres. These devices had been designed and manufactured at the San Bartolomeo torpedo establishment, a part of the great naval arsenal at Le Spezia. Named for their inventor, Naval Lieutenant (*tenente di vascello*) Carlo Cipelli, *granate Cipelli* (Cipelli Grenades) were fabricated from thin steel into a sphere weighing about half a kilogram when filled with picric acid. The grenades had fabric ribbons attached which, when air-dropped, provided a 'parachute' effect and helped to neutralise any horizontal travel. The presence of the ribbons led to them being nicknamed 'ballerinas.' They were difficult to deploy as a firing cap had to be inserted into them immediately prior to use; not an easy task for a solo pilot. Other, similar, ordnance available was of Norwegian origin though manufactured in Denmark. Designed by Nils Waltersen Aasen, who is generally credited with creating the first functioning hand grenade, the device was fitted with a cloth skirt attachment. It was armed by a long cord that burned through as it was thrown or dropped. Consequently, as a contemporary British source stated it: 'The chief property of the Aasen grenade is that it cannot explode prematurely during the first 11 yards [10 metres] of its flight, for the safety pin is only withdrawn after the burning of a strip of wool, 11 yards long, with which it is secured.'[8] According to some sources, the

Italians had seized a consignment of these weapons during the course of their blockade. The British airman and author, Edgar C Middleton, was to write in 1917 that 'the war in Tripoli was of immense advantage to the Italians both in the matter of experience and development in aerial warfare.'[9] Epitomising this reflection was the development of purpose-built bombs and devices for launching them from aircraft. An artillery officer, Lieutenant Aurelio Bontempelli, constructed finned cylindrical bombs containing explosive and shrapnel that could be launched through a tube affixed to the aircraft fuselage. In the early stages of the conflict, and certainly during November 1911, the Italian aviators had to make do with what they had or could contrive whilst they learned, or invented, techniques of air warfare.

These included the difficulties of photographing or bombing accurately from the air, which was rendered problematical due to the nature of the machines they were flying. According to an account by Piazza, the camera was mounted under the pilot's seat, and, as the nose of the aeroplane prevented a clear view of the ground under a given angle, the target became invisible as it was approached. In order then to take a photograph, or indeed drop a bomb, it was necessary to calculate the length of the interval between losing sight of the objective and being in a position to photograph or hit it. Presumably after a good deal of trial and error, the interval between no longer seeing 'the point to hit and the instant in which to drop the bomb,' or trigger the camera, was calculated at 35 seconds whilst flying at an altitude of 700 metres at a speed of 72 kilometres per hour.[10]

The pilots usually flew their machines at an altitude of between 600 and 800 metres but, as they discovered, the range of the Ottoman Mauser rifles when fired vertically was some 1700 metres. Consequently, the aeroplanes were frequently hit by fire from the ground, Moizo merely being the first to encounter this. Inevitably there came a time when the fire from the Ottoman Mausers hit one of the aviators. This occurred on 31 January 1912 when a two-seater Farman piloted by Captain Giuseppe Rossi and with one of the volunteer airmen, Captain Carlo Montu, as 'bombardier' took off from Tobruk. Their mission involved reconnoitring an enemy encampment some 30 kilometres distant and testing the Aasen grenade. According to Rossi's report:

> We flew at an altitude of 600 metres and had covered 15 kilometres when we spotted the first group of Arab tents. These welcomed us with such a volley of accurate fire that I had half a mind to give up continuing the mission. But I immediately felt ashamed of my timidity and headed directly toward the Turkish camp, giving my companion the first signal to make ready the bomb, which had to be suspended over the side for dropping.

> At 100 metres away from the centre of the camp I gave the second signal to Montu to drop the bomb and, to observe the effect, I turned immediately to the left. I saw a thick dust cloud rise from the ground and people, horses and camels scattered in every direction. It was a wonderful sight: the bomb had erupted with the intended effect. But the joy of this perception was severely impaired by the incessant crackle of the volley of fire aimed at us. I endeavoured to escape from this by turning to the right, but had to turn away again after seeing that this would take me right over the enemy camp. I steered back to the left, only to discover to my horror that a bullet had struck my aeroplane. I tried to climb but was unsuccessful, and so was passing over the left side of the camp when my companion shouted that he was wounded. I had turned around to look at him when the engine stopped and we began to descend. Happily it started again, but we were struck by two more bullets.

The engine was causing me great difficulties and to add to my misfortunes the wind, which was unfavourable, began to drive me off course. The Arabs never ceased firing for a moment whilst my machine hung in the air swaying as if in pain and almost stationary in the wind. I had an engine that was unreliable and feared that Montu might be fatally wounded, and that if he was no longer in control of himself he might unbalance the aeroplane. I expected death every minute but we managed gradually to return to our headquarters, when Captain Montu's injuries were attended to. He was not fatally wounded.[11]

Captain Montu, the President of the Aero Club of Italy and the commander of the volunteer airmen at Tobruk, thus became the first ever casualty of ground to air fire in the history of warfare.[12] Despite the experience of Rossi and Montu however, aeroplanes had already proven remarkably difficult to damage with rifle fire, and they had consequently become extremely useful to the Italians. This had been exemplified when Frugoni deployed all his airborne assets, both in reconnaissance roles and attempts at ground attack, during the advance to Ain Zara of 4 December 1911, where the enemy were estimated to number several thousand. Ain Zara in Italian hands would become an outpost giving advanced warning of any manoeuvres towards Tripoli and the coast that might be made by Ottoman forces. It would also protect the flank of Italian movements and communication eastward

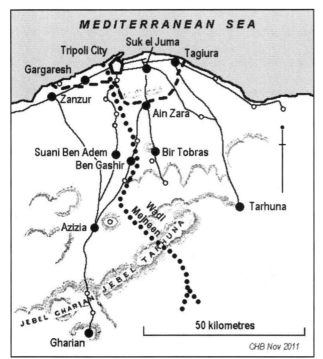

Tripoli and the occupied zone, together with the hinterland to the south, following the advance to Ain Zara.
After the arrival of substantial reinforcements and the formation of the *I° Corpo d'Armata Speciale* (1st Special Army Corps) the occupied zone around Tripoli City was expanded somewhat. Ain Zara was taken in early December 1911. The eastern portion of the Tripoli Oasis was also occupied, and the Ottoman forces withdrew. Initially they went to Azizia, some 40 kilometres to the south-west, but once the Italians began strongly fortifying Ain Zara moved their main position some 20 kilometres to Suani Ben Adem. Untrained for, and ill-equipped to wage, desert warfare the Italians were unable to make any further substantial advances for the duration of the conflict. Their enemy, consisting largely of irregulars unable to wage conventional warfare, could not eject them from their entrenched positions. The result was deadlock.
(© Charles Blackwood).

from Tripoli, particularly with regards to the coastal town of Tagiura (Tajura, Tajoura) situated on Cape Tagiura, which it was intended to advance to through the oasis. Tagiura was situated at what may be considered the far eastern extremity of the Oasis of Tripoli. The verdant area between Tagiura and Tripoli, some 18 kilometres in length and 5 kilometres wide, was described in 1817 as 'a tract of coast [...], which abounds with palm trees.' Little had changed in the intervening period, though the population of Tagiura that had then been enumerated as about three thousand 'chiefly Moors and Jews' was now greatly expanded by anti-Italian forces.[13] Amongst these was one of the officers that had managed to travel to Tripoli; Ali Fethi Bey (Fethi Okyar) an Albanian and the former Ottoman Military 'Attaché in Paris. Fethi had his HQ at a place named Suk el Juma, so called because a market was held there on Fridays. This consisted, unsurprisingly, of a large marketplace and little else. There were however some shops on one side of the marketplace, whilst facing them on the other were two government buildings where the Ottoman HQ was established. The war correspondent for Central News, Henry Charles Seppings Wright, visited the HQ which he described as being 'right under the guns of Tripoli.' He described the work there as dangerous, and communication between it and Ain Zara difficult because 'the alertness of the Italians render[ed] it unsafe to ride there during the day.' Travelling at night was preferable, because 'one can get through without having to dodge big shells.'[14] Just to the north of Suk el Juma was the village of Amruz (Amruss), described as being 'surrounded by gardens, and containing many habitable houses, in which the Turkish soldiers were comfortably lodged.'[15]

Ain Zara is a small oasis about 6.5 kilometres south east of Tripoli, at which the Ottoman forces had, to some degree, concentrated; Nesat Bey had his headquarters near there some 5 kilometres to the south. The oasis itself was described by the British journalist Alan Ostler, who was employed as a war correspondent for the *Daily Express*. He travelled to Tripoli via Tunisia and spent several months with the Ottoman forces and their commander. According to Ostler, Ain Zara consisted of:

> [...] a short street of tents along the side of a sandy hollow. Horses, tethered in a line behind the tents, snuffed the ground for stray grains of barley. [...] At the bottom of the hollow, disposed in a sort of square, were barley sacks and camel saddles, boxes of cartridges, and three light waggons taken from the Bersaglieri only a few days ago. They were commissariat wagons, with the numbers of their companies and the name of the regiment stencilled in white upon their sides.[16]

Around the oasis, and screened from view from the north by sand ridges, were 'many scattered villages of tents' including one where the Ottoman cavalry were bivouacked. Further out to the west there were also two *fenduks* (*fendukes, fondouks*), *Fenduk Sharki* and *Fenduk Gharbi*.[17] *Fenduk Sharki* was about one kilometre away from Ain Zara and had been converted into a hospital, over which flew the flag of the Red Crescent. The whole area, including the hospital, was within range of the Italian naval artillery. George Frederick Abbott, who had 'decided to join the main Turkish and Arab forces in the desert round Tripoli town, with the object of collecting material for a book on the campaign,' later wrote that the patients of the hospital, 'while waiting for the overworked surgeon to dress their wounds, amused themselves by squatting under the arched gateway and watching the Italian shells swish in the air, burst, and drop, digging deep pits in the ground around them. Some of these projectiles dropped on the hospital itself, despite

Italian Trenches at Ain Zara. Though probably a posed photograph, it illustrates well the difficulties the Ottoman forces faced in attempting to attack the Italian positions. Essentially composed of irregulars, the attackers might at best be classed as light infantry with little in the way of artillery to support them. On the other hand, the Italian forces had abundant artillery further supported by naval gunfire so long as they remained within range of the coast. When the Italians did advance inland they did so in such strength as to be irresistible, which had the concomitant effect of rendering their manoeuvres ponderous in the extreme. The advance to Ain Zara, a small oasis about 6.5 kilometres south east of Tripoli, on 4 December 1911 exemplifies this. Under the cover of artillery support from both naval and land-based guns, more than half of Frugoni's *i° Corpo d'Armata Speciale* were deployed; the 1st Infantry Division enlarged by a third brigade and extra artillery. The objective was taken, but the enemy forces easily escaped. (Author's Collection).

the Red Crescent flag that flew over its roof.'[18] Nesat had around 700 regular troops, including 60 cavalrymen and about 1,500 irregulars under his command as well as eight artillery pieces. In terms of supplies, particularly food, they were reasonably well off. Fethi Bey remarked to Ostler that, 'No doubt it pleases the Italians to picture us as starving in the desert, but before they bring us to that stage, they must cut off our line of communication. And, as yet, they have not ventured inland beyond the range of their own naval guns.'[19] The Italian reinforcements had though included heavy artillery, and for the advance on Ain Zara, Frugoni utilised batteries of 152 mm guns and 203 mm howitzers emplaced at Messri and Bulemiana. These batteries were certainly capable of reaching most of the Ottoman positions.

The nearest of these were around three kilometres from the Italian line and consisted of trenches and other excavations. The left of the Ottoman position was to the south-west of Bulemiana and was composed of trenches, described by Abbott as 'primitive ditches following the up-and-down, in-and-out curves of the dunes, and providing very indifferent cover.'[20] These had been augmented by shelters dug into the sand behind the trenches, though connected to them by zigzag saps, and roofed over with planks covered with sand. Each of these could provide shelter for about ten men, protect them from shelling, and conceal them from accurate observation from the air. Manning these defences were around thirty regular soldiers and about two hundred Arab irregulars under a lieutenant; their only heavy weapon was a German manufactured machine gun, probably an MG-09, the 7.65 mm export version of the Maxim machine gun. Farther to the east about opposite to the Tomb of Sidi Messri at some three kilometres distance, was a battery of three field guns and about twenty regular infantry under the command of a captain. Some three hundred irregulars were stationed to the south-west of this position, whilst to the south-east was another field piece opposite Fort Sidi Messri. A further battery of four guns was positioned just to the north of Ain Zara. Curiously both sides were armed with Krupp field artillery; the Italians had the 75 mm 1906 model and the Ottomans the 87 mm 1897 model. The range of the latter was however much inferior. Other than the troops, regular and irregular, mentioned above, Nesat had another similar sized body in front of Ain Zara and a fourth positioned some four kilometres to the west, which included some cavalry.

Frugoni's plan was relatively simple. Under the cover of artillery support from both naval and land-based guns he would attack using more than half of his *i° Corpo d'Armata Speciale,* or, in other words, overwhelming force. The manoeuvre was structured around the 1st Infantry Division under Lt. Gen. Count *Conte* Guglielmo Pecori Geraldi, which was enlarged by a third brigade and extra artillery. The battle was to be fought by brigades; on the left was the 1st Brigade under Rainaldi, augmented by the 93rd Regiment from the 5th Brigade of de Chaurand's 3rd Infantry Division. The task of the strengthened 1st Brigade was to operate within the oasis to the east, and apply pressure to the Ottoman forces there in order to fix them in position and prevent them manoeuvring or redeploying; the 93rd Regiment being tasked with advancing on Amruz. This would prevent the forces in the oasis from interfering with the main Italian forces operating to the south, or indeed vice-versa. Earmarked with a special duty in this regard were two battalions of the 52nd Regiment from the 6th Brigade, stationed at Fort Sidi Messri under Colonel Amari. Amari's command was not part of the operation in the oasis, but was, if necessary, to advance from Fort Messri to interdict the road from Ain Zara to Suk el Juma should the enemy attempt to move any of their forces along it.

The other two brigades were to advance in column; the centre column, consisting of an ad-hoc Mixed Brigade (*Brigata Mista*), was commanded by Major-General Clemente Lequio. This brigade was formed from the 11th Bersaglieri Regiment, one battalion of Alpine Troops (the *Fenestrelle*), and the 2nd Battalion of Grenadiers (*granatieri*), together with supporting mountain artillery. With his left flank protected by Rainaldi and Amari, Lequio's objective was Ain Zara itself, upon which he was tasked with approaching directly. This would hopefully fix the defenders in position whilst the right-hand column, the 2nd Brigade under Giardina, with two squadrons of the 15th Light Cavalry Regiment (*Cavalleggeri di Lodi*) on his extreme right, attempted to flank the defences and circle around behind the oasis.

In all, about 15,000 troops were to take part in the advance to the south, whilst another 3,000 or so were engaged in the oasis. Several field and mountain artillery batteries were in direct support, whilst the newly-landed heavy guns and howitzers, and the naval artillery aboard the ships, offered more distant support. The terrain over which the Mixed and 2nd Brigade were to advance was such as to make it almost impossible to conduct conventional military operations. Charles Wellington Furlong described the conditions and the difficulties they caused as follows:

> It is a land essentially of shifting sand dunes, into which the narrow boots of the Italian soldiers sink deeply, and which can only be traversed by sticking to narrow, winding trails between sand mounds, which average thirty feet [nine metres] and which are sometimes ten times as high. The winding trails are only as broad as a city street. The columns of the Italian army of invasion can't deploy or spread out in open order. The men in front are picked off as they come up on the Arabs, who lurk behind the dunes or who – a favourite trick with them – bury themselves in the sand so that even their heads cannot be seen.

> Cavalry movements are impossible in such a country, and no artillery larger than a three-pounder or machine gun can be drawn. All food, water and even fodder must be transported by the invading army, because there is no such thing as 'living on the country' in Tripoli. The only places where vegetables, fruit and water can be obtained are the oases. And the Arabs take care that there is little left in the oases for the enemy to live on. All the fruit and vegetables are taken away and dead camels or mules are thrown into the wells to pollute the enemy's water supply. The only method of transportation which is practical in that country is by camel. But the Italians have no camels, the Arabs having been careful to leave none behind them.[21]

The ground between Tripoli and Ain Zara was even more hazardous, being intersected with *wadis*; dry, and not so dry, riverbeds. Indeed, the night of 3-4 December had seen severe rain and there was a heavy storm at daybreak. Accordingly it is somewhat paradoxical to note that because the rains had filled many of the riverbeds, as well as creating several deep pools, one of the potential dangers faced by those advancing into the desert was drowning. One particularly large *wadi* that had been in flood since the advent of the rains, *wadi Mejneen*, was to mark the demarcation line between the two brigades; the Mixed Brigade to the east and the 2nd Brigade to the west. The latter, deployed in column by regiments, had the furthest distance to travel and set off first when the sun rose at about 08:05 hrs, preceded by the cavalry. The central column deployed into marching order shortly afterwards, with the *Bersaglieri* in the van and the *Alpini* bringing up the rear, and began moving due south. It was a stormy morning, but the weather that soaked the troops was not bad enough to prevent flying over the desert, which wore 'a look of desolation most depressing in the morning twilight' according to Irace who was with the *Bersaglieri*. He wrote in heroic terms of 'Captain Moizo's aeroplane flying on the storm against the lurid background of the great clouds which the wind whirls and twists.' Moizo, who had attached the Italian national flag to the rear of his craft, was not merely there to raise the morale of the damp soldiery. When he spotted concentrations of the enemy he attacked them. According to Irace again:

> [...] we see him circling in great sweeping rings over a special point, like a hawk which has sighted its prey below. Five minutes more and we mark in the far distance, rising from the ground one after the other, in a straight line right ahead of us, eight towering black columns of smoke, like gigantic solitary trees sprung up by magic on the horizon. The master of the sky has sighted the enemy's trenches and bombarded them, vanishing shortly afterwards towards Ain-Zara.[22]

Whether Moizo, and his fellow pilots, were responsible for the 'towering black columns of smoke' is debatable. Because they had very small charges and tended to bury themselves in the sand before exploding, the grenades utilised were largely ineffective unless they dropped amongst a group of people. As the Ottoman forces had learned to scatter upon the approach of an aircraft, the pilots concentrated on what they could see and, according to some sources, *Fenduk Sharki*, being large and therefore obvious was a favourite target.[23] The soft sand also mitigated the effects of the heavy artillery shells; these sometimes penetrated to the depth of a metre or more before exploding.[24]

Though the fire of the heavy and naval artillery would have been the most damaging had it been able to hit its target accurately, this was rendered problematical because it could only fire indirectly. As an aid to spotting, a captive observation balloon (*drachen-ballon*) was sent up from one of the ships to a height of some 1300 metres. From this lofty position the observers were able, to some extent, to correct the fire of the big guns. What would have made a real difference were using aircraft for this service. However, whilst they were eminently suited for the task, they lacked any means of real time communication, or near so, between the aviators and the gunners. Thus observers in aircraft could only communicate by landing to deliver a report, or dropping weighted notes in small metal containers, either of which meant flying away from whatever was being observed. Guglielmo Marconi himself was to argue that whilst the aeroplane had 'demonstrated in Tripoli its usefulness for scouting purposes in wartime' this usefulness would 'be greatly multiplied if the aeroplanes could carry wireless telegraph instruments and operators so that information gathered on scouting trips could be instantly communicated to the operating forces.'[25]

To counter the Italian advance Nesat ordered the troops stationed to the west of Ain Zara to advance and cover the left flank of the trenches in front of Bulemiana. He also ordered the guns near Ain

'*The New Arm's Fearful Strength: Death from the Air*': this drawing appeared in *The Illustrated London News* on 13 January 1912 and was derived from a sketch made by Henry Seppings Wright. Despite the effects depicted, he was to write that 'bombs from the aeroplanes were small; quite sufficient to create a scare, but not so deadly and destructive [as those launched from dirigibles]. Also the great elevation at which they flew presented the camp as a very small target.' The first ever delivery of ordnance from an aeroplane occurred on 5 November 1911.
(Author's Collection).

Zara to advance and support the defenders facing Sidi Messri, but great difficulty was encountered in moving them across the desert and each needed ten pairs of horses to drag it through the sand. It took three hours to get three of the guns forwards and these, together with about fifty regulars, were positioned slightly to the west of the extant battery.

With these reinforcements the Ottoman front was about 5 kilometres wide and manned by approximately 500 regulars and 1,000 irregulars. The Italian infantry advanced slowly and carefully under the cover of the overwhelming artillery superiority that the pitifully few Ottoman guns could do little to counter. Ordinarily Ain Zara would have been about two hours march from Tripoli, but it was some four hours later that the position on the right of the Ottoman line, its commanding officer having been killed, began to give way and the troops to retire leaving their dead and carrying their wounded. With the left retiring, the centre of the line had also to give way and begin to fall back slowly.

The Ottoman infantry, though forced from its first line of trenches, did not quit the field but rather fired at the Italian infantry from whatever cover could be found. However, as Irace put it, 'They cannot long resist the fire of our artillery and the menace of the enveloping movement.'[26] The enveloping movement by the 2nd Brigade had indeed forced the Ottoman left to give ground, whilst the reinforcements sent by Nesat had become entangled with the Italian cavalry and were also forced to retreat. In withdrawing the Ottomans were required to abandon their artillery through an inability to tow the guns away. One observer reckoned that it took no fewer than 19 horses to drag a gun through the desert sand. This problem also affected the Italians, though they had a way around the worst of it in the shape of mountain artillery.

Attached to the army in Tripoli were three groups (gruppi), each of three batteries, of mountain artillery. The 2nd (Mondovì) and 3rd (Torino-Susa) groups were part of the 1st Mountain Artillery Regiment (1° Reggimento Artiglieria da Montagna), whilst the 2° Reggimento Artiglieria da Montagna had provided its 3rd (Vicenza) group. These artillery regiments formed the organic artillery component of the Alpini, the army's mountain warfare force. Incongruous though it might appear, the Alpini had extensive experience of operating in North Africa. The 1st African Alpine Battalion (1° Battaglione Alpini d'Africa) had been formed in 1887 and campaigned in Eritrea and Ethiopia. The mountain artillery were equipped with the 70 mm Cannone da 70/15, which weighed nearly 400 kg when assembled, but could be broken down into four loads for transporting by mule.[27] The ammunition was also loaded onto mules. The mobility conferred allowed the 2nd Brigade to emplace mountain guns under Colonel Besozzi on a large dune to the south-west of Bulemiana and, from roughly 14:00 hrs, direct enfilade fire onto the enemy positions to their east. Under fire from two directions, the Ottoman forces facing the left of the Italian advance were obliged to retire southwards.

The Italian infantry moved forward as the Ottomans began to retreat, though they did not press hard. By this time the 2nd Brigade and the cavalry were advancing to the west of the wadi Mejneen and Nesat at Ain Zara perceived that his forces were in danger of being encircled, and ordered a general retirement to the south west in the direction of Kasr Azizia some 40 kilometres away. As he later explained to Abbott:

There was nothing else to do. When I saw the enemy coming on - regiment after regiment - my only thought was to save my men. I feared the Italians might take it into their head to send a regiment round our left, and take us all prisoners![28]

Attached to the army in Tripoli were three groups (*gruppi*), each of three batteries, of mountain artillery, which ordinarily formed the organic artillery component of the *Alpini*, the army's mountain warfare force. The possession of such weaponry - guns that could be broken down and transported on the backs of mules or camels – proved invaluable due to the desert terrain. Field artillery was extremely difficult to move with up to 19 horses required to drag a single piece through the sand. (George Grantham Bain Collection/Library of Congress)

At about 15:00 hrs the majority of the Ottoman forces had conducted a fighting withdrawal towards Ain Zara. However, a previously unengaged contingent that had been stationed some 6.5 kilometres to the west of Tripoli, near Gargaresh, and had been summoned by Nesat, appeared near the *wadi* to the west of the oasis. Seemingly oblivious to the presence of the 2nd Brigade, or that his command was in its path, the commanding officer led his men towards the *wadi* until he was intercepted by a messenger who warned him of the situation. This information must have caused the officer to panic, as instead of taking up a position whereby he could impede the advancing Italian brigade, if only for a time, he instead led his command in a dash southwards. According to Abbott 'he was the only Turk who on that day failed to do his duty, and he was subsequently cashiered for his incompetence.'[29] Not that it would have made any difference, for there was no, or very little, fighting between the infantry of the two sides. Whenever the Italians encountered resistance, and the Ottoman forces sniped at them incessantly, rather than engage in infantry attacks they made the defenders retreat by bombarding their position.

The vast majority of the Ottoman forces being irregular, they had their families and other non-combatants camped around Ain Zara. The order to retreat obviously applied to them too, but as Ostler discovered they seemed reluctant to up sticks:

> Beyond the ridge that shelters the greatest of the many scattered villages of tents, I came to the straggling encampment of the Arab women, children, and camp-followers. Here were the

markets that supplied the army with fodder, meat and flour, and milk and eggs. Already the market was afoot, and the thoughtless Arabs chattered and haggled and brawled, heedless as ever of the rumbling guns; though here and there upon the crests of the rolling dunes sat groups of men intently watching clouds and rings of smoke far to the north. At little distances, too, upon the ridges, sentinels in Turkish uniform kept watch upon the fight, but in the hollows noisy Arab commerce ruled the day.[30]

It was one of the local leaders, Suleiman el Barouni, who with his colleague Farhat al-Zawi had been a deputy in the Ottoman Parliament, that roused them: 'The Italians have come against our left in thousands; but on the right we still hold them back. I go to Suk el Juma.' One of the reasons el Barouni went to the HQ of Fethi Bey was to order or help organise the Ottoman retreat from the Oasis of Tripoli, where the retreat order also applied. With Ain Zara in Italian hands Ottoman communications with their forces in the oasis would be effectively severed. The 1st Brigade had not made much headway in penetrating the Ottoman-held part of the oasis due to the difficulty of the terrain. Italian artillery preponderance was of much less utility when they were fighting in what was, effectively if not actually, a built up area with its 'maze of deep, tortuous lanes, winding among gardens and groves, the trees and enclosures of which afforded ample cover to the defenders.'[31] Elements of the brigade, supported by marines – 'men in white' landing from warships[32] – had managed to get forward along the coast, avoiding the worst of the 'maze,' nearly as far as the Ottoman HQ at Suk el Juma, a distance of 5 kilometres or so. But being unsupported on their right flank through the inability of the rest of the brigade to advance, they could not consolidate, and were forced back to their original position.

Nor had the two battalions of the 52nd Regiment under Colonel Amari had an easy time of it. They had advanced from Fort Sidi Messri to interdict the Suk el Juma-Ain Zara road as per plan, but had come under fire from their own artillery. They took some casualties and their advance was halted whilst a messenger was sent back to the fort. When they resumed their advance they were opposed. Abbott got the tale from 'Ismail Effendi, a middle-aged Lieutenant of infantry – the Turkish officer in command at that point:'

> I was stationed in the Fenduk Jemel, opposite Fort Sidi Misri, on the Ain Zara road, with fourteen Turks and two hundred Arabs. An Italian regiment attacked us furiously, shouting 'Hurrah! Hurrah!' and drove us out of the fenduk. Then my Arabs made a counter-attack, yelling 'Allah! Allah!' and forced the Italians to fall about one hundred and fifty metres back. These attacks and counter-attacks went on till evening, and at sunset the enemy withdrew into their trenches. About an hour and a half later we made an offensive reconnaissance to see if there were any Italians in front of us or not. We found the field deserted and covered with knapsacks, water-flasks, caps, shovels, rifles, and cartridges. We picked up as much of the loot as we could, and returned to the fenduk, where we rested and slept till midnight. About an hour after midnight two horsemen came to tell us that the headquarters had moved from Ain Zara to Ben Gashir, where we were ordered to follow at once. We could not make out why.[33]

Nesat's order to withdraw was also greeted with something approaching incredulity at Suk el Juma. Like Ismail Effendi's command, they were unaware of the precise nature of the events to their south and had similarly more than held their own against the Italian attacks. Accordingly, those Arab irregulars who were so minded refused to obey and remained in the oasis. The others moved along the Ain Zara road, which of course remained open, and joined the exodus, first to Ben Gashir, around 28 kilometres south of Ain Zara, and then a further 31 kilometres to the south west to El Azizia (Kasr Azizia, Al 'Aziziyah). The forces at Ain Zara had begun to retreat at about 16:00 hrs and, rather remarkably, this manoeuvre was carried out in a leisurely manner, at least by the regulars. Abbott likened their attitude to that of:

> [...] an East End mob going home after a day on Hampstead Heath. There was no hurry [...] The soldiers just strolled away, passed Ain Zara, and got to the headquarters. The first to arrive there were the artillerymen with some of their horses, but without any artillery. The infantry followed. Then came the Staff officers.[34]

This would have been leaving it too late had not the 2nd Brigade swung eastwards towards Ain Zara at about 15:30 hrs, more or less at the same time as the Mixed Brigade was approaching the oasis from the north-west. From the peak of some of the higher ridges around the place they were able to see the last of the fighters and the camp followers evacuating the place in a disorderly mass. Ostler, who was with them, described the sight thus:

> The retreating columns marched across sands now glowing rosy in the sunset [sunset was a little after 18:00 hrs]. Belated Arabs straggled beside the ranks of marching Turks. Arab women, carrying huge loads, staggered wearily through the loose sand, but would not bate a whit of their burdens. One passed me bearing on her head a shallow wooden dish of mighty size, inverted, hat-wise. There were tiny children, hardly old enough to walk. I saw a pair of new-born calves, yoked together at the neck. Frail as they were they must bear some household burden; and even sheep and goats had packs and nets of fruit on their backs. A fainting rabble followed in the army's wake, and the desert way for close on twenty miles was strewn with discarded horse-gear, cooking pots, a chair or two, and miscellaneous litter from the Arab tents.[35]

It seems probable that the 2nd Brigade had mismanaged its swing to the east, and so rather than cutting off Ain Zara it merely approached it from that direction. This left the south uncovered and allowed the former occupants to escape. This was not unobserved as has already been noted, and why the Italians, and particularly their cavalry, made no attempt to intercept this mass is a mystery. Little resistance would have been encountered, since to cover the retreat, or at least to give warning of Italian intentions, only a small detachment of cavalry under Captain Ismail Hakki had been deployed. They were not called upon to do any fighting, but according to Abbott, who got the story from him later, Hakki observed the Italians from the top of a high dune. From a distance of some 150 metres he had a good view of at least the vans of both brigades in the moonlight, and he saw them deploy outposts whilst the battalions behind them remained massed. There was much shooting by the sentries at shadows and bushes swayed by the breeze, but his conclusion was that the Italians had settled down for the night. Once he had established that there was no danger of any further activity from the Italians, Hakki returned to Ain Zara at around 21:00 hrs and calmly dined. The Italian decision allowed several parties of Ottoman combatants from north of Ain Zara to pass through it during the night without hindrance, and the last contingent from the oasis left at 04:30 on the morning of 5 December with a small caravan of camels. The oasis was occupied by the Italian forces at daybreak without fighting and work on constructing entrenchments immediately began.

The capture of Ain Zara was undoubtedly a useful victory, though not perhaps of quite the stature that the Italian army made of it. Reports based on a communiqué issued from Tripoli on 6 December told their version of the battle:

> The fighting lasted from daylight to dusk. When darkness began to fall, 8,000 Turks and Arabs disappeared rapidly to the south-east. A long line of camels was with them, bearing their wounded. The Turks lost several hundred killed, while the Italian casualties are estimated at 100. The headquarters staff of the Italian Army asserts that the battle was a decisive one for the possession of the country, as it has almost entirely cleared the oasis around the town of Tripoli and forced the Turks from the coast and away from their bases of supplies.[36]

This pronouncement, as with all similar types issued during the conflict, must be treated with some scepticism. Though there are no accurate reports of, and no way of calculating accurately, the number of those who evacuated Ain Zara, it seems highly unlikely that they numbered anything like 8,000. The best estimates, made from the observations of the various foreigners, mainly correspondents, who retreated with the Ottomans reckon the numbers to have been less than 4,000, including non-combatants. Neither did the capture force the enemy 'away from their bases of supplies'; these, such as they were, were not on the coast, which was already dominated by Italian naval supremacy. The claim about the battle clearing the enemy from the Oasis of Tripoli was however accurate, or mainly so. Although a number of irregulars had declined to obey Nesat's order to evacuate, they were few, and when the eight battalions of Rainaldi's strengthened 1st Brigade resumed the offensive they made swift headway. Tagiura was occupied on 13 December without serious opposition.

Frugoni had then, by the use of a military force ill-equipped and poorly trained to deal with the terrain, manoeuvred his enemy out of their position at Ain Zara without serious fighting; the total Italian casualties are reckoned to have been 17 killed and 94 wounded. This can be viewed as tactically skilful, however at the operational level the battle was a failure inasmuch as it did little to diminish the Ottomans capacity to resist. The main factor in this was that, by accident or design (and probably the former), the 2nd Brigade and the cavalry had turned too soon to cut off the enemy and prevent their retreat. Had Ain Zara been encircled from the south then it is at least possible that a large number of Ottoman regular troops might have been captured, which would have severely weakened the ability to resist Italian occupation. Pursuit of the retreating enemy was also rendered difficult, if not impossible, because the traditional main arm of pursuit, the cavalry, were weak (two squadrons at 142 men per squadron).[37] Also, and like the infantry and artillery, they were unable to operate properly in such difficult terrain. Indeed, the fact that such a small force of cavalry was attached to the right wing of the brigade suggests that using them in pursuit was not envisaged, and that their task was confined to screening the flank of the advance.

The Ottomans retired initially to Azizia, some 40 kilometres to the south-west, but once the Italians began strongly fortifying Ain Zara they advanced their main position some 20 kilometres to Suani Ben Adem (Senit Beni-Adam). This place was, as McClure noted, close enough to threaten the surroundings of Tripoli, whilst being 'far enough away to admit of an easy retreat [...] if that course should seem politic.'[38] That a retreat, easy or otherwise, would not become politic was quickly to become evident.

CHAPTER NINE

Deadlock

When Europe knows how few were the men who for months kept the great and splendidly equipped Italian army cooped up, so that it hardly dared to venture forth from the town of Tripoli, and is even now confined to a very few miles of coast-line, the standing of Italy as a military power must surely be forever lost.

Alan Ostler, *The Arabs in Tripoli*, 1912[1]

EXPECTATIONS that Frugoni would prove an aggressive general seemed to have been confirmed with the advance on Ain Zara. The former Ottoman HQ was turned into 'a miniature fortress; planks by hundreds were formed into rough parallel stockades and the space between filled with sand and rubble.'[2] The garrison for this stronghold was powerful, consisting of the 1st Infantry Division under Lieutenant-General Count *Conte* Pecori-Giraldi, and arrangements were made to construct a railway between it and Tripoli. It was first proposed that this be a 'Decauville Railway' – a 600 mm narrow gauge line made up of easily portable pre-assembled sections[3] – but this was upgraded to a 950 mm gauge line before work started.

As originally conceived, the taking and fortification of Ain Zara was but a first step in a scheme for further advances. Caneva and Frugoni were planning a divisional-strength advance into the 'Jaws of the Sahara' in order to clear the enemy from the oases that lay on the Tripolitanian coastal plain (the Jefara plain), the southern boundary of which was marked by the Nafusa Mountains.[4] One of the primary targets would be Al 'Aziziyah (El Azizia, Azizia) some 55 kilometres south-west of Tripoli, a major waypoint on the route from the coast to the mountains and beyond to the Fezzan. Though the term desert implies a trackless expanse of sand and rock this was not quite the case. There were routes through it that had been used for centuries, perhaps millennia, by camel caravans. Such caravan routes, or *masrabs* as they were sometimes termed, were observed and studied by a New Zealander who had enlisted in the British Army and was stationed in Western Egypt in 1916, Captain Claud H Williams:

> The *masrabs* consist of wavy camel tracks a few feet apart, running parallel to one another, and vary in number from 5 or 6 to 50 or 60 according to the importance of the route. In one case 120 distinct camel tracks were counted and the *masrab* was consequently over 100 yards in

width. The *masrabs* appear to be of great antiquity, for the tracks are, in some places, deeply worn into solid rock; the constant traffic over a period of hundreds of years has rendered them much firmer and more solid than the surrounding unbeaten desert. A little study of the map will show the system in which they are laid out, and how connection can be made between almost any part of the coast and the important places in the interior [...] they help define one's position on the map in travelling across their course.[5]

The purpose of Williams' study was in relation to the use of motor vehicles for penetrating the desert, using the ancient routes for travel and reference points. Prior to the advent of reliable vehicles, which were just coming into being in 1911, the only way to move through the desert was on foot or on the back of an animal. The desert inhabitants knew these routes and their waypoints intimately, whereas of course the invaders did not and the difficulty the Italians faced was based on getting their forces through, and maintaining them in, the desert over large distances. There were precedents for such operations, though study of them probably offered little in the way of practical advice for Caneva and Frugoni. Even the much vaunted Imperial German army had found itself stymied by the guerilla tactics employed, perforce, by the Nama people during the colonial war in *Deutsch-Südwestafrika* (Namibia) between 1904 and 1909. Despite adopting a process of extermination towards the Herero and Nama, the German troops sent to the colony were unable to effectively penetrate the desert regions where the Nama survivors of the German genocide continued to fight. Jakobus (Jacob) Morenga, the Nama leader in the insurrection, was interviewed in the *Cape Times* and was asked if he knew that 'Germany is one of the mightiest military powers in the world?' Morenga replied 'Yes, I am aware of it; but they cannot fight in our country. They do not know where to get water, and do not understand guerrilla warfare.'[6]

The most recent successful large-scale attempt had probably been the British reconquest of the Sudan in 1897-98, when an Anglo-Egyptian force some 25,000 strong had travelled to Omdurman under Major-General Herbert Kitchener and won the eponymous battle there on 2 September 1898. One of the officers that had taken part in the campaign was Charles à Court Repington, who had since been forced to resign his commission after being named in a divorce case. Repington, who had seen extensive wartime military service in India, Afghanistan, Egypt, the Sudan and South Africa, then became military correspondent for the London *Times* in 1902. He had applied his not inconsiderable intellect to the problems facing the Italians, and proffered advice, albeit in a rather negative tone, in one of his columns:

> The crossing of the desert can be accomplished in one of three ways: by throwing a light railway into the interior – a very long and difficult undertaking – by establishing posts at intervals for the storage of water, or by forming a huge system of camel transport to accompany the army. The posts would have to be very strong, and the establishing of them would be a long and very considerable enterprise in itself. As for camel transport, the thousand camels said to be at General Caneva'a disposal would be utterly insufficient. Napoleon preferred deserts to mountains or rivers as the natural protection of a State, and he had good reason.[7]

Kitchener's force had of course the benefit of the Nile to aid his communications, hence Churchill's account of the campaign being called *The River War*. Nonetheless, because of the various cataracts and meanderings of this artery they also had to construct the 600-kilometre long Sudan Military Railway from Wadi Halfa to Atbara.

More pertinently, the Sudanese forces chose to fight conventionally. Their error in so doing was revealed at Omdurman, where Winston Churchill observed that the technological superiority of the Anglo-Egyptian force ensured that destroying the enemy was merely a 'matter of machinery.'[8] The forces resisting the Italians would make no such error, but in attempting to penetrate the interior the Italian army seemed to be contemplating using a combination of all three of Repington's stated methods. The beginning of the railway to Ain Zara, the wells of which could perhaps be considered as the first of the 'posts,' coincided with the beginning of a scheme to purchase and import some 2,000 camels from Tunisia and *Somalia Italiana*. There was an additional component, and one that had only recently became available; McClure noted the presence in one of the Tripoli markets of 'Fifty motor wagons, each carrying between 1-1.5 tonne […] and it was reported that Italian firms were working night and day to treble the number.'[9]

Something of a consensus seems to have emerged amongst the foreign war correspondents with the Italians, to the effect that large-scale operations would commence around March 1912. The weather would be better then, and the facilities for operating the semi-rigid dirigible airships, P1 and P3, would have been repaired; the two hangars, one complete and one nearly so, at the aviation facility near the Jewish Cemetery had been destroyed on 16 December by a storm. Without the enhanced endurance and communication facilities of these craft, compared with aeroplanes, any advanced operations would be rendered more difficult.

If large-scale advances were seemingly on hold, then the same did not apply to more minor manoeuvres designed to disrupt Ottoman communications. The Italians had not occupied two villages on the coast to the west of Tripoli which lay just outside their lines. The nearest of these was Gargaresh (Gargaresch, Girgarish) at some 4 kilometres distance, whilst Zanzur (Janzur, Sansur) was around another 4 kilometres away. There was little that was remarkable about these places; the contemporary edition of *Baedeker's Mediterranean* described a 'monotonous sandy coast […] with the little port of Sansur, and the watch-tower of [Gargaresh] [being] scarcely visible till we are nearing Tripoli.'[10] Zanzur though was one of the few decent anchorages between Tripoli and the Tunisian frontier, albeit only able to accommodate small vessels. According to Irace: 'Here the roads meet that come from Tunis, and from it start good caravan routes for Azizia and Garian to the south. Through it naturally passes a double stream of contraband from the sea and from Tunis.'[11]

It is then difficult to understand why the Italians had not occupied the place, though both it and Gargaresh were highly vulnerable, inasmuch as they lay directly under the guns of the fleet with Gargaresh being within range of land-based artillery as well. There was also a telegraph station at Janzur that the Italians believed formed a link in the communication chain between Zuwarah (Zuara, Zuwara, Zwara, Zouara), a coastal town about 105 kilometres west of Tripoli, and the Ottoman forces at Gharian and Azizia. They therefore decided to mount an operation with the objective of destroying 'telegraphic communication between Zuwarah and the Turkish headquarters.' Zuwarah was also an important link in the trade route from Tunisia. In an attempt at interdicting this route an amphibious landing was attempted there on 16 December when four transports with naval support appeared offshore. The town and surrounding area was subjected to a heavy bombardment under cover of which advance parties of marines landed on the beach. Following their securing of a beachhead the intention was to land the 10th Brigade of infantry that had been transported from Italy for the purpose. A combination of bad weather and unexpectedly stiff resistance from the defenders, who forced the marines back to their boats carrying their dead and wounded, prevented the operation being carried out. According to Abbott:

> The Arabs kept quiet until several boats had disembarked their passengers. Then the sheikh in command gave the order 'Fire!' The Arabs poured volley after volley down upon the hapless marines. [...] They tried to repel the attack, and, supported by the big guns from the warships, they answered the Arab fire. But they had to fire from low and open ground at an enemy whom they could not see. After a time they gave up their futile fusillade and fled back to their boats, carrying off half a dozen dead with them, and leaving a quantity of rifles, ammunition, and other loot, to make glad the heart of the Arabs, who, having picked up these spoils, retired from the fray with only one wounded. The warships went on bombarding the sand dunes.[12]

Thwarted thus in their efforts to take the more distant target, the Italians determined on securing the closer. Consequently a land-based thrust against Janzur began on the morning of 17 December with the advance of the now experienced 50th Regiment, augmented by one battalion of the newly arrived 73rd Regiment. The infantry were supported by a regiment (five squadrons) of the 9th Regiment of Florence Lancers (*Lancieri di Firenze*) also newly arrived, and a battery each of mountain and field artillery. Covering the desert flank of this force was a smaller column, consisting of two battalions of infantry, two squadrons of cavalry, and one battery of mountain-guns. This force moved south-west towards el-Togar, where there was a small party of Ottoman regulars about twenty strong. The force was described as 'advancing gingerly to the south' by eyewitnesses and it halted completely when fired on by the nineteen remaining troops; one had been sent to Suani Ben Adem to report the movement. Bennett, the former MP and fellow of Hertford College, Oxford, later reported:

> I was in the Turkish lines at the time, and everybody, officers and men alike, was highly amused at the almost incredible timidity of the assailants. We were all longing to see them advance against [Suani Ben Adem]. No such luck! All we saw was fifteen shells rushing over the desert from the retiring mule battery and bursting 1,000 yards in front of the camp – a sheer waste of ammunition.[13]

There was an even smaller Ottoman force, consisting of four men according to some sources, at Janzur, which wisely retreated inland at the approach of the column. They were accompanied by many of the inhabitants, as the appearance of the Italians heralded a bombardment of the village from the sea. Possession of the village was thus undisputed; most of the male Arabs of military age had vanished. The remaining women, children, and old men offered no resistance as the invaders carried out a thorough search for weapons and suchlike and cut down the telegraph-line.

What then happened, as so often in the conflict, is subject to partisan dispute. According to the Italian version, which was reported in communiqués and reproduced in the international press, the column remained in Janzur throughout the rest of the day before retiring back to Tripoli in the evening with their work done. It was stated that 'the importance of this advance lies in the fact that by it the smuggling of arms into Tripoli from the west has been rendered impossible for the future.' The anti-Italian account argued that whilst engaged in Janzur the force was subject to an attack by tribesmen from the south, who eventually prevailed by driving them back to Tripoli at sunset. The Italian version is in general terms the most plausible, though the particular claim that it had made an impact on the movement of arms is risible.

There is though one point on which both narratives agree. When they withdrew the Italians took with them four senior tribesmen, variously described as notables or sheikhs. These either went willingly, because they had 'submitted' to Italian rule, or, as the counter argument has it, were captives and taken as prisoners. Both version agree in that whilst in Tripoli they paid formal homage to Italian power, though one version has it that they did this out of good sense, whilst the other maintains they dissimulated in order to get back to Zanzur. Whatever their motives, they were issued with paperwork so that they could fetch their families to Tripoli and returned to Zanzur.

Neither the notables nor their families travelled to Tripoli. However, it was reported by 'spies' to, and believed by, the Italians (and their supporters) that when Ottoman forces returned they did not find them at Zanzur either. According to this account, the Ottomans refused to accept the explanation that they had been made prisoners. They must then have gone to, and presumably stayed at, Tripoli willingly. Therefore they were traitors and, accordingly, their families were duly executed. This, according to McClure, demonstrated the folly of the Italians in 'taking submission without giving protection' as the results of 'this untoward incident must have helped to rivet wavering Arabs to the Turkish cause.' McClure admits that 'the source of this story perhaps makes it suspect' yet also argues that 'it fits entirely with the probabilities.'[14] According to Abbott, who was with the Ottoman forces at Azizia at the time, there was a very good reason the notables were not at Zanzur, or at Tripoli either for that matter. Instead of returning to Zanzur and taking themselves and their families to Tripoli, they instead 'fetched their families away to the interior, and they themselves joined our camp, bringing the Italian permits with them.'[15]

The anti-Italian tale is undoubtedly the more convincing, and the story, whilst of little moment of itself, surely demonstrates the Italian's continuing capacity for wishful thinking. It is though something of a mystery as to why they did not extend their occupation westwards the 8-10 kilometres necessary to enclose Zanzur and Gargaresh, given that the former was such an important hub in the Ottoman communication network. The excuse offered by Irace, 'The fact that it is still in possession of the enemy merely means that we do not wish them to be relieved of the obligation of extending their forces from Azizia to the coast, a length of lines which is a continued source of weakness to them strategically', seems flimsy. This is particularly so if one balances the Ottoman effort expended on defending it against the likely cost of having an important route closed down. The rationale behind the after-the-event Italian declaration that 'the oasis of Zanzur has been occupied, and the population has submitted' is also obscure. This is even more puzzling since the same communiqué also announced that the reason for withdrawal was because the operation had succeeded in its mission of destroying the telegraph.[16] Even pro-Italian commentators were critical, McClure arguing that:

> [...] on broad principles, the whole episode of the reconnaissance to Janzur must be regarded as an error. [...] A mere raid, followed by withdrawal, was of doubtful value at the best; in view of the accompanying circumstances and the inevitable sequel, the step cannot escape condemnation. These Janzur sheikhs were the first, outside the occupied towns, to make

submission to the Italians. The precedent set by their experience was not favourable to the prospect of further defections from the Turkish cause.[17]

The belief that there were pro-Italian elements within the Arab population requiring rescue from Ottoman influence was one of the factors that led to a near disaster two days after the action at Zanzur. Again, interpretations of the affair were much disputed, both at the time and later, ranging across a spectrum of opinion from 'a successful fight,' to an event that was merely a 'repulse' of Ottoman attempts to harass a reconnoitring party, through to a situation that 'nearly attained the rank of a regrettable incident,' and on to a 'crushing' Italian defeat.[18]

The origins of it appear to have been when news was conveyed to Ain Zara on 18 December to the effect that a body of Arabs, some 2-300 strong, had occupied a small oasis called Bir Tobras, about 15 kilometres to the south. This information was supposedly brought by five Arabs, who claimed that the usual inhabitants of the oasis were being mistreated by the occupiers and were appealing for protection from the Italians. When this news was conveyed to *Conte* Pecori-Giraldi he determined to send a column to force the occupiers to disperse and to rescue the inhabitants. The core of this force was to consist of two battalions of the 11th *Bersaglieri* Regiment reinforced with a battalion of Grenadiers. In support was a machine gun section of two guns, a squadron of light cavalry, and two mountain guns. The whole amounted to 1,500 men and it was put under the command of the 'ambitious' Colonel Gustavo Fara, hero of the defence at al-Hani on 23 October.[19]

Fara set out at 02:00 hours on the morning of 19 December with the object of arriving at Bir Tobras at 06:00 hours in order to attack at dawn. To guide him through

Mountain Artillery at Bir Tobras with, inset, Colonel Gustavo Fara. Bir Tobras is a small oasis about 15 kilometres to the south of Ain Zara. On 19 December 1911 two battalions of the 11th *Bersaglieri* reinforced with a battalion of Grenadiers plus a machine gun section of two guns, a squadron of light cavalry, and two mountain guns amounting to some 1,500 men under the command of Colonel Gustavo Fara, set out to disperse an Ottoman detachment reported to be there. Upon engaging the enemy, however, it soon became apparent to Fara that they were far too strong and he sought to disengage. This proved impossible when the enemy pressed forward, flanking the Italian force on both sides so that it was in danger of being completely cut off. The retreat was in danger of turning into a rout as Fara attempted to manoeuvre his force through the dunes, with incipient panic becoming evident amongst the troops. Only by exercising decisive leadership did Fara rescue his command though they were forced to abandon much of their equipment. Fara was feted for his courage and coolness under fire and promoted to Major-General, but it was claimed that an 'inclination to rashness' and a 'failure to see difficulties' made him somewhat suspect. Any further such ventures were thereafter banned. (Author's Collection).

the unfamiliar terrain, and in the dark, Fara took three of the five Arabs who had reported the enemy at Bir Tobras whilst the other two were kept at Ain Zara. Four hours would, under ideal circumstances, have been plenty of time to cover the required distance. The circumstances were very far from ideal however, and the column was distant from its objective at 06:00 hours, having become, perhaps predictably, disoriented in the difficult topography. With daylight the Arab guides were able to establish their position and successfully guided the force towards its objective. The delay occasioned meant that it was though another four hours before the Italians sighted the oasis and elements of the enemy contingent. These small groups were immediately brought under fire and they retreated towards Bir Tobras, followed by the column which was now itself under harassing fire from the flanks. The more they pressed forward however the more resistance they came up against and Fara realised that the enemy were in greater strength than had been calculated. Nevertheless he was confident that his command could still deal with them, though he took the precaution of sending a report of his progress and situation back to Ain Zara.

By 12:00 hours, and still moving forward, Fara came to realise that his previous impression had been in error and that he was in fact up against a force that was far too large to engage with, and contained numbers of regular troops. Accordingly he ordered disengagement and withdrawal. The enemy though refused to allow him to disengage and pressed forward in turn, flanking the Italian force on both sides so that it was in danger of being completely cut off. The retreat was in danger of turning into a rout as Fara attempted to manoeuvre his force through the dunes, with incipient panic becoming evident amongst the troops.

Realising this, and with commendable coolness, he ordered the column to halt and entrench whilst he despatched further messengers back to Ain Zara for reinforcements. These were urgently required; his men were running short of ammunition and water and sand ingress had rendered his machine guns inoperable. Once the ammunition was gone then the column was finished. At least three concerted attacks were made by the enemy at 17:00, 20:00 and 23:00 hours, but while each was repulsed it was at the cost of depleting the ammunition. Indeed, it was fortunate in the extreme for the Italians that the enemy did not press home their attacks with more vigour, or move to completely surround their force. Given that his messengers had got through at all, which was by no means certain, Fara calculated that reinforcements should have arrived at midnight or so. However, with no sign, or even news, of them whatsoever he determined that he would have to evacuate his position before dawn on 20 December. If not he would then face certain destruction as the Ottomans were certain to renew their offensive, probably in greater strength, and his force would quickly run out of ammunition.

This withdrawal began at 03:00 hours and succeeded in moving silently through the dunes in a northward direction. They were completely unmolested and at about 07:00 hours they came across a camp containing a brigade strength contingent under Major-General Clemente Lequio that had entrenched for the night. This combined force then returned to Ain Zara, meeting on the way virtually the entire strength of the rest of the 1st Division under the personal command of *Conte* Pecori-Giraldi. The divisional commander was in search of his two subordinates and was undoubtedly mightily relieved to find them, and their forces, both largely intact; Fara's casualties, announced at the time as six killed and 78 wounded, amounted to eleven dead and 91 wounded.[20]

The corresponding enemy casualties were according to Bennett, eleven killed and 40 wounded.[21]

There is no question that the Italians had been both foolhardy and extremely lucky. The sole creditable facet of the entire affair was the behaviour of Colonel Fara, who displayed a superlative presence of mind and quality of leadership without which the column would have been destroyed. Indeed, the decision to send the column seems of itself somewhat curious. The word of the five Arabs seems to have been taken at face value, at least by Pecori-Giraldi. That it was not a trap seems self-evident in retrospect inasmuch as the column escaped, whereas if the Ottomans had been waiting for it then they would have pre-deployed a much larger force and surrounded it properly. The bodies of the three who acted as guides were subsequently found riddled with bullets, and it seems practically certain that Fara, convinced of their treachery, had seen that they were shot. The two who remained at Ain Zara are believed to have been hanged.

According to Abbott, who was with the Ottoman forces and witnessed much of the fighting at Bir Tobras, the five Arabs were actually genuine. They were acting on behalf of a sheikh called Mukhtar, 'a rich man who owned […] a large estate, consisting of a dozen palm-groves, with many mud dwellings and wells […]' in the vicinity of Bir Tobras. At first he supported resistance to the Italian occupation, but suspected that the advance to Ain Zara presaged further movement:

> When that came to pass, his property, owing to its position, would be the first to be seized, ravaged, and confiscated. He saw in fancy his noble palm-trees cut down, his mud dwellings demolished, his wives and his children, if not slain, driven to starvation and mendacity. He determined to avert this fate from himself, while there was yet time, by entering into secret negotiations with the enemy, and offering not only his submission, but also his assistance.[22]

Bennett, who was also there, admitted he did not know whether or not 'these Arabs were mere Decoys' or 'were actually seeking the protection of the invaders.'[23] He went on to make the point that 'If the arrival of the five Arabs at Ain Zara was part of a carefully planned ruse, one can only say that no military trap ever caught a more gullible enemy.'[24] On the other hand, and Pecori-Giraldi was to argue this when his decision to despatch the force came under criticism, the column was a powerful unit that was well able to take care of itself under foreseeable circumstances. It was not expected to operate at any great distance from its base and neither the troops nor their commander were inexperienced. The 11th *Bersaglieri* in particular had extensive recent experience of fighting the *Saraceni*, and they were supported by artillery and machine guns, albeit the latter were difficult to keep working in the sandy conditions. Against this the Ottomans were able to bring together a force, albeit in a piecemeal fashion, that was probably not greatly superior in numbers. The Italians estimated them as being 3,000 strong, whilst the Ottoman side reckoned there were only about five or six hundred. Undoubtedly both were inaccurate, but no reliable figure can be arrived at. The peril that the column found itself in was not then caused by weakness as such, but rather to the extreme difficulties of moving across the terrain combined with the lack of a reliable system of communications, and thus the ability to summon support. That it was not expected to have to do any serious fighting is evidenced by the limited supplies of ammunition, food, and water, it carried.

Despite its outcome, the Bir Tobras affair was condemned by the Italian high command in Tripoli, and Frugoni in particular. Indeed there was no aspect of the operation that Frugoni did not find fault with. He complained that he had not been consulted by his divisional commander and knew nothing of the despatch of Fara's column, and he censured Pecori-Giraldi for initiating an operation, particularly as it escalated to embrace the entire 1st Division, without his knowledge and consent. Frugoni was also censorious of the tactics employed, especially with regard to night marches across the desert. The divisional commander was reminded that Frugoni had forbidden such manoeuvres during the advance on Ain Zara some two weeks previously, and that Pecori-Giraldi should therefore have known of, and respected, this decision. Damning criticism was directed at the planning and support of the operation, inasmuch as no provision had been made for keeping in communication with Fara's column, and that no preparations had been made to have a reserve force ready to move in case of an emergency. Therefore when news reached Ain Zara at about 15:00 hours on 19 December, to the effect that the enemy were in greater strength than had been calculated, the divisional commander was unable to immediately initiate steps to get in touch with Fara. Astonishingly, neither did he bring his command to a state of readiness for going to his relief. The composition and strength of the column was also found wanting. Frugoni considered it too weak for independent operations and stated that it should have had at least a whole battery (six guns) of mountain artillery in support instead of just two guns.

Pecori-Giraldi defended himself against the majority of the charges, though he did acknowledge that the despatch of the column on the say-so of the five Arabs demonstrated a lack of prudence. He did, however, argue that the operation differed only slightly from the reconnaissance missions that had been carried out from Ain Zara on an almost daily basis since its capture. He also, as already explained, disputed Frugoni's points about the strength of the unit, and claimed that if the enemy's strength was greatly in excess of what he expected then the failure lay with army intelligence, upon whose information he had to rely, rather than him. The failure to maintain adequate communication he blamed on Fara, who, he claimed, had been assigned cavalry for just such a purpose. He also held Fara responsible for failing to make a surprise attack at dawn on the oasis, and held that he should have abandoned the attack after arriving at the oasis so late in the day. Carrying on with it was a major departure from the expected mission, and he should have sent word back to Ain Zara immediately he began the attack, instead of waiting two hours until he discovered the opposition was stronger than at first thought. Fara's message to this effect, despatched at noon, did not arrive until after 15:00 hours, by which time, Pecori-Giraldi claimed, any relieving force would have to travel in the dark and would likely get lost in the desert. Further, he stated, Fara had informed him in the message that the column could take care of itself. When some hours later he was informed that the column was in trouble and had been forced to entrench, the two hour delay in sending Lequio and his brigade was explained by the need to try and prepare such a manoeuvre in the darkness. That General Lequio did get lost has already been noted, and because he could hear no firing from the south towards which to march he, perhaps wisely, decided to encamp and wait for daylight.[25]

There can be little doubt that Pecori-Giraldi's arguments were as weak as his performance; nor can there be an excuse for his failure to at least ensure that reinforcements were on standby. This is particularly the case following the arrival of Fara's morning message at around 15:00 hours stating that the enemy were in greater strength than anticipated. The outcome of this lack of preparation meant that when the message requesting urgent relief was received this had to be organised from scratch. As McClure was to state it: 'General Pecori seems to have launched Fara's column into the desert, and then ceased to have troubled himself about it any further.'[26]

The Bir Tobras affair was, of itself, of minor importance. One of the immediate outcomes was that the Ottomans claimed a victory and salvaged a great deal of booty from the battlefield. The most important of this was the two hundred rifles or so recovered. Abbott's account offers an explanation for the large number of these:

> [...] there were scores and scores of them, and as I could not believe that every rifle represented a dead enemy, I was obliged to accept the explanation which everybody gave - namely, that the Italians, knowing the Arabs' unquenchable thirst for plunder, throw their rifles and cartridges away as they flee, so that they may escape while their pursuers waste time in picking them up.[27]

Gustavo Fara was feted for his courage and coolness under fire and promoted to Major-General, but it was claimed that an 'inclination to rashness' and a 'failure to see difficulties' made him somewhat suspect. If Fara came out of the affair with credit, the same cannot be said of Pecori-Giraldi. His position became untenable and early in January the inevitable 'General Pecori-Giraldi has returned to Italy owing to ill health' notice appeared. His replacement was the former commander of the 13th Division at Ancona, Count Vittorio Camerana. None of this was particularly significant in the grand scheme of things, but what was of great importance was the effect the whole business seems to have had on the minds of Caneva and Frugoni.

The plan for a powerful advance to the south in divisional strength, still very much in play in December, was quietly shelved. On 4 January 1912 the politicians and staff in Rome were told that any such offensive would be too costly and hazardous and would in any case be unlikely to bring about a decisive battle. Operational strategy defaulted to consolidation of territory already occupied, localised and small scale military operations, and to 'ally ourselves with time.'[28] The relationship between the Bir Tobras affair and the abandonment of what might be termed a forward strategy is impossible to determine with any certainty; it cannot be claimed that it was indisputably one of cause and effect. Nevertheless observers noted that progress on the railway to Ain Zara was not pursued with any great urgency. The specialised material and labour for the construction did not arrive at Tripoli until the middle of January 1912, suggesting that an advance early in 1912 was not a high priority. At some 14 kilometres in total length the line was of single track, with double track at six locations to provide passing places, and laid directly onto an excavated sand base with iron sleepers. The first train steamed into Ain Zara on 17 March 1912.

It was of course not perceived immediately that the lack of advance movement was a matter of policy rather than a matter imposed by military difficulties or 'that tendency to wait upon events which must be held to have marked the Italian conduct of hostilities.'[29] Repington noted towards the end of December that 'the failure to turn the enemy out of Bir Tobras is one of the various symptoms that little progress is being made.'[30] Retrospectively, McClure adjudged that 'the most interesting points' revealed by the events at Bir Tobras were 'the obvious determination of the supreme command to avoid all the ordinary risks of war and, with that end in view, its conception of the proportionate military strength requisite for given operations.' He perceived that this heralded the first indication of a policy that proscribed any action 'involving the minimum of risk or more than the minimum of loss.' The corollary of this required that 'no operation should be undertaken without the assurance of a strong numerical superiority over the forces of the enemy.' Despite being avowedly pro-Italian in outlook he was critical, arguing that: 'The adoption of such principles of action gives ground for surprise; the enunciation of the second certainly seems to call for criticism.'[31]

This hesitant and risk-free philosophy was demonstrated in the Battle of Gargaresch, which took place on 18 January 1912. The decision to finally take the village seems to have been a reaction to the Ottoman forces operating openly in the area and, according to Italian sources, terrorizing the 'loyal' inhabitants. In any event on the morning of 18 January a powerful force was despatched westward from Tripoli consisting of the entire 57th Regiment of Infantry, reinforced with a battalion of Grenadiers and supported by a battery of mountain artillery, a half-battery of field artillery, a force of engineers, and the 2nd and 4th squadrons of the 19th Cavalry (Guide) Regiment (*Cavalleggeri Guide* 19°) – about 3000 men in total under the regimental commander, Colonel Giuseppe Amari. This force, arrayed in column, reached the oasis surrounding Gargaresch at about 09:00 hours and encountered an enemy force estimated to be about 100 strong lurking amongst the foliage.

Being greatly outnumbered and under threat of being outflanked to the south, the defenders soon abandoned their positions and retreated to the west, allowing the column to occupy the village and its oasis. The construction of a series of strong entrenchments was immediately begun. By late morning the defenders to the south were deployed in deep trenches at a distance of around two kilometres from the outskirts of the oasis whilst the Grenadiers were similarly placed to the west. According to some sources there were three lines of trenches, but all accounts agree that there were two at least.

Around noon an Ottoman force, estimated by the Italians to be about 2,000 strong and comprising both men on foot and on horseback, became visible to the south and was watched as it moved towards the defensive perimeter. Those on horseback attempted to exploit a gap between the right-wing of the Grenadiers and the shore, but were thwarted when the defenders shortened their line somewhat and extended it to cover the weak point. Soon afterwards the whole Italian line was engaged in the battle supported by the artillery. The Ottomans advanced in open order, skilfully utilising the ground for cover, to approach the earthworks.

As is usual, the subsequent events were subject to partisan interpretation. Pol Tristan, a French war correspondent, was on the scene with the Ottoman forces and described what he saw:

> [the attackers] were obliged to cross the zone that was swept by the Italian artillery which had taken up position in front of the oasis. They managed this without heavy loss, and so this kill zone did not prevent the Arabs making contact with the enemy, and they attempted, with a superb contempt of danger, to turn their left wing.

> The Italian infantry, buried, as usual, to the shoulders in trenches [dug the previous day] seemed at first, in my view, to be well protected from the Turkish fire. I was then amazed to see them all of a sudden leap from these works, and retreat three hundred yards only to disappear again in a new trench; their first line of defence had become untenable. In this first trench, which was immediately occupied, wide and plentiful pools of blood abundantly proved the efficient shooting of the Turkish-Arab attackers. Moreover, several dead soldiers, who they had not had time to remove, still lay there.

This first retreat was to be followed a quarter of an hour later by a second, when the defenders withdrew another three hundred yards into the defences close around the oasis itself. The Italian troops were unsteady and I saw distinctly through my telescope, the officers attempting in vain to rally them under fire. Upon entering the second trench line twelve more dead bodies were found, as well as crates of ammunition, camping equipment and a considerable quantity of clothing.

Until the evening and even three quarters of an hour after sunset, the fire persisted without interruption on both sides. In the afternoon, we had seen arriving in a hurry along the road from Tripoli, several squadrons of cavalry and a number of Infantry battalions, supported by a battery of Artillery. These troops took up positions on the same front on the edge of the oasis, without attempting a forward movement or a march on the left, which would have undoubtedly given them fire superiority.[32]

The reinforcements were under the command of Major General Gustavo Fara, the hero of Bir Tobras, and with their arrival the Italian situation was stabilised. Tristan's account is largely supported by those of other correspondents with the Ottoman forces, though their timings differ somewhat, but all agree that the attackers almost succeeded in breaking through the defences and that the Italians had suffered a severe shock.

Official Italian reports of the time stated only that the 'enemy was attacked and defeated by our troops' but accounts by pro-Italian correspondents such as McClure told a very different tale of how 'by sunset the Turks and Arabs were in full retreat and the Italians were left in undisputed occupation of the position they had come to fortify.' Tristan's account concurs with the point about the Italians being left in occupation of the position, but he goes on to relate that during the night a reconnaissance was made of the Italian position, and this revealed that the entire force had withdrawn:

> The oasis was completely abandoned! The disorder that had reigned in the Italian trenches, with abandoned equipment and eighteen corpses that had not been removed, allowed us to suppose that the fire of the Arabs had been very deadly for the second phase of the battle and that the Italian losses were considerable.[33]

An 'Arab Joan of Arc': Selima bent Mogos, or Salima bint Mughus, was a female warrior believed to have been from the nomadic Nuwayil tribe of western Tripolitania from an area close to the Tunisian border. She enjoyed the reputation of being a ferocious fighter who had 'taken part in all the battles around Tripoli and had been wounded by a bullet in the chest.'

One somewhat remarkable facet of the battle of Gargaresch concern reports that the Ottoman attack was led by a woman. Alan Ostler of the *Daily Express* had his account of this 'War Goddess in Tripoli' syndicated by many papers. He wrote that as the attackers broke into the first line of trenches:

> At their head was a figure, cloaked and hooded in russet brown, who carried no weapon but a staff of olive wood, and whose voice rang high and shrill above the shouts and rattling rifle fire. The face beneath the russet hood was of so deep a brown as to be almost black. [...] The desert men swept up and over the earthworks, and their fearless leader, leaping into the trenches, stooped, plunged an arm elbow deep in blood, and then stood, with a dripping right hand flung upwards, a statue of the Goddess of African Battle. For it was a woman, a Soudanese she warrior [...][34]

His tale had been toned down a little when it came to be published in *The Arabs in Tripoli,* but the presence of this woman is confirmed by other witnesses. The Frenchman Georges Remond, correspondent of the Parisian *L'Illustration*, had crossed the Tunisian border on 17 January 1912 and was an observer of the attack on Gargaresch. He published an account of this in his 1913 book, and identifies the female warrior as 'Selima bent Mogos, guerrière de la tribe des Naouaïl.' He wrote that:

> She had taken part in all the battles around Tripoli and had been wounded by a bullet in the chest. After fifteen days rest with her tribe she came back to take her place among the fighters. Pol Tristan gave her a sabre, which she branded fiercely while singing her war song.[35]

Remond also published a photograph of this 'Arab Joan of Arc,' as Ostler had called her, with the sword. She has been identified by Richard Pennell as Salima bint Mughus who, he argues, was not from the Sudan but was rather from the Nuwayil tribe. These were a nomadic clan whose territory was based in western Tripolitania around the Tunisian border, and were noted for their history of raiding and resistance.[36]

In terms of the battle, there is no definitive account of why the Italians withdrew from a position that they had just fought so hard to keep, other than it was ordered by Frugoni. The implications for morale amongst the Italian soldiery caused by such a withdrawal are not hard to fathom, and of course the opposite held true amongst the Ottoman forces. The decision is made all the more mysterious when it is considered that two days later, on 20 January, Gargaresch was reinvaded. This time the 1st Brigade – the 82nd and 84th Infantry Regiments complete with two batteries of artillery and an engineering battalion and supported by six squadrons of cavalry – traversed the few kilometres to the town and oasis under the command of Lieutenant General Felice de Chaurand. There was no opposition, and the engineers began constructing a defensive system of trenches and redoubts that would be too strong for any force the Ottomans might muster to take on.

The Italian's Fabian-like strategy of making only tactical moves in irresistible force was also to be applied in the eastern theatre of the former *vilayet*, Cyrenaica. There had been no really notable battles or military manoeuvres in that portion of the war zone and, following the initial landings, the invaders did very little beyond consolidate themselves in the coastal enclaves. Nevertheless the principle of overwhelming strength was observed; Caneva's request for reinforcements at the end of October 1911 saw the 4th Division under Lieutenant General *Conte* Vittorio Trombi, less the 50th Regiment of the 8th

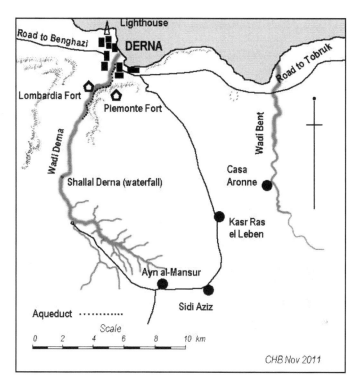

Derna and hinterland. The commander of Ottoman forces in Cyrenaica was the later infamous Enver Bey (Enver Pasha), who established his general headquarters at Ayn al-Mansur some 15 kilometres south-east of Derna. The fighting before Derna was centred around possession of the Wadi, and thus control of the water supply which depended upon an aqueduct extending some 3-5 kilometres south of the town. The Italian defences were sited to protect the aqueduct, and two large forts, Piemonte and Lombardia, were constructed. There was some fierce fighting and on occasion the garrison had to depend on water shipped from Italy, but, as elsewhere, the situation became essentially deadlocked with neither side able to prevail. Among the Ottoman officers was Mustafa Kemal, later the Empire's greatest general and then Atatürk, the founder of modern Turkey. Reassigned to Ayn al-Mansur on 30 December 1911 he was to command the forces before Derna and Tobruk while Enver oversaw the whole Cyrenaican theatre. (© Charles Blackwood).

Brigade, despatched to Cyrenaica. Further reinforcements brought Italian numbers there to the 40,000 mark with the largest contingent being some 20,000 strong at Benghazi under Lieutenant General Ottavio Briccola. There were about 15,000 men under Trombi and Major-General Vittorio Zuppelli at Derna, where the former had been appointed governor, and 5,000 at Tobruk under Major-General Vittorio Signorile. (The western theatre got the lion's share; 55,000 at Tripoli City and environs and 5,000 at Al Khums).

The reinforcements were not confined to conventional forces. Three further aviation units were raised for the Cyrenaica theatre, the first to arrive being the 2nd Aeroplane Flotilla (*2a Flottiglia aeroplani*) at Benghazi with three aircraft; a Blériot, a Farman and an Italian-made Asteria. Five pilots were assigned to the unit, which left the Italian army

somewhat short of qualified aviators. This situation was remedied via an intervention by
the Italian sports magazine *La Stampa Sportiva* at the end of November. The magazine
offered to pay for a group of civilian pilots to take part in the war. This unusual measure
was approved by the army and eight civilians, together with eight army pilots, were
deployed to Tobruk and Derna together with nine Blériot aeroplanes and one Farman.
The four civilian pilots sent to Tobruk included the sportsman and politician, Carlo
Montu, who was given the rank of captain. As has already been related, Captain Montu
made aviation history on 31 January 1912 when he became the first casualty of
anti-aircraft fire.

Meanwhile, the Ottoman forces in Cyrenaica became progressively better led,
organised and equipped under the auspices of Enver Bey. According to his account dated
9 January 1912:

> Despite all the unexpected difficulties that are revealed on every side, little by little the situation
> is stabilized. The organization begins to function. Supply columns of ten thousand camels
> ensure the provisioning of our forces. [...] Each tribe is now commanded by officers.
> I hope soon to be able to set up a special company of picked Arabs, these will be trained as
> regular troops.[37]

Enver was impressed with the calibre of the tribesmen he encountered, stating they
were contemptuous of the infidel soldiers. He became of a similar opinion himself,
writing after the battle that took place on 27 December 1911 (see below) that the 'Italian
soldiers are cowards and unwilling or reluctant to fight [*kampfunlustig*], but I admire their
officers who sacrifice themselves.'[38] He had little money or equipment to kit out his
'army' but developed the technique of living off the enemy to some extent. After the
battle referred to above, the booty obtained following the Italian retreat behind the
defences at Derna amounted to: two machine guns, 600,000 cartridges, two mountain
guns, twenty-five boxes of grenades and ten mules, which, Enver pointed out, 'I can very
well use to tow my guns.'[39]

The tribesmen were organised as units under their traditional chiefs, but the higher
command devolved onto regular Ottoman officers. Enver was to be promoted to
command of the whole of Cyrenaica[40] and a general headquarters at Ayn al-Mansur (Ain
al-Mansur, Ain Mansur), some 15 kilometres south-east of Derna was established by him.

> My camp is on a high plateau [...] In the east there is a deep gorge with almost vertical walls
> and down a narrow valley shaded by evergreen trees the water of Ain-el-Mansur spring flows
> to the sea. On the steep slopes on either side of the valley can be seen here and there, cave
> entrances, which serve as places of concealment for the local tribes. Another wadi, borders the
> plateau from the west. The plateau is about 300 metres above Derna and covered with huge
> boulders, between which wild thorny shrubs grow. [...] In the middle of our campsite are the
> white tents of our soldiers, well-ordered in rows, whilst the dark or sand-coloured tents of the
> Arabs are scattered irregularly, often very cleverly hidden amongst the rocks and bushes. Further
> back, behind a hill, the tents of the Red Crescent are set up. I have my own tent, which actually
> consists of two Egyptian tents [...] one I use as a bedroom, whilst the other is a reception
> room. Two rugs cover the ground and a white sheepskin form the seat - the furniture of the
> 'salon.' The bedroom is much more elegant: a portable bed, a small Turkish leather suitcase, and
> a stone slab that serves as a sink [...].[41]

This is not quite the 'great tent with carpets spread on the floor and hung with draperies' that some have claimed.[42] Nevertheless his was a sophisticated administration, and a factory to produce ammunition, a training camp for the tribesmen, and a school for their sons were also set up whilst a printing press produced a propagandist news sheet entitled *Al-Jihad*.[43] Derna and its environs was a fertile area, and its topography had been described in 1864 by two British explorers, Captain R Murdoch Smith of the army and Commander E A Porcher of the navy. Their description gives an excellent indication of the likely course of any struggle for control of the area:

> The town of Derna, with its gardens, covers a small triangular plain, formed by a projection of the seashore from the base of the range of hills […]. The shingly bed of a deep wady, which recedes several miles into the range, divides the small plain and the town into two distinct portions. On the eastern side are the two villages of Upper and Lower Bou Mansour; and on the western, a village on a spur of the hills called II Maghar, Derna proper lying immediately below, and a small detached village, called Gebeli, near the projecting headland. The whole assemblage of villages constitutes the town of Derna […] The beauty and fertility of the little plain of Derna are owing to the copious stream of fresh water which flows down the bed of the wady. Some two or three miles [3-5 kilometres] above the town the water is collected into an artificial aqueduct, by which it is led into the town, and thence distributed over the surrounding fields and gardens by means of small lateral branches. To insure the regular supply to every man's property, a 'Chief of the Water' is appointed, whose duty it is to see that a supply is sent to every district in succession, and to prevent any one from diverting for his own use the stream that for the time belongs to his neighbour. Water-stealing is very properly considered a serious crime, and is punished accordingly.[44]

Once the Italians had occupied Derna then it was fairly obvious that any attempts to dislodge or discomfit them would begin with attempts at 'water stealing.' In order to prevent or mitigate this, the Italian defences were sited south of the town to protect the aqueduct and water flow, which followed the course of the Wadi Derna, the steep sides of which were filled with vegetation. To facilitate the defence two forts, christened *Piemonte* and *Lombardia,* were constructed on the plateau overlooking Derna, east and west of the watercourse respectively.

Until these forts and the other works were completed, and they were not finished until March–April 1912, the Italian defences were considered somewhat vulnerable and accordingly were subject to attacks by the Ottomans. Probing attacks were recorded on 17 November, and the Italians reckoned that efforts were made to raise a revolt amongst the inhabitants of Derna. These were unsuccessful, but the occupiers believed that the attackers were massing troops for a large scale operation.

In an attempt to gain further information, and possibly disrupt the attack, powerful reconnaissance units were despatched along the Wadi Derna. On 24 November one of these was advancing along the eastern side of the Wadi when it was ambushed by a large force. The difficulties of the terrain meant that disengagement and retreat was rendered difficult, but the despatch of a battalion of *Alpini* as reinforcements allowed the column to escape. In an engagement lasting some eight hours the Italians lost 15 killed and 37 wounded.

The next serious engagement took place on 27 December, when the Ottoman forces destroyed part of the aqueduct and cut off the water supply. Engineers were sent to effect repairs and to cover them three strong columns of infantry with mountain artillery were despatched; one on each side of the ravine of the Wadi Derna and one along the watercourse. This meant, of course, that each of the three columns was isolated from the other two, and when the right hand column on the west of the ravine was attacked there could be little cooperation from the centre or left. Despite its possession of mountain artillery, the right hand column came very close to being overrun by the Ottoman force and it was only with difficulty that reinforcements were able to reach it. Nevertheless, one battalion of *Alpini* were able to cross from the left column and strengthen the defenders, and this tipped the balance. The slackening of the Ottoman attack was not however the signal for an Italian forward movement, and the column began to retreat back towards Derna as part of a general withdrawal. Both left and right columns were fiercely attacked during this retreat, but managed to gain the safety of the main defences. The left column though was forced to abandon its machine guns and much other equipment as related above. This abandonment was also noted by foreign correspondents.[45] The Italians unquestionably lost this encounter, and the cutting of the aqueduct forced them to rely on water shipped in from Italy. Captain Mahan would almost certainly have been impressed with this example of what 'Command of the Sea' could achieve. On the other hand, it is doubtful if he would have equally regarded the strategy that had got Italy into such a mess; reliance on imported water proved a very expensive and cumbersome business that caused serious inconvenience. An intense effort was made then to restore the water supply, and on 30 December a reinforced regiment advanced up the Wadi and managed to clear the area of the enemy. Repairs were made to the aqueduct, but without a large permanent force stationed in the vicinity it remained vulnerable to further attack.

Ottoman Artillery at Derna. Taken by Georges Remond, this photograph shows what appear to be mountain artillery in the Ottoman camp. Both the Italian and Ottoman armies were equipped with Krupp 75mm 1904 mountain guns, but it seems possible that these are captured weapons.

If the fighting around Derna was centred around possession of the Wadi, and hence control of the water supply, the terrain around Benghazi was rather less difficult, at least in terms of defence, with a fairly flat plain between the coast and the hills. Although frequent small-scale skirmishes occurred, there was no real attempt at an attack for weeks after the Italian occupation of the town, giving the occupiers time to construct strong earthworks and blockhouses. The Benghazi defences were sophisticated, and a ten-kilometre 'Decauville Railway' was constructed to provide communication between the various parts. An artificial airstrip was also built as, due to the soft nature of the ground around the chosen area of construction near the Wells of Sabri, it was necessary to lay down a wooden platform some 100 x 12 metres for the machines to take-off and land.

As at Tripoli City, the artillery had been reinforced with a number of heavy, 152 mm, guns by the middle of November. Provided that the Italians did not venture outside these defences then they were safe even though the Ottoman forces, estimated to number around 15,000, constantly attacked them, or pretended to. Following the movement of Ottoman officers into the *vilayet* the forces around Benghazi were under the command of Aziz Ali Bey El-Masri, an officer of Egyptian descent, of whom more later. According to the Italians, the tactics he often employed revolved around simulated nocturnal attacks, with the object of the exercise being twofold; the defenders would be unnerved and they would waste a great deal of ammunition in repelling these 'attacks.' Whether the first object was attained is difficult to judge, but the second was certainly achieved as these excursions usually resulted in a huge artillery barrage, from both land-based and, often, naval artillery. Tittoni describes such an action in what he calls a 'general attack upon the city:'

> This action involved only the artillery, as the Arab-Turks advanced cautiously and kept a great distance from the lines. The other arms, ready and on the watch, consequently participated neither in the action nor in the defense of the trenches nor in the counter-attacks.

> The artillery opened up an efficacious and continuous fire at 3800 to 4000 metres [...] using 29 pieces, each one firing on an average of 39 shots.

> There were no appreciable losses; and when it is taken into consideration that the firing kept up all day, the expenditure of that amount of ammunition was justified. The batteries gave proof of their perfect fire-discipline, excellent technical and professional preparation, efficacy, and coordination of action.[46]

In November reconnaissance revealed that substantial elements of the Ottoman force were located to the north-east of Benghazi, principally at the oases of al Kuwayfiya (el-Coefia, al-Kwaifiya, Koefia, el Coef) and Sidi Khalifa (Sidi Chalifa, Sidi Califa); some 10 and 15 kilometres away respectively. Because these oases were close to the sea they were well within range of naval gunfire, therefore any advance on them would be well supported and thus less hazardous than an inland manoeuvre that went beyond the range of the warships. Accordingly, on 28 November Major General Raynaldo de'Amico led his 3rd Brigade, supported from offshore by the armoured cruiser *San Marco* and the destroyer *Agordat,* on a march along the coast towards the two oases.[47] The brigade reached both objectives but came into conflict with a large Ottoman force. As usual, accounts of the fighting and its outcome differ greatly according to the proclivities of the author. Tittoni, quoting from the reports of the Italian General Staff, puts it thus: '[...] our troops, after ably overcoming the difficulty of the terrain, and giving proof of their vigor and ardor, surprised and dispersed a large force of Bedouins, who left on the field 21 dead [...]. McClure, who admits he was not a witness of any of the events which took place in Cyrenaica, reported, from Italian sources, 'a sharp but indecisive action' whilst most non-Italian accounts describe a defeat, with twenty-two killed and fifty wounded, followed by retreat to Benghazi.

Minor combats of this nature, with no larger purpose other than to consolidate gains already made, were much in evidence at Tobruk, the third Cyrenaican port in Italian hands. Indeed the only notable feature of the conflict there, other than perhaps the airborne wounding of Carlo Montu, was the presence on the Ottoman side of Mustafa Kemal, who went on to become the Ottoman Empire's greatest general and Atatürk (Father of the Turks), the founder of modern Turkey. Kemal had left Istanbul on 15 October and arrived in Alexandria, Egypt, on 29 October (the dates vary dependant on source).[48] Travelling as either a journalist named Sherif (Serif) Bey, or a carpet salesman, or conceivably a mixture of the two, he was taken ill and delayed in the city. He eventually reached Benghazi on 8 December and was sent on to Tobruk, where the main Ottoman camp was situated at el-Mdàuar (Ras Mdauar, Mdawar) some 20 kilometres to the south.

The commander there was Edhem Pasa, who had requested the services of Kemal and quickly oversaw his promotion to the rank of major. Kemal, according to one of his biographers, stressed discipline and order to the men under his command, and divided them into small units.[49] As soon as he arrived he personally reconnoitred the Italian positions and recommended a small-scale attack. This, his first engagement with the enemy, took place outside Tobruk on 22 December, and was deemed a victory.[50] It was though, as elsewhere, impossible to do more than attempt to hold the Italians within their defences. As Tittoni related it: 'the adversary was growing in numbers, and made a great many attacks against our works and skirmished with our troops on reconnaissance, but all the engagements were limited in importance.'[51] On 30 December Kemal was reassigned to Ayn al-Mansur (Ain Mansur), where he was to command the forces before Derna and Tobruk while Enver commanded the whole Cyrenaican theatre from the same place. He was to write to a friend about how he had 'crossed the Mediterranean Sea' and 'covered distant deserts to confront an enemy based on his Fleet, and how the Ottoman-led forces had 'managed to keep the enemy at bay at certain points on the coast.'[52] If his later account to his biographer, Hikmet Bayur, is to be believed, he realized from the start that doing anything more than containing the Italians in their enclaves 'was hopeless.' He had to stay and make the effort however in order 'to keep my material and moral position in the army and amongst the officers who were my contemporaries.'[53] It is often said that Kemal and Enver did not get on and this is borne out by the former's 1926 reminiscence:

'How his (Enver's) designs were to be carried out was for him a matter of detail. He was generally ignorant in military matters, as he had not progressed step by step from the command of a battalion to that of a regiment, and so on.'[54]

At Al Khums in Tripolitania it became evident by the end of December 1911 that an advance, albeit one tactical in nature, was necessary. The port and town, complete with its 18-metre lighthouse, was surrounded on its landward side by an oasis, whilst some

6 kilometres to the east were the ancient ruins of Leptis Magna (Neapolis, Lebda). However the feature of most importance in the military context was Ra's al Marqab (al-Markib, Markib, Colline del Mercheb, Mergheb), a steep-sided hill some 213 metres high and about 6 kilometres to the south-west. Dominating the town as it did, this was the key strategic feature of the landscape. Elements of the 8th *Bersaglieri* that had landed on 21 October under Colonel Giovanni Maggiotto to occupy Al Khums had penetrated as far as the hill, but without support could not take and hold it. Upon the withdrawal of the *Bersaglieri*, Ottoman forces had swiftly occupied the position, which was topped with a structure dating from antiquity, probably a blockhouse, that was then adapted for modern military purposes.[55] According to Irace, this had 'always been a well-known refuge of brigands, who, ensconced amongst the ruins of an old Roman castle, defied from this mountain eyrie the Turkish authority.'[56]

The modern adaptation might have been of only minor import had it not eventually included the emplacing of two artillery pieces; probably the Krupp 87 mm 1897 model though they might have been the more potent 75 mm 1906 model captured from the Italians. The usual inconclusive skirmishes and minor actions had taken place around the periphery of the defences ever since the occupiers had taken possession of Al Khums, and following the sending of large-scale reinforcements there were about 5,000 troops in the garrison under Major-General Ezio Reisoli. This garrison was apparently surprised when early in the New Year the Ottoman guns began a sporadic bombardment, firing several shells a day into Al Khums. This was little more than a nuisance, and was countered by the emplacing of a counter battery of 149 mm howitzers near the lighthouse that silenced the Ottoman guns on 12 January. It became clear to Reisoli though that to make the occupation secure Ra's al Marqab would have to be taken and held. As well as mounting the two guns, it provided a secure base from which to mount harassing attacks.

Assaulting the position would be no easy task however, as the Ottomans had entrenched themselves around the prominence and were present in significant numbers. In order to weaken the defenders Reisoli devised and implemented a cunning and audacious plan. On 26 February 1912 two Italian vessels, a warship and a passenger steamer, appeared off the coast at Zliten (Sliten), some 40 kilometres east of Al Khums. Activity aboard these vessels indicated to those watching from shore that a landing was imminent. Accordingly, substantial reinforcements were hurried from the Ra's al Marqab area to oppose the manoeuvre. It was however merely an Italian ruse, and during the early morning of 27 February almost the entire garrison of Al Khums left the defences and, divided into three columns, made towards the mountain in the pre-dawn darkness.

The centre column was composed of a battalion from the 89th Infantry Regiment, a battalion of *Alpini*, and a company of engineers, with a mountain battery in support. This was the assault column, tasked with making a frontal attack on Ra's al Marqab in an attempt to take it by storm. The left and right columns, composed of battalions from the 8th *Bersaglieri* and two infantry battalions drawn from the 6th and 37th Regiments respectively, together with supporting elements, had the task of protecting the flanks and rear of the assaulting troops from any enemy interference. At daylight the artillery at Al Khums began a heavy bombardment of the Ottoman position and the troops of the centre column attacked the mountain. It was, according to reports issued from Rome the following day, 'an all day battle' but the Italians prevailed and by the evening of 27 February they held the summit of Ra's al Marqab. Reisoli, through a combination of guile and daring, had won an important, if relatively minor, victory at the cost of 26 dead and 130 wounded; the Italian occupation of Al Khums was made secure.

Italian innovation was not restricted to tactical matters however. Mention has already been made of the collecting of motor wagons at the market at Tripoli City, and the use of lorries to carry and distribute supplies, and later infantry, became widespread. It had not at first been thought that such vehicles would prove useful due to the lack of proper roads in the theatre. A trial of two light FIAT lorries fitted with twin pneumatic tyres on the rear wheels was undertaken. Despite much of the terrain over which they operated consisting of rough, loose sand and gravel-type material strewn with rocks, interspersed with dunes that they could not negotiate, they quickly established their superiority over animal transport. Thirty more of the same type were then despatched followed by larger consignments. Sources differ as regards to numbers, but around 300 light 'auto-trucks' were sent to the theatre with around half being deployed in and around Tripoli City – heavier vehicles were excluded because they used solid rubber tyres, which would have been of no use given the ground.

The idea of using self-propelled vehicles in warfare was not novel and had been long encouraged by proponents of the devices. Indeed between the years 1873-1883 the Italian Army had conducted extensive experiments in using traction engines, or road locomotives (*locomotive stradali*) as they were termed, to haul artillery, but had concluded that they were too unwieldy and not reliable enough at that time.[57] This was undoubtedly correct, but late nineteenth century technological evolution by no means discarded steam power. *The Horseless Age,* the first US automotive magazine, had carried an article in 1897 entitled 'Motor Vehicles in Warfare' which had identified deficiencies in internal combustion engine powered vehicles, and therefore argued that the future of such vehicles lay in steam power:

> […] since the petroleum motors at present are not satisfactory above ten horse power […] a motor vehicle for military service must be a carefully designed steam traction engine, planned to haul artillery and supply trains anywhere where horses can go; the questions of speed and personal comfort, so important in pleasure vehicles, need hardly be considered […] and it is not at all unlikely that motors in warfare may soon enter the field service as extensively as they have already entered other departments.[58]

They were indeed used in small number during the Second Boer War when the British despatched 24 of them to South Africa in 1899 followed by six armoured versions; the latter being equipped with four armoured trailers apiece.[59] Used to tow heavy guns and their impedimenta the British named them 'steam sappers,' but the Italian experience was replicated according to Major General Sir John Headlam of the Royal Artillery who served with them. He concluded that they were 'too cumbersome for general use on ordinary roads, and quite unsuited for taking guns into action.'[60]

Technological advances though led to much improved internal combustion engines, and by 1911 the objections to utilising vehicles powered by them had been largely overcome. Italy thus scored another military first by making large-scale use of motorised lorries to transport supplies. According to Renato Tittoni:

> This new method of transportation resulted in the rapid clearing of the wharves and transmitting the stores to the troops, transporting construction materials, removal of camp equipage, and carrying ammunition and rations to the firing-line. We therefore had

A Fabbrica Automobili Isotta Fraschini armour-plated car. By 1911 technological advances in internal combustion engines had led to their widespread adoption in vehicles. The Italian Army scored a military first by making large-scale use of motorised lorries to transport supplies, though the convoys thus formed of these thin-skinned vehicles were of necessity slow moving and thus somewhat vulnerable to small arms fire. In order to offer some protection, and to be able to retaliate against attack, armoured versions were constructed armed with machine guns. The first of these, designed by Giustino Cattaneo of the Milanese company Isotta Fraschini, was ready for deployment by the end of 1911. It was of an advanced design armed with two 6.5 mm Vickers-Maxim machine guns, one in a turret mounting that could swivel and one rear-firing. Plated with 4 mm steel for crew protection, the vehicle weighed some 3 tonnes and was fitted with steel extension rims for the wheels to prevent it sinking into the ground. It was a success, and several more of similar designs were ordered from various manufacturers. Though the concept was not entirely new, these were the first armoured fighting vehicles ever to be deployed in a combat situation. (Author's Collection).

ample proof from this complex work – the long daily trips made over desert and variable ground – that inspired complete faith in this mode of transportation to follow the troops, under any circumstances and for long distances, with great saving of time and fatigue, besides the ordinary services required by the presence of many troops on a warlike mission.[61]

The convoys thus formed of these thin-skinned vehicles were of necessity slow moving and thus somewhat vulnerable to small arms fire. In a similar manner to their steam-powered ancestors, and in order to offer some protection and to be able to retaliate against attack, armoured versions equipped with machine guns were developed. Again this was not a totally new idea, and armoured cars powered by internal combustion engines had been both mooted and built previously; Austria-Hungary and France had constructed working, albeit experimental, models in 1900-6.[62]

Working quickly, and probably sensing a commercial opportunity, the Milanese company Fabbrica Automobili Isotta Fraschini had a model designed by its engineer Giustino Cattaneo ready for use by the end of 1911. It was of an advanced design armed with two 6.5mm Vickers-Maxim machine guns, one in a turret mounting that could swivel and one rear firing. Plated with 4mm steel for crew protection the vehicle weighed some 3 tonnes and was fitted with steel extension rims for the wheels to prevent it sinking into the ground. It can safely be concluded that the concept was considered successful, inasmuch as several more of similar design were ordered from various manufacturers.

The mobility conferred by the use of vehicular transport was first put to use in a military operation during another advance towards Zanzur (Janzur) that took place on 8 June 1912. This was undertaken by the heavily reinforced 1st Division comprising 13,494 infantry including troops from Eritrea (*ascari*), 8 squadrons of cavalry, 12 machine guns, and 50 artillery pieces now under the command of *conte* Vittorio Camerana, which departed from the Italian lines near Gargaresh at 03:30 hours with its two core Brigades each in column.[63] These two columns advanced in echelon, with Giardina's 2nd Brigade (the 6th and 40th Regiments and two batteries of mountain artillery) on the right nearest the sea being slightly ahead of the 1st Brigade (the 82nd and 84th Regiments, with three batteries of field artillery) under Rainaldi.

Accompanying the advance were 54 motor lorries divided into four transport columns, the whole of this mechanical transport being under the command of Captain Corazzi. One of these columns, consisting of ten vehicles, formed an ambulance train under the command of a surgeon, whilst the other three (under the command of Lieutenants Milani, Bosio and Marocco) carried engineering equipment such as barbed wire, sand bags, and shovels together with a large quantity of dynamite. The ambulance column followed directly behind the advancing troops whilst the engineering supplies

waited until called upon.

The objective was a small hill topped with a shrine or tomb (*marabutto*) marking the eastern extremity of the Zanzur Oasis. This high ground was considered

'After the battle of Zanzur: General Frugoni with other senior officers visited the conquered enemy trenches filled with the dead.' The small village of Zanzur lay about eight kilometres beyond the Italian occupied zone around Tripoli City and was remarkable only because it was one of the few decent anchorages between there and the Tunisian frontier. The Italians believed that it was a nodal point for the 'contraband' that succoured the Ottoman-led forces in the interior, but left it until 8 June 1912 before despatching an overwhelmingly strong force to occupy it. This ponderous manoeuvre was successful, though the great number of enemy dead depicted was more the result of artistic licence rather than an accurate rendition. From *La Domenica del Corriere* 23-30 June 1912. (Author's Collection).

to be the key to the whole position, and it was defended by a considerable Ottoman force that was well protected in narrow and deep trenches that sheltered them from rifle fire and all but direct hits from artillery. Against the nearly invisible enemy manning these defences the 2nd Brigade could not at first prevail, despite an outflanking move along the shore by a battalion of the 40th Regiment and heavy support from the mountain artillery and the 152 mm guns of the armoured cruiser *Carlo Alberto* stationed offshore. However the weight of fire eventually told and the infantry were able to advance over the open ground and into the trenches where some hand-to-hand fighting took place. Numbers prevailed and the clearance of the trenches meant that that the Ottoman forces as a whole were obliged to fall back into the Oasis of Zanzur and the position was taken. Having taken the hill the Italians now set out to fortify it against any counter-attack, and the 44 lorries conveyed the engineering equipment the *circa* 15 kilometres to the requisite positions. Having been unloaded the three columns returned to Gargaresh, where two of them were redeployed as ambulances whilst one was employed in conveying rations and equipment to the 6th and 40th Regiments atop their recently conquered position.

Frugoni's report on the battle stated that out of the total manpower deployed the losses had amounted to one officer and 38 troops (including ten *ascari*) killed and 13 officers and 278 troops (including 75 *ascari*) wounded. Of these categories, 70 wounded Italian soldiers were carried to forward hospitals by the ambulances, whilst the dead were conveyed to the cemetery.[64] In these matters, and in carrying the engineering materials to the object of the attack which would otherwise have had to be moved using horses or mules, the lorries had proven useful if not decisive. It was, though, a pointer of things to come, and the writer Horace Wyatt quoted an Italian newspaper in this regard:

> The motor lorry was ubiquitous; it transported ammunition or succoured the wounded, fetched fodder for the horses and other animals, or money for the troops and for the Arabs; it brought new boots for the soldiers or delivered urgent messages, as well as being used for the transport of troops from the various bases right up to the first fighting line in battle. Only the advent of the autocar rendered possible many of the daring moves of this war, as it solved the difficulties of desert transport.[65]

This perhaps overstates the case somewhat, but nevertheless there can be no doubt that the Italians had at least begun the process of solving the difficulties of desert mobility by demonstrating that light lorries and similar vehicles could, in the main, handle the terrain and climatic conditions.

Mobility and the resultant ability to project power was assisted by the redeployment of airships to the theatre. This occurred at the end of February as, according to an eye-witness account, one of the dirigibles was test-flown about a week before first operational usage, the wind direction and speed at various heights being ascertained by sending up tethered kites. The observer was the British artist and experienced war correspondent, Henry Charles Seppings Wright, who recounted the sighting in his 1913 book:

> One peaceful morning about eight o'clock a strange phenomenon presented itself in the sky. Over Tripoli was hovering what appeared to be an indistinct moon. The sky was heavy, and a purple haze obscured the horizon. We were not left long in doubt as to what this strange new object was, for gradually it turned and presented the long ovoid body of an airship, a new

The airships P 2 and P 3 in their hangar at Tripoli. The P Type (*modello piccolo*) semi-rigid airship consisted of a gas-filled envelope 63 metres in length and 11.6 metres in diameter containing 4400 cubic metres of hydrogen. From the internal hinged keel was slung a boat-shaped car or gondola, with two 75 hp Fiat engines, one on either side, equipped with reversible propeller blades. The aircraft were fitted with dual controls and had a four or five man crew, which, despite the airships being army machines, consisted of both naval and military officers. The petrol for the engines was carried in the car as was the water ballast, whilst additional sand ballast was contained in bags and a number of bombs could also be carried. The first operational usage of the two airships occurred during the attack on Zanzur on 5 March 1912. Seppings Wright related how the two 'ballons,' as the Ottomans called them, 'proceeded slowly and gracefully to Zanzur, manoeuvring like a couple of battleships.' (Author's Collection).

terror for frightening these unconquerable desert men. I had seen it before manoeuvring above the lagoons at Venice earlier in the year. We all watched its motions with intense interest; the Turks showed little concern, and the Arabs seemed to think that the Italians were providing a new target for them to practise at. Rifles were immediately discharged, in their usually excited and erratic manner, although the ship was a good fifteen miles away. This first ascent was evidently only a trial trip, or perhaps the kites had shown that the wind was set in a wrong direction, for she continued to hover over Tripoli. Probably, too, they were testing the engines.[66]

This vessel was either the P 2 or P 3. The P Type (*modello piccolo*) semi-rigid airship consisted of a gas filled envelope 63 metres in length and 11.6 metres in diameter containing 4400 cubic metres of hydrogen. From the internal hinged keel was slung a boat-shaped car or gondola, with two 75hp Fiat engines, one on either side, equipped with reversible propeller blades. The aircraft were fitted with dual controls and had a four or five man crew, which, despite the airships being army machines, consisted of both naval and military officers. The petrol for the engines was carried in the car as was the water ballast, whilst additional sand ballast was contained in bags and, although this was not apparent at the time, a number of bombs could also be carried.[67] The aviators who manned these craft included several who went on to higher things. Perhaps most notable were Salvatore Denti di Piraino, who became an admiral and commander in chief of the Italian Navy and Giulio Valli, who as a rear admiral was to argue for the construction of Italian aircraft carriers to provide organic air power for the Italian fleet.

The first operational usage of the two airships (a third slightly smaller P Type – 60 metres in length and 11.6 metres in diameter containing 4200 cubic metres of hydrogen

– P 1, was deployed at Benghazi from 11 May 1912) occurred in an attack on Zanzur on 5 March 1912. Seppings Wright related how the two 'ballons,' as the Ottomans called them, 'proceeded slowly and gracefully to Zanzur, manoeuvring like a couple of battleships.'[68] Though obviously useful for reconnaissance the dirigibles also had an embryonic strike capability. According to Abbott, who was in the vicinity, they aimed six bombs at 'a hillock between Girgaresh and Zanzur, where a body of fifteen Arab horsemen were gathered at the time.' Only one of these devices exploded whilst the rest embedded themselves in soft sand, allowing the Ottoman forces to recover them. Abbott described one he saw thus:

> They consist of an outer iron cylinder, about nine inches long and four inches in diameter, and a narrower concentric cylinder inside. The latter is charged with dynamite, the former with about three hundred shrapnel bullets embedded in brittle resin. On the top of the cylinder is a wooden cap; through its centre passes a tube about two feet six inches long. The upper and longer portion of this tube serves to suspend and direct the bomb. The portion that goes through the bomb contains a detonator. From below projects a needle resting on a spring. When the lower end of the tube, which for equipoise is armed with a small linen parachute, has struck a hard substance, the needle gets loose, shoots upward, and hits the detonator, thus bringing about the explosion.[69]

According to reports issued from Rome shortly after the event these bombs had 'terrific effect.'[70] Later reports, having digested the operations in Tripoli as a whole, gave a different view; 'The dropping of bombs, while they did no material damage, had a wonderful moral effect.'[71]

According to Italian sources, the dirigibles had an important effect on the advance towards Zanzur that took place on 8 June 1912. Drawn by the sounds of battle, Ottoman forces moved towards the Italian forces and hoped to surprise the 1st Brigade which was inland covering the flank of the main advance. This was spotted by the observers in the airships, who not only reported the movement but also bombed the advancing force. Though the bombing had little or no effect the warning was invaluable to Rainaldi's brigade as it allowed it to deploy in good time and repulse the Ottoman attack.[72]

Another area of novel technology that the Italians utilised was in communications. Radio, or wireless, telegraphy (*radiotelegrafici*) was not new to the Italian forces, and they despatched a wireless detachment to Tripoli under the command of Lieutenant Luigi Sacco on 9 October. Nor was this was the first time wireless communication had been used in land warfare as the German forces in *Deutsch-Südwestafrika* had employed the technique during their campaign there in 1904-7. There it was discovered that it was possible to send Morse messages successfully at distances of over 150 kilometres using the portable *Telespark* apparatus. However, other than installation in permanent land-based stations, the apparatus was only really suitable for use on board ships because in that application the weight and size of the apparatus could easily be accommodated; such factors meant that developing portable apparatus for military use was problematical.

Sacco was joined at Tripoli City by none other than Guglielmo Marconi and they carried out a series of experiments on 16 December in the presence of Caneva and Frugoni at the airfield near the Jewish Cemetery. They established that with small-scale equipment using four 1.5-metre length antennae it was possible to communicate over a distance of 15-20 kilometres. The next day a further experiment was performed near the cavalry barracks. During the course of these tests Sacco and Marconi 'accidentally made a discovery of the greatest importance.' They discovered that they did not have to rig up an antenna on masts in order to send or receive a signal. Rather the insulating properties of the dry desert sand meant the running of a 200-metre cable on the ground allowed the apparatus to function 'without interruption, exactly the same as if the usual system were employed.'

Messages sent from Tripoli were received at Coltano, near Pisa, in Italy, and as Sacco put it in his report it meant 'a simple and safe communication with Italy although in only one direction.' In terms of military applications he noted that the removal of the need for tall masts, which Marconi reckoned to be a grave danger as they could be seen by an enemy from a long distance, would allow greater flexibility in the field. He also noted that although it would be possible to intercept enemy wireless transmissions, the same applied in reverse and that therefore it would be necessary to encrypt all transmission by *radiotelegrafici*. Tactically, the Italians did manage to produce wireless sets that were small enough to be carried by animal transport and which were used by gunfire direction parties to communicate with ships close offshore. The use of these sets allowed close support naval gunfire to the army.[73] The utilisation of these new technologies, though they were not without interest or import and reflected the Italian search for, and deployment of, technological solutions to the difficulties of terrain they faced, did not alter the fact that at the theatre or operational level the war was stalled. It was becoming impossible to disguise the fact that at the political and strategic level, the Italian government was in difficulties.

CHAPTER TEN

'Nations have no friends, they only have interests'

(Attributed to Lord Palmerston)

'The German Powers disapproved of Italy's adventure in Tripoli, but to check it would have been to drive her into the Triple Entente.'
H N Brailsford, *The War of Steel and Gold*, 1914[1]

'If the Powers of the Triple Entente wish to secure the goodwill of Italy, they must acquiesce in her designs on Tripoli. If they do this they must presumably pro tanto alienate the sympathy of Turkey and throw her more and more into the arms of Germany.'
Joseph Heller, *British policy towards the Ottoman Empire, 1908–1914*, 1983[2]

AS has already been pointed out, the last strand of Italian pre-war strategy had collapsed with the mutual alienation engendered by the Battle of Tripoli and its aftermath. Consequentially, all hopes of the conflict being a short, victorious war on the Italian side had vanished. When the in-theatre leadership decided that there could be no military resolution in the medium, or perhaps even long term, and that waiting upon events was the only option, then Italian strategy was paralysed. It could be argued that deadlock prevailed, inasmuch as the same applied to the Ottoman Empire. However time was very much on the Ottoman side. An unnamed Ottoman Senator who visited Britain in early 1912 was quoted by W T Stead as arguing:

> We cannot make peace with Italy for two very good reasons. If we made peace signing away Tripoli, we should immediately be confronted with a far more serious war, a war of the Arabs against the Power which had betrayed them to their foes. The other reason why we cannot make peace is because it costs us less to make war than it did to govern Tripoli in time of peace. The war at present costs us nothing. Tripoli in time of peace was a burden upon our finances. Tripoli carries on the war without asking from us one *piastre*. But an Arab war would cost us much. To ask us to make peace, therefore, is to ask us to exchange a war with Italy, which costs us nothing and cannot possibly do us any serious harm, for a war with the Arabs which will cost millions and might entail the loss of the whole of Arabia and Mesopotamia. So far as we are concerned there will be no peace until the summer comes, when the cholera and perhaps the Senoussi may clear the invaders out of Tripoli.[3]

On the Italian side the conflict was becoming if not unaffordable then exorbitantly expensive; in the financial year 1912-13 it was reckoned to have absorbed nearly 47 per cent of total state expenditure.[4] By March 1912 Italian strength in Tripolitania and

'La fucilazione degli Arabi traditori (Shooting the treacherous Arabs).' According to one Italian of the Bersaglieri, Lieutenant-Colonel Gherardo Pàntano: 'Our officers demonstrate feelings of great resentment, hostility, and hatred against the Arabs, and do not know how to distinguish between friends and foes, or, rather, between those who we should fight and those we should protect [...] Arabs found seriously injured are covered in gasoline and burned, or thrown into wells [...] others are shot with no other reason than that of a cruel whim.' These types of actions met with the general approval of a section of the Italian Press. Giuseppe Bevione was to put it thus following the Battle of Tripoli: 'Executions that lasted for three days in the oasis and have sent to Allah more than a thousand faithful were indispensable. Only a generous return of killings could establish in the Arab soul a sense of justice and the certainty of our strength.' Photograph from: Antonio de Martino, *Tripoli Italiana: La Guerra Italo-Turca, Le Nostre Prime Vittorie* (New York; Sociata Libraria Italiana, 1911).

Cyrenaica was around 100,000 strong and the campaign had seriously depleted the army's stocks of weapons, ammunition, and equipment. The need to provide these reinforcements seriously disrupted the training and force levels of almost every unit in the army.

Certain reservations also began to be expressed by the Italian press, which had, with the exception of anarchist and socialist organs, been generally supportive. Senator Maggiorino Ferraris, a former government minister and proprietor and chief editor of *La Nuova Antologia,* the oldest and most prestigious organ of Italy's cultured press, 'admitted frankly' in the February 1912 edition of the magazine, that the Italian nation was deceived as to the probable attitude of the Arabs towards them. He noted that the resistance of the latter had introduced an entirely new element into the military situation, and argued for a policy of remaining on the coast and not venturing upon any hazardous expeditions. The conservative *Rassegna Nazionale,* whilst deploring the actions of the Socialist Party in opposing the campaign and the foreign press likewise, nevertheless conceded that the conquest would prove a far longer and more difficult task than the nation had imagined.

The Socialist Party that the more conservative press excoriated had indeed been strongly opposed to the war, and was outspoken about it from the start. On 1 October the Socialist organ *Avanti (Forward)* published an editorial on the matter:

> Some people tell us that this will not be really a war at all, that there will be a few shots, a blockade by the fleet, the simple landing of an army corps, and that all will then be over. And perhaps this thought is behind the whole enterprise; doubtless this conviction led to the war being prepared and decided upon. By exalting the prowess of Italy's military forces and ridiculously under-estimating the Turkish forces, our rulers have, as it were, administered

morphia to a section of public opinion in this country and have rendered it insensible to the direct and indirect perils of the situation.[5]

Avanti was not then a large circulation paper. This was to change largely thanks to one, then little known, socialist named Benito Mussolini. When the war began he was editing another much smaller Socialist newspaper, *La Lotta di Classe* (*Class Struggle*) at Forli in the north-east of Italy. He was forthright in his opposition to the war and campaigned for a general strike. This led to him being arraigned for obstructing the public authorities in the performance of their duties, advocating violence against persons and property, and inciting people to cause specific damage. He was sentenced on 23 November 1911 to one year in prison, subsequently reduced to five months. His fame spread because of the conviction and on his release in April 1912 he was appointed as editor of *Avanti* in Milan. He increased the circulation and, because he wrote a great deal of the content personally, greatly expanded his influence.[6] It is unsurprising that *Avanti* increased its circulation. The anti-war message had begun to resonate among the working class and the conscripts that had to fight it were drawn from their ranks. Many attempted to avoid military service and, for example, the Italian community in Australia 'increased markedly, especially as a result of an influx of men trying to avoid call up.'[7]

Domestically unpopular as the war might have been in certain quarters, this opposition was in no way powerful enough to deflect the government. The problem was the government did not really have a policy in respect of bringing the Ottoman government to terms, and felt constrained in formulating one. As long as the war was confined to the territory of the Tripoli *vilayet* then it was, from the point of view of the Great Powers, considered generally containable. With Italy, in Lowe's words, 'straddling the Triple Alliance-Triple Entente confrontation' neither of the blocs, or their members, would act in such a way as to push her into the arms of the opposing bloc; no power was willing to risk seriously offending Italy.[8] Nevertheless, the Italo-Ottoman War had considerable potential to upset the delicate equilibrium of European politics should it spread.

The views of the most disinterested of the Great Powers, Russia, had been made known right at the outset: 'So long as France does not protest it is a matter of indifference to Russia who occupies the North African coast [...] Russian diplomacy will remain passive unless Turkey should seek compensation, leading to disturbances in the Balkans.'[9] It was of course a cardinal point of Italian diplomacy that who occupied the North African coast remained 'a matter of indifference' to Russia and the other powers, insofar as it allowed Italy to be that occupier. On the other hand, and particularly after the situation there became militarily stalemated, Italy sought to involve the other powers in such a way as to pressure the Ottoman Empire to make peace on Italian terms. The Ottomans of course sought international aid for precisely the opposite reason, and had done so from the beginning of hostilities by making unsuccessful appeals for intervention and for one or other of the Great Powers, or a combination of them, to broker a deal. These approaches even included the offer of a formal Alliance with Britain, made on 30 October 1911. In return for this alliance Britain was expected to guarantee the integrity of the Ottoman Empire and use her power to intervene with Italy. The object of this last exercise being to get the Italians to accept a settlement which would recognize some version of Ottoman sovereignty in Tripoli and Cyrenaica.

Such an action was though unpalatable to Sir Edward Grey, Britain's Foreign Secretary, and he refused to countenance a departure from the policy of strict neutrality that he had proclaimed at the start of hostilities.[10] As has already been noted, Italy could have had the substance of what she wanted from the outset, though this would have involved compromises over the form. The Italian declaration of sovereignty over the *vilayet* on 5 November prevented any further dubiety on that score, and so the situation became one of diplomatic, as well as military, stalemate.

Though all the powers sought to avoid estranging Italy, none of them wished their relations with the Ottoman Empire to be damaged either, or for the Empire to be greatly weakened. All the powers wanted to avoid disturbances in the Balkans, which were notoriously unstable, whilst, as has been noted, Austria–Hungary was particularly sensitive to any Italian action in the Adriatic that might precipitate this. Of all the Great Powers that wished an end to the Italo–Ottoman conflict, the one with perhaps the most compelling reasons was probably Germany. German–Ottoman links were several and seemingly deep. Such figures as the revered German Field-Marshal Count Helmuth von Moltke (the Elder) had, as a young officer, served with the Ottoman army from 1836 to 1839 as an adviser. Though undoubtedly he became the most famous German commander to have strong associations with the Ottoman army, he was not the first such, nor the last, and military ties between the two empires were to become very close.[11]

In a similar vein Ottoman armaments were supplied by German companies, and Karl Küntzer calculated that in 1897 the profits on these arms sales, mainly accrued by Krupp and Mauser, were around 80 million Marks.[12] Indeed, these two firms had a 'virtual monopoly' on the supply of arms and ammunition to the Ottoman army after 1885.[13] The main heavy units of the Ottoman navy, such as it was in the early twentieth century, were also ex-German, though new construction was being pursued in Britain. Nevertheless, between 1890 and 1910, trade with Germany increased from 6 per cent to 21 per cent of all Ottoman trade.

Apart from armaments, the most famous example of German–Ottoman ties came in the shape of railways. German capital and expertise built the Anatolian Railway, which was begun in May 1889, and the better known Baghdad Railway, started in 1904, whilst the rolling stock for these networks was provided by German enterprises.[14] These were not just business deals; the German government pressurised the Deutsche Bank, the financial institution behind the business, to carry them through as part of German foreign policy.[15]

The attractions of being friendly with, if not allied to, the Ottoman Empire were obvious to Germany. If, in the event of a great European war involving Germany and Russia, the Ottoman Empire were opposed to the latter then a huge shift in Russian military attention from Germany's east to the Balkans and Caucasus would take place. This would be of immense benefit to Germany whose war plan for dealing with Russia and her ally France had, since the early years of the century, envisaged massing her forces overwhelmingly in the west whilst leaving those in the east with the bare minimum. This policy was probably aided by Germany being the only one of the Great Powers that did not have any obvious ambitions as regards annexing or otherwise claiming Ottoman territory. However, Germany's policy had its limits cruelly exposed by the Italian precipitation of war. Germany, in common with the other powers, could and would do nothing to jeopardize the international balance of power. But neither did Germany want to lose Italy as an ally nor the Ottomans as friends; a devilish conundrum for the German foreign office to attempt to solve.

Russia, the state that had proclaimed 'indifference' over the war whilst it remained confined to North Africa, and who probably had most to gain by any rupture in German-Ottoman relations, was however to be greatly interested by one gambit that was proposed separately and for differing reasons by both sides; the closure of the Dardanelles. The Dardanelles (the Hellespont of antiquity) formed the southern portion, from the Aegean Sea in the north-eastern part of the Mediterranean Basin to the Sea of Marmara, of the Turkish Straits. The northern portion consists of the Bosphorus (Bosporus), which links the Sea of Marmara to the Black Sea. The Turkish Straits were of immense strategic importance internationally, with some forty per cent of all Russian trade passing through them on, largely, British owned ships. They were also of huge import to the Ottoman Empire, with its capital Istanbul (Constantinople), located at the southern entrance to the Bosphorus. One recent analysis of Turkish foreign policy stated it thus: 'The foreign relations of Turkey, and the Ottoman Empire before her, have been in the large part, governed since the eighteenth century by the attempts of the Russians to gain control of the Straits, and the efforts of Britain and France (and lately the United States) to stop them.'[16]

The Straits were regulated by international treaty. The Treaty of Paris in 1856, which brought to an end the Crimean War, de-navalised the Black Sea by prohibiting the Ottoman Empire and Russia from deploying warships there. Further, the passage of warships of any nationality through the Straits was forbidden. Revision to this agreement was made by the 1871 Treaty of London (sometimes called the Pontus Treaty after the ancient Greek name for the Black Sea: *Pontos Euxeinos*) under which Russia and the Ottoman Empire could again deploy warships in the Black Sea. Such vessels were however excluded from passing through the Straits, except when in time of peace the Ottoman Sultan should deem it necessary in order to enforce the provisions of the Treaty of Paris. Russia had suffered from this prohibition during the Russo-Japanese War. The Black Sea Fleet had been unable to join the Second and Third Pacific Squadrons as they sailed around the world from the Baltic. Russia did ask the Ottoman Empire for permission to send the fleet through the Straits, but the British, who were allied with Japan, had argued that such action would be considered a breach of the treaty.

The right of merchant vessels of all nations to pass through the Straits, other than those of belligerents during a period of conflict, was affirmed by Article III. These various instruments had been signed by Austria, Britain, France, Germany, the Ottoman Empire, Italy, and Russia. British interest in the Straits and the prevention of Russian control of them had been elucidated by Lord Beaconsfield (Benjamin Disraeli) in 1876. He reckoned that possession of the Ottoman capital constituted the 'key to India.'[17] Disraeli may have exaggerated, but there is no doubt that the future of the Turkish Straits became a major concern for British defence planners and policy-makers throughout the rest of the long nineteenth century.

The first intimation that the closure of the Turkish Straits was in the offing came from the Ottoman government. Concerned by reported Italian naval activity in the Aegean Sea, which was actually confined to small-scale patrolling, the garrisons at several of the Dodecanese Islands were strengthened. Beehler states that these reinforcements amounted to sending 2,000 troops to Lesbos and 1,500 each to Rhodes, Samos and

Chios (Khíos). Weapons were also issued to the Muslim population of the islands, though not to the majority Orthodox population.[18] On 10 November 1911 a new Foreign Minister, Mustafa Assim Bey, had been appointed in Istanbul. He lost no time in asking his ambassadors to the five Great Powers to point out that the threat of Italian attacks in the Aegean could lead to the paralyzing of 'general commerce.' This was a less than subtle reference to the closure of the Straits, but it could be prevented if the Powers were able to persuade Italy not to extend the war.[19] The Powers were unwilling to pressure Italy, and nothing came of the initiative; in any event the Straits remained open. Italy made the next move, or perhaps 'hesitant step' would be a better description, by informing the Austro-Hungarian and Russian governments on 20 November that it would set up a naval blockade of the Dardanelles.

The Russian Foreign Minister at the time was Sergei Sazonov, but he had been taken seriously ill and so foreign policy was in the hands of his deputy, Anatoli Neratov. The Russian reply, delivered to Istanbul as well as Rome on 22 November, was to the effect that any interference with neutral shipping was a violation of Article III of the 1871 Treaty of London. Also protested was the strengthening of the Ottoman defences, which involved the placing of mines in the southern portion of the Dardanelles.

When Sazanov resumed active control of the Foreign Ministry in December 1911 he immediately changed the policy of 'indifference' to a more pro-Italian approach, the emphasis being on improving relations with Italy in order to weaken her ties with the Triple Alliance. His first proposals were based on the Great Powers intervening with the Ottoman Empire in order to get her to accept the Italian conquest and annexation. This initiative, which was not taken up, was followed by others, also unsuccessful. Sazanov's view with respect to the Italians blockading the Dardanelles was also benign at first. He knew that the Italians, for all that they were superior to the Ottomans in naval strength, did not have the ability to undertake sustained operations in the area; they were 'the only power which could go there without staying there.'[20] Indeed, Sazonov went further and encouraged the Italians. Giolitti's memoirs record that the Italian ambassador to St Petersburg was told by Sazonov that 'he would be happy if we did something that hit Turkey in a vital part, and we gave a good lesson to the Young Turks in order to reduce their unbearable arrogance.'[21] That such an operation might sink or damage part of the Ottoman fleet was, for him, a bonus. Sazonov wanted an Italian victory, and a quick one at that, for several reasons. According to Bobroff's analysis, these included the value of Italian friendship as a counterpoise to Austria-Hungary in the Balkans, and the possibility of using Italian penetration of the Straits as an excuse for demanding Russian access.[22] However, Italy was not to mount any naval operations against the Dardanelles until April 1912, and then British and Russian policy was found to be rather at odds.

If Russian policy was somewhat pro-Italian after December 1911, then events conspired to make that of France and Britain appear the opposite, at least to Italian popular opinion. The border between Egypt and Cyrenaica had never been accurately or officially delimitated; there had been little need as it ran through a region of seemingly little value. In 1907 this had been reiterated by Sir Edward Grey. He had been asked in Parliament whether he considered that a military position established at Sidi Barani, half-way between Sollum and Mersa Matru to prevent smuggling, would give rise to friction with the Ottoman garrison at Sollum. Further, would he advise the Egyptian government to enter negotiations 'for the proper delimitation of the western frontier of Egypt.' Grey confirmed the establishment of a 'coastguard post' but went on to state that there was 'nothing in this act which renders delimitation necessary, or is likely to give rise to friction.'[23]

Sollum (Solum, Sallum, as-Sallum) was a small town situated on the Bay of Sollum (Khalij as-Sallum), and the Ottoman Empire had claimed it since 1840. Supposedly, this had been established following the Convention of London of that year. Two maps detailing the border were drafted, and it was believed that one was destroyed during a fire in Egypt whilst the other, apparently in Istanbul, is believed to have disappeared. Arthur Silva White visited the area in 1898 and reckoned that he could pinpoint the boundary, but it was of almost academic interest and the exact whereabouts were, and remained, unknown.[24]

British interest became heightened when the Italians declared a blockade of the coast of Ottoman territory. They notified the British on 3 October 1911 that this had been established between the Tunisian and Egyptian frontiers. This demarcation included the whole of the Bay of Sollum, and the British objected. Italy deferred to the objection, and the eastern extremity of the blockade was moved west to exclude Sollum on 25 October. The question remained somewhat hypothetical, but this changed following the Italian occupation of Tobruk when the possibility of Italy converting it into a naval base arose. A naval force based there would be able to dominate the adjacent coastline and local sea area, including the only other decent anchorage for several hundred kilometres at the Bay of Sollum. Accordingly, the logic went, if Italy had Tobruk then Britain, via Egypt, would have to have the use of Sollum.

Italy was not popular with Egyptians at the time. Pier Luigi Grimani, the *chargé d'affaires* at the Italian embassy in Cairo, telegraphed San Giuliano on 17 November complaining of the hostile articles that appeared in the press there. This, he argued, had reached a stage where there was almost a competition amongst the newspapers concerning which could write the most antagonistic articles against Italy. He reckoned that the most popular papers were 'those that demonstrate Italy as hostile and Turkey as victorious.'[25] Nevertheless he liaised with the Egyptian Khedival government (effectively Lord Kitchener) on the subject, reporting on 19 November that he had communicated the 'conditions imposed by Italy to accept the change.' These were essentially minor, and related to adjustments in favour of Italy, or at least Cyrenaica, further inland that would be agreed in detail at a later date. The British Foreign Office issued a statement on the same day, stating that the Ottoman government had been informed in November 1904 that the line of the Egyptian frontier ran some 15 kilometres to the west of Sollum. This statement was also communicated to the Italian Government.

There was an Ottoman garrison at Sollum, a fact that Grimani in a telegraph communication of 6 December considered an 'embarrassment' to Lord Kitchener given that Sollum was claimed by Egypt. However, the British government, to the intense annoyance of Italy, did not move to occupy Sollum until after it had negotiated the matter with the Ottoman government. Indeed, it was not until 15 December that the Ottoman Sultan announced that he had ceded the area to Egypt. Only then did an Anglo-Egyptian force relieve the Ottoman garrison, and on 9 January 1912 the cruiser HMS *Suffolk* anchored in the bay.[26]

Officially, the Italian government underplayed the matter, preferring to remain on as friendly terms with Britain as possible. This was a wise move as one of the reasons given for the British/Egyptian occupation was the suppression of cross-border smuggling. This was successful to an extent, but resulted in the smuggled goods being routed further south. Indeed, shortly after the takeover a caravan of some 175 camels was able to cross into Cyrenaica carrying a large amount of contraband. Bennett records however that the Italian newspapers were 'full of frenzied indignation' at what they saw as British perfidy. He quoted one of the many outraged missives contributed to the press, which 'came from the pen' of Benedetto Cirmeni, a well-known journalist and parliamentary deputy:

> As Sollum is a part of Cyrenaica, over which Italy has proclaimed her full and complete sovereignty, how can Egypt and England accept it as a gift from the Sultan? What is the meaning of this incessant alteration of the Egyptian frontier to the detriment of Cyrenaica during the progress of the Turco-Italian War?
>
> First of all, England made the successful demand that the blockade by our warships, which extended up to the Egyptian frontier, as marked on all the maps, should be withdrawn, because, forsooth, we had blockaded that part of Tripolitan territory upon which Egypt had seen fit to encroach. And now, to-day, by a gracious concession from the Sultan, who has no longer any right to dispose of a single yard of territory in the *vilayet* he has lost, the Egyptian frontier has been advanced so as to include the port of Sollum. Why should England derive such vast profit from the war between ourselves and Turkey?[27]

Britain was not the only state to indulge in a spot of boundary revision. In the far south-west of Fezzan France took the opportunity of occupying the Oasis of Djanet (Ganat). This was an area that had long been in contention; France claimed that it was in Algeria, whilst the Ottoman government argued that it was a part of Tripoli. Situated in an incredibly remote area some 2300 kilometres south of the Mediterranean coast, the Oasis of Djanet derived its importance from its being situated on an important trade route that ran from the Fezzan to the western Sahara. This trade, it was believed, included slaves kidnapped from the eastern regions of Morocco and it was in an attempt to stop this that France had occupied the area in 1905. The following year both France and the Ottoman Empire had reached an understanding that neither would place military forces in the region prior to reaching a final settlement of the matter. However, France claimed that this agreement had been broken in 1908 and 1910 when Ottoman troops were found to have been deployed in the area.[28] These forces were recalled to the north when Italy invaded, but to prevent 'insecurity' a small column of Algerian troops and cavalry under the command of Captain Edouard Charlet was despatched. The oasis was occupied on 27 November 1911 and a small fort constructed to defend it. Djanet was renamed Fort Charlet in 1916 in memory of the captain who was killed on the Western Front in 1915.[29] France also quietly moved small forces based in Chad into the areas that were to become the Borkou, Ennedi, and Tibesti regions of that colony, itself a part of French Equatorial Africa. The border between Ottoman and French territory was amorphous and disputed, and an attempt at settling it was to have taken place in late 1911. Small Ottoman garrisons had been established at oases such as Bardaï, Tibesti, Aïn Galakka and Borkou, but they were steadily withdrawn following the Italian invasion. The news of these manoeuvres took months to reach Rome.[30]

If Italy had a bone of contention with France over these areas there was some consolation in the fact that they were located in little known places that were thousands of kilometres away from areas of Italian occupation. Any disputes could then be resolved out of the public eye. This was not to be the case however with what the British ambassador to Rome, Sir James Rennell Rodd, was to term 'an unfortunate incident' that occurred in January 1912. It was actually the first of a series, and occurred at 06:30 hours on the morning of 16 January in the open sea some 27 kilometres off the coast of Sardinia. The French mail steamer *Carthage*, of the Compagnie Générale Transatlantique, was on its regular voyage between Marseilles and Tunis when it was intercepted and stopped by the protected cruiser *Agordat*. Aboard the French vessel was an aeroplane and an aviator named Emile Duval, who had received his pilot's licence in 1910.[31] Italian agents at Marseilles had notified their masters that Duval and his cargo were aboard the vessel, and it was believed that both man and machine were heading to Tripoli for service with the Ottoman forces. The captain of *Agordat* informed his opposite number on the mail ship that the aeroplane was contraband of war, and that the *Carthage* was therefore to proceed under escort to Cagliari, the capital of Sardinia. Once berthed, the Italian authorities ordered the aeroplane to be offloaded. The captain refused to comply with this order and thereupon the Italians declared the ship had been sequestered and proceeded to seal up the hatches.

This news, telegraphed from the French vice-consul at Cagliari, landed on the desk of Raymond Poincaré, who had become head of the French Government and Foreign Minister on 13 January. In the latter capacity he immediately telegraphed the French Ambassador in Rome, the Italophile Camille Barrère, instructing him to demand the release of the ship and Duval. The next day Poincaré summoned the Italian Ambassador, who explained that his government's attitude was based on the belief that Duval had signed a contract to serve with the Ottoman forces. The ship would be allowed to leave and to proceed to Tunis after the aeroplane had been offloaded.

Negotiations between Barrère, who counselled caution throughout the affair, and the Italian government were proceeding when at 08:00 hours on 18 January the *Agordat* intercepted another French ship off Sardinia. Aboard this vessel, the Marseilles-Tunis mail steamer *Manouba* of the Compagnie de Navigation Mixte, were twenty-nine citizens of the Ottoman Empire. Having ascertained this fact, the commander of the Italian warship escorted the *Manouba* to Cagliari. Upon arrival the Italian authorities requested the French captain to deliver the Ottoman passengers to them, and upon his refusal to do so the *Manouba* was seized. The French vice-consul at Cagliari again became involved and, following instructions from his embassy in Rome, he ordered the Captain to disembark the passengers. The embassy had been assured by the Italian authorities that they carried weapons and were soldiers, so the next day they were taken into Italian custody. The *Manouba* was then allowed to proceed, leaving Cagliari at 19:20 hours on 19 January.

The *Carthage* was released the next day with Duval and his aeroplane aboard, the Italians having been satisfied that it was not intended for the Ottoman forces in Tripoli.[32] If they really believed this then they were mistaken, though the publicity ensured that Duval never got to fly against the Italians. However, the Ottoman War Ministry made at least two further attempts to get aeroplanes and mercenary pilots into the *vilayet*. These efforts included recruiting the noted French aviators, Jules Vedrines and Marc Bonnier, and procuring two Deperdussin aircraft. This particular attempt came to nothing when, according to Ottoman sources, the pilots got cold feet and flew to Algeria where their machines were impounded. Quite what might have been achieved had any of these attempts been successful is another matter, but it seems likely that another aviation first, that of air-to-air combat, might not have had to wait until the German-Japanese confrontation over eastern China in late 1914.[33]

There remained the question of the *Manouba* passengers, of whom France also demanded the release. Their passage had been negotiated by the Ottoman and French governments on 5 January. They were not combatants, but members of the Ottoman Red Crescent Society, a humanitarian organisation equivalent to the Red Cross Society that had been formed in 1867 and formally recognised ten years later. The Italian ambassador to Paris had been informed of this and had telegraphed his government explaining their status. This message had seemingly miscarried or been delayed, and in any event the French Foreign Office, urged by the Ottoman Ambassador, made pressing representations for their release and demanded compensation for the detention of both ships. They also demanded that the Italian navy cease the interception of French vessels. Italy replied to the effect that the right of search for contraband of war would not be renounced.

Poincaré made his first significant speech on foreign affairs to the French parliament on 22 January relating the incidents. He argued that it was for the French authorities, and not the Italian, to establish the status of passengers aboard its ships, and that the aeroplane was not an instrument of war. His language throughout was moderate; he described the incidents as painful though argued that they would not change the friendly relations between the two countries.[34] That same morning, Prime Minister Giolitti had in the absence of Barrère discussed the matter with Albert Legrand, the First Secretary of the French Embassy at Rome. According to Giolitti's memoirs he, Giolitti, then proposed that the matter would best be resolved by referring it to the adjudication of the Permanent Court of Arbitration at The Hague. Legrand asked if he might telegraph this proposed referral to his government, and Giolitti asked that it be done immediately. Accordingly the telegram was sent at 13:00 hours. Poincaré made his speech at 15:00 hours, and the Italian Prime Minister was unprepared for what he termed the 'rather harsh and almost threatening' content, in which the arbitration proposal was not mentioned.[35] According to Rennell Rodd, Poincaré's words 'aroused strong resentment in Italy, and the cordial relations which had prevailed since the outbreak of the war, were inevitably compromised.'[36] On the other hand, if it aroused the ire of some Italians, the address was acclaimed by many in France. As one 'Veteran Diplomat' wrote:

> [...] Poincaré has by his prompt action [...] imbued his fellow countrymen with confidence in his ability and determination to conduct the foreign relations of France with a greater degree of vigour and dignity than his predecessors in office. [...] The Caillaux administration was turned out of office the other day in the most ignominious manner conceivable, on account of its foreign policy, which was held by Frenchman of every party to have impaired the self respect of the nation and its dignity abroad.[37]

Italian sensibilities were further outraged by the reception given to the two mail ships when they arrived at Tunis. Large crowds and military bands were on the quayside as if welcoming them home from some great victory. Newspapers reported that sections of the crowd chanted '*down with Italy*' and '*long live Turkey,*' as well as '*viva le aeroplane.*' Nevertheless, and despite the frothing of the press in both countries, San Guiliano and Barrère managed to defuse the situation at governmental level by finding a formula whereby the matter was referred to the Permanent Court of Arbitration. This was arrived at despite San Guiliano taking the position that the French insistence on handing over what the Italian's considered prisoners of war amounted to a surrender of Italian rights and was a blow to their prestige. The agreement was published as a *note commune* on 26 January 1912 and amongst its provisions the Ottoman passengers were to be delivered to the French consul in Cagliari. Under his care and responsibility they would then be sent back to Marseilles. France also agreed to verify their identity as Red Crescent personnel and take all necessary measures to prevent any Ottoman military personnel from entering Tunisia.[38]

In retrospect it seems surprising that the note was published at all. On 25 January the Italian destroyer *Fulmine* accompanied by the torpedo-boat *Canopo* seized another Compagnie de Navigation Mixte vessel, the *Tavignano*, some 14 kilometres to the east of Zarzis, Tunisia. Based at Tunis, the *Tavignano* was a coaster used for carrying mail between its home port and other Tunisian towns. In proximity to the steamer at the time were two Tunisian *mahones*, large sailing vessels approximating to galleasses, that the Italians believed were preparing to carry material to shore. These vessels, the *Camouna* and *Gaulois,* were fired on by the *Canopo,* though not seemingly damaged, and driven off. The *Tavignano* was then escorted to Tripoli under suspicion of containing contraband of war, though this suspicion was proven unfounded after a search and she was released the next day.

When news of the incidents, particularly the detention of the *Tavignano,* reached the French Government, Poincaré fired off a 'stiff telegram' to Barrère demanding that he seek an 'immediate' resolution of the matter. The reply came on 26 January stating that the ship had been searched and released, which earned Barrère a 'stinging rebuke' from Poincaré:

> I ask myself how you could accept the suspicions of the Italian Government. I also ask myself why you did not protest against the clear violation of the Franco-Italian Convention of 1875, the *Tavignano* being a mail-boat. You seem entirely to misconceive the state of French opinion. If these incidents recur, we cannot guarantee order at Marseilles or in Tunis. It appears, moreover, that the *Tavignano* was stopped in territorial waters. Finally it is strange that she was taken to Tripoli, which Europe has not yet recognised as an Italian port and where there is no Prize Court. For all these reasons I beg you to make to the Italian Government the most express reserves on the consequences of this new and annoying incident.[39]

Poincaré's mention of the ship being a mail-boat under the 1875 Convention had some political significance. According to the terms of the Convention a mail-boat enjoyed the same honours and privileges as a national ship, which was considered to be a part of the territory of the state to which it belonged. In other words, the taking of the *Tavignano* could be considered an assault on a portion of French sovereign territory, which was an act of war. Poincaré hardly wanted conflict, but he was concerned at the pro-Italian slant that he perceived Barrère had with regards to Franco-Italian relations. This he wished to discourage, for the reason that, in adopting it, he perceived that Barrère was formulating his own foreign policy and attempting to extract Italy from the Triple Alliance.[40] This was not Poincaré's policy; he later claimed his 'philosophy' on the matter was that of Sir Edward Grey, who put it thus in his memoirs: 'If we intrigued to break up the Triple Alliance, our contention that the Entente was defensive and was not directed against Germany would cease to be true.'[41]

Public opinion in Italy, which Barrère reported as viewing 'the surrender of the [Manouba] Turks as a national humiliation,' continued to be outraged at the apparent disregard of Italy's 'greatness.' The same could be said about Tunisia, and such was the anger directed at Italian residents that a large number were forced to leave the country.[42] High politics trumped the low version, and once again, the matter was defused. The French Government's claim for indemnity, on the grounds that the vessels when encountered were within Tunisian territorial waters and were not thus liable to be attacked or captured, was, like the *Carthage* and *Manouba* incidents, referred to the Permanent Court of Arbitration.

The affair of the mail-boats coincided with a visit to Rome of the German Foreign Minister, Alfred von Kiderlen, who arrived on Friday, 20 January. Rumours abounded among the diplomatic community that the visit was arranged so that the Triple Alliance could be renewed a year early. The British Ambassador believed, as did a wide section of the press, that the rift that had occurred in the formerly cordial Franco-Italian relationship would encourage Kiderlen, with Austro-Hungarian approval, to press for an early renewal. It was not to be. According to Rennell Rodd:

> Giolitti, while expressing his cordial appreciation of the offer, insisted that recognition of the annexation of Libya must be a condition of signature. As Germany and Austria had proclaimed their neutrality on the outbreak of the war, they could not, while it was still in progress, recognize as already determined the very issue which stood in the way of peace.[43]

Childs points out that Italy refused all attempts to discuss specifics relating to the renewal of the alliance, wanting to wait until after the war had been decided, from the Italian point of view, satisfactorily.[44] Kiderlen-Waechter did however propose to San Guiliano that the only reasonable basis for negotiations leading to a settlement of the conflict was to split the *vilayet*. The Ottoman Empire would retain Cyrenaica whilst Italy would take Tripolitania. San Guiliano replied that the only basis for settlement was the annexation decree of the previous November.[45]

Italy's refusal to compromise meant that a negotiated peace was unobtainable. Therefore, in an attempt to impose terms upon the Ottoman Empire, Italy was left with no choice but to broaden the war. It became a cardinal belief amongst the Italian leadership that once the Ottomans had been removed from the scene, then peace could be achieved in Tripoli. If the resistance there had no outside source upon which it could rely for support, then it would come to terms. This thinking was encapsulated by Irace:

> The opposition of the Turks and Arabs to the Italian occupation of Tripoli would speedily be at an end if the trade in contraband of war were effectually stopped on the Tunisian and Egyptian frontiers, by means of which our enemies receive fresh supplies of arms, ammunition, and provisions.[46]

The difficulties of identifying and attempting to interdict contraband travelling via Tunisia have been seen. That which travelled via Egypt was discouraged by the authorities there, but given the nature of the terrain and the sympathies of many of the Egyptians it was impossible to stop completely whilst the Ottoman Empire remained in the war.

This was the crux of the Italian problem. Since the forces in Tripoli could not be defeated, or at least not quickly, then an attack had to be made at some other point. The problem was where? Any attack on Ottoman European possessions, or in Anatolia

(Asia Minor), would incur horrendous international complications. It would also involve large scale warfare with the Ottoman Army in strength. Thus, attacks in these places were not realistic prospects. There remained only those places that were vulnerable to naval attack and were not in particularly sensitive areas. There were few locations that fell within such parameters, and these obviously had the disadvantage of not being areas the loss of, or damage to, which would compel the Ottoman government to sue for peace. Nevertheless one such had already been earmarked by Italy, and it was announced that, from 22 January, a blockade would be established off Yemen on the Ottoman Red Sea coast.

CHAPTER ELEVEN

Navalism

'*Unforgettable the thunder of the guns shaking the golden blue of sky and sea while not a breath stirred the palm-trees, not a cloud moved on the swanlike snows of Lebanon.*'

James Elroy Flecker and Sir John Squire (Ed.), *The Collected Poems of James Elroy Flecker*, 1947[1]

THE Italian naval contingent in the Red Sea was reinforced in early January with four modern destroyers of the 'Soldati Artigliere' class; the *Artigliere* (1907), *Granatiere*, (1906) *Bersagliere* (1906) and *Garibaldino* (1910). These vessels were attached because of intelligence reports that the Ottoman Navy was attempting to redeploy a number of its ships from the Persian Gulf into the area. The Italians were seemingly concerned that these might be used to transport Ottoman troops across the Red Sea to attack Eritrea. In retrospect this seems rather far-fetched. Though mainly modern, the Ottoman ships hardly constituted a formidable force. They were: the 240-tonne German-built gunboat, *Kastamonu* (1905) the name-ship of its class, and the French constructed 315-tonne 'Taskopru' class *Gokcedag* (1908), *Refahiye* (1908), *Ayintab* (1908), *Ordu* (1908), and *Bafra* (1908). Their largest calibre weapon was one 75 mm gun on the *Kastamonu,* whilst the rest mounted nothing heavier than 47 mm but were possessed of one 450 mm torpedo tube apiece. Accompanying these were two British-built vessels; the steam yacht *ipka* (constructed as the *Fauvette* in 1892) and the tug *Muha* of unknown age. None of this heterogeneous flotilla could steam at more than 12 knots. The Italians believed that these vessels had arrived in the Red Sea and had secreted themselves in and around the Farsan (Farasan) Islands (Jaza'ir Farasan). Accordingly they began searching the area and the adjacent littoral zone.

On the afternoon of 7 January the *Artigliere* in company with the *Garibaldino* and protected cruiser *Piemonte,* found the enemy ships anchored at Al Qunfidhah. The Italians did not know it, but they were more or less stranded there having run short of coal. The supply vessel carrying their fuel, the *Kaiserieh*, had been masquerading as a hospital ship flying the Red Crescent, and had been stopped by the *Puglia* on 16 December. Upon boarding the ship however, the Italians could find no sign of any hospital beds or

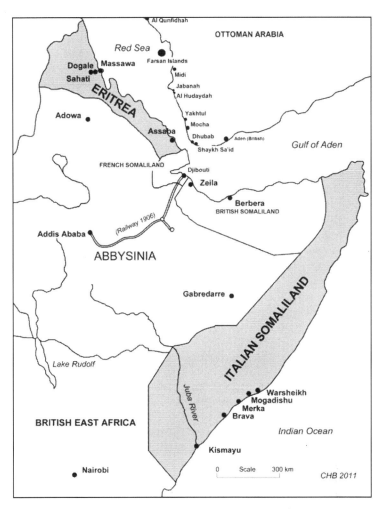

Italian East Africa and the Red Sea. The Italian naval contingent in the Red Sea was reinforced in January 1912 with four modern destroyers. These vessels were deployed because of intelligence reports that the Ottoman Navy was attempting to redeploy a number of its ships from the Persian Gulf into the area. The Italians were seemingly concerned that these might be used to transport Ottoman troops across the mostly modern, the Ottoman ships hardly constituted a formidable force, being small gunboats in the main. Several Ottoman ports were subjected to naval bombardment, but there were no battles worthy of the name. (© Charles Blackwood).

other medical provisions or arrangements, merely a cargo of coal. Accordingly the ship was taken as a prize.

The *Artigliere* opened fire on the Ottoman ships, which replied as best they could, assisted by the shore defences. The engagement, which was quickly joined by the *Piemonte* and *Garibaldino,* took place at fairly long range, about 4500-6000 metres, giving the advantage to the larger Italian guns. After some three hours firing, the entire Ottoman flotilla had been sunk, run aground or, in the case of the *ipka,* scuttled, whilst the shore defences were silenced. The Italians landed the next morning, completed the destruction of the three beached gunboats, and refloated the *ipka,* which they were able to tow off as a prize.

With these last remnants of Ottoman naval power in the area destroyed, Italian naval action was restricted to bombarding the easily accessible ports; Al- Aqabah (Aqaba, Akaba), Jabanah (Djebana), Cheikh Saïd (Sheik Said), Mocha (Mocca) and Midi (Midy).[2] A blockade was also declared from 24 January along the Ottoman coast on the Red Sea, stretching a distance of some 75 kilometres on each side of Al Hudaydah (Hodeida). Neutral vessels would be given five days in which to clear from the blockaded ports.

Neutral ships had been stopped by the Italians before the blockade came into being. One such was the *Africa,* a British registered vessel. On 20 January she was intercepted by *Volturno* en route from Al Hudaydah to Aden and a boarding party discovered twelve Ottoman officers aboard, including the distinguished Colonel Riza Bey. They were taken prisoner and removed from the ship. On 23 January the Österreichischer Lloyd vessel *Bregenz* was stopped and again a number of Ottoman officers were removed.

No protests were made regarding these, and other similar, actions (and according to Sir Edward Grey, about 61 per cent of the vessels passing through the Suez Canal and Red Sea at the time were British[3]), but the imposition of the blockade in general caused British objections. As has already been noted, Italian actions in Tripoli occasioned 'immense ferment' amongst Britain's Islamic subjects in India, and their actions in the Red Sea exacerbated this. It was argued by, for example, the All India Muslim League that the blockade threatened to prevent pilgrims from the sub-continent performing *Hajj.*[4] Also exacerbating this situation was the Italian encouraged seizure of the Farsan Islands by the followers of the rebellious Sayyid Muhammad Ibn Ali al-Idrisi in early February. Situated on the main island was a quarantine centre through which those pilgrims travelling to Mecca on ships were obliged to pass. This centre, together with a similar station at El-Tor (El Tur) in Sinai on the Gulf of Suez, had been established following an outbreak of cholera in 1865. The disease originated in India and was spread to Arabia by pilgrims before moving on to Europe, causing the death of some 200,000 people worldwide. Thus quarantine procedures, supervised by Britain and the Ottoman Empire, now became part of the sea-going pilgrim's experience.[5] There was an element of hyperbole in these protests inasmuch as the last *Dhu al-Hijjah,* the month of pilgrimage, as calculated by the Gregorian calendar occurred between 23 November and 21 December 1911. The next was due to occur between 12 November and 10 December 1912. Nevertheless, the British government quietly protested about the matter and was, in a similar manner, reassured by Italy that interference with the *Hajj* would not be permitted.[6]

France, as well as making similar protests over the potential disruption to those of her subjects who wanted to undertake the *Hajj,* had another more particular complaint against Italian actions. A French syndicate, the 'Ottoman Hodeida-Sana'a and Branch Line Railway Company,' led by the Banque Française pour le Commerce et de l'Industrie had begun to construct a short 17-kilometre railway between a planned new harbour at Ra's Kath b (Rw-el-Ketib) and Al Hudaydah in 27 March 1911. As the name of the syndicate suggests, this was to be the start of a line from the port to Sana'a, the largest and most important inland city in southern Arabia (and now the capital of the Republic of Yemen), and situated about 160 kilometres inland. This first section ran along a long spit that connected the harbour and town, and a little less than half had been completed by January 1912. This spit lay between the open sea and Jabanah (Djebana) and unfortunately during a bombardment by the *Piemonte*, the railway was severely damaged and the project had to be abandoned. The syndicate sued the Italian government for 200,000 lira for the damage to French property.[7]

Though the destruction of Ottoman naval assets in the Red Sea was undoubtedly a useful operation of war in itself, it did not of course bring much pressure to bear on the Ottoman government with respect to the wider conflict. Ottoman complaints about Italy's actions were unceasing, but, as must have been very clear to them by now, no Great Power intervention against Italy was likely to take place until some Great Power vital interest was threatened. The Ottoman government believed that one such area of vital interest related to Syria, where France had long standing and internationally recognised ambitions.[8] At the time, the boundaries of the area termed 'Syria' were imprecise, but in the current context it roughly meant the coast of modern Syria and Lebanon. The Ottoman government believed any Italian naval action along this coast was likely to provoke French intervention. Such was the information conveyed to Giolitti by one of his sources in Istanbul, Giuseppe Volpi.[9] As Giolitti stated it in his memoirs: 'Notwithstanding the state of war, indirect relationships of an absolutely private character were maintained between us and important members of the Ottoman government regime.' Volpi, with his 'wide network of knowledge and relationships,' thus acted as an unofficial conduit between the two governments.[10] This then was the political context within which the Italian Navy mounted an attack on Beirut on 24 February, which, as Childs points out, may have been made in an attempt to disabuse the Ottomans of any prospect of such intervention.[11] The ostensible reason sometimes given for it, that the two Ottoman warships at anchor there might 'interfere with the transportation of Italian troops to the Red Sea,' is unconvincing.[12] The larger vessel was the *Avnillah* (*Avn-Illah*), which had been constructed in Britain in 1869 as a casemate corvette; at some 2,300 tonnes a lighter version of a central battery ship. She was, literally, an ironclad and had been obsolete for decades although, according to the London *Times* correspondent in Beirut, she was 'interesting as a naval antiquity.'[13] Although rebuilt in 1907, her engines were worn out and so she was unmanoeuvrable under her own steam. The smaller ship was the 165-tonne 'Antalya' class torpedo-boat *Ankara*, constructed in Italy in 1906. Armed with two 450 mm torpedo tubes, she was undoubtedly a more potent force than her harbour-mate, but hardly a threat to Italian naval supremacy.

To despatch these two warships Vice-Admiral Luigi Faravelli sent half the 4th Division of his 2nd Squadron, the armoured cruisers *Giuseppe Garibaldi* (flag) and *Francesco Ferruccio*, taking the command himself. According to his official report, the Italian ships 'surprised' the Ottoman ships at daybreak in the Port of Beirut, and ordered them to surrender before 09:00 hours. No sign of this being manifested at the expiration of the deadline, a signal demanding surrender was hoisted, and when this elicited no response fire was opened upon the *Avnillah*, which the report throughout calls a 'gunboat.' This vessel 'replied energetically' until 09:20 hours when it was seen that it had been set alight and firing ceased. The Italian flagship then proceeded to the mouth of the harbour and engaged the *Ankara*, which was 'badly damaged' before being destroyed by a torpedo. The report ended by stating that 'The report that the town of Beirut was bombarded is absolutely false.'[14]

A credible neutral observer generally confirms Faravelli's report, though demonstrates that he was somewhat economical with the truth. Howard Bliss, since 1903 the President of the American University of Beirut (founded 1866), had a panoramic view of the action from the campus overlooking the Mediterranean: 'From the College grounds we could easily see the firing, and from the College tower the view was still more clear.' One of his colleagues, Mrs. Professor Nickoley, was near the waterfront when the 'serious firing' began, and he recounted her story:

> She said that the excitement was indescribable. Shops were closed. Hundreds of people poured into the streets. Animosity against suspected Italians was fierce. She saw two persons fall as a result of revolver or gun shots or other attacks. A Russian Jew, supposed to be an Italian, was attacked, but he was not killed. It is probable, however, that the people were more frightened for their own safety than bent upon revenge.

Bliss noted that 'before long', presumably at 09:20 hours, the firing from the vessels ceased, 'but one of them proceeded slowly to the opening of the port, coming within a few rods [1 rod = 5.0292 metres] of the breakwater.' His account continued:

> The breakwater runs east and west and then at right angles with it another portion runs north and south leaving an opening between the two portions for the entrance of vessels. The Italian vessel took up its position just at this opening and soon began firing upon the Turkish gun-boat which was lying in the harbor. [...]

> Huge columns of water rose up from where the shells or torpedoes struck, and a great volume of smoke arose from the attacked gun-boat. [...] After firing quite a number of shots the Italian warship withdrew, and with its companion went off in a northerly and then a northwesterly direction, to a point eight or ten miles away.

Another pair of his colleagues who ventured to the telegraph office reckoned that they saw the bodies of 'fifteen or twenty' people who had been killed by the explosion of a shell near the port. At least some of them had become victims when the balcony of a hotel near to the Custom House had collapsed, presumably after being hit by a shell. Probably thinking that with the retirement of the ships the excitement was over, Bliss went for luncheon. However, at about 14:00 hours, he interrupted his meal and went out to see 'whether the vessels had changed their position.' He was 'surprised' to note that they were returning and that one of them, the *Giuseppe Garibaldi,* was 'making its way to the entrance of the inner harbor.' As he put it:

> For some unexplained reason the morning's work had not destroyed the small Turkish torpedo boat, and this second visit was for the purpose of finishing the morning's work. [...] The warship directed its fire against the torpedo boat and soon sunk it. Among the five or six shots that were fired was another shell that went screeching over the city and landed, presumably, on the sands near the Municipal Hospital. [...] Immediately after firing the shots the Italian warship withdrew, and together with her sister ship sailed away, remaining, however, within sight of the College, fifteen miles to the northwest.[15]

Contemporaneous official communications from the authorities at Beirut reckoned that 50 sailors that had been aboard the *Avnillah* were missing presumed dead, and 30 civilians had been killed and another 100 wounded during the attack. The total number of sailors and civilians killed was later amended to a round figure of 100.[16] The civilian casualties had mainly occurred because a large crowd had gathered on the quayside to watch the attack and these were hit by 'splinters from ricocheting shells.'[17]

The Austro-Hungarian Ambassador immediately protested over the action, in the 'erroneous' belief that the target of the bombardment had been the city rather than the warships. Barrère too made representations, but according to Giolitti these were put forward in a 'friendly' way.[18] Perhaps slightly less friendly was the deployment of the armoured cruiser *Amiral Charner* (1894) from Crete to Beirut; as one newspaper put it: 'there is £6,000,000 of French capital invested in Beirut.'[19] Italy did attract criticism for bombarding the city, an act which it denied. Bliss's report seems to confirm the Italian position in that the material damage, and the deaths and injuries, were the result of stray, rather than aimed, shells. Perhaps ironically, those who paid the highest price for the Italian attack at Beirut were those Italians that resided in the Ottoman Levant. The Ottoman Government announced on 26 February that, following the action, it had been decided to expel Italian subjects from the *vilayets* of Aleppo, Beirut and Damascus, plus the *mutasarrifiyya* (district) of Jerusalem, within fifteen days. The expulsion was only partial however, inasmuch as those in religious orders were exempted.[20]

The attack on the ships at Beirut, though relatively insignificant in itself, may nevertheless be viewed as something of a turning point. If it was meant to demonstrate to the Ottoman government that it could not rely on France, or indeed any of the other Great Powers, to deter Italy militarily then it worked. Conversely, the non-response of those powers sent much the same message to Giolitti and his government. This served to embolden them somewhat, and this at a time when they were becoming impatient at the frustrating refusal of the Ottoman regime to accept the Italian version of reality in North Africa. Romano argues that the Navy too was developing a sense of frustration and resentment at its lack of action, and wanted to be allowed to up the ante.[21]

The prospect of an expansion of the naval war had occurred to the Ottoman Government. Despatches from Istanbul on the day of the attack stated that the Ambassadors to the Great Powers had been instructed to inform these powers that should the Italian fleet appear off the Dardanelles then this seaway would be immediately closed by mine defences. On 27 February reports indicated that the Ambassadors had handed notes to the Great Powers protesting against the sinking at Beirut 'without the usual notices.' The note also announced that the Dardanelles would be closed if hostilities spread to the Aegean.[22]

This lurking though as yet unrealised threat to the Aegean generally and the Dardanelles specifically exercised the mind of the British Foreign Secretary. He circulated a message to the British Ambassadors to Austria-Hungary, France, Germany and Russia in an effort to coordinate action:

> In view of the very serious injury which would be caused to commerce should the Turkish Government in self-defence proceed to close the Dardanelles by mines, I would like to know if the Government to which you are accredited would consider it desirable to approach Italy and ask her if she would be disposed to give an assurance that she would undertake no hostile operations in the Dardanelles and neighbouring waters.[23]

Sir George Buchanan at St Petersburg replied on 5 March, relaying the views of Sazanov. The Russian Foreign Minister argued that such an action would be incompatible with neutrality, and that he was most anxious to avoid taking any step to which the Italian Government could possibly take exception.[24] The Austro-Hungarian view was essentially similar despite the death of Foreign Minister Count Lexa von Aehrenthal and his replacement, on 17 February 1912, by Count Leopold Berchtold. Berchtold continued his predecessor's policy, writing to his Ambassadors in Berlin, Constantinople, London, Paris, Rome and St. Petersburg on 3 March of his reply to Sir Edward Grey's approach:

> Sir F[airfax] Cartwright [the British Ambassador] called on me yesterday and reiterated verbally the proposal [..] I told the Ambassador that, in my opinion, the Italian Government would not entertain the demand for a declaration that she will not undertake any warlike operations in the Dardanelles and the adjacent waters; it was our duty as neutrals to avoid all that might give the appearance that we wish to impede the freedom of action of either of the belligerent parties. In support of his representations Sir F. Cartwright asked whether the Italian Government had not previously made to the Vienna Cabinet a declaration coinciding in principle with the one which the five Powers were to demand now from Italy on Sir Edward Grey's initiative. I replied to the Ambassador that I had never heard of such a declaration by Italy.[25]

Austria-Hungary was, as has been already noted, sensitive in the extreme to any disturbance of the status quo in the Balkans and Eastern Mediterranean. Moreover, relations with Italy over the matter were regulated by treaty; Article VII of the Triple Alliance as renewed in 1902 stated the obligations imposed on the two states quite clearly:

> Austria-Hungary and Italy, being desirous solely that the territorial status quo in the near East be maintained as much as possible, pledge themselves to exert their influence to prevent all territorial modification which may prove detrimental to one or the other of the Powers signatory of this Treaty. To that end they shall communicate to one another all such information as may be suitable for their mutual enlightenment, concerning their own dispositions as well as those of other Powers.

> Should, however, the status quo in the regions of the Balkans, or of the Turkish coasts and islands in the Adriatic and Aegean Seas, in the course of events become impossible; and should Austria-Hungary or Italy be placed under the necessity, either by the action of a third Power or otherwise, to modify that status quo by a temporary or permanent occupation on their part, such occupation shall take place only after a previous agreement has been made between the two Powers, based on the principle of reciprocal compensation for all advantages, territorial or otherwise, which either of them may obtain beyond the present status quo, a compensation which shall satisfy the legitimate interests and aspirations of both Parties.[26]

This Article had been clarified further by an agreement reached between Austria-Hungary and Italy 'explaining and supplementing Article VII of the Treaty of the Triple Alliance of 1887.' Signed on 30 November 1909 at Vienna and on 15 December at Rome this agreement rendered Article VII, which remained in force in its entirety, 'more specific and complete'

Each of the two Cabinets binds itself not to conclude with a third Power any agreement whatsoever concerning Balkan questions without the participation of the other Cabinet on a footing of absolute equality; likewise, the two Cabinets bind themselves to communicate to each other every proposition which may be made to the one or to the other by a third Power, running contrary to the principle of non-intervention and tending to a modification of the status quo in the regions of the Balkans or of the Ottoman coasts and islands in the Adriatic and of the Aegean Sea.[27]

Thus by withholding agreement to any modification of the status quo Austria-Hungary was, under the terms of Article VII and its subsequent clarification, virtually granted a power of veto over any Italian move to widen the war. Whether or not this extended to an attack on the Dardanelles was another matter, but in order to bring diplomatic pressure to bear on Austria-Hungary to allow Italy to extend hostilities into the area concerned, Giolitti's government invoked the assistance of the senior partner in the Triple Alliance.

Kaiser Wilhelm II habitually reserved the last half of March and the whole of April each year for trips to Italy and the Mediterranean, including his Aechilleion estate on Corfu which he had purchased in 1907. During his 1912 visit he stopped off at Venice for two days on 24-25 March, and whilst there he was visited by Victor Emmanuel III.[28] The Kaiser was personally sympathetic to the Ottomans, although these sentiments were not fully shared by his Foreign Minister who wanted an end to the conflict. Generally, the two monarchs did not get on, but nevertheless the King was able to persuade the Emperor that Austro-Hungarian opposition to an extension of the conflict was harming the prospects of renewal of the Triple Alliance. Kaiser Wilhelm had never been averse to intervening in foreign affairs or indeed any aspect of the governance of Imperial Germany, though his influence had been severely curtailed following the embarrassing 'Daily Telegraph Affair' of 1908. However, on this occasion his inclinations were in line with those of Kiderlen, who began to apply diplomatic pressure on Berchtold.[29] This was revealed in a telegraph message from Berchtold to Kajetan von Mérey, the Austro-Hungarian Ambassador at Rome, of 6 April. In this he related that Heinrich von Tschirschky, the German Ambassador, acting on instructions had 'made to me the following declaration:'

In consequence of the long duration of the Italo-Turkish conflict, the situation is beginning to become serious for Italy, and both military circles and public opinion urge that a decisive blow be delivered. It is not a question of action in the Aegean Sea, but in the Dardanelles.

The Ambassador added in strict confidence that the King of Italy had approached Emperor William on the subject at Venice. The question now arising for Germany is, what attitude the Allies [i.e. Austria-Hungary and Germany] will take toward these intentions of Italy. You will please seek an occasion to converse with the Marchese di San Giuliano and tell him that you have perceived, from information received from Vienna, that it was a matter of great surprise to me to learn that von Tschirschky had been instructed by his Government to make the aforesaid intimation.

In consideration of our alliance, as well as of the friendly manner in which I have met Italy heretofore, I would have thought a direct discussion more natural and more expedient. At the same time you will hint that for conspicuous reasons I was obliged to adhere in principle to the standpoint which my predecessor had taken up in respect of an eventual extension of the hostilities.

Von Tschirschky explicitly designated an Italian action in the Dardanelles; the apprehension is easy to understand, that such action might find its echo in Constantinople and in the Balkans, the consequence of which may not be gauged to-day, but which would be diametrically opposed to the maintenance of the status quo—the policy pursued by both Italy and Austria-Hungary.

Should, nevertheless, the Italian Government find an extension of the region of her warlike operations indispensable, then I would certainly consider a direct discussion of the matter the most natural course to take. Without obtaining a decided consent from me, which would to a certain extent imply our participation in the responsibilities for the consequences, Italy may secure our tacit passivity in the event of an intended temporary warlike action, confined to such territories as would not involve the danger of a reaction in the Balkans.

If the Marchese di San Giuliano enters upon a discussion of any specific Italian operation, you will lead the conversation into other channels with the intimation that you consider such discussion inopportune. In fact, we must positively avoid every appearance that any specific warlike action had received our previous consent.[30]

Giuseppe, *Duc* d'Avama, the Italian Ambassador to Vienna, pursued this theme with Berchtold following von Tschirschky's approach. The foreign minister related the course of this meeting to von Mérey on 15 April:

The Duke of Avama again broached the subject of a possible extension of the Italian naval operation, though pointing out with emphasis that he spoke without instructions.

I pointed out in the first place that, to my mind, an action by the Italian Navy outside of the North-African war theatre could accomplish its purpose only if it caused a strong enough impression in Constantinople to be felt in the Balkans. Such reaction, however, could not leave us, Italy's allies, indifferent. A minor operation and a less extensive reaction would bring Italy no nearer to her aim, while it would still create a feeling of uneasiness with us if the scene of action comprised the territories referred to in Article VII of the Alliance Treaty.

Under these circumstances I could not *give my express consent to any similar action* whatsoever. The Duke of Avarna had not asked me to give such consent; but I, on my part, was determined to leave the responsibility for the consequences upon Italy's shoulders.

Concerning the islands of Rhodos, Karpathos and Stampalia, I expressed my willingness to consider it disputable whether or not they pertain to the islands of the Aegean Sea. The Duke of Avarna replied that he felt convinced that his Government would give us its express assurances, in the event of their occupation, that such occupation would be only temporary.[31]

Indeed Stampalia (Astipalea, Astypalaia), whether or not it was diplomatically 'removed' from its normal geographic position, had been earmarked by the Italian navy as a forward base for any operations in the Aegean or Eastern Mediterranean. The fleet now had a new commander in Vice-Admiral Luigi Faravelli. He had succeeded to the post following the death through illness of the former C-in-C Vice-Admiral Augusto Aubry. Aubry had died aboard his flagship at Taranto on 4 March.

Faravelli was not long in position, for on 7 April he asked to be relieved on medical grounds as he was suffering from a 'severe nervous ailment.' He was succeeded on 9 April by Vice-Admiral Leone Viale and so it was under his auspices that, on 13 April, the Italian fleet sailed from Taranto. It arrived off Stampalia on 15 April and, with the arrival of additional vessels, concentrated there over the next two days. When Viale steamed eastwards on 17 April he had under his command the 1st Squadron – the battleships *Vittorio Emanuele III* (flag), *Roma* and *Napoli* (1st Division) and the armoured cruisers *Pisa* (flag), *Amalfi*, and *San Marco* (2nd Division). Also in hand was the 4th Division of the 2nd Squadron – the armoured cruisers *Giuseppe Garibaldi* (flag), *Francesco Ferruccio, Varese* and *Marco Polo*.

The battleship *Roma* of the Regina Elena (sometimes categorised as *Vittorio Emanuele*) class. The four ships of this class, *Regina Elena, Vittorio Emanuele, Napoli,* and *Roma,* were commissioned between 1901 and 1903 and were considered extremely fast. They were somewhat lightly armed, however, with a main battery of only two 305 mm guns each in single turrets. Because the Ottoman Navy refused battle, none of the Italian heavy ships saw any major action during the conflict. (Author's Collection).

The fleet was accompanied by the destroyers *Aquilone, Borea, Nembo,* and *Turbine,* and the torpedo-boats, *Calipso, Climene, Pegaso, Perseo,* and *Procione,* under the command of the Duke of Abruzzia. The Duke flew his flag aboard the *Vettor Pisani,* and also had in his command two auxiliary cruisers and a cable ship. This latter vessel, the British-constructed *Citta di Milano,* was the first into action. During the night of the 17th/18th it grappled for, and then cut, the cable between the Dardanelles and Imbros (Gökçeada), the Ottoman island some 25 kilometres west of the southern tip of the Dardanelles. Also dredged up and severed were the cables that connected Lemnos with Tenedos (Bozcaada) and Salonica (Thessalonica), thus effectively disrupting Ottoman communications.

The main body of the fleet, less the torpedo boats which had been forced to seek shelter during the night because of rough seas, remained well out of range, whilst the armoured cruisers of Rear-Admiral Ernesto Presbitero's 2nd Division approached the entrance to the strait at sunrise. If he was trying to lure out the Ottoman fleet then the manoeuvre failed, and at 09:00 hours, the whole fleet concentrated and steamed towards the Dardanelles in line ahead. An Ottoman destroyer was spotted near the entrance and Viale signalled the armoured cruisers of the 4th Division under Rear-Admiral Paolo Thaon di Revel to move ahead and engage it. Unsurprisingly, the destroyer rapidly withdrew and the Italian ships were fired on by Fort Ertogrul (Ertrogrul, Ertugrul), situated at Cape Helles on the the south-westernmost tip of the Gallipoli peninsula and Fort Orhaniye (Orchanie) on the Asian shore. These two positions commanded the approaches and entrance to the strait, though what ordnance they were equipped with is the subject of much disagreement. Probably the most authoritative source for the defences of the Turkish Straits is that provided by the British Lieutenant J K L Fitzwillams, who translated an article that had appeared in the *Russian Artillery Journal* for August 1912. The translation appeared in the *Journal of the Royal Artillery* in January 1913 and the January-June edition of the *Journal of the United States Artillery* in 1915. In between these times it was used extensively by Commodore William H. Beehler, U.S.N. (retired) for his 1913 history. According to Fitzwilliams, the coastal defence artillery were nearly all made by Krupp and 'did not need to be of particularly long range.' He stated that Fort Ertogrul and Fort Orhaniye were armed with eight and seven 238 mm guns respectively.[32]

Further forts and batteries were arranged over the whole length of the Dardanelles, but since they do not figure in the story they may be ignored for the moment. Indeed, the defences in general had been greatly boosted as an attack was expected. These measures included some 350 guns relocated from the forts on the Bosphorus, strengthened and improved minefields, and the deployment of some 40,000 troops in the Dardanelles district. Because of the dangers from the mines the passage of merchant ships at night was prohibited, and during the day all had to be navigated by pilots.

Undoubtedly aware of these hazards, Viale made no attempt to send any of his ships into the entrance and upon being fired upon he moved the fleet around to the western side of Cape Helles. At about 10:30 hours the heavy units began a bombardment of the forts on the Asiatic side of the strait, firing over the tip of the Gallipoli peninsula. Fire was returned with 'great accuracy' according to the Italian official account, but despite this no serious hits were recorded on any of the ships. In any event, the fleet did not venture any closer than about nine kilometres, which was at the outer range of the coastal artillery. This long-range duel continued until about 13:30 hours when, after discharging 180 shells, the fleet withdrew. Though claims and counter-claims about the amount of damage inflicted on both sides were made, there is little doubt that no significant injury was inflicted on either ships or defences.

It is difficult to see what military objective was served by this action. It is almost certainly the case that what had been originally contemplated by the Italians was an attack on the Ottoman fleet. This was anchored at Nagara Point (Nara Burnu, Abydos) some 30 kilometres north of the entrance and just above the narrows at Çanakkale. Indeed Giolitti claimed at the time that the Ottoman fleet was the objective, and in his memoirs revealed that the Italians had picked up a 'secret agent' at Stampalia who was to act as a pilot during any action in the Dardanelles.[33] The presence of the Duke of Abruzzi's command, the 'Division of the Torpedo Boat Inspector,' lends credence to this conclusion, though why the operation was not delayed when the weather proved too heavy for the torpedo boats to operate is something of a mystery. The objective may not have been military at all. Luigi Albertini, editor of the influential Milanese paper *Corriere della Sera*, posited that the operation was a feint, and mounted in order to distract attention from the Southern Sporades where Italy planned her next naval moves.[34] Whatever the aim of the attack might have been it brought immediate political consequences when the Ottoman government proclaimed a blockade of the Dardanelles.

This caused instantaneous protests from the Austro-Hungarian, the British, and the Russian governments. On 19 April the Italian chargé d'affaires, Gaetano Manzoni, visited the Permanent Under Secretary for Foreign Affairs, Sir Arthur Nicolson, at the Foreign Office in London. He explained that the action the previous day had been caused when the Italian squadron, which had been cruising off the entrance to the Dardanelles in an effort to entice out the Ottoman fleet, had been fired on by the defences. Manzoni was told that Britain took the view that it was Italian actions that had compelled the closure of the Dardanelles, and that the Ottoman government could not be blamed. He reiterated that the blockade was a most serious matter for Britain and would cause much discontent. This was restated the next day to the Ottoman government by Sir Edward Grey, who telegraphed to the British Ambassador in Istanbul, Sir Gerard Lowther, pointing out that he recognised the rights of the Ottoman Government to 'adopt such legitimate means of defence as they may consider necessary.'[35]

Also on 22 April Nicolson had a further meeting this time with the Italian Ambassador, Marquis Guglielmo Imperiali, and told him that the closure of the waterway was causing grave injury to British commercial and shipping interests. Around 150 merchant vessels manned by about 4,000 British personnel were being held up by the closure and it was costing the shipowners some £9,000 per day. When the Ambassador suggested that such protests would better be directed towards the Ottoman Government, Nicolson demurred. British policy, as he explained personally and as was stated publicly in Parliament by Viscount Morley the same day, was to express the 'hope' that, whilst the British recognised the right of the Ottoman Empire 'to adopt measures of self-defence,' they would nevertheless 'open a passage through the straits to foreign commerce as soon as possible.' Imperiali replied that he 'trusted' the Italian Government would not be asked for assurances that they would abstain from hostilities near the Straits. The answer came that whilst Britain did not wish to contemplate anything 'disagreeable' to Italy, there could be no pledges as to what measures the British might be compelled to take in the interests of maintaining their trade.[36] Though these exchanges were couched in exquisite diplomatese, the Italians were left in absolutely no doubt that Britain blamed them for the whole affair.

Conversely, Russia held the Ottoman Government responsible. Count Alexander Benckendorf, the Russian Ambassador to Britain, informed Nicolson on 22 April, that 'very strong pressure had been put upon the Russian Government to take strong measures for opening the Dardanelles, as their closure was causing the greatest injury to Russian commerce.' A note had therefore been delivered in Istanbul to 'the following effect:'

> The Russian Government were unaware how the Turkish Government could reconcile the free passage of the Straits accorded to merchant vessels by Treaty with the present measures of closing the Straits. They, therefore, expressed the 'firm hope' that, as soon as the imminent danger of hostile attack had passed by, the Turkish Government would open the Straits to foreign commerce. Otherwise the Russian Government would have to consider the question of indemnities for the losses incurred.[37]

The Austro-Hungarian government, though not affected as directly as Britain and Russia, was at one with the former in respect of attributing blame. Called to explain, d'Avama argued that the action had been a demonstration to illustrate Italian naval superiority and freedom of action to the Ottoman Government. Berchtold expressed his displeasure and warned that if any similar operation were attempted in future, it would carry with it 'grave consequences.' This warning took place within the context of, as it was perceived by Berchtold, the rights conferred by the Triple Alliance treaty. He was later to reiterate his previously stated argument that although Austria-Hungary made representations in an 'unequivocal manner' this in no way hindered Italy's actions: 'We refused our expressed consent to actions, from which we apprehended dangerous consequences for the Balkans, and because we would not share the responsibility for these, but all we did, was to warn Italy with regard to the threatening consequences.'[38] In any event, Giolitti himself had ensured that the 'grave consequences' would not come to pass when he ordered the fleet to suspend any further operations in the upper Aegean on the day that they took place.

Russia and Britain, though at odds in apportioning blame for the closure of the Dardanelles still had a shared interest in getting them reopened. The cargo aboard the stranded vessels consisted largely of Russian grain, which was essentially a perishable commodity. On 30 April with the strait still closed Grey telegraphed to Lowther instructing him to urge the Ottoman Government to open the Straits temporarily so that the detained ships could recommence their voyages.[39] In order to support this initiative, Grey tasked Rodd with putting the point to San Guiliano that the reopening of the Dardanelles would be facilitated if the Italian Government would agree that the British could say to the Ottomans that there would be no further attacks there 'for a reasonable period.'[40] Giuliano was, as might have been expected, somewhat evasive. According to Rodd's reply on 1 May, he had been told that because Russia had protested to the Ottomans about the closure, any such promise from Italy would have the effect of weakening the effect of those protests. Guiliani further argued that because Russia had shown 'goodwill' to Italy, it would be difficult for Italy to take any step until it was certain that the Russian protest had failed.[41] This Russian 'goodwill' was further demonstrated when Sazanov refused entreaties to become involved in Grey's 'friendly representations' to Rome; when Buchanan approached him on the matter he 'absolutely declined' to become involved. Upon being asked by the British Ambassador 'what he hoped to gain by so assiduously courting Italy[?]' Sazanov replied that he didn't want 'Italy to send, as she had undertaken to do, [an] Army Corps into Galicia, in the event of a Russo-German war.' Buchanan added that 'after a moment's pause' he then added that 'she won't do this now.'[42]

These exchanges illustrate a growing difference in political strategy between Britain and Russia. Grey wished above all to maintain the delicately poised equilibrium of Europe, more or less divided between the Alliance and Entente blocs. Hence he deprecated any attempts to detach Italy from its Alliance partners lest it disturb this equilibrium and precipitate a European conflict. Sazanov, given his policy of 'assiduously courting' Italy, was of a different opinion, and his remark to Buchanan indicates why. Which of the two views was the more accurate was not put to the test as it happened, for on 1 May the Ottoman Government indicated that the straits would indeed be reopened as soon as the mines were cleared. As long as the conflict lasted though, and because it had the potential to destabilise European politics, Grey considered it to be dangerous in the wider context.[43]

Italy for her part seemed ready to steer between the two blocs, and to push to the limit the constraints of Article VII of the treaty with Austria-Hungary. The decision to extend the war into the Eastern Mediterranean and Aegean required some careful consideration. As had become obvious, action at the Dardanelles caused international diplomatic ructions and any actions on the Anatolian mainland or in the Balkans were militarily and politically problematical to say the least. The Southern Sporades were then, almost by default, the only option and had been recognised and suggested as a suitable place for operations as far back as the 19 October 1911. On that occasion the army Chief of Staff, General Alberto Pollio, had raised the issue with his naval opposite number, Admiral Carlo Rocca Rey via a letter. They met on 9 November and agreed that if the navy intervened in the area, the army would also be required to participate although at that time no plans had been prepared. The chiefs agreed that the best way to proceed would be for the two services to reach agreement on the feasibility of occupying the islands and, if this were settled, only then would the proposal be put forward for political consideration. There could be no question of taking action unilaterally without careful deliberation of the political ramifications as Article VII of the Triple Alliance specified Austro-Italian pledges to maintain the status quo regarding Ottoman possessions in the

Adriatic and Aegean Seas. Any modification was dependent upon previously agreed mutual consent, and promises of compensation between Austria-Hungary and Italy.[44]

Rocca Rey was to have doubts concerning the wisdom of carrying out any such operation, believing that the results would not be commensurate with the effort required and that it would likely cause an intervention by the Great Powers. Pollio, on the other hand, argued that taking the islands from the Ottoman Empire would be an effective military operation. Pollio's superior, the Minister of War Paulo Spingardi, was also cautious arguing in a letter of 12 January 1912 that any action would require very careful consideration due to the possible political repercussions.[45] In the immediate term, and in respect of Austria-Hungary, Italy had received a grudging acquiescence towards occupying the islands of Rhodes, Karpathos and Stampalia on a temporary basis. What prompted this concession was German pressure. San Giuliano's constant theme in this context was based around how difficult it would be for Italy to remain a friend and ally of Austria-Hungary if it were perceived that the latter state was not acting in a friendly way. Rather, by attempting to prevent Italy from bringing the conflict with the Ottoman Empire to a close, Austria-Hungary was breaching the duties of neutrality in favour of Italy's enemy. If it became known to public opinion in Italy that operations against the Ottomans were being hampered by Austria-Hungary, then the future of their alliance would be at stake.[46] Since the maintenance and renewal of the Triple Alliance was a prime German foreign policy objective, Italy was able to continue to use the influence of the senior member as leverage. Accordingly, the German government brought strong pressure to bear to make the Austro-Hungarian foreign minister agree to Italian wishes, pointing out that any refusal 'not merely complicated the renewal of the Triple Alliance (as Kiderlen said on 31 March 1912) but even risked its breaking up.'[47] This ploy was successful.

Where such action might lead though was obviously unknowable, but given the failure of all previously attempted efforts, whether military, naval, or political, to force the Ottoman Empire to come to terms the politicians, when the option was put to them, decided that on balance the risk was worth taking. Rocca Rey remained unconvinced however, sending two 'confidential and personal' memoranda to Spingardi on 16 and 18 April 1912 in which he set out his doubts. The admiral pointed out that Rhodes, the main island of the archipelago, was only around 17 kilometres from the southern coast of Anatolia (Asia Minor), whilst the nearest Italian naval base was at Tobruk, over 1000 kilometres distant. He also cautioned that the Ottomans had a 'fleet in being' in the Dardanelles, near to their supply base and to dockyards (though also around a 1000 kilometres away). These vessels, should they be put into good order, could sortie and attack southward through the Aegean, necessitating the Italians keeping a squadron at least as strong permanently on station to repel any possible attack. This squadron would have to be constantly cruising in order to be effective, and would risk becoming worn out. Therefore it would have to be relieved regularly, and the deployment would then tie up two naval squadrons, a total of ten ships and forty torpedo boats. Furthermore, whilst the Ottoman vessels remained a threat Italian shipping to and from the area would have to be convoyed and escorted. Rocca Rey also argued that since Rhodes had no military or economic value, it was unlikely that the loss of it would force the enemy to make peace. Additionally, the Ottoman government would undoubtedly believe that Italian occupation could only be temporary, and that the island would return to being a possession of the Sultan in any event. The enterprise would therefore wear out the Italian fleet, be expensive, and only provide a diversion from the main theatre where all efforts should be concentrated.[48] His protests fell on deaf ears; Giolitti and San Giuliano had decided 'resolutely' to go ahead, and on 23 April the Italian navy 'occupied the island of Stampalia (Astipalea), set up our own naval base, and took prisoner the Turkish garrison.'[49]

Apart from extending the conflict into totally new areas, the Italian navy also had a significant part to play in the maintenance and extension of the occupation of Tripoli. Chief among these was the interdiction of the coastal route from Tunisia via which it was believed the Ottoman forces were receiving large amounts of supplies. This route began at Ben-Gardane on the Tunisian side of the frontier and then along the road to Zuwarah in Tripoli. Zuwarah is situated around 110 kilometres to the west of Tripoli City and about 60 kilometres from the border, and from there the supplies went on to Azizia. Zuwarah was also provided with an anchorage suitable for coastal shipping at least, and *mahones,* such as the *Camouna* and *Gaulois* involved in the incident of 25 January 1912, and other vessels were able to moor there and discharge their cargoes.

That there was much traffic through Zuwarah is beyond dispute, though whether it was all 'contraband of war' as the Italians claimed is uncertain. Ernest Bennett related how whilst crossing the border from east to west over the new-year period of 1911-12, he caught sight of an immense caravan of 1,240 camels laden with around 150 tonnes of flour travelling in the other direction. This caravan had been delayed at Ben-Gardane by the French authorities for 15 days before being allowed to proceed. The French, he argues, had for some time been acting 'in a curiously erratic fashion as regards the passage over the frontier of food and necessaries.'[50] Supplies such as he describes were not of course necessarily contraband of war unless they were destined for those engaged in fighting, and of course a large portion of the population of Tripoli could not be described thus. The Italians however made no distinction, and determined to at least gain control of the route, which the Ottomans, indicating that it was of considerable importance to them, made great efforts to prevent.

Previous attempts at interdiction had mainly been restricted to the naval bombardment of Zuwarah and surrounding areas, and a decision to attempt a landing there with a brigade of infantry in late December 1911 had to be abandoned due to the poor weather and the 'energetic' defence put up by the Ottoman defenders, as already related.[51] By April 1912 the weather had settled enough for another attempt to be made, this time in much greater strength. The naval component comprised the 'Training Division' under Rear-Admiral Borea Ricci, with the obsolete, though still adequate for the task, battleships *Re Umberto, Sicilia* (flag) and *Sardegna* forming its core. The landing force consisted of the 5th Special Division under Lieutenant-General Vincenzo Garioni. One brigade, commanded by Major-General Clemente Lequio, was drawn from forces based in Tripoli City, the 11th Regiment of *Bersaglieri* plus an extra battalion (the 28th), two battalions of Grenadiers, and the 6th and 7th Eritrean Battalions. The other was under Major-General Alberto Cavaciocchi and mainly comprised the 60th Infantry Regiment, which sailed directly from Italy. There were also three batteries of artillery and a company of engineers.

The plan was much more sophisticated this time, demonstrating the respect that the Italians had for the Ottoman forces and the learning process attendant on the difficulties of amphibious warfare at that time. The Training Division, including the three battleships and the armoured cruisers *Carlo Alberto* and *Marco Polo* left the port of Tripoli with three transport ships on 8 April 1912. The three transports and the two armoured cruisers arrived off Zuwarah on 9 April and anchored some two kilometres offshore. The warships began a desultory bombardment of the town until nightfall, resuming with a much fiercer barrage the next morning. The resumption of the fire from the cruisers coincided with the approach of some twenty boats from the transports towards the landing beach. This was however all a feint to fix the attention of the Ottomans whilst the real landing took place some 40 kilometres to the west on the El Faru (Farwa, Farwah, Ra's al Makhbaz, Macabez) peninsula. Running more or less parallel to the coast some three kilometres to the south, this small uninhabited spit of land is about twelve kilometres in length and about 1 kilometre at its broadest. During the night of 9–10 April seven transports, escorted by those warships not engaged at Zuwarah, with the vast majority of the 5th Division aboard (about 10,000 men) appeared off this peninsula and began landing advance parties of troops at around 03:00 hours. There was no sign of any opposition and so the the Italians secured the landing ground without difficulty. At daybreak the main body began to disembark and some four hours later, at about 12:00 hours, it was also safely ashore despite choppy conditions on the water.

Landings on the mainland opposite El Faru were undertaken on the morning of 11 April by a mixed force of marines and army troops. This operation was unopposed and by 12:00 hours large contingents had moved inland and the whole area had been secured with the occupation of Abu Kammash (Bu Kamez, Bu Kamech), a small Berber village

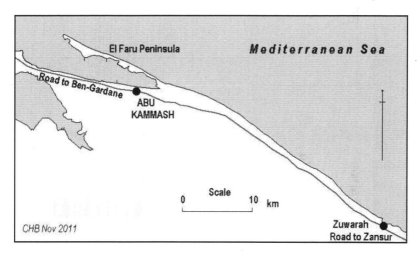

Abu Kammash. The Italians decided to occupy the small village of Abu Kammash in order to interdict the coastal route from Tunisia via which it was believed the Ottoman forces were receiving large amounts of supplies. This route began at Ben-Gardane on the Tunisian side of the frontier and then along the road to Zuwarah, which is situated around 110 kilometres to the west of Tripoli City and about 60 kilometres from the border. From there the supplies went on to Azizia. With total command of the sea, and having acquired expertise in the techniques of amphibious warfare, the landing was a sophisticated affair. With the defenders lured away via a ruse, landings on the mainland opposite the El Faru Peninsula were undertaken on the morning of 11 April 1912 by a mixed force of marines and army troops. This operation was unopposed and by 12:00 hours large contingents had moved inland and the whole area had been secured. The Ottoman forces could then only try and contain the invaders, and a good deal of the supplies were forced to take a less convenient route some 150 kilometres inland. (© Charles Blackwood).

on the shore just west of where the peninsula joins the mainland. The village featured a small and obsolete 'Turkish Fort' and this was occupied by a detachment of marines and Eritrean *ascari*. The first Ottoman forces did not appear on the scene until later in the day to find the Italians well dug in and covered by the guns of the fleet. By 12 April Garioni estimated that there were around 1,000 men in the dunes around Abu Kammash who kept up a constant sniping at the Italian positions and at the various boats working in the bay between the peninsula and mainland. The Ottoman positions were cleared by a flank attack carried out by Eritrean troops who moved off the peninsula during a sandstorm on the morning of 13 April and thus had the element of surprise. Once the dunes overlooking the bay had been cleared of the enemy they were incorporated into the Italian defences, which, given their great strength backed by the guns of the Training Division, made the whole area secure.

Once again Italian naval supremacy had allowed Italian forces to descend upon the coast at a time and place of their own choosing in overwhelming force. The landing at El Faru and the occupation of Abu Kammash had an effect on the Ottoman supply situation. Because the road between Ben-Gardane and Zuwarah was now vulnerable, though not yet completely cut, a good deal of the contraband trade was forced to take a less convenient route some 150 kilometres inland. Further, with torpedo-boats able to use Abu Kammash as a temporary base – the bay was found to be deep enough for torpedo-boats to shelter in, and was utilised as their anchorage – the passage of contraband by sea to Zuwarah was also threatened, though not entirely stopped.

CHAPTER TWELVE

The Southern Sporades, the Dardanelles, and the Limits of Navalism

'A cardinal factor [of British Mediterranean policy] has naturally been that no strong Naval Power should be in effective permanent occupation of any territory or harbour East of Malta.'
Rear-Admiral ECT Troubridge in a Memorandum of 29 June 1912[1]

'The water boiled around the torpedo boats from stem to stern, and jets of water flew high as shells fell with horrible thuds, as if volcanic eruptions were flashing inexhaustibly beneath the water [...] The air was full of flashes, of flames, explosions, and splinters. Convulsive, foaming, full of glare and reflections, the sea seemed to become a huge fiery furnace. But at the zenith shone always the star of Italy.'
Giuseppe Bevione in *La Stampa*, 25 July 1912[2]

AS originally conceived, the military component of the expedition to Rhodes was to be some 3,000 strong taken from the units around Tobruk, together with 350 horses and mules. This special detachment was to carry with it four weeks' worth of rations and supplies, plus enough water to last two weeks, and 600 rounds of ammunition per rifle. Subsequently however it was greatly strengthened, which necessitated the use of units from Italy. The force thus created was to be termed the 6th Aegean Special Division (*6° Divisione Speciale dell'Egeo*) with Giovanni Ameglio, who had recently been promoted to Lieutenant General, in command. The concentration points for the division were Tobruk and Benghazi, where seven steamships (*Sannio, Europa, Verona, Toscana, Bulgaria, Cavour* and *Valparaiso*) to transport it were despatched. Protection for the convoy was provided by the heavy units of the 2nd Division of the 1st Squadron and torpedo boats, which would operate close by the troop carriers during the landing.[3]

The military contingent sent from Italy consisted of ten battalions of infantry, organised as the 34th and 57th Infantry Regiments, with two batteries of field artillery, eight machine gun sections, plus engineering and support troops. Also included were a group of *Carabinieri* and the 4th Regiment of *Bersaglieri*. The force drawn from the North African theatre consisted of the *Fenestrelle* Battalion of *Alpini* with its machine gun section and four-gun mountain battery, together with support. Also sent were two wireless telegraphy sections and two field hospitals. The 57th Infantry and 4th *Bersaglieri* were sent to Benghazi whilst the 34th Infantry concentrated at Tobruk. The total strength of the 6th Special Division amounted to between 8,494-9,282 officers and men, and 1,186-1,309 transport animals, dependent upon source. Also loaded aboard the ships were a number of civilians whose task would be to oversee civil administration.[4]

In order to maintain secrecy as to the destination of the expeditionary force, misinformation was disseminated to the effect that a landing was planned at Bomba, a

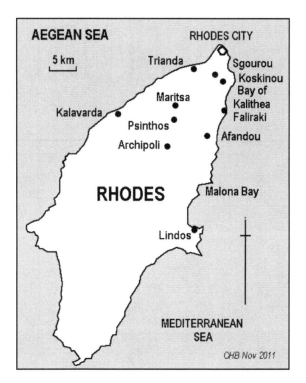

Rhodes. The Italian decision to expand and extend the campaign against the Ottoman Empire to the Southern Sporades (Dodecanese) was prompted by the wish to increase pressure on the Ottoman government. Opening another theatre of operations was fraught with diplomatic dangers, but the way was eventually cleared for a 'temporary' occupation of the islands of Rhodes, Karpathos and Stampalia. Once again utilising their command of the sea and expertise in amphibious warfare, the navy successfully landed a large force at the Bay of Kalithea (Baia di Catilla) on the east coast on 4 May 1912. This force advanced on Rhodes City and occupied it with little resistance, and after a short campaign of some twelve days the Ottomans throughout the island were forced to surrender. It had been a dramatic victory made possible by Italian naval supremacy, and it was followed by the occupation of the several other islands of the Southern Sporades. However, whilst an operational success the venture was a strategic failure as it did little or nothing to force the Ottoman government to terms. It also threatened a diplomatic rupture with Austria-Hungary as Italy occupied many more islands than the agreed three. (© Charles Blackwood).

village on the Gulf of Bomba some 60 kilometres from Derna. Secrecy was maintained to the extent that Ameglio forbade any reconnaissance of the target and strict censorship was imposed on all communications, particularly with respect to those of journalists. This led to the force being tagged as the Bomba detachment.

The 1st Division of the 1st Squadron left Taranto on 30 April for Stampalia en route to Rhodes, whilst destroyers and torpedo-boats began to patrol the seas around the island and seize any Ottoman shipping found there. Ameglio, who it may be remembered had commanded the amphibious operation that seized Benghazi, had been granted complete tactical freedom by Pollio, though the Bay of Trianda, an area on the north-west coast near to the village of Trianda (Trianta, Ialyssos), which had a level shingle beach some two kilometres in length, had been suggested as the best area to land the troops. Furthermore it was also only around two or three kilometres from Rhodes City, the key objective of the invasion.

The Ottoman garrison on Rhodes was estimated to be somewhere between 2,000-5,000 strong and equipped with artillery. Should this force be in the right place at the right time then it could cause severe difficulties to the landing operation. Since the Trianda Bay area was obviously the most likely candidate for an amphibious attack Ameglio had decided to land elsewhere. Instead he chose to put his force ashore at the Bay of Kalithea (*Baia di Catilla*) on the east coast, which was about ten kilometres from Rhodes City and just north of the modern resort of Faliraki.[5] On 1 May the cable between Rhodes City and the Anatolian mainland was dredged up and cut whilst the expeditionary force left the following day aboard the steamships. Escorted by the warships and accompanied by a hospital ship the *Re d'Italia* the fleet first steamed eastward at around ten knots. Even the crews were not aware of the true destination and only once it was out of sight of land was the course altered northwards.

This force was off Kalithea early on the morning of 4 May whilst diversionary tactics were employed by vessels off Trianda and several other places. The Italian navy had no specialist amphibious equipment, and the troops and their equipment had to be ferried to the landing beach aboard ships boats. After initial reconnaissance parties had landed and verified that there were no Ottoman forces in the vicinity the landing of the main force began at 04:00 hours. It was some ten hours later that Ameglio had his main body ashore, and so at 14:00 hours the north-eastern advance from the landing beach towards Rhodes City began, protected by the guns of the fleet.

There was to be very little opposition, and the only resistance encountered was from a small Ottoman detachment, estimated to be 400 strong, some five kilometres from the beachhead on high ground around the villages of Koskinou (Koskino) and Sgourou (Asguru, Arguru) The former village was deemed to be inhabited by 'Greeks' whilst the latter was 'Turkish.' This resistance only slowed the advance slightly, and by nightfall the main Italian body was about two kilometres from its objective where it camped for the night.

The advance resumed the next morning and Ameglio sent a deputation under his Chief of Staff, Major Ernesto Mombelli of the *Alpini* battalion, into Rhodes City to arrange terms of surrender with Ali Subhi (Subhy, Soubhy) Bey, the *vali* (governor) of the island. The terms were simple; capitulate immediately or the city would be bombarded. The navy was making similar demands. Captain Gustavo Nicastro took his destroyer *Alpino* into the harbour and also demanded that the governor surrender.

Subhi Bey had fled however, and his deputy prevaricated, arguing that he could not surrender the Ottoman military component as all the troops had left the city, leaving it undefended. Accordingly there was no resistance when both Italian army and navy detachments entered and took possession; at about 14:00 hours the Italian flag was raised above the old fortifications. Unnoticed by the invaders, the Ottoman *vali* escaped by boat and made his way along the coast. He was captured at Lindos whilst waiting to be transported to the Anatolian mainland on 28 May.

The Ottoman forces, the strength of which the Italians had greatly overestimated, had meanwhile concentrated around the village of Psinthos (Psithos, Psindos, Psitos) on a plateau some twenty kilometres south-west of Rhodes under the command of Lieutenant-Colonel (*bimbashi*) Abdullah Bey. According to Italian sources they numbered 1,300 in total, whilst Ottoman records indicate about 950, though this figure may only include regular fighting troops. In any event, they were greatly outnumbered, had very little artillery, and no hope of escape.

Ameglio moved to deal with them on 15 May, dividing his force into three. Under his personal command the main body, Column A, consisting of the two infantry regiments with artillery support, would advance toward the enemy position overland. This advance would be supported by two amphibious operations in order to cut off any attempt at retreat. The *Bersaglieri* formed Column B and would embark on the *Sannio* landing on the beach at Kalavarda on the north-west of the island before moving south-east towards Kalopteri. Column C, the *Alpini,* would use the *Bulgaria* to land at Malona Bay on the south-east and then advance north-west. In order to preserve security rumours were spread to the effect that the two steamers were conveying troops to the other islands, and both left the harbour at Rhodes City at around 19:00 hours.

Both columns were safely ashore some two to three hours later, and guided by local people, they began to move towards their objectives along roads that were little better than mule tracks. At about 02:00 hours on 16 May the main body under Ameglio, which had advanced over half the distance between Rhodes City and Psinthos on the previous day, resumed its forward movement, arriving at Afandou to the east of the objective at 05:00 hours. The column then split, one of the regiments moving west to Archipoli whilst the other advanced directly towards Psinthos. By 09:00 hours the enemy were effectively surrounded and appeared to have been taken by surprise, though the barren and rocky terrain made any rapid movement difficult.

The defenders, once they observed the advancing Italians, began to fire upon them from around 09:30 hours, to which the Italian artillery replied. Under cover of the bombardment the infantry advanced towards the Ottoman positions, and the defenders began to slowly fall back. The broken nature of the ground made it difficult for the various attacking units to keep in proper contact with each other, but given the disparity in strength there could be little doubt of the outcome of the struggle. As the Italians gained ground they began to occupy the higher features of the terrain, and consequently were able to make the Ottoman positions increasingly untenable. Some of them began to withdraw north-east along the track to Maritsa, whilst attempts to suppress the Italian artillery with counter battery work was hopeless in the face of the much heavier rate of fire.

By 15:00 hours the Ottoman force had been largely driven from its positions and was attempting to retire in some disorder towards Maritsa along the only route not completely blocked by Italian units. A large number were able to shelter from the Italian fire in the broken ground, though could make little progress towards their goal because the *Bersaglieri* were positioned to interdict the track. Ameglio had already decided that he would deploy an entire regiment across this line of retreat the following day, which would have completely surrounded the Ottoman force. However, at 23:00 hours he despatched an officer under a flag of truce to call for surrender. Realising that his position was ultimately hopeless Abdullah sent a representative to Ameglio to negotiate terms. These were simple and straightforward; the entire Ottoman force would give itself and its weapons up at 08:00 hours the next morning, the only exceptions being the officers who would keep their swords as a mark of respect for them having fought bravely and with honour. This was accepted and the emissary returned.

Though Ameglio remained suspicious that some of the enemy would try to escape or even continue to fight, and so made his dispositions for resuming operations accordingly, the enemy did indeed lay down their arms as agreed. The Ottoman commander-in-chief, accompanied by the commander of the gendarmerie, called on Ameglio to observe the formalities and their forces accordingly handed over their arms. Also captured was a section of mountain artillery, together with an ammunition train complete with draft animals and much other equipment was also taken after being found abandoned. The total number of prisoners amounted to about 1,300 including 38 officers and they were sent to Rhodes City. The Italians estimated that around 200 of the enemy had been killed or wounded, whilst their own casualties amounted to one officer and seven soldiers killed, and 26 soldiers wounded. This casualty list demonstrates that although the fighting had been somewhat lengthy, it had certainly not been hard.

It had though, by any standards, been a dramatic military victory made possible, of course, by Italian naval supremacy, and it was this that allowed the occupation of several other islands of the Southern Sporades. On 12 May the islands of Karpathos (Scarpanto), Kasos (Caso), Tilos (Piscopi), Nisyros (Nisiro), Kalymnos (Calino), Leros (Lero), and Patmos (Patmo) were seized by landing parties from individual ships. There was no resistance and having left small garrisons the vessels departed. The island of Kos (Coo) was likewise taken on 21 May and the islands of Leipsoi (Lisso), Symi (Simi), and Halki (Calchi) soon followed.

This was, of course, going well beyond the occupation of Rhodes, Karpathos and Stampalia that had been reluctantly accepted by Austria-Hungary. That Berchtold was becoming somewhat exasperated by Italian actions in the Aegean, or at least by requests concerning them, is made plain in his communication with the Austro-Hungarian ambassador at Rome, Kajetan von Merey, dated 23 May 1912.

> The question of occupation of islands in the Aegean Sea has repeatedly been the subject of conversations between me and the Italian Ambassador in the last few days.

> The Duke of Avarna resumed the discussion yesterday. He especially expressed the apprehension that the decision we had promised in respect of the occupation of several unimportant islands (he referred to Chios and the isles whence the Turkish officials had first been removed) might be such as to arouse profound ill-feeling in Italy.

> He further observed that it impressed him strangely to see that of all Europe, including Germany, it was Austria-Hungary, Italy's ally, who caused her the greatest difficulties in the attainment of her aim, which consisted in a speedy conclusion of the war.

> I pointed out, that in this case we were in a peculiar situation in two respects: Firstly, because we had entered into bilateral agreements with Italy concerning the matter in question; secondly, because we were directly adjacent neighbours of Turkey, and consequently were the most

closely concerned of all. Besides, I failed to understand his apprehension, inasmuch as there never had been a question of a 'protest' against the occupation of the islands referred to. Yet, we were compelled to specify our legitimate claim at this time in order to avoid possible future misunderstandings.

I finally specified our standpoint on this question as follows: We have been painfully impressed by the news of the occupation of additional islands by Italian troops. Because of the consequences to be feared from such operations, we are compelled to express our most serious misgivings. At the same time it is our duty to point out that in our opinion the occupations in question are contrary to the provisions of Article VII of the Treaty of Triple Alliance, and give us the right to demand compensation on our part.

True, for the time being we do not wish to make use of this right, out of a desire to avoid complicating Italy's position. However, we must declare emphatically that if Italy perseveres in this policy the responsibility for it will rest with her, while we would be constrained to reserve the right to compensation which we are at liberty to use according to our own judgment.[6]

The 'right to compensation' as enshrined in Article VII of the Triple Alliance, was probably the motive force behind Austro-Hungarian concerns. Indeed, Austria–Hungary was the only Great Power to raise protests at Italian actions. As Giolitti recalled:

The occupation of the islands did not rise to any comments from the Powers, except Austria-Hungary. Berchtold renewed his complaints over our occupation, because it was not limited to those islands over which he had reluctantly expressed consent. [...] He intended, however, that the occupations carried marked the final limit that he would accept.[7]

Austro-Hungarian forbearance was being prompted by the senior partner in the Triple-Alliance, who was accordingly grateful, as is revealed by messages passed between Austria-Hungary's Ambassador to Berlin and Berchtold in Vienna. For example:

Von Kiderlen-Waechter assured me that he gratefully acknowledged our conciliatory attitude in the matter of Italian action in the Archipelago. He still entertained hopes that the occupation of several islands in the Aegean Sea by Italy would not provoke a dangerous reaction in the Balkans.[8]

Austro-Hungarian concerns were the only ones expressed directly, if in somewhat muted form, but the British Admiralty was certainly exercised by the Italian actions and their potential. Rear-Admiral Ernest Troubridge, the chief of the Admiralty War Staff, had the responsibility at the time for drawing up plans for naval strategy in the event of war. On 29 June 1912 he authored a memorandum entitled 'Italian occupation of Aegean Islands and its effect on naval policy,' which he circulated to the foreign office and other interested government departments. His analysis and conclusions were clear:

A cardinal factor of [of British policy] has naturally been that no strong Naval Power should be in effective permanent occupation of any territory or harbour East of Malta, if such harbour be capable of transformation into a fortified Naval base. [...] None can foresee the developments of material in warfare, and the occupation of the apparently most useless island should be resisted equally with the occupation of the best. The geographical situation of these islands enables the Sovereign Power, if enjoying the possession of a Navy, to exercise a control over the Levant and Black Sea trade and to threaten our position in Egypt in an unprecedented degree. It may be confidently asserted that the possession by Italy of naval bases in the Aegean

Sea would imperil our position in Egypt, would cause us to lose our control over our Black Sea and Levant trade at its source, and would in war expose our route to the East via the Suez Canal to the operations of Italy and her allies.[9]

A naval base in the area would be even more significant if, as the Admiralty suspected they might, the other members of the Triple Alliance were to have access to it. A combined Austro-Hungarian and Italian fleet would be 'a much more formidable opponent than the feeble Italy' and could have profound effects on British interests.[10] Winston Churchill, the political head of the Royal Navy noted on 15 June that Britain's rivals in the Mediterranean 'may be said to be Italy and Austria, separately or together.'[11] This was all the more so as many units of the Royal Navy's Mediterranean fleet were being withdrawn to counteract the increasing German threat in the North Sea. It is then no surprise that the Admiralty were disquieted, or that Sir Edward Grey made it his unstated policy to prevent Italy gaining a permanent hold on the islands. The policy was tacit at that time because of the repeated Italian assurances that the occupation was temporary. For example, Giolitti declared in Parliament on 5 December 1912 that the occupation was temporary and had been undertaken for 'purely military purposes.'[12] Nevertheless, just over a year later on 12 August 1913, after Italy proved somewhat reluctant to quit, Grey stated the policy, as agreed between the Great Powers, concerning the islands in an official statement to the UK Parliament:

> The destiny of these Aegean Islands – all of them including those in the temporary occupation of Italy – is a matter which concerns all the Great Powers, and must be settled eventually by them and no Great Power is to retain one of these islands for itself.[13]

Italy was to have different ideas of course, but there is no evidence to suggest that Giolitti, San Giuliano, or indeed anyone else in a position of influence or power in Italy was being deliberately insincere in 1912 when they stated that the islands would be returned. There was however one complicating factor; the people of the occupied islands. In 1912 the population was around 143,000 of whom some 45,000 lived on Rhodes, whilst Halki, Astypalea, Tilos, Patmos and Kasos averaged under 3,000. It was not however a homogenous population. According to a study published in 1912 the population of Rhodes was mainly Greek (37,777) with a smaller number of Muslims (4,854), and the rest (2,445) categorised as Jews and 'others.' Over half of these lived in Rhodes City and its environs, whilst the rest were divided amongst 44 rural villages.[14] This preponderance of Greeks, or rather those who thought of themselves as Greek, was more or less replicated amongst the other islands.

This population had been outraged when the Ottoman government had re-established the 1876 constitution, since, by establishing a common citizenship, it had removed their 'privileges' and made them liable for conscription into the army. According to Skevos Zervos, this had been proclaimed in a telegram dated 27 July 1909, which:

> [...] revoked the whole of the privileges of the Dodecanese, demanded the payment of new taxes, insisted upon the use of the Turkish language in the courts of judicature, at once imposed the obligation to serve in the Turkish armies, and endeavoured, in fine, to assimilate the islands in all respects to the other Ottoman provinces.[15]

The response to this was to be found in political protest and, amongst men of military age in particular, large-scale migration to Greece. There was then little disappointment amongst the majority of the population when the Italians landed and made prisoners or fugitives of the Ottoman officials and soldiers. Indeed, the Italians were welcomed as liberators throughout the islands and there was no shortage of those happy and willing to assist them. Right from the first days of the occupation Ameglio had made clear that Italy would not greatly interfere with the way of life of any of the inhabitants, provided they did not resist. On 5 May, the day the Italian forces entered Rhodes City, he had issued a decree addressed to the inhabitants stating this:

> Inhabitants of the island of Rhodes! Italy, tied to you by the glorious memories and affinity of civilization, is forced by the events of the war to occupy your island. On the order of H M the King I assume the chief civil and military powers, declaring that Italy is at war with the Ottoman government and army, but considers the unarmed and peaceful population of Rhodes friendly and will ensure the utmost respect to your religious beliefs, your customs, and your traditions.[16]

That their former rulers were not going to be back in the near future became plain once the Ottoman forces had surrendered, not just on Rhodes but throughout the islands that Italy had captured. Whilst this process was still ongoing Ameglio issued another decree on 20 May, basically restating the Italian position as previously enunciated:

> The people of Rhodes can be confident in the feelings of justice and fairness that are characteristic of the Italian Government. Do not be afraid, for respect for your religion, your families, and for your properties will be meticulously observed. Italy welcomes you under her protection, which always was and always will be a symbol of civilization and progress.[17]

The Muslim population in general, and those who were supporters of the Committee of Union and Progress in particular, were hostile to the occupation, but they were very much in the minority. On the other hand the Orthodox, or Greek, majority were well pleased to be rid of their Ottoman masters, seeing the Italian invasion as a means to an end. That end however was not one the Italians would necessarily subscribe to. Dr Skevos George Zervos described the assistance given to Ameglio at the Battle of Psinthos, and the reason why it was offered:

> In this engagement the Rhodians preceded and guided the Italians, for whom they performed invaluable service […] risking their lives in the fighting line with dauntless bravery and the conviction that when they had driven out the Turks they would at last be free and united with Mother Greece.[18]

Zervos, who had been born on Kalymnos, was an eminent medical practitioner and ardent patriot in the cause of the Dodecanese; this name, from the Greek *dodeca* (twelve) and *nesos* (island), being what the Greek population called the islands under Italian occupation from now on. This section of the population already had a functioning civic society, and their leaders wasted no time in setting out their desires and expectations. On 17 June 1912 a meeting was held at the Monastery of St John the Divine on Patmos with the leaders and representatives from all the islands attending. There they convened 'a General Assembly of the Dodecanese' and under its auspices issued a declaration:

> We hereby make known the steadfast determination of the Dodecanesian people to undergo any sacrifice rather than again fall beneath the horrible despotism of the Turks. We further proclaim the age-long national yearning of the Dodecanesians for union with their Mother Country, Greece.[19]

They also proclaimed the 'Autonomous state of the Dodecanese' sometimes referred to as the 'Autonomous state of the Aegean Sea,' even approving a design for a flag according to some sources; a proposal 'strongly discountenanced by Italy.'[20] Indeed, a little later Ameglio was to ban any manifestation of Greek irredentism on the grounds that it could disturb public order, and removed from office Savvas Pavlides, the elected Mayor of Rhodes, for attempting to stir up a rebellion against the Italian occupation. The new, appointed, mayor was Attilio Brizi, an Italian.[21]

At this time, as has been pointed out, the Italian government had only a practical interest in occupying the islands, inasmuch as they could be used as leverage to force the Ottoman government to terms. Even if this was problematical in the extreme, the archipelago being, as Bosworth described it, 'ethnically Greek and economically valueless,' there was no purpose beyond this other than their usefulness in helping to interdict the seaborne passage of 'contraband of war' to Cyrenaica.[22]

Unfortunately for the Italians, and as Rocca Rey had argued, the occupation of the islands had no immediate apparent effect on what the Italian government considered to be Ottoman intransigence, leaving Italy in an awkward position. The accuracy of Albert Legrand's observation in November 1911 that the war was 'a cruel embarrassment' to Italian politicians was becoming ever more apparent.[23] The problems were not all Italian, as the Ottoman government had troubles aplenty. To quote Childs on the matter: 'the Ottoman Empire at the beginning of 1912 was in a state of turmoil and disarray, its government in an ever more precarious position [...] further complicated by the endemic unrest in northern Albania.'[24] The problems in Albania, though they had deep roots, were exacerbated by the same factors that had alienated the population that cleaved to the notion of the 'Autonomous state of the Dodecanese.' This led, in May 1912 to what the Austro-Hungarians termed the *Malissorenaufstand* – a Christian Albanian uprising.

These ongoing, and increasing, Ottoman problems in Albania would appear to have been one of the motivating factors behind a document dated 29 June 1912 and sent by Pollio to his chief, Spingardi. This 'Memorandum Regarding our Political and Military Situation' (*Promemoria sulla nostra situazione politico-militare*) contains an analysis of the 'internal crisis' of the Ottoman Empire with particular reference to the recent events in Albania, which Pollio saw as having 'enormously worsened the politico-military situation of the enemy.'[25] Now, he argued, was an excellent time to strike them hard because their collapse was probable in any case, and Italy could profitably exploit the opportunity. Demonstrating the degree to which Giolitti and San Giuliano kept the military and naval leadership in the dark as regards the international political situation, he also admitted that he was unaware of the situation as regards the other members of the Triple Alliance, or indeed Britain and France, and did not know the reasons behind the paralysis of 'our action in the eastern Mediterranean.' He also reasoned that if the Empire did not collapse, 'through foreign gold or the support of the Powers,' then the prolongation of the war would cause Italy 'great damage' and require an even greater effort in the future.

The methodology by which Italy could finally shatter the Ottoman Empire he saw as twofold; a landing of an Italian expeditionary force at Smyrna (Izmir) and the support of the Christian insurgents in the Balkans. Pollio suggested that an army of 100,000 men be landed, though raising, equipping, transporting and maintaining a force of this size would have been unworkable given the amount of effort being expended in North Africa. In any event, the proposal was politically impossible and both at the time, and later in his memoirs, Giolitti was dismissive. He wrote that such an attack would be engaging an enemy where its strength was greatest, and that 'unfortunately there are very few who can remain immune to the particular excitement that accompanies war.'[26]

The navy leadership, who might have baulked at having to mount an expedition such as proposed by Pollio, were however somewhat exercised at the incipient threat posed by the Ottoman 'fleet in being' sheltering in the Dardanelles. Rocca Rey had, it may be recalled, expressed his concerns before the operations to take the Dodecanese regarding the extra work Italian occupation would throw upon the Italian fleet. The need to maintain a force powerful enough to deal with any Ottoman sortie, unlikely as it was, and the necessity of escorting convoys in the area took their toll, not least in the admiral's mind. He was to argue that, despite the 'poor state' of its ships and the similarly depressed morale of the crews, the Ottoman squadron 'continued to pose a threat to our command of the sea.' Furthermore it forced Italy 'to keep defences on the islands and a vast number of ships at sea [...] at large expense, putting great strain (forte logorio) on both personnel and material. We must put an end to this state of things.'[27]

There was only one way to achieve this and that was to sink or disable the offending ships, which had remained at anchor at Nagara Point (Nara Burnu, Abydos) some 30 kilometres north of the entrance and about 10 kilometres above the narrows at Çanakkale following the first attempt on them on 17-18 April. The Duke of Abruzzi's command, the 'Division of the Torpedo-Boat Inspector,' would furnish the means, and his chief-of-staff, Captain Enrico Millo, would lead the enterprise. Millo was summoned to Rome to discuss the matter. The plan arrived at was relatively simple; five torpedo-boats were to enter the Dardanelles under cover of darkness and attempt to travel unseen over the distance to the Ottoman anchorage. Millo hand-picked the boats and their commanders; Spica, Perseus, Astore, Climene, and Centaur, commanded respectively by Umberto Bucci, Giuseppe Sirianni, Stanislao di Somma, Carlo Fenzi and Italo Moreno, all holding the rank of lieutenant (tenente di vascello). With Millo in tactical command aboard the Spica, the attack would not be closely supported and the boats would rely on going unnoticed. General support would be afforded by the Vettor Pisani and two destroyers, the Nembo and Borea, and the eight-vessel flotilla assembled at Stampalia before sailing on 14 July for Leros (Lero). Normally each boat was commanded by two officers but on this occasion each was given a third for the mission, and a pilot.

At Leros the torpedo-boats were prepared for the attack, with extraneous equipment being removed and camouflage paint applied, before sailing north to the Ottoman-ruled, but sparsely inhabited, island of Agios Efstratios (Saint Eustratius) near Lemnos on 17 July. From this position they were around 100 kilometres from the entrance to the strait, and on the afternoon of the next day Millo led his command, escorted by the three larger vessels, northwards towards the target. At 23:30 hours the flotilla split up, with the escort remaining out of sight whilst the torpedo-boats headed towards the strait.

According to Millo's report of the action, 'the weather was good and the sea calm, with only a light haze on the horizon.' He also noted that the entrance to the Dardanelles was clearly identified by searchlights at Cape Helles and Kum Kale and that despite these the boats were able to enter unobserved a little after midnight. The flotilla was arranged in line ahead, with Spica leading them in the order Perseus, Astore, Climene, and lastly Centaur. They advanced at 12 knots at first, then increased to 15 as they passed through the entrance, keeping to the Asiatic side, in order to counteract the effects of the current. At around 00:40 hours the middle boat, Astore, was however fixed by one of the two searchlights at Cape Helles and followed for several minutes, during which time the alarm was raised and gunfire directed at the intruders. This fire was inaccurate, and despite being discovered Millo decided to continue the mission:

> Since the defences appeared weak, I decided to continue the reconnaissance and advance further into the straits before deciding what to do depending on the circumstances. Speed was increased to 20 knots and the boats headed towards the European side to avoid the bombardment. Many other searchlights came into action, and from the illumination provided by that at Fort Suandare I was able to see that the squadron was in an orderly line ahead with the commanders bravely leading their units in precise formation despite the enemy fire.

Incredibly the boats managed to penetrate to within about ten kilometres of the anchorage without taking any serious hits before being forced to a halt off Çanakkale at the narrows, where the lead vessel fouled an underwater obstacle.

> The *Spica* reached at great speed the promontory of Kilid-Bahr when it was suddenly halted. The abrupt manner of the stop, and the fouling of the two propellers, led us to believe that we had run into steel cables. The commander of the *Spica* immediately tried to manoeuvre us off the obstacle whilst the battery at Kilid-Bahr began a rapid fire.

> Under such conditions, and after achieving the intended results of the reconnaissance, but with no chance to torpedo the enemy, and knowing that the torpedo boats under my command would be destroyed by enemy short-range fire […] I therefore considered any further advance an unnecessary sacrifice of men and torpedo boats. […] I then judged it my duty to stop the reconnaissance and retreat.

Lieutenant Bucci did manage to free his boat from the obstruction and the flotilla began the return journey at high speed. Remarkably, and despite being under fire the whole way, all the craft survived the journey more or less unscathed. Millo was to report that the total damage to his command was negligible with only *Spica*, *Astore* and *Perseus* suffering minor hits. The other two boats were not touched and there were no injuries whatsoever to any of the personnel that undertook the mission. It will be noted that Millo's report referred to the mission as primarily a reconnaissance, and he had made clear to his superiors beforehand that if he adjudged the attack had no prospect of success then he would withdraw and call it just that. This was greeted with derision in certain quarters. For example, Captain Arthur Courtenay Stewart, the British Naval Attaché at Rome, was scathing, arguing that to claim the mission was a reconnaissance was 'scarcely believable as everyone already knew precisely where the Turkish fleet was!'[28]

Whilst the enterprise was undoubtedly hazardous, and there can be little doubt that Millo made the correct decision to withdraw after becoming caught up on the defences, it was depicted in the Italian press, and government propaganda, as a stunning victory. Alfredo Frassati, the editor of the widely circulated Piedmontese daily *La Stampa*, published a piece in his paper on 21 July entitled .'Five Italian torpedo-boats advance for 20 kilometres in the Dardanelles in strong Turkish crossfire.' To Frassati the success of the mission restored the navy to glory and expunged the memories of the Battle of Lissa:

> The recent fearful suspicions both moral and strategic of the value of our navy have disappeared: we breathe freely, free from all the care cultivated over the years of waiting defenceless […] Italy's navy has entered into [parity with those of] the great powers: it can count its sailors among the best trained and the most fearless in the world.[29]

Captain Enrico Millo and the Dardanelles: a graphic that featured in *L'illustrazione Italiana* on 24 July 1912 following the mission by five torpedo-boats six days earlier. The story it illustrated was entitled *'The Bold Action of our Torpedo-Boats in the Dardanelles'* and even though the mission to damage or sink the enemy 'fleet in being' was unsuccessful, it was nevertheless depicted in the Italian press, and in government propaganda, as a stunning victory. (Author's Collection).

Giuseppe Bevione wrote a long account of the mission in the same paper four days later, entitling it 'The Wonderful Adventure in the Dardanelles.' He explained that because the Ottoman fleet refused to leave its base, the torpedo boats had set out to hunt them. These vessels, he told his readers, were almost without guns, were protected only with a 'hint' of steel armour, and for their protection relied on speed and audacity. His description of the escape is worth recounting:

> The water boiled around the torpedo boats from stem to stern, and jets of water flew high as shells fell with horrible thuds, as if volcanic eruptions were flashing inexhaustibly beneath the water […] The air was full of flashes, of flames, explosions, and splinters. Convulsive, foaming, full of glare and reflections, the sea seemed to become a huge fiery furnace. But at the zenith shone always the star of Italy.[30]

Such overblown rhetoric may perhaps be forgiven, or at least is understandable, coming from the same press that had done so much to bring about the conflict, and was now desperate for victories to proclaim. The politicians were also keen to talk up the affair, and Millo and his fellow officers were promoted and bemedalled. Some ten years later Giolitti was still claiming the event as a naval triumph, stating that 'steel nets' made an attack impossible and that 'the retreat was conducted in perfect order, without any harm, and ensuring that the enemy did not dare to chase, although our torpedo boats were not protected by any larger ships.'[31]

The Ottoman response was muted because the raid coincided with a political upheaval when Sait Pasa had resigned on 17 July following the collapse of his cabinet. Indeed, and according to the British *chargé d'affaires* at Constantinople Charles M Marling, it was popularly believed that the whole affair was a sham engineered by the CUP. In a message of 23 July he opined that the 'Young Turks' would not have been averse to 'arranging a scenic display on the Dardanelles and attempting, by the expenditure of a little gunpowder, to draw off public attention from the very tight corner in which [they] found [themselves].'[32] The fact that there was political instability perhaps explains why, although the Ottoman Government improved the defences in the Dardanelles by narrowing the channels through the barricades and mine fields, they did not close the straits.

With the occupation of the islands in the Southern Sporades and Millo's 'reconnaissance' the limits of Italian navalism, and its ability to influence the outcome of the conflict with the Ottoman Empire, had been reached. There were to be no further notable actions, other than the occasional exchange of fire with Ottoman coastal defences, in the eastern Mediterranean or Aegean, but in the main theatre of the war the navy continued to assist in the occupation of key points. Perhaps chief amongst these was the operation to take Misrata (Misratah, Misurata), probably the most important commercial centre in the Tripoli *vilayet* after Tripoli City. It was a substantial town with a population estimated at about 10,000, surrounded by a large oasis with a population calculated to be some 35,000 strong.

The amphibious operation once again involved a feint by vessels of the Training Division. On the evening of 15 June and the next morning a demonstration was made at Zliten, about 60 kilometres west of Misrata by three auxiliary cruisers, the *Duca di Genova, Citta di Messina* and *Citta di Siracusa*, accompanied by three transports. The real landing however took place on the morning of 16 June at Qasr Ahmed (Bu-Sceifa, Misurata Marina), some 12 kilometres to the east of the target, under cover of the guns of the major units of Borea Ricci's command. The military force, aboard nine transports, was made up of a composite division under Major-General Count Vittorio Camerana drawn from formations stationed in Italy, Tripoli, Derna and Benghazi. Three regiments of infantry formed the core of his command, the 35th, 50th, and 63rd, together with the *Mondovi* and *Verona* battalions of *Alpini,* a battalion of the 40th Infantry, a company of the 5th Eritrean, a squadron of *Lucca* cavalry, and artillery and engineer support. The whole force totalled about 10,000 men, and in command of the second of the two mixed brigades (*II Brigata Mista*) was Major-General Gustavo Fara, the hero of the actions at el-Hani on 23 October and Bir Tobras on 20 December.

The landing was accomplished without major incident, and by the evening of 16 June a secure bridgehead had been established ashore. Easily repulsed piecemeal attacks were made on the defensive perimeter during 17 June, but Camerana had decided on remaining on the defensive for the moment and so he made no attempt to exploit the lodgement. Indeed, the next week was spent by the Italians in consolidating their position on what was a barren stretch of coast, and building up supplies there for use as a base of operations. The cavalry squadron was used for reconnaissance towards the target and surrounding areas, and reported that there was no sign of the enemy in any force. This changed on 23 June when signs of Ottoman activity in the oasis of Misrata were detected and a concerted attack by a force reckoned to have been 5,000 strong was repulsed on 2 July.

At 04:00 hours on 9 July Camerana moved over to the offensive, advancing on Misrata in three columns supported by the Training Division steaming slowly offshore. The right and centre columns advanced directly towards the town whilst that on the left, commanded by Fara, swept around it to the south with his flank protected by the cavalry. According to official Italian reports, the column closest to the coast encountered stiff resistance from the start from enemy troops entrenched on the eastern edge of the Oasis of Misrata. The centre and left-hand columns bypassed much of this resistance, though the centre column also encountered enemy forces entrenched at the village of Az Zarrug on the eastern outskirts of the town, and Misrata itself was entered and taken by 18:00 hours that evening. It took until 20 July for the oasis to be completely cleared of enemy combatants, but the final Italian casualty list, 9 killed and 121 wounded (including 4 *ascari*) since landing, again suggests that the fighting had not been particularly hard. The figures for Ottoman casualties are impossible to compute, the Italians as always estimated several hundred, but a strong force remained congregated at the village of Al Ghiran (Gherem) southwest of Misrata. This village was attacked by Fara on 20 July and, relatively speaking, he suffered heavy casualties with 19 killed and 87 wounded and was almost overwhelmed; a manifestation of his supposed 'inclination to rashness' perhaps.

In any event, with the capture of Misrata the sole port on the entire coastline of the *vilayet* not in Italian hands was Zuwarah. The landing at El Faru and subsequent capture of Abu Kammash on 10 April had served notice that the usefulness of this coastal village as a node in the contraband route was threatened, but it had not completely negated it as there was an alternative, parallel, route some 15 kilometres inland. Ottoman forces still retained control of the village of Bi'r Sidi Sa'id (Sidi Said), situated some two kilometres along the coast from the base of the El Faru peninsula. Retention of this position gave the holders a flanking position in respect of any move on Riqdalin (Regdalin) which sat astride the inland road.

Accordingly, on 26 June 1912 Garioni had moved in two columns on Bi'r Sidi Sa'id from Abu Kammash and the peninsula and, after three days fighting, had taken possession. The next step was the taking of Zuwarah itself, and this was accomplished on 4 August via a two-pronged assault utilising control of the sea. Escorted by the battleships of the Training Division, together with two destroyers and six torpedo-boats, a brigade strength force, 5,000 men in 6 battalions with 2 artillery batteries, under Major-General Giulio Cesare Tassoni was conveyed in seven transports and landed at a small bay some 3.5 kilometres to the east of Zuwarah. Once ashore this force began to advance on the town hoping to time its arrival to coincide with an advance from the west by a brigade under Major-General Lequio. This force had set out during the night, but despite having to traverse rough terrain, covered the 18 kilometres in good time and arrived outside Zuwarah before Tassoni's command at about 09:00 hours. Here they halted until 13:00 hours when Tassoni arrived, and the two brigades then entered the oasis and town; both were deserted.

The last significant port in the *vilayet*, albeit a very small and poor one, available to the Ottoman forces had fallen into Italian hands, cutting off any kind of meaningful marine trade. The road to the south was not to remain open much longer either; on 15 August Garioni directed both brigades southwards and they occupied and fortified high ground around Riqdalin. From here the road could be interdicted and so the trade had to be moved to the southern route where the Italians could not venture.

The amphibious warfare practised by Italy was sophisticated, and the various feints and ruses employed to ensure that the landing forces met with no opposition were an essential part of it. Perhaps the landing at Rhodes was the most prominent of these, achieved as it was with minimal cost. That operation, together with the occupation of the other islands, represented, according to General Ameglio, 'the first major and successful combined operation between the army and the navy.'[33] One may quibble at that statement, inasmuch as other landings such as the Benghazi operation of 21 October under Ameglio were similar, but he did identify a major point; that of the necessity of cooperation. This had the potential to be problematical, and historical examples abound of inter-service rivalry, but Italy seems to have had little trouble in 1911-12.

The other main problem was of course tactical. The only way of getting men from transport ships to the landing beach was by putting them in small boats, usually ships' boats but almost anything that would float could be pressed into service. Before the First World War no army or navy possessed any specialised equipment to facilitate landing operations, the first such being the British 'Beetle.' These were armoured and each could carry about four hundred men; 'They have a long gangway which lets down in front to enable troops to jump ashore across deep water, the gangway acting like a drawbridge.'[34]

The most hazardous parts of the operation from the point of view of the attackers was when they were still in the boats and completely powerless, or, having successfully made the journey from the ships, just after landing when they are weak and exposed. If Ottoman forces were present at or near the landing site in any significant number, then they would wreak havoc on the unprotected troops, and although the guns of the warships could lend support they were of little utility against nearly invisible defenders stationed in sand dunes and the like.

Unless they had the element of surprise, Italian amphibious operations were then hazardous and likely to fail. As the famous military theorist and historian, Basil Liddell Hart, was to put it in 1939 when considering the forthcoming war with Germany: 'A landing on a foreign coast in face of hostile troops has always been one of the most difficult operations of war.'[35] The need for surprise is an enduring principle; the modern doctrine of the US Marine Corps, whose knowledge and abilities in the matter are unrivalled, emphasises this element.[36]

Mostly then, through cooperation between their army and navy, combined with good intelligence and thus their use of surprise, or 'landing where the enemy wasn't' as it might be termed, the Italians were successful in most of their amphibious enterprises and scored some notable achievements. However, as has been noted, the Italians never admitted to suffering any setbacks and consequently their records show no indication of overt failure. In the amphibious context it is probably the case that two operations had to be aborted because of the presence of defenders, though because of the way the Italians conducted their operations casualties were slight. Italian practice devolved around landing parties of marines or sailors to reconnoitre and, if there were no resistance, secure the beach. These were then followed by the main body of the landing force. If resistance was met, then the initial landing parties would withdraw. This is what happened at Zuwarah on 16 December 1911, though the Italians blamed poor weather. Another hazard revolved around disinformation. This is what seems to have occurred on 1 June 1912 when landing parties were lured ashore under a false pretext, at least according to Enver Pasa. His diary entry for that day is as follows:

> It was reported that the Italians had landed at Susa. That would be an excellent opportunity for us. They will run up against insurmountable difficulties in the terrain and fierce resistance from the Bedouin.[37]

Susah (Susa) is located some 70 kilometres to the west of Derna, on the Cyrenaican coast and was described in 1854 by 'Mediterranean Smyth' as 'a mere boat cove, though once the port of the potent city of Cyrene.'[38] A slightly fuller account of the event was given by Enver in his entry for the following day:

> The landing of the Italians at Susa went as I had hoped. A native of Derna that served the Italians as a spy, was put ashore in order to ask the Bedouin around to a meeting with the

Italians, where they would be persuaded by words and deeds of Italian generosity. The local Bedouin chief sent the spy back with a message agreeing to meet. Some Italians then left the ships and came to the beach in boats. After they had landed they were immediately put under a heavy fire and flew headlong back into their boats. In response to this friendly reception, the warship fired on the coast for the rest of the day.[39]

Nevertheless, the majority of Italian amphibious operations were successful, and the experienced gained made the Italian armed forces skilled in this form of warfare. Indeed, until the British and French operations at Gallipoli in 1915 were undertaken, amongst the European nations it was Italy that possessed the most knowledgeable and experienced forces in the technique. Skills in the military and naval spheres could not though resolve the conflict with the Ottoman Empire in Italy's favour, and so it remained to be seen whether Italian politicians and diplomats could succeed where force had failed.

CHAPTER THIRTEEN

The Iron Dice Roll

*'In Europe, the opinion is widespread that the Italians found it impossible to penetrate
into the interior, due to the resistance, of the Turks and Arabs that opposed them.
That is completely erroneous. The Italians have not penetrated into the interior,
because they have not had the courage to act.'*
From an article in Rome's *La Tribuna*, 1912[1]

IF Italian strategy vis-à-vis war with the Ottoman Empire was paralysed, then the
Ottoman strategy of waiting in the hope of gaining Great Power support in order to
force Italy to an acceptable compromise had also failed. Ottoman approaches to various
of the Great Powers had been rebuffed, and the focus of attention had begun to shift from
the North African *vilayet* to trouble in areas far closer to home. Chief amongst these was
the Albanian issue. The Ottoman *vilayets* of Janina, Kosovo and Iskodra had a majority
population that considered themselves Albanian, and a large proportion of the *vilayet* of
Monastir was likewise. Albanian nationalists, though not necessarily hostile to Ottoman
rule as such, desired the amalgamation of the four *vilayets* into an autonomous homeland.

The advent of the CUP-supported regime following the revolution and counter-
revolution of 1908 led the nationalists to hope that their aim of autonomy within the
empire would be realised. As stated, they were not anti-Ottoman inasmuch as they shared
the Islamic faith and culture, but the ramshackle nature of the empire, and its various ad
hoc expedients over time, had allowed the Albanian people certain privileges.
The arrangements by which they were governed were shambolic. Sir John Hobhouse
accompanied Lord Byron on a tour through the area in the early years of the nineteenth
century and put it thus:

> Specimens of almost every sort of government are to be found in Albania. Some districts and
> towns are commanded by one man [...]; others obey their elders; others are under no
> subjection, but each man governs his own family. The power in some places is in abeyance, and
> although there is no apparent anarchy, there are no rulers.[2]

Things had not altered much a century later, but the CUP aimed to change all this
by imposing centralised government with equal citizenship rights for all. Such policies

discountenanced the notion of autonomous 'national' homelands and, accordingly, discontent manifested itself in armed revolts in many areas where Albanians resided. The Sultan himself visited Albanian areas in 1911 but to little effect, and the continuing and growing discontent not only consumed more and more Ottoman military resources, but fed political tensions in the whole Balkan region. A large-scale uprising occurred in May 1912 and was more successful than many previous efforts inasmuch as the city of Skopje, now in the modern Republic of Macedonia but at the time the administrative centre of Ottoman rule in the *vilayet* of Kosovo, fell to the insurgents.

By the summer of 1912 Ottoman control of the whole Balkan region had begun to deteriorate badly and the government in Istanbul seemed impotent. The situation was exploited by groupings other than Albanian nationalists with agendas of their own, and several of these most definitely did want to throw off Ottoman rule. Further, concessions made to Albanian nationalism in respect of Kosovo, were highly provocative to Serbian nationalists. They regarded the *vilayet* as unredeemed Serbian territory, the acquisition of which was pivotal in their struggle for national reunification and the reconstitution of 'Old Serbia.'[3] The question of unredeemed territory currently under Ottoman control was also central to the ambitions of Bulgaria, Greece, and Montenegro, and in 1912 these independent states had begun to form themselves into an alliance or coalition in order to pursue their shared interests. A 'Treaty of Coalition' was signed between Serbia and Bulgaria on 29 February 1912, followed by a 'Military Convention' on 12 June. Likewise Greece and Bulgaria came to an agreement, signing a 'Treaty of Coalition' on 16 May, which was followed by a 'Military Convention' on 22 September.[4] These bilateral arrangements included an informal agreement between Montenegro and Bulgaria, which was concluded in April, but no formal treaty was signed.

Attempts were made to keep the formulation and existence of these treaties and agreements secret. However the inevitable rumours did the diplomatic rounds particularly as Russia – the Protector of the Slavs – was perceived, correctly, to be complicit in the creation of a bloc to counterbalance the expansive moves of Austria-Hungary.[5] Rumours of impending conflict were also fuelled by military purchases; both the Ottoman and Serbian governments began making large-scale purchases of horses in Austria-Hungary and Russia during the month of May. The following month the Serb Parliament voted a special credit of twenty million francs for war purposes. Whether or not they knew of the alliances in detail, the Ottoman government was certainly aware of increased instability; 'chaos was increasing in the Balkans day by day' following the agreements. 'After the formation of the Serbian-Bulgarian alliance, demonstrations against the Ottoman state had begun in Bulgaria. Through the provocations of Serbia and Bulgaria, militia activities in Macedonia suddenly increased, and anarchy broke out.'[6]

Balkan unrest, or at least unrest that led to Austro-Hungarian or Russian advantage, was very much against Italian interests. This was particularly so in respect of the area that encompassed the Albanian *vilayets*, which Italian politicians and businessmen had viewed through imperialist eyes for some time. Italian economic penetration in the area, including the presence of banks and railway construction, might be said to have been greater than it had managed in Tripoli. The ties went even deeper than that though; Italy also had a substantial population of Italo-Albanians (*Schipetaro, Arbëreshë*) living mainly in the south and it was from this community that Francesco Crispi had hailed. Indeed none other than San Giuliano, before he became foreign minister, had published a book advocating Italian expansion in the area.[7] There were also dynastic ties in that the King of Montenegro, Nikola (Nicholas) I, was the father-in-law of Vittorio Emmanuel III of Italy.

Whether Italy's war with the Ottoman Empire was a contributory factor in bringing about the Balkan turmoil, and if so to what extent, has long been debated. According to the British Ambassador to Rome in 1912, Sir James Rennell Rodd, it was 'generally accepted' at the time that it was a direct cause. This is perhaps overstating the case. For example, Sir George Young, writing in 1915, argued that the Italo-Ottoman war 'brought no material contribution to the conjunction of political forces that was to cause the war of the Balkan Coalition.' He did though go on to contend that:

> [I]n the moral sphere of international relations, it was of great effect. It radically changed the moral situation in Eastern Europe by breaking the ice for the plunge into war, on the brink of which the Balkan Governments were shivering.[8]

This is a point of view echoed by Childs, who opines that the Balkan states were 'encouraged […] to speed up and to coordinate their own preparations to take over the Ottoman Empire in Europe.' He also points out that the Great Powers who had formerly acted in concert to one degree or another in order to maintain the status quo were no longer capable of so doing. Indeed, at that time and in that place, Austria-Hungary and Russia were mutually hostile and suspicious.[9]

Indeed, to posit that the Italian decision to go to war with the Ottoman Empire led unswervingly to the war in the Balkans might, ultimately, lead on to arguing that Giolitti and San Giuliano were then directly responsible for setting in train events that led to the First World War. Such a position would be ridiculously simplistic and completely untenable. Certainly the First Balkan War was in all essentials a continuation of the struggle for independence from the Ottoman Empire, and which would almost certainly have occurred irrespective. Nevertheless, there can be little doubt that those scholars who have placed the Italo-Ottoman conflict in the context of a prelude to the First and then Second Balkan Wars, themselves a prime cause of the general European conflict that erupted in 1914, have a point.[10]

This belief in the interrelationship between the Tripoli and Balkan wars was no doubt reinforced because of the one conflict following hard on the heels of the other. Another factor in this regard was the time of year when the Balkan League began their operations. According to Rennell Rodd, 'experts had pronounced it as contrary to precedent in that incalculable region that the crisis should have occurred at the beginning of winter.' He then went on to undermine the arguments of the experts:

> It is true that the *Comitadjis* [irregular soldiers or fighters] and mountain peoples were more disposed to take the warpath in the spring and summer, but the Bulgarians, to whom the gathering of their harvest was a paramount consideration, had been trained to winter warfare.

He also dismissed the notion that the North African campaign had damaged the strength of the Ottoman armed forces:

> In so far as any weakening of Ottoman resources might have acted as a stimulus to the Balkan States, a connection with the war in Tripoli might be sustained. But the military strength of the Ottoman Empire had not really been much affected by a campaign which was strictly localized, and in which only insignificant forces were engaged.[11]

This is pretty much self evidently the case, and if the Ottoman senator who argued in early 1912 that 'the war at present costs us nothing'[12] might be reasonably accused of exaggerating somewhat, it can be said in mitigation that he at least had a point.

There is one other factor to consider in respect of the formation of the Balkan League and its subsequent military action; that of the policy, or perceived policy, of the CUP and Ottoman government towards the Independent Balkan States. The Bulgarian government published an account of its activities, and the rationale behind them, in both the Balkan Wars and the First World War in 1919. This document, *The Bulgarian Question and the Balkan States*, was aimed at the leaders of the victorious powers that were then gathered at the Peace Conference at Versailles. It was then hardly objective. However, it does contain a mention of the Bulgarian perception of the Ottoman attitude towards Bulgaria and the other independent Balkan states, which followed on from the CUP seizure of power.

> The new regime undertook nothing in the direction of liberty; the only thing to which it devoted itself sincerely was the military power of the empire. The plan of the Young-Turk Committee was really to provoke one by one all the Balkan States, and beat them separately.[13]

This of course was a retrospectively adopted viewpoint that was self justifying. However, there was undoubtedly at least some truth in it. The CUP leaders were extremely vocal about the need to recover 'lost territories,' and of course they may have been in a position to replace the talk with action when their reforms were complete, a situation that the governments of the Balkan States could hardly have viewed with equanimity.[14]

Whatever the cause of it, the increasing tension and unrest was beyond the power of the Ottoman government to control, a factor that was greatly exacerbated by the ongoing reorganisation of the Ottoman Army. The CUP, being composed largely of army officers, had begun to modernise the Ottoman army along Prussian lines. This unfinished process had, in the words of the Turkish General Staff historian Re at Halli, led to 'the most disastrous results.' The military was at an interim stage of transformation in which the pre-existing system had been more or less dismantled whilst the new was as yet unready.[15] Service in the Ottoman army, which had a fearsome reputation based mainly on its wars with Russia in the nineteenth century and before, had been based on the conscription of Muslims solely. Those of the Jewish or Christian faiths, and there were many within the boundaries of the empire, were exempt. The CUP changed this system so that all faiths became common citizens of the empire and were, in theory at least, equally liable to bear arms. Colonel Herbert Conyers Surtees, the British Military Attaché in Constantinople, observed the antipathy this 'equality' caused amongst the Islamic population. He reckoned that the degree of resentment was akin to that which would have been felt by the white population of the Deep South of the United States had enfranchisement of the black population been decreed from above.[16] Whether or not this was an exaggeration is impossible to tell, but the effectiveness of the army was certainly impaired by the reforms in general and by their effects on the 'Prussianisation' of the officer corps in particular. According to Ellis Ashmead-Bartlett, the former officer and war correspondent for the *Daily Telegraph* who had reported extensively on the Russo-Japanese War, the results of this policy were disastrous in the short term:

In their dealings with the old type of regimental officer the Young Turks made the most fatal mistake of all. Because they saw European armies with young regimental officers who enjoyed steady promotion, they said, 'We must get rid of all these old subalterns and captains who were promoted from the ranks, and who are old enough to be colonels and generals, and replace them by young officers.' Therefore, with a stroke of the pen they placed all the regimental officers over a certain age in retirement before they had a sufficiency of young officers to take their place. Thus for the last three years the Turkish Army has been woefully short of officers, and when the war broke out [October 1912] it was no fewer than two thousand below its proper establishment.[17]

It was the opinion of the British Director of Military Operations, Sir Henry Wilson, 'that with the re-organisation of her forces completed [the Ottoman Empire] will, in the near future, be infinitely stronger than she is at the present moment.'[18] Given in 1911 in a 'Memorandum on Coercive Action against Turkey' this forecast was to be proven substantially correct some three years later. Whilst it was still in process however, Ashmead-Bartlett's assessment of officer shortage and inexperience in 1912 was essentially correct. This was confirmed by later Turkish military historians, and it was a situation moreover that was greatly exacerbated by the situation in North Africa.[19] Some of the best, and youngest, Ottoman officers had been despatched there to lead the military campaign against the Italians, including most famously Enver and Mustafa Kemal, and by the middle of 1912 there were several hundred in action.[20] Indeed, it is somewhat ironic to note that if the CUP had decided that it would change the 'glue' that bound the Ottoman Army from religion to nationalism, then, according to one of their most high profile leaders, the successes obtained by Ottoman officers in raising and maintaining Arab forces was largely to do with their common religion. Indeed, Enver's diary entry for 9 October 1911 gives his reason for travelling to fight as 'to fulfil a moral duty; the entire Islamic world expects it of us.'[21]

If the removal of Enver, Kemal, and other skilled officers to North Africa, combined with the disruption caused to the army by the ongoing attempts at reorganisation, and not forgetting the deployment of some 30,000 troops to tackle the instability in Yemen, left the Ottoman military in a potentially parlous state, all cannot be said to have been well with the political scene either. This owed more to domestic than foreign politics, and arose from factionalism in the army.

A constitutional issue had arisen in December 1911 concerning the proroguing of parliament. According to the restored 1876 constitution, in the event of a dispute between the government and parliament it was the government that had to resign. If any new government found itself still at loggerheads with the parliament, then the Sultan could dissolve the latter and new elections would take place. The leader of the government at the time was Grand Vizier Sait Pasa, who had taken over following the resignation of its predecessor following the Italian invasion of Tripoli. Sait was highly experienced, having been Grand Vizier no fewer than eight times over his career, and was generally well respected and not seen as merely a CUP stooge. His government wanted to modify the constitution, so that in the event of a disagreement between parliament and government, the government would remain and parliament would be prorogued. Parliamentary elections however would not automatically follow.

Sait was unable to persuade parliament of his case and, in accordance with the constitution, he and his government resigned on 30 December 1911. He was charged by the Sultan with forming a new government on 1 January 1912, but was still unable to get parliament to agree the reform. Accordingly, and in full compliance with constitutional requirements, he again resigned and elections were scheduled. These took place in April and resulted in a CUP landslide; only six opposition members, out of a total of 275 deputies, were elected. The new parliament met on 18 April 1912, and with the overwhelming majority now enjoyed by the CUP, there was no doubt that the constitutional amendment would pass comfortably. The new parliament was however tainted; the election that brought it into being became known as the 'big-stick election' because of the degree of manipulation and intimidation involved with it. As well as gerrymandering, these included arresting opposition candidates on unconvincing charges or suddenly calling them up for military service. These practices not only alarmed the opposition, but also caused discontent within a section of the officer corps.

Many army officers combined membership of the CUP, and concomitant political activities, with their military duties. Another grouping however held the view that the two were incompatible, and that military and political matters should be kept separate, apart from the army having an overarching responsibility for defending the restored constitution. They also blamed the CUP, whose centralising policies could not be said to have proven noticeably effective in ensuring the territorial integrity of the empire, for the Italian invasion of Tripoli and generally deprecated the dictatorial methods practiced by the government, which now commanded a chamber packed with compliant deputies.

Known as the 'Saviour Officers' (*Haliskar Zabitan*) this group was formed from officers based mainly in the Ottoman capitol but was allied with others stationed in the European *vilayets*. The 'Saviour Officers' published papers stating their aims in late June and early July 1912, and heavily criticised the government for the deteriorating situation in the Albanian areas. This division within the officer corps put the government in a difficult position, particularly at a time when the army might be needed shortly.

The Minister of War, Mahmud Sevket Pasa, introduced a bill into parliament with a revised military code that introduced provisions concerning the separation of military and political roles. This eventually passed, but on the same day, 9 July 1912, Sevket resigned from his post. His resignation precipitated a crisis, which led eventually to something approaching a military coup on the part of the army units commanded by the disaffected officers. On 16 July Sait Pasa resigned the premiership and the process of forming a new government began.

The new regime was in place by 21 July with Field-Marshal Ahmet Muhtar Pasa, a military hero of the 1877-8 war with Russia, at its head; his prestige as a military hero perhaps giving him influence over the army in general. The accession of this 'Great Cabinet' as it became known because it contained three former Grand Viziers, was not universally acclaimed.[22] When Enver learned of the events he was perturbed, writing on 24 July:

> The thought of the events at home do not leave me a moment. The old government was replaced by a feebler one. Only the ministry of war remains in energetic hands, and the army, I hope, will benefit. I myself can only continue the work begun.[23]

The Minister of War was another military man, Hussein Nazim Pasa, who had served in the post previously, but for only two days in February 1909.[24] His tenure was not to prove a resounding success, and he was to perish in a shooting incident the following year in which Enver was involved. His first days in office cannot have filled him with confidence over the situation in North Africa; telegrams from Tripolitania of 17 and 21 July awaited him reporting acute shortages of ammunition and advocating the cessation of operations unless supplies were rapidly shipped.[25] This of course could not be accomplished. Gabriel Noradungiyan (Gabriel Effendi), the newly appointed Foreign Minister was also regaled with news of the most unsettling kind. On 27 July the ambassador to Imperial Germany, Osman Nizami Pasa, who had been appointed in 1908 by the CUP dominated regime,[26] telegraphed with intelligence on the Balkan alliances. After reiterating that there was no doubt that anti-Ottoman military moves were afoot, he advised Gabriel that the Ottoman government must find a solution to its conflict with Italy.[26] A military solution was obviously out of the question, whilst a political arrangement was fraught with difficulty given the reluctance of the army in particular to concede anything to a foe that could not conquer. Enver in Cyrenaica bemoaned the military situation, recording on 16 August his thoughts on the matter: 'Had these accursed Italians the courage to attack us! It is sad that we are forced to wage a war of siege!' The same entry also revealed his unhappiness with the events at home:

> The events in Constantinople take an ever more evil course whilst I stand here, trying to save a corner of my country, powerless. As for the agitators among the officers, I telegraphed to the Secretary of War that here we all curse these miserable wretches, whose actions will lead to the ruin of the army and country. [28]

In fact moves, albeit tentative in the extreme, towards a negotiated settlement had been underway under the previous government. Talks had been taking place at the Hotel Gibbon (named for the British Historian who finished his epic work there in 1787) at Lausanne, Switzerland. The Italian delegation comprised of Volpi, the 'unofficial conduit' between the two governments, and two parliamentary deputies, Pietro Bertolini and Guido Fusinato. This trio had been discussing, negotiating even, an end to the conflict with a representative of the Ottoman government Sait Halim Pasa (not to be confused with the similarly named Grand Vizier) since 12 July.[29] Though these discussions had been undertaken in the strictest secrecy, rumours concerning them inevitably surfaced in the press causing San Giuliano a great deal of nervousness. He feared that should the talks become widely known about then Italian 'public opinion,' as expressed through the nationalist press and via jingo politicians, would perceive them as a sign of weakness and that Italy was suing for peace. Indeed, his nervousness may well have been increased, as Childs points out, by the fact that none of the trio at Lausanne came under his authority, but reported directly to Giolitti.[30]

Peace efforts were also being made through more formal channels. Sait Pasa had sent Poincare a four-point proposal for onward transmission to Italy. This though had been rejected out of hand by the Italians because it did not have, as its very basis, recognition of Italy's annexation of the North African *vilayet*.[31] In his memoirs Giolitti discusses a briefing letter he had received from Fusinato, in which he was informed that the Italians were convinced that Sait had no official instructions, but that they were also certain that the Ottoman government really desired peace and that Sait was there in good faith.

The stumbling block was of course the Ottoman reluctance to abandon a Muslim province and population to foreign domination, and the associated difficulties this would cause amongst the Ottoman people. On the other hand there was the Italian determination that nothing less would suffice. As Giolitti stated it: 'Italy demanded the recognition of our sovereignty by Turkey, and would not accept any formula that disregarded this.'[32] Efforts to get around this apparent impasse might have continued, but with the resignation of Sait Pasa on 16 July the talks were suspended.

That this was a temporary state of affairs was ascertained following two meetings between an employee of Volpi's, Bernardino Nagara, and Gabriel Effendi in Constantinople on 30 July. According to Giolitti's account, during the course of the first meeting Gabriel agreed to urge the Ottoman Council of Ministers to continue the negotiations and, by the time of the second held in the evening, had received assent to this. Two delegates would be sent to meet the Italian negotiators with fresh instructions, but in order not to inflame domestic opinion regarding the Tripoli *vilayet* Gabriel asked that Italy abstain from hostile military operations. Giolitti agreed to this in respect of the Aegean, but ordered that operations in Tripoli should be intensified in general and in Cyrenaica in particular. Advances in the latter would serve to 'remove the Turkish illusion that, because of the limited extent of our occupation there, Italy would eventually renounce [the annexation of] Cyrenaica.'[33] Later historians have confirmed that this statement is supported by contemporary evidence, though as Childs points out Giolitti was only prepared to concede a *temporary* cessation of hostilities outside the North African theatre.[34]

The two Ottoman delegates chosen by Gabriel were experienced diplomats of senior rank, Nabi Bey and Fahreddin Bey (Rumbeyoglu Fahr al-Din Bey), but they did not have plenipotentiary powers. Thus they would have to refer any agreement they might arrive at back to their government for approval.[35] Because of intensive interest, and thus intrusions, from journalists the negotiations were moved to the Grand Hotel at Caux-sur-Montreux, and both parties met there in secret on 12 August 1912 whilst reporters searched the vicinity for any sign of them.[36]

Because Giolitti and San Giuliano were prisoners of the jingo right and nationalist press, Italy could not shift position on absolute sovereignty for Italy over Tripoli even if they had wanted to. Benedetto Cirmeni, whilst contemporaneously complaining about the British acquisition of Sollum, put the matter succinctly in a Vienna newspaper:

> The only peace condition of Italy is the recognition of its complete and absolute sovereignty over the entire African *vilayet* [...] If this condition is not accepted, then Italy will continue the war, even if it were convinced that the continuation would bring the dissolution of Turkey in Europe.[37]

Giolitti's lack of room to manoeuvre translated into Italian intransigence, which in turn inevitably meant that the process of arriving at an agreement was to be tedious and long-drawn.

If progress in the diplomatic sphere was agonisingly slow, then something fundamentally indistinguishable might be said to apply to the military operations undertaken to 'disillusion' the enemy. Perhaps the first step taken towards a more aggressive policy was the replacement of the military commanders and the splitting of the theatre into two separate commands. Frugoni had been recalled in July 1912 and replaced with Lieutenant-General Ottavio Ragni. Caneva was recalled in early September, and following his departure his former command was divided; Ragni became Commander in Chief in Tripolitania whilst Lieutenant-General Ottavio Briccola held the same position in Cyrenaica. Neither of the recalled commanders was held to have been superseded for failure, and Giolitti explained the rationale behind the decision as being necessary because the war had entered a new phase, one requiring a combined military and police style of operation which 'demanded freedom of initiative and speed.'[38] Accordingly, the new commanders, who had control in both the military and civil spheres, had the 'implicit mandate' of reversing the ultra-cautious methods of Caneva and Frugoni.[39] In the tactical sphere this had, as has been noted, generally manifested itself in the use of ponderous movements in overwhelming force. Frugoni and Caneva were averse to exposing their forces to even the slightest risk, ensuring that they suffered no chance of even a minor defeat or reverse, and if they did then this was concealed by propaganda. According to the press release put out in Rome on 5 September announcing the promotion of Briccola and Ragni; 'they have been appointed to separate commands [...] with a view to pushing on operations in the interior.'[40]

Changes were made lower down the command structure as well, amongst them being the replacement of Major-General *conte* Trombi, whose tenure at Derna was not considered to have been creditable, with Major-General Ezio Reisoli in August. The Italian occupation of Derna had always been somewhat uncertain due to the extremely difficult ground to the south of the town and the precariousness of the water supply. The Ottoman forces surrounding them were also large in number, and were of course commanded ultimately by Enver, who reported that he had been promoted to the rank of lieutenant-colonel (*Oberstleutnant*) on 17 June.[41]

That the relative insecurity of Derna was unacceptable was made evident by it being the place chosen for the first manifestation of the new Italian policy of pushing on operations into the interior with initiative and speed. The garrison there had been depleted somewhat in order to provide troops for the expeditions to Rhodes and Misurata, but early in September it was reinforced by a number of units, many of which had recent battle experience. These included two battalions of *Alpini,* the *Mondovi* and *Fenestrelle,* the 43rd and 34th Infantry Regiments, and an *ascari* battalion. Also drafted was one of Italy's most experienced general officers, Tommaso Salsa, who had been occupying an administrative post in Tripoli City. Salsa had been involved in the campaign that terminated at Adua and had commanded the 1st Infantry Brigade during the international intervention in China during the Boxer War. He was put in charge of a mixed brigade consisting of the *Alpini* and *ascari* battalions.

On the morning of 14 September, before first light, Reisoli's command began to move. On the western side of the Wadi Derna a brigade-strength column of troops under Major General Luigi Capello debouched from the entrenchments near to the fortification known as the *ridotta Lombardia* (Lombardia Fort) and, extended into line, began spreading out to the west and north-west of this work towards the Wadi Bu Msafer supported by a heavy artillery bombardment. This movement had the effect of drawing enemy forces towards the slowly advancing troops, which was the intent behind it. Having advanced to draw the enemy's attention to the west of the town, the real operation began in the east about an hour afterwards. Two brigades, one under Major-General Francesco Del Buono and the other under Salsa, moved to the east and south east simultaneously. Salsa's command marched in column parallel to the shore until it reached the point where it was intersected by the Wadi Bent, then turned right and moved up the river bed until reaching Casa Aronne, a large white house that dominated the surrounding terrain.

Del Buono meanwhile had moved from the Italian lines slightly to the north-east of the *ridotta Piemonte* and advanced across the difficult ground to the south-south-west on the position known as Kasr Ras el Leben (Kasr el Leben), where the ruins of an old fortification were sited. Like that at Casa Aronne, this was on high ground that could dominate the local terrain, and both positions were therefore of some importance. By virtue of their manoeuvres the Italians had extended their forward line by some 4.5 kilometres and had, largely through the feint by Capello's brigade, achieved these objectives without loss or serious opposition. Work was immediately set in motion to consolidate these gains with the construction of strong entrenchments. Thus the left of the Italian position east of the Wadi Derna was held by Salsa's mixed brigade, with the centre, based on Kasr Ras el Leben, defended by Del Buono's infantry.

If Reisoli's intention was to bring about an offensive-defensive battle then he succeeded. On 17 September the Ottoman forces counter-attacked under the command of Enver and, as always, accounts of the subsequent battle are highly partisan in nature.[42] According to Enver's own account, dated 18 September, his intention was to 'break through the centre' of the Italian position. This, he claimed, had been achieved and the Italians were totally surprised; the attackers however were unable to fully exploit their success due to difficulties on the flanks of the attack. After fighting for sixteen hours, they withdrew, but, despite their numerical superiority, the Italians remained on the defensive. He concluded: 'Our artillery has proved to be excellent [and] it is a pity that the final outcome of the battle has not quite met my expectations.'[43] In his diary entry for 21 September however, beginning 'I will attempt to describe our last battle' he gives a fuller description of the action from his perspective:

At 5 o'clock, the appointed hour, the attack was announced on our right wing by brisk infantry and machine gun fire. The Italian artillery replied a few moments later with the utmost severity. Except for the flash of the guns firing we could see nothing, and had to follow the course of the battle from its confused sounds.

After a quarter of an hour it became relatively quiet, and I concluded that our troops had penetrated into the enemy positions. At first light our artillery opened fire on the small Italian fort opposite. To get a better view of the situation, I went further forward just as the sun rose above the horizon. In the centre everything was good, the Italian position had been pierced. On our right flank however our troops had been forced back into the Italian first line, which was already behind them. Two companies of the Guards with two machine guns brought the enemy counter-attack to a halt.[44] The left wing seemed endangered by the enemy forces; around midday however it pressed once more in a furious and dashing assault in order to gain a breathing space. [...] As I stood motionless and watched the comings and goings of the battle, I suddenly received from an Italian battery which had been fired upon our artillery, heavy shrapnel fire. [...]

On the right wing the enemy [counter-attacks] gained the upper hand [and] our men were forced to retire somewhat initially. But when I made a quick advance in the centre, which was joined in by the right wing, the enemy attacks immediately stopped. We also parried the attack on our left wing and our troops took up new positions there, without the enemy venturing to disturb them. […]

Towards evening we galloped to the right wing, pursued by a hailstorm of Italian shrapnel. Here the attackers had established themselves around 100 meters in front of the Italian positions, after having to give up the trenches following their initial capture. Their position was unfavourable, as they were not only shelled from the flank by an Italian armoured cruiser, but also threatened by Italian forces disembarked from the sea. I realized that any further attacks on this wing were no longer promising of success. Also a telephone call from the commander of the forces west of the Wadi Derna informed me that a large enemy formation, of about brigade strength, was concentrating in front of our right wing. I found myself therefore forced break off the struggle and commanded the attackers to break off and retreat as darkness fell taking along all the dead and wounded.

It was a bloody day; a new page was written in the history of this war. The outposts remained in touch with the enemy, who with his 24 battalions, four field and 6 mountain guns did not dare to interfere with our movements, and even today still does not show himself. If only such strength available to us!

Our artillery has stood up to artillery ten times as heavy and silenced a series of hostile batteries. Our casualties were 185 wounded and 98 dead. Unfortunately, these battles have no influence on the outcome of the war.[45]

Accounts of the battle appeared in the various newspapers of the European states, and, as has become tediously obvious, reflected the viewpoint of the writer. The Italian General Staff issued a report that, perhaps naturally, magnified the Italian contribution. This was reproduced by Tittoni:

The battle was composed of three distinct actions: a weak one early in the morning on our extreme left, in which the enemy was easily repulsed; the other two respectively heavy, at the head of the [Wadi] Bent in the morning, and again on our extreme left in the afternoon; but in the evening the enemy was defeated and left the field covered with dead and wounded.

On that memorable day the Arab-Turk forces, several thousand strong, with plenty of well-commanded artillery, conducted by Enver Bey, arrayed themselves against the solidity, calmness, and vigour of the counter-attacks of our troops, white and native, conducted by the conspicuous ability of our officers and guided by a clear conception of tactics, with harmonious and effectual opportune dispositions of troops.

Our losses of 10 officers and 174 men, dead and wounded, were small compared with those of the enemy, of whom 1,135 were found dead near our lines.[46]

By the time the encounter came to be written up by the pro-Italian correspondents it had turned into a total disaster for the Ottoman forces. McClure had it thus:

On the extreme left the Arabs advanced with splendid daring, but as they drew near they were staggered by an irresistible counter-attack from a battalion of *Alpini* and the Eritrean battalion. The Arabs broke and fled, pursued by a steady and pitiless fire, which dropped many of them before they could reach cover. […] By nine o'clock in the morning the battle was virtually over […][47]

It matters little whose version of events was the more accurate, and the battle, both in course and in result, differed hardly at all from any of the other small-scale encounters between the Italian army and the Ottoman forces that occurred during the conflict. However, if it is seen in the context of the 'new phase' of the war identified by Giolitti, the type that 'demanded freedom of initiative and speed,' and was a step towards 'pushing on operations in the interior' then it must be accounted as an Italian failure. Indeed, it is difficult to distinguish it from the style of operation pursued by Caneva and Frugoni. This point is reinforced when considering that further advances in early October around Derna meant that when Italy and the Ottoman Empire finally came to terms, the territory controlled by the Italian army there stretched along the coast some 6.5 kilometres and extended inland some 5 kilometres; a total area of about 30 square kilometres. If the example of Derna were used as a yardstick to compute how long it would take to occupy Cyrenaica, the answer would be a most unfeasibly long time. The point Enver made, that 'these battles have no influence on the outcome of the war,' was then undoubtedly correct.

The same held true in Tripolitania. The operations that took place in June against the area around Zanzur had failed to prevent Ottoman forces from operating there as the oasis itself had not been occupied. Therefore, and as part of the new forward policy, Ragni decided to mount an attack in order to rectify this, thus denying it to the enemy. The advance was to be made in overwhelming force in reinforced divisional strength, and was to take place on 20 September. The core of the force consisted of a Special Division (*Divisione special*). This comprised two brigades of infantry; one from the 1st Division under Major-General Michele Salazar and one from the 3rd Division under Major-General Massimo Tommasoni. This force was placed under the commander of the 3rd Division, Lieutenant-General *Conte* Felice de Chaurand. In support were four batteries of mountain guns, a battery of field guns, an engineer battalion, two squadrons of the Lodi cavalry, and an *ascari* battalion. There was also a reserve force under Major-General Giovanni Maggiotto consisting of the second brigade from the 1st Division supported by an engineer battalion and two field batteries. In addition, a flying, or mobile, column was assembled under the command of Major-General *Conte* Coardi di Carpeneto. Consisting of the 11th Regiment of *Bersaglieri* and squadrons of the Lodi Cavalry and Firenze Lancers it was to operate on the left flank of the advance.[48]

Lieutenant-General Ragni took tactical command on the day, the whole force amounting to nearly 12,000 infantry, 550 cavalry, and 34 artillery pieces. Naval support was also forthcoming if necessary. Subterfuge had been employed; announcements to the effect that the troops had been concentrated to hold a parade were made. Credence was lent to this by the fact that 20 September was the anniversary of the fall of Rome to the Italian army. Whether anyone was taken in by this seems doubtful, and in any event when the whole force moved off on the morning of the anniversary it was met with attacks from the desert on its left flank. If, as with Reisoli's tactic at Derna, Ragni's preferred option was to fight an offensive-defensive battle, then he was disappointed.

It is not proposed to enumerate the details of this battle, in which the Ottoman forces eventually came to number about 7,000. Suffice to say that at that at the end of the day's fighting, which was dubbed the Battle of Sidi Balil, the Italians had managed to entrench themselves in and around the Zanzur Oasis and hold onto the ground they had won, albeit after suffering over 500 casualties. These included 115 officers and men killed, including the commander of the Lodi Cavalry Major Giuseppe De Dominicis, and 431 wounded. The Ottoman casualties, as estimated by the Italians, were reckoned to have been over 2,000. The Italian advance had also been marked by errors, inasmuch as the two regiments of Salazar's brigade lost touch with each other and risked having to fight in isolation.

The Italians could however award themselves a victory, though, as in Cyrenaica, if this was evidence of the 'new phase' of warfare then it was exceedingly difficult to discern any substantial difference between it and the previous version. One may perhaps quote Francis McCullagh, who wrote in the introduction of his 1913 book that: 'A glance at the map of Tripolitania will show that, at their present rate of progress, the Italians will take about fifty years to get to Gharian [the main Ottoman base, some 80 kilometres to the south].'[49] Fortunately, for the Italians, at least they did not have to wait until 1963 to get the Ottoman Empire to agree terms.

The site of the negotiations had moved on 3 September from Caux-sur-Montreux to the Beau Rivage Palace Hotel at Ouchy, south of Lausanne, on the shore of Lake Geneva, due to the prospect of better weather.[50] This had no effect on progress or the lack thereof, but if they were moving at an agonisingly slow pace they were nevertheless advancing more rapidly than the Italian military. The crux of the problem revolved around Gabriel's desire to avoid a humiliating peace. Conversely, it was politically necessary for Giolitti to inflict one, or at least be in a position to tell Italian 'public opinion' that he had. Whilst it is not proposed to enter into a detailed study of the peace talks (and anyone interested in the definitive account should consult Chapters IX and X of Timothy W Childs excellent work – see Bibliography) it was largely in the area of perception that the necessary 'wriggle room' was found.

Gabriel, and the Ottoman government in general, was also under pressure from the Balkan situation; respected newspapers were captioning their articles on the region with headlines such as 'The War Cloud' and 'The Balkan Peril' during September and the hugely respected London *Times* carried authoritative reports of Ottoman excesses against innocent Christians.[51] Whether the latter reports were entirely accurate (Childs makes the pertinent point that Christians in the Ottoman Balkans were always considered 'innocent' by most Europeans no matter how far from the truth this was) is largely irrelevant.[52] What mattered was they were believed, and were merely symptomatic of the inflamed situation in the region.

Whilst the build-up of tension in the Balkans gave an incentive to Gabriel and the Ottoman government to come to terms, it was also a worry to Giolitti. Should the Italian conflict with the Empire become intertwined with a Balkan conflict, then it was entirely possible that the Great Powers would intervene and propose some means of settling the outstanding issues by negotiation. Such an eventuality could easily lead to Italy getting less than she wanted in respect of Tripoli, which would likely have been the end of the Giolitti government. Accordingly, from the Italian Prime Minister's perspective, the process had to be terminated in a satisfactory manner as quickly as possible. On 2 October he authorised the negotiators at Ouchy to deliver an ultimatum to the effect that if at least a preliminary treaty had not been signed within eight days, then the negotiations would be suspended.

The same thought about a Great Power intervention settling the war with Italy had naturally enough also occurred to Gabriel. Indeed, the Ottoman ambassador in London,

Ahmet Tevfik Pasa, had urged just such a course on him on 29 September.[53] Gabriel declined to pursue the matter, and on the same date that Giolitti issued the ultimatum, he decided that the war had to be brought to a close. It is undoubtedly the case that Gabriel was right to ignore Tevfik's advice, because it soon became clear that the peace that the Great Powers sought basically involved the Ottoman Empire conceding on Italy's terms. That this was so became clearly evident when the negotiations stalled yet again on 12 October. Giolitti immediately notified the Great Powers that the Ottoman government was prevaricating, and that the talks were in danger of collapse. This caused a flurry of diplomatic activity, with Herbert Dering, the British chargé d'affaires at Rome, telegraphing Sir Edward Grey that he had been informed by the Italian Ambassador that the Ottoman delegation had withdrawn from the negotiations and that Italy might, using her navy, broaden the conflict.[54] A cable from Paris to the *New York Tribune*, dated 12 October, outlined the situation rather well, albeit from a somewhat pro-Italian perspective:

> The threatened rupture of the negotiations between the Italian and Turkish representatives at Ouchy has occupied the diplomats of Europe today almost to the exclusion of the Balkan Imbroglio. The powers have concentrated their efforts to prevent Turkey from placing in the hands of the Balkan federation such a trump card as would be the failure of the *pourparlers*, which have been a large factor in causing the hesitation of Bulgaria, Greece and Servia to declare war.

> It is pointed out that while Italy is still fighting the Mussulmans the position of the Balkan States is so enormously strengthened that the powers feel that nothing could restrain them. But with Turkey free from the Italian danger an entirely new perspective is created. The Greek fleet then would be practically put out of action, and large contingents of the Greek army would be tied up guarding the coasts, while Turkey would be able, without restriction, to move hordes of her finest fighting men from Asia Minor against the Balkan invaders.

> Italy, in granting a fresh delay in the peace settlement, is seconding the efforts of the powers. The Italian Ambassador, Signor Tittoni, had no fewer than three conferences today with M. Poincare, the French Premier. Italy's desire for peace is explained on the ground that she fears complications might follow an attack by her on a port in European waters, or in the vicinity of those waters.[55]

The non-mention of Montenegro amongst the Balkan states that were 'hesitating' to declare war is accounted for by the fact that Montenegro had already declared war on the Ottoman Empire on 8 October; the first shot of the war being fired the next day.[56] It had become very clear to Gabriel, as to all other European politicians, that war in the Balkans was imminent and that peace with Italy must be secured. Accordingly on 14 October he gave his team at Ouchy instructions to settle, though to attempt to extract some last minute compromises from the Italians.[57] These were unsuccessful.

Peace between the Ottoman Empire and Italy came via two separate, though intimately related, treaties. The first, signed on 15 October 1912, was a preliminary, and secret, treaty that established a sequence of events. Under Article 1, the Ottoman government, in the name of the Sultan, would within three days issue an imperial command (*ferman*) addressed to the populations of Cyrenaica and Tripolitania. A draft of this edict was attached, and it basically granted autonomy to the *vilayet*, though the Sultan would nominate a representative to safeguard Ottoman interests in the country. These would essentially consist of maintaining and adjudicating the *sharia* amongst the Islamic population. The identity of this representative, and other religious leaders, 'must be agreed to in advance' by the Italian government.

The Italian government agreed under Article III that, after a delay of no more than three days following the issuing of the Sultan's command, it would issue a Royal Decree. Again the draft text of this was attached, and the crucial sentence as far as the Italians were concerned, and one that had proved an obstacle in the negotiations, was the opening line after the preamble. It read: 'In view of the Law of 25 February 1912 […] with which Tripolitania and Cyrenaica were placed under the full and entire Sovereignty of the Kingdom of Italy […].' Article 1 of this decree stipulated that a 'full and entire amnesty' was granted to the inhabitants who had participated in the hostilities, and that individuals detained or deported 'will immediately be liberated.' Religious freedom was also granted to the population, and the Sultan's representative recognised as 'safe-guarding the interests of the Ottoman State and of Ottoman subjects.'

Article IV concerned Rhodes and the other islands occupied by Italy. The Ottoman government agreed, no more than three days after issuing the imperial command referred to in Article 1, to issue a decree granting 'administrative and judicial reforms' to the 'inhabitants of Islands of the Aegean Sea' so that they would have 'equal enjoyment of justice, security, and well being, without distinction of cult or religion.' An amnesty was also granted to those inhabitants who had sided with the Italians, worded in almost exactly the same terms as was granted to those in Article III.

The Ottoman edicts under the treaty were promulgated on 18 October as agreed, and the delegates then moved to sign the public treaty of peace at 15:45 hours that afternoon. Under Article 1, the two governments agreed to 'take the necessary dispositions for the immediate and simultaneous cessation of hostilities' and to despatch 'Special Commissioners' to ensure that this occurred. Article 2 specified that the two governments would, 'immediately after the signature of the present Treaty,' order the return of their armed forces and civil functionaries from, in the Ottoman case, Tripolitania and Cyrenaica, and, in the Italian, of 'the islands it has occupied in the Aegean Sea.' There was however an apparently minor caveat to this; the 'effective evacuation' of the islands would only take place *after* the removal of Ottoman personnel from North Africa. The next two articles dealt with the return of prisoners of war and hostages and reiterated the terms of amnesty as set out in the Secret Treaty, whilst Article 5 stated that the various treaties and agreements that had applied between the two states prior to the outbreak of hostilities were reinstated as if there had been no war. The remaining six articles related to commercial and other matters, though under Article 10 Italy agreed to pay an annual 'annuity' to the Ottoman Empire that 'cannot be less than two million Italian Lire.'[58] When the representatives of both sides signed the Treaty it was deemed to have come into force, and the Italo-Ottoman War was formally over.

CHAPTER FOURTEEN

Peace?

'*Know that the great Italy, after having conquered your mother Tripoli, has become your father.*'
Italian proclamation to the Arabs [1]

Take up the white man's burden – The savage wars of peace.
Rudyard Kipling, *The White Man's Burden: A Poem*, 1899 [2]

*According to European international law, Libya is now under the undisputed and entire
sovereignty of Italy. On the other hand, the firman of the Sultan agreed to at Ouchy,
and the subsequent Royal Decree of 17 October 1912, have gravely hampered the entire exercise
and led the native population to consider that they are jointly governed in an Italian-Turkish
condominium. […] It is clear that the state of affairs created by the arrangements between Italy
and Turkey creates uncertainty concerning our governing of Libya.*
Aldobrandino Malvezzi, *L'Italia e L'Islam in Libia*, 1913 [3]

I T is doubtful if the news of the peace agreed at Ouchy gave much cause for concern
to the Ottoman government and peoples; they had much greater matters to grapple
with. What became known as The First Balkan War had effectively begun on 8 October
1912 with the Montenegrin attack on Ottoman positions at Podgoritza. It became
general following the demand by the Balkan League that the European *vilayets* be granted
autonomy and divided according to nationality on 13 October. This was followed the
next day by the Greek government signalling that the union of Crete with Greece was
imminent. In response to these 'provocations' the Ottomans declared war on 17 October
and the Balkan League responded by beginning military action the following day.[4]
The League also had a naval arm, courtesy of the Greek Navy, and of course Greece had
a separate agenda of its own. This quickly manifested itself when the Hellenic fleet was
dispatched to the Aegean and began landing on the Ottoman islands that had not been
occupied by Italy. Eleven of them were taken by the end of November; Lemnos
(21 October), Imbros (31 October), Thasos (31 October), Samothrace (1 November),
Psara (4 November), Tenedos (7 November), Nikaria (17 November), Mytilene
(21 November), Chios (24 November), Samos (24 November), and Agios Efstratios
(24 November).[5] Once again, the Ottoman Navy did not seek to contest matters, not
even leaving the Dardanelles until December. To be fair however it did deploy into the
Sea of Marmara and the Black Sea, supporting the successful defence mounted by the
army at Catalca and harassing the Bulgarian coast.[6]

The Ottoman military plan in the case of a concerted attack by the states of the Balkan League was relatively simple; to defend from prepared positions and await reinforcements. It failed comprehensively and the army was routed, retreating in disorder to strong fortified lines at Çatalca, which extended from the Black Sea to the Sea of Marmara but were only some thirty kilometres to the west of Constantinople. Thus virtually all of the European portions of the Empire were overrun. These areas, which included some of the most developed and economically profitable *vilayets*, had been Ottoman territory for over five hundred years and contained over four million inhabitants or about 16 per cent of the population of the Empire. There was massive suffering amongst the civil population as the 'innocent' Christians turned on their neighbours:

> […] the Moslem population endured during the early weeks of the war a period of lawless vengeance and unmeasured suffering. In many districts the Moslem villages were systematically burned by their Christian neighbours. […] In the province of Monastir, occupied by the Serbs and Greeks, the agents of the (British) Macedonian Relief Fund calculated that eighty per cent of Moslem villages were burned. Salonica, Monastir, and Uskub were thronged with thousands of homeless and starving Moslem refugees, many of whom emigrated to Asia.[7]

The arrival of these emigrant refugees produced, according to Arnold J Toynbee, 'an unexampled tension of feeling in Anatolia and a desire for revenge.'[8] Indeed, the cycle was to be repeated when some of the lost Ottoman territory was subsequently regained. Powerful forces had been unleashed, and to quote Richard C Hall: 'The Balkan Peninsula was aflame, a conflagration that would rage for the next six years.'[9] There were other implications for the future; the CUP openly stated that they would never have countenanced peace with Italy.[10] They were of course in opposition in October 1912, but that would change.

The Great Powers were also deeply concerned over the Balkan situation, but nevertheless took the step of recognising Italian sovereignty over the North African former *vilayet*; both Britain and France soon followed the example of Austria-Hungary, Germany and Russia. Whilst Italian occupation of Tripoli was of little or no consequence in terms of the 'Balance of Power' between the Great Power groupings, the Italian acquisition of the islands, even if ostensibly at least this was only on a temporarily basis, had major implications. Whilst it would be untrue to assert that neither Austria-Hungary nor Germany had any interests in the Mediterranean area, it was undoubtedly the case that they were relatively weak there in the naval context. On the other hand the French and British fleets exercised almost complete control of the Mediterranean. This was achieved by the deployment of significant naval assets, which together with the necessary bases to support them and the fact that the two states acted in concert guaranteed superiority. That there was effective liaison was exemplified by the withdrawal of British forces to northern waters to face the growing strength of Germany's High Seas Fleet, and their replacement by French squadrons. Newspapers in September and October 1912 carried reports of the French Government transferring a third battle squadron from Brest to the Mediterranean 'with the scarcely concealed intention of carrying out an understanding with Great Britain that the North Sea should be left to the care of that power.'[11]

This reallocation of resources and division of responsibility made little difference to the naval balance in the Mediterranean, which remained overwhelmingly on the side of

The Boiling Point. This cartoon, taken from the 2 October 1912 edition of the British magazine Punch, depicts figures representing Russia, Britain, Germany, and Austria-Hungary attempting to prevent the pot containing the 'Balkan Troubles' from boiling over. The Italian figure looks on having, in contemporaneous opinion, materially contributed to the turbulence within by initiating war with the Ottoman Empire the previous year. When the pot did boil over the Ottomans lost most of their European territory to members of that ad hoc formation, the Balkan League. (Author's Collection).

THE BOILING POINT.

Britain and France. Indeed, the British navy still intended to deploy significant force there including, from the end of October 1912, the eight pre-Dreadnoughts of the 'King Edward' class and, from July 1913, four battle-cruisers.[12] When combined with virtually all the heavy units of the French Navy, *Entente* superiority was overwhelming. Even a combined Italian and Austro-Hungarian fleet would have struggled to prevail. This of course also meant that, in terms of the recently acquired territories at least, Italian interests would probably be best served by remaining friendly with Britain and France. If this were taken to its logical conclusion by an Italian Government, then a realignment of Italian foreign policy was implied at some point. That though was for the future, and the most immediate effect of the treaty was on the Italian domestic scene.

Italian 'public opinion,' as expressed through the various press organs, took a generally favourable view of the outcome. The *Corriere della Sera* ran an editorial arguing that the struggle had succeeded in restoring Italian pride and confirming its position amongst the Great Powers.

> We wished to confirm to ourselves, and have Europe attest to, our national progress, to our energy and the great revival of our power, and to have full consciousness of our place in the world and our strength and ability to enforce it.[13]

There were however dissenting voices. In his memoirs, Giolitti characterised some amongst these as being 'humanitarians' who wished Italy to undertake a 'crusade' against the Ottoman Empire in order to liberate all the oppressed peoples, with particular emphasis on those who were Christian. There were also the nationalists of the jingo-right. They were disappointed that the war had been terminated with a negotiated peace and had wanted an all-out struggle with no holds barred. This would have involved attacking the Ottomans at vital points, including those in the Aegean and on the European and Anatolian mainland, ignoring all international complications that might have arisen. They also criticised the inaction of the army in North Africa, arguing that it should have advanced inland and conducted military operations 'with greater speed and energy.' This viewpoint, of course, ignored the realities pertaining on the ground. Giolitti also made the point that conducting operations in Europe or Asia Minor would have resulted in a great loss of life, and argued that whilst such considerations might be ignored in a struggle for national survival it was a 'strict duty' to avoid bloodshed in a colonial war.[14] The nationalists also disapproved of the government's willingness to evacuate the Aegean islands. If, in their somewhat febrile imagination, the venture in North Africa offered a modern parallel to Roman imperialism, then Italian conquests in the Eastern Mediterranean and Aegean demonstrated an analogous resurgence of the Venetian Empire.[15] Other aspects of the treaty also caused some concern, one being the payment of an indemnity; victors did not indemnify those they had vanquished.[16]

Whilst much of the criticism can be discounted, there is no doubt that the Treaty of Ouchy, or of Lausanne as it was also known, was somewhat ambiguous. It was, as the modern Italian historian Mariano Gabriele has noted, 'rather strange and full of implications.'[17] Other contemporary scholars have tended to agree that the treaty had major flaws. Mario Montanari has written that the government wholly underestimated the importance to the inhabitants of Tripoli of the Sultan's official representative (Naib es-Sultan) and the judges (Cadi) who were to oversee the sharia. He notes that the intimate linkage between political and religious authorities and civil and religious law inherent in Islamic societies, completely escaped them and quotes approvingly the observation that 'history probably does not record another example of a treaty discussed and concluded with such complete ignorance of the opponent's institutions.'[18] Indeed, under its terms as published, both Italy and the Ottoman Empire were 'two states which appear, at the same time, to be sovereign over the territory and people of Libya.'[19] Giolitti simply ignored such matters when, on 26 November 1912, he presented the treaty to those assembled for the reopening of the Chamber of Deputies. His references to Italian successes and the 'happy conclusion' of peace was greeted with 'great cheering,' and when he read out the various protocols he emphasised 'the complete recognition by Turkey of Italian sovereignty [over] Libya.'[20] Under the Italian constitution the treaty had to be approved by parliament because it involved financial responsibilities, and to this end a committee of deputies was appointed by the Speaker to examine it. When the matter of sovereignty was submitted for parliamentary approval 431 of 470 Deputies voted in favour, whilst it passed through the senate unanimously.[21]

The costs incurred by Italy during the war are not easy to reckon. The casualty figures for the Italian Army vary dependant on source and the way they are calculated, but generally a figure of about 10,000 killed and wounded is usually accepted. It is probably about right, though almost certainly on the low side. The reports of the General Staff produced more or less contemporaneously give the figure for September 1911-January 1912 as 1,432 killed and 4,220 wounded in combat operations, plus 1,948 that died of disease. From January-October 1912 a total of 4,292 dead and wounded were recorded. These total to 11,892 for all casualties from all causes, but do not seem to include prisoners. Taking everything into account, it is likely that about 4,000 Italians died during the period of the conflict and about 8,000 were wounded.[22] Such low casualty figures for just over a year of war demonstrate what had become apparent as the conflict went on; the Italian Army had not engaged in heavy fighting. Conversely, if the price of victory had been relatively cheap in terms of blood then the same could not be said of treasure. It was calculated in January 1914 that the total cost of the acquisition of the former *vilayet* amounted to 957,000,000 francs, or £38,260,000. The army accounted for the greater portion of this, £31,440,000, whilst naval costs amounted to a figure of £4,840,000 at the time.[23] Indeed, as has already been pointed out, in the financial year 1912-13 the adventure was reckoned to have absorbed nearly 47 per cent of total state expenditure.[24] This precipitated an economic crisis which sent the cost of foodstuffs, unemployment, and poverty levels, rocketing. There was a political uproar when the costs of the war thus far were revealed in November 1913 by Finance Minister Luigi Facta; parliament had been kept in the dark by Gioitti's government concerning the enormous financial costs.[25] Indeed, it had not proved cheap, in any sense of the word, for Giolitti and San Giuliano to extricate their donkey from the tip of the Tripoli minaret.

The terms of the Treaty of Ouchy were by no means welcomed by those peoples who found themselves involuntarily bound up with them. Without a doubt the inhabitants of the Aegean Islands occupied by Italy, or the 'Autonomous state of the Dodecanese' as they had proclaimed themselves, were in a somewhat invidious situation. Dr. Skevos Zervos put the matter succinctly:

> Italy [...] undertook in a special article to restore the Twelve Islands to the Ottoman tyranny. Stirred by the report of this unholy compact, the Dodecanesians held mass meetings and national congresses, and, by universal resolutions addressed to the European Governments, reasserted their immemorial desire, their single and unalterable determination [for union with the Greek State].[26]

To add to their discomfiture, upon the outbreak of the Balkan War in October 1912 the Greek navy had almost immediately taken possession of many of the other Aegean islands:

> Thus the Balkan Wars [...] found the Dodecanese diplomatically a Turkish province, but *de facto* under the power of Italy, who continued to hold it provisionally until the execution of the terms of the treaty by the Porte. For this reason the Hellenic Fleet, which within a few hours of the commencement of the Helleno-Turkish hostilities had freed all the great sister islands and close neighbours of the Dodecanese [...] was unable to act as the liberator of the Dodecanesians because they were still in Italian hands.[27]

The frustration felt by the Dodecanesians, who had welcomed the Italians as liberators, must have been excruciating. Had the Italians not invaded in May then Greece undoubtedly would have in October, and their 'immemorial desire' would have been satisfied. In order to try to influence the Italians and other Great Powers, plebiscites were held between December 1912 and February 1913 on all of the islands occupied by Italy. The results of these were sent to the Italian, Greek and British governments, together with pleas for assistance. One of the shorter addresses, from the inhabitants of Kalymnos, may serve to give the flavour of these resolutions:

> The people of the Island of Calymnos [...] are in great anxiety because – owing to the temporary Italian occupation of their island – they cannot participate in the struggle [against the Ottoman Empire] in this island, held a mass meeting this Sunday, February 3rd, 1913, in the premises of the Holy Church of Christ, and have decided the following:

1. They proclaim the union of their most Greek island with the motherland Greece.

2. They declare their unswerving decision that they will not accept any other settlement of the fate of the island. They are ready in the contrary case to follow the brilliant example of their sister island Crete.

3. They solicit the favour of all the great Powers for the realization of their national establishment.

[Follow the signatures of the people.]

The Holy Metropolis and the Town Council confirm the contents of the above resolution.[28]

This was not though an age when the democratically expressed wishes of a people were reckoned of much, if any, importance, and the desires of the islanders were ignored. They did perhaps have one crumb of comfort inasmuch as it soon became apparent that the Dodecanese would not be handed back to the Ottoman Empire. That the Italians would keep them became more and more evident as the months passed; 'within a year of their occupation […] they [the Italians] had introduced martial law, prohibited assemblies, forbidden the display of the national symbols of Greece, meddled in the affairs of the local Orthodox Church and deported some of the most vocal champions of *enosis* [union with Greece].'[29] The Italian justification for this change of policy and apparent breach of the terms of the Treaty of Ouchy related to the precise wording and meaning of the relevant article. This had specified that the withdrawal from the Dodecanese would only take place following the removal of Ottoman personnel from North Africa, and, the Italians argued, this had not taken place. It must be conceded that, in this at least, they had a point.

It was of course the peoples of the former Tripoli *vilayet* that had the most to lose, or gain, from the settlement. The reactions of these peoples, as well as the Ottoman officers and regular forces that led their resistance, differed somewhat between Tripolitania and Cyrenaica. In the former area reports that the Italians and the Ottomans had come to terms at Ouchy arrived, in Angelo del Boca's words 'like a bolt out of the blue.' He quotes one of the tribal leaders as stating that the news caused 'alarm and confusion among the rank and file of the *mujahedeen* formations' and further split the already fragile unity of the resistance.[30] Upon learning of the peace treaty, Nesat Bey withdrew the Ottoman regulars, estimated to number some 2,600, southwards away from the Italian lines, and the Arab and Berber irregulars felt they were being more or less left to fend for themselves. They had not been totally abandoned however. Before he left with his command on 8 December 1912, aboard ships provided by Italy, the Ottoman commander addressed them and, according to an Italian source, informed them that:

A peace treaty has been signed: the Turkish government can no longer provide any official aid to you for your continuation of the war, but there is someone who can: the Committee for Union and Progress. I can make available to you the victuals that have already been ordered and 20,000 Turkish liras; other sums will be sent to you from the committees of Tunis and Egypt. I cannot give you munitions, but I can let you take them, likewise with rifles, and I will report that you simply carried them off.[31]

In order to decide what their course of action might be, the tribal leaders met at Kasr Azizia. There is no doubt that the withdrawal of the Ottoman commander and his troops, and the removal of the administrative and logistical structure they had created and fostered, inflicted a devastating blow to the Arab resistance movement, and they could not reach agreement on what to do and split along tribal and regional lines. According to the memoirs of Mohamed Fekini, who was later to become the most notable and effective leader of the resistance to Italian occupation in Tripolitania, the chiefs from the coastal region and its hinterland were in favour of coming to terms with the Italians. On the other hand, those from further inland were more inclined to continue the struggle using Kasr Azizia as their base of operations. The Ottoman deputy, or former deputy as he now was, Sulyman al-Baruni (Sulaiman al-Barouni) was one of the most fervent supporters of continuing to resist the Italians. He argued that the Ottoman government was almost bound to continue sustaining them in one way or another and that they would have the support of the Islamic world. He also advocated continuing the fight for its moral effects, and, more prosaically, because they might then get more concessions from Italy were they forced to come to terms. His motives were not purely derived from hatred of the Italians or solidarity with his fellow resistance fighters. Sulyman al-Baruni was a Berber, and his political goal was to set up a Berber territory within the framework of Tripolitania. This had been resisted by Ottoman governments over the years, particularly since the advent of the CUP who sought to suppress such ideas and followed a policy of amalgamation. With their departure from Tripolitania he saw an opportunity with the potential at least to realise his ambition.[32]

Given his later status it is perhaps ironic to note that it was Mohamed Fekini who was amongst the most vociferous in arguing against the general thrust of Sulyman's position. He made the point that the vast majority of the inhabitants of Tripolitania were living a hand-to-mouth existence, were largely without weapons, and could not hope to defeat Italy given that the Ottoman Empire, with all its resources, had failed to do so. This analysis was also in accord with the viewpoint expressed by al-Baruni's fellow former Ottoman parliamentarian, Farhat al-Zawi.[33] These arguments were rejected or ignored by el-Baruni, who also managed to take possession of the munitions, food, and money left behind by Nesat Bey and withdrew southwards to the mountains. He claimed that he was in possession of a secret order from the Ottoman Sultan appointing him the leader of the forces charged with continuing the *jihad* against the invaders. He issued proclamations to this effect in the expectation that the tribes would follow him in to the renewed conflict. This response was, in the opinion of Mohamed Fekini and others, premature. He issued an appeal urging caution, arguing that it would be sensible to discover what the Italians intended before coming to any final decisions. Fekini believed at this point that there was a chance of some autonomy for the Tripolitanian peoples similar to that which he believed pertained in Tunisia and Egypt. Even given that the 'autonomy' that France and Britain accorded to Tunisia and Egypt had far more form than substance, it is clear that Fekini was somewhat over optimistic in this regard. Having said that, both of the countries he looked to as potential models were, albeit, nominally still under the sovereignty of the Ottoman Sultan. As has been repeatedly noted, Italy had continually and specifically rejected any settlement of the conflict on anything even approaching similar terms, though had eventually accepted a settlement that could be interpreted as so doing. It depended of course on whose interpretation could be made to stick.

On the other hand, if Mohamed Fekini was responsible for over-optimism, or in retrospect even naivety, then the same charge may certainly be made in respect of

Sulyman al-Baruni. Described even by Fekini as standing head and shoulders above all the other chiefs, he took the autonomy granted by the Sultan at face value. He proclaimed an independent mini-state in the mountains of the Gharyan region, a predominantly Berber populated area, around 100 kilometres to the south of Tripoli. His words on the matter are quoted by Del Boca:

> His Majesty the Sultan granted to the inhabitants of Tripolitania complete and entire self-government, we have decided to maintain that autonomy in accord with the inhabitants, who have invited me to accept the presidency of the government. Many requests in writing and signed by the people were presented to me for that purpose, and I accepted, and hastened to telegraph the news to the Great Powers and the most respected newspapers. [...] I formed a regiment of soldiers, consisting of infantry and cavalry on horseback and camels, uniformed in the European style. I organized a mail system over the entire territory. Telegraph and telephone offices were instituted that extended to the border of Tunisia. I established a war zone in front of the Italian forces.[34]

Such developments were of course deeply unwelcome to the occupiers. This was particularly so given their long standing belief that it was only the presence of Ottoman forces and their logistical arrangements that had prevented the tribes conceding Italian dominance. The Italian strategy of coming to terms with the Ottoman Empire in order to remove its forces from the theatre had developed from this, and it appeared, on the face of it, to be working. Following the withdrawal from combat and eventual departure of the Ottoman forces under Nesat Bey, General Ottavio Ragni had begun successfully extending the area of occupation. The three former Ottoman strongholds of Suani Ben Adem, el-Azizia, and Funduq Ben Ghashir were occupied without major effort. For the majority of the Tripolitanian tribes the motivation for fighting had been to preserve their way of life, on which the Ottomans had hardly impinged; they were at that time 'unencumbered by any sense of nationhood.'[35]

With some misgivings, the majority of the tribal leaders from the regions in the coastal hinterland and the northern areas of the mountains to the south decided to go, or send emissaries, to Tripoli City. Some 6,000 irregulars accompanied this delegation, and somewhat unexpectedly they were welcomed and treated with honour though required to surrender their arms. A measure of the distrust felt by the tribes is perhaps indicated by the fact that only some 800 weapons were handed over, and fewer than 500 of these were modern and suitable for combat. Nevertheless, whilst undoubtedly worried by this, General Ragni expressed his friendship for the various leaders and confirmed that Italy was determined on a path of reconciliation. To this end, the Italian government was prepared to invest significant funds in the region, and was happy to answer all the questions that the tribesmen might care to put. Indeed, at this time the Italian administration appeared happy to leave the tribesmen much to their own devices, and Fekini noted that whilst the position of *mutasarrif* (governor of a district) that he had held under Ottoman rule was no longer recognised, he was held to be a *kaymakam* (sub-governor or communal leader). By virtue of this rank he was able to appoint judges and teachers in his area of responsibility, and ensure adherence to Islamic sharia law throughout his jurisdiction.[36]

From the Italian perspective then, the first few weeks following the signing of the Treaty of Ouchy boded tolerably well in Tripolitania. The Italian regime in Tripoli City and the majority of the tribal peoples within easy reach of the seat of government had reached an accommodation of sorts, albeit with a great deal of mutual suspicion. Moreover, the Ottoman forces had been removed from the theatre. This latter success formed the culminating point of Italian initial operational strategy, and led to the fracture of whatever solidarity the Tripolitanian population had previously displayed. This was of course a phenomenon that could hardly be to Italy's disadvantage in future.

From the initial viewpoint of the tribal peoples, the outlook also appeared reasonable. Those tribes that had decided to attempt an accommodation with the Italians had been courteously received and no particularly onerous conditions had been imposed upon them. Those that had no wish to come to terms with Italy were reasonably free from interference in the interior. Even the statelet proclaimed by Sulyman al-Baruni, which continued to not only proclaim war on the Italian invaders but also began attacking areas where the leaders were in favour of compromise with them, was ostensibly tolerated. Indeed, a two-man delegation sent to Rome by al-Baruni was cordially greeted by Pietro Bertolini, head of the newly constituted Colonial Ministry, and their requests for an autonomous relationship with Italy were seemingly well received. In reality however, the Italian military in Tripoli was merely biding its time before moving against him. Ragni informed Bertolini on 19 January 1913 that 'al-Baruni was truly a megalomaniac, not a man of war' and that 'only in his imagination' does he believe that he could be Emir of the polity he had created.[37] This view was entirely in accordance with the wishes of Giolitti in Rome, who upbraided Bertolini on 23 March 1913 for giving al-Baruni's ideas any consideration whatsoever, and arguing that only 'vigorous action' would convince him of the futility of his goal.[38] Indeed, this vigorous action had already begun by the time Bertolini received Giolitti's missive, for on the day that he wrote it a divisional-strength force won a substantial victory as it moved to assert Italian control.

Consisting of the 1st Brigade under Major General Domenico Mazzoli (23rd and 82nd Regiments), the Mixed Brigade under Major General Luca Montuori (the 11th *Bersaglieri*, 8th *Alpino*, and a battalion of the 52nd Infantry), and supported by a battalion of Eritrean *ascari* plus camel-transported artillery, engineers and cavalry, this powerful force consisting of 259 officers and 8,014 troops, was commanded by Major-General Clemente Lequio. Since there were now no regular Ottoman forces in the theatre there was little to oppose them, and on 23 March the Battle of Assaba (Asàbaa, also Asabaa-Rabta) saw Sulyman al-Baruni's force routed. The autonomy of his 'tiny alpine state' lasted a mere five months.[39] Lequio's force moved further inland and on 27 April a small detachment of about 530 colonial troops, mainly recruited from around Tripoli, under the command of Captain Alessandro Pavoni arrived at Ghadames. En route he had received a welcome from the leaders of many of the local tribes, which led the Italians to the conclusion that they had submitted their rule.[40] This belief was bolstered when several of the Tuareg leaders visited him there and likewise acquiesced in accepting Italian rule.[41] However, if, from the Italian point of view, the situation in Tripolitania seemed relatively favourable then the same could not be said in respect of Cyrenaica. There, the Italo-Ottoman War morphed into what came to be called the First Italo-Senussi War, and, as an appreciation by the British Foreign Office put it, 'the peace was merely nominal.'[42]

Enver's diary entry for 22 October 1912, quoting a 'letter to a friend,' says that on the previous day he had received a message from the Italian commander informing him that the two sides were now at peace. Further, during the night of 21-22 October he 'received a telegram from the War Minister, which ordered me to cease hostilities, as His Majesty the Sultan had signed the peace treaty. You can imagine my thoughts.' Indeed in the same missive Enver raged that he and his fellow Ottoman soldiers have 'done our duty in vain, and the new government has destroyed everything again. A shameful peace, and further war with an uncertain end. This is the final result!' However, despite both his knowledge of the 'shameful' peace and the orders from his superiors in Istanbul Enver nevertheless determined on continuing to fight the Italians. His verdict was perhaps spurred on by the similar decision made by the Senussi leader and communicated to him on the same date as he wrote to his unknown friend. Indeed, despite arriving at the decision to continue fighting Enver found himself suffering from 'an unspeakable inner dilemma.' In his own words: 'I cannot abandon this land, but on the other hand I cannot let down my homeland which urgently needs me.'[43] Orders from the Ottoman capital reached him on 25 October summoning him home, but despite this direct command he seems to have hesitated. On the other hand news of the disasters visited upon the Ottoman Empire in the Balkans was also reaching him and his understanding of the dire situation there was reinforced on 30 October. He records that on that date, and perhaps with a view to unsettling him, 'the Italians now had the kindness to send me recent newspapers.' He concluded after perusing them that 'the situation in Rumelia seems to be very serious for us.' Having weighed up the matter, Enver determined that the crisis in the Balkans was of such magnitude that he was bound to travel home to attempt to ease it:

It is increasingly disgraceful and intolerable to be a powerless spectator able merely to watch the deteriorating situation. Despite my wishes and all my pledges I must travel as quickly as possible to Constantinople, where the war for us has taken an unfavourable turn. I am deeply sad, especially because I must remain inactive [untätig].[44]

The last entry in the diary is dated 8 November 1912, but a postscript states that soon afterwards Enver surreptitiously left Cyrenaica via Egypt, where he was hunted by the police. However, he disguised himself and, ironically, succeeded in boarding an Italian steamship to Brindisi before eventually travelling to the Ottoman capital. This was then a departure completely different from that undertaken by Nesat Bey in Tripolitania, and not only did Enver appoint a successor but some 800 Ottoman regulars also remained. The inheritor of Enver's command was the *circa* 34-year old Aziz Ali al-Masri (or Misri), usually referred to as Aziz Bey, an Ottoman officer of Egyptian origin later to become famous as a champion of Arab nationalism.[45] He had made an impression on his superiors during the campaign to settle the 1911 Yemeni revolt, not just with his military but also with his political skills; the campaign ended with an agreement in which Aziz Bey had a large part in negotiating.

His tenure as commander in Cyrenaica was relatively short, and during it the first battles of the First Italo-Senussi War were fought. Unlike the Tripolitanian situation, Italian attempts to expand their coastal enclaves were bitterly contested and several battles of the type that characterised the Italo-Ottoman campaign were fought. Given their preponderance of military technology the Italians usually prevailed, but if their progress was painfully slow then it almost came to a complete halt following the Battle of Sidi el-Garbàa (Sidi al-Qarbaa, Sidi Garbàa, Sidi Garba) that took place on 16 May 1913 about 12 kilometres south of Derna.

Details of what happened at Sidi el-Garbàa were suppressed contemporaneously by the Italian government but some reports did leak out. A recently arrived officer of colonial experience (he had survived the Battle of Adua), Major-General Ettore Mambretti, was in command at Derna and intelligence reached him that there were a number of enemy entrenched at Sidi el-Garbàa and nearby Ettangi. He despatched a strong force of infantry, plus the usual supporting arms, divided into three columns. The centre column, consisting of six (some sources say seven) battalions of infantry plus artillery and engineers under the command of Colonel Nicolò Maddalena, was to advance directly onto the enemy position at Sidi el-Garbàa.

The attack began at 03:30 hours following a march through the night without breaks for food or water so that in consequence the troops were tired and weary. Nevertheless their attacks were initially successful inasmuch as they penetrated the enemy entrenchments. The enemy were however present in far greater strength than had been estimated, with the result that Maddalena's command was then surrounded and had to attempt a fighting retreat back to Derna. According to some press reports the entire operation had been a trap into which the Italians had unknowingly walked. This had been unwittingly triggered by an 'escaped prisoner,' appropriately named Angelo Machiavelli, who had been duped into delivering misinformation to the command at Derna. An alternative tale had Machiavelli genuinely escaping and warning his superiors that the enemy was present in strength, but being disbelieved.[46]

Whatever the truth of the matter, the column was forced to retire in disorder and was harried to the outskirts of Derna, losing most of its artillery and accoutrements into the bargain. The Italian socialist newspaper *Avanti!* complained about the 'lying official communications' and published an account claiming that Italian casualties included 400 killed, 700 wounded and over 100 taken prisoner. Harrowing accounts of the wounded being abandoned also appeared, with one officer, Lieutenant Alfredo Monarelli, quoted as admitting that this was so, but arguing that there was no alternative due to a lack of transport.[47] Later scholarship has established that the casualty figures were greatly exaggerated, amounting to some 79 killed, including Colonel Maddalena, and 284 wounded, with an unknown number taken prisoner.[48] In the grand scheme of things the affair at Sidi el-Garbàa was a minor affair, but it demonstrated beyond any doubt that the conquest of Cyrenaica was to be a difficult and lengthy business.

The Italians attributed blame on the continued presence of Ottoman officers who remained, despite this being a breach of the Ouchy Treaty. There is no question that some did indeed stay behind, but Aziz Bey left the theatre for Egypt on 23 July 1913 where he was interviewed by the Cairo-based Egyptian newspaper *Al-Ahram*. Described as 'the hero of Benghazi' he revealed that he would have preferred to remain in Benghazi 'in order to inflict as much damage as possible upon the Italians because they are my enemy.' He was compelled to withdraw from the fray however due to a shortage of *matériel*; 'I needed ammunition, supplies and money. These things are essential for fighters and I had none.' The Bedouin tribes came in for high praise for remaining loyal to the cause, but he was much more critical of the Senussi leadership:

> Sanusis are like Russian priests – their only interest is in putting food in their mouths. Some of them had already concluded a truce with the Italians while others had stopped fighting them a long time ago […] The misguided policies of the Sanusis forced me to leave the general command to their elders.[49]

If the populations of Tripolitania and even Cyrenaica were indeed somewhat divided in their loyalties at this juncture, and all the evidence collected by scholars who have studied the matter suggests that this was indeed the case, then from the Italian point of view the situation was advantageous, or at least potentially so. Any student of western colonialism would be well aware that a strategy of divide and conquer, though clichéd, had nevertheless often proved effective. However a combination of internal policy and external shock were to radically change this and trigger what became termed The Great Arab Revolt (*La Grande Rivolta Araba*).[50]

One of the things that provoked hatred of the Italians was their seeming refusal to honour their commitment, under the terms of the Ouchy Treaty, to release those removed and incarcerated on the Italian islands; none had been released by January 1913. Those detained for deportation had been chosen in a random and haphazard fashion; they included males and females, both adult and juvenile. The elderly were not exempt and they came from every, and any, social strata, and even their identities were not established until they arrived at their destinations. Some 1,410 of these unfortunates were exiled on the Tremiti archipelago (*Isole Tremiti*). By 9 January 1912 it has been calculated that 198 of them had perished from disease, starvation, and cold. Many of these were elderly with 35 of the dead being aged between 60 and 70, seven between 70 and 80, and one aged over 90. Two ten-year old children also perished. Six months later a total of 437 people had died, a death-rate amounting to 31 per-cent of the deportee population on the islands.[51]

However, of perhaps more immediate concern to those still inhabiting the area claimed by Italy, and the policy that proved effective in providing an impetus towards solidarity against their rule, was the repressive and brutal behaviour of the occupiers. As has been noted (see Chapter Eight), the attitude of the Italians towards the inhabitants had undergone a profound change following the 'betrayal,' as they perceived it, of Shara Shatt and this outlook was generally maintained as was the brutality that accompanied it. One group that had constantly opposed the Tripoli venture were the Socialists. Their newspaper *Avanti!* published a photograph captioned '*The fourteen strangled in Piazza del Pane*' (*I quattordici strangolati in piazza del Pane*) following the execution of that number of 'rebels' after the Battle of Tripoli.[52] These multiple executions in the daily bread market, a place obviously visited by a large number of people, were intended to provide 'a salutary example' to others who might be inclined to emulate them.[53] Such behaviour was deprecated by those on the left of Italian politics. Arcangelo Ghisleri, atheist, republican, geographer, author and prolific founder of reviews, was coruscating in his criticism:

> Can you imagine Garibaldi, instead of Caneva, ordering the 'clearing of the oasis' and raising gallows in the Piazza del pane? [...] This war in Tripoli has been more fatal for us – morally - than a barbarian invasion. A barbarian wind has devastated and continues to devastate all kinds of minds; it blew unnoticed through the reports of all the large newspapers, no longer distinguishable from each other, all pervaded by the same folly. [...] Every elementary desire for justice and integrity was overturned; every abuse and excess was praised and justified in the name of "historical fate"; and anyone from Tripoli who intended to tell the truth was forced into silence and threatened with exile. The Italy of the Tripolists lost every sense of morality. [...] Unfortunately every offense to the principles of justice and morality must be paid for! This wretched war will bear fruits of ash and poison. It has already begun to bear them. The frenzy of the massacres, the debasement of human life, the exaltation of savagery, the reinstatement of the gallows (the war has even provided us with this macabre resurrection of our painful past!) will have their repercussions in the homeland.[54]

Such behaviour is perhaps explicable, though certainly not excusable, given the panic that arose amongst the occupiers following the events of Shara Shatt. That it had not only continued but had become institutionalised – 'the gallows flourished everywhere in Libya, like ineradicable weeds'[55] – was demonstrated by, once again, *Avanti!* The 5 December 1913 edition carried a series of photographs documenting the hanging of Arabs as carried out by Italian soldiers. The matter was raised by the Socialist deputy, Filippo Turati, in the Italian parliament on 18 December. Turati was unambiguous in his denunciation of the barbarity inherent in the colonial policy of the government.

> I heard the King speak, a few days ago, of how the acquisition of Libya by Italy gives us a great mission of civilization, and we have as a first goal to make friends with the people, with respect to religion, property and the family and to let them learn the benefits of civilization. But everywhere I see the shadow of the gallows reaching out [...] I wonder if this is really Italy, and if the government knows that Cesare Beccaria was born in Italy.[56]

The reference to Cesare Beccaria can be construed as a swipe at the claim that Italian colonial rule was at all civilised. Beccaria was an eighteenth century jurist and politician whose name came to be 'indissolubly linked with opposition to the death penalty and with efforts to create a more reasoned, effective, and humane approach to punishment' via his 1764 work entitled *Dei delitti e delle pene (On Crimes and Punishments)*.[57] According to William Schabas, 'the modern abolitionist movement establishes its paternity' with Beccaria, and his influence was one of the factors in the abolition of capital punishment in Tuscany, though all of the other pre-unification Italian states retained it.[58] Capital punishment had been abolished throughout the unified Kingdom of Italy since 1889, though had been the subject of a general pardon since 1877. However, if Turati's shafts went home in respect of the more cerebral deputies, they were certainly ineffective in influencing the policies pursued in the colonial sphere.

The raising of such matters by socialists and their ilk was of course attributed to the bleating of the usual suspects. There were though accounts from those that could hardly be so called. One such was an officer of the *Bersaglieri*, Lieutenant-Colonel Gherardo Pàntano, the *commissario del Gebel*. As a young officer he had become a prisoner of the Ethiopians following Adua and he later went on to command, as a Lieutenant-General, an Infantry Division during the First World War. He had extensive colonial experience in East Africa and was also something of a scholar and author of several books. His 1910 monograph, *Nel Benadir: La Citta de Merca e la Regione Bimal,*[59] provided virtually the only source for later studies of the social and political organisation, and the resistance against Italian colonialism, of Somali society in the late nineteenth and early twentieth century.[60] Unlike many of his fellow officers, he neither underrated nor despised the tribesmen that Italy claimed to rule, nor did he fail to appreciate the difficulties of campaigning against them should such an eventuality arise. After the event, he recorded meeting in the second half of February 1914 with one of their leaders, Ahmed es-Sunni, who had been willing to reach an accommodation with the Italians:

> I found myself in front of a young man of fair complexion, with a sensitive expression that was mild and gentle, almost feminine. [...] That young man of such delicate appearance was able to dominate the vast desert and I felt that even with so many forces at my disposal, with my fast motor trucks and my radio equipment keeping me in contact with Tripoli, I was not master of what he was. The silent desert was hostile to us but obedient to him. Whilst for us it was pain

and difficulty, he was defended and protected; for us it was all about mystery and danger […] we were prisoners of that immensity where he could move freely.[61]

Some 17 months after that meeting, on 29 July 1915, he submitted a confidential memorandum to the Colonial Ministry, explaining why, in his opinion, The Great Arab Revolt had broken out:

> Our officers demonstrate feelings of great resentment, hostility, and hatred against the Arabs, and do not know how to distinguish between friends and foes, or, rather, between those who we should fight and those we should protect […] They tell you with pleasure amazing things: Arabs found seriously injured are covered in gasoline and burned, or thrown into wells […] others are shot with no other reason than that of a cruel whim. There are officers who boast of personally ordering such executions. There are others that systematically prey on non-rebels, thus feeding Sennusi propaganda in the best possible way. I cannot understand why our officers display such blind ferocity, so much thirst for blood, and so refined a cruelty. […] We take revenge on the Arabs for our errors, our retreats, and the checks we suffer, but the cause of these is not their skill but our ineptitude. Indeed, unable to avenge ourselves on those who obtain such conspicuous results with such little means, we vent our humiliation on the weak and helpless and those unfortunates who look to us for protection. The consequence was that all of those we want to be with us hate us.[62]

By this time, of course, the external shock to Italian rule had made its impact in the shape of the First World War. Italian participation in the conflict, when it came on 23 May 1915, was not on the side of its allies of 30 years in the Triple-Alliance, but rather on the side of Britain, France and Russia against Austria-Hungary (but not yet Germany). 'Perfidy, like history does not know' was how Kaiser Franz Joseph described it. Whether perfidy or not, this political and strategic realignment necessitated a similar operational rearrangement, with Italian forces shifting their focus from the north-west border with France to the north and north-east frontier with Austria-Hungary. Even before this, from about the summer of 1914, the threat of large-scale armed resistance to Italian rule was beginning to manifest itself and by August the Fezzan had become entirely Italian free. The influence of the Senussi in fomenting this resistance is well documented, and of course, as Pàntano was to write, their propaganda had been well underpinned by Italian acts.[63]

The response to this resurgence of resistance, from the occupiers' point of view, would have been to crush it. The Italian government however, under the premiership of Antonio Salandra since 21 March 1914, had its eyes fixed elsewhere since the outbreak of hostilities between the Central and Entente Powers. The new Chief of Staff of the army, who had taken office following the sudden death of Alberto Pollio on 1 July 1914, was General Luigi Cadorna. Cadorna was expecting that Italy would honour its commitments to the Triple Alliance and immediately began pressing for measures to be taken in anticipation of this. When he discovered that Italy was to remain neutral he sought an audience with Salandra, and asked what – if war alongside Austria-Hungary and Germany was not going to take place – he should prepare for. Though the politicians had yet to make up their mind, the impression he was given was that Austria-Hungary would be the enemy.[64] Cadorna thus had the enormous task of recasting Italy's long-standing strategic planning; however, upon assuming office he claimed that the 'serious deficiencies' that he found with the army were 'much greater than he had imagined.'[65]

Cadorna's account of his early days in office as Chief of Staff sometimes reads as if he had no idea of the state of the organisation of which he had been a member since 1866, a general officer since 1898 and had become a senior corps commander of in 1910. Nevertheless there can be little doubt that his inheritance was unenviable. The reforms that Pollio and Spingardi had been attempting to carry out had been disrupted by the campaign in North Africa, and the effects of this were still very much in evidence. The equipment and stores needed for a European campaign were in disarray following the need to deploy far larger forces in North Africa than had been anticipated and supply them adequately for a far longer period than had been foreseen. As well as absorbing a huge amount of *matériel*, a large proportion of the army's artillery was also located in the theatre leaving a critical shortage to the home-based forces. One further factor was that most of the best officers were stationed in Tripolitania and Cyrenaica, and their units had been assembled piecemeal from the forces based in Italy, leaving what remained in a state of disarray.[66]

To Cadorna the need to reorganise for a European war overrode all other considerations and he began withdrawing units and equipment from Tripoli and Cyrenaica in order to bring the army up to strength.[67] The result could be little more than to encourage the resistance, and by April 1915 the revolt had spread over the entire Tripoli region and the Italian hold, such as it was, was becoming tenuous. An example of this was the Battle of Gasr Bu Hadi (al-Qardabiya) near Sirte fought on 29 April 1915 when a column some 3,000 strong, about two-thirds of which were *ascari,* led by Colonel Antonio Miani marched out to attack the Senussi camp at Gasr Bu Hadi, south of Sirte. The Italian force was attacked relentlessly almost the whole day whilst marching in close formation and was eventually pushed into a narrow defile. By evening the Italians were surrounded and attempted to retreat to Sirte. The retreat was chaotic and severe casualties were inflicted; out of 84 officers, 19 were killed, and 23 were wounded, whilst 479 of the troops (237 Italian and 242 *ascari*) were killed and 407 (127 Italian and 280 *ascari*) wounded. All the impedimenta was abandoned to the attackers, including the machine guns, six batteries of artillery, and all the ammunition and the provisions.[68]

Faced with the double blow of a rapidly swelling revolt and a shrinking force with which to counter it, the Italians simply retreated. Between mid-June and mid-July 1915 all the outlying garrisons and forces began perforce to withdraw into the coastal enclaves, and even some of these were abandoned. The whole retreat was carried out under continuous attack, and the *matériel* losses were enormous; Del Boca calculates that the resistance captured '37 cannons, 20 machine guns, 9,048 rifles, 28,021 cannon shells, 6,185,000 cartridges for rifles and machine guns, 37 trucks, and 14 broadcasting and receiving stations.'[69] The casualties were also grim, and according to the best estimates calculated afterwards amounted to '5,600 dead, several thousand wounded, and about 2,000 prisoners.'[70]

The seriousness of the situation as viewed by the head of government is perhaps revealed in a letter of 3 July 1915 from Salandra to the minister for colonies, Ferdinando Martini. In his missive Salandra refers to the massacre that had taken place on 18 June 1915 when an Italian column, in attempting to evacuate Tarhuna some 80 kilometres to the south-east of Tripoli City, had been surrounded. He further notes that a similar fate was expected to befall those garrisoning Beni Ulid, which was a further 70 kilometres away than Tarhuna. He asks Martini, rhetorically perhaps, if we can 'passively allow events to run their course?' Martini and the local commanders in North Africa would, of course, have liked to have deployed reinforcements to the theatre. Cadorna however would have none of it and is alleged to have responded to such requests by remarking that 'the war will be won in the Alps and not in the African deserts' (*La guerra si vince sulle Alpi e non nei deserti d'Africa*). Though there seems to be no evidence that he actually said this, it nevertheless encapsulates his strategic view. Whilst this was undoubtedly a correct position, in the grand scheme of things it was a disaster for Italy's position in Tripoli and Cyrenaica; as Salandra put it to Martini: 'our losses in terms of material and morale are almost as great as those of Adowa.'[71] For an Italian Prime Minister to have used the 'A' word to a former governor of Eritrea – Martini had been appointed in 1897 and served for ten years – is perhaps evidence of how bad he thought things were. They were however to get worse. Cyrenaica and Tripolitania were, as far as Italy was concerned, reunited in the gubernatorial sense when General Giovanni Ameglio, who had been appointed governor of Cyrenaica in October 1913, also took over Tripolitania at the end of July 1915. He ordered the evacuation of all interior positions and several of the coastal enclaves as well. When Italy declared war on the Ottoman Empire on 21 August 1915 both states found themselves in an almost identical situation to that which had pertained following the initial landings in 1911. It was indeed back to square one with a vengeance, though this time those stirring up the locals had been reinforced. According to a post-war appraisal by Colonel Arturo Vacca Maggiolini:

> [The] Germans and Turks worked to great effect throughout the European war, conducting an active and skilful campaign which destroyed the last shreds of Italian prestige and fanned the flames of the most ferocious hatred and the blindest fanaticism, against us. We became for the Arabs of Tripolitania the most despicable creatures in all creation, and it became a just and meritorious action to exterminate us and expel us from the sacred soil of Islam.[72]

Although Italy and Germany had been 'unofficially' at war since the former's declaration against Austria-Hungary of 23 May 1915, the matter became official on 28 August 1916. Though the main military effect of this was to be felt in the Alpine region in the Battle of Caporetto (Twelfth Battle of the Isonzo), fought 24 October-19 November 1917, it also had an impact on the North African theatre.[73] This was mainly via the Mediterranean U-Boat campaign of the German and Austro-Hungarian navies, which not only allowed small numbers of, mainly Ottoman, officers to be landed in Tripolitania and Cyrenaica, but also supplies of weapons and munitions. Indeed, the situation in Cyrenaica was if anything worse because the Senussi were better organised, or at least rather less fragmented, than the resistance fighters in Tripolitania. Del Boca quotes an Italian prisoner, Lieutenant Ettore Miraglia, captured at Beni Ulid, who later wrote that he had seen submarines arriving every fifteen days carrying Ottoman officers who were sent to assist the resistance.[74] This is almost certainly a gross exaggeration, and though they were undoubtedly useful in the transport role the primary mission of the U-Boats was to sink Allied ships. In that they proved deadly until, in 1917, convoy systems and other measures, including a flotilla of Japanese destroyers, were introduced to the theatre. One aspect of this campaign was the near starvation level to which the Italian garrisons were reduced at times. According to Pàntano: 'The troops were in an incredibly physically depressed state [...] food was so short that they resorted to eating the dogs and cats found in the oasis [...] The meat ration was reduced to 200 grams per week.'[75] Since it is certain that the Arab inhabitants were not eating better than the Italians one can only imagine their state.

One effect of the arrival of Ottoman officers in Cyrenaica was the opening of a western front against Egypt. The senior Ottoman officer despatched was Nuri Killigil (Nuri Pasha), the brother of the former commander in Cyrenaica and now Ottoman Minister of War, Enver Pasha. He was joined by another officer of Mesopotamian origin, referred to as 'Gaafer, a Germanised Turk of considerable ability' by Lieutenant-General Sir John Maxwell in a 1916 report.[76] The person in question is now better known as Jafar Pasha Al-Askari and whilst Maxwell was certainly correct about his abilities, he was less accurate about his background.[77] Jafar was to lead the Senussi in an attack on Egypt from Cyrenaica, the idea being to exert pressure on the western border thus expediting an attack on the Suez Canal in the east from the Ottoman territory of Palestine. They also hoped to cause an uprising among the overwhelmingly Muslim population of Egypt against what had become the Sultanate of Egypt when the British deposed the Khedive in 1914 and proclaimed a Protectorate.[78]

That trouble was brewing in respect of the Senussi, and western Egypt had become evident to the British in late 1915. On 5 November the German submarine U35 torpedoed the British auxiliary patrol boat HMS *Tara* (formerly the London & North Western Railway passenger steamer SS *Hibernia* used on the Holyhead to Kingstown (Dun Laoghaire) route) off Sollum. There were 93 survivors from a crew of 104 and these were rescued by the commander of the U-Boat, the all-time greatest submariner in terms of sunken targets, Lothar von Arnauld de la Perière, who towed their lifeboats to Port Bardia (Bardiyah) some 20 kilometres to the north-east. There the unfortunate Holyheadians, for most of the crew had transferred with the steamer, were handed over to Nuri Bey and the Senussi. Two of the senior officers, the former captain of the *Hibernia*, Lieutenant Edward Tanner RNR and the captain of the *Tara*, Captain Rupert Gwatkin-Williams RN, were taken to visit Nuri along with their interpreter, Vasili Lanbrimidis. Gwatkin-Williams later left a description of Nuri: 'a dark-eyed gentle-looking man, somewhat slightly built, and with a straggling black beard; he is an ardent antiquarian and naturalist, and spoke much of the ancient ruins in the interior.' He also noted that the Ottoman commander 'did what he could for us, but it did not amount to much.'[79] Indeed, the prisoners, together with four of the crew of the horse transport *Moorina*, sunk on 7 November by the U35, were to be held by the Senussi until St Patrick's Day (17 March) 1916, whilst the strong representations made to the Senussi for their release immediately following their capture were greeted by 'feigned ignorance.'

Ignorance on the part of the British as to the intentions of the Senussi could not however be maintained, for in the middle of the month they made active hostile moves. Sollum was attacked by the Senussi regular troops, originally trained by Enver, on the night of 14 November, and on 17 November attacks were made against positions at Sidi Barrani some 95 kilometres east of the border with Cyrenaica.[80] The campaign, whilst it did succeed in tying up some British and Allied forces was ultimately a disaster for the Senussi for several reasons. One of the foremost was that they attempted to engage in modes of warfare, such as taking and holding ground, more suited to a regular army. As was observed by a certain Archibald Wavell, who wrote a history of the Great War campaigns in the theatre, this was a grave error: 'It is usually a fatal mistake for irregular leaders to cramp their natural methods of warfare by adopting the training and tactics of regular armies. The Senussi's so-called regulars were no match for the British troops, and were easily defeated.'[81] Another reason for their failure concerned technology and in particular the advent of reliable motorised vehicles and aircraft. Indeed, the campaign against the Senussi saw some of the earliest successful usage of methods of penetrating the desert using airpower, mainly for reconnaissance, and armoured vehicles.[82] The British Royal Naval Air Service famously developed their Rolls Royce Armoured Car in 1914 for use in Belgium, but because they were unsuitable for the conditions that developed on the Western Front most were transferred to Army control and found themselves in the Middle East in 1915. There they became of great utility; according to T E Lawrence 'a Rolls in the desert was above rubies' and 'they were worth hundreds of men to us.'[83] They were though quite heavy, and because they could not easily cross stony areas of desert lighter vehicles, based on the Ford Model T chassis and armed with Lewis Guns, were also extemporised.[84]

One example demonstrating that the old style of warfare was being superseded by a new methodology came with the rescue of the prisoners from *Tara* and *Moorina*, which could not have been accomplished in any other way. Following the defeat of the Senussi forces and the reoccupation of Sollum on 14 March 1916, during which manoeuvre aircraft directed the light armoured car battery under Major the Duke of Westminster onto an enemy force completely smashing them, a number of prisoners fell into British hands. Intelligence gathered from interrogation suggested that the unfortunate seamen were being held at Bir Hakeim (Abyar al Hakim), a remote oasis in the desert and the site of an old Ottoman fort. As the crow flies, the oasis is about 160 kilometres west of Sollum and some 60 kilometres south-west of Tobruk. It was decided to attempt to rescue them, a task which was entrusted to the armoured car battery (sometimes referred to as a Brigade), which would be accompanied by a number of unarmoured vehicles; forty-three in all. It was stuff from a '*Boy's Own*' adventure; the vehicular column covered nearly 200 kilometres before it found the oasis, whose exact location was largely a matter of conjecture, at 15:00 hours and totally surprising the Senussi guards. Most of these perished whilst attempting to flee, according to Gwatkin-Williams, but there were no casualties amongst the 92 surviving prisoners or the rescuers and the entire column, complete with the former prisoners, returned safely to British-held territory.[85] It was most definitely one of those 'Deeds that thrilled the Empire' and the Duke of Westminster certainly deserved the Distinguished Service Order that he was awarded for leading the mission.

There was though a much larger implication. The Western Desert Force in general, and the Duke of Westminster in particular, had demonstrated unequivocally that Pàntano's words of only a year or so previously, about 'the silent desert' being 'hostile' to outsiders, no longer applied. No longer were Europeans 'prisoners of that immensity' where the desert tribes could find sanctuary. The perhaps primitive vehicles originally manufactured by FIAT and Isotta Fraschini were capable of evolution, and what could be done with Rolls Royce and Ford vehicles could also be done with improved Italian designs. Likewise, and particularly following the technological quantum leap consequent upon the Great War, the basic aircraft types of 1911-12 led to hugely improved machines. That these technologies rendered penetration of the desert a practical proposition to Italian arms was something that the peoples of what would become Libya in 1934 were to find out to their immense cost. The Italian reconquest (*reconquista*) that began in the 1920s and continued into the 1930s was a brutal campaign. Some indication of the harshness of it may be adjudged by noting that, according to figures compiled by Italy, the population of Cyrenaica dropped from 225,000 in 1928 to 142,000 in 1931.[86] Giorgio Rochat calculates that between 1923 and 1936 the number of dead in Cyrenaica was between a lower limit of 30,000 and an upper of 70,000.[87] Angelo Del Boca estimates that the total deaths in both Tripolitania and Cyrenaica were in the order of 100,000.[88] Whichever figures are the more accurate it is indisputable that, in any event, the slaughter was on a large scale. It is then perhaps ironic, though hardly surprising, to note that during the majority of this period Italy was governed by the ex-socialist and former campaigner against the Tripoli War, Benito Mussolini now reinvented as *Il Duce*.

CHAPTER FIFTEEN

Retrospect: The Italian Army and the Politicians, 1911-1912

'When I was military attaché in Rome an impressive Alpini brigadier asked me who were the ten greatest British generals. I thought for a moment then answered that there wouldn't be much debate about the top five, but for the rest…
He stopped me and with a sigh said: "The point is, we don't have a single one. How do you think that makes an Italian officer feel?"'
Brigadier Allan Mallinson quoted in *History Today*, July 2011[1]

A Regiment of Italians well entrenched, under cover of the Fleet big guns, see on the horizon a frieze of wandering Bedouins. Arrives, with orders to attack, the Colonel. He takes off his helmet and shouts Eviva L'Italia! *All the regiment follow suit. Then he shouts:* Avanti! *Avanti! The entire regiment rises as one man, shouts* Avanti *and… remains where it was! Somehow it reminds me of railway travel in Italy.*
Rudyard Kipling writing to Colonel H W Feilden, 29 January 1913[2]

THOUGH it was by any standards something of a military sideshow in terms of what had gone before it, and particularly so in relation to what came later, the Italian Army, despite seemingly winning, did not emerge from the Italo–Ottoman War with any great credit. This was recognised within some of the more thoughtful branches of the Italian military, perhaps most notably by Luigi Capello, considered by some to have been Italy's best general during the First World War.[3] Though his reputation was largely destroyed in 1917 following the Battle of Caporetto, Capello later wrote of the campaign in North Africa as disastrous because of the 'enormous waste of materials.' He went on to point out the 'no less disastrous devaluation of our military reputation.'[4] Luigi Cadorna compared his own position as Chief of Staff unfavourably with those of his Prussian/German counterparts. Whereas they led an ever victorious army, he was 'the leader of the army of Custoza and Adua.'[5] Cadorna's reputation disappeared at the same time as Capello's and from much the same cause. However, to quote Paul Kennedy, 'the general antimilitarism of Italian society, the poor quality of the officer corps, and the lack of adequate funding for modern weaponry raised doubts about Italian military effectiveness long before the disasters of Caparetto.'[6] 'Long before' could of course encompass the pre-unification era and the famous, and inaccurate, 'Italians don't fight' quip.[7] In reality, the entire history of the struggle to attain Italian unification comprises military struggles of varying kinds, though they were not of the sort that led to decisive battles with overwhelming victories and were often against other 'Italians.'

The army that was sent to North Africa was in need of modernisation and reorganisation. This had been recognised and a process of improvement begun, when it was interrupted by the decision to go to war. Italy's army was organised, trained, and equipped, albeit poorly in the latter context, to fight a European style conflict in conjunction with its allies in the Triple Alliance. The conflict that developed in Tripoli was very different, and unsurprisingly it found some difficulty in adapting to it at the tactical level. At the operational level the plans drawn up for intervening, as reviewed in August 1911, did not envisage moving beyond the seizure of the coastal towns. The occupation of the hinterland and beyond was to follow via political action. Intelligence, both political and military, was hopelessly misleading in predicting that there would be little resistance and therefore fighting, and when combat became necessary it is hardly surprising that the army as constituted was unable to undertake it effectively. The rising in and around the Oasis of Tripoli, the Battle of Tripoli, came as a very unpleasant shock to the invaders, and the repression and atrocities that followed it further alienated the two sides. Indeed, the last strand of Italian pre-war strategy had collapsed with the mutual fear and hatred engendered by the battle and its aftermath and, consequently, all hopes of the conflict being a short, let alone victorious, war.

The other major Italian miscalculation was that it would be fairly simple to knock the Ottoman Empire out of the war, and when this element of strategy misfired the Italians were left at a strategic loss. The whole operation to take Tripoli had been predicated on it not disturbing the 'balance of power' in Europe, particularly in the Balkan region, and so attempting to find somewhere where pressure could be applied on the Ottoman government, but not cause intervention by either of the Great Power blocs or their members, became a priority. For want of better the Dodecanese were eventually chosen, and the operation to occupy them proceeded smoothly. Indeed, the amphibious capability displayed during the several joint army and navy operations undertaken was, by any standards, impressive. One of the factors that made such operations possible was the withdrawal of the inferior Ottoman Navy into the Dardanelles at the very beginning of the war, leaving the Italian fleet with total command of the sea. Whilst the lack of an opponent left the navy in a state of frustration at being unable to give battle, which it would undoubtedly have won, it did allow it to land military forces more or less where it chose. That virtually none of these landings was against significant opposition, and an opposed amphibious landing was always, and remains, one of the most hazardous operations of war, was deliberate on the part of the Italians. Where there was opposition, or the likelihood of it, then landings were either not attempted or abandoned; the abortive attempt at Zuwarah in late December 1911 being one such example. When the time came to attempt the operation again in April 1912 it was a much more sophisticated affair, with feints and ruses to confuse any potential defenders. Not all the Italian amphibious operations were successful. The flanking operation attempted on 6 November 1911 to retake Fort Hamidije for example had been foreseen and a force deployed to counter it. Some 200 Italians managed to disembark, but they were immediately attacked and very few escaped alive. The operation against the Dodecanese also involved deception as did that to take Misrata in June 1912, when the landing force was put ashore some 12 kilometres to the east of the target – where the enemy were not in other words. Once firmly ashore, and protected by the guns of the fleet, the Italians could not be dislodged and they only had to wait to build up their strength before moving on their objective.

Though the Italians could hold the coastal enclaves that they conquered relatively easily, attempts to occupy territory inland were fraught with danger. Conversely, the guerrilla style of resistance envisaged by Enver Pasa, whereby attempts to lure Italian detachments from behind their defences in order that small numbers of them could be overwhelmed, was not entirely successful. This was largely due to the Italian policy of risk avoidance; the affair at Bir Tobras of 19-20 December 1911 had demonstrated the dangers of attempting to project power into the desert using unsupported columns. Only the cool-headedness and leadership skills of Colonel Gustavo Fara had averted disaster on that occasion and, whether coincidentally or not, Italian operations thereafter operated on the principle of minimum risk. This meant the use of large forces that were strong enough to defend themselves against anything that the Ottoman led resistance might assemble against them. The inevitable corollary of this was that, tactically, Italian moves were ponderous. Junior officers were prevented from being, as the Italian phrase has it, *impetuoso*. On the rare occasions when one did act impetuously, such as demonstrated by the now Major-General Gustavo Fara on 9 July 1912 during the operations to take Misrata, the result was an unacceptably high casualty list; another demonstration of his supposed 'inclination to rashness' and a 'failure to see difficulties' perhaps.

Fighting in desert conditions is, in any event, a specialised business because of the hostility of the environment. This is an enduring situation, and though the advent of mechanical vehicles did much to alleviate it the nub of the problem remained. As well as the difficulties of terrain there are factors such as the extreme heat and insect life – flies, sand flies, ticks, lice, and fleas – to consider. The question of water is paramount, and this matter can perhaps be encapsulated in a quote from a late 20th century study:

> Inhabitants of temperate zones do not appreciate the importance of water to everyday life as do the inhabitants of equatorial deserts. For example, there is no one word in the English language that means 'to die of thirst,' yet in Arabic there are eight degrees of thirst [...] Arabs express thirst in terms of simple thirst, burning thirst, vehement thirst, burning thirst with dizziness, and lastly excessive thirst – the thirst that kills.[8]

Given the difficulties of conducting desert warfare against a foe that was, literally, quite at home there, and noting that for political reasons avoidance of casualties and therefore risk was of paramount concern, then the apparent ineffectiveness of the Italian Army is explicable. The extreme difficulties experienced by the Italian military in physically traversing the desert terrain wherein the enemy lived was a problem further compounded by the amorphous nature of the foe they sought to fight. The Ottoman formations had, as General Caneva acknowledged within three weeks of the initial landings, become 'meagre detachments' some six hours march from the main Italian position at Tripoli City. The ability of such 'detachments' to concentrate if required, and then disperse again when necessary, was an enduring problem. The answer, from the invaders side, was to be found in vehicular technology. This however was not far removed from its infancy in 1911-12, but nevertheless the Italians were not slow in making the attempt to utilise it. Mobility in desert terrain would eventually be conferred by the use of motorised vehicles, and these were first used in military operations on a significant scale during the advance on Zanzur of 8 June 1912. Armoured cars were also developed, and from these beginnings more powerful and reliable models would evolve. The circa 400-kilometre round trip made by the Duke of Westminster's command of forty-three vehicles through the desert on St Patrick's Day 1916, to rescue the shipwrecked prisoners from *Tara* and *Moorina*, demonstrated how far the potential of such methods had developed in just a few years.

The same might be said of aircraft. The Italians were the first to use aircraft in a military context, though of course the models available were extremely basic. Nevertheless the experience of, and developments in, aerial warfare were of much value to them. Aircraft were used initially in the context of reconnaissance, and as deserts are mostly devoid of vegetation and offer virtually no natural concealment from aerial observation they were fairly effective in that role. With rather less success they were also used for bombardment. There were 712 sorties by aeroplanes during the course of the war, whereby 'several hundred' bombs were dropped, whilst the airships sortied on 136 occasions and released 360 bombs.[9] The conclusion in respect of aviation reached after the conflict was that aeroplanes, although representative of a younger and less proven technology, were nevertheless faster, more manoeuvrable, and much more versatile than airships, and thus had more to offer in the field of war in the future.[10] This was prophetic, and when combined with armed, and armoured, vehicles able to traverse the terrain they were to provide the key to successful penetration of the desert. Indeed, drawing on their experiences, the Italians were the first to use integrated mobile air and ground units, dubbed *compagnie auto-avio sahariane* for desert warfare in the 1930s.

Another technology that was to become vital to successful desert warfare was radio, or wireless telegraphy as it was termed at the time. Guglielmo Marconi, the father of the science, was deeply interested in this development and noted in an interview in 1912 how advances in the technology had begun to make it semi-portable:

When the Italian warships bombarded the Turks, scouting parties equipped with wireless apparatus were sent ashore. The sending instruments that they carried were no bigger than [a medium sized travelling bag] and the masts and their antennae were no bigger than fishing rods. Yet with this apparatus the scouts sent messages five and eight miles [8-13 kilometres] – the range of modern naval guns.[11]

The science had not yet advanced to a stage where the sending and receiving apparatus were combined in one unit, and neither was the equipment entirely reliable, but undoubtedly the ability to give targeting instructions in real time to artillery beyond the line of sight was another valuable addition to Italy's war-making capability. The Italian forces were not the pioneers in respect of using radio in war; that had been done in 1900 during the Boxer War in China. It had also figured in the Russo-Japanese War of 1904-05 and had been used in colonial warfare by the German army in German South-West Africa (Namibia) during the 1904-09 campaign against the Herero and Nama people.[12]

It is also worth recalling that during the South-West African campaigns the German Army – which was, contemporaneously, the ideal against which others were measured – found itself stymied. According to the East German historian, Horst Drechsler, the leader of the resistance, Jacob Morenga, '[…] stood head and shoulders above the Germans in the art of guerrilla warfare, and even the Kaiser's top brass had to acknowledge his tactical skill.' He quotes Hauptmann M Bayer who served on the General Staff on the matter:

[…] a major European power, with about 15,000 soldiers in the field, was locked for years in a struggle with what were even initially only 1,000 to 2,000 and later no more than some hundred Nama whose methods of warfare proved unanswerable.[13]

In contradistinction to the Italian example, this apparent failure of arms did not lead to accusations of military ineptitude. Neither have the German commanders in South-West Africa, Major-Generals Lothar von Trotha and Berthold von Deimling successively, been charged with timidity and incompetence (as opposed to barbaric brutality and genocide). Nor was the overall reputation of the German Army called into question by its inability to prevail in the given circumstances. Of course the German Army, or at least its Prussian predecessor and allies, had not fought since 1871 if one discounts the contribution made to the Boxer War in China, but had then done so with great success against France. No such success had attended Italian efforts which had experienced some spectacular failures at Custoza and Adowa as ruefully noted by Luigi Cadorna.

Though Cadorna, and Capello, wrote with hindsight and most certainly had an axe to grind, both were no more than reflecting a good deal of contemporary domestic criticism of the apparent timidity of the Italian Army during the Italo-Ottoman War. This was however dwarfed by foreign criticism, which was sometimes nasty in the extreme and reached denigratory levels. Indeed, great indignation was expressed by Italian, and pro-Italian, commentators and journalists on the scathing criticisms of Italian military prowess made by some foreign writers in their accounts of the campaign. Many of these, both Italian and Italophile, stressed the martial qualities of the Italian soldiers and General Emilio De Bono, who served on the General Staff during the conflict and was appointed Governor of Tripolitania in 1925, argued in 1931 that the successful outcome of the campaign had a morally uplifting effect; 'after more than forty years non-commissioned officers and soldiers with medals on their breasts could be seen again.'[14] The vast majority of the soldiers who fought in Italy were poorly educated conscripts and probably had little motivation for the conflict over an immense and valueless box of sand (*immenso ed inutile scatolone di sabbia*) as Gaetano Salvemini, and then other opponents of the war, termed it.[15] Many tried to escape military duty and, as has been noted, the Italian community in Australia 'increased markedly during the course of the conflict especially as a result of an influx of men trying to avoid call up.'[16] Enver Bey, whose forces fought against them for nearly the whole course of the campaign, considered that the ordinary Italian soldiers were cowardly and 'unwilling to fight [*kampfunlustig*]' but he considered the junior officers that led them admirable and willing to 'sacrifice themselves.'[17]

The contemporaneous reporting of the war, as has already been shown, became extremely partisan, and opinions of the effectiveness of the Italian Army likewise. Francis McCullagh, probably the most prominent of all the critics of the Italian venture, condemned the Italians as possessing 'the one and only European army which ever showed twenty thousand clean pairs of heels to niggers.'[18] This was vicious stuff, and almost explicitly propounded the concept that there was something inherently unmilitary about Italy and Italians.[19] Such nationalist stereotyping would be dismissed without further argument by the late 20th century, but at the time and later was held to have some validity. It should have been completely discounted during the First World War. The numerous gruelling battles along the Isonzo between 1915-1917, when the Italian army attempted to breach the Austro-Hungarian defences first begun by Conrad von Hötzendorf in the Dolomites before the Italo-Ottoman War, proved this. Despite the near impossibility of campaigning in the hostile Alpine territory, the Italian army fought eleven major battles in an attempt to breach the enemy lines. They were unsuccessful, incurring huge casualties, and during the twelfth battle, the Italians were severely defeated by a combined Austro-Hungarian and German offensive. This was, according to Gaetano Cavallaro, an 'army that knew how to fight and how to die.'[20]

Italian military incapacity was again amplified by British propaganda during the Second World War following the defeat of the unmotorised and unarmoured Italian forces in Cyrenaica and in Somaliland. No doubt Japanese propaganda made many of the same claims following the defeat of the British in Malaya and Singapore in 1942 – the 'largest capitulation' in British history according to Churchill.[21] The causes of the debacle in both cases were much the same; the defeated were poorly trained and ill-equipped to fight the type of campaign imposed upon them by their enemies and their own political leaders. The belittling of Italian military prowess did not of course go down too well with the British forces that had fought them, whose achievements were correspondingly downgraded 'and whose experience often suggested otherwise.'[22] As the historian John Whittam put it: 'the fighting qualities of the Italian soldier have been very severely judged in the twentieth century.' Whittam went on to argue that this judgment has to be considered in relation to a defective high command, inadequate economic resources and a sometimes inept political leadership.[23]

Major Eric G Hansen of the US Marine Corps, in studying the subject of Italian military capabilities and performance, is much in agreement, arguing however that the 'most important aspect' lay in Italy's political system: 'Throughout her history, this confused governing body has been responsible, in large part, for getting Italy involved in conflicts which she was not prepared to fight.'[24] That it was the government of Giolitti and San Giuliano that plunged the Italian Army into just such a conflict in 1911 has, hopefully, been demonstrated.

Giolitti and San Giuliano retained complete control of military and naval strategy throughout the course of the war with the Ottoman Empire, steering a narrow course between bringing pressure to bear on the enemy and bringing on Great Power arbitration. The impetus behind the decision to invade the Ottoman *vilayet* was a form of social imperialism, inasmuch as Giolitti and his Foreign Minister hoped to outflank, and indeed harness, a growing right wing nationalist current as expressed by various organisations and press organs. Having made the move however, the two politicians found themselves captured by the jingo right and unable to adopt any policy other than outright military victory over the Ottomans and the inhabitants of the Tripoli province. Conversely, and no doubt with the example of Francesco Crispi and Adowa some fifteen years before firmly in mind, they exercised a close control over the Italian Army and ensured that it followed a tactical no-risk policy.

Although this was a case of making a virtue out of a necessity, inasmuch as the army was neither equipped nor trained for desert warfare, it was largely successful since it prevented any disasters that might have attended a bolder policy; the near miss of Bir Tobras being an object lesson in this regard. On the other hand, the apparent passivity of Italian arms, and the protracted resistance of the Ottoman Empire and the inhabitants of Tripoli, led to criticism of Government policy for not being bold enough. Indeed, the unexpected difficulties that arose from what had been expected to be a walkover completely paralysed Italian strategy. As the Ottoman politician interviewed by the British journalist W T Stead put it in 1912: 'a war with Italy […] costs us nothing and cannot possibly do us any serious harm.'[25]

It was, of course, an attempt to indeed cause 'serious harm' to the Ottomans that led to the decision to widen the war into the eastern Mediterranean and Aegean, utilising the Italian naval supremacy that could not be challenged. This was though a course fraught with difficulties, particularly in respect of Italy's partner in the Triple Alliance, Austria-Hungary, who had effectively vetoed earlier action in the Adriatic. France too had been provoked by the attack at Beirut in February 1912. Any such action also had the potential to, at the very least, annoy the British who were very sensitive to any latently hostile naval presence on the flank of the Suez Canal route. Sir Edward Grey, in whose hands British foreign policy lay, was determined to maintain strict neutrality between the combatants, whilst San Giuliano was able to get Germany, the senior partner in the Triple Alliance, to apply discrete pressure on the Austro-Hungarians to allow Italy to widen the conflict. Being seriously disadvantaged by their lack of a navy, the Ottomans had attempted to get the Great Powers involved, and, when diplomatic attempts had proven unsuccessful, had sought to provoke such intervention by closing the Dardanelles following the half-hearted Italian attack. Britain and Russia, the two powers most directly affected, had taken differing positions on this closure, with Britain complaining to Italy whilst Russia held the Ottoman Empire to blame. Neither power made any move to directly intervene though, to Italian satisfaction and Ottoman disappointment.

The operation to occupy the islands of the Southern Sporades (Dodecanese) was sanctioned somewhat reluctantly by Austria-Hungary after German pressure, and the British were able to tolerate it publicly because they understood that it was only a temporary measure. As an operation of war it was carried out in an efficient manner, with Giovanni Ameglio being able to land his forces, defeat the enemy, and occupy the whole island of Rhodes between 4-17 May 1912.

The other smaller islands were all occupied before the end of the same month with the willing assent of most of their populations, as the Italian invasion was initially viewed as liberation from Ottoman rule by the majority, who wished to be united with Greek State. This view was soon to change when it became apparent that the Italians were going to stay, and it must have been heartbreaking for the Orthodox population to observe the genuine liberation of other Aegean islands when the Greek Navy easily took them following the outbreak of the First Balkan War in October 1912. This conflict had become general, with offensive military action by Greece, Bulgaria, and Serbia, on the same day that Italy and the Ottoman Empire had made their peace with the signing of the Treaty of Ouchy on 18 October.

To claim that the relationship between the Italo-Ottoman and First Balkan War was one of cause and effect is stretching the available evidence beyond what it can bear. Conversely, it would probably be going too far to argue that it had no effect at all. Certainly, the military operations in North Africa did not absorb much in the way of Ottoman military strength, though the logistics and support activities of the *Teskilat-i-Mahsusa* (Special Organisation) must have absorbed a great deal of resources. There were also several hundred officers, including the most able, in action in Tripoli by the middle of 1912 (though they were recalled once the peace treaty was signed and the Balkan conflict erupted). This was a commitment that would not have been impossible to maintain had the political will been there, but the events of July 1912, and the formation of the new government with its 'Great Cabinet' changed this. The new foreign minister, Gabriel Noradungiyan (Gabriel Effendi), was of the opinion that, because of the trouble now looming following the formation of the Balkan League, the war with Italy must be brought to an end. Agreeing a peace treaty was though difficult for the new government, as the CUP and the Ottoman army were reluctant to concede territory to a foe that could not conquer it.

Eventually, as we have seen, a formula was arrived at which allowed something to both sides; in other words rather a fudge. As the Italian author of works on law, politics and government, Aldobrandino Malvezzi, explained it in 1913: 'It is clear that the state of affairs created by the arrangements between Italy and Turkey creates uncertainty concerning our governing of Libya.'[26] Giolitti ignored any dubiety in the Ouchy Treaty and proclaimed a clear victory. Others were not so sure, and these included the unfortunate populations of the former Tripoli *vilayet*, who were to find that Italian occupation meant that 'the gallows flourished everywhere in Libya.'[27] This was of course under the rule of so-called 'Liberal Italy.' The reaction caused by Italy's methods, combined with Italian participation in the First World War and subsequent withdrawal of most forces to the Alpine Front, led to the Great Arab Revolt. When the reconquest, or, more accurately the conquest of the peoples of the interior of Libya (as it became in 1934) began following the defeat of the Central Powers in 1918, technology had advanced to an extent that the desert no longer provided the same degree of protection to its peoples as had previously applied. Using a devastating combination of motor vehicles, aeroplanes, and radio communications, the Italian army was able to penetrate the forbidding terrain. However, to quote Angelo Del Boca again: 'With the advent of Fascism and the elimination of an opposition capable of criticizing the excesses of colonialism, the reconquest of Libya took on a more intense pace and an unprecedented scale.' It was thus that the peoples of Libya, much more so than those of the Dodecanese, paid the greatest price for the war started by Giolitti and San Giuliano.

The Italo-Ottoman War was above all else an unnecessary war, only entered into to satisfy the nationalist and jingo right wing that had become a powerful force in Italian domestic politics. Italy could have had effective control of the Tripoli *vilayet*, in much the same style as Britain and France were effective rulers of Egypt and Tunisia respectively, up to the point of the invasion. Whether this would have resulted in the local population being more accepting of the Italian presence is unknown. But had the local Ottoman forces been withdrawn peacefully, and had the logistical support furnished by the Ottoman government never been forthcoming, and had the Italians attempted to rule with the same light-touch that the Ottoman Empire had employed, then it is conceivable that the outcome might have been considerably more peaceful than it turned out to be. Italy had long coveted the territory as has been shown, and had taken pains diplomatically to try to ensure that it would eventually get it. It was though not enough for Giolitti and San Giuliano to satisfy this long-standing territorial ambition by diplomacy. It had to be done by force of arms with famous victories reflecting the glory of Italy. That the Italian army in particular had made no plans to do anything other than what it eventually did do and occupy strategic locations on the coast, and that political and military intelligence concerning the nature of what was likely to be the reception offered were not factors that seemed to figure in the political calculation.

Neither did the virtual worthlessness of the territory being conquered. McCullagh might have been heavily biased against the Italian venture, but the title of his 1913 book on the conflict, *Italy's War for a Desert*, was nevertheless accurate. The Italo-Ottoman War was entirely a conflict of choice on Italy's part and may be reasonably viewed as a strategic blunder of massive proportions. This was recognised by at least one of Giolitti's successors. Francesco Nitti, who served as the 36th Prime Minister of Italy between 1919 and 1920, opined thus in 1921:

> The Libyan adventure, now considered serenely, cannot be looked on as anything but an aberration. Libya is an immense box of sand which never had any value, nor has it now. Tripolitania, Cyrenaica and Fezzan cover more than one million one hundred thousand square kilometres and have less than nine hundred thousand inhabitants, of whom even now, after ten years, less than a third are under the effective control of Italy.[28]

That the Italo-Ottoman War in general, and the Tripoli campaign in particular, ended as favourably as it did from the Italian perspective was entirely due to circumstances outside its control. No advice as to local conditions seems to have been solicited and no intelligence sought as to what conditions would be encountered in the theatre. No assessment as to the likely response of the enemy was carried out. Consequently the venture was launched with the invaders having little or no idea of what they were getting themselves into, and no idea of how to bring it to an end once their initial strategy collapsed.

From a distance of 100 years it should seem incredible that any responsible government would launch itself and its armed forces into such an ill-conceived campaign. However, the early years of the 21st century have surely demonstrated that the Giolitti government was by no means unique in this regard.

APPENDIX A

ULTIMATUM FROM ITALY TO TURKEY
REGARDING TRIPOLI, 28 SEPTEMBER 1911

Throughout a long series of years the Italian Government has never ceased to represent to the Porte the absolute necessity that the state of disorder and neglect in which Tripoli and Cyrenaica are left by Turkey should come to an end, and that these regions should be allowed to enjoy the same progress as that attained by other parts of Northern Africa. This transformation, which is required by the general exigencies of civilization, constitutes, so far as Italy is concerned, a vital interest of the very first order, by reason of the small distance separating these countries from the coasts of Italy.

Notwithstanding the attitude maintained by the Italian Government, which has always loyally accorded its support to the Imperial Government on the different political questions of recent times, notwithstanding the moderation and patience displayed by the Italian Government hitherto, not only have its views in regard to Tripoli been misunderstood by the Imperial Government, but what is more, all enterprises on the part of Italians, in the aforesaid regions, constantly encounter a systematic opposition of the most obstinate and unwarranted kind.

The Imperial Government, which has thus up to now displayed constant hostility towards all legitimate Italian activity in Tripoli and Cyrenaica, quite recently, at the eleventh hour, proposed to the Royal Government to come to an understanding, declaring itself disposed to grant any economic concession compatible with the treaties in force and with the higher dignity and interests of Turks; but the Royal Government does not now feel itself in a position to enter upon such negotiations, the uselessness of which is demonstrated by past experience, and which, far from constituting a guarantee for the future, could but afford a permanent cause of friction and conflict.

On the other hand, information received by the Royal Government from its consular agents in Tripoli and Cyrenaica represents the situation there as extremely dangerous on account of the agitation prevailing against Italian subjects, which is very obviously fomented by officers and other organs of the authorities. This agitation constitutes an imminent danger not only to Italian subjects but also to foreigners of any nationality who, justly perturbed and anxious for their safety, have commenced to embark and are leaving Tripoli without delay. The arrival at Tripoli of Ottoman military transports, the serious consequences of the sending of which the Royal Government had not failed to point out previously to the Ottoman Government, cannot but aggravate the situation and impress on the Royal Government the strict and absolute obligation of providing against the perils resulting therefrom.

The Italian Government, therefore, finding itself forced to think of the guardianship of its dignity and its interests, has decided to proceed to the military occupation of Tripoli and Cyrenaica. This solution is the only one Italy can decide upon, and the Royal Government expects that the Imperial Government will in consequence give orders so that it may meet with no opposition from the present Ottoman representatives, and that the measures which will be the necessary consequence may be effected without difficulty. Subsequent agreements would be made between the two governments to settle the definitive situation arising therefrom. The Royal Ambassador in Constantinople has orders to ask for a peremptory reply on this matter from the Ottoman Government within twenty-four hours from the presentation of the present document, in default of which the Italian Government will be obliged to proceed to the immediate execution of the measures destined to ensure the occupation.

Pray add that the reply of the Porte within the aforesaid limit of twenty-four hours must be communicated to us through the intermediary of the Turkish Embassy in Rome also.

San Giuliano.[1]

THE TURKISH REPLY TO ITALIAN ULTIMATUM
REGARDING TRIPOLI, 29 SEPTEMBER 1911

The Royal Embassy understands the many difficulties of the circumstances which made it impossible for Tripoli and Cyrenaica to share in the benefit of progress. An impartial examination of conditions does, in effect, suffice to establish that the constitutional Ottoman Government could not be held responsible for the existence of a situation created by the former regime. This being accepted, the Sublime Porte, in reviewing the course of events of the past three years seeks, but without avail, those circumstances in which it is claimed she has shown herself hostile to Italian enterprises relating to Tripoli and Cyrenaica. On the contrary it has always appeared to her normal and reasonable that Italy should cooperate with her capital and industrial activity to the regeneration of that part of the Empire. The Imperial Government is conscious of having shown favourable disposition each time it was confronted by propositions conceived in that spirit.

The Ottoman Government also has examined and generally settled in the most friendly way every claim and all other questions laid before it by the Royal Embassy. Is it necessary to add that in doing this it obeyed dictates so often manifested to cultivate and maintain relations of trust and of friendship with the Italian Government? In short, it was this sentiment alone which again inspired it, when it proposed most recently to the Royal Embassy an arrangement based upon economic concessions likely to furnish to Italian activity a vast field for operation in said provinces; in setting as the only limitation to these concessions the dignity and the superior interests of the Empire, as well as the treaties actually in force, the Ottoman Government gave expression to its sentiments of conciliation without, however, losing sight of the treaties and conventions that pledge the Ottoman Government to other Powers, and whose international worth would be forfeited by the will of one party.

Regarding the question of order and of security, both in Tripoli and in Cyrenaica, the Ottoman Government, well posted to appreciate the situation, can only prove, as it has already had the honour to do, all lack of reason which might justify apprehension regarding the fate of Italian subjects and of other foreigners therein established. Not only is there at this time no agitation in these countries and even less of inflaming propaganda, but the officers and other agencies of Ottoman authority have as their mission the safeguarding of order, a mission which they perform conscientiously.

As regards the presence in Tripoli of Ottoman military transports, which the Royal Embassy takes for its text to deduce from it the possibility of ominous consequences, the Sublime Porte believes it necessary to observe that it is question of a single transport whose expedition antedates by several days the note of September 26, independent of the fact that this expedition had no troops on board, could have had no other but a reassuring effect upon the people.

Reduced to its essential terms the actual disagreement resides in the absence of guarantee likely to reassure the Italian Government regarding the economic expansion of interests in Tripoli and in Cyrenaica. By not resorting to an act so grave as a military occupation, the Royal Government will find the Sublime Porte quite agreeable to the removal of the disagreement.

Therefore, in an impartial spirit, the Imperial Government requests that the Royal Government be good enough to make known to it the nature of these guarantees, to which it will readily consent if they are not to affect its territorial integrity. To this end it will refrain, during the parleys from modifying in any manner whatever the present situation of Tripoli and of Cyrenaica in military matters; and it is to be hoped that, yielding to the sincere disposition of the Sublime Porte, the Royal Government will acquiesce in this proposition.[2]

---

[1] Translation taken from: 'Ultimatum from Italy to Turkey Regarding Tripoli' in *The American Journal of International Law*, Volume 6, No. 1. Supplement: Official Documents (January 1912). pp. 11–12.

[2] Translation taken from: 'The Turkish Reply to Italian Ultimatum Regarding Tripoli' in *The American Journal of International Law*, Volume 6, No. 1. Supplement: Official Documents (January 1912). pp. 12–14.

APPENDIX B

THE CURIOUS CASE OF OSMAN MAHDI

On Tuesday, 7 May 1912 an account of a minor skirmish that had occurred outside Derna appeared in the Italian *Gazzetta Ufficiale*. It related how a nocturnal patrol of *Alpini* under Lieutenant Vialini had encountered a group of Bedouin under the command of a Turkish officer in some caves in no man's land between the Ottoman and Italian lines. Fire had been exchanged, causing the death of one of the Arabs and the wounding of the officer whilst the remainder of the group fled. According to the report the wounded officer then shouted for help in Italian but, as Vialini approached to offer this, the Turk produced a revolver and fired at the lieutenant who responded, mortally wounding his opponent. The dead Bedouin and the wounded officer were then carried inside the defences where the latter expired after being identified as one Mahdi Osman.[1]

This episode was later used by Tullio Irace as evidence of inherent Arab and Turkish treachery:

> Underneath the Arab bravery lies a substratum of cowardice. When fanaticism dies down, their habitual deceit and lying come again to the top. Treachery seems an essential part of their nature. […] The Turks are not much better, as the following incident will prove. An Italian patrol was suddenly fired on from an ambush, by Bedouins under a Turkish officer, who discharged a revolver at the Italian lieutenant (Violini) who was in command. The Italians returned the fire, wounding the officer and killing a few Arabs. The wounded officer begged for assistance, but when the Italian lieutenant advanced towards him to give him help, the Turk fired two more shots at him, but without effect. The Italian was obliged to use his own revolver in self-defence. The Turk, who expired shortly afterwards, was identified as an officer named Osman Mahdi.[2]

That there was a little more to the story was shortly revealed. For example the weekly *La Domenica del Corriere* informed its readership in the 19-26 May edition that the enemy protagonist in the incident was not what he seemed. Osman Mahdi, it had been discovered, was 'in fact British journalist John Warren Stuart Smallwood of *The Daily Chronicle* in disguise.'[3] The same information had been released to the foreign press on 14 May and many newspapers worldwide carried accounts, which also indicated that there was more to Smallwood than had at first been thought:

> Found on the body were several notebooks filled with sketches of the Italian positions, and literary matter evidently intended for newspaper articles. His binoculars, a large photographic apparatus of German make, and a Browning pistol with 211 cartridges were afterwards discovered in the recesses of the grotto, besides a military order signed by the commander of the Turkish camp furnishing him with a Bedouin escort for reconnoitring near the Italian lines.[4]

Perhaps naturally, the English language papers within the British Empire gave the most coverage, including, of course, the paper that had employed him, though it studiously avoided labelling him as a combatant:

> We have to announce with profound regret that Mr Stuart Smallwood, *Daily Chronicle* correspondent, has been killed in Tripoli. The news reached the office of the paper in a telegram from its Rome correspondent, who states that while reconnoitring in the environments of Derna, a patrol, led by Lieutenant Vitalini, was set upon, by a band of Arabs. In the ensuing fighting a distinguished looking person, first thought to be a Turkish officer, was mortally wounded. Upon him were found papers issued by the British Consulate at Cairo in October last bearing the name John Warren Stuart Smallwood, British subject, aged 29 described as a professional journalist.[5]

Though these articles were syndicated throughout the world, there were few further embellishments in respect of John Smallwood, alias Osman Mahdi, available until Georges Remond, correspondent of the Parisian *L'Illustration,* published his articles in book form, *Aux Camps Turco-Arabes: Notes de Route et de guerre en Cyrénaïque et en Tripolitaine,* in November 1912. Remond's journey through the desert had coincidentally brought him to Enver's headquarters at Ayn al-Mansur at the pertinent time, and he met Smallwood. His physical description of this *officier anglais* is interesting and, in terms of what might have been expected with regards to the majority of English officers, untypical: blonde and thin with a flat, boxer's, nose he was covered from head to toe in tattoos. In terms of temperament, Smallwood was a 'hothead,' who had no fear and viewed life as sport.[6]

Furthermore, far from being a mere correspondent, and therefore a non-combatant, Remond's account confirms that Smallwood was active on the Ottoman side when he perished. In a section entitled *mort d'un officier Anglais,* Remond relates how Smallwood had taken a Kodak camera in order to photograph the Italian works, promising the Frenchman that he would supply him with pictures for publication in *L'Illustration.* He would achieve this by setting up the camera on a tripod and utilising a long exposure time in order to get a decent picture in the bright moonlight. Unfortunately, the reflection of this on the metal parts of the camera aroused the attention of the defenders and they opened fire. He was popular with the Arabs it seems, for following his disappearance and death a poet of the local Barassa tribe sang to the Ottoman camp of him (*Le soir, le poète des 'Barassa' a chanté pour Osman effendi devant toute l'armée!*)[7]

When the, by then, German-exiled Enver Pasa published the diary recounting his participation in the Italo-Ottoman war in 1918, he included more information on Smallwood in his entry for 8 May 1912:

> In the camp we had a British officer who had converted to Islam before he had joined us as a volunteer. He was a brave fellow of a boldness I have not encountered before. It was sport for him to slip under the Italian wire and scout and record the enemy's entrenchments. A few days ago he went deep with an Arab guard into the Italian positions, was discovered, attacked and killed. Tonight I remember that dead Osmanli, whose real name was Stuart Smallwood, I see his ugly features and his jerky movements. People loved him in the camp.[8]

For those who might have been interested in learning more of this curious individual who had converted to Islam and fought and died for the Ottoman Empire, it was to be another three decades or so before more information came within the public purview. This was via a book by the equine expert Carl Raswan entitled *Drinkers of the Wind* which related the journeying of the nineteen-year old Carl Reinhard Schmidt, as Raswan then called himself, in search of the origins of the famous Arabian horse.[9] He found himself in Egypt in 1911 when, one morning at the end of August, he witnessed a British officer involved in an accident whilst out riding and from which he became unhorsed. His steed then bolted but was caught by Schmidt and returned to the unhurt former rider. According to the German, this officer then introduced himself as 'John Stuart Smallwood of the Mounted Police.' Despite some linguistic difficulties the two became good friends thereafter, and Schmidt recalled his appearance as being of a 'fine young cavalry officer' whose 'firm features had been tanned by the sun' and who possessed a 'lithe but soldierly bearing.' The account went on:

> John Stuart Smallwood was as interesting as I had hoped he would be. For two years he had been a Boundary Guard officer in Australia; later he served as a colonial cavalry officer in India. Only lately he had returned from the Sudan where he had a commission in the Camel Corps. In spite of his wide experience he was only twenty-nine years of age. He sympathised with the Arabs and was enthusiastic about the Egyptian nationalist movement.[10]

'Though quite a scholar and linguist' his greatest interest was geology, and he was at the time concerned with the investigation of gold mines between the Nile and the Red Sea, and turquoise mines in the Sinai. The young Schmidt later discovered that Smallwood had, rather unusually for a European officer, become a Muslim and was decidedly more than merely 'enthusiastic' about Egyptian nationalism. Indeed, he had actually joined the Egyptian Nationalist Party and took an active, though inevitably secret, part in their councils, particularly as these related to organising aid for the resistance following the Italian invasion of Tripoli. Whilst these latter activities were concealed from his English colleagues they were nevertheless still somewhat shocked at his religious conversion, but rationalised it by considering that it had probably occurred at the request of the British Foreign Office; that he was working undercover as a spy or agent of some description.[11]

According to Schmidt's account, over the 1911 Christmas period Smallwood contracted diphtheria and was quarantined at Victoria Hospital in Cairo meaning he was effectively incommunicado for a period of time. Schmidt thus rather lost touch with him, and was surprised to discover that after recovering from the disease the Englishman had not only resigned from the police but had also disappeared completely without leaving word of his whereabouts. It was only 'many weeks later' that Schmidt received four letters from his errant friend revealing that he had journeyed to Derna in Cyrenaica, where he was 'helping the Turks to organise artillery positions, establish observation points and train volunteers.' Also related was that, accompanied by an 'heroic Arab' named Sheykh Sassi 'who was his guide and constant companion,' he was in the habit of reconnoitring the Italian defences at night by surreptitiously crawling amongst them.[12]

At Smallwood's prompting, and with the cooperation of the movement to aid the Ottoman resistance which he had also joined, Schmidt made the lengthy and complex journey to join his friend at Derna. Arriving on the evening of 7 May 1912, he found that the Englishman and his colleague were not at Ayn al-Mansur,

Ridotta Lombardia (the Lombardia redoubt or fort) was constructed to anchor the western side of the defences of Derna, to a design obviously influenced by the fact that the Ottoman forces were in possession of much inferior artillery. Though not visible in this photograph, the work was protected by 18-metre wide belts of interwoven barbed wire. It was in the vicinity of this work that the Muslim Englishman, John Smallwood (Osman el-Mahdi), met his death on the night of 7 May 1912. (Author's Collection).

whilst the sound of gunfire, and the activity of Italian searchlights, indicated that a firefight of some kind was taking place on the left of the Ottoman lines close to the Italian strongpoint of *ridotta Lombardia*. The very intensity of the fire, the 'incessant strafing of the machine guns,' indicated that something out of the ordinary was in the offing and, as Schmidt learned, Smallwood and Sheykh Sassi were abroad somewhere in that very area.

Permission to proceed having been received from Ottoman headquarters, Schmidt and two Arabs, Aziz and Marzuki, set out to see if they could locate the errant pair by heading towards the sound of the guns:

> Aziz, familiar with every foot of the surrounding countryside, led us directly to the last Turkish trench, where he spoke with the officers in charge.

> No report of Osman el-Mahdi or Sheykh Sassi had been received at the front, nor could any telephonic contact be made with the old ruined blockhouse hidden in the gully between the Turkish and Italian lines. Smallwood had lately installed [telephone] wires there, and he kept a store of arms and ammunition in the place. [...]

> After leaving the Turkish trench, we crossed a narrow valley. On the opposite height our real task began. Before us lay a sector about a third of a mile [*circa* 500 metres] in width, leading over level ground right up to the Italian barbed wire defences, behind which the masonry of the fortress of *Lombardia* could plainly be distinguished. From time to time the Italian searchlights flared up and groped about the tangled mass of wires in front of us.[13]

By creeping forward, and using camouflaged burlap sheets to cover themselves where necessary, the three men reached a small patch of dead ground at the outer edge of the Italian wire without being discovered. The trio then split up. Marzuki remained under cover whilst the other two went left and right in an attempt to ascertain if there were any signs of Smallwood and Sheykh Sassi. Schmidt went to the right [easterly] but after venturing some sixty metres decided it was unlikely the pair would have gone that way as the ground sloped away steeply and offered no cover at all. Reversing his course he passed Marzuki before continuing after Aziz. The Italians were obviously on high alert, 'flooding the landscape with their light beams,' so he had to proceed with extreme caution. He discovered electrical wires used to trigger mines that had been cut and taped back. This was work he attributed to Smallwood who, he had been told, made a habit of appropriating Italian mines by installing control wires that allowed them to be triggered from the Ottoman positions.

Eventually he came across Aziz, who told him that he had discovered the body of Sheykh Sassi lying at the edge of the barbed wire. The Italian defenders could see the corpse too, and were illuminating and scrutinising the area in the expectation that where there had been one man then there would likely be more. With there still being no sign of Smallwood, the two crawled further along the defensive perimeter; 'an almost impregnable girdle of interwoven barbed wire at least sixty feet [18 metres] wide.' His account continued:

> The moonlight was now so bright that we could see to the western end of the fortification where it turned to the north. Along this line, but not more than fifty feet [15 metres] away, inside the defence – as if in the cobweb of a spider – hung the lifeless, broken form of a human being.

> The body had fallen into the wire entanglement against a wooden post. [...] The part of the face I was able to see [and the brown khaki uniform of an officer] left no doubt in my mind that this was Smallwood. [...] The left sleeve of his brown khaki shirt was torn by bullets, and the broad leather belt around his waist was furrowed and split. There could not be life in him.[14]

In this Schmidt was mistaken, as he was later to discover. However in withdrawing to the Ottoman lines he came under fire, and was wounded severely enough to require hospitalisation. After recovering somewhat he was told that Aziz had made it safely back, but had then returned with another Bedouin in the hope of recovering the bodies of Sheykh Sassi and Smallwood, or at least bringing them within the Ottoman sector before sunrise (when there was an hour's truce whilst both sides recovered any dead and wounded). The two Arabs had managed at least part of this task, but discovered that the Englishman, despite suffering eleven wounds, was somehow still alive. Indeed, they managed to drag him to the ruined blockhouse where he recovered consciousness.

This was not safety however, as the Italians were by this stage thoroughly aroused and were pushing out patrols under the cover of artillery which shelled any points where an enemy might be lurking. It was one of these patrols, led by Enrico Vitalini, that approached the blockhouse. The unnamed Bedouin managed to slip away and later stated that 'when he last saw Aziz and Smallwood, they were still alive, and – incredibly – even Smallwood, propped up against a wall, was firing at the enemy!' Their ultimate fate was communicated via a note sent to the Ottoman headquarters by Vitalini: Aziz had been found dead, his life taken by an Italian revolver bullet but the other man had been taken alive and 'carried to the hospital in the fortress of Lombardia, where 'Osman el-Mahdi' died late at night in his [Vitalini's] arms.'[15]

This is undoubtedly a tale with more than a hint of romance, and one moreover that ended tragically. However, there is a little more known about Smallwood that perhaps somewhat undermines the romanticism. It might be the case that, rather than being quarantined with diphtheria in December 1911, Smallwood had fled Cairo to avoid the authorities. This was because of an incident at the Heliopolis Palace Hotel that occurred on the evening of 16 December.[16] Further to this, on 19 December, a summons was issued by His Britannic Majesty's Provincial Court at Cairo to 'Mohamed Sherif Smallwood, otherwise known as John Warren Stuart Smallwood.'[17] According to this document, Smallwood was charged with causing a disturbance 'at or about eight in the evening' by threatening 'to kill Hassib Ydlibi and use abusive language to and of him.'[18] In order to answer this charge he was commanded to appear before the court on Saturday, 23 December 1911 at 10 o'clock in the morning.

He did not turn up, and may have had a good excuse not to do so, for it appears that there were two guests at the hotel that night named Smallwood, and the summons was delivered to the other one; Arthur Smallwood. The latter wrote to A D Alban, the British Consul who would preside over the hearing, on 21 December pointing out that he was not the person named on the document and would send his advocate, John Walker, to return it and clarify the situation. He explained that he could not stay in Cairo as he had 'made arrangements to leave for the Soudan to-day.'

Demonstrating that J W S Smallwood had yet another alias is probably the only point of interest that arises from this inconsequential incident. Whether or not he did leave Egypt because of it, or after recovering from diphtheria as he told Schmidt, can only be a matter of speculation. Indeed, I have been unable to discover much more about the man, other than that he was probably born in Droitwich, Worcestershire, in 1882.[19]

Quite what, undoubtedly twisting, path led Smallwood from Droitwich to Derna, via his identities of Mohamed Sherif and Osman Mahdi and decision to join the Ottoman resistance, remains a total mystery. His is indeed a curious case and he appears to have been one of those eccentric and colourful adventurers that occasionally surface in studies of European imperialism. Unfortunately, the amount of work that would be required to unearth any more information on this intriguing character would be disproportionate to the probable results and his historical importance.

I took the liberty of giving Smallwood a small role in the second book of The Samson Plews Collection, *The Niagara Device*, (shortly available via all main book outlets in both electronic and hard copy), where the main character accompanies him on the journey to Derna. In this portion of the adventure the protagonist is on the trail of what becomes known as The Voynich Manuscript.

However, if anyone who reads this knows anything more about Smallwood, or can point me in the right direction, then I would be most interested to hear from them.

---

[1]   *Gazzetta Ufficiale del Regno D'Italia,* Martedì, 7 maggio 1912.

[2]   Tullio Irace, *With the Italians in Tripoli: The Authentic History of the Turco-Italian War* (London; John Murray, 1912) pp. 155-6.

[3]   *La Domenica del Corriere,* 19-26 maggio 1912.

[4]   Official Report issued from Rome and syndicated internationally.

[5]   *The Daily Chronicle,* 15 May 1912.

[6]   Georges Remond, *Aux Camps Turco-Arabes: Notes de Route et de guerre en Cyrénaïque et en Tripolitaine* (Paris; Hachette, 1913) p. 182.

[7]   Remond. pp. 182-3.

[8]   Enver Pascha, *Um Tripolis* (München; Hugo Bruckmann, 1918) pp. 45-6.

[9]   Carl R Raswan, *Drinkers of the Wind* (New York; Creative Age Press, 1942).

[10] Raswan. p. 51.

[11] Raswan. p. 61. There may have been, at least to some extent, a grain of truth in this. Smallwood was definitely in contact with Arthur Wavell (Arthur John Byng Wavell), a cousin of the future Field Marshal Lord Wavell, who was almost certainly a British agent operating in Ottoman territory and was deported from Yemen in June 1911. See: Önder Kocatürk, *Hacı Ali (Wavell) Olayı* (an article which 'aims to shed light on the incident in which Arthur Wavell (1882-1916) was caught in Yemen and taken into custody by the Ottoman authorities and later developments from then on). Available from stanbul Üniversitesi website: http://www.istanbul.edu.tr/enstituler/ataturk/kisiler/docs/onderkocaturk-Wavell.pdf

[12] Raswan. p. 66.

[13] Raswan. p. 145.

[14] Raswan. p. 147.

[15] Raswan. p. 155.

[16] The Heliopolis Place Hotel was no ordinary establishment. Opened on 1 December 1910 it was advertised as the 'most luxurious and comfortable hotel in the world' containing '500 rooms with private bath' and a 'first class restaurant.' Samir Raafat, 'The Heliopolis Palace Hotel: A Desert Taj Mahal' in the *Cairo Times,* 19 March 1998. Available online at: www.egy.com/landmarks/98-03-19.php

[17] The records are in the National Archives at Kew. FO 841/121 Consular Court Cases. Hassib Ydlibiv (sic). Mohd. Sherif Smallwood k/a John Warren Stuart Smallwood.

[18] Hasib, or Hassib, Ydlibi (Ydlabi) was a person of some substance: 'One of the most intriguing foreign personalities involved in Ethiopian trade and politics at the turn of the 20th century. He was born in 1866 of a Syrian father and a Circassian mother. As of 1897, Ydlibi served as an interpreter for the British Expeditionary Force in the Sudan. After leaving the service, his trading in gum brought him to Kordofan, which was followed in 1905 by his trip to Ethiopia as a representative of the Kordofan Trading Company. After discovering rubber trees in the south of the country, Hasib Ydlibi was granted monopoly rights for the trading of gum by Emperor Menelik II and gradually became involved in Ethiopian state matters and the politics of the Empire.' Hanna Rubinkowska, Review of May Ydlibi and Bahru Zewde (Ed.), *With Ethiopian Rulers: a Biography of Hasib Ydlibi* (Addis Ababa; Addis Ababa University Press, 2006) in *Aethiopica: International Journal of Ethiopian and Eritrean Studies,* Volume 11, 2008. pp. 283-85. He was domiciled in Britain and had been a partner in a rubber importation business at 56 Bloom Street, Manchester; Hassim, Ydlibi & Rehan. See: 'The India-Rubber Trade in Great Britain' in *The India Rubber World,* Vol. XXXV No. 2. 1 November 1906. p. 47.

[19] John Warren S Smallwood born June 1882 in Droitwich, Worcestershire. Information from Ancestry.com. Retrieved 27 January 2013.

APPENDIX C

THE ITALIAN CAMPAIGN AND THE PRINCIPLES OF WAR

Clausewitz is often quoted as stating that war is the continuation of politics by other means. If this is so, then the Italian campaign to gain Tripoli cannot be said to have conformed to the maxim. Making war was not a means to an end but rather an end in itself, because all that Italy hoped and wanted to gain could have been achieved politically without fighting. Further, it may be argued, having decided to ignore Clausewitzean principle in that context and fight for the sake of military glory, the Italians went on to disregard other, much more important, principles; the Principles of War.

There are no universally accepted Principles of War as such because different states, military organizations, and cultures have codified them (if they have done so at all) according to circumstance; the needs of time and place. Having said that, those principles that have evolved, however they may be articulated, represent an attempt to grapple with fundamental truths, and serve as basic guidelines, in relation to the practice of the art or science of military affairs. Indeed, many writers have argued that, however expressed, the Principles of War are essentially timeless; that there is *Nothing New under the Sun Tzu*.[1] There have been many attempts at writing them down. The first, and perhaps the most famous, being the treatise by Sun Tzu known as *The Art of War* which dates from around 500 years BCE. The somewhat more recent works by Clausewitz, Jomini, et al have also been well studied.

Current thinking, certainly in western militaries, has decocted all the various theories, wisdom, and experiences into a few general principles (doctrine). For example, the United States military has nine whilst the British have ten. Current US doctrine, and the ruling principles underlying it, has been tabulated as follows:[2]

PRINCIPLE	DEFINITION
Mass	Concentrate combat power at the decisive place and time
Objective	Direct every military operation towards a clearly defined, decisive, and attainable objective
Offensive	Seize, retain, and exploit the initiative
Surprise	Strike the enemy at a time, at a place, or in a manner for which he is unprepared
Economy of force	Allocate minimum essential combat power to secondary efforts
Maneuver	Place the enemy in a position of disadvantage through the flexible application of combat power
Unity of command	For every objective, ensure unity of effort under one responsible commander
Security	Never permit the enemy to acquire an unexpected advantage
Simplicity	Prepare clear, uncomplicated plans and clear, concise orders to ensure thorough understanding

There are no doubt many others, and it may be an interesting, if entirely academic, diversion to take whichever rendition most appeals and compare and contrast it with the conduct of the Italian campaign in Tripoli. So, to steal a line from the unknown author of *The Beale Papers*, 'when your day's work is done, and you are comfortably seated by your good fire, a short time devoted to the subject can injure no one, and may bring its reward.'

---

[1]   Commander Jacques P Olivier, *Nothing New Under the Sun Tzu: Timeless Principles of the Operational Art of War*. Available from www.journal.forces.gc.ca/vol14/no1/PDF/CMJ141Ep55.pdf

[2]   The nine Principles of War, as defined in the Army Field Manual FM-3 Military Operations. Available from:www.wpi.edu/academics/military/prinwar.html

CHAPTER NOTES

CHAPTER ONE

[1] Quoted in Walter K Kelly, *The History of Russia: From the Earliest Period to the Present Time*. Two Volumes. (London; Henry G Bohn, 1855). Vol. II. p. 421.

[2] Sevket Süreyya Aydemir, *Makedonya'dan Ortaasya'ya Enver Pa a*, Vol. II 1908-1914 (Istanbul; Remzi Kitabevi, 1981) p. 552.

[3] There had been a long period of steady erosion. Since 1878 the Ottoman Empire had lost, or lost control of, a great deal of territory. In that year Cyprus came under British administration, though the Sultan retained sovereignty, whilst Montenegro, Romania, and Serbia became independent and Bosnia-Herzegovina was occupied by Austria-Hungary. Tunisia became a French protectorate in 1881 and the British took effective control of Egypt the following year. Cretan autonomy was imposed, via Great Power intervention, in 1898 and Britain declared a protectorate over Kuwait in 1899. In 1908 Austria-Hungary formally annexed Bosnia-Herzegovina and Bulgaria gained independence.

[4] Walter K Kelly, *The History of Russia: From the Earliest Period to the Present Time*. Two Volumes. (London; Henry G Bohn, 1855). Vol. II. p. 421.

[5] For a brief version of this see: Richard C Hall, *The Balkan Wars, 1912-1913: Prelude to the First World War* (London; Routledge, 2000) pp. 7-8. For an in depth account: D W Sweet, 'The Bosnian Crisis' in F H Hinsley (Ed.), *British Foreign Policy Under Sir Edward Grey* (Cambridge; Cambridge University Press, 1977) pp. 178-92.

[6] Richard Millman, 'The Bulgarian Massacres Reconsidered,' in *The Slavonic and East European Review*, Vol. 58, No. 2, (April, 1980), p. 230.

[7] J A MacGahan, *The Turkish Atrocities in Bulgaria, Letters of the Special Commissioner of the Daily News [. . .]. With an Introduction and Mr. Schuyler's Preliminary Report* (London; Bradbury, Agnew, 1876).

[8] There is a huge literature on this subject. See for example: Alan Palmer, *The Decline and Fall of the Ottoman Empire* (London; Barnes and Noble, 1994) and Suraiya Faroqhi, *The Ottoman Empire and the World Around It* (London; I B Tauris, 2005).

[9] L S Stavrianos, *Balkan Federation: A History of the Movement Toward Balkan Unity in Modern Times* (Hamden, CT; Archon, 1964).

[10] The evidence that Bismarck actually said this is at several removes, and seems to originate in a speech made by Winston S Churchill in the House of Commons on 16 August 1945. According to Churchill: 'I remember that a fortnight or so before the last war, the Kaiser's friend, Herr Ballin, the great shipping magnate, told me that he had heard Bismarck say it towards the end of his life. Churchill was thus recalling a second-hand remark made to him some 31 years previously, which was itself a recollection of a comment made around 17 years before that. Robert Rhodes James (Ed.), *Winston S Churchill: His Complete Speeches, 1897-1963*, 8 Vols. (New York; Chelsea House Publishers, 1974) Vol. VII 1943-1949. p. 7214.

[11] 'The ancient geographic term of 'Macedonia' underwent a restoration in the era of modern nationalism. Historically, it denoted a territory the extent of which had varied through the ages. For example, the tenth-century Byzantine province [of] Macedonia, which covered the Thracian districts of modern Bulgaria, had little to do with the Macedonia of antiquity. In the medieval Bulgarian and Serbian kingdoms the term was totally meaningless, nor did it have any place within the administrative vocabulary of the Ottoman Empire. But by the beginning of the twentieth century, Macedonia was frequently in the headlines of the European press: it was now understood to correspond roughly to the Ottoman *vilayets* of Salonika and Monastir (Bitola), as well as the sanjak of Oskiib (Skopje) in the *vilayet* of Kosov.' Fikret Adanir, 'The Socio-Political Environment of Balkan Nationalism: the Case of Ottoman Macedonia 1856-1912' in Heinz-Gerhard Haupt, Michael G. Mulle, Stuart Woolf (Eds.), *Regional and national identities in Europe in the XIXth and XXth centuries/Les identites regionales et nationales en Europe aux XIXe et XXe siecles* (The Hague; Kluwer Law International, 1998) pp. 240-1. See also: Fikret Adanir, 'The Macedonians in the Ottoman Empire. 1878-1912' in Andreas Kappeler in collaboration with Fikret Adanir and Alan O'Day (eds.), *The Formation of National Elites* (New York; New York University Press, 1992). pp. 161-91.

[12] Adolf Vischer, 'Tripoli' in *The Geographical Journal*, Vol. 38, No. 5 (November 1911) p. 487. Sükrü Hanioglu, 'The Second Constitutional Period, 1908-1918' in Re at Kasaba (Ed.), *The Cambridge History of Turkey: Volume 4, Turkey in the Modern World* (Cambridge; Cambridge University Press, 2008) p. 86.

[13] Ali Abdullatif Ahmida, *The Making of Modern Libya: State Formation, Colonization, and Resistance* (Albany, NY; State University of New York Press, 2009) p. 74.

[14] W S Cooke, *The Ottoman Empire and Its Tributary States* (B. R. Grüner, Amsterdam, 1968) p. 64.

[15] The CIA World Factbook. https://www.cia.gov/library/publications/the-world-factbook/geos/ly.html

[16] Libya was not formally adopted as the collective term for the three provinces until 1929. Lisa Anderson,

'The Development of Nationalist Sentiment in Libya, 1908-1922' in Rashid Khalidi, Lisa Anderson, Muhammad Muslih and Reeva S Simon (Eds.) *The Origins of Arab Nationalism* (New York; Columbia University Press, 1991) p. 241.

[17] E W Bovill (Ed.), *Missions to the Niger Volume I: The Journal Of Friedrich Hornemann's Travels From Cairo To Murzuk In The Years 1797-98; The Letters Of Major Alexander Gordon Laing 1824-26* (London: Hakluyt Society, 1964) p. 150. Bornu was a region on the south-west shore of Lake Chad and an important source of slaves.

[18] See: Joseph Wheelan, *Jefferson's War: America's First War on Terror 1801-1805* (New York; Carroll & Graf, 2003) and Frederick C Leiner, *The End of Barbary Terror: America's 1815 War Against the Pirates of North Africa* (Cary, NC; Oxford University Press USA, 2007).

[19] Kola Folayan, 'Tripoli-Bornu Political Relations, 1817-1825' in *Journal of the Historical Society of Nigeria.* Volume 5 No. 4, June 1971. pp. 463-71. Kola Folayan, *Tripoli During the Reign of Y suf P sh Qaram nl* (Ilé-If , Nigeria; University of Ife Press, 1979).

[20] James Henry Skene, *The Three Eras of Ottoman History: A Political Essay on the Late Reform of Turkey, Considered Principally as Affecting her Position in the Event of a War Taking Place* (London; Chapman and Hall, 1851) p. 77.

[21] 'Tripoli was always a main Mediterranean outlet of black slaves traded across the Sahara. [...] The abolition of slavery and the slave trade in Tunis and Algiers in the 1840s only confirmed this predominance. But it was short lived, for by the late 1850s Tripoli, too, was falling victim to European abolitionist fervour, leaving only Benghazi and lesser Turkish North African anchorages as the sole, unmolested, Saharan slaving outlets on the Mediterranean. They continued quietly to ship slaves to Levantine markets until the beginning of the twentieth century.' John L Wright, *The Trans-Saharan Slave Trade* (London; Routledge, 2007) p.114.

[22] Leonhard Schmitz, *A Manual of Ancient Geography* (Philadelphia, PA; Blanchard and Lea, 1857) p. 114.

[23] A H Keane, *Asia: Vol. II, Southern and Western Asia* (London; Edward Stanford, 1909). Ritter zur Helle von Samo, *Das Vilajet der Inseln des Weissen Meeres (Bahr i setid dschezairi), das privilegirte Beylik Samos (Syssam) und das Mutessariflik Cypern (Kybris). Statistische und militärische Notizen aus den Papieren des früheren Militär-Attaches der k.u.k. österreichisch-ungarischen Botschaft in Constantinopel* (Wien, C Gerold's sohn, 1877).

[24] Edouard Driault and Michel Lheritier, *Histoire diplomatique de la Grèce de 1821 a nos jours,* 5 vols. Vol. II, E Driault, *La règne d'Othon. La Grande Idée (1830-1862)* (Paris; Les Presses Universitaires de France, 1925) pp. 252-253.

[25] H P Willmott, *The Last Century of Sea Power: Volume I, From Port Arthur to Chanak, 1894-1922* (Bloomington, IN; Indiana University Press, 2009) pp. 32-33.

[26] Theodore Ropp and Stephen S Roberts (Ed.), *The Development of a Modern Navy: French Naval Policy 1871-1904* (Annapolis, MD; Naval Institute Press, 1987) p. 203.

[27] Gabor Agoston, *Guns for the Sultan: Military Power and the Weapons Industry in the Ottoman Empire* (Cambridge; Cambridge University Press, 2005) pp. 49-50, 178. See also: Gabor Agoston and Bruce Masters, *Encyclopedia of the Ottoman Empire* (New York; Facts On File, 2007).

[28] Bernd Langensiepen and Ahmet Güleryüz (James Cooper Ed. and Trans.), *The Ottoman Steam Navy, 1828-1923* (London; Conway Maritime Press, 1995) pp. 8-9.

[29] The date according to the Gregorian calendar.

[30] Michelle U Campos, *Ottoman Brothers: Muslims, Christians, and Jews in Early Twentieth-Century* Palestine (Stanford, CA;: Stanford University Press, 2011) p. 110.

[31] Ali Abdullatif Ahmida, *The Making of Modern Libya: State formation, Colonization, and Resistance, 1830-1932* (Albany, NY; State University of New York Press, 1994) pp. 111- 3.

[32] See: Aykut Kansu, *The Revolution of 1908 in Turkey* (Leiden; Brill Academic Publishers , 1997). Feroz Ahmad, *The Young Turks: The Committee of Union and Progress in Turkish Politics, 1908-1914* (Oxford; University Press, 1969); M ükrü Hanio lu, *The Young Turks in Opposition* (Cary, NC; Oxford University Press USA, 1995) N Naim Turfan, *Rise of the Young Turks: Politics, the Military and Ottoman Collapse* (New York; I B Tauris, 2000); M ükrü Hanio lu, *Preparation for a Revolution: The Young Turks, 1902-1908* (New York; Oxford University Press, 2001).

[33] Bernd Langensiepen and Ahmet Güleryüz (James Cooper Ed. and Trans.), *The Ottoman Steam Navy, 1828-1923* (London; Conway Maritime Press, 1995) p. 17.

[34] Mark Kerr, *Land, Sea, and Air: Reminiscences of Mark Kerr* (New York; Longmans, Green, 1927) p. 122.

[35] Francis Yeats-Brown, *Bloody Years: A Decade of Plot and Counter-Plot by the Golden Horn* (New York; Viking Press, 1932) p. 43.

[36] G P Gooch and H W V Temperley (Eds.), *British Documents on the Origins of the War: 1898-1914,* Volume V, *The Near East, the Macedonian Problem and the Annexation of Bosnia, 1903-1909* (London; HMSO, 1928) p. 282-3.

[37] Minute by HC Norman (Quoting Harold Nicolson to Hugh O'Beirne), War Office, September 12, 1910. G P Gooch and H W V Temperley (Eds.), *British Documents on the Origins of the War: 1898-1914,* Volume IX, *The Balkan Wars,* Part I, *The Prelude: The Tripoli War* (London; HMSO, 1933) No 177, p. 202.

[38] Miranda Vickers, *The Albanians: A Modern History* (London: I B Tauris, 2000) pp. 63-5. Erik Jan Zürcher, Turkey: a Modern History (London: I B Tauris, 2004) p. 104.

CHAPTER TWO

[1] Suzanne Stewart-Steinberg, *The Pinocchio Effect: On Making Italians, 1860-1920* (Chicago; University of Chicago Press, 2007) p. 1.
[2] Quoted in: Luciano Cheles and Lucio Sponza, 'Introduction: National Identities and Avenues of Persuasion' in Luciano Cheles and Lucio Sponza (Eds.), *The Art of Persuasion: Political Communication in Italy from 1945 to the 1990s* (Manchester; Manchester University Press, 2001) p. 1.
[3] The Holy Alliance was formed to preserve reactionary powers. See: William Penn Cresson, *The Holy Alliance: The European Background of the Monroe Doctrine* (Oxford; Oxford University Press, 1922).
[4] Paul Ginsborg, *Daniele Manin and the Venetian Revolution of 1848-49* (Cambridge; Cambridge University Press, 1979) p. 324.
[5] Jonathan Sperber, *The European Revolutions, 1848-1851* (Cambridge; Cambridge University Press, 2005) pp. 242-4.
[6] See: Denis Mack Smith, 'The Revolutions of 1848-1849 in Italy' in R J W Evans and Hartmut Pogge von Strandmann (Eds.) *The Revolutions in Europe, 1848-1849: From Reform to Reaction* (Oxford; Oxford University Press, 2000) pp. 55-82.
[7] See: Bernard Reardon, *Liberalism and Tradition: Aspects of Catholic Thought in Nineteenth-Century France* (Cambridge; Cambridge University Press, 1975).
[8] Edyth Hinkley, *Mazzini: The Story of a Great Italian* (New York; G P Putnam's, 1924.) p. 123.
[9] Arnold Whitridge, *Men in Crisis: The Revolutions of 1848* (New York; Charles Scribner's Sons, 1949) pp.114-193.
[10] A J P Taylor, *The Habsburg Monarchy, 1809-1918: A History of the Austrian Empire and Austria-Hungary* (London; Hamish Hamilton, 1948) p. 93.
[11] J A S Grenville, *Europe Reshaped, 1848-1878* (Oxford; Blackwell, 2000) p. 151.
[12] For accounts of this episode, and for the next section generally, unless otherwise stated, see: Christopher Duggan, *The Force of Destiny: A History of Italy Since 1796* (London; Allen Lane, 2007) pp. 199-200. Alan Cassels, *Ideology and International Relations in the Modern World* (London; Routledge, 1996) pp. 72-3. Michael Graham Fry, Erik Goldstein and Richard Langhorne, *Guide to International Relations and Diplomacy* (London; Continuum, 2002) pp. 123-4. Shepard B Clough and Salvatore Saladino, *A History of Modern Italy: Documents, Readings, and Commentary* (New York; Columbia University Press, 1968) p. 101. Frank J Coppa, *The Origins of the Italian Wars of Independence* (London; Longman, 1992). William Roscoe Thayer, *The Life and Times of Cavour* (Boston, MA; Houghton Mifflin, 1911) Vol. I. pp. 527-532. Arnold Blumberg, *A Carefully Planned Accident: The Italian War of 1859* (Cranbury, NJ; Associated University Presses, 1990). Mack Walker (Ed.), *Plombières: Secret Diplomacy and the Rebirth of Italy* (New York; Oxford University Press USA, 1968)
[13] William Roscoe Thayer, *The Life and Times of Cavour* (Boston, MA; Houghton Mifflin, 1911) Vol. II. p. 52-3.
[14] Richard Brooks, *Solferino 1859: The Battle for Italy's Freedom* (Oxford; Osprey, 2009) p. 87.
[15] A Correspondent of the New York Times, 'Battle of Solferino,' in *The Advocate of Peace,* March, 1860 p. 48. The British diplomat Sir Edward Charles Blount visited the battlefield on 1 July, and left a description in his memoirs: '[I] shall never forget the sight. The carnage had been frightful. [. . .] Even at a distance of seven miles, the stench was horrible, and imagination at its best, or worst, could scarcely exaggerate the horror of the scene.' Sir Edward Blount, *Memoirs of Sir Edward Blount* (London; Longman Green, 1902) pp. 140-1. Others agreed, and one of them, the Swiss, Henry Dunant, who assisted with the care of the wounded, later published an account of what he had seen. In this book, *A Memory of Solferino,* he proposed the creation of national relief societies of trained volunteers to provide neutral and impartial help to wounded soldiers. This later segued into the International Committee of the Red Cross. Henry Dunant, *A Memory of Solferino* (Geneva; International Committee of the Red Cross, 1986).
[16] Gary P. Cox, *The Halt in the Mud: French Strategic Planning from Waterloo to Sedan* (Boulder, CO; Westview, 1994) pp. 164-5.
[17] Robert Sencourt, *Napoleon III: The Modern Emperor* (London; Ernest Benn, 1933) p. 220. Christopher Duggan, *The Force of Destiny: A History of Italy Since 1796* (London; Allen Lane, 2007) p. 205.
[18] Erik Goldstein, *Wars and Peace Treaties, 1816-1991* (London; Routledge, 1992) p. 16.
[19] The 'foolish, kind, old Grand-Duke Leopold of Tuscany' had been deposed in April 1859, and, following the victory of Magenta, the 'fiercer despots of Modena and Parma fled from their territories with the Austrian garrisons, and the simultaneous [Austrian] withdrawal [. . .] from Bologna was the signal for the rising of the Pope's [Romagnol] subjects.' George Macaulay Trevelyan, *Garibaldi and the Thousand* (London; Longmans Green, 1912) p. 111.

20 Christopher Duggan, *The Force of Destiny: A History of Italy Since 1796* (London; Allen Lane, 2007) p. 206. Perhaps Pius IX particularly; following the rising in the Umbrian city of Perugia in early June 1859, a 2000 strong contingent of the Swiss Guard (*guardia svizzera*) under the command of Colonel Antonio Schmid was sent to restore Papal authority. These troops succeeded in gaining entry to the city on 20 June 1859, but then ran amok, looting and killing the citizenry in what became known as the 'Massacre of Perugia.' In an astonishingly insensitive move Pius IX promoted Schmid to the rank of brigadier-general for re-establishing 'the legitimate Government to the satisfaction of all good men.' Further, he 'ordered due encomiums to be given to the troops who took part in the action, and so highly distinguished themselves.' [*Giornale di Roma*, 21 June 1860]. The Holy See, and Catholic opinion generally, denied of course that the Papal Troops had misbehaved. Unfortunately for such apologists an American family had been non-fatal victims of the Swiss Guard. This led to an intervention by the US Government. [James Buchanan, *Message of the President of the United States, communicating [. . .] papers in relation to an alleged outrage on an American family at Perugia, in the Pontifical States* (36th Congress, 1st Session. Ex. Doc. No. 4) (US Government; Government Printing Office, 1860)]. The British Prime Minister, Gladstone, 'crushed' the Papal apologist Sir George Bowyer in the House of Commons on 4 March 1861 by quoting to him the report of what occurred at Perugia sent to Brigadier Giuseppe Agostini of the Papal Army. 'The soldiers [. . .] took by assault the houses and the convent, where they killed and wounded all they could, not excepting some women and, proceeding forward, they did the same thing at the inn in the Borgo San Pietro.' [*The Spectator*, 9 March 1861]. Agostini was involved in the Edgardo Mortara case. See: David Kertzer, *The Kidnapping of Edgardo Mortara* (London; Picador, 1997).
21 Johannes Mattern, *The Employment of the Plebiscite in the Determination of Sovereignty: A dissertation Submitted to the Board of University Studies of The Johns Hopkins University in conformity with the Requirements for the degree of Doctor of Philosophy* (Baltimore, MD; John Hopkins University. 1922) pp. 94-5.
22 Johannes Mattern, *The Employment of the Plebiscite in the Determination of Sovereignty: A dissertation Submitted to the Board of University Studies of The Johns Hopkins University in conformity with the Requirements for the degree of Doctor of Philosophy* (Baltimore, MD; John Hopkins University. 1922) p. 89.
23 At least some of those who cast doubt on them were fervent partisans of the status quo. The English Sir George Bowyer MP, for example, was a passionate defender of the temporal power of the Popes. He is recorded as shouting 'hear, hear' to the notion that to 'take the Romagna from the Pope is not an aggression, is not a robbery, but is a sacrilege.'[Hansard, *House of Commons Debates*, 04 May 1860. Vol. 158. Columns 685-9.] The French Félix Dupanloup was a Catholic bishop, so perhaps is is not surprising that he wrote an often-quoted book denouncing the means whereby the Pope was shorn of his territories: F A P Dupanloup, *La souveraineté pontificale selon le droit catholique et le droit européen, par Mgr. l'évêque d'Orléans* (Paris; Lecoffre, 1860). For a more detailed discussion of the issue see: George Martin, *The Red Shirt and the Cross of Savoy* (London; Eyre & Spottiswoode, 1969) p. 616.
24 Christopher Duggan, *The Force of Destiny: A History of Italy Since 1796* (London; Allen Lane, 2007) p. 206.
25 Alfonso Scirocco (Trans. Allan Cameron) *Garibaldi: Citizen of the World* (Princeton, NJ; Princeton University Press, 2007) pp. 236-7.
26 There is a vast literature devoted to Garibaldi. Personal favourites include those works by Alfonso Scirocco and George Macaulay Trevelyan.
27 Lieut. Colonel Chambers [Osborne William Samuel Chambers], *Garibaldi and Italian Unity* (London; Smith Elder, 1864) pp. 32-3.
28 George Macaulay Trevelyan, *Garibaldi and the Thousand* (London; Longmans Green, 1912) p. 175. The Mincio is a river in northern Italy. In 1860 its course delineated the border between (Italian) Lombardy and (Austrian) Venetia.
29 D Mack Smith (Ed.), *Plombieres: Secret Diplomacy and the Rebirth of Italy* (New York; Oxford University Press, 1968) p. 248. J A R Marriott, *The Makers of Modern Italy* (London; Macmillan, 1901) p. 49.
30 George Macaulay Trevelyan, *Garibaldi and the Thousand* (London; Longmans Green, 1912) pp. 175-6. Some sources say the ballot boxes were to be smashed before the vote: William Roscoe Thayer, *The Life and Times of Cavour* (Boston, MA; Houghton Mifflin, 1911) Vol. II. p.252.
31 Laurence Oliphant, *Episodes in a Life of Adventure: Or, Moss from a Rolling Stone* (Edinburgh: William Blackwood, 1887) pp. 177-8. Oliphant goes on to state: 'I will not vouch for these being the very words he used, but this was their exact sense.' Certainly the mention of 'Bomba' seems strange, as Ferdinand II, aka Re Bomba (King of Bombs), had died on 22 May 1859 and was succeeded by Francis II (Francesco II). See: Harold Acton, *The Last Bourbons of Naples* (1825-1861) (London; Methuen, 1961). For information on Oliphant see: Philip Henderson, *The Life of Laurence Oliphant: Traveller, Diplomat, Mystic,* (London; Robert Hale, 1956).
32 Nice: For 25,743 – Against 160. Savoy: For 130,533 - Against 235. William Roscoe Thayer, *The Life and Times of Cavour* (Boston, MA; Houghton Mifflin, 1911) Vol. II. p. 222.
33 Lucy Riall, *Sicily and the Unification of Italy: Liberal Policy and Local Power, 1859-1866* (Oxford; Oxford University Press, 2002) p. 80.

34 Lucy Riall, *Sicily and the Unification of Italy: Liberal Policy and Local Power, 1859-1866* (Oxford; Oxford University Press, 2002) p. 68.

35 Lucy Riall, *Garibaldi: Invention of a Hero* (New Haven, CT; Yale University Press, 2007) p. 184. F Britten Austin, *The Red Flag* (London; Eyre and Spottiswoode, 1932) p. 255

36 Whilst the Marsala landings took place, two Royal Navy warships, the *Intrepid* and *Argus* were in the vicinity. It has been claimed that the presence of these two vessels inhibited the Neopolitan navy who came upon the scene during the landing from engaging the invaders' ships. This does seem to have been the case, but there seems little evidence to suggest that the Royal Navy 'protected' Garibaldi's enterprise. See, for example: [Rear-Admiral Sir] Rodney Mundy, *HMS Hannibal at Palermo and Naples During The Italian Revolution, 1859-1861, With Notices of Garibaldi, Francis II, and Victor Emanuel* (London; John Murray, 1863) pp. 23, 85.

37 The body of literature on Garibaldi and 'the Thousand' is vast. Personal favourites include the following, upon which this section is primarily based: Giuseppe Cesare Abba (Trans. ER Vincent) *The Diary of One of Garibaldi's Thousand* (Westport, CT; Greenwood Press, 1981); Thomas de Angelo, *Garibaldi's Ghosts: Essays on the Mezzogiorno and the Risorgimento* (Park Ridge, NJ; First Line Publishing, 2006); Alexandre Dumas (Trans. Richard Garnett), *On Board the Emma: Adventures with Garibaldi's 'Thousand' in Sicily* (New York; D Appleton and Company, 1929); Alexandre Dumas, *Viva Garibaldi! Une Odyssée en 1860* (Paris; Fayard, 2002); Christopher Hibbert, *Garibaldi: Hero of Italian Unification* (London; Palgrave Macmillan, 2008); Alfonso Scirocco (Trans. Allan Cameron), *Garibaldi: Citizen of the World: A Biography* (Princeton NJ; Princeton University Press, 2007); George Macaulay Trevelyan, *Garibaldi and the Thousand, May 1860* (London; Phoenix Press, 2002).

38 A fine, if no doubt embroidered, account of this episode can be found in Conder: 'It had been known for some time, that the convention with the Swiss Cantons, by virtue of which the fine Swiss regiments that formed the Corps de Elite of the Neapolitan army and the real guard of the king was about to terminate. The Swiss authorities were unwilling to incur the odium thrown upon them as the main supporters of an effete tyranny. But there was an attempt made to reconstitute these regiments, not as under the direction of the Swiss Government, but as individual volunteers in the Neapolitan service. Brand new flags were therefore substituted for the torn and tattered rags which were the pride and glory of the martial Swiss. This they would not stand. The matter was conducted with the usual official clumsiness, and the Swiss broke into mutiny. Word came to Queen Marie Therese that there was a mutiny among the troops. "Send for the Swiss," cried her Majesty, "send instantly for the Swiss." "Majesty it is the Swiss that are in mutiny." The Queen fell in a faint General Nunziante promptly brought up his chasseurs, his artillery loaded with grapeshot There was no public account given of the bloodshed of that day, but the brilliant red coats of the Swiss, disappeared from the forts and barracks of Naples. There was perhaps not another man in the service of the king, of promptitude, pluck, and military capacity able to deal with such an emergency.' An English Civilian (Frances Roubiliac Conder), *The Trinity of Italy, or, the Pope, the Bourbon, and the Victor; Being Historical Revelations of the Past, Present, and Future of Italy* (London; Edward Moxon, 1867) pp. 209-10. See also: Genova Thaon Di Revel, *Il 1859 E L'Italia Centrale: Miei Ricordi* (Charleston, SC; BiblioLife, 2009) p. 81.

39 Clara Tschudi (Trans. Ethel Harriet Hearn), *Maria Sophia, Queen of Naples: A Continuation of The Empress Elizabeth* (London; Swan Sonnenschein, 1905) p. 132.

40 D Mack Smith, *Cavour and Garibaldi, 1860: A Study in Political Conflict* (Cambridge; Cambridge University Press, 1986) p. 436.

41 Paul Bew, *Ireland: The Politics of Enmity 1789-2006* (Oxford; Oxford University Press, 2007) p. 253. C.T. McIntire, *England Against the Papacy 1858–1861: Tories, Liberals and the Overthrow of Papal Temporal Power during the Italian Risorgimento* (Cambridge; Cambridge University Press, 1983) p. 202.

42 R de Cesare (Trans. Helen Zimmern) *The Last Days of Papal Rome 1850-1870* (London; Constable, 1909) p. 247.

43 John Whittam, *The Politics of the Italian Army 1861-1918* (London; Croon Helm, 1977) pp. 97-99.

44 Maggior Generale Alberto Pollio, *Custoza 1866* (Torino; Roux e Viarengo, 1903) p. 419.

45 For the Battle of Custoza see: G B Malleson, *The Refounding of the German Empire 1848 – 1871* [Facsimile reprint of the 1898 edition] (London; R J Leach, 1992) pp. 175-82; Geoffrey Wawro, *The Austro-Prussian War* (Cambridge; University Press, 1998) pp. 100-24. For accounts of the Battle of Lissa see: E B Potter (Ed.) *Sea Power: A Naval History* (Annapolis MD; Naval Institute Press, 1982) pp. 156-7; Geoffrey Regan, *The Brassey's Book of Naval Blunders* (Dulles, VA; Brassey's, 2000) pp. 154-64. For a potted history of the Italian Navy, see: *Conway's All the world's fighting ships, 1860-1905*, pp. 344-36.

46 For details of the battle and the strategy behind it see: Julian Corbett, *Principles of Maritime Strategy* [Reprint of 1911 edition] (London; Dover Publications, 2004) pp. 298-9; John Richard Hale, *Famous Sea Fights from Salamis to Tsu-shima* (London, Methuen, 1911) pp. 231-51; Lawrence Sondhaus, *Naval Warfare, 1815-1914 (London;* Routledge, 2001) pp. 94-6.

47 Aldo Fraccaroli, 'Italy' in Robert Gardiner, Roger Chesneau and Eugene M Kolesnik (Eds), *Conway's All the World's Fighting Ships 1860-1905* (London; Conway Maritime Press, 1979) p. 336.

48 Victor Emmanuel II to Pius IX, 8 September 1870. Karl Samwer and Jules Hoff (Eds), *Nouveau recueil général de traités, conventions et autres transactions remarquables, servant à la connaissance des relations étrangères des puissances et états dans leurs rapports mutuels.* 20 Vols. (Göttingen; J C Dietrich, 1843-75) Vol.V. p. 33.

49 Antonio Di Pierro, *L'ultimo giorno del papa re: 20 settembre 1870, la breccia di Porta Pia* (Milan; Mondadori, 2007) p. 6.

50 Kanzler was born at *Weingarten, Baden, in 1822. See: Francis X. Blouin (Ed.), Vatican Archives: an Inventory and Guide to Historical Documents of the Holy See (New York; Oxford University Press USA, 1998) p. 369.*

51 Antonio Di Pierro, *L'ultimo giorno del papa re: 20 settembre 1870, la breccia di Porta Pia* (Milan; Mondadori, 2007) p. 167.

52 See: Michael Howard, *The Franco Prussian War* (St Albans; Granada, 1979) p. 275.

53 A. E. J. Morris, *History of Urban Form: Before the Industrial Revolutions* (Harlow; Pearson, 1994) p. 44.

54 Quoted in Charles Stephenson (Charles Blackwood Ed.) *'Servant to The King for His Fortifications:' Paul Ive and The Practise of Fortification* (Doncaster; DP&G, 2008) p. 2.

55 Edmondo de Amicis, 'L'entrata dell'esercito italiano in Roma' in R De Mattei (Ed.), *XX settembre 1870: Tre testimonianze. G Guerzoni, A M Bonetti, E De Amicis* (Roma; Istuto di Studi Romani, 1972) pp. 132-8.

56 Roberto De Mattei, *Pius IX* (Leominster; Gracewing, 2004) p. 74.

57 Antonio Di Pierro, *L'ultimo giorno del papa re: 20 settembre 1870, la breccia di Porta Pia* (Milan; Mondadori, 2007)

58 Philippe Levillain (Ed.), *Dictionnaire historique de la papauté* (Paris; Librairie Arthème Fayard, 2003) Vol. II. p. 1107. Joseph McCabe, *Crises in the History of the Papacy: A Study of Twenty Famous Popes whose Careers and whose Influence were Important in the History of the World* (New York; G P Putnam, 1916) p. 408 n. 1. Christopher Duggan, *Francesco Crispi, 1818-1901: From Nation to Nationalism* (Oxford; Oxford University Press, 2002) p. 326. Antony Alcock, *A History of the Protection of Regional Cultural Minorities in Europe: From the Edict of Nantes to the Present Day* (Basingstoke; Macmillan, 2000) p. 35.

59 David Kertzer, *Prisoner of the Vatican: The Popes' Secret Plot to Capture Rome from the New Italian State* (Boston; Houghton Mifflin, 2004).

60 Dennis Mack Smith, *Italy: A Modern History.* (Ann Arbor MI; University of Michigan Press, 1969) pp. 25, 66-7. Raphael Zariski, *Italy: the Politics of Uneven Development* (Hinsdale, Ill; Dryden, 1972) p. 19. Tim Chapman, *The Risorgimento: Italy 1815-1871* (Penrith; Humanities-Ebooks, 2008) pp. 80-1. Alan Cassels, *Ideology and International Relations in the Modern World* (London; Routledge, 1996.) p. 73.

61 Sondra Z Koff and Stephen P Koff, *Italy: from the First to the Second Republic* (London; Routledge, 2000) pp. 10-11.

62 Susan A Ashley, *Making Liberalism Work: The Italian Experience, 1860-1914* (Westport CT; Praeger, 2003) p. 14.

63 Cardinal Manning, *The Independence of the Holy See* (London; Henry S King, 1877) p. xiii.

64 Robert C Fried, *The Italian Prefects. A Study in Administrative Politics* (New Haven CT; Yale University Press, 1963).

65 Christopher Seton-Watson, *Italy From Liberalism to Fascism, 1870-1925* (London; Methuen, 1967) p. 319.

66 Christopher Seton-Watson, *Italy From Liberalism to Fascism, 1870-1925* (London; Methuen, 1967) p. 24. See also: Max Henninger, 'Italy, peasant movements, 19th-20th centuries,' in Immanuel Ness (Ed.) *The International Encyclopaedia of Revolution and Protest* available from: http://www.blackwellreference.com/public/tocnode?id=g9781405184649_chunk_g9781405184649807#citation

67 Daniela Del Boca and Alessandra Venturini, *Italian Migration: Discussion Paper No. 938* (Bonn; Institut zur Zukunft der Arbeit, 2003) pp. 4-5. This work is available at: http://ftp.iza.org/dp938.pdf

68 See Chapter 9, 'The Italian Exodus,' in Maldwin A Jones, *Destination America* (London; Weidenfeld and Nicolson, 1976) pp. 192-219.

69 Adrian Lyttelton, 'Politics and Society 1870-1915' in George Holmes (Ed.) *The Oxford Illustrated History of Italy.* (Oxford; Oxford University Press, 1997) pp.238-240.

70 Vera Zamagni, *The Economic History of Italy, 1860-1990: Recovery After Decline* (Oxford; Clarendon Press, 1997) p. 188.

71 Susan A Ashley, *Making Liberalism Work: The Italian Experience, 1860-1914* (Westport CT; Praeger, 2003) p. 13.

72 Kevin G Kinsella, 'Changes in life expectancy 1900-1990' in *The American Journal for Clinical Nutrition* Vol 55 June 1992. p. 1197S. Ralph Spence, 'Italy' in Ann Wall (Ed.), *Health Care Systems in Liberal Democracies* (London; Routledge, 1996) p. 49.

73 The Carabinieri were a gendarmerie under the jurisdiction of the War Ministry in terms of recruitment, training, discipline and administration but were theoretically responsible to the Interior Ministry for policing matters. Founded in pre-unification Italy in Turin on 13 July, 1814, the force had a dual function; national defence, and policing. On 24 January 1861 the Carabinieri became, in effect, the nucleus of the military forces of the Kingdom of Italy and were dubbed the 'First Force' of the newly founded national army. They were also entrusted with the policing of rural areas, where the mainly

urbanised Interior Ministry civilian police, had little influence. Their presence was, and still is ubiquitous, extending to the smallest rural villages.

See: http://www.carabinieri.it/Internet/Multilingua/EN/HistoricalReferences/01_EN.htm. Also see: http://www.history.ac.uk/resources/e-seminars/dunnage-paper

[74] Martin Clark, *Modern Italy 1871-1995* (London; Longman, 1996) p. 126.

[75] Benedetto Croce (Cecilia M Ady Trans.) A history of Italy, 1871-1915 (New York; Russell & Russell, 1963) p. 187. Marc Brianti, *Bandiera rossa: un siècle d'histoire du Mouvement ouvrier italien du Risorgimento (1848) a la republique (1948)* (Paris; Connaissances et savoirs, 2007) pp. 163-5. Carl Levy, *Gramsci and the Anarchists* (New York; Berg, 2000) p. 37.

[76] It can perhaps be argued that Crispi had good, and personal, reasons for adopting these illiberal measures. He had been the victim of an assassination attempt on 16 June 1894 when Paolo Lega, an anarchist, had unsuccessfully shot at him from close range.

[77] John Gooch, *Army, State and Society in Italy, 1870-1915* (London; Palgrave Macmillan, 1989) p. 71.

[78] Jonathan Dunnage, 'Continuity in Policing Politics in Italy, 1920-1960' in Mark Mazower (Ed.), *The Policing of Politics in the Twentieth Century: Historical Perspectives* (Oxford; Berghahn, 1997) pp. 60-1. See also: Jonathan Dunnage, *The Italian Police and the Rise of Fascism: A Case Study of the Province of Bologna, 1897-1925* (Westport CT; Praeger, 1997); Richard Bach Jensen, *Liberty and Order: The Theory and Practice of Italian Public Security Policy, 1848 to the Crisis of the 1890s* (New York: Garland, 1991); Romano Canosa and Amedeo Santosuosso, *Magistrati, anarchici e socialisti alla fine dell'ottocento in Italia* [Magistrates, Anarchists and Socialists at the end of the Eighteen Hundreds in Italy] (Milan: Feltrinelli, 1981).

[79] Nunzio Pernicone, 'Luigi Galleani and Italian Anarchist Terrorism in the United States,' in David C Rapoport (Ed.), *Terrorism: Critical Concepts in Political Science* (Abingdon; Routledge, 2006) p. 193. The term 'subversive' (*sovversivo*) has somewhat different connotations in Italian than it does in English, and, whilst almost impossible to accurately define, might best be expressed as dislike, even hatred, of officialdom rather than of the state itself. Indeed, there was a long tradition of subversiveness (*sovversivismo*) within Italian society, and the working class particularly, that preceded the foundation of an Italian socialist party in 1892. This has been said to date back to, and have evolved from, Italy's 'pre-industrial' and 'pre-urban' society, and was an attitude that was not confined to the political left. See: Kate Crehan, *Gramsci, Culture and Anthropology* (Los Angeles; University of California Press, 2002) p. 99-100. Franco Andreucci, '"Subversiveness" and Anti-Fascism in Italy' in Raphael Samuel (Ed.) *People's History and Socialist Theory* (London; Routledge & Kegan Paul) p. 200. Richard Bessel, *Fascist Italy and Nazi Germany: Comparisons and Contrasts* (Cambridge; Cambridge University Press, 1996) p. 41. See also: Carl Levy, '"Sovversivismo": The Radical Political Culture of Otherness in Liberal Italy,' in the *Journal of Political Ideologies*, Volume 12, Issue 2 June 2007 , pp. 147-161.

[80] Aldobrandino Malvezzi, *L'Italia e L'Islam in Libia* (Firenze-Milano; Fratelli Treves, 1913) p. x.

[81] Benjamin C Fortna, 'The Reign of Abdülhamid II,' in Re at Kasaba (Ed.), *The Cambridge History of Turkey: Volume 4, Turkey in the Modern World* (Cambridge; Cambridge University Press, 2008) p. 47.

[82] Thomas Palamenghi-Crispi (Ed.) (Trans. Mary Prichard-Agnetti) *The Memoirs Of Francesco Crispi: Compiled from Crispi's Diary and other Documents*. Vol. II The Triple Alliance (London; Hodder and Stoughton, 1912) p 347.

[83] William I. Shorrock, 'The Tunisian Question in French Policy toward Italy, 1881-1940' in *The International Journal of African Historical Studies*, Vol. 16, No. 4 (1983), pp. 631-651, Arthur Marsden, 'Britain and her Conventional Rights in Tunis, 1888-1892' in *Revue de l'Occident musulman et de la Méditerranée*, Vol. 8, No. 1. (1970) pp. 163-173. See also: Ezio M Gray, *Italy and the Question of Tunis* (Milan; A Mondadori, 1939).

[84] Okbazghi Yohannes, *Eritrea, a Pawn in World Politics* (Gainesville, FL; University Press of Florida, 1991) pp. 46-7, 74.

[85] Festus Ugboaja Ohaegbulam, *Towards an Understanding of the African Experience from Historical and Contemporary Perspectives* (Lanham, MD; University Press of America, 1990) pp. 185-7. Saheed A Adejumobi, *The History of Ethiopia* (London; Greenwood, 2006) p. 29.

[86] For the history of the territory see: Guido Corni (Ed.), *Somalia italiana* (Milan; Editoriale Arte e Storia, 1937); Robert L Hess, *Italian Colonialism in Somalia* (Chicago; University of Chicago Press, 1966).

[87] Hess, *Italian Colonialism in Somalia*. p. 101.

[88] Quoted in Paulos Milkias and Getachew Metaferia (Eds.), *The Battle of Adwa: Reflections on Ethiopia's Historic Victory Against European Colonialism* (New York; Algora, 2005) p. 126. The description of the battle is taken from this work.

[89] Thomas Pakenham, *The Scramble for Africa 1876-1912* (London; Abacus, 1992) p. 475.

[90] Richard Bellamy and Darrow Schecter, *Gramsci and the Italian State* (Manchester; Manchester University Press, 1993) p. 14.

[91] Charles Klopp, *Sentences: The Memoirs and Letters of Italian Political Prisoners from Benvenuto Cellini to Aldo Moro* (Toronto; University of Toronto Press, 1999) p. 113.

[92] This section, unless otherwise stated, is taken from the following: Paolo Valera, *I cannoni di Bava Beccaris* (Milano; Giordano, 1966). Hubert Heyriès, 'L'armée italienne et le maintien de l'ordre dans les villes de 1871 à 1915 d'après les attachés militaires français: Guerre de rue, guerre dans la rue' in *Guerres mondiales et conflits contemporains.* avril-juin 2002, No 206. pp. 11-28.

[93] Thomas Okey, 'United Italy' in A W Ward, G W Prothero and Stanley Leathes (Eds.) *The Cambridge Modern History* (Cambridge; Cambridge University Press, 1910) Vol. XII. p. 220.

[94] Milan's Central Station was, at that time, situated next to the modern station of Porta Garibaldi. A new Central Station was officially inaugurated in 1931. Andrea Giuntini 'Downtown by the Train: The Impact of Railways on Italian Cities in the Nineteenth Century – Case Studies' in Ralf Roth and Marie-Noëlle Polino (Eds.) *The City and the Railway in Europe* (Aldershot; Ashgate, 2003) p .124

[95] Abraham Ascher, *The Revolution of 1905: A Short History* (Stanford CA; Stanford University Press, 2004) p. 27.

[96] Arthur James Whyte, *The Evolution of Modern Italy* (Oxford; Basil Blackwell & Mott, 1959) p. 207.

[97] James Joll, *The Second International, 1889-1914* (London; Routledge & Kegan Paul, 1974) p. 87.

[98] Luciano Regolo, *Jelena: tutto il racconto della vita della regina Elena di Savoia* (Milano; Simonelli Editore, 2003) p. 309. Arthur James Whyte, *The Evolution of Modern Italy* (Oxford; Basil Blackwell & Mott, 1959) p. 207.

[99] Percentages of total population amongst the European Great Powers enfranchised for lower chambers in 1900: France 29, Germany 22, Austria 21, Hungary 6 (Austria and Hungary had separate legislatures and governments), UK 18, Russia 15, Italy 8. Niall Ferguson, *The Pity of War* (London; Allen Lane, 1998) p. 29.

[100] See: Christopher Seton-Watson, *Italy From Liberalism to Fascism, 1870-1925* (London; Methuen, 1967) pp. 193-5; John Whittam, Fascist Italy (Manchester; Manchester University Press, 1995) pp. 11-2.

[101] Humbert L Gualtieri, *The Labor Movement in Italy* (New York; S F Vanni, 1946) p. 245.

[102] Christopher Duggan, *The Force of Destiny: A History of Italy Since 1796* (London; Allen Lane, 2007) p. 349.

[103] Bava-Beccaris retired in 1902, but continued to involve himself in politics. He supported Italain participation in World War I, and in 1922 he recommended that power be handed Mussolini. He wrote a book on the army; F Bava-Beccaris, *Esercito Italiano: Sue origini, suo successivo ampliamento, suo stato attuale* (Roma; Accademia dei Lincei, 1911).

[104] T.Boston Bruce, 'The New Italian Criminal Code' in *Law Quarterly Review*, Vol. 5, 1889. p. 287.

[105] Maria Sophia Quine, *Population Politics in Twentieth Century Europe* (London; Routledge, 1996) p. 23. J Bowyer Bell, *Assassin: Theory and Practice of Political Violence* (New Brunswick, NJ; Transaction Publishers, 2005) p. 31. Perhaps surprisingly, the city council at Carrara in northern Italy decided, in the mid 1980s, to donate public land for a monument honouring Bresci. As may be imagined, much controversy ensued. See the *Los Angeles Times* of 7 December 1986 http://articles.latimes.com/1986-12-07/news/mn-1250_1_king-umberto and the 4 May 1990 edition of *La Republica* http://ricerca.repubblica.it/repubblica/archivio/repubblica/1990/05/04/gaetano-bresci-gli-anarchici-in-piazza.html

[106] Arthur James Whyte, *The Evolution of Modern Italy* (Oxford; Basil Blackwell & Mott, 1959) p. 212.

[107] Richard Drake, *Apostles and Agitators: Italy's Marxist Revolutionary Tradition* (Cambridge, MA; Harvard University Press, 2003) pp. 93-4.

[108] Report of a speech made by Ferri at Suzzara, Lombardy; reported in *La Stampa* 27 December 1909. Ferri, editor of the party paper *Avanti!*, was an intellectual, an eminent criminologist, and 'the architect of a remarkably vulgar Darwinian Marxism.' Geoff Eley, *Forging Democracy: The History of the Left in Europe, 1850-2000* (Oxford; Oxford University Press, 2002) p. 45.

[109] Oda Olberg, 'Der italienische Generalstreik,' in *Die Neue Zeit*, 23:1 (1904-05), p. 19.

[110] As Karl Kautsky put it: 'The political general strike succeeds more frequently if it be sudden and unexpected, brought about spontaneously by some plainly outrageous act of the bourgeois government.' E. Pataud and E. Pouget: *Syndicalism and the Co-operative Commonwealth* (Oxford: New Internationalist Publications, 1913) p. 227.

[111] André Tridon, *The New Unionism* (New York; B W Huebsch, 1913) p. 149.

[112] James Joll, *The Second International, 1889-1914* (London; Routledge & Kegan Paul, 1974) p. 88.

[113] For the history of the general strike and subsequent events see: Zeev Sternhell with Mario Sznaidr and Maia Asheri (Trans. David Maisel), *The Birth of Fascist Ideology: From Cultural Rebellion to Political Revolution* (Princeton NJ; Princeton University press, 1994) 133-5. Carl Levy, 'Currents of Italian Syndicalism before 1926' in *International Review of Social History* (2000), Vol. 45, Issue 2. pp. 209-250. Oda Olberg, 'Der italienische Generalstreik,' in *Die Neue Zeit*, 23:1 (1904-05), pp. 18-21. One recruit to the revolutionary wing of the PSI was Benito Mussolini; in 1909 he was working as a journalist for the paper *L'Avvenire del Lavoratore* (The Future of the Worker) in the Trentino, then a part of *Italia Irredenta* under austro-Hungarian rule. His espousal of revolutionary methods saw him imprisoned on several occasions and eventually expelled from the area. Peter Neville, *Mussolini* (London; Routledge, 2004) p. 28. R N L Absalom, *Mussolini and the Rise of Italian Fascism* (London; Methuen, 1969) p. 21.

[114] William C Askew, *Europe and Italy's acquisition of Libya, 1911-1912* (Durham, NC; Duke University Press, 1942) p. 4.

[115] He actually said 'Unfortunately we have made Italy, but we have not created Italians.' Luciano Cheles and Lucio Sponza, 'Introduction: National Identities and Avenues of Persuasion' in Luciano Cheles and Lucio Sponza (Eds.), *The Art of Persuasion: Political Communication in Italy from 1945 to the 1990s* (Manchester; Manchester University Press, 2001) p. 1.

[116] Paolo Varvaro, *L'orizzonte del Risorgimento: l'Italia vista dai prefetti* (Napoli; Dante & Descartes, 2001) p. 47.

[117] Don H Doyle, *Nations Divided: America, Italy, and the Southern Question* (Athens, GA; University of Georgia Press, 2002) p. 39.

[118] 'Blood, sacrifice, revenge, martyrdom and slaughter of the tyrannous foreigner were all crucial themes in Italian patriotic writings in the mid-nineteenth century' Christopher Duggan, 'Nation-Building in 19th Century Italy: The Case of Francesco Crispi' in *History Today*, Volume 52 (2) February 2002. p. 13.

CHAPTER THREE

[1] Leonard Woolf, *Empire & Commerce in Africa: A Study In Economic Imperialism* (London; Labour Research Department, 1920) p. 121

[2] Lady Gwendolen Cecil, *Life of Robert Marquis of Salisbury, Volume IV 1887-1892* (London; Hodder and Stoughton, 1932) p. 323.

[3] C E Callwell, *Field-Marshal Sir Henry Wilson: His Life and Diaries,* (London: Cassell, 1927) Volume I. p. 105.

[4] Cesare Balbo, *Delle speranze d'italia* (Firenze [Florence]; Felice le Monnier, 1855) p. 133. Naples, at the time of his writing, was the capital of the Kingdom of the Two Sicilies; a polity that had been formed at the Congress of Vienna in 1815 by combining the kingdoms of Naples and Sicily. For an account of Balbo's political viewpoint see: Ettore Passerin d'Entreves, *La giovinezza di Cesare Balbo* (Firenze [Florence]; Felice Le Monnier, 1940.) pp. 22-26.

[5] Stefano Recchia and Nadia Urbinati (Eds.) (Trans. Stefano Recchia) *A Cosmopolitanism of Nations: Giuseppe Mazzini's Writings on Democracy* (Princeton NJ; Princeton University Press, 2009) p. 238.

[6] Stefano Recchia and Nadia Urbinati (Eds.) (Trans. Stefano Recchia) *A Cosmopolitanism of Nations: Giuseppe Mazzini's Writings on Democracy* (Princeton NJ; Princeton University Press, 2009) p. 239.

[7] Alan Cassels, 'Reluctant Neutral: Italy and the Strategic Balance in 1939' in B J C McKercher and Roch Legault (Eds.), *Military planning and the origins of the Second World War in Europe* (Westport CT; Praeger, 2001) p. 38. James Muldoon, *Empire and Order: The Concept of Empire, 800-1800* (Basingstoke; Palgrave Macmillan, 1999) p. 22.

[8] George B Manhart, *Alliance and Entente, 1871–1914* (New York; F S Crofts, 1932) p. 27.

[9] Supplement to Secret Dispatch No. 496, Rome, 1 July 1902. 'Copy of the declaration transmitted to the Royal Italian Government with regard to Tripoli.' Alfred Franzis Pribram, *The Secret Treaties of Austria-Hungary 1879-1914* (Cambridge; Harvard University Press, 1920) Vol. I. pp. 232-3. Quoted in part in: George B Manhart, *Alliance and Entente, 1871–1914* (New York; F S Crofts, 1932) p. 34.

[10] Andre Tardieu, *France and the Alliances: The Struggle for the Balance of Power* (New York; Macmillan, 1908) p. 91.

[11] 'Naval Notes: The French Mediterranean and Italian Squadrons at Toulon' in *The RUSI Journal*, Volume 45, Issue 277, 1901. p. 613.

[12] 'King of Italy in Paris: Victor Emmanuel and Queen Helena Warmly Welcomed', in *The New York Times,* 15 October, 1903.

[13] Bernard de Montferrand, *Diplomatie: des volontés françaises* (Versailles; Alban, 2006) p. 178.

[14] Wedel to Holstein, 12 April 1901. Norman Rich And M H Fisher (Eds), *The Holstein Papers: Volume 4: Correspondence 1897-1909* (London; Syndics of the Cambridge University Press, 1963) p. 221.

[15] Sidney B Fay, *The Origins of the World War* (New York; Macmillan, 1928) Vol. I. p. 145.

[16] For a description of the results of the rapprochement in a European context, see: Dwight E Lee, *Europe's Crucial Years: The Diplomatic Background of World War I, 1902-1914* (Hanover, NH; University Press of New England for Clark University Press, 1974) pp. 43-5. Edward E McCullough, *How the First World War Began: The Triple Entente and the Coming of the Great War of 1914-1918* (Montreal; Black Rose, 1999) p. 26. Denna Frank Fleming, *The Origins and Legacies of World War I* (London; Allen & Unwin, 1969) pp. 79-80.

[17] George B Manhart, *Alliance and Entente, 1871–1914* (New York; F S Crofts, 1932) p. 33.

[18] Gino J Naldi, 'The Aouzou Strip Dispute-A Legal Analysis' in *Journal of African Law*, Vol. 33, No. 1 (Spring, 1989), p. 72.

[19] Thomas Palamenghi-Crispi (Ed.) (Trans. Mary Prichard-Agnetti) *The Memoirs Of Francesco Crispi: Compiled from Crispi's Diary and other Documents.* Vol. III *International Problems* (London; Hodder and Stoughton, 1914) p. 22.

[20] Zeev Sternhell with Mario Sznajder and Maia Ashéri (Trans. David Maisel), *The Birth of Fascist Ideology: From Cultural Rebellion to Political Revolution* (Princeton, NJ; Princeton University Press, 1994) p. 21.

[21] Donald F Busky, *Communism in History and Theory: The European Experience* (Westport, CT; Praeger, 2002) p. 93. A selection of Labriola's writings can be viewed at: http://www.marxists.org/archive/labriola/index.htm

[22] John Rees, *The Algebra of Revolution: The Dialectic and the Classical Marxist Tradition* (London; Routledge, 1998) p. 259.

[23] Gian Mario Bravo, 'Antonio Labriola e la questione coloniale' in *I sentieri della ricerca: Rivista di storia contemporanea*, No.1 /June 2005. p. 58.

[24] Nino Valeri, *La lotta politica in Italia dall'unità al 1925: Idee e documenti* (Firenze [Florence]; Le Monnier, 1945) p. 327.

[25] Francis McCullagh, *Italy's War For A Desert: Being Some Experiences Of A War Correspondent With The Italians In Tripoli* (Chicago, IL; F G Browne, 1913) p. 41.

[26] For a brief overview of these matters see: Charles Stephenson, *The Fortifications of Malta, 1530-1945* (Oxford; Osprey, 2004) pp. 29-37.

[27] Paul G Halpern, *The Naval War in the Mediterranean, 1914-1918* (Boston; Allen & Unwin, 1986) p. 1.

[28] Quoted in Holger H Herwig, *'Luxury' Fleet: The German Imperial Navy 1888–1918* (London: George Allen & Unwin, 1980) p. 1.

[29] Hew Strachan, *The First World War. Volume One: To Arms* (Oxford: Oxford University Press, 2003.) p. 376.

[30] Paul G Halpern, *The Mediterranean Naval Situation, 1908-1914* (Cambridge, MA; Harvard University Press, 1971) p. 45.

[31] *Inflexible* transferred to the theatre as flagship in November 1912; *Indomitable* and *Invincible* joined in August 1913. Dennis Castillo, *The Maltese Cross: A Strategic History of Malta* (Westport, CT; Praeger, 2006) p. 132.

[32] Richard Wilkinson, 'Lord Lansdowne and British Foreign Policy 1900-1917' in *History Today*, Issue 36, March 2000, p. 9.

[33] J L Glanville, *Italy's Relations with England* (Baltimore; John Hopkins Press, 1934) p. 118.

[34] R J B Bosworth, *Italy the Least of the Great Powers: Italian Foreign Policy before the First. World War* (London: Cambridge University Press, 1979) p. 138

[35] Tommaso Tittoni (Trans. Bernardo Quaranta di San Severino), *Italy's Foreign and Colonial Policy: A Selection From the Speeches Delivered in the Italian Parliament by the Italian Foreign Affairs Minister Senator Tommaso Tittoni during his Six Years of Office (1903-1909)*, (London; Smith, Elder,1914) p. 20.

[36] Tommaso Tittoni (Trans. Bernardo Quaranta di San Severino), *Italy's Foreign and Colonial Policy: A Selection From the Speeches Delivered in the Italian Parliament by the Italian Foreign Affairs Minister Senator Tommaso Tittoni during his Six Years of Office (1903-1909)*, (London; Smith, Elder,1914) p. 20.

[37] The 'Sublime Porte' was the term used for the Ottoman Government, in much the same way as the 'Wilhelmstrasse' was sometimes a metonym for the German Foreign Office and 'Westminster' was, and is, similarly applied to the British government.

[38] Tommaso Tittoni (Trans. Bernardo Quaranta di San Severino), *Italy's Foreign and Colonial Policy: A Selection From the Speeches Delivered in the Italian Parliament by the Italian Foreign Affairs Minister Senator Tommaso Tittoni during his Six Years of Office (1903-1909)*, (London; Smith, Elder,1914) p. 21.

[39] Tommaso Tittoni (Trans. Bernardo Quaranta di San Severino), *Italy's Foreign and Colonial Policy: A Selection From the Speeches Delivered in the Italian Parliament by the Italian Foreign Affairs Minister Senator Tommaso Tittoni during his Six Years of Office (1903-1909)*, (London; Smith, Elder,1914) p. 27.

[40] Tommaso Tittoni (Trans. Bernardo Quaranta di San Severino), *Italy's Foreign and Colonial Policy: A Selection From the Speeches Delivered in the Italian Parliament by the Italian Foreign Affairs Minister Senator Tommaso Tittoni during his Six Years of Office (1903-1909)*, (London; Smith, Elder,1914) p. 29.

[41] Tommaso Tittoni (Trans. Bernardo Quaranta di San Severino), *Italy's Foreign and Colonial Policy: A Selection From the Speeches Delivered in the Italian Parliament by the Italian Foreign Affairs Minister Senator Tommaso Tittoni during his Six Years of Office (1903-1909)*, (London; Smith, Elder,1914) p. 26.

[42] For the involvement of the bank with the papacy and the role of Ernesto Pacelli see: John F Pollard, *Money and the Rise of the Modern Papacy: Financing the Vatican, 1850-1950* (Cambridge; Cambridge University Press, 2005) pp. 65-78. For Eugenio Pacelli see: Richard A Webster, *The Cross and the Fasces: Christian Democracy and Fascism in Italy* (Stanford, CA; Stanford University Press, 1960) p. 29. Manus I Midlarsky, *The Killing Trap: Genocide in the Twentieth Century* (Cambridge; Cambridge University Press, 2005) p. 220. See also: Peter Hertner, 'Modern Banking in Italy' in European Association for Banking History, *Handbook on the History of European Banks* (Aldershot, UK; Edward Elgar, 1994) pp. 631, 635.

[43] Richard A Webster (Trans. Mariangela Chiabrando), *L'imperialismo industriale italiano 1908-1915: Studio sul prefascismo* (Turin; Giulio Einaudi, 1974) p. 213. See also Luigi De Rosa, *Storia del Banco di Roma* (Rome; Banco di Roma,1982) Vol. I, Chapter 5.

[44] Luigi De Rosa, *Storia del Banco di Roma* (Rome; Banco di Roma,1982) Vol. I, p. 252.

[45] Ali Abdullatif Ahmida, *The Making of Modern Libya: State formation, Colonization, and Resistance, 1830-1932* (Albany, NY; State University of New York Press, 1994) p. 64.

[46] Charles Lapworth and Helen Zimmern, *Tripoli and Young Italy* (London; Stephen Swift, 1912) p. 69.

[47] Arthur Silva White, *The Development of Africa* (London; George Philip, 1890) p. 221. For details of Italian investments see: Eugene A Staley, *War and the Private Investor: A Study in the Relations of International Politics and International Private Investment* (Garden City, NY; Doubleday Doran, 1935) pp. 62-70.

[48] Charles Wellington Furlong, *The Gateway to the Sahara: Observations and Experiences in Tripoli* (New York; Charles Scribner's Sons, 1909) p. 171.

[49] Francis McCullagh, *Italy's War for a Desert: Being Some Experiences of a War-Correspondent with the Italians in Tripoli* (London; Herbert & Daniel, 1913) p. 18.

[50] Gioacchino Volpe, *Italia moderna: Volume III 1910-1914* (Firenze; Le lettere, 2002) p. 81

[51] Charles Wellington Furlong was an explorer, anthropologist, painter, teacher, writer, lecturer, and soldier. His papers are held at the Rauner Special Collections Library, Dartmouth College, Hanover, NH. http://ead.dartmouth.edu/html/stem197.html

[52] Charles Wellington Furlong, *The Gateway to the Sahara: Observations and Experiences in Tripoli* (New York; Charles Scribner's Sons, 1909) pp. 181-2.

[53] Charles Wellington Furlong, *The Gateway to the Sahara: Observations and Experiences in Tripoli* (New York; Charles Scribner's Sons, 1909) p. 32.

[54] Charles Wellington Furlong, *The Gateway to the Sahara: Observations and Experiences in Tripoli* (New York; Charles Scribner's Sons, 1909) pp. 39-40.

[55] Arthur Silva White, Fellow of the Royal Society of Edinburgh, was the first secretary of the Royal Scottish Geographical Society and editor of the Scottish Geographical Magazine. See: David N Livingstone, 'Tropical Climate and Moral Hygiene: The Anatomy of a Victorian Debate' in *The British Journal for the History of Science,* 1999, Volume 32, pp. 93-110; Dalvan M. Coger, 'Africana in the Scottish Geographical Magazine, 1885-1914' in *African Studies Bulletin,* Vol. 9, No. 3 (December 1966), pp. 88-102.

[56] Arthur Silva White, *The Development of Africa* (London; George Philip, 1890) p. 62.

[57] Arthur Silva White, *The Development of Africa* (London; George Philip, 1890) pp. 221-2.

[58] Charles Wellington Furlong, *The Gateway to the Sahara: Observations and Experiences in Tripoli* (New York; Charles Scribner's Sons, 1909) p. 296. Furlong was prescient; large reserves of fossil water fairly near the surface were serendipitously discovered in Libya during the 1950's whilst drilling for oil. Omar Salem, 'Management of Shared Groundwater Basins in Libya' in *African Water Journal* Volume I, Number 1, March 2007, pp. 106-117. Patrick E Tyler, 'Libya's Vast Pipe Dream Taps Into Desert's Ice Age Water' in *The New York Times,* 2 March 2004.

[59] Douglas J Forsyth, *The Crisis of Liberal Italy: Monetary and Financial Policy, 1914-1922* (Cambridge; Cambridge University Press, 1993) p. 47.

[60] Timothy W Childs, *Italo-Turkish Diplomacy and the War over Libya, 1911-1912* (Leiden; E J Brill, 1990) p. 32. Francesco Malgeri, *La Guerra Libica 1911-1912* (Roma; Edizioni di storia e letteratura, 1970) pp. 15-20.

[61] Eugene A Staley, *War and the Private Investor: A Study in the Relations of International Politics and International Private Investment* (Garden City, NY; Doubleday Doran, 1935) p. 67.

[62] Louis Leo Snyder, *Historic Documents of World War I* (Westport, CT; Greenwood Press, 1977) p. 44.

[63] Statement by San Giuliano of 24 September 1910. Quoted in Charles Lapworth and Helen Zimmern, *Tripoli and Young Italy* (London; Stephen Swift, 1912) pp. 66-7. Also quoted in part, without attribution, in: Paolo De Vecchi, *Italy's Civilizing Mission in Africa* (New York, Brentano's, 1912) p. 27

[64] Adrian Lyttelton (Ed. and Intro), *Italian Fascisms from Pareto to Gentile* (New York; Harper & Row, 1975) pp. 146-7. Martin Blinkhorn, *Fascism and the Right in Europe, 1919-1945* (Harlow; Pearson Education, 2000) p. 120.

[65] Mussolini opined in a similar manner: 'War alone keys up all human energies to their maximum tension and sets the seal of nobility on those peoples who have the courage to face it.' He is also recorded, whilst at a conference with Hitler at the Brenner Pass on 18 March 1940, as stating that 'To make a people great it is necessary to send them to battle [. . .].' He added, 'even if you have to kick them in the backside.' Benito Mussolini, *Fascism: Doctrine and Institutions* (Rome; Ardita, 1935) p. 19; Hugh Gibson, *The Ciano Diaries, 1939-1943: The Complete, Unabridged Diaries of Count Galeazzo Ciano, Italian Minister for Foreign Affairs, 1936-1943* (Garden City, NY; Doubleday, 1946) pp. 235-6.

[66] See: Giulio Benedetti, *Enrico Corradini; Profilo* (Piacenza; Presso la Società tipografica editoriale Porta, 1922). For an overview of the rise of nationalism up to the outbreak of war in 1911 see: Salvatore Saladino, 'Italy' in Hans Rogger and Eugen Weber (Eds.), *The European Right: a Historical Profile* (Berkeley, CA; University of California Press, 1974) pp. 208-240.

[67] Bosworth. pp. 143-5.

[68] Ronald S Cunsolo, 'Libya, Italian Nationalism, and the Revolt against Giolitti' in *The Journal of Modern History,* 37, June 1965. p. 189.

[69] Ronald S Cunsolo, 'Libya, Italian Nationalism, and the Revolt against Giolitti' in *The Journal of Modern History,* 37, June 1965. p. 190.

[70] Bosworth. p. 145. Alan Cassels, *Fascist Italy* (Arlington Heights, IL; H Davidson, 1985) p. 9.

[71] *The Times,* 30 September 1911

[72] Bosworth. p. 149.

[73] Mark I Choate, *Emigrant Nation: The Making of Italy Abroad* (Cambridge, MA; Harvard University Press, 2008) p. 168.

[74] Ciro Paoletti, *A Military History of Italy* (Westport, CT; Praeger Security International, 2008) p. 134.

[75] Timothy W Childs, *Italo-Turkish Diplomacy and the War over Libya, 1911-1912* (Leiden; E J Brill) p. 39.

[76] Bosworth. p. 150.

[77] Timothy W Childs, *Italo-Turkish Diplomacy and the War over Libya, 1911-1912* (Leiden; E J Brill) p. 36.

[78] For a detailed study of the affair see: Geoffrey Barraclough, *From Agadir to Armageddon: Anatomy of a Crisis* (New York; Holmes & Meier, 1982). Also: Ima C Barlow, *The Agadir Crisis* (Hamden CT; Archon Books, 1971).

[79] Memorandum by Kiderlen-Wächter, 3 May 1911. in E T S Dugdale (Selected and Trans.) *German Diplomatic Documents, 1871-1914.* Vol. IV *The Descent to the Abyss, 1911-14* (London: Methuen, 1931) pp. 2-4.

[80] Edward Crankshaw, *The Fall of the House of Hapsburg* (New York; Viking, 1963) p. 369.

[81] Konrad H Jarausch, *The Enigmatic Chancellor: Bethmann Hollweg and the Hubris of Imperial Germany* (New Haven CT; Yale University Press, 1973) p. 126.

[82] Roughly the area of the present-day Republic of the Congo, Gabon, Chad and the Central African Republic.

[83] Ernst Jäckh, (Ed.) *Kiderlen-Wächter, der Staatsmann und Mensch: Briefwechsel und Nachlaß.* Two Volumes (Stuttgart; Deutsche Verlags-Anstalt, 1924) Vol. II. p. 128.

[84] Winston S Churchill, *The World Crisis 1911-1918* Volume I (London; Odhams Press, 1938) p. 29.

[85] Sir James Rennell Rodd, *Social and Diplomatic Memories, Third Series* [Volume 3] *1902-1919* (London; Edward Arnold, 1925) p. 141.

[86] Charles Lapworth and Helen Zimmern, *Tripoli and Young Italy* (London; Steven Swift, 1912) pp. 18-19.

[87] Charles Lapworth and Helen Zimmern, *Tripoli and Young Italy* (London; Steven Swift, 1912) p. 92.

[88] Jay Spaulding and Lidwien Kapteijns, *An Islamic Alliance: Ali Dinar and the Sanusiya, 1906-1916* (Evanston, IL; Northwestern University Press, 1994) p. 35.

[89] Ian Mugridge, *The View from Xanadu: William Randolph Hearst and United States Foreign Policy* (Montreal; McGill-Queen's University Press, 1995) pp. 7-18. Denis Brian, *Pulitzer: A Life* (New York; John Wiley and Sons, 2001) pp. 2, 390.

[90] W Joseph Campbell, *Yellow Journalism: Puncturing the Myths, Defining the Legacies* (Westport, CT; Praeger, 2001) p. 97.

[91] Francesco Malgeri, *La Guerra Libica 1911-1912* (Roma: Edizioni de Storia e Letteratura, 1970) p. 66.

[92] San Giulano to Giolotti and Victor Emmanuel III. 28 July 1911. Quoted in: Claudio Pavone, (ed.), *Dalle carte di Giovanni Giolitti: Quarant'anni di politica italiana,* Volume III, *Dai prodromi della grande guerra al al fascismo* (Milano; Feltrinelli 1962) pp. 52-56.

[93] Handan Nezir Akme e, *The Birth of Modern Turkey: The Ottoman Military and the March to World War I* (London; Tauris, 2005) p. 112. Lawrence Sondhaus, *Naval Warfare, 1815-1914* (Abingdon; Routledge, 2001) p. 220. Robert Gardiner and Randal Gray (Eds.), *Conway's All the World's Fighting Ships, 1906-1921* (Annapolis, MD; Naval Institute Press, 1985) p. 391. M J Whitley, *Battleships of World War Two: An International Encyclopaedia* (Annapolis, MD; Naval Institute Press, 1998) p. 237.

[94] See also: Theodore Ropp, 'The Modern Italian Navy' [since 1900] in *Military Affairs,* Vol. 5, No. 2 (Summer, 1941), pp. 104-116.

[95] Grey to Rodd. 28 July 1911. UK NA CAB 37/107/112.

[96] Grey to Lowther. 30 August 1911. UK NA CAB 37/107/112.

[97] Timothy W Childs, *Italo-Turkish Diplomacy and the War over Libya, 1911-1912* (Leiden; E J Brill) p. 49.

[98] Giovanno Giolotti, *Memorie della mia vita, con uno studio di Olindo Malagodi* (Milano; Fratelli Treves, 1922) Volume II. pp. 335-7.

[99] Giovanno Giolotti, *Memorie della mia vita, con uno studio di Olindo Malagodi* (Milano; Fratelli Treves, 1922) Volume II. p. 334.

[100] Giovanno Giolotti, *Memorie della mia vita, con uno studio di Olindo Malagodi* (Milano; Fratelli Treves, 1922) Volume II. p. 327.

[101] Francesco Malgeri, *La Guerra Libica 1911-1912* (Roma: Edizioni de Storia e Letteratura, 1970) pp. 126-7.

[102] Rodd to Grey. 4 September 1911. G P Gooch and H W V Temperley (Eds.), *British Documents on the Origins of the War: 1898-1914,* Vol. IX, *The Balkan Wars,* Part I, *The Prelude: The Tripoli War* (London; HMSO, 1933) pp. 267-8.

[103] Paolo Maltese, *La terra promessa: La guerra italo-turca e la conquista della Libia 1911-12* (Milano; Mondadori, 1976) pp. 73-4; Francesco Malgeri, *La Guerra Libica 1911-1912* (Roma: Edizioni de Storia e Letteratura, 1970) pp. 61-2.

[104] Francesco Malgeri, *La Guerra Libica 1911-1912* (Roma: Edizioni de Storia e Letteratura, 1970) p. 131. R
      J B Bosworth, *Italy the Least of the Great Powers: Italian Foreign Policy before the First. World War* (London:
      Cambridge University Press, 1979) p. 160.

[105] Timothy W Childs, *Italo-Turkish Diplomacy and the War over Libya, 1911-1912* (Leiden; E J Brill) p. 60.

[106] San Giuliano to Giolotti. 2 September 1911. Quoted in: Claudio Pavone, (ed.), *Dalle carte di Giovanni
      Giolitti: Quarant'anni di politica italiana*, Volume III, *Dai prodromi della grande guerra al al fascismo* (Milano;
      Feltrinelli 1962) p. 59. Brian R Sullivan, 'The Strategy of the Decisive Weight: Italy, 1882-1922' in
      Williamson Murray, MacGregor Knox, and Alvin Bernstein (Eds.) *The Making of Strategy: Rulers, States,
      and War* (Cambridge; Cambridge University Press, 1994) p. 324.

[107] Timothy W Childs, *Italo-Turkish Diplomacy and the War over Libya, 1911-1912* (Leiden; E J Brill) p. 60.

[108] Giovanno Giolotti, *Memorie della mia vita, con uno studio di Olindo Malagodi* (Milano; Fratelli Treves, 1922)
      Volume II. p. 355.

[109] Pansa to San Giuliano. 23 September 1911. Quoted in Timothy W Childs, *Italo-Turkish Diplomacy and the
      War over Libya, 1911-1912* (Leiden; E J Brill) p. 62.

[110] Giovanno Giolotti, *Memorie della mia vita, con uno studio di Olindo Malagodi* (Milano; Fratelli Treves, 1922)
      Volume II. p. 357.

[111] David G Herrmann, *The Arming of Europe and the Making of the First World War* (Princeton, NJ; Princeton
      University Press, 1997) pp. 137-8.

[112] This documentation is contained in the Archivio dell'Ufficio Storico dello Stato Maggiore dell'Esercito:
      Carteggio Libia and was utilized by David G Herrmann for his groundbreaking work on Italian Strategy.
      See: David G Herrmann, 'The Paralysis of Italian Strategy in the Italian-Turkish War, 1911-1912' in *The
      English Historical Review*, Vol. 104, No. 411, April 1989. p. 335.

[113] Archivio dell'Ufficio Storico dello Stato Maggiore dell'Esercito: Carteggio Libia, 215/2: 'Studio per
      l'occupazione della Tripolitania, Agosto 1911.' Campagna di Libia, Volume 1 p. 269.

[114] Giovanni Giolitti, *Memorie della mia vita, con uno studio di Olindo Malagodi* (Milano; Fratelli Treves, 1922)
      Volume II. p. 358.

[115] For a complete history up until 1918 see: Odoardo Marchetti, *Il servizio informazione dell'esercito italiano
      nella grande Guerra* (Roma; Tipografia Regionale, 1937).

[116] Giuseppe De Lutiis, *Storia dei servizi segreti in Italia [History of the Secret Services in Italy]* (Roma: Riuniti,
      1984) p. 303.

[117] Giuseppe De Lutiis, *Storia dei servizi segreti in Italia [History of the Secret Services in Italy]* (Roma: Riuniti,
      1984) p. 8. Marco Meini, *Il decimo corridoio [The Tenth Corridor]* (Roma: Robin, 2005) pp. 343-4. n. 8.

[118] Paolo Maltese, *La terra promessa: La guerra italo-turca e la conquista della Libia 1911-12* (Milano; Mondadori,
      1976) p. 85-6.

[119] San Giuliano circular telegram to Ambassadors at Berlin, London, Madrid, Paris, St. Petersburg and
      Vienna. 24 September 1911. Quoted in Francesco Malgeri, *La Guerra Libica 1911-1912* (Roma; Edizioni
      di storia e letteratura, 1970) p. 106.

[120] *The New York Times.* 25 September 1911.

[121] W H Beehler, *The History of the Italian-Turkish War, September 29, 1911, to October 18, 1912* (Annapolis,
      MD; William H Beehler, 1913) pp. 12-3. Childs. p. 25.

[122] William C Askew, *Europe and Italy's Acquisition of Libya, 1911-1912* (Durham, NC; Duke University Press,
      1942) p. 55.

[123] Orhan Kolo lu, *500 Years In Turkish-Libyan Relations: SAM Paper 1/2007* (Ankara; Stratejik Arastirmalar
      Merkezi (SAM), 2007) p. 174.

[124] Timothy W Childs, *Italo-Turkish Diplomacy and the War over Libya, 1911-1912* (Leiden; E J Brill) p. 64.

[125] Francesco Malgeri, *La Guerra Libica 1911-1912* (Roma; Edizioni di storia e letteratura, 1970) pp. 125,
      138, 140.

[126] Timothy W Childs, *Italo-Turkish Diplomacy and the War over Libya, 1911-1912* (Leiden; E J Brill) p. 64.

[127] Raymond Poincaré (Trans. Sir George Arthur), *The Memoirs of Raymond Poincaré, Volume I: 1912*
      (London: William Heinemann, 1926) p. 19.

[128] Translation taken from: 'Ultimatum from Italy to Turkey Regarding Tripoli' in *The American Journal of
      International Law*, Volume 6, No. 1. Supplement: Official Documents (January 1912), pp. 11-12.

[129] The 'surprise' evinced by Hakki comes from an account by the well-connected Marquess Alberto
      Theodoli, the Italian delegate on the Ottoman Public Debt Council who had lived in Istanbul since
      1905. Alberto Theodoli, 'La preparazione dell'impresa di Tripoli. Ricordi di una missione in Turchia' in
      Nuova Antologia, 16 July 1934. p. 242. His account is used by Childs and Del Boca: Timothy W Childs,
      Italo-Turkish Diplomacy and the War over Libya, 1911-1912 (Leiden; E J Brill) p. 66. Angelo Del Boca, *Gli
      Italiani in Libia: Tripoli bel suol d'amore: 1860-1922*, Vol. I (Millan; Mondadori, 1986) p. 73.

[130] Translation taken from: 'The Turkish Reply to Italian Ultimatum Regarding Tripoli' in *The American
      Journal of International Law*, Volume 6, No. 1. Supplement: Official Documents (January 1912). pp. 12-14.

[131] Sir Thomas Barclay, (With an Additional Chapter on Moslem Feeling by Ameer Ali), *The Turco-Italian
      War and its Problems, with Appendices Containing the Chief State Papers Bearing on the Subject* (London;
      Constable, 1912) pp. 112-13.

CHAPTER FOUR

1   Prime Minster Antonio Salandra on Italy's entry into the Great War on the side of the Entente Powers. 23 May 1915. Charles F Horne, Walter F Austin and Leonard P Ayres (Eds.), *Source Records of the Great War, Volume 3, AD 1915* (Indianapolis, IN; The American Legion, 1931) p. 224.

2   Machiel Kiel, *Ottoman Architecture in Albania, 1385-1912* (Istanbul; Research Centre for Islamic History, Art and Culture, 1990) p. 90.

3   For a discussion on whether or not Bismarck said it: Charles Stephenson, *Germany's Asia-Pacific Empire: Colonialism and Naval Policy 1885–1914* (Woodbridge; Boydell Press, 2009) p. 220.

4   Cartwright to Nicolson. 12 October 1911. G P Gooch and H W V Temperley (Eds.), *British Documents on the Origins of the War: 1898-1914*, Volume IX, *The Balkan Wars*, Part I, *The Prelude: The Tripoli War* (London; HMSO, 1933) p. 307. Sir Arthur Nicolson was the British Permanent Under-Secretary of State for Foreign Affairs from 1910–1916.

5   Edward J. Erickson, *Defeat in Detail: the Ottoman Army in the Balkans, 1912-1913* (Westport, CN; Praeger, 2003) pp. 47-8. Hasan Kayalı, *Arabs and Young Turks: Ottomanism, Arabism, and Islamism in the Ottoman Empire, 1908–1918* (Berkeley, CA; University of California Press, 1997) p. 111-12.

6   Giovanni Giolitti, *Memorie della mia vita, con uno studio di Olindo Malagodi* (Milano; Fratelli Treves, 1922) Volume II. p. 373-4.

7   Charles F Horne, Walter F Austin and Leonard P Ayres (Eds.), *Source Records of the Great War, Volume 3, AD 1915* (Indianapolis, IN; The American Legion, 1931) p. 224.

8   E Alexander Powell, *The New Frontiers Of Freedom: From The Alps To The Aegean* (New York; Charles Scribner's Sons, 1920) p. 138.

9   Giovanni Giolitti, *Memorie della mia vita, con uno studio di Olindo Malagodi* (Milano; Fratelli Treves, 1922) Volume II. p. 374.

10 Despatch dated 7 October 1911 from Vienna. *The Pittsburg Press.* 8 October 1911.

11 For accounts of this incident see: Samuel R Williamson, *Austria-Hungary and the Origins of the First World War* (London; Macmillan, 1991) pp. 789. Alfred von Wittich (Trans. Oliver L Spaulding), *Marshal Conrad in the Preparation for War* (Washington, DC; Army War College, 1936) pp. 6-7. Morris Beatus, *The Views of Conrad von Hötzendorf: Politics, Diplomacy, and War, 1906-1914* [MA Thesis] (Madison, WI; University of Wisconsin, 1970) pp. 44-5. Lawrence Sondhaus, *The Naval Policy of Austria-Hungary, 1867 - 1918: Navalism, Industrial Development, and the Politics of Dualism* (West Lafayette, IN; Purdue University Press, 1994) p. 205. Gunther E Rothenberg, *The Army of Francis Joseph* (West Lafayette, IN; Purdue University Press, 1998) pp. 163-4.

12 Lawrence Sondhaus, *The Naval Policy of Austria-Hungary, 1867-1918: Navalism, Industrial Development, and the Politics of Dualism* (Lafayette, IN; Purdue University Press, 1994) p. 205.

13 Sergio Romano, *La quarta sponda: la guerra di Libia, 1911-1912* (Milano; Bompiani, 1977) p. 67.

14 See: Mirella Tenderini and Michael Shandrick, *The Duke of the Abruzzi: An Explorer's Life* (Seattle, WA; The Mountaineers, 1997).

15 Sergio Romano, *La quarta sponda: la guerra di Libia, 1911-1912* (Milano; Bompiani, 1977) p. 66.

16 Wm Morton Fullerton, *Problems of Power: A Study of International Politics from Sadowa to Kirk-Kilisse* (New York, NY; Charles Scribner's Sons, 1913) p. 290.

17 Prime Mnister Antonio Salandra on Italy's entry into the Great War on the side of the Entente Powers. 23 May 1915. Charles F Horne, Walter F Austin and Leonard P Ayres (Eds.), *Source Records of the Great War, Volume 3, AD 1915* (Indianapolis, IN; The American Legion, 1931) p. 224.

18 Haroon-ur Rasheed, *Pakistan: The Successful Culmination* (Lahore; Publishers Emporium, 1996) p. 478.

19 Rajendra Prasad, *India Divided* (Bombay; Hind Kitabs, 1947) p. 18.

20 Hardinge to Crewe. Letter dated 12 October 1912. Quoted in P Hardy, *The Muslims of British Indian* (Cambridge; Cambridge University Press, 1972) pp.182-83.

21 See: Muhammad Yusuf Abbasi, *The Political Biography of Syed Ameer Ali* (Lahore; Wajidalis, 1989).

22 According to the 1911 census, the total population of India amounted to 315,156,396, 244,267,542 or 77.5 per cent of which resided in directly ruled British territory and 70,888,854 or 22.5 per cent in the 'native states.' The Muslim population was calculated at 65,921,820, or just under 21 per cent, of the total. http://censusindia.gov.in/Census_And_You/old_report/Census_1911.html

23 Reproduced in: Shan Muhammad (Ed.), *The Right Honourable Syed Ameer Ali: Political Writings* (New Delhi; Ashish, 1989) pp. 244-5.

24 See: Azmi Özcan, *Pan-Islamism: Indian Muslims, the Ottomans and Britain (1877-1924)* (Leiden; Brill, 1997) pp. 139-145.

25 Abu Yusuf Alam, *Muslims and Bengal Politics (1912-24)* (Kolkata [Calcutta]; Raktakarabee, 2005) p. 155.

26 Azmi Özcan, *Pan-Islamism: Indian Muslims, the Ottomans and Britain (1877-1924)* (Leiden; Brill, 1997) p. 140.

27 Ishtiaq Ahmad, 'Turkish-Pakistan Relations: Continuity and Change' in Mehmet Tahiroglu and Tareq Y Ismael (Eds.), *Turkey in the 21st Century: Changing Role in World Politics* (Gazimagusa; Eastern Mediterranean University Press, 2000) pp. 143-144.

[28] M Naeem Qureshi, *Pan-Islam in British Indian Politics: A Study of the Khilafat Movement, 1918-1924* (Leiden; Brill, 1999) p. 55. See also: Stuart E Brown, 'Modernism, Association, and Pan-Islamism in the Thought of Ali Bash Hanbah' in Donald P Little (Ed.), *Essays on Islamic Civilization: Presented to Niyazi Berkes* (Leiden; Brill, 1976) p. 76.

[29] Hardinge to Nicolson. 15 October 1911. UK NA FO 800/351, Miscellaneous Correspondence Volume 5, September-November 1911.

[30] John Charmley, Splendid Isolation?: Britain and the Balance of Power 1874-1914 (London; Hodder & Stoughton, 1999) p. 325.

[31] David Lloyd George, War Memoirs. Two-volume edition (London; Odhams, 1938) Vol. I pp. 27-8.

[32] Winston S Churchill, *The Grand Alliance* (Boston, MA; Houghton Mifflin, 1950) p. 71.

[33] For details see: C J Lowe, 'Grey and the Tripoli War' in F H Hinsley (Ed.), *British Foreign Policy under Sir Edward Grey* (Cambridge; Cambridge University Press, 1977) pp. 315-323.

[34] Grey to Rodd. 29 September 1911. G P Gooch and H W V Temperley (Eds.), *British Documents on the Origins of the War: 1898-1914*, Volume IX, *The Balkan Wars*, Part I, *The Prelude: The Tripoli War* (London; HMSO, 1933) p. 285.

[35] Raymond Poincaré (Trans. Sir George Arthur), *The Memoirs of Raymond Poincaré, Volume I: 1912* (London: William Heinemann, 1926) p. 19.

CHAPTER FIVE

[1] Enver Pasa, *Um Tripolis* (Munchen, Hugo Bruckmann, 1918) p. 9.

[2] John Baldry, 'Anglo-Italian Rivalry in Yemen and As r 1900-1934' in *Die Welt des Islams*, New Series, Vol. 17, Issue 1/4 (1976 - 1977) p. 155.

[3] Mehmed Selahaddin, *ttihad ve Terakki'nin Kurulu u ve Osmanlı Devleti'nin Yıkılı ı Hakkında Bildiklerim* (Istanbul; nkilab, 1989) p. 38.

[4] Joshua Teitelbaum, *The Rise and Fall of the Hashimite Kingdom of Arabia* (New York; New York University Press, 2001) p. 64.

[5] For brief accounts see: Sergio Romano, *La quarta sponda: la guerra di Libia, 1911-1912* (Milano; Bompiani, 1977) p. 64. n. 3. Giorgio Giorgerini and Augusto Nani (Eds.), *Gli incrociatori italiani, 1861-1975* (Roma; Ufficio storico marina militare, 1976) pp. 144, 180.

[6] One, *Regina Elena,* did not join his command until 5 October 1911.

[7] Unless otherwise stated, all information on naval operations is derived from: Giovanni Roncagli and Camillo Manfroni (Eds.), *Guerra italo-turca (1911-1912): Cronistoria delle operazioni navali.* Two Volumes: Vol. I: *Dalle origini al decreto di sovranità su la Libia.* Vol. II: *Dal decreto di sovranità su la Libia alla conclusione della pace.* (Milano/Roma; Hoepli/Poligrafico Editorial, 1918/1926).

[8] Tullio Irace, *With the Italians in Tripoli: The Authentic History of the Turco-Italian War* (London; John Murray, 1912) p. 3.

[9] Gianpaolo Ferraioli, *Politica e diplomazia in Italia tra XIX e XX secolo: Vita di Antonino di San Giuliano (1852-1914)* (Soveria Mannelli; Rubbettino, 2007) p. 357.

[10] Enver Pasa, *Um Tripolis* (Munchen, Hugo Bruckmann, 1918). Written in German, a language in which Enver was competent, and couched in terms of a diary with dated entries, it is not however thought that it was compiled contemporaneously. Rather it was probably constructed later using reports and letters that Enver had sent to colleagues and friends in Germany during his time in the theatre of war. This perhaps accounts for the fact that there appears to be no original Turkish text, despite an acknowledgment to 'Friedrich Perzynski' for transcription and, possibly, translation. It was translated into Turkish and published as part of a larger work on the Ottoman forces during the war by Orhan Kolo lu in 1979 [*Trablusgarp Sava ı ve Türk Subaylan 1911-12* (Ankara; Basın Yayın Genel Müdürlü ü, 1979) and then into Arabic by Abdelmola Salah al-Hariri the following year. An Italian translation by Salvatore Bono, with additional notes and appendices, appeared in 1986 [*Enver Pascià: diario della guerra libica* (Bologna; Cappelli, 1986)] but so far no English language edition has been published.

[11] Enver Pasa, *Um Tripolis* (Munchen, Hugo Bruckmann, 1918) pp. 9-10.

[12] *The New York Times*, 30 September 1911.

[13] Sukru Hanioglu (Ed.), *Kendi Mektuplarinda Enver Pasa* (Istanbul; Der Yayınları, 1989) pp. 75-6.

[14] Francis McCullagh, *Italy's War for a Desert: Being Some Experiences of a War-Correspondent with the Italians in Tripoli* (London; Herbert & Daniel, 1913) p. 48.

[15] Harvey E Goldberg, *Jewish Life in Muslim Libya: Rivals & Relatives* (Chicago, IL; University of Chicago Press, 1990) p. 50.

[16] Mordecai ha Cohen, *Higgid Mordecai* (Jerusalem: Ben-Zvi Institute, 1978) pp. 185, 340-343, 348.

[17] For an account of these troops during the initial phases of the 'Libyan enterprise' see: L Fulvi, T Marcon, and O Miozzi, *Le fanterie di marina italiane* (Roma; Ufficio storico della Marina militare, 1998). pp. 37-54.

[18] Great Britain Naval Intelligence Division, *A Handbook of Libya* (London; HMSO, 1917) p. 138.

[19] William C Askew, *Europe and Italy's Acquisition of Libya: A study in Mediterranean Politics and European*

Alignments, 1911-1912 (Durham, NC; Duke University Press, 1942) p. 28. Lisa Anderson, *The State and Social Transformation in Tunisia and Libya, 1830-1980* (Princeton, NJ; Princeton University Press, 1986) pp. 189-90.

[20] Chris B. Rooney, 'The international significance of British naval missions to the Ottoman Empire, 1908-14' in *Middle Eastern Studies*, Volume 34, Issue 1 January 1998. pp. 1-29. Bernd Langensiepen and Ahmet Güleryüz (James Cooper Ed. and Trans.), *The Ottoman Steam Navy, 1828-1923* (London; Conway Maritime Press, 1995) p. 197.

[21] Benito Mussolini in the *Popolo d' Italia*, 14 January 1915.

[22] Augustus Henry Keane, *Africa Volume I: North Africa* (London; Edward Stanford, 1895) p 169.

[23] *Daily Express*. 11 October 1911.

[24] Pollio, 'Memoria sulla occupazione della Tripolitania e della Cirenaica,' 19 September 1911. Archivio dell'Ufficio Storico dello Stato Maggiore dell'Esercito: Carteggio Libia. Raccoglitore I, Fascicolo 14.

[25] San Giuliano to Spingardi. 24 September 1911. Ministero degli Affari Esteri, Archivio di Gabinetto Casella 44, No. 40.

[26] Archivio dell'Ufficio Storico dello Stato Maggiore dell'Esercito: Carteggio Libia, 215/2: *Studio per l'occupazione della Tripolitania*, August 1911.

[27] See: 'The Landing at Derna ' in *The RUSI Journal*, Volume 56, Issue 413 July 1912, page 890.

[28] Ali Abdullatif Ahmida, *The Making of Modern Libya: State formation, Colonization, and Resistance, 1830-1932* (Albany, NY; State University of New York Press, 1994) pp. 75-6.

[29] Tullio Irace, *With the Italians in Tripoli: The Authentic History of the Turco-Italian War* (London; John Murray, 1912) pp. 35-36.

[30] Mohammed Bescir Fergiani, *The Libyan Jamahiriya* (Tripoli; Dar Al-Fergiani, 1976) p. 99

[31] W K McClure, *Italy in North Africa: An Account of the Tripoli Enterprise* (London; Constable, 1913) pp. 56-7.

[32] Tullio Irace, *With the Italians in Tripoli: The Authentic History of the Turco-Italian War* (London; John Murray, 1912) p. 51.

[33] *The Parliamentary Debates (Official Report), Fifth Series, Volume XXX* (London; HMSO, 1911) p. 1794.

[34] Lord Keyes, *Amphibious Warfare and Combined Operations* (Cambridge; Cambridge University Press, 1943) p. 7.

[35] Arianna Sara De Rose, *Marcello Piacentini: opere 1903-1926* (Modena; Panini, 1995) p. 117.

[36] Guido Bonsaver, *Censorship and Literature in Fascist Italy* (Toronto; University of Toronto Press, 2007) p. 15.

[37] Caneva to Spingardi. 18 October 1911. Archivio dell'Ufficio Storico dello Stato Maggiore dell'Esercito. 2/10.

[38] Reuters Telegram from Tripoli. 13 October 1911. Reproduced internationally.

[39] Francis McCullagh, *Italy's War for a Desert: Being Some Experiences of a War-Correspondent with the Italians in Tripoli* (London; Herbert and Daniel, 1913) p. 72

[40] David Nicolle, *The Italian Army of World War I* (Oxford; Osprey, 2003) p. 3.

[41] Francis McCullagh, *Italy's War for a Desert: Being Some Experiences of a War-Correspondent with the Italians in Tripoli* (London; Herbert and Daniel, 1913) p. 72

CHAPTER SIX

[1] H W Halleck, *International Law: or, Rules Regulating the Intercourse of States in Peace and War* (San Francisco; H H Bancroft, 1861) p. 442.

[2] "Kepi," 'The Italians at Tripoli,' in *Blackwood's Magazine* No. MCLIV, December 1911. Vol. CXC. p. 832.

[3] Angelo Del Boca, *A un passo dalla forca: atrocita e infamie dell'occupazione italiana della Libia nelle memorie del patriota Mohamed Fekini* (Milano, Baldini Castoldi Dalai, 2007) p. 16.

[4] Angelo Del Boca, *Gli Italiani in Libia: Tripoli bel suol d'amore: 1860-1922*, Vol. I (Millan; Mondadori, 1986) p. 74; *Sergio Romano, La quarta sponda: la guerra di Libia, 1911-1912* (Milano; Bompiani, 1977) p. 162; Francis McCullagh, *Italy's War for a Desert: Being Some Experiences of a War-Correspondent with the Italians in Tripoli* (London; Herbert & Daniel, 1913) pp. 238-240.

[5] W T Stead, 'Francis McCullagh of Tripoli' in W T Stead (Ed.) 'The Reviews Reviewed' in *The Review of Reviews for Australasia*, February 1912, p. 611.

[6] W K McClure, *Italy in North Africa: An Account of the Tripoli Enterprise* (London; Constable, 1913) p. 60.

[7] Tullio Irace, *With the Italians in Tripoli: The Authentic History of the Turco-Italian War* (London; John Murray, 1912) p. 118.

[8] Francis McCullagh, *Italy's War for a Desert: Being Some Experiences of a War-Correspondent with the Italians in Tripoli* (London; Herbert & Daniel, 1913) pp. 124-5, 127.

[9] Francis McCullagh, *Italy's War for a Desert: Being Some Experiences of a War-Correspondent with the Italians in Tripoli* (London; Herbert & Daniel, 1913) p. 132.

[10] Angelo Del Boca, *A un passo dalla forca: atrocita e infamie dell'occupazione italiana della Libia nelle memorie del patriota Mohamed Fekini* (Milano, Baldini Castoldi Dalai, 2007) p. 24.

11 Francis McCullagh, *Italy's War for a Desert: Being Some Experiences of a War-Correspondent with the Italians in Tripoli* (London; Herbert & Daniel, 1913) p. 218. The General Staff had issued a handbook for officers on how to conduct themselves in respect of the local population. Although paternalistic ('The natives are like children: they should be treated with kindness, correctly but firmly) it had stressed the need to respect local customs, particularly those associated with religion, and that it was 'absolutely necessary to respect the women.' It had though also remarked that it was necessary to severely punish 'any attempt, however small, to avoid European authority.' *Campagna di libia,*Volume I: *Parte generale – operazione in Tripolitania dall'inizio della campagna alla occupazione di Punta Tagiura (ottobre-dicembre 1911)* (Roma, Stabilimento Poligrafico per l'Amministrazione della Guerra, 1922). p. 369.

12 "Kepi," 'The Italians at Tripoli,' in *Blackwood's Magazine* No. MCLIV, December 1911. Vol. CXC. p. 835.

13 Felice Picciole, *Diario di un bersagliere* (Milano, formichiere, 1974) p. 26.

14 "Kepi," 'The Italians at Tripoli,' in *Blackwood's Magazine* No. MCLIV, December 1911. Vol. CXC. p. 837.

15 Francis McCullagh, *Italy's War for a Desert: Being Some Experiences of a War-Correspondent with the Italians in Tripoli* (London; Herbert & Daniel, 1913) p. 202.

16 "Kepi," 'The Italians at Tripoli,' in *Blackwood's Magazine* No. MCLIV, December 1911. Vol. CXC. p. 837.

17 *Daily Mirror,* 2 November 1911.

18 H W Halleck, *International Law: or, Rules Regulating the Intercourse of States in Peace and War* (San Francisco; H H Bancroft, 1861) p. 442.

19 The United Nations War Crimes Commission, *Law Reports of Trials of War Criminals* Volume IV. (London: HMSO, 1948) p. 33.

20 Quinto Poggioli, 'Aeroplanes at Tripoli' in *Flight* magazine, 11 November 1911, p. 989. Walter J Boyne, *The Influence of Air Power upon History* (Gretna, LA; Pelican, 2003) p. 37.

21 McCullagh, *Italy's War for a Desert: Being Some Experiences of a War-Correspondent with the Italians in Tripoli* (London; Herbert & Daniel, 1913) p. 202.

22 Tullio Irace, *With the Italians in Tripoli: The Authentic History of the Turco-Italian* War (London; John Murray, 1912) p. 144.

23 An 'anglais Israelite' according to one who met him there. See: Guy d'Aveline, *La guerre à Tripoli, par un témoin oculaire [The War in Tripoli, by an Eyewitness]* (Paris; Charles Amat, 1912) p. 208. Guy d'Aveline was the pen name of Jeanne Gazala *nee* Kieffer, the wife of Dr Suleiman Gazala, or Gazala Bey, who had been a medical student in Paris, and then a doctor who studied, and wrote about, outbreaks of cholera and plague in Mesopotamia (Iraq). She later translated his memoirs from Arabic and published them in France. See: Guy d'Aveline, *Mémoires d'un délégué sanitaire* [Memoirs of a Sanitary Delegate] (Paris; N Maloine, 1931).

24 *The New York Times,* 13 January 1912.

25 Ernest N Bennett, *With the Turks in Tripoli: Being Some Experiences in the Turco-Italian War of 1911* (London; Methuen, 1912) p. 95.

26 McCullagh, *Italy's War for a Desert: Being Some Experiences of a War-Correspondent with the Italians in Tripoli* (London; Herbert & Daniel, 1913) p. 202.

27 Ernest N Bennett, *With the Turks in Tripoli: Being Some Experiences in the Turco-Italian War of 1911* (London; Methuen, 1912) p. 95.

28 Ashmead Bartlett's despatch is reproduced in: W K McClure, *Italy in North Africa: An Account of the Tripoli Enterprise* (London; Constable, 1913) pp. 253-259.

29 Quoted in: McCullagh, *Italy's War for a Desert: Being Some Experiences of a War-Correspondent with the Italians in Tripoli* (London; Herbert & Daniel, 1913) p. 228.

30 Quoted in: McCullagh, *Italy's War for a Desert: Being Some Experiences of a War-Correspondent with the Italians in Tripoli* (London; Herbert & Daniel, 1913) p. 292.

31 Quoted in: McCullagh, *Italy's War for a Desert: Being Some Experiences of a War-Correspondent with the Italians in Tripoli* (London; Herbert & Daniel, 1913) pp. 253-59.

32 McCullagh, *Italy's War for a Desert: Being Some Experiences of a War-Correspondent with the Italians in Tripoli* (London; Herbert & Daniel, 1913) p. 250.

33 "Kepi," 'The Italians at Tripoli,' in *Blackwood's Magazine* No. MCLIV, December 1911. Vol. CXC. p. 838-9.

34 Angelo Del Boca, *A un passo dalla forca: atrocita e infamie dell'occupazione italiana della Libia nelle memorie del patriota Mohamed Fekini* (Milano, Baldini Castoldi Dalai, 2007) p. 27. Commodore W H Beehler, *The History of the Italian-Turkish War* (Annapolis, MD; United States Naval Institute, 1913) p. 34.

35 See: Mohamed al-Jefa'iri et al, *The Libyan Deportees in the Prisons of the Italian Islands: Documents, Statistics, Names, Illustrations* (Tripoli: Libyan Studies Centre, 1989). Eliana Calandra, 'Prigionieri arabi a Ustica: un episodio della guerra italo-turca attraverso le fonti archivistiche' in Carla Ghezzi (Ed.), *Fonti e problemi della politica coloniale italiana* (Roma; Ministero per i Beni Culturali e Ambientali,1996) Volume II, pp. 1150-1167.

36 Angelo Del Boca, *A un passo dalla forca: atrocita e infamie dell'occupazione italiana della Libia nelle memorie del patriota Mohamed Fekini* (Milano, Baldini Castoldi Dalai, 2007) p. 45.

37 Tullio Irace, *With the Italians in Tripoli: The Authentic History of the Turco-Italian War* (London; John Murray, 1912) pp. 163-4.

38 Quoted in: W T Stead, *Tripoli and the Treaties or Britain's Duty in this War* (London; Stead's Publishing, 1911) pp. 62-4.

39 W T Stead, 'Francis McCullagh of Tripoli' in W T Stead (Ed.) 'The Reviews Reviewed' in *The Review of Reviews for Australasia*, February 1912, p. 563.

40 F T Marinetti, *La battaglia di Tripoli 26 ottobre 1911: vissuta e cantata da F.T. Marinetti* (Milano; Edizioni Futuriste di Poesia, 1912).

41 Angelo Del Boca, *Gli Italiani in Libia: Tripoli bel suol d'amore: 1860-1922*, Vol. I (Milano; Mondadori, 1986) p. 118.

42 Quoted in McCullagh, *Italy's War for a Desert: Being Some Experiences of a War-Correspondent with the Italians in Tripoli* (London; Herbert & Daniel, 1913) p. 304.

43 *Grey River Argus*, 6 March 1912

44 Quoted in McCullagh, *Italy's War for a Desert: Being Some Experiences of a War-Correspondent with the Italians in Tripoli* (London; Herbert & Daniel, 1913) p. 394.

CHAPTER SEVEN

1 Domenico Tumiati, 'Le fauci del Sahara' in *Tripolitania* (Milano; Fratelli Treves, 1911) p. 90.

2 Johannes Lepsius, Albrecht Mendelssohn-Bartholdy, Friedrich Thimme (eds), *Die Große Politik der Europäischen Kabinette 1871 bis 1914I*, Vol. XXX part 1 (Berlin; Deutsche Verlaggesellschaft fur Politik und Geschichte, 1926).

3 Geoffrey A Haywood, *Failure of a Dream: Sidney Sonnino and the rise and fall of Liberal Italy 1847-1922* () p. 396.

4 Giovanni Giolotti, *Memorie della mia vita, con uno studio di Olindo Malagodi* (Milano; Fratelli Treves, 1922) Volume II. pp. 380-82.

5 Foreign Office Historical Section, *Italian Libya* (London; HMSO, 1920) p. 58.

6 W T Stead, *Tripoli and the Treaties: or Britain's Duty in This War* (London; Stead's, 1911) p. 17.

7 Lassa Oppenheim and Ronald F Roxburgh (Ed.), *International Law: A Treatise, Vol. I. Peace* (London; Longmans, Green, 1920) p. 397.

8 Charles E P Brome Weigall, *A History of Events in Egypt from 1798 to 1914* (London; William Blackwood, 1915).

9 Taner Akçam. *Insan Haklari ve Ermeni Sorunu: Ittihat ve Terakki'den Kurtulus Savasina* (Ankara; IMGE Kitabevi, 1999) pp. 92-3. See also: Philip Hendrick Stoddard (Trans. Tansel Demirel), *Te kilat-ı Mahsusa: Osmanlı Hükümeti ve Araplar 1911-1918 Te kilat-ı Mahsusa üzerine bir ön çalı ma* (Istanbul; Arba Yayinlari, 1994). A translation of Hendrick's PhD thesis, *The Ottoman Government and the Arabs, 1911 to 1918: A Preliminary Study of the Teskiat-i Mahsusa* (Ann Arbor, MI; University Microfilms, 1963)]

10 Ottoman titles have no direct European equivalents, but men could be granted the right to be known as Effendi, Bey, and Pasa (Pasha), in ascending order.

11 Robert Graves, *Lawrence and the Arabs* (London; Jonathan Cape, 1934) p. 14.

12 Salvatore Bono, *Enver Pascià: diario della guerra libica* (Bologna; Cappelli, 1986) p. 74. n. 10.

13 Enver Pasa, *Um Tripolis* (Munchen, Hugo Bruckmann, 1918) pp. 15-16.

14 A zavia or zawia 'is, at the same time, a religious seminary and a pious and gratuitous hotel.' The abode of a *marabout*, a religious leader and teacher, man devoted to the religious observance of the Koran, and to the edification of the faithful. See: Amos Perry, *Carthage and Tunis, Past and Present: In Two Parts* (Providence, RI; Providence Press, 1869) pp. 262, 275.

15 Enver Pasa, *Um Tripolis* (Munchen, Hugo Bruckmann, 1918) p. 23.

16 Andrew Mango, *Ataturk: The Biography of the Founder of Modern Turkey* (Woodstock, NY; Overlook Press, 2002) p. 105.

17 Andrew Mango, *Atatürk: The Biography of the Founder of Modern Turkey* (London; John Murray, 2004) p. 105.

18 Sukru Hanioglu (Ed.), *Kendi Mektuplarinda Enver Pasa* (Istanbul; Der Yayınları, 1989) p. 88.

19 Sukru Hanioglu (Ed.), *Kendi Mektuplarinda Enver Pasa* (Istanbul; Der Yayınları, 1989) pp. 75-6.

20 Philip Hendrick Stoddard (Trans. Tansel Demirel), *Te kilat-ı Mahsusa: Osmanlı Hükümeti ve Araplar 1911-1918 Te kilat-ı Mahsusa üzerine bir ön çalı ma* (Istanbul; Arba Yayinlari, 1994) [*The Special Organisation: The Ottoman Government and the Arabs, 1911 to 1918 a Preliminary Study of the Special Organisation*. A translation of Hendrick's PhD thesis, *The Ottoman Government and the Arabs, 1911 to 1918: A Preliminary Study of the Teskiat-i Mahsusa* (Ann Arbor, MI; University Microfilms, 1963)] p. 84.

21 E E Evans-Pritchard, *The Sanusi of Cyrenaica* (Oxford; Clarendon Press, 1949). Muhammad Khalil, 'Renaissance in North Africa: The Sanusiyyah Movement' in M M Sharif (Ed.) *A History of Muslim Philosophy with Short Accounts of Other Disciplines and the Modern Renaissance in Muslim Lands*, Volume II (Wiesbaden; Otto Harrassowitz, 1966). Knut S Vikør, *Sufi and Scholar on the Desert Edge: Muhammad b. Ali*

Al-Sanusi and His Brotherhood (Evanston, Ill; Northwestern University Press, 1995). N.A. Ziadeh, *Sanusiya: A Study of a Revivalist Movement in Islam* (Leiden; Brill, 1958). Mahmood Ahmad Ghazi, *The Sanusiyyah Movement Of North Africa: An Analytical Study* (Islamabad; Shariah Academy, 2001).

22   Knut S Vikør, *Sufi and Scholar on the Desert Edge: Muhammad b. Ali Al-Sanusi and His Brotherhood* (Evanston, Ill; Northwestern University Press, 1995) p. 1.

23   Hanns Vischer, *Across the Sahara from Tripoli to Bornu* (London; Edward Arnold, 1910) p. 69.

24   Hanns Vischer, *Across the Sahara from Tripoli to Bornu* (London; Edward Arnold, 1910) p. 68.

25   Rosita Forbes, *The Secret of the Sahara: Kufara* (New York; George H Doran, 1921) p. 331.

26   Ali Abdullatif Ahmida, *The Making of Modern Libya: State Formation, Colonization, and Resistance* (Albany, NY; State University of New York Press, 2009) p. 1.

27   Amal Obeidi, *Political Culture in Libya* (Richmond UK; Curzon, 2001). Abdulmola El-Horeir, *Social and Economic Transformations in the Libyan Hinterland during the Second Half of the 19th Century: The Role of Sayyid Ahmad al-Sharif al-Sanusi* (Los Angeles, CA; University of California, 1981). Mohamed Zahi El-Mogherbi, *Tribalism, Religion and the Challenge of Political Participation: The Case of Libya.* (A Paper presented to Conference on Democratic Challenges in the Arab World, Centre for Political and International Development Studies, Cairo, 22–27 September 1992). Ernest Gellner and Charles Micaud, *Arabs and Berbers: from Tribe to Nation in North Africa* (London; D C Heath, 1973).

28   Gerhard Rohlfs, *Kufra: Reise von Tripolis nach der Oase Kufra* (Leipzig; F A Brockhaus, 1881).

29   Lisa Anderson, 'The Development of Nationalist Sentiment in Libya, 1908-1922' in Rashid Khalidi, Lisa Anderson, Muhammad Muslih and Reeva S Simon (Eds.) *The Origins of Arab Nationalism* (New York; Columbia University Press, 1991) p. 229.

30   Abdul-mola al-Horeir, *Social and Economic Transformations in the Libyan Hinterland during the Second Half of the Nineteenth Century: The Role of Sayyid Ahmad al-Sharif al-Sanusi* (Los Angeles; University of California, 1981) pp. 224-5.

31   Muhammad Khalil, 'Renaissance in North Africa: The Sanusiyyah Movement' in M M Sharif (Ed.) *A History of Muslim Philosophy with Short Accounts of Other Disciplines and the Modern Renaissance in Muslim Lands*, Volume II (Wiesbaden; Otto Harrassowitz, 1966)

32   Mesut Uyar and Edward J Erickson, *A Military History of the Ottomans: From Osman to Ataturk* (Westport, CT; Praeger, 2009) p. 223.

33   Archivio dell'Ufficio Storico dello Stato Maggiore dell'Esercito, *Studi per un'eventuale occupazione dell'isola di Rodi o altre isole turche*, L8, R1, C18.

34   Tullio Irace, *With the Italians in Tripoli: The Authentic History of the Turco-Italian War* (London; John Murray, 1912) p. 200.

35   Ernest Nathaniel Bennett for the *Manchester Guardian* and George Frederick Abbott left London together on 23 November for Tunis. Bennett was an experienced hand and the author of several books detailing his experiences, including *The Downfall of the Dervishes: Being a Sketch of the Final Sudan Campaign of 1898* (1898) and *With Methuen's Column on an Ambulance Train* (1900). Abbott was also well travelled and had written widely. His books included *Songs of Modern Greece* (1900), *Macedonian Folk-Lore* (1903), *The Tale of a Tour in Macedonia* (1903), *Through India with the Prince* (1906), *Greece in Evolution* (1909), *Turkey in Transition* (1909), *The Philosophy of a Don* (1911), and *The Ambassador of Loss* (1911).

36   W K McClure, *Italy in North Africa: An Account of the Tripoli Enterprise* (London; Constable, 1913) pp. 96-7.

37   F Abbott, *The Holy War in Tripoli* (London; Edward Arnold, 1912) p. 50.

38   W K McClure, *Italy in North Africa: An Account of the Tripoli Enterprise* (London; Constable, 1913) pp. 102-3.

39   *Le Matin*. 30 November 1911.

40   Quoted in: Duncan Anderson, *Glass Warriors: The Camera at War* (London; Collins, 2005) p. 78.

41   W K McClure, *Italy in North Africa: An Account of the Tripoli Enterprise* (London; Constable, 1913) p. 103.

42   Richard Bagot, *The Italians of To-Day* (London; Mills & Boon, 1912) p. 98.

43   Nicola Labanca, 'The Embarrassment of Libya: History, Memory, and Politics in Contemporary Italy' in *California Italian Studies Journal*, Volume 1, Issue 1, 2010.

44   Salvatore Bono, 'Lettere dal fronte libico (1911-1912)' in *Nuova Antologia* No. 2052. December 1971.

45   Lucia Re, 'Italians and the Invention of Race: The Poetics and Politics of Difference in the Struggle over Libya, 1890-1913' in *California Italian Studies Journal* 1.1. (2010). p. 28.

46   Carolina Invernizio, *Odio di araba [The Hatred of Arabs]* (Firenze; Salani, 1912) p. 5.

47   Tullio Irace, *With the Italians in Tripoli: The Authentic History of the Turco-Italian War* (London; John Murray, 1912) p. 313.

CHAPTER EIGHT

1   Charles Wellington Furlong, 'Italy finds Tripoli a Hard Nut to Crack' in *The New York Times*, 4 May 1912.

2   Quinto Poggioli, 'Aeroplanes at Tripoli' in *Flight* magazine, 11 November 1911, p. 989.

3   Leslie Gardiner, *Lunardi: The Story of Vicenzo Lunardi* (Shrewsberry; Airlife, 1963).

4   Lieutenant General [Gugliemo] Pepe, *Narrative of Scenes and Events in Italy from 1847 to 1849, Including the Siege of Venice*, Volume II (London; Henry Colburn, 1850) p. 116.

5   Angelo Lodi, *Storia delle origini dell'aeronautica militare, 1884-1915: aerostieri, dirigibilisti, aviatori dell'Esercito e della Marina in Italia nel periodo pionieristico* (Roma; Bizzarri, 1976) Volume 1. Gaetano V Cavallaro, *The Beginning of Futility: Diplomatic, Political, Military and Naval Events on the Austro-Italian Front in the First World War 1914-1917* (Bloomington, IN; Xlibris, 1999) Volume I, p. 107.

6   Andrea Curami, 'La nascita dell'industria aeronautica' in Paolo Ferrari (Ed.), *L'aeronautica italiana: una storia del Novecento* (Milano; Franco Angeli, 2004) pp. 22-23

7   Sebastiano Licheri, 'Gli ordinamenti dell 'aeronautica militare italiana dal 1884 al 1918' in Ministero per i beni culturali e ambientali Ufficio centrale per i beni archivistici, *Le fonti per la storia militare italiana in età contemporanea. Atti del III seminario, Roma, 16-17 dicembre 1988* (Roma; Ediprint, 1993) p. 479.

8   RUSI Journal, 1911.

9   Edgar C Middleton, *Airfare of To-Day and of the Future* (London; Constable, 1917) p. 30.

10 C Canovetti 'L' Aviazione in Libia' in *Emporium: rivista mensile illustrata d'arte, letteratura, scienze e varietà*, Vol. XXXV (Bergamo; Istituto Italiano d'Arti Grafiche, 1912) pp. 456-7.

11 Quoted in: Bertha von Suttner. 'Randglossen zur Zeitgeschichte' in Alfred M Fried (Ed.), *Die Friedens-Warte: Zeitschrift für zwischenstaatliche Organisation* (Berlin; Zeitschrift für zwischenstaatliche Organisation, 1912) pp. 99-100.

12 http://www.aeci.it/

13 Anthony Aufrere (Trans.), *Narrative of an Expedition from Tripoli in Barbary to the Western Frontier of Egypt, in 1817, by the Bey of Tripoli; in letters to Dr Viviani of Genoa, by Paolo Della Cella, Physician Attendant on the Bey; with an Appendix containing Instructions for Navigating the Great Syrtis* (London; John and Arthur Arch, 1822) pp. 15-18.

14 H C Seppings Wright, *Two Years Under the Crescent* (Boston; Small, Maynard and Co., 1913) p. 59.

15 G F Abbott, *The Holy War in Tripoli* (London; , 1912) p. 46.

16 Alan Ostler, *The Arabs in Tripoli* (London; John Murray, 1912) p. 48.

17 A *Fenduk,* or *Caravanserai*, was a type of inn or lodging house consisting of a more or less square enclosure surrounded by a wall and pierced by an arched gateway. Built on the inside of the wall were a number of bare windowless rooms with doors that opened into the square, which contained a well or water source. Animals, such as camels or horses, would remain tethered in the square whilst their owners could store their possessions, and sleep, in the rooms. The gate was locked during the night affording some security, and whilst no charge was made to stay, those who could afford to were expected, on leaving, to leave a small gratuity to the porter.

18 G F Abbott, *The Holy War in Tripoli* (London; Edward Arnold, 1912) p. 1.

19 Alan Ostler, *The Arabs in Tripoli* (London; John Murray, 1912) p. 55.

20 G F Abbott, *The Holy War in Tripoli* (London; Edward Arnold, 1912) p. 45.

21 Charles Wellington Furlong, 'Italy finds Tripoli a Hard Nut to Crack' in *The New York Times*, 4 May 1912.

22 Tullio Irace, *With the Italians in Tripoli: The Authentic History of the Turco-Italian War* (London; John Murray, 1912) pp. 248-9.

23 Herbert Gerald Montagu, despatch to The Central News dated 14 January 1912. Alan Ostler, *The Arabs in Tripoli* (London; John Murray, 1912) pp. 68-9.

24 G F Abbott, *The Holy War in Tripoli* (London; Edward Arnold, 1912) p. 51.

25 Interview with Marconi, *New York Times* 24 March 1912.

26 Tullio Irace, *With the Italians in Tripoli: The Authentic History of the Turco-Italian War* (London; John Murray, 1912) p. 249.

27 Diario storico del Comando I Gruppo Artiglieria da Fortezza di Tripoli (28 settembre 1911-16 ottobre 1912). Gianni Oliva, *Storia degli alpini* (Milano; Rizzoli, 1985).

28 G F Abbott, *The Holy War in Tripoli* (London; Edward Arnold, 1912) p. 54.

29 G F Abbott, *The Holy War in Tripoli* (London; Edward Arnold, 1912) p. 55.

30 Alan Ostler, *The Arabs in Tripoli* (London; John Murray, 1912) p. 76.

31 G F Abbott, *The Holy War in Tripoli* (London; Edward Arnold, 1912) p. 56.

32 G F Abbott, *The Holy War in Tripoli* (London; Edward Arnold, 1912) p. 50.

33 G F Abbott, *The Holy War in Tripoli* (London; Edward Arnold, 1912) p. 56.

34 G F Abbott, *The Holy War in Tripoli* (London; Edward Arnold, 1912) p. 57.

35 Alan Ostler, *The Arabs in Tripoli* (London; John Murray, 1912) p. 82.

36 Reuters despatch from Tripoli City. 6 December 1911.

[37] David Nicolle and Raffaele Ruggeri, *The Italian Army of World War I* (Oxford; Osprey, 2003) p. 34.

[38] W K McClure, *Italy in North Africa: An Account of the Tripoli Enterprise* (London; Constable, 1913) p. 122.

CHAPTER NINE

[1] Alan Ostler, *The Arabs in Tripoli* (London; John Murray, 1912) p. 58.

[2] Ernest N Bennett, *With the Turks in Tripoli: Being Some Experiences in the Turco-Italian War of 1911* (London; Methuen, 1912) p. 108.

[3] The inventor was French farmer Paul Decauville, who conceived the idea after visiting the narrow gauge Rheilffordd Ffestiniog (Ffestiniog Railway) between Blaenau Ffestiniog and Porthmadog in North Wales. He originally devised it as a means of improving access to his land, but realised that it could be adapted for other purposes. He formed a company to produce track and rolling stock in 1875. The French Army adopted the system in 1888 and it had become standardised equipment for the militaries of several countries by 1914. See: 'Portable Railways' in *Scientific American Supplement No. 446* New York, 19 July 1884; Pascal Ory, *1889 La Mémoire des siècles: L'Expo universelle* (Paris; Editions Complexe, 1989) p. 119; Ffestiniog Railway Company, *Rheilffordd Ffestiniog Guide Book* (Porthmadog; Ffestiniog Railway Company, 1997); Jim Harter, *World Railways of the Nineteenth Century: A Pictorial History in Victorian Engravings* (Baltimore MD; John Hopkins University Press, 2005) p. 141.

[4] Archivio dell'Ufficio Storico dello Stato Maggiore dell'Esercito: Carteggio Libia 180/5: Caneva to Pollio, 19 Dec. 1911; AUSSME 180/5: Intendenza, Corpo di Spedizione in Libia, reports of 19 & 27 Dec. 1911.

[5] Claud H Williams, *Report on the Military Geography of the North-Western Desert of Egypt* (London; HM Government, 1919) p. 60. See also: Jim Harold, 'Cars, Deserts, Maps and Naming: An Analysis of Captain Claud H Williams' Report on the Military Geography of the North-Western Desert of Egypt, (1917).' A paper presented to the Fifth Biennial ASTENE (Association for the Study of Travel in Egypt and the Near East) Conference, held on Friday 11 July - Monday 14 July 2003 at Worcester College, Oxford.

[6] Cape Times, 29 May 1906.

[7] Charles à Court Repington, 'Italy's Difficulties' in *The Times*, 30 December 1911.

[8] Winston S Churchill, *The River War: The Reconquest of the Sudan* (London; New English Library, 1985) p. 262.

[9] W K McClure, *Italy in North Africa: An Account of the Tripoli Enterprise* (London; Constable, 1913) p. 132.

[10] *Baedeker's Mediterranean: Seaports and Sea Routes including Madeira, The Canary Islands, The Coast of Morocco, Algeria, and Tunisia* (Leipzig; Karl Baedeker, 1911) p. 404.

[11] Tullio Irace, *With the Italians in Tripoli: The Authentic History of the Turco-Italian War* (London; John Murray, 1912) p. 264.

[12] G F Abbott, *The Holy War in Tripoli* (London; Edward Arnold, 1912) p. 130.

[13] Ernest N Bennett, *With the Turks in Tripoli: Being Some Experiences in the Turco-Italian War of 1911* (London; Methuen, 1912) pp. 106-7.

[14] W K McClure, *Italy in North Africa: An Account of the Tripoli Enterprise* (London; Constable, 1913) pp. 112-3.

[15] G F Abbott, *The Holy War in Tripoli* (London; Edward Arnold, 1912) p. 132.

[16] G F Abbott, *The Holy War in Tripoli* (London; Edward Arnold, 1912) p. 132.

[17] W K McClure, *Italy in North Africa: An Account of the Tripoli Enterprise* (London; Constable, 1913) p. 113.

[18] Respectively: Ciro Paoletti, *A Military History of Italy* (Westport, CT; Praeger Security International, 2008) p. 134; Tullio Irace, *With the Italians in Tripoli: The Authentic History of the Turco-Italian War* (London; John Murray, 1912) p. 263; W K McClure, *Italy in North Africa: An Account of the Tripoli Enterprise* (London; Constable, 1913) p. 114; Francis McCullagh, *Italy's War For A Desert: Being Some Experiences Of A War Correspondent With The Italians In Tripoli* (Chicago, IL; F G Browne, 1913) p. 30.

[19] Angelo Del Boca, *Gli Italiani in Libia: Tripoli bel suol d'amore: 1860-1922 [The Italians in Libya: Tripoli Beautiful Land of Love]*, Vol. I (Millan; Mondadori, 1986) p. 135.

[20] Angelo Del Boca, *Gli Italiani in Libia: Tripoli bel suol d'amore: 1860-1922 [The Italians in Libya: Tripoli Beautiful Land of Love]*, Vol. I (Millan; Mondadori, 1986) p. 136.

[21] Ernest N Bennett, *With the Turks in Tripoli: Being Some Experiences in the Turco-Italian War of 1911* (London; Methuen, 1912) p. 115.

[22] G F Abbott, *The Holy War in Tripoli* (London; Edward Arnold, 1912) p. 137.

[23] Ernest N Bennett, *With the Turks in Tripoli: Being Some Experiences in the Turco-Italian War of 1911* (London; Methuen, 1912) pp. 108-9.

[24] Ernest N Bennett, *With the Turks in Tripoli: Being Some Experiences in the Turco-Italian War of 1911* (London; Methuen, 1912) p. 117.

[25] The correspondence between Frugoni and Peccori-Giraldi was published as 'Il Memoriale di Pecori-Giraldi' in *La Stampa*. 12 March 1912.

[26] W K McClure, *Italy in North Africa: An Account of the Tripoli Enterprise* (London; Constable, 1913) p. 120.

[27] G F Abbott, *The Holy War in Tripoli* (London; Edward Arnold, 1912) p. 143.

28 Archivio dell'Ufficio Storico dello Stato Maggiore dell'Esercito: Carteggio Libia 2/15: Maj. Gen. Gaetano Giardina to Giolitti, San Giuliano, Spingardi, and Pollio. 4 January 1912.

29 W K McClure, *Italy in North Africa: An Account of the Tripoli Enterprise* (London; Constable, 1913) p. 123.

30 Charles à Court Repington, 'Italy's Difficulties' in *The Times*, 30 December 1911.

31 W K McClure, *Italy in North Africa: An Account of the Tripoli Enterprise* (London; Constable, 1913) p. 121.

32 Pol Tristan, 'Le combat de Gargaresch' in *L'Ouest-Éclair*, 24 Fevrier 1912.

33 Pol Tristan, 'Le combat de Gargaresch' in *L'Ouest-Éclair*, 24 Fevrier 1912.

34 Alan Ostler, 'An Arab Joan of Arc' in the *New York Daily Tribune* 10 March 1912.

35 Georges Remond, *Aux Camps Turco-Arabes: Notes de Route et de guerre en Cyrénaïque et en Tripolitaine* (Paris; Hachette, 1913) p. 56.

36 C R Pennell, 'Women and Resistance to Colonialism in Morocco: the Rif 1916–1926' in *The Journal of African History*, Volume 28, 1987. p. 115.

37 Enver Pascha, *Um Tripolis* (München; Hugo Bruckmann,1918) p. 32.

38 Enver Pascha, *Um Tripolis* (München; Hugo Bruckmann,1918) p. 35.

39 Enver Pascha, *Um Tripolis* (München; Hugo Bruckmann,1918) p. 35.

40 Andrew Mango, *Ataturk: The Biography of the Founder of Modern Turkey* (Woodstock, NY; Overlook Press, 2002) p. 105.

41 Enver Pascha, *Um Tripolis* (München; Hugo Bruckmann,1918) p. 30.

42 Wilfred T P Castle, *Grand Turk: An Historical Outline of Life and Events, of Culture and Politics, of Trade and Travel during the Last Years of the Ottoman Empire and the First Years of the Turkish Republic* (London; Hutchinson, 1943) p. 90.

43 Andrew Mango, *Atatürk: The Biography of the Founder of Modern Turkey* (Woodstock, NY; Overlook Press, 2002) p. 106.

44 Captain R Murdoch Smith RE and Commander E A Porcher RN, *History of the Recent Discoveries at Cyrene, made during an Expedition to the Cyrenaica in 1860-61, under the Auspices of Her Majesty's Government* (London; Day & Son, 1864) pp. 59-60.

45 *Berliner Lokal-Anzeiger* of 28 January 1912.

46 Renato Tittoni, *The Italo-Turkish War (1911-12): Translated and Compiled from the Reports of the Italian General Staff* (Kansas City, MO; Franklin Hudson, 1914) pp. 43-4.

47 Relazione sul combattimento di Koefia del Generale d'Amico, Comandante la 3a Brigata di Fanteria (28 novembre 1911). Archivo Storico Stato Maggiore Esercito. 144. 6.

48 Ilhan Aksit (Ed.), *Mustafa Kemal Ataturk* (Istanbul; Cagaloglu, 1998) p. 33.

49 Jacob M Landau, *Atatürk and the Modernization of Turkey* (Boulder, CO; Westview Press, 1984) p. 22.

50 Andrew Mango, *Atatürk: The Biography of the Founder of Modern Turkey* (Woodstock, NY; Overlook Press, 2002) p. 105.

51 Renato Tittoni, *The Italo-Turkish War (1911-12): Translated and Compiled from the Reports of the Italian General Staff* (Kansas City, MO; Franklin Hudson, 1914) p. 81.

52 Patrick Kinross, *Atatürk: The Rebirth of a Nation* (New York; Morrow, 1965) p. 63.

53 Quoted in *Andrew Mango, Atatürk: The Biography of the Founder of Modern Turkey (Woodstock, NY; Overlook Press, 2002) p. 106.*

54 Quoted in *Andrew Mango, Atatürk: The Biography of the Founder of Modern Turkey (Woodstock, NY; Overlook Press, 2002) p. 106.*

55 Massimiliano Munzi, 'Italian Archaeology in Libya: From Colonial Romanita to Decolonization of the Past' in Michael L Galaty and Charles Watkinson, *Archaeology under Dictatorship* (New York, NY; Springer, 2004) p. 79.

56 Tullio Irace, *With the Italians in Tripoli: The Authentic History of the Turco-Italian War* (London; John Murray, 1912) p. 267.

57 Otfried Layriz and R B Marston (Trans.), *Mechanical Traction in War for Road Transport with Notes on Automobiles Generally* (London; Sampson Low, Marston, 1900) pp. 26-7, 69-71. L Giletta, 'Le locomotive stradali e la mobilitazione dell'esercito' in *Rivista Militare Italiana*, September 1876, p. 404. P Mirandoli, 'Le locomotive stradali' in *Rivista Militare Italiana*, January 1883, p. 73 and February 1883, p. 293.

58 'Motor Vehicles in Warfare' in *The Horseless Age: A Monthly Journal Devoted to Motor Interests*, Volume 11, Number 9, July 1897. p. 14.

59 J F C Fuller, *The Conduct of War 1789-1961* (London; Eyre & Spottiswoode, 1961) p. 136. For some splendid photographs see: Richard Willcox, *The Traction Engine Archive* (Stonehouse, UK; The Road Locomotive Society, 2004).

60 Major General Sir John Headlam, *The History of the Royal Artillery from the Indian Mutiny to the Great War, Volume II 1899-1914* (Woolwich; Royal Artillery Institution, 1937) p. 260.

61 Renato Tittoni, *The Italo -Turkish War (1911-12): Translated and Compiled from the Reports of the Italian General Staff* (Kansas City, MO; Franklin Hudson, 1914) p. 109.

62 E Bartholomew, *Early Armoured Cars* (Oxford; Shire Publications, 1988).

63 Cesare Causa, *La guerra italo-turca e la conquista della Tripolitania e della Cirenaica dallo sbarco di tripoli alla pace di losanna* (Firenze; Salani, 1912) p. 668.

64 Cesare Causa, *La guerra italo-turca e la conquista della Tripolitania e della Cirenaica dallo sbarco di tripoli alla pace di losanna* (Firenze; Salani, 1912) p. 668. Ispettorato generale della motorizzazione, *L'Albo d'Onore del Servizio della Motorizzazione* (Roma; Ispettorato generale della motorizzazione, 1966) p. I.
65 Horace Wyatt, *Motor Transports in War* (London; Hodder and Stoughton, 1914) pp. 67-8.
66 H C Seppings Wright, *Two Years Under the Crescent* (Boston; Small, Maynard, 1913) p. 105. Seppings Wright (1849-1937) worked for *The Pictorial World* from about 1883, before joining the *Illustrated London News* in 1888. He covered the Ashanti and Dongola Campaigns and Spanish-American War for them, and was Armstrong-Whitworth's representative in the Russo-Japanese War. He went out to Tripoli, for the Central News. R Wilkinson-Latham, *From Our Special Correspondent: Victorian War Correspondents and their Campaigns* (London; Hodder & Stoughton, 1979).
67 Carlo Rinaldi, *I dirigibili italiani nella campagna di Libia*, Storia Militare N° 18/marzo 1995 pag 38-49.
68 H C Seppings Wright, *Two Years Under the Crescent* (Boston; Small, Maynard, 1913) p. 106.
69 G F Abbott, *The Holy War in Tripoli* (London; Edward Arnold, 1912) pp. 291-2.
70 *The New York Times,* 7 March 1912.
71 Renato Tittoni, *The Italo-Turkish War (1911-12): Translated and Compiled from the Reports of the Italian General Staff* (Kansas City, MO; Franklin Hudson, 1914) p. 100.
72 Report on Italian Aviation in the Turco-Italian War, 1912, Air 1/2133/207/154/ 12, PRO. Amadeo Chiusano and Maurizio Sapotiti, *Palloni, dirigibili ed aerie del Regio Esercito (1884-1923)* (Roma; Ufficio Storico dello Stato Maggiore dell'Esercito, 1998).
73 Luigi Sacco's report, *Relazione circa le esperienze compiute dal Comm. Marconi nei giorni 16 e 17 dicembre 1911 a Tripoli*, can be viewed at http://luigisacco.bonavoglia.eu/relazione_19111220.pdf Interview with Marconi, reported on 30 December 1911 in *The New York Times.* Franco Soresini, *90 anni di trasmissioni nell'esercito italiano: segnalazioni, telegrafia, telefonia e radio* (Maser; Mose, 1998)

CHAPTER TEN

1 H N Brailsford, *The War of Steel and Gold* (London; G Bell, 1914) p. 169.
2 Joseph Heller, *British policy towards the Ottoman Empire, 1908-1914* (London; Frank Cass, 1983) p. 53.
3 Quoted by W T Stead, in an untitled posthumously published piece dated 1 April 1912 in *The Review of Reviews* for June 1912.
4 Giorgio Rochat and Giulio Massobrio, *Breve storia dell'esercito italiano dal 1861 al 1943* (Turin; Einaudi, 1978) p. 163.
5 *Avanti* 1 October 1911.
6 A James Gregor, *Young Mussolini and the Intellectual Origins of Fascism* (Berkeley, CA; University of California Press, 1979) p. 129.
7 J Gentilli, *Italian Roots in Australian Soil: Italian Migration to Western Australia 1829-1946* (Marangaroo, Western Australia; Italo-Australian Welfare Centre, 1983) p. 58.
8 C J Lowe, 'Grey and the Tripoli War, 1911-1912' in F H Hinsley (Ed.), *British Foreign Policy under Sir Edward Grey* (Cambridge; Cambridge University Press, 1977) p. 315
9 A despatch from St Petersburg dated 29 September 1911, quoted in the Novoe Vremya.
10 G P Gooch and H W V Temperley (Eds.), British Documents on the Origins of the War: *1898-1914, Volume IX, The Balkan Wars*, Part I, *The Prelude: The Tripoli War* (London; HMSO, 1933) p. 780.
11 Helmuth von Moltke, *Briefe über Zustände und Begebenheiten in der Türkei aus den Jahren 1835-39* (Berlin; Mittler, 1841).
12 Karl Küntzer, *Abdul Hamid II und die Reformen in der Türkei* (Dresden/Leipzig; Carl Reissner, 1897) p. 22.
13 Merwin Albert Griffiths. *The Reorganization of the Ottoman Army under Abdülhamid II, 1880-1897* (Los Angeles, CA; University of California, 1968) p. 67.
14 Rifat Önsoy, *Türk-Alman iktisadî münasebetleri (1871-1914)* (Istanbul; Ünal Matbaası, 1982); *Andreas Birken, Die Wirtschaftsbeziehungen zwischen Europa und dem Vorderen Orient im ausgehenden 19. Jahrhundert* (Wiesbaden; L Reichert, 1980).
15 Boris Barth, *Die deutsche Hochfinanz und die Imperialisten: Banken und Aussenpolitik vor 1914* (Stuttgart: Franz Steiner, 1995).
16 Mustafa Aydin, *Turkish Foreign Policy: Framework and Analysis* (Ankara; Center for Strategic Research, 2004) p. 6.
17 Milos Kovic, *Disraeli and the Eastern Question* (Oxford; Oxford University Press, 2011) p. 165.
18 Commodore W H Beehler, *The History of the Italian-Turkish War* (Annapolis, MD; United States Naval Institute, 1913) p. 46.
19 Timothy W Childs, *Italo-Turkish Diplomacy and the War over Libya, 1911-1912* (Leiden; E J Brill) p. 96.
20 Luigi Albertini, *Le origini della guerra del 1914: Vol. I, Le relazioni europee dal Congresso di Berlino all'attentato di Sarajevo* (Milano; Bocca, 1941)p. 358.
21 Giovanno Giolotti, *Memorie della mia vita, con uno studio di Olindo Malagodi* [*Memories of My Life, with a study by Olindo Malagodi*] (Milano; Fratelli Treves, 1922) Volume II. p. 392.

22 Ronald P Bobroff, *Roads to Glory: Late Imperial Russia and the Turkish Straits* (London; I B Tauris, 2006) pp. 29-31.

23 *Hansard's Commons Debates*, 4 July 1907, Volume 177 columns 863-4.

24 A Silva White, *The Expansion of Egypt under Anglo-Egyptian Condominium* (London; Methuen, 1899)

25 Agenzia Diplomatica, 2013/752. Archivio Centrale del Stato, Presidenza Consiglio Ministero collection, Archivio Centrale del Stato, Roma.

26 Reuters Telegram 10 January 1912.

27 Ernest N Bennett, *With the Turks in Tripoli: Being Some Experiences in the Turco-Italian War of 1911* (London; Methuen, 1912) p. 15.

28 *Questions diplomatiques et coloniales: revue de politique extérieure paraissant le 1er et le 16 de chaque mois quatorzieme. Année – 1919 tome XXX* (Juillet-Décembre) (Paris; Rédaction at administration, 1910) p. 432.

29 Anthony Clayton, *Histoire de l'armée française en Afrique: 1830-1962* (Paris; Albin Michel, 1994) p. 104.

30 Brian R Sullivan, 'The Strategy of the Decisive Weight: Italy, 1882-1922' in Williamson Murray, MacGregor Knox and Alvin Bernstein (Eds.) *The Making of Strategy: Rulers, States, and War* (Cambridge; Cambridge University Press, 1994) p. 326.

31 *Flight: A Journal Devoted to the Interests, Practice, and Progress of Aerial Locomotion and Transport*, Volume 2, Part 2 1910, p. 585.

32 Cour Permanente D'arbitrage, *Affaire du Carthage*. France contre Italie. Sentence Arbitrale, La Haye, Le 6 Mai 1913. Cour Permanente D'arbitrage, *Affaire du Manouba*. France contre Italie. Sentence Arbitrale, La Haye, Le 6 Mai 1913.

33 See: Yavuz Kansu, Sermet Sensoz, Yılmaz Oztuna, *Havacılık Tarihinde Türkler* (Ankara; Hava Kuvvetleri Basım ve Nesriyat Mud, 1971) p. 124. Bülent Yilmazer, 'Ottoman Aviation, Prelude to Military Use of Aircraft' Appendix A of Edward J Erickson, *Defeat in Detail: the Ottoman Army in the Balkans, 1912-1913* (Westport, CN; Praeger, 2003) p. 350-51. Süreyya lmen, *Turkiye'de Tayyarecilik ve Balonculuk Tarihi* (Istanbul; brahim Horoz Basımevi, 1947) pp. 51-54. For the German-Japanese combat see Charles Stephenson, *Germany's Asia-Pacific Empire: Colonialism and Naval Policy, 1885-1914* (Woodbridge; Boydell Press, 2009) pp. 153-176.

34 Raymond Poincaré and Sir George Arthur (Trans.), *The Memoirs of Raymond Poincaré*, Volume I (London; Heinemann, 1926); J F V Keiger, Raymond Poincaré (Cambridge; Cambridge University Press, 1997).

35 Giovanno Giolotti, Memorie della mia vita, con uno studio di Olindo Malagodi [Memories of My Life, with a study by *Olindo Malagodi]* (Milano; Fratelli Treves, 1922) Volume II. p. 387.

36 Sir James Rennell Rodd, *Social and Diplomatic Memories, Third Series* [Volume 3] *1902-1919* (London; Edward Arnold, 1925) p. 153.

37 *The New York Times,* 28 January 1912.

38 'Note commune du 26 Janvier 1912 concernant le règlement des affaires du "Carthage" et du "Manouba"' in James Brown Scott (Ed.), *Les travaux de la Cour permanente d'arbitrage de La Haye: recueil de ses sentences, accompagnees de resumes des differentes controverses, des compromis d'arbitrage et d'autres documents soumis a la cour et aux commissions internationales d'enquete en conformite des conventions de 1899 et de 1907 pour le reglement pacifique des conflits internationaux* (New York; Oxford University Press, 1921).

39 Quoted in: G P Gooch, *Before the War: Studies in Diplomacy, Vol. II: The Coming of The Storm* (London; Longmans, Green, 1938) p. 143.

40 J F V Keiger, Raymond Poincaré (Cambridge; Cambridge University Press, 1997) p. 135.

41 Viscount Grey of Falloden, *Twenty-Five Years: 1892-1916* (London; Hodder & Staughton, 1925) Vol. I. p. 195.

42 Commodore W H Beehler, *The History of the Italian-Turkish War* (Annapolis, MD; United States Naval Institute, 1913) p. 56.

43 Sir James Rennell Rodd, *Social and Diplomatic Memories, Third Series* [Volume 3] *1902-1919* (London; Edward Arnold, 1925) p. 153.

44 Timothy W Childs, *Italo-Turkish Diplomacy and the War over Libya, 1911-1912* (Leiden; E J Brill) p. 142.

45 Timothy W Childs, *Italo-Turkish Diplomacy and the War over Libya, 1911-1912* (Leiden; E J Brill) p. 112.

46 Tullio Irace, *With the Italians in Tripoli: The Authentic History of the Turco-Italian War* (London; John Murray, 1912) p. 313.

CHAPTER ELEVEN

1 James Elroy Flecker and Sir John Squire (Ed.), *The Collected Poems of James Elroy Flecker* (London; Secker & Warburg, 1947) p. xvii.

2 Achile Rastelli, 'les operations navales durant la de guerre de 1911 entre l'Italie et la Turquie' in *revue Navires et Histoires,* No.s 22 and 23 fevrier and mars 2004.

3 *Hansard's Commons Debates,* 14 March 1912, Volume 35, Columns 1243-4.

4 Muhammad Yusuf Abbasi, *London Muslim League, 1908-1928: An Historical Study* (Islamabad; National Institute of Historical and Cultural Research, 1988) p. 262.

[5] John Slight, *The British Empire and the hajj 1865-1939*. http://hdl.handle.net/10036/82014

[6] Azmi Özcan, *Pan-Islamism: Indian Muslims, the Ottomans and Britain (1877-1924)* (Leiden; Brill, 1997) p. 141.

[7] Ufuk Gülsoy, *Hicaz Demiryolu* (stanbul, Eren, 1994)

[8] Edmund Burke III, 'A Comparative View of French Native Policy in Morocco and Syria, 1912-1925' in *Middle Eastern Studies* Vol. 9, No. 2 (May, 1973). William I Shorrock, 'The Origin of the French Mandate in Syria and Lebanon: The Railroad Question, 1901–1914' in *International Journal of Middle East Studies* (1970), 1. Jan Karl Tanenbaum, 'France and the Arab Middle East, 1914-1920' in *Transactions of the American Philosophical Society*, New Series, Vol. 68, No. 7 (1978).

[9] Timothy W Childs, *Italo-Turkish Diplomacy and the War over Libya, 1911-1912* (Leiden; E J Brill) p. 121.

[10] Giovanno Giolotti, *Memorie della mia vita, con uno studio di Olindo Malagodi* (Milano; Fratelli Treves, 1922) Volume II. pp. 416-7. Sergio Romano, *Giuseppe Volpi: Industrie e finanza fra Giolitti e Mussolini* (Milan: Bompiani, 1979).

[11] Timothy W Childs, *Italo-Turkish Diplomacy and the War over Libya, 1911-1912* (Leiden; E J Brill) p. 121.

[12] Commodore W H Beehler, *The History of the Italian-Turkish War* (Annapolis, MD; United States Naval Institute, 1913) p. 56.

[13] *The Times*, 26 February 1912.

[14] 26 February 1912. *The New York Times*.

[15] Howard Bliss, 'Report Sent to the Board of Trustees, New York, 27 February 1912' in *Main Gate, American University of Beirut Quarterly Magazine*, Fall 2006 Vol. V, No. 1.

[16] Sergio Romano, *La quarta sponda: la guerra di Libia, 1911-1912* (Milano; Bompiani, 1977) p. 208.

[17] Report in *The Times*, 26 February 1912.

[18] Giovanno Giolotti, *Memorie della mia vita, con uno studio di Olindo Malagodi* (Milano; Fratelli Treves, 1922) Volume II. p. 393-4.

[19] 'Beirut Affair' in the *Evening Post*, 27 February 1912.

[20] Report in *The Times*, 26 February 1912.

[21] Sergio Romano, *La quarta sponda: la guerra di Libia, 1911-1912* (Milano; Bompiani, 1977) p. 208.

[22] Various news agency reports, 24 and 27 February 1912.

[23] Circular telegram from Foreign Office to British Ambassadors to France, Austria-Hungary, Germany and Russia. 28 February 1912. G P Gooch and H W V Temperley (Eds.), *British Documents on the Origins of the War: 1898-1914*, Volume IX, *The Balkan Wars*, Part I, *The Prelude: The Tripoli War* (London; HMSO, 1933) p. 368.

[24] Buchanan to Grey. 5 March 1912. G P Gooch and H W V Temperley (Eds.), *British Documents on the Origins of the War: 1898-1914*, Volume IX, *The Balkan Wars*, Part I, *The Prelude: The Tripoli War* (London; HMSO, 1933) p. 373.

[25] James Brown Scott (Ed.), *Diplomatic Documents Relating to the Outbreak of the European War, Part I* (New York; Oxford University Press, 1916) p. 342.

[26] Alfred Franzis Pribram (Ed.), *The Secret Treaties of Austria-Hungary 1879-1914* (Cambridge; Harvard University Press, 1920) Vol. I. p. 225.

[27] Alfred Franzis Pribram (Ed.), *The Secret Treaties of Austria-Hungary 1879-1914* (Cambridge; Harvard University Press, 1920) Vol. I. p. 243.

[28] Lamar Cecil, *Wilhelm II Volume II: Emperor and exile, 1900-1941* (Chapel Hill, NC; University of North Carolina Press, 1996) p. 15. Lamar Cecil, *Wilhelm II Volume II: Emperor and exile, 1900-1941* (Chapel Hill, NC; University of North Carolina Press, 1996) p. 15. Isabel V Hull, *The Entourage of Kaiser Wilhelm II, 1888-1918* (Cambridge; Cambridge University Press, 2004) p. 34.

[29] Luigi Albertini, *Le origini della guerra del 1914: Vol. I, Le relazioni europee dal Congresso di Berlino all'attentato di Sarajevo* (Milano; Bocca, 1941) pp. 358-9.

[30] James Brown Scott (Ed.), *Diplomatic Documents Relating to the Outbreak of the European War, Part I* (New York; Oxford University Press, 1916) p. 342-3.

[31] James Brown Scott (Ed.), *Diplomatic Documents Relating to the Outbreak of the European War, Part I* (New York; Oxford University Press, 1916) p. 344.

[32] J K L Fitzwilliams, 'The Coast Defenses of Turkey' in the *Journal of the United States Artillery* Vol. 43 No. 1 January-February 1915.

[33] Giovanno Giolotti, *Memorie della mia vita, con uno studio di Olindo Malagodi* (Milano; Fratelli Treves, 1922) Volume II. p. 399.

[34] Luigi Albertini, *Le origini della guerra del 1914: Vol. I, Le relazioni europee dal Congresso di Berlino all'attentato di Sarajevo* (Milano; Bocca, 1941) pp. 359-60.

[35] Grey to Rodd. 19 April, and Grey to Lowther, 20 April 1912. G P Gooch and H W V Temperley (Eds.), *British Documents on the Origins of the War: 1898-1914*, Volume IX, *The Balkan Wars*, Part I, *The Prelude: The Tripoli War* (London; HMSO, 1933) pp. 387-8.

[36] Grey to Rodd. 22 April 1912. G P Gooch and H W V Temperley (Eds.), *British Documents on the Origins of the War: 1898-1914*, Volume IX, *The Balkan Wars*, Part I, *The Prelude: The Tripoli War* (London; HMSO,

1933) p. 388.Viscount Morley, reply to the Marquess of Lansdowne. House of Lords Debates, 22 April 1912,Volume 11, Columns 797-8.

[37] Bilâl N im ir (Ed.), *Ege Sorunu: Belgeler Cilt-1 1912-1913* (Ankara :Türk Tarih Kurumu Yayınları, 1976) p. 75.

[38] Berchtold to von Merey (Rome) and Szogyeny (Berlin). 24 July 1914. *Austrian Red Book: Official Files Pertaining to Pre-War History, Part I, 28 June to 23 July 1914* (London; George Allen & Unwin, 1920) p. 110.

[39] Grey to Lowther. 30 April 1912. G P Gooch and H W V Temperley (Eds.), *British Documents on the Origins of the War: 1898-1914*,Volume IX, *The Balkan Wars*, Part I, *The Prelude:The Tripoli War* (London; HMSO, 1933) p. 390.

[40] Grey to Rodd. 30 April 1912. G P Gooch and H W V Temperley (Eds.), *British Documents on the Origins of the War: 1898-1914*,Volume IX, *The Balkan Wars*, Part I, *The Prelude:The Tripoli War* (London; HMSO, 1933) p. 390.

[41] Rodd to Grey. 1 May 1912. G P Gooch and H W V Temperley (Eds.), *British Documents on the Origins of the War: 1898-1914*,Volume IX, *The Balkan Wars*, Part I, *The Prelude:The Tripoli War* (London; HMSO, 1933) p. 391.

[42] Buchanan to Nicolson (Private Letter). 2 May 1912. G P Gooch and H W V Temperley (Eds.), *British Documents on the Origins of the War: 1898-1914*,Volume IX, *The Balkan Wars*, Part I, *The Prelude:The Tripoli War* (London; HMSO, 1933) p. 394.

[43] C J Lowe, 'Grey and the Tripoli War, 1911-1912' in F H Hinsley (Ed.), *British Foreign Policy under Sir Edward Grey* (Cambridge; Cambridge University Press, 1977)

[44] Minutes of meeting of 9 November 1911. Archivio dell'Ufficio Storico dello Stato Maggiore dell'Esercito, L8, R1.

[45] Spingardi to Pollio. Letter dated 12 January 1912. Archivio dell'Ufficio Storico dello Stato Maggiore dell'Esercito, L8, R2.

[46] Giovanni Giolitti, *Memorie della mia vita, con uno studio di Olindo Malagodi* (Milano; Fratelli Treves, 1922) Volume II. p. 403.

[47] Fritz Fischer, *War of Illusions: German Policies from 1911 to 1914* (London: Chatto and Windus, 1975) p. 145.

[48] M G Pasqualini, *L'esercito italiano nel Dodecaneso 1912-1943, speranze e realtà, i documenti dell'Ufficio Storico dello Stato Maggiore dell'Esercito* (Roma;Archivio dell'Ufficio Storico dello Stato Maggiore dell'Esercito, 2006) pp. 18-34.

[49] Giovanni Giolitti, *Memorie della mia vita, con uno studio di Olindo Malagodi* (Milano; Fratelli Treves, 1922) Volume II. p. 402.

[50] Ernest N Bennett, *With the Turks in Tripoli: Being Some Experiences in the Turco-Italian War of 1911* (London; Methuen, 1912) p. 294.

[51] W H Beehler, *The History of the Italian-Turkish War, September 29, 1911, to October 18, 1912* (Annapolis, MD;William H Beehler, 1913) p. 53.

CHAPTER TWELVE

[1] Rear-Admiral ECT Troubridge, Memorandum of 29 June 1912: 'Italian occupation of Aegean Islands and its effect on naval policy'

[2] Giuseppe Bevione, 'La meravigliosa avventura nei Dardanelli narrate do Guiseppe Bevione' in *La Stampa*, 25 luglio 1912.

[3] Mariano Gabriele, *La marina nella guerra italo-turca: il potere marittimo strumento militare e politico (1911-1912)* (Roma; Ufficio Storico della Marina Militare, 1998) p. 164. M G Pasqualini, *L'esercito italiano nel Dodecaneso 1912-1943, speranze e realtà, i documenti dell'Ufficio Storico dello Stato Maggiore dell'Esercito* (Roma;Archivio dell'Ufficio Storico dello Stato Maggiore dell'Esercito, 2006) p. 39.

[4] *Memoria sulla costituzione del Distaccamento di Bomba*, in *Direttive per l'occupazione dell' isola di Rodi*, 22 aprile 1912, L8 R 180.

[5] *Direttive per l'occupazione dell' isola di Rodi*, 22 aprile 1912. Archivio dell'Ufficio Storico dello Stato Maggiore dell'Esercito, L8 R61.

[6] Count Berchtold to Kajetan von Merey. (Telegram) Vienna, 23 May 1912. James Brown Scott (Ed.), *Diplomatic Documents Relating to the Outbreak of the European War, Part I* (New York; Oxford University Press, 1916) p. 345.

[7] Giovanni Giolotti, *Memorie della mia vita, con uno studio di Olindo Malagodi* [*Memories of My Life, with a study by Olindo Malagodi*] (Milano; Fratelli Treves, 1922) Volume II. p. 403.

[8] Ladislaus Count von Szögyény-Marich, the Austro-Hungarian ambassador in Berlin, to Count Berchtold. (Telegram.) Berlin, May 21, 1912. James Brown Scott (Ed.), *Diplomatic Documents Relating to the Outbreak of the European War, Part I* (New York; Oxford University Press, 1916) p. 344.

[9] Rear-Admiral ECT Troubridge, Memorandum of 29 June 1912: 'Italian occupation of Aegean Islands

and its effect on naval policy' in G P Gooch and H W V Temperley (Eds.), *British Documents on the Origins of the War. 1898-1914, Vol. IX, The Balkan Wars*, Part I, *The Prelude: The Tripoli War* (London; HMSO, 1933) no. 430, pp. 413–15.

[10] C J Lowe, 'Grey and the Tripoli War, 1911-1912' in F H Hinsley (Ed.), *British Foreign Policy under Sir Edward Grey* (Cambridge; Cambridge University Press, 1997) p. 322.

[11] Randolph S Churchill, *Winston S Churchill, Companion Volume II, Part 3 1911-1914* (London; Heinemann, 1969) p. 1565.

[12] Joseph S Roucek, 'The Legal Aspects of Sovereignty over the Dodecanese' in *The American Journal of International Law,* Vol. 38, No. 4 (Oct., 1944) p. 701.

[13] HC Deb 12 August 1913 vol 56 cc2281-352.

[14] Jeanne Z Stephanopoli, *Les Iles de l'Egee Leurs Privileges (avec documents et notes statistiques)* (Atene; Apostolopoulos, 1912) p. 147.

[15] Dr Skevos Zervos, *The Dodecanese: The History of the Dodecanese through the Ages - Its Services to Mankind and its Rights* (No Place; No Publisher, 1918-19) p. 65.

[16] Quoted in Renzo Sertoli Salis, *Le isole italiane dell'Egeo dall'occupazione alla sovranità* (Roma; Vittoriano, 1939) p. 19.

[17] Quoted in Renzo Sertoli Salis, *Le isole italiane dell'Egeo dall'occupazione alla sovranità* (Roma; Vittoriano, 1939) p. 20.

[18] Dr Skevos Zervos, *Le Dodécanèse: l'histoire du Dodécanèse à travers les siècles - les services qu'il a rendus à l'humanité ses droits* (London; no publisher, no date –probably 1920) p. 71.

[19] Joseph S Roucek, 'The Legal Aspects of Sovereignty over the Dodecanese' in *The American Journal of International Law,* Vol. 38, No. 4 (Oct., 1944) p. 701. Dr Skevos Zervos, *Le Dodécanèse: l'histoire du Dodécanèse à travers les siècles - les services qu'il a rendus à l'humanité ses droits* (London; no publisher, no date –probably 1920) pp. 72-3.

[20] L Divanis, F Constantopoulou *et al, The Dodecanese: The long road to union with Greece. Diplomatic Documents from the Historical Archives of the Ministry of Foreign Affairs* (Athens; Kastaniotis, 1997) p. 17. William Miller, *The Ottoman Empire 1801-1913* (Cambridge; Cambridge University Press, 1913) p. 497.

[21] M G Pasqualini, *L'esercito italiano nel Dodecaneso 1912-1943, speranze e realtà, i documenti dell'Ufficio Storico dello Stato Maggiore dell'Esercito* (Roma; Archivio dell'Ufficio Storico dello Stato Maggiore dell'Esercito, 2006) p. 72. For a Greek perspective see: Αυτώνη Σεβ. Μαίλλη, Ή κατάληψη της Ρόδου: Χρονικό της πολεμικής επιχείρησης του ιταλικών στρατιωτικών δυνάμεων' in Επτα Ημερεσ. Κυριακη 30 Νοεμβριου 1997. p. 4.

[22] R J B Bosworth, 'Italy and the End of the Ottoman Empire' in M Kent (Ed.) *The Great Powers and the End of the Ottoman Empire* (London: Allen and Unwin 1984) p. 64. Cesare Cesari, *Colonie e possedimenti coloniali. Cenni storici e geografici. Con 15 tavole ed una breve appendice riassuntiva delle varie questioni d'Oriente* (Roma; Libreria di Scienze e Lettere, 1926) . p. 161.

[23] Albert Legrand to Justin de Selves, 20 November 1911. Commission de publication des documents relatifs aux origines de la guerre de 1914, *Documents diplomatiques francais 1871-1914. 3. serie (1911-1914) tome 1* (Paris; Imprimerie nationale, 1929) p. 161.

[24] Timothy W Childs, *Italo-Turkish Diplomacy and the War over Libya, 1911-1912* (Leiden; E J Brill) p. 114.

[25] Generale Alberto Pollio, *promemoria sulla nostra situazione politico-militare trasmesso a Paolo Spingardi il 30 giugno 1912*, in Carte Giolitti, Sottofasc c/5, Archivio Centrale dello Stato.

[26] Giovanno Giolotti, *Memorie della mia vita, con uno studio di Olindo Malagodi* [*Memories of My Life, with a study by Olindo Malagodi*] (Milano; Fratelli Treves, 1922) Volume II. p. 471.

[27] Camillo Manfroni (Ed.), *Guerra italo- turca (1911-1912): Cronistoria delle operazioni navali,* Vol. II: *Dal decreto di sovranità su la Libia alla conclusione della pace* (Roma; Poligrafico, 1926) p. 171. The whole story of the attack can be found in this work on pp. 168-179, and unless otherwise stated it is the source of this section. Millo's report can be found in the Archivo Storico Stato Maggiore Esercito, 223, *Forzamento dei Dardanelli - Telegrammi del Comandante Millo e dell'Amiraglio Viale* (19-20 luglio 1912).

[28] Report from Naval Attaché Rome, to Sir Rennell Rodd. 23 July 1912. UK National Archives. PRO ADM 116/1154.

[29] Alfredo Frassati, 'Cinque torpediniere italiane s'inoltrano per 20 chilometri nei Dardanelli sotto il fuoco incrociato dei forti turchi' in *La Stampa*, 21 luglio 1912.

[30] Giuseppe Bevione, 'La meravigliosa avventura nei Dardanelli narrate do Guiseppe Bevione' in *La Stampa*, 25 luglio 1912.

[31] Giovanno Giolotti, *Memorie della mia vita, con uno studio di Olindo Malagodi* [*Memories of My Life, with a study by Olindo Malagodi*] (Milano; Fratelli Treves, 1922) Volume II. p. 406.

[32] Marling to Grey. No. 624. 23 July 1912, UK National Archives. PRO ADM 116/1154.

[33] Mariano Gabriele, *La marina nella guerra italo-turca: il potere marittimo strumento militare e politico (1911-1912)* (Roma; Ufficio Storico della Marina Militare, 1998) p. 170

[34] E Ashmead-Bartlett, *The Uncensored Dardanelles* (London; Hutchinson, 1928) p. 177.

[35] B H Liddell Hart, *The Defence of Britain* (London; Faber and Faber, 1939) p. 130.

[36] Chairman of the Joint Chiefs of Staff, *Joint Publication 3-02; Amphibious Operations.* 10 August 2009. Available at http://www.dtic.mil/doctrine/new_pubs/jp3_02.pdf

37 Enver Pasa, *Um Tripolis* (Munchen, Hugo Bruckmann, 1918) p. 48.

38 Rear-Admiral William Henry Smyth, *The Mediterranean: A Memoir Physical, Historical, and Nautical* (London; John Parker, 1854) p. 87.

39 Enver Pasa, *Um Tripolis* (Munchen, Hugo Bruckmann, 1918) pp. 48-9.

CHAPTER THIRTEEN

1   'La Misura,' an article in Rome's *La Tribuna*. Quoted in Carl Ludwig Siemering, 'Artikel Rundschau' in Alfred M Fried (Ed.), *Die Friedens-Warte: Zeitschrift für zwischenstaatliche Organisation* (Berlin; 1912) p. 360.

2   J C Hobhouse, *A Journey through Albania and Other Provinces of Turkey in Europe and Asia to Constantinople during the Years 1809 and 1810*, Volume I (London; James Cawthorn, 1813) Letter XIV pp. 159-60.

3   Jovan M Jovanovi , *Borba za narodno ujedinjenje 1903–1908* (Belgrade; Geca Kon, 1938) pp. 81–4.

4   For the text of these agreements see: 'Diplomatist' [Sir George Young] and Lord Courtney of Penwith (Ed.), *Nationalism and War in the Near East* (Oxford; Clarendon Press, 1915) pp. 387-400.

5   Imre Ress, 'The Value System of Serb Liberalism' in Iván Zoltán Dénes (Ed.), *Liberty and the Search for Identity: Liberal Nationalisms and the Legacy of Empires* (Budapest; Central European University Press, 2006) p. 354

6   Murat Ocak, Hasan Celâl Güzel, Cem O uz, Osman Karatay (Eds.), *The Turks,* 6 Volumes, Volume 4, *Ottomans* (Ankara; Yeni Turkiye, 2002).

7   Antonino di San Giuliano, *Lettere sull'Albania: pubblicate nel Giornale d'Italia* (Roma; Giornale d'Italia, 1903).

8   'Diplomatist' [Sir George Young] and Lord Courtney of Penwith (Ed.), *Nationalism and War in the Near East* (Oxford; Clarendon Press, 1915) p. 160

9   Timothy W Childs, *Italo-Turkish Diplomacy and the War over Libya, 1911-1912* (Leiden; E J Brill, 1990) p. 234.

10 Other than those already mentioned, George Gooch and Harold Temperley, the editors of *British Documents on the Origins of the War: 1898-1914*, placed their treatment of the Italo-Ottoman War firmly within the context of, and as a prelude to, the Balkan Wars. See: Gooch, G P and Temperley, H W V (Eds.). *British Documents on the Origins of the War: 1898-1914, Vol. IX, The Balkan Wars*, Part I, *The Prelude: The Tripoli War* (London; HMSO, 1933).

11 Sir James Rennell Rodd, *Social and Diplomatic Memories, Third Series* [Volume 3] *1902-1919* (London; Edward Arnold, 1925) p. 160.

12 Quoted by W T Stead, in an untitled posthumously published piece dated 1 April 1912 in *The Review of Reviews* for June 1912.

13 [Ministry of Foreign Affairs], *The Bulgarian Question and the Balkan States* (Sofia; State printing Press, 1919) p. 22.

14 Celal Bayar, *Ben de Yazdım: Milli Mücadeleye gidi* ,Vol III (stanbul: Sabah Kitapları, 1997) p. 814.

15 Re at Halli, *Balkan Harbi (1912-1913): I.Cilt* [Volume I], *Harbin Sebepleri, Askeri Hazirliklar ve Osmanli Devletinin Harbe Giri i* (Ankara; Genelkurmay, 1970) p. 119.

16 Report by H Conyers Surtees, military attaché, Constantinople. 20 June 1909. PRO/FO 195/2323.

17 Ellis Ashmead-Bartlett, *With the Turks in Thrace* (New York; George H Doran, 1913) p. 55.

18 Brigadier Henry Wilson, *War Staff Memorandum on Coercive Action against Turkey*, 24 April 1911. UK NA WO 106/43.

19 Re at Halli, *Balkan Harbi (1912-1913): I.Cilt* [Volume I], *Harbin Sebepleri, Askeri Hazirliklar ve Osmanli Devletinin Harbe Giri i* (Ankara; Genelkurmay, 1970) pp. 130-31.

20 Cemal Kutay, *Trablus Garb'de Bir Avuç Kahraman* (Istanbul; Kutay, 1978) pp. 86–111. Hamdi Ertuna, *Türk Silahlı Kuvvetleri Tarihi, Osmanlı Devri, Osmanlı- talyan Harbi* (Ankara; Genelkurmay Basımevi, 1981) pp. 152-58.

21 Enver Pascha, *Um Tripolis* (München; Hugo Bruckmann, 1918) p. 10.

22 The main source for this section dealing with the fall of the Sait Pasa government and its replacement is Childs. Timothy W Childs, *Italo-Turkish Diplomacy and the War over Libya, 1911-1912* (Leiden; E J Brill, 1990) pp. 168-70.

23 Enver Pascha, *Um Tripolis* (München; Hugo Bruckmann, 1918) pp. 61-2.

24 List of Ottoman Ministers of War 1908-1914 in Edward J Erickson, *Defeat in Detail: The Ottoman Army in the Balkans 1912-1913* (Westport, CT; Greenwood, 2003) p. 22.

25 Paolo Maltese, *La terra promessa: La guerra italo-turca e la conquista della Libia 1911-12* (Milano; Mondadori, 1976) pp. 297-8.

26 *Vossische Zeitung* 31 August 1908.

27 Timothy W Childs, *Italo-Turkish Diplomacy and the War over Libya, 1911-1912* (Leiden; E J Brill, 1990) pp. 171-2.

28 Enver Pascha, *Um Tripolis* (München; Hugo Bruckmann, 1918) p. 67.

29 Giovanno Giolitti, *Memorie della mia vita, con uno studio di Olindo Malagodi* (Milano; Fratelli Treves, 1922) Volume II. p. 425.

[30] Timothy W Childs, *Italo-Turkish Diplomacy and the War over Libya, 1911-1912* (Leiden; E J Brill, 1990) pp. 160-1.

[31] William C Askew, *Europe and Italy's Acquisition of Libya, 1911-1912* (Durham, NC; Duke University Press, 1942) p. 239.

[32] Giovanno Giolitti, *Memorie della mia vita, con uno studio di Olindo Malagodi* (Milano; Fratelli Treves, 1922) Volume II. p. 429.

[33] Giovanno Giolitti, *Memorie della mia vita, con uno studio di Olindo Malagodi* (Milano; Fratelli Treves, 1922) Volume II. pp. 435-6.

[34] Timothy W Childs, *Italo-Turkish Diplomacy and the War over Libya, 1911-1912* (Leiden; E J Brill, 1990) p. 172. n. 60.

[35] William C Askew, *Europe and Italy's Acquisition of Libya, 1911-1912* (Durham, NC; Duke University Press, 1942) p. 241.

[36] Luigi Albertini and Ottavio Bari (Ed.), *Epistolario 1911-1926*,Vol. I *Dalla guerra di Libia alla Grande Guerra* (Milano; Mondadori, 1968) p. 132.

[37] Benedetto Cirmeni in an article in Vienna's *Neue Freie Presse,* 18 January 1912.

[38] Giovanno Giolitti, *Memorie della mia vita, con uno studio di Olindo Malagodi* (Milano; Fratelli Treves, 1922) Volume II. p. 408.

[39] Sergio Romano, *La quarta sponda: la guerra di Libia, 1911-1912* (Milano; Bompiani, 1977) p. 248.

[40] Cable Press Association despatch. Rome 5 September 1912.

[41] Enver Pascha, *Um Tripolis* (München; Hugo Bruckmann, 1918) p. 53.

[42] Preparations for assaulting the Italian defences had been ongoing for several months. See Appendix B for example.

[43] Enver Pascha, *Um Tripolis* (München; Hugo Bruckmann, 1918) p. 77.

[44] Enver had formed units of Arab volunteers, 'the sons or relatives of influential sheikhs,' into infantry companies under the command of regular Ottoman officers. These were trained in conventional infantry tactics, armed with Mauser rifles, and wore the uniform of the Ottoman army. A company thus constituted he termed a *Gardekompagnie.* Enver Pascha, *Um Tripolis* (München; Hugo Bruckmann, 1918) pp. 37, 38, 42, 43, 45, 56, 59, 79, 99.

[45] Enver Pascha, *Um Tripolis* (München; Hugo Bruckmann, 1918) pp. 79-83.

[46] Renato Tittoni, *The Italo-Turkish War (1911-12): Translated and Compiled from the Reports of the Italian General Staff* (Kansas City, MO; Franklin Hudson, 1914) pp. 75-6.

[47] W K McClure, *Italy in North Africa: An Account of the Tripoli Enterprise* (London; Constable, 1913) pp. 204-5.

[48] Dario Temperino, *Cavalleggeri di Lodi 1859-1995* (www.bibliomil.com/pdf/cavalleggeri_lodi.pdf, 2009) pp. 27-28.

[49] Francis McCullagh, *Italy's War For A Desert: Being Some Experiences Of A War Correspondent With The Italians In Tripoli* (Chicago, IL; F G Browne, 1913) p. xxvii.

[50] Baron Bernardo Quaranta di San Severino, 'The Peace Negotiations between Italy and Turkey' in *The New York Times,* 24 November 1912.

[51] Correspondent at Andrievitza, 'Berane Massacre' in *The Times,* 3 September 1912.

[52] Timothy W Childs, *Italo-Turkish Diplomacy and the War over Libya, 1911-1912* (Leiden; E J Brill, 1990) p. 195.

[53] Timothy W Childs, *Italo-Turkish Diplomacy and the War over Libya, 1911-1912* (Leiden; E J Brill, 1990) p. 206.

[54] Herbert Dering to Sir Edward Grey. 13 October 1912. G P Gooch and H W V Temperley (Eds.), *British Documents on the Origins of the War: 1898-1914, Volume IX, The Balkan Wars,* Part I, *The Prelude: The Tripoli War* (London; HMSO, 1933) p. 428.

[55] 'Italy Grants 3 Days' Grace to Turkey' in the *New York Tribune,* 13 October 1912.

[56] Richard C Hall, *The Balkan Wars, 1912-1913: Prelude to the First World War* (London; Routledge, 2000) p. 56.

[57] Timothy W Childs, *Italo-Turkish Diplomacy and the War over Libya, 1911-1912* (Leiden; E J Brill, 1990) p. 224.

[58] The text of both treaties can be found in: Timothy W Childs, *Italo-Turkish Diplomacy and the War over Libya, 1911-1912* (Leiden; E J Brill, 1990) pp. 246-253.

CHAPTER FOURTEEN

[1] Italian proclamation to the Arabs. Quoted in: G F Abbott, *The Holy War in Tripoli* (London; Edward Arnold, 1912) p. 195.

[2] Lines taken from: Rudyard Kipling, *The White Man's Burden: A Poem* (New York; Doubleday and McClure, 1899).

3   Aldobrandino Malvezzi, *L'Italia e L'Islam in Libia* (Firenze; Fratelli Treves, 1913) p. 186.
4   Carnegie Endowment for International Peace, *Report of the International Commission to Inquire into the Causes and Conduct of the Balkan Wars* (Washington DC; Carnegie Endowment for International Peace, 1914) p. 49.
5   Deniz Bölükba 1, *Turkey and Greece: The Aegean Disputes: A Unique Case in International Law* (London; Cavendish, 2004) p. 832.
6   Bernd Langensiepen and Ahmet Guleryuz, *The Ottoman Steam Navy: 1828-1923* (Annapolis, MD; Naval Institute Press, 1995) pp. 19–21, 25.
7   Carnegie Endowment for International Peace, *Report of the International Commission to Inquire into the Causes and Conduct of the Balkan Wars* (Washington DC; Carnegie Endowment for International Peace, 1914) p. 72.
8   Arnold J Toynbee, *The Western Question in Greece and Turkey: A Study in the Contact of Civilisations* (London; Constable, 1922) p. 139.
9   Richard C Hall, The Balkan Wars, 1912-1913: Prelude to the First World War (London; Routledge, 2000) p. 15.
10 Fabio Gramellini, *Storia della guerra italo-turca 1911-1912* (Milano; CartaCanta, 2010) p. 222.
11 *The New York Times*, 17 October 1912.
12 Winston S Churchill, First Lord of the Admiralty, in response to a question in the UK Parliament on 10 October 1912. *Hansard's Commons Debates*, 10 October 1912, Vol. 42, Column 506.
13 Luigi Albertini, *Corriere della Sera*. 16 October 1912.
14 Giovanno Giolitti, *Memorie della mia vita, con uno studio di Olindo Malagodi* (Milano; Fratelli Treves, 1922) Volume II. pp. 469-71.
15 David Nicolle, *The Venetian Empire 1200–1670* (Oxford; Osprey, 1989).
16 Sergio Romano, *La quarta sponda: la guerra di Libia, 1911-1912* (Milano; Bompiani, 1977) p. 235; Paolo Maltese, *La terra promessa: La guerra italo-turca e la conquista della Libia 1911-12* (Milano; Mondadori, 1976) pp. 333-4, 350-1.
17 Mariano Gabriele, *La marina nella guerra italo-turca: il potere marittimo strumento militare e politico (1911-1912)* (Roma; Ufficio Storico della Marina Militare, 1998) p. 198.
18 Mario Montanari, *Politica e strategia in cento anni di guerre italiane; vol. II: il periodo liberale; tomo I: le guerre d'Africa* (Roma; Ufficio storico delleo stato Maggior dell'Esercito, 1999) p. 463.
19 Mariano Gabriele, *La marina nella guerra italo-turca: il potere marittimo strumento militare e politico (1911-1912)* (Roma; Ufficio Storico della Marina Militare, 1998) p. 195.
20 'Deputies Cheer Giolitti' in *The New York Times*, 27 November 1912.
21 Guido Mussolini and Filippo Giannini, *Benito Mussolini, l'uomo della pace: Da Versailles al 10 giugno 1940* (Milano; Greco & Greco, 1997) p. 71.
22 Sources include: The 'Correlates of War' project, an academic study of the history of warfare by the University of Michigan. www.correlatesofwar.org/; Renato Tittoni, *The Italo-Turkish War (1911-12): Translated and Compiled from the Reports of the Italian General Staff* (Kansas City, MO; Franklin Hudson, 1914).
23 'Diplomatist' [Sir George Young] and Lord Courtney of Penwith (Ed.), *Nationalism and War in the Near East* (Oxford; Clarendon Press, 1915) p. 158.
24 Giorgio Rochat and Giulio Massobrio, *Breve storia dell'esercito italiano dal 1861 al 1943* (Turin; Einaudi, 1978) p. 163.
25 Antonella Randazzo, *Roma predona: Il colonialismo italiano in Africa, 1870-1943* (Milano; Kaos, 2006) p. 45.
26 Dr Skevos Zervos, *The Dodecanese: The History of the Dodecanese through the Ages - Its Services to Mankind and its Rights* (No Place; The Executive Committee of the Dodecanesians, 1918-19) p. 75.
27 Dr Skevos Zervos, *The Dodecanese: The History of the Dodecanese through the Ages - Its Services to Mankind and its Rights* (No Place; The Executive Committee of the Dodecanesians, 1918-19) p. 76.
28 Dr Skevos Zervos and Paris J Roussos, *The Dodecanese: Resolutions and Documents concerning the Dodecanese 1912-1919* (No place; The Executive Committee of the Dodecanesians, 1920?) p. 25.
29 Alexis Rappas, 'National Allegiance and Imperial Loyalty: Greeks under European Colonial Rule.' *University Seminar #703: Modern Greek Studies* held on 25 March 2010 at Columbia University. http://www.columbia.edu/cu/hellenicstudies/seminar_papers/2008-2009/Rappas%20Santarelli-Greek%20under%20Europeans.pdf
30 Angelo Del Boca, *A un passo dalla forca: atrocita e infamie dell'occupazione italiana della Libia nelle memorie del patriota Mohamed Fekini* (Milano; Baldini Castoldi Dalai, 2007) p. 57.
31 From a report, *Questione del Gebel. Situazione politica,* by General Ottavio Ragni to the Colonial Ministry dated 19 January 1913. Luigi Tuccari (Ed.), *I governi militari della Libia, 1911-1919: Documenti* (Roma; Stato maggiore dell'esercito, Ufficio storico, 1994) p. 51. Also quoted in Angelo Del Boca, *A un passo dalla forca: atrocita e infamie dell'occupazione italiana della Libia nelle memorie del patriota Mohamed Fekini* (Milano; Baldini Castoldi Dalai, 2007) p. 57.

[32] Francesco Corò, 'Una interessante pagina di storia libica. Suleiman el-Baruni. Il sogno di un principato berbero e la battaglia di Asàbaa 1913' in *Gli Annali dell'Africa Italian,* anno I, n. 3-4, dicembre 1938, p. 960. Angelo Del Boca, *A un passo dalla forca: atrocita e infamie dell'occupazione italiana della Libia nelle memorie del patriota Mohamed Fekini* (Milano; Baldini Castoldi Dalai, 2007) p. 58.

[33] Lisa Anderson, 'The Development of Nationalist Sentiment in Libya, 1909-1922' in Rashid Khalidi, Lisa Anderson, Muhammad Muslih and Reeva S Simon (Eds.), *The Origins of Arab Nationalism* (New York; Columbia University Press, 1991) p. 231.

[34] Angelo Del Boca, *A un passo dalla forca: atrocita e infamie dell'occupazione italiana della Libia nelle memorie del patriota Mohamed Fekini* (Milano; Baldini Castoldi Dalai, 2007) p. 60.

[35] Helen Chapin Metz, Libya (Whitefish, MT; Kessinger, 2004) p. 43.

[36] Angelo Del Boca, *A un passo dalla forca: atrocita e infamie dell'occupazione italiana della Libia nelle memorie del patriota Mohamed Fekini* (Milano; Baldini Castoldi Dalai, 2007) p. 63.

[37] General Ottavio Ragni to Minister Pietro Bertolini. 19 January 1913. Position 150/14, file 55. Archivio Storico del Ministero dell'Africa Italiana.

[38] Angelo Del Boca, *A un passo dalla forca: atrocita e infamie dell'occupazione italiana della Libia nelle memorie del patriota Mohamed Fekini* (Milano; Baldini Castoldi Dalai, 2007) p. 66.

[39] Angelo Del Boca, *A un passo dalla forca: atrocita e infamie dell'occupazione italiana della Libia nelle memorie del patriota Mohamed Fekini* (Milano; Baldini Castoldi Dalai, 2007) p. 67.

[40] Cesira Filesi, *L'archivio del Museo africano in Roma: presentazione e inventario dei documenti* (Roma; Istituto italiano per l'Africa e l'Oriente, 2001.) p. 88. Angelo Del Boca, *Gli Italiani in Libia: Tripoli bel suol d'amore: 1860-1922*, Vol. I (Milan; Mondadori, 1986) p. 218.

[41] Paolo Soave, *Fezzan: il deserto conteso (1842-1921)* (Milano; Giuffre, 2001) p. 277.

[42] G W Prothero (Ed.) for the Historical Section of the Foreign Office, *Peace Handbooks: Spanish and Italian Possessions: Independent States*, Volume XX (London; HMSO, 1920) p. 24.

[43] Enver Pascha, *Um Tripolis* (München; Hugo Bruckmann, 1918) p. 93-4.

[44] Enver Pascha, *Um Tripolis* (München; Hugo Bruckmann, 1918) p. 95.

[45] Majid Khadduri, 'Aziz Ali Misri and the Arab Nationalist Movement' in Albert Hourani (Ed.), *St Antony's Papers, 17: Middle Eastern Affairs, 4* (Oxford; Oxford University Press, 1965) pp. 140-163.

[46] 'Arab Ruse Duped Italians' by cable from Chiasso, Switzerland dated 25 May 1913 in *The New York Times,* 26 May 1913. 'General Disregards Danger Warning' by Special Cable from Benghazi dated 25 May 1913 in *The San Francisco Call,* 26 May 1913.

[47] Press Association Cable, dated 29 May 1913 from Rome.

[48] Luigi Tuccari (Ed.), *I governi militari della Libia, 1911-1919* (Roma; Stato maggiore dell'Esercito, 1994) p. 143. See also: Renzo Catellani and Giancarlo Stella, *Soldati d'Africa: storia del colonialismo italiano e delle uniformi per le truppe d'Africa del Regio Esercito 1897-1913* (Parma; Ermanno Albertelli, 2004) p. 126; Giuliano Bonacci, *Da Tolmetta a Marsa Susa e da Derna a Sidi Garbaa: discorso letto in Roma all'Associazione della stampa il 30 Maggio 1913* (Roma; Bontempelli e Invernizzi, 1913). '

[49] Yunan Labib Rizk, 'Aziz Al-Masri's was a legend in his own time: The Ottoman officer of Egyptian origin with the heart of a lion was hailed as a hero by Egyptians' in *Al-Ahram Weekly On-line,* Issue No 386, 16 - 22 July 1998. Available at: http://weekly.ahram.org.eg/1998/386/chrncls.htm Anna Baldinetti, 'Aziz Ali al-Misri: un ufficiale egiziano al fronte libico (1911-1913)' in *Africa: Rivista trimestrale di studi e documentazione dell'Istituto italiano per l'Africa e l'Oriente,* Anno 47, No. 2 (Giugno 1992), pp. 268-275.

[50] Angelo Del Boca, *Gli Italiani in Libia: Tripoli bel suol d'amore: 1860-1922,* Vol. I (Milan; Mondadori, 1986) p. 261. See also: Mario Isnenghi, *I luoghi della memoria: Simboli e miti dell'Italia unita* (Roma; Laterza, 1996) 421.

[51] Habib Wada'ah el-Hasnawi, 'Effetti psico-sociali delle operazioni di deportazione dei libici nelle isole italiane sugli esiliati e i loro parenti in epoca coloniale (1911–1943)' in Francesco Sulpizi and Salaheddin Hasan Sury, *Primo convegno su Gli esiliati libici nel periodo coloniale: 28-29 ottobre 2000, Isole Tremiti* (Roma; Istituto italiano per l'Africa e l'Oriente, 2002) pp. 31-32, 67.

[52] Romain Rainero, *Paolo Valera e l'opposizione democratica all'impresa di Tripoli* (Roma; L'Erma di Bretschneider, 1983) pp. 87-89.

[53] Angelo Del Boca, *Italiani, brava gente?: un mito duro a morire* (Vicenza; Neri Pozza, 2005) p. 112.

[54] Quoted in Salvatore Bono, *Tripoli bel suol d'amore: Testimonianze sulla guerra italo-libica* (Roma: Istituto italiano per l'Africa e l'Oriente, 2005) p. 84.

[55] Angelo Del Boca, *Italiani, brava gente?: un mito duro a morire* (Vicenza; Neri Pozza, 2005) p. 112.

[56] Camera dei Deputati, Atti parlamentari, legislazione XXIV, sessione I, tornata del 18 dicembre 1913, pp. 555-557.

[57] Aaron Thomas in the preface to Cesare Beccaria (Aaron Thomas (Ed.). Trans. By Aaron Thomas and Jeremy Parzen), *On Crimes and Punishments and Other Writings* (Toronto; University of Toronto Press, 2008) p. xv.

[58] William Schabas, *The Abolition of the Death Penalty in International Law* (Cambridge; Cambridge University Press, 2002) p. 5.

[59] Gherardo Pàntano, *Nel Benadir: La Citta de Merca e la Regione Bimal* (Livorno; Belforte, 1910).

[60] Lee V Cassanelli, *The Shaping of Somali Society: Reconstructing the History of a Pastoral People, 1600-1900* (Philadelphia, PA; University of Pennsylvania Press, 1982) p. 223.

[61] Gherardo Pàntano, *Ventitré anni di vita Africana* (Firenze; Casa editrice militare italiana, 1932) p. 268.

[62] Gherardo Pàntano, Rapporto del 29 Luglio 1915. 'Memoria confidenziale del Ministry delle Colonie' in Ministero delle Colonie (Ed.), *Libia: La ribellione in Tripolitania nell'anno 1915* (Roma, Tipografia del Senato, 1916) p. 122. Quoted in part in: Romain Rainero, *Paolo Valera e l'opposizione democratica all'impresa di Tripoli* (Roma; L'Erma di Bretschneider, 1983) p. 116.

[63] See Chapter 5 of Angelo Del Boca, *A un passo dalla forca: atrocita e infamie dell'occupazione italiana della Libia nelle memorie del patriota Mohamed Fekini* (Milano; Baldini Castoldi Dalai, 2007).

[64] Gianni Rocca, *Cadorna* (Milano; Mondadori, 1985) p. 47.

[65] Giorgio Rochat, *L'esercito italiano da Vittorio Veneto a Mussolini* (Bari; Laterza, 1967) p. 234. Luigi Cadorna, *Altre pagine sulla grand guerra* (Milano; Mondadori, 1925) pp. 13-14.

[66] Luigi Cadorna, *La guerra alla fronte italiana: fino all'arresto sulla linea della Piave e del Grappa. (24 Maggio 1915 - 9 Novembre 1917)* Volume I (Milano; Fratelli Treves, 1921) pp. 6, 7, 14-15, 20, 43, 44.

[67] Angelo Del Boca, *Gli Italiani in Libia: Tripoli bel suol d'amore: 1860-1922*, Vol. I (Milan; Mondadori, 1986) pp. 261-271.

[68] Angelo Del Boca, *A un passo dalla forca: atrocita e infamie dell'occupazione italiana della Libia nelle memorie del patriota Mohamed Fekini* (Milano; Baldini Castoldi Dalai, 2007) p. 78-9. For a detailed account of the battle see:
      Angelo Del Boca, *La disfatta di Gasr Bu Hadi 1915: il colonnello Miani e il più grande disastro dell Italia colonial* (Milano; Mondadori, 2004).

[69] Angelo Del Boca, *A un passo dalla forca: atrocita e infamie dell'occupazione italiana della Libia nelle memorie del patriota Mohamed Fekini* (Milano; Baldini Castoldi Dalai, 2007) p. 80.

[70] Vincenzo Giovanni Di Meo in Istituto coloniale italiano, *Atti del Convegno nazionale coloniale per il dopoguerra delle colonie: Roma 15-21 gennaio 1919, relazioni, comunicazioni e resoconti delle sedute* (Roma; Unione, 1920) p. 286. Angelo Del Boca considers De Meo's estimates to be the most accurate. Angelo Del Boca, *Gli Italiani in Libia: Tripoli bel suol d'amore: 1860-1922*, Vol. I (Milan; Mondadori, 1986) p. 298.

[71] Antonio Salandra to Ferdinando Martini, letter of 3 July 1915. Ferdinando Martini and Gabriele de Rosa (Ed.), *Diario 1914–1918* (Milano; Mondadori, 1966) p. 462.

[72] Arturo Vacca Maggiolini, 'La situazione in Tripolitania' in *Rivista Militare Italiana*, January 1922, pp. 41–45.

[73] Mario Morselli, *Caporetto 1917: Victory or Defeat?* (London; Frank Cass, 2001).

[74] Ettore Miraglia, *Tra le quinte della rivolta libica*, an unpublished account quoted in Angelo Del Boca, *A un passo dalla forca: atrocita e infamie dell'occupazione italiana della Libia nelle memorie del patriota Mohamed Fekini* (Milano; Baldini Castoldi Dalai, 2007) pp. 86-7.

[75] Gherardo Pàntano, *Ventitré anni di vita Africana* (Firenze; Casa editrice militare italiana, 1932) p. 332.

[76] J G Maxwell, General, Commanding the Force in Egypt. Despatch No. III. Army Headquarters, Cairo. 1 March, 1916. Quoted in: Everard Wyrall, *The Die-Hards in the Great War: A History of the Duke of Cambridge's own (Middlesex Regiment) Volume I, 1914 - 1916* (London; Harrison and Sons, 1926) p. 191. See also: http://www.naval-history.net/WW1NavyBritishLGDispatchesArmy1916-17.htm#29632c

[77] See: Jafar Pasha Al-Askari and Mustafa Tariq Al-Askari (Trans.), *A Soldier's Story: From Ottoman rule to Independent Iraq: The Memoirs of Jafar Pasha Al-Askari* (London; Arabian Publishing, 2003).

[78] Malak Badrawi, *Political Violence in Egypt, 1910-1924: Secret Societies, Plots and Assassinations* (Richmond, UK; Curzon, 2000) p. 116.

[79] R S Gwatkin-Williams, *Prisoners of the Red Desert: Being a Full and True History of the Men of the 'Tara'* (London; Thornton Butterworth, 1919) pp. 25, 26.

[80] Russell McGuirk, *The Sanusi's Little War: The Amazing Story of a Forgotten Conflict in the Western Desert, 1915-1917* (London; Arabian Publishing, 2007).

[81] Lieutenant-General Sir Archibald Wavell, *The Palestine Campaigns* (London; Constable, 1928) p. 38.

[82] See particularly Chapter 2, 'The Penetration of the Desert', in John W Gordon, *The Other Desert War: British Special Forces in North Africa, 1940-1943* (New York; Greenwood, 1987).

[83] T E Lawrence, *Seven Pillars of Wisdom: A Triumph* (Garden City, NY; Doubleday, 1938) pp. 544, 545.

[84] E Bartholomew, *Early Armoured Cars* (Oxford; Shire Publications, 1988) p. 18.

[85] For the fate of the guards see R S Gwatkin-Williams, *Prisoners of the Red Desert: Being a Full and True History of the Men of the 'Tara'* (London; Thornton Butterworth, 1919) p. 295 in particular, and also for the entire episode generally. See also: S C Rolls, *Steel Chariots in the Desert: The First World War Experiences of a Rolls Royce Armoured Car Driver with the Duke of Westminster in Libya and in Arabia with T.E. Lawrence* (London; Jonathan Cape, 1937); William Davies, *The Sea and the Sand: The Story of HMS Tara and the Western Desert Force* (Caernarfon; Gwynedd Archives and Museums Service, 1988). For the official

documentation pertaining to the Senussi Campaign see: http://www.naval-
history.net/WW1NavyBritishLGDispatchesArmy1916-17.htm

[86] Claudio G Segrè, *Italo Balbo: A Fascist Life* (Berkeley, CA; University of California Press, 1987) p. 322.
[87] Giorgio Rochat, 'La repressione della resistenza in Cirenaica' in Enzo Santarelli, Giorgio Rochat, Romain H Rainero and Luigi Goglia, *Omar al-Mukhtar e la riconquista fascista della Libia* (Milano; Marzorati, 1981) pp. 82-83.
[8] Angelo Del Boca, *A un passo dalla forca: atrocita e infamie dell'occupazione italiana della Libia nelle memorie del patriota Mohamed Fekini* (Milano; Baldini Castoldi Dalai, 2007) p. 10.

CHAPTER FIFTEEN

[1] Brigadier Allan Mallinson, 'At Ease with their Heritage' in *History Today*, Volume 61, Issue 7, July 2011, p. 38.
[2] Rudyard Kipling writing to Colonel H W Feilden on 29 January 1913 relating a tale told to him by 'young Garnier' about the Italian army in Tripoli. See: Thomas Pinney (Ed.) *The Letters of Rudyard Kipling, Volume 4: 1911-19* (Iowa City, IA; University of Iowa Press, 1999) pp. 145-6.
[3] Camillo Pavan, *Caporetto: storia, testimonianze, itinerari* (Treviso; Camillo Pavan, 1997) p. 74. See also: Dario Ascolano, *Luigi Capello: Biografia militare e politica* (Ravenna; Longo, 1999).
[4] Luigi Capello, *Per la Verita* (Milano; Fratelli Treves, 1920) p. 7.
[5] Quoted in John Whittam, *The Politics of the Italian Army, 1861-1918* (London; Croom Helm, 1977) p. 193.
[6] Paul M Kennedy, *The Rise and Fall of the Great Powers: Economic Change and Military Conflict from 1500 to 2000* (New York; Random House, 1988) p. 205.
[7] Edyth Hinkley, *Mazzini: The Story of a Great Italian* (New York; G P Putnam's, 1924.) p. 123.
[8] Allan R Becker, *Problems in Desert Warfare* (Quantico, VA; Marine Corps Combat Development Command, 1990) p. 4.
[9] See: Ferdinando Pedriali, 'Aerei italiani in Libia (1911-1912)' in *Storia Militare* N° 170 - novembre 2007 pp. 31- 40 and Carlo Rinaldi, 'I dirigibili italiani nella campagna di Libia' in *Storia Militare* N° 18 - marzo 1995 pp. 38-49.
[10] Sebastiano Licheri, 'Gli ordinamenti dell 'aeronautica militare italiana dal 1884 al 1918' in Ministero per i beni culturali e ambientali Ufficio centrale per i beni archivistici, Le fonti per la storia militare italiana in età contemporanea. *Atti del III seminario, Roma, 16-17 dicembre 1988* (Roma; Ediprint Service, 1993) p. 480
[11] 'Marconi Plans New Inventions as Useful as Wireless' in *The New York Times*, 24 March 1912.
[12] C L Fortescue, *Wireless Telegraphy* (Cambridge; Cambridge University Press, 1913) p. 117. Sebastian Mantei, *Von der Sandbüchse zum Post-und Telegraphenland: Der Aufbau des Kommunikationsnetzwerks in Deutsch-Südwestafrika* (Windhoek; Namibia Wissenschaftliche Gesellschaft, 2007).
[13] Horst Drechsler (Trans. Bernd Zollner), *Let us Die Fighting: The Struggle of the Herero and Nama against German Imperialism 1884-1915* (Berlin; Akademie, 1980) pp. 193, 186.
[14] Emilio De Bono, *Nell'esercito nostro prima della guerra* (Milano; Mondadori, 1931) p. 391.
[15] The expression was derived from an article by Gaetano Salvemini, 'Perché non si deve andare a Tripoli' in *La Voce*, Anno III, n 33, 17 agosto 1911, pp 631-632. Salvemini was an historian, journalist, and founder of the socialist journal *L'unita*. See: Luigi Scoppola Iacopini, 'Capitolo Terzo. Le vicende della comunita italiana in Libia 1956-1974' in Gianluigi Rossi (Ed.), *Italia-Libia. Storia di un dialogo mai interrotto* (Roma; Apes, 2012) p. 111.
[16] J Gentilli, *Italian Roots in Australian Soil: Italian Migration to Western Australia 1829-1946* (Marangaroo, Western Australia; Italo-Australian Welfare Centre, 1983) p. 58.
[17] Enver Pascha, *Um Tripolis* (München; Hugo Bruckmann, 1918) p. 35.
[18] Francis McCullagh, *Italy's War for a Desert* (London; Herbert & Daniel, 1913) p. 91.
[19] Napoleon Bonaparte (1769-1821) was famously from Corsica, which only became French territory in 1768 following purchase from the Republic of Genoa. His parents were members of the Genoese nobility; Napoleon was then very nearly Genoese. Genoa was incorporated into the Kingdom of Piedmont-Sardinia in June 1815 by the Final Act of the Treaty of Vienna.
[20] Gaetano V Cavallaro, *The Beginning of Futility: Diplomatic, Political, Military and Naval Events on the Austro-Italian Front in the First World War 1914-1917* (Bloomington, IN; Xlibris, 1999) Volume I, p. xxi.
[21] Winston S Churchill, *The Hinge of Fate* (London; Cassell, 1951) p. 81.
[22] H P Wilmot, *The Great Crusade: A New Complete History of the Second World War* (Dulles, VA; Potomac, 2008) p. 116. John Strachey, the British Secretary of State for War 1950-51, addressed the matter in a speech in Parliament in 1953: '[...] when I was at the War Office I remember asking Sir William Slim the then CIGS about the disasters suffered by the Italians against which he had fought during much of the War. He at once replied that the Italian troops were just as brave as the troops of any other country

and that the failure was in their selection of officers. They had never succeeded in recruiting an effective officer corps. We can never expect an army to be any better than its officers. That is one of the absolute limiting factors in the efficiency of an armed Service.'

[23] John Whittam, *The Politics of the Italian Army, 1861-1918* (London; Croom Helm, 1977) p. 24.

[24] Eric G Hansen, *The Italian Military Enigma* (Quantico, VA; Command and Staff College, Education Center, 1988) p. 46.

[25] Quoted by W T Stead, in an untitled posthumously published piece dated 1 April 1912 in *The Review of Reviews* for June 1912.

[26] Aldobrandino Malvezzi, *L'Italia e L'Islam in Libia* (Firenze; Fratelli Treves, 1913) p. 186.

[27] Angelo Del Boca, *Italiani, brava gente?: un mito duro a morire* (Vicenza; Neri Pozza, 2005) p. 112.

[28] Francesco Nitti, *L'Europa senza pace* (Firenze; Bemporad & Figlio, 1921) p. 87.

SOURCES AND BIBLIOGRAPHY

Documents

The records of the Italian Army relating to the invasion of Tripoli are held in the *Carteggio Libia* at the *Archivio dell'Ufficio Storico dello Stato Maggiore dell'Esercito* in Rome. The archive also holds material relating to the invasion of the Aegean Islands.

Documents from the political arena, can be found in the *Carte Giolitti* at the *Archivio Centrale dello Stato*, and in the *Ministero degli Affari Esteri, Archivio di Gabinetto Casella*, also in the Italian capital.

Many of the documents from the Italian Archives appear in the official history of the *Campagna di libia*, published in five volumes between 1922 and 1927, by the Ministry of War and the historical office of the Army General Staff:

Volume I: *Parte generale – operazione in Tripolitania dall'inizio della campagna alla occupazione di Punta Tagiura (ottobre-dicembre 1911)* (Roma, Stabilimento Poligrafico per l'Amministrazione della Guerra, 1922).

Volume II: *Operazioni in Tripolitania dal Dicembre 1911 (dopo l'occupazione di Punta Tagiura) alla fine dell'agosto 1912* (Roma, Stabilimento Poligrafico per l'Amministrazione della Guerra, 1923).

Volume III: *Le operazioni a Homs, al confine tunisino e a Misurata* (periodo ottobre 1911-agosto 1912) (Roma: Stabilimento Poligrafico per l'Amministrazione della Guerra, 1924).

Volume IV: *Le operazioni in Cirenaica (periodo ottobre 1911-agosto 1912)* (Roma: Stabilimento Poligrafico per l'Amministrazione della Guerra, 1925).

Volume V: *Appendice (periodo ottobre 1911-Agosto 1912)* (Roma; Stabilimento Poligrafico per l'Amministrazione della Guerra, 1927).

Documents relating to Italian naval operations are covered in two volumes published in 1918 and 1926 entitled *Guerra italo-turca (1911-1912): Cronistoria delle operazioni navali*.

Volume I: Roncagli, Giovanni (Ed.). *Dalle origini al decreto di sovranità su la Libia* (Milano; Ulrico Hoepli, 1918).

Volume II: Manfroni, Camillo (Ed.). *Dal decreto di sovranità su la Libia alla conclusione della pace.* (Roma; Stabilimento Poligrafico Editorial Romano, 1926).

In relation to the Aegean Islands, much of the documentation has been published in: Pasqualini, M G. *L'esercito italiano nel Dodecaneso 1912-1943, speranze e realtà, i documenti dell'Ufficio Storico dello Stato Maggiore dell'Esercito* (Roma; Archivio dell'Ufficio Storico dello Stato Maggiore dell'Esercito, 2006).

There is of course a problem respecting Ottoman documents from the period inasmuch, to quote the modern Turkish historian Taner Akcam, 'these sources are in the Ottoman language – Turkish written in Arabic script, with a strong influence from Persian and Arabic – and require special skills to read.' Fortunately many of the relevant sources have been read and used in the Turkish Armed Forces history of the conflict: Ertuna, Hamdi. *TSK [Türk Silahlı Kuvvetleri] Tarihi Osmanli Devri, Osmanli-Italyan Harbi (1911-1912)* (Ankara; Genelkurmay Basimevi, 1981). Similarly, documents relating to the Aegean Islands can be found in im ir, Bilâl N (Ed.). *Ege Sorunu: Belgeler Cilt-1 1912-1913* (Ankara; Türk Tarih Kurumu Yayınları, 1976). Greece has also published documents relating to these islands: Divanis, L, Constantopoulou, F et al. *The Dodecanese: The Long Road to Union with Greece. Diplomatic Documents from the Historical Archives of the Ministry of Foreign Affairs* (Athens; Kastaniotis, 1997). See also: Stephanopoli, Jeanne Z. *Les Iles de l'Egee Leurs Privileges (avec documents et notes statistiques)* (Atene; Apostolopoulos, 1912).

The UK National Archives at Kew hold the records of Consular Court Cases in Egypt. FO 841/121 Hassib Y dlibiv (sic). Mohd. Sherif Smallwood k/a John Warren Stuart Smallwood.

Documents pertaining to the conflict in relation to the other European Great Powers can be found in various published works, the most important of which are:

Commission de publication des documents relatifs aux origines de la guerre de 1914. *Documents diplomatiques francais 1871-1914. 3. serie (1911-1914) tome 1* (Paris; Imprimerie nationale, 1929).

Dugdale, E T S (Selected and Trans.). *German Diplomatic Documents, 1871-1914.* Vol. IV *The Descent to the Abyss, 1911-14* (London: Methuen, 1931).

Gooch, G P and Temperley, H W V (Eds.). *British Documents on the Origins of the War: 1898-1914,*Volume V, *The Near East, the Macedonian Problem and the Annexation of Bosnia, 1903-1909* (London; HMSO, 1928).

Gooch, G P and Temperley, H W V (Eds.). British Documents on the Origins of the War: *1898-1914, Vol. IX, The Balkan Wars,* Part I, *The Prelude: The Tripoli War* (London; HMSO, 1933).

Horne, Charles F, Austin, Walter F, and Ayres, Leonard P (Eds.). *Source Records of the Great War, Volume 3, AD 1915* (Indianapolis, IN; The American Legion, 1931).

Pribram, Alfred Franzis. *The Secret Treaties of Austria-Hungary 1879-1914* (Cambridge; Harvard University Press, 1920) Vol. I.

Scott, James Brown (Ed.). *Diplomatic Documents Relating to the Outbreak of the European War, Part I* (New York; Oxford University Press, 1916).

Internet

Cour Permanente D'arbitrage, *Affaire du Carthage.* France contre Italie. Sentence Arbitrale, La Haye, Le 6 Mai 1913. http://untreaty.un.org/cod/riaa/cases/vol_XI/449-461.pdf

Cour Permanente D'arbitrage, *Affaire du Manouba.* France contre Italie. Sentence Arbitrale, La Haye, Le 6 Mai 1913. http://untreaty.un.org/cod/riaa/cases/vol_XI/463-479.pdf

Indian Census of 1911.
http://censusindia.gov.in/Census_And_You/old_report/Census_1911.html

Accounts by participants and eyewitnesses

Abbott, G F. *The Holy War in Tripoli* (London; Edward Arnold, 1912).

d'Aveline, Guy. *La guerre à Tripoli, par un témoin oculaire* (Paris; Charles Amat, 1912).

Bennett, Ernest N. *With the Turks in Tripoli: Being Some Experiences in the Turco-Italian War of 1911* (London; Methuen, 1912).

Enver Pascha, *Um Tripolis* (München; Hugo Bruckmann,1918).

Giolitti, Giovanni. *Memorie della mia vita, con uno studio di Olindo Malagodi* (Milano; Fratelli Treves, 1922) Volume II.

Irace, Tullio. *With the Italians in Tripoli: The Authentic History of the Turco-Italian War* (London; John Murray, 1912).

McClure, W K. *Italy in North Africa: An Account of the Tripoli Enterprise* (London; Constable, 1913).

McCullagh, Francis. *Italy's War For A Desert: Being Some Experiences Of A War Correspondent With The Italians In Tripoli* (Chicago, IL; F G Browne, 1913).

Marinetti, F T. *La battaglia di Tripoli 26 ottobre 1911: vissuta e cantata da F T Marinetti* (Milano; Edizioni Futuriste di Poesia, 1912).

Ostler, Alan. *The Arabs in Tripoli* (London; John Murray, 1912).

Pàntano, Gherardo. Rapporto del 29 Luglio 1915. 'Memoria confidenziale del Ministry delle Colonie' in Ministero delle Colonie (Ed.), *Libia: La ribellione in Tripolitania nell'anno 1915* (Roma; Tipografia del Senato, 1916)

Picciole, Felice. *Diario di un bersagliere* (Milano; Formichiere, 1974).

Remond, Georges. *Aux Camps Turco-Arabes: Notes de Route et de guerre en Cyrénaïque et en Tripolitaine* (Paris; Hachette, 1913).

Rossi, Captain Giuseppe. 'Beschießung eines Aeroplans bei Tripolis' in Bertha von Suttner. 'Randglossen zur Zeitgeschichte' in Alfred M Fried (Ed.), *Die Friedens-Warte: Zeitschrift für zwischenstaatliche Organisation* (Berlin; Zeitschrift für zwischenstaatliche Organisation, 1912).

Seppings Wright, H C. *Two Years Under the Crescent* (Boston; Small, Maynard, 1913).

Theilhaber, Felix A. *Beim roten Halbmond vor Tripolis: Reiseerlebnisse von einer Fahrt ins türkisch-italienische Kriegsgebiet* (Köln; Schaffstein, 1915).

Internet

Sacco, Luigi. *Relazione circa le esperienze compiute dal Comm. Marconi nei giorni 16 e 17 dicembre 1911 a Tripoli.* http://luigisacco.bonavoglia.eu/relazione_19111220.pdf

Accounts in Journals and Newspapers

Avanti
Berliner Lokal-Anzeiger
Cape Times
Daily Chronicle
Daily Express
Daily Mirror
La Domenica del Corriere
Evening Post
Flight: A Journal Devoted to the Interests, Practice, and Progress of Aerial Locomotion and Transport
Gazzetta Ufficiale del Regno D'Italia.
Grey River Argus
Los Angeles Times
Le Matin
New York Times
Neue Freie Presse
L'Ouest-Éclair
Pittsburg Press
Popolo d' Italia
La Republica
The Review of Reviews
La Stampa
The Times
La Tribuna
La Voce
Vossische Zeitung

Secondary Sources

Abba, Giuseppe Cesare (Trans. ER Vincent). *The Diary of One of Garibaldi's Thousand* (Westport, CT; Greenwood Press, 1981).

Abbasi, Muhammad Yusuf. *London Muslim League, 1908-1928: An Historical Study* (Islamabad; National Institute of Historical and Cultural Research, 1988).

Abbasi, Muhammad Yusuf. *The Political Biography of Syed Ameer Ali* (Lahore; Wajidalis, 1989).

Acton, Harold. *The Last Bourbons of Naples (1825-1861)* (London; Methuen, 1961).

Adanir, Fikret. 'The Macedonians in the Ottoman Empire. 1878-1912' in Andreas Kappeler in collaboration with Fikret Adanir and Alan O'Day (eds.), *The Formation of National Elites* (New York; New York University Press, 1992).

Adanir, Fikret. 'The Socio-Political Environment of Balkan Nationalism: the Case of Ottoman Macedonia 1856-1912' in Heinz-Gerhard Haupt, Michael G. Mulle, Stuart Woolf (Eds.), *Regional and national identities in Europe in the XIXth and XXth centuries/Les identites regionales et nationales en Europe aux XIXe et XXe siecles* (The Hague; Kluwer Law International, 1998).

Adejumobi, Saheed A. *The History of Ethiopia* (London; Greenwood, 2006).

Agoston, Gabor. *Guns for the Sultan: Military Power and the Weapons Industry in the Ottoman Empire* (Cambridge; Cambridge University Press, 2005)

Agoston, Gabor and Masters, Bruce. *Encyclopedia of the Ottoman Empire* (New York; Facts On File, 2007).

Ahmad, Feroz. *The Young Turks: The Committee of Union and Progress in Turkish Politics, 1908-1914* (Oxford; University Press, 1969).

Ahmad, Ishtiaq. 'Turkish-Pakistan Relations: Continuity and Change' in Mehmet Tahiroglu and Tareq Y Ismael (Eds.), *Turkey in the 21st Century: Changing Role in World Politics* (Gazimagusa; Eastern Mediterranean University Press, 2000).

Ahmida, Ali Abdullatif. *The Making of Modern Libya: State Formation, Colonization, and Resistance* (Albany, NY; State University of New York Press, 2009).

Akme e, Handan Nezir. *The Birth of Modern Turkey: The Ottoman Military and the March to World War I* (London; Tauris, 2005).

Akçam, Taner. *Insan Haklari ve Ermeni Sorunu: Ittihat ve Terakki'den Kurtulus Savasina* (Ankara; IMGE Kitabevi, 1999).

Aksit, Ilhan (Ed.). *Mustafa Kemal Ataturk* (Istanbul; Cagaloglu, 1998).

Alam, Abu Yusuf. *Muslims and Bengal Politics (1912-24)* (Kolkata [Calcutta]; Raktakarabee, 2005).

Albertini, Luigi. *Le origini della guerra del 1914: Vol. I, Le relazioni europee dal Congresso di Berlino all'attentato di Sarajevo* (Milano; Bocca, 1941).

Albertini, Luigi and Bari, Ottavio (Ed.). *Epistolario 1911-1926*,Vol. I *Dalla guerra di Libia alla Grande Guerra* (Milano; Mondadori, 1968).

Alcock, Antony. *A History of the Protection of Regional Cultural Minorities in Europe: From the Edict of Nantes to the Present Day* (Basingstoke; Macmillan, 2000).

American Journal of International Law,Volume 6, No. 1. Supplement: Official Documents (January 1912).

Amicis, Edmondo de. 'L'entrata dell'esercito italiano in Roma' in R De Mattei (Ed.), *XX settembre 1870: Tre testimonianze. G Guerzoni, A M Bonetti, E De Amicis* (Roma; Istuto di Studi Romani, 1972).

Anderson, Duncan. *Glass Warriors: The Camera at War* (London; Collins, 2005).

Anderson, Lisa. *The State and Social Transformation in Tunisia and Libya, 1830-1980* (Princeton, NJ; Princeton University Press, 1986).

Anderson, Lisa. 'The Development of Nationalist Sentiment in Libya, 1908-1922' in Rashid Khalidi, Lisa Anderson, Muhammad Muslih and Reeva S Simon (Eds.) *The Origins of Arab Nationalism* (New York; Columbia University Press, 1991).

Anon. 'Portable Railways' in *Scientific American Supplement No. 446* New York, 19 July 1884.

Anon. 'Motor Vehicles in Warfare' in *The Horseless Age: A Monthly Journal Devoted to Motor Interests*,Volume 11, Number 9, July 1897.

Anon. 'Naval Notes: The French Mediterranean and Italian Squadrons at Toulon' in *The RUSI Journal*, Volume 45, Issue 277, 1901.

Anon. 'The India-Rubber Trade in Great Britain' in *The India Rubber World*, Vol. XXXV No. 2. 1 November 1906.

Anon. 'The Landing at Derna' in *The RUSI Journal*,Volume 56, Issue 413 July 1912.

Andreucci, Franco. '"Subversiveness" and Anti-Fascism in Italy' in Raphael Samuel (Ed.) *People's History and Socialist Theory* (London; Routledge & Kegan Paul).

Angelo, Thomas de. *Garibaldi's Ghosts: Essays on the Mezzogiorno and the Risorgimento* (Park Ridge, NJ; First Line Publishing, 2006).

Ascher, Abraham. *The Revolution of 1905: A Short History* (Stanford CA; Stanford University Press, 2004).

Ascolano, Dario. *Luigi Capello: Biografia militare e politica* (Ravenna; Longo, 1999).

Ashley, Susan A. *Making Liberalism Work: The Italian Experience, 1860-1914* (Westport CT; Praeger, 2003).

Ashmead-Bartlett, Ellis. *With the Turks in Thrace* (New York; George H Doran, 1913).

Ashmead-Bartlett, Ellis. *The Uncensored Dardanelles* (London; Hutchinson, 1928).

Askew, William C. *Europe and Italy's acquisition of Libya, 1911-1912* (Durham, NC; Duke University Press, 1942).

Austrian Red Book: Official Files Pertaining to Pre-War History, Part I, 28 June to 23 July 1914 (London; George Allen & Unwin, 1920).

Aydemir, evket Süreyya. *Makedonya'dan Ortaasya'ya Enver Pa a*,Vol. II 1908-1914 (Istanbul; Remzi Kitabevi, 1981).

Aydin, Mustafa. *Turkish Foreign Policy: Framework and Analysis* (Ankara; Center for Strategic Research, 2004).

Baedeker's Mediterranean: Seaports and Sea Routes including Madeira, The Canary Islands, The Coast of Morocco, Algeria, and Tunisia (Leipzig; Karl Baedeker, 1911).

Bagot, Richard. *The Italians of To-Day* (London; Mills & Boon, 1912).

Balbo, Cesare. *Delle speranze d'italia* (Firenze; Felice le Monnier, 1855).

Baldry, John. 'Anglo-Italian Rivalry in Yemen and As r 1900-1934' in *Die Welt des Islams*, New Series,Vol. 17, Issue 1/4 (1976 - 1977).

Barclay, Sir Thomas (With an Additional Chapter on Moslem Feeling by Ameer Ali). *The Turco-Italian War and its Problems, with Appendices Containing the Chief State Papers Bearing on the Subject* (London; Constable, 1912).

Barlow, Ima C. *The Agadir Crisis* (Hamden CT; Archon Books, 1971).

Barraclough, Geoffrey. *From Agadir to Armageddon: Anatomy of a Crisis* (New York; Holmes & Meier, 1982).

Barth, Boris. *Die deutsche Hochfinanz und die Imperialisten: Banken und Aussenpolitik vor 1914* (Stuttgart: Franz Steiner, 1995).

Bartholomew, E. *Early Armoured Cars* (Oxford; Shire Publications, 1988).

Bava-Beccaris, F. *Esercito Italiano: Sue origini suo successivo ampliamento, suo stato attuale* (Roma; Accademia dei Lincei, 1911).

Bayar, Celal. *Ben de Yazdım: Milli Mücadeleye gidi* ,Vol III (stanbul: Sabah Kitapları, 1997).

Beatus, Morris. *The Views of Conrad von Hötzendorf: Politics, Diplomacy, and War, 1906-1914* [MA Thesis] (Madison, WI; University of Wisconsin, 1970).

Becker, Allan R. *Problems in Desert Warfare* (Quantico, VA; Marine Corps Combat Development Command, 1990).

Beehler, Commodore W H. *The History of the Italian-Turkish War, September 29, 1911, to October 18, 1912* (Annapolis, MD; William H Beehler, 1913).

Bellamy, Richard and Schecter, Darrow. *Gramsci and the Italian State* (Manchester; Manchester University Press, 1993).

Benedetti, Giulio. *Enrico Corradini; Profilo* (Piacenza; Presso la Società tipografica editoriale Porta, 1922).

Bessel, Richard. *Fascist Italy and Nazi Germany: Comparisons and Contrasts* (Cambridge; Cambridge University Press, 1996).

Bevione, Giuseppe. 'La meravigliosa avventura nei Dardanelli narrate do Guiseppe Bevione' in *La Stampa*, 25 luglio 1912.

Bew, Paul. *Ireland: The Politics of Enmity 1789-2006* (Oxford; Oxford University Press, 2007).

Birken, Andreas. *Die Wirtschaftsbeziehungen zwischen Europa und dem Vorderen Orient im ausgehenden 19. Jahrhundert* (Wiesbaden; L Reichert, 1980).

Blinkhorn, Martin. *Fascism and the Right in Europe, 1919-1945* (Harlow; Pearson Education, 2000).

Bliss, Howard. 'Report Sent to the Board of Trustees, New York, 27 February 1912' in *Main Gate, American University of Beirut Quarterly Magazine*, Fall 2006 Vol. V, No. 1.

Blouin, Francis X (Ed.). *Vatican Archives: an Inventory and Guide to Historical Documents of the Holy See* (New York; Oxford University Press USA, 1998).

Blount, Sir Edward. *Memoirs of Sir Edward Blount* (London; Longman Green, 1902).

Blumberg, Arnold. *A Carefully Planned Accident: The Italian War of 1859* (Cranbury, NJ; Associated University Presses, 1990).

Bobroff, Ronald P. *Roads to Glory: Late Imperial Russia and the Turkish Straits* (London; I B Tauris, 2006).

Boca, Angelo Del. *Gli Italiani in Libia: Tripoli bel suol d'amore: 1860-1922*, Vol. I (Millan; Mondadori, 1986).

Boca, Angelo Del. *Italiani, brava gente?: un mito duro a morire* (Vicenza; Neri Pozza, 2005).

Boca, Angelo Del. *A un passo dalla forca: atrocità e infamie dell'occupazione italiana della Libia nelle memorie del patriota Mohamed Fekini* (Milano, Baldini Castoldi Dalai, 2007).

Bono, Emilio De. *Nell'esercito nostro prima della guerra* (Milano; Mondadori, 1931).

Bono, Salvatore. 'Lettere dal fronte libico (1911-1912)' in *Nuova Antologia* No. 2052. December 1971.

Bono, Salvatore. *Enver Pascià: diario della guerra libica* (Bologna; Cappelli, 1986).

Bonsaver, Guido. *Censorship and Literature in Fascist Italy* (Toronto; University of Toronto Press, 2007).

Bosworth, R J B. *Italy the Least of the Great Powers: Italian Foreign Policy before the First. World War* (London: Cambridge University Press, 1979).

Bovill, E W (Ed.). *Missions to the Niger Volume I: The Journal of Friedrich Hornemann's Travels From Cairo To Murzuk In The Years 1797-98; The Letters Of Major Alexander Gordon Laing 1824-26* (London: Hakluyt Society, 1964).

Bowyer Bell, J. *Assassin: Theory and Practice of Political Violence* (New Brunswick, NJ; Transaction Publishers, 2005).

Boyne, Walter J. *The Influence of Air Power upon History* (Gretna, LA; Pelican, 2003).

Brailsford, H N. *The War of Steel and Gold* (London; G Bell, 1914).

Bravo, Gian Mario. 'Antonio Labriola e la questione coloniale' in *I sentieri della ricerca: Rivista di storia contemporanea*, No.1 /June 2005.

Brian, Denis. *Pulitzer: A Life* (New York; John Wiley and Sons, 2001).

Brianti, Marc. *Bandiera rossa: un siècle d'histoire du Mouvement ouvrier italien du Risorgimento (1848) a la republique (1948)* (Paris; Connaissances et savoirs, 2007).

Britten Austin,, F. *The Red Flag* (London; Eyre and Spottiswoode, 1932).

Brooks, Richard. *Solferino 1859: The Battle for Italy's Freedom* (Oxford; Osprey, 2009).

Brown, Stuart E. 'Modernism, Association, and Pan-Islamism in the Thought of Ali Bash Hanbah' in Donald P Little (Ed.), *Essays on Islamic Civilization: Presented to Niyazi Berkes* (Leiden; Brill, 1976).

Bruce, T Boston. 'The New Italian Criminal Code' in *Law Quarterly Review*, Vol. 5, 1889.

Buchanan, James. *Message of the President of the United States, communicating [. . .] papers in relation to an alleged outrage on an American family at Perugia, in the Pontifical States* (36th Congress, 1st Session. Ex. Doc. No. 4) (US Government; Government Printing Office, 1860).

Burke III, Edmund. 'A Comparative View of French Native Policy in Morocco and Syria, 1912-1925' in *Middle Eastern Studies* Vol. 9, No. 2 (May, 1973).

Busky, Donald F. *Communism in History and Theory: The European Experience* (Westport, CT; Praeger, 2002).

Calandra, Eliana. 'Prigionieri arabi a Ustica: un episodio della guerra italo-turca attraverso le fonti archivistiche' in Carla Ghezzi (Ed.), *Fonti e problemi della politica coloniale italiana* (Roma; Ministero per i Beni Culturali e Ambientali, 1996) Volume II.

Callwell, C E. *Field-Marshall Sir Henry Wilson: His Life and Diaries,* (London: Cassell, 1927) Volume I.

Campbell, W Joseph. *Yellow Journalism: Puncturing the Myths, Defining the Legacies* (Westport, CT; Praeger, 2001).

Campos, Michelle U. *Ottoman Brothers: Muslims, Christians, and Jews in Early Twentieth-Century Palestine* (Stanford, CA;: Stanford University Press, 2011).

Canosa, Romano and Santosuosso, Amedeo. *Magistrati, anarchici e socialisti alla fine dell'ottocento in Italia* (Milan; Feltrinelli, 1981).

Capello, Luigi. *Per la Verita* (Milano; Fratelli Treves, 1920).

Cassels, Alan. *Fascist Italy* (Arlington Heights, IL; H Davidson, 1985).

Cassels, Alan. *Ideology and International Relations in the Modern World* (London; Routledge, 1996).

Cassels, Alan. 'Reluctant Neutral: Italy and the Strategic Balance in 1939' in B J C McKercher and Roch Legault (Eds.), *Military planning and the origins of the Second World War in Europe* (Westport CT; Praeger, 2001).

Castillo, Dennis. *The Maltese Cross: A Strategic History of Malta* (Westport, CT; Praeger, 2006).

Castle, Wilfred T P. *Grand Turk: An Historical Outline of Life and Events, of Culture and Politics, of Trade and Travel during the Last Years of the Ottoman Empire and the First Years of the Turkish Republic* (London; Hutchinson, 1943).

Causa, Cesare. *La guerra italo-turca e la conquista della Tripolitania e della Cirenaica dallo sbarco di tripoli alla pace di losanna* (Firenze; Salani, 1912).

Cavallaro, Gaetano V. *The Beginning of Futility: Diplomatic, Political, Military and Naval Events on the Austro-Italian Front in the First World War 1914-1917* (Bloomington, IN; Xlibris, 1999) Volume I.

Cecil, Lady Gwendolen. *Life of Robert Marquis of Salisbury, Volume IV 1887-1892* (London; Hodder and Stoughton, 1932).

Cecil, Lamar. *Wilhelm II Volume II: Emperor and exile, 1900-1941* (Chapel Hill, NC; University of North Carolina Press, 1996).

Cesare, R de (Trans. Helen Zimmern). *The Last Days of Papal Rome 1850-1870* (London; Constable, 1909).

Cesari, Cesare. *Colonie e possedimenti coloniali. Cenni storici e geografici. Con 15 tavole ed una breve appendice riassuntiva delle varie questioni d'Oriente* (Roma; Libreria di Scienze e Lettere, 1926).

Chambers, Lieut. Colonel [Osborne William Samuel Chambers], *Garibaldi and Italian Unity* (London; Smith Elder, 1864).

Chapman, Tim. *The Risorgimento: Italy 1815-1871* (Penrith; Humanities-Ebooks, 2008).

Charmley, John. *Splendid Isolation?: Britain and the Balance of Power 1874-1914* (London; Hodder & Stoughton, 1999).

Cheles, Luciano and Sponza, Lucio. 'Introduction: National Identities and Avenues of Persuasion' in Luciano Cheles and Lucio Sponza (Eds.), *The Art of Persuasion: Political Communication in Italy from 1945 to the 1990s* (Manchester; Manchester University Press, 2001).

Childs, Timothy W. *Italo-Turkish Diplomacy and the War over Libya, 1911-1912* (Leiden; E J Brill).

Chiusano, Amadeo and Sapotiti, Maurizio. *Palloni, dirigibili ed aerie del Regio Esercito (1884-1923)* (Roma; Ufficio Storico dello Stato Maggiore dell'Esercito, 1998).

Choate, Mark I. *Emigrant Nation: The Making of Italy Abroad* (Cambridge, MA; Harvard University Press, 2008).

Churchill, Randolph S. *Winston S Churchill, Companion Volume II, Part 3 1911-1914* (London; Heinemann, 1969).

Churchill, Winston S. *The River War: The Reconquest of the Sudan* (London; New English Library, 1985).

Churchill, Winston S. *The World Crisis 1911-1918* Volume I (London; Odhams Press, 1938).

Churchill, Winston S. *The Grand Alliance* (Boston, MA; Houghton Mifflin, 1950).

Churchill, Winston S. *The Hinge of Fate* (London; Cassell, 1951).

Clark, Martin. *Modern Italy 1871-1995* (London; Longman, 1996).

Clayton, Anthony. *Histoire de l'armée française en Afrique: 1830-1962* (Paris; Albin Michel, 1994).

Clough, Shepard B and Saladino, Salvatore. *A History of Modern Italy: Documents, Readings, and Commentary* (New York; Columbia University Press, 1968).

Coger, Dalvan M. 'Africana in the Scottish Geographical Magazine, 1885-1914' in *African Studies Bulletin*, Vol. 9, No. 3 (December 1966).

Cohen, Mordecai ha. *Higgid Mordecai* (Jerusalem: Ben-Zvi Institute, 1978).

Conder, Frances Roubiliac [aka 'An English Civilian']. *The Trinity of Italy, or, the Pope, the Bourbon, and the Victor; Being Historical Revelations of the Past, Present, and Future of Italy* (London; Edward Moxon, 1867).

Cooke, W S. *The Ottoman Empire and Its Tributary States* (B. R. Grüner, Amsterdam, 1968).

Coppa, Frank J. *The Origins of the Italian Wars of Independence* (London; Longman, 1992).

Corbett, Julian. *Principles of Maritime Strategy* [Reprint of 1911 edition] (London; Dover Publications, 2004).

Corni, Guido (Ed.). *Somalia italiana* (Milan; Editoriale Arte e Storia, 1937).

Correspondent of the New York Times, 'The Battle of Solferino,' in *The Advocate of Peace,* March, 1860.

Cox, Gary P. *The Halt in the Mud: French Strategic Planning from Waterloo to Sedan* (Boulder, CO; Westview, 1994).

Crankshaw, Edward. *The Fall of the House of Hapsburg* (New York; Viking, 1963).

Crehan, Kate. *Gramsci, Culture and Anthropology* (Los Angeles; University of California Press, 2002).

Cresson, William Penn. *The Holy Alliance: The European Background of the Monroe Doctrine* (Oxford; Oxford University Press, 1922).

Croce, Benedetto (Cecilia M Ady Trans.). *A history of Italy, 1871-1915* (New York; Russell & Russell, 1963) p. 187.

Cunsolo, Ronald S. 'Libya, Italian Nationalism, and the Revolt against Giolitti' in *The Journal of Modern History*, 37, June 1965.

d'Aveline, Guy. *Mémoires d'un délégué sanitaire* [Memoirs of a Sanitary Delegate] (Paris; N Maloine, 1931).

'Diplomatist' [Sir George Young] and Courtney of Penwith, Lord (Ed.). *Nationalism and War in the Near East* (Oxford; Clarendon Press, 1915).

Doyle, Don H. *Nations Divided: America, Italy, and the Southern Question* (Athens, GA; University of Georgia Press, 2002).

Drake, Richard. *Apostles and Agitators: Italy's Marxist Revolutionary Tradition* (Cambridge, MA; Harvard University Press, 2003).

Drechsler, Horst (Trans. Bernd Zollner). *Let us Die Fighting: The Struggle of the Herero and Nama against German Imperialism 1884-1915* (Berlin; Akademie, 1980).

Driault, Edouard and Lheritier, Michel. *Histoire diplomatique de la Grèce de 1821 a nos jours*, 5 vols. Vol. II, E Driault, *La règne d'Othon. La Grande Idée (1830-1862)* (Paris; Les Presses Universitaires de France, 1925).

Duggan, Christopher. *Francesco Crispi, 1818-1901: From Nation to Nationalism* (Oxford; Oxford University Press, 2002).

Duggan, Christopher. 'Nation-Building in 19th Century Italy: The Case of Francesco Crispi' in *History Today*, Volume 52 (2) February 2002.

Duggan, Christopher. *The Force of Destiny: A History of Italy Since 1796* (London; Allen Lane, 2007).

Dumas, Alexandre (Trans. Richard Garnett). *On Board the Emma: Adventures with Garibaldi's 'Thousand' in Sicily* (New York; D Appleton and Company, 1929).

Dumas, Alexandre. *Viva Garibaldi! Une Odyssée en 1860* (Paris; Fayard, 2002).

Dunant, Henry. *A Memory of Solferino* (Geneva; International Committee of the Red Cross, 1986).

Dunnage, Jonathan. 'Continuity in Policing Politics in Italy, 1920-1960' in Mark Mazower (Ed.), *The Policing of Politics in the Twentieth Century: Historical Perspectives* (Oxford; Berghahn, 1997).

Dunnage, Jonathan. *The Italian Police and the Rise of Fascism: A Case Study of the Province of Bologna, 1897-1925* (Westport CT; Praeger, 1997).

Dupanloup, F A P. *La souveraineté pontificale selon le droit catholique et le droit européen, par Mgr. l'évêque d'Orléans* (Paris; Lecoffre, 1860).

Eley, Geoff. *Forging Democracy: The History of the Left in Europe, 1850-2000* (Oxford; Oxford University Press, 2002).

Erickson, Edward J. *Defeat in Detail: the Ottoman Army in the Balkans, 1912-1913* (Westport, CN; Praeger, 2003).

Evans-Pritchard, E E. *The Sanusi of Cyrenaica* (Oxford; Clarendon Press, 1949).

Faroqhi, Suraiya. *The Ottoman Empire and the World Around It* (London; I B Tauris, 2005).

Fay, Sidney B. *The Origins of the World War* (New York; Macmillan, 1928).

Fergiani, Mohammed Bescir. *The Libyan Jamahiriya* (Tripoli; Dar Al-Fergiani, 1976).

Ferguson, Niall. *The Pity of War* (London; Allen Lane, 1998).

Ferraioli, Gianpaolo. *Politica e diplomazia in Italia tra XIX e XX secolo: Vita di Antonino di San Giuliano (1852-1914)* (Soveria Mannelli; Rubbettino, 2007).

Ffestiniog Railway Company, *Rheilffordd Ffestiniog Guide Book* (Porthmadog; Ffestiniog Railway Company, 1997).

Fischer, Fritz. *War of Illusions: German Policies from 1911 to 1914* (London: Chatto and Windus, 1975).

Fitzwilliams, J K L. 'The Coast Defenses of Turkey' in *The Journal of the United States Artillery* Vol. 43 No. 1 January-February 1915.

Flecker, James Elroy and Squire, Sir John (Ed.). *The Collected Poems of James Elroy Flecker* (London; Secker & Warburg, 1947).

Fleming, Denna Frank. *The Origins and Legacies of World War I* (London; Allen & Unwin, 1969).

Folayan, Kola. 'Tripoli-Bornu Political Relations, 1817-1825' in *Journal of the Historical Society of Nigeria*. Volume 5 No. 4, June 1971.

Folayan, Kola. *Tripoli During the Reign of Y suf P sh Qaram nl* (Ilé-If , Nigeria; University of Ife Press, 1979).

Forsyth, Douglas J. *The Crisis of Liberal Italy: Monetary and Financial Policy, 1914-1922* (Cambridge; Cambridge University Press, 1993).

Foreign Office Historical Section, *Italian Libya* (London; HMSO, 1920).

Fortescue, C L. *Wireless Telegraphy* (Cambridge; Cambridge University Press, 1913).

Fortna, Benjamin C. 'The Reign of Abdülhamid II,' in Re at Kasaba (Ed.), *The Cambridge History of Turkey: Volume 4, Turkey in the Modern World* (Cambridge; Cambridge University Press, 2008).

Fraccaroli, Aldo. 'Italy' in Robert Gardiner, Roger Chesneau and Eugene M Kolesnik (Eds), *Conway's All the World's Fighting Ships 1860-1905* (London; Conway Maritime Press, 1979).

Frassati, Alfredo. 'Cinque torpediniere italiane s'inoltrano per 20 chilometri nei Dardanelli sotto il fuoco incrociato dei forti turchi' in *La Stampa*, 21 luglio 1912.

Fried, Robert C. *The Italian Prefect: A Study in Administrative Politics* (New Haven CT; Yale University Press, 1963).

Fry, Michael Graham, Goldstein, Erik and Langhorne, Richard. *Guide to International Relations and Diplomacy* (London; Continuum, 2002).

Fuller, J F C. *The Conduct of War 1789-1961* (London; Eyre & Spottiswoode, 1961).

Fullerton, Wm Morton. *Problems of Power: A Study of International Politics from Sadowa to Kirk-Kilisse* (New York, NY; Charles Scribner's Sons, 1913).

Fulvi, L, Marcon, T, and Miozzi, O. *Le fanterie di marina italiane* (Roma; Ufficio storico della Marina militare, 1998).

Furlong, Charles Wellington. *The Gateway to the Sahara: Observations and Experiences in Tripoli* (New York; Charles Scribner's Sons, 1909).

Gabriele, Mariano. *La marina nella guerra italo-turca: il potere marittimo strumento militare e politico (1911-1912)* (Roma; Ufficio Storico della Marina Militare, 1998).

Gardiner, Robert and Gray, Randal (Eds.). *Conway's All the World's Fighting Ships, 1906-1921* (Annapolis, MD; Naval Institute Press, 1985).

Gellner, Ernest and Micaud, Charles. *Arabs and Berbers: from Tribe to Nation in North Africa* (London; D C Heath, 1973).

Gentilli, J. *Italian Roots in Australian Soil: Italian Migration to Western Australia 1829-1946* (Marangaroo, Western Australia; Italo-Australian Welfare Centre, 1983).

George, David Lloyd *War Memoirs.* Two-volume edition (London; Odhams, 1938) Vol. I.

Ghazi, Mahmood Ahmad. *The Sanusiyyah Movement of North Africa: An Analytical Study* (Islamabad; Shariah Academy, 2001).

Gibson, Hugh. *The Ciano Diaries, 1939-1943: The Complete, Unabridged Diaries of Count Galeazzo Ciano, Italian Minister for Foreign Affairs, 1936-1943* (Garden City, NY; Doubleday, 1946).

Giletta, L. 'Le locomotive stradali e la mobilitazione dell'esercito' in *Rivista Militare Italiana*, September 1876.

Ginsborg, Paul. *Daniele Manin and the Venetian Revolution of 1848-49* (Cambridge; Cambridge University Press, 1979).

Giorgerini, Giorgio and Nani, Augusto (Eds.). *Gli incrociatori italiani, 1861-1975* (Roma; Ufficio storico marina militare, 1976).

Giuliano, Antonino di San. *Lettere sull'Albania: pubblicate nel Giornale d'Italia* (Roma; Giornale d'Italia, 1903).

Giuntini, Andrea. 'Downtown by the Train: The Impact of Railways on Italian Cities in the Nineteenth Century – Case Studies' in Ralf Roth and Marie-Noëlle Polino (Eds.) *The City and the Railway in Europe* (Aldershot; Ashgate, 2003).

Glanville, J L. *Italy's Relations with England* (Baltimore; John Hopkins Press, 1934).

Goldberg, Harvey E. *Jewish Life in Muslim Libya: Rivals & Relatives* (Chicago, IL; University of Chicago Press, 1990).

Goldstein, Erik. *Wars and Peace Treaties, 1816-1991* (London; Routledge, 1992).

Gooch, G P. *Before the War: Studies in Diplomacy, Vol. II: The Coming of The Storm* (London; Longmans, Green, 1938).

Gooch, John. *Army, State and Society in Italy, 1870-1915* (London; Macmillan, 1989).

Graves, Robert. *Lawrence and the Arabs* (London; Jonathan Cape, 1934).

Gray, Ezio M. *Italy and the Question of Tunis* (Milan; A Mondadori, 1939).

Great Britain Naval Intelligence Division, *A Handbook of Libya* (London; HMSO, 1917).

Gregor, A James. *Young Mussolini and the Intellectual Origins of Fascism* (Berkeley, CA; University of California Press, 1979).

Grenville, J A S. *Europe Reshaped, 1848-1878* (Oxford; Blackwell, 2000).

Grey of Falloden, Viscount. *Twenty-Five Years: 1892-1916* (London; Hodder & Staughton, 1925) Vol. I.

Griffiths, Merwin Albert. *The Reorganization of the Ottoman Army under Abdülhamid II, 1880-1897* (Los Angeles, CA; University of California, 1968).

Gualtieri, Humbert L. *The Labor Movement in Italy* (New York; S F Vanni, 1946).

Gülsoy, Ufuk. *Hicaz Demiryolu* (stanbul, Eren, 1994).

Hale, John Richard. *Famous Sea Fights from Salamis to Tsu-shima* (London, Methuen, 1911).

Halli, Re at. *Balkan Harbi (1912-1913): I.Cilt* [Volume I], *Harbin Sebepleri, Askeri Hazirliklar ve Osmanli Devletinin Harbe Giri i* (Ankara; Genelkurmay, 1970).

Hall, Richard C. *The Balkan Wars, 1912-1913: Prelude to the First World War* (London; Routledge, 2000).

Halleck, H W. *International Law: or, Rules Regulating the Intercourse of States in Peace and War* (San Francisco; H H Bancroft, 1861).

Halpern, Paul G. *The Mediterranean Naval Situation, 1908-1914* (Cambridge, MA; Harvard University Press, 1971).

Halpern, Paul G. *The Naval War in the Mediterranean, 1914-1918* (Boston; Allen & Unwin, 1986).

Hanioglu, Sukru (Ed.). *Kendi Mektuplarinda Enver Pasa* (Istanbul; Der Yayınları, 1989).

Hanio lu, M Sükrü. *The Young Turks in Opposition* (Cary, NC; Oxford University Press USA, 1995).

Hanio lu, M ükrü. *Preparation for a Revolution: The Young Turks, 1902-1908* (New York; Oxford University Press, 2001).

Hanioglu, M Sükrü. 'The Second Constitutional Period, 1908–1918' in Re at Kasaba (Ed.), *The Cambridge History of Turkey: Volume 4, Turkey in the Modern World* (Cambridge; Cambridge University Press, 2008).

Hansen, Eric G. *The Italian Military Enigma* (Quantico, VA; Command and Staff College, Education Center, 1988).

Hardy, P. *The Muslims of British India* (Cambridge; Cambridge University Press, 1972).

Harold, Jim. 'Cars, Deserts, Maps and Naming: An Analysis of Captain Claud H Williams' Report on the Military Geography of the North-Western Desert of Egypt, (1917).' A paper presented to the Fifth Biennial ASTENE (Association for the Study of Travel in Egypt and the Near East) Conference, held on Friday 11 July - Monday 14 July 2003 at Worcester College, Oxford.

Harter, Jim. *World Railways of the Nineteenth Century: A Pictorial History in Victorian Engravings* (Baltimore MD; John Hopkins University Press, 2005).

Haupt, Heinz-Gerhard, Mulle, Michael G, and Woolf, Stuart (Eds.). *Regional and national identities in Europe in the XIXth and XXth centuries / Les identites regionales et nationales en Europe aux XIXe et XXe siecles* (The Hague; Kluwer Law International, 1998).

Haywood, Geoffrey A. *Failure of a Dream: Sidney Sonnino and the rise and fall of Liberal Italy 1847-1922* (Florence; Leo S Olschki, 1999).

Headlam, Major General Sir John. *The History of the Royal Artillery from the Indian Mutiny to the Great War, Volume II* 1899-1914 (Woolwich; Royal Artillery Institution, 1937).

Heller, Joseph. *British Policy Towards the Ottoman Empire, 1908-1914* (London; Frank Cass, 1983).

Henderson, Philip. *The Life of Laurence Oliphant: Traveller, Diplomat, Mystic,* (London; Robert Hale, 1956).

Herrmann, David G. 'The Paralysis of Italian Strategy in the Italian-Turkish War, 1911-1912' in *The English Historical Review*, Vol. 104, No. 411, April 1989.

Herrmann, David G. *The Arming of Europe and the Making of the First World War* (Princeton, NJ; Princeton University Press, 1997).

Hertner, Peter. 'Modern Banking in Italy' in European Association for Banking History, *Handbook on the History of European Banks* (Aldershot, UK; Edward Elgar, 1994).

Herwig, Holger H. *'Luxury' Fleet: The German Imperial Navy 1888–1918* (London: George Allen & Unwin, 1980).

Hess, Robert L. *Italian Colonialism in Somalia* (Chicago; University of Chicago Press, 1966).

Heyriès, Hubert. 'L'armée italienne et le maintien de l'ordre dans les villes de 1871 à 1915 d'après les attachés militaires français: Guerre de rue, guerre dans la rue' in *Guerres mondiales et conflits contemporains.* avril-juin 2002, No 206.

Hibbert, Christopher. *Garibaldi: Hero of Italian Unification* (London; Palgrave Macmillan, 2008).

Hinkley, Edyth. *Mazzini: The Story of a Great Italian* (New York; G P Putnam's, 1924).

Hinsley, F H (Ed.). *British Foreign Policy under Sir Edward Grey* (Cambridge; Cambridge University Press, 1997).

Hobhouse, J C. *A Journey through Albania and Other Provinces of Turkey in Europe and Asia to Constantinople during the Years 1809 and 1810,* Volume I (London; James Cawthorn, 1813).

Horeir, Abdulmola S El. *Social and Economic Transformations in the Libyan Hinterland during the Second Half of the Nineteenth Century: The Role of Sayyid Ahmad al-Sharif al-Sanusi* (Los Angeles, CA; University of California, 1981).

Howard, Michael. *The Franco Prussian War* (St Albans; Granada, 1979).

Hull, Isabel V. *The Entourage of Kaiser Wilhelm II, 1888-1918* (Cambridge; Cambridge University Press, 2004).

lmen, Süreyya. *Turkiye'de Tayyarecilik ve Balonculuk Tarihi* (stanbul; brahim Horoz Basımevi, 1947).

Ispettorato generale della motorizzazione, *L'Albo d'Onore del Servizio della Motorizzazione* (Roma; Ispettorato generale della motorizzazione, 1966).

Invernizio, Carolina. *Odio di araba* (Firenze; Salani, 1912).

Jäckh, Ernst (Ed.). *Kiderlen-Wächter, der Staatsmann und Mensch: Briefwechsel und Nachlaß.* Two Volumes (Stuttgart; Deutsche Verlags-Anstalt, 1924) Vol. II.

Jarausch, Konrad H. *The Enigmatic Chancellor: Bethmann Hollweg and the Hubris of Imperial Germany* (New Haven CT; Yale University Press, 1973).

Jefa'iri, Mohamed al, *et al. The Libyan Deportees in the Prisons of the Italian Islands: Documents, Statistics, Names, Illustrations* (Tripoli: Libyan Studies Centre, 1989).

Jensen, Richard Bach. *Liberty and Order: The Theory and Practice of Italian Public Security Policy, 1848 to the Crisis of the 1890s* (New York: Garland, 1991).

Joll, James. *The Second International, 1889-1914* (London; Routledge & Kegan Paul, 1974).

Jones, Maldwin A. *Destination America* (London; Weidenfeld and Nicolson, 1976).

Jovanovi , Jovan M. *Borba za narodno ujedinjenje 1903–1908* (Belgrade; Geca Kon, 1938).

Kansu, Aykut. *The Revolution of 1908 in Turkey* (Leiden; Brill Academic Publishers , 1997).

Kansu, Yavuz, Sensoz, Sermet, and Oztuna, Yılmaz. *Havacılık Tarihinde Türkler* (Ankara; Hava Kuvvetleri Basım ve Nesriyat Mud, 1971).

Kayali, Hasan. *Arabs and Young Turks: Ottomanism, Arabism, and Islamism in the Ottoman Empire, 1908–1918* (Berkeley, CA; University of California Press, 1997).

Keane, Augustus Henry. *Africa Volume I: North Africa* (London; Edward Stanford, 1895).

Keane, Augustus Henry. *Asia: Vol. II, Southern and Western Asia* (London; Edward Stanford, 1909).

Keiger, J F V. *Raymond Poincaré* (Cambridge; Cambridge University Press, 1997).

Kelly, Walter K. *The History of Russia: From the Earliest Period to the Present Time.* Two Volumes. (London; Henry G Bohn, 1855). Vol. II.

Kennedy, Paul M. *The Rise and Fall of the Great Powers: Economic Change and Military Conflict from 1500 to 2000* (New York; Random House, 1988).

Kepi. 'The Italians at Tripoli,' in *Blackwood's Magazine* No. MCLIV, December 1911. Vol. CXC.

Kerr, Mark. *Land, Sea, and Air: Reminiscences of Mark Kerr* (New York; Longmans, Green, 1927).

Kertzer, David. *The Kidnapping of Edgardo Mortara* (London; Picador, 1997).

Kertzer, David. *Prisoner of the Vatican: The Popes' Secret Plot to Capture Rome from the New Italian State* (Boston; Houghton Mifflin, 2004).

Keyes, Lord. *Amphibious Warfare and Combined Operations* (Cambridge; Cambridge University Press, 1943).

Khalil, Muhammad. 'Renaissance in North Africa: The Sanusiyyah Movement' in M M Sharif (Ed.) *A History of Muslim Philosophy with Short Accounts of Other Disciplines and the Modern Renaissance in Muslim Lands,* Volume II (Wiesbaden; Otto Harrassowitz, 1966).

Kiel, Machiel. *Ottoman Architecture in Albania, 1385-1912* (Istanbul; Research Centre for Islamic History, Art and Culture, 1990).

Kinross, Patrick. *Atatürk: The Rebirth of a Nation* (New York; Morrow, 1965).

Kinsella, Kevin G. 'Changes in life expectancy 1900-1990' in *The American Journal for Clinical Nutrition* Vol 55 June 1992.

Klopp, Charles. *Sentences: The Memoirs and Letters of Italian Political Prisoners from Benvenuto Cellini to Aldo Moro* (Toronto; University of Toronto Press, 1999).

Koff, Sondra Z and Koff, Stephen P. *Italy: from the First to the Second Republic* (London; Routledge, 2000).

Kolo lu, Orhan. *Trablusgarp Sava ı ve Türk Subayları 1911-12* (Ankara; Basın Yayın Genel Müdürlü ü, 1979).

Kolo lu, Orhan. *500 Years In Turkish-Libyan Relations: SAM Paper 1/2007* (Ankara; Stratejik Arastirmalar Merkezi (SAM), 2007).

Kovic, Milos. *Disraeli and the Eastern Question* (Oxford; Oxford University Press, 2011).

Küntzer, Karl. *Abdul Hamid II und die Reformen in der Türkei* (Dresden/Leipzig; Carl Reissner, 1897).

Kutay, Cemal. *Trablus Garb'de Bir Avuç Kahraman* (Istanbul; Kutay, 1978).

Labanca, Nicola. 'The Embarrassment of Libya: History, Memory, and Politics in Contemporary Italy' in *California Italian Studies Journal,* Volume 1, Issue 1, 2010.

Landau, Jacob M. *Atatürk and the Modernization of Turkey* (Boulder, CO; Westview Press, 1984).

Langensiepen, Bernd and Güleryüz, Ahmet (James Cooper Ed. and Trans.). *The Ottoman Steam Navy, 1828-1923* (London; Conway Maritime Press, 1995).

Lapworth, Charles (In Collaboration with Miss Helen Zimmern), *Tripoli and Young Italy* (London; Stephen Swift, 1912).

Layriz, Otfried and Marston, R B (Trans.). *Mechanical Traction in War for Road Transport with Notes on Automobiles Generally* (London; Sampson Low, Marston, 1900).

Lee, Dwight E. *Europe's Crucial Years: The Diplomatic Background of World War I, 1902-1914* (Hanover, NH; University Press of New England for Clark University Press, 1974).

Leiner, Frederick C. *The End of Barbary Terror: America's 1815 War Against the Pirates of North Africa* (Cary, NC; Oxford University Press USA, 2007).

Lepsius, Johannes, Mendelssohn-Bartholdy, Albrecht, and Thimme, Friedrich (Eds.). *Die Große Politik der Europäischen Kabinette 1871 bis 1914I,* Vol. XXX part 1 (Berlin; Deutsche Verlaggesellschaft fur Politik und Geschichte, 1926).

Levillain, Philippe (Ed.). *Dictionnaire historique de la papauté* (Paris; Librairie Arthème Fayard, 2003) Vol. II.

Levy, Carl. *Gramsci and the Anarchists* (New York; Berg, 2000).

Levy, Carl. 'Currents of Italian Syndicalism before 1926' in *International Review of Social History* (2000), Vol. 45, Issue 2.

Levy, Carl. '"Sovversivismo": The Radical Political Culture of Otherness in Liberal Italy,' in the *Journal of Political Ideologies,* Volume 12, Issue 2 June 2007.

Licheri, Sebastiano. 'Gli ordinamenti dell 'aeronautica militare italiana dal 1884 al 1918' in Ministero per i beni culturali e ambientali Ufficio centrale per i beni archivistici, *Le fonti per la storia militare italiana in età contemporanea. Atti del III seminario, Roma, 16-17 dicembre 1988* (Roma; Ediprint Service, 1993).

Liddell Hart, B H. *The Defence of Britain* (London; Faber and Faber, 1939).

Lindley, M F. *The Acquisition and Government of Backward Territory in International Law: Being a Treatise on the Law and Practice Relating to Colonial Expansion* (London: Longmans, Green, 1926).

Livingstone, David N. 'Tropical Climate and Moral Hygiene: The Anatomy of a Victorian Debate' in *The British Journal for the History of Science,* 1999, Volume 32.

Lowe, C J. 'Grey and the Tripoli War' in F H Hinsley (Ed.), *British Foreign Policy under Sir Edward Grey* (Cambridge; Cambridge University Press, 1977).

Lutiis, Giuseppe De. *Storia dei servizi segreti in Italia* (Roma: Riuniti, 1984).

Lyttelton, Adrian (Ed. and Intro). *Italian Fascisms from Pareto to Gentile* (New York; Harper & Row, 1975).

Lyttelton, Adrian. 'Politics and Society 1870-1915' in George Holmes (Ed.) *The Oxford Illustrated History of Italy*. (Oxford; Oxford University Press, 1997).

MacGahan, J A. *The Turkish Atrocities in Bulgaria, Letters of the Special Commissioner of the Daily News [. . .]. With an Introduction and Mr. Schuyler's Preliminary Report* (London; Bradbury, Agnew, 1876).

McCabe, Joseph. *Crises in the History of the Papacy: A Study of Twenty Famous Popes whose Careers and whose Influence were Important in the History of the World* (New York; G P Putnam, 1916).

McCullough, Edward E. *How the First World War Began: The Triple Entente and the Coming of the Great War of 1914-1918* (Montreal; Black Rose, 1999).

McIntire, C T. *England Against the Papacy 1858–1861: Tories, Liberals and the Overthrow of Papal Temporal Power during the Italian Risorgimento* (Cambridge; Cambridge University Press, 1983).

Μαίλλη, Αυτώνη Σεβ. Ἡ κατάληψη της Ρόδου: Χρονικό της πολεμικής επιχείρησης του ιταλικών στρατιωτικών δυνάμεων' in Επτα Ημερεσ, Κυριακη 30 Νοεμβριου 1997.

Malgeri, Francesco. *La Guerra Libica 1911-1912* (Roma; Edizioni di storia e letteratura, 1970).

Malleson, G B. *The Refounding of the German Empire 1848 – 1871* [Facsimile reprint of the 1898 edition] (London; R J Leach, 1992).

Mallinson, Brigadier Allan. 'At Ease with their Heritage' in *History Today*, Volume 61, Issue 7, July 2011.

Maltese, Paolo. *La terra promessa: La guerra italo-turca e la conquista della Libia 1911-12* (Milano; Mondadori, 1976).

Malvezzi, Aldobrandino. *L'Italia e L'Islam in Libia* (Firenze-Milano; Fratelli Treves, 1913).

Mango, Andrew. *Ataturk: The Biography of the Founder of Modern Turkey* (Woodstock, NY; Overlook Press, 2002).

Manhart, George B. *Alliance and Entente, 1871 –1914* (New York; F S Crofts, 1932).

Manning, Cardinal. *The Independence of the Holy See* (London; Henry S King, 1877).

Mantei, Sebastian. *Von der Sandbüchse zum Post-und Telegraphenland: Der Aufbau des Kommunikationsnetzwerks in Deutsch-Südwestafrika* (Windhoek; Namibia Wissenschaftliche Gesellschaft, 2007).

Marchetti, Odoardo. *Il servizio informazione dell'esercito italiano nella grande Guerra* (Roma; Tipografia Regionale, 1937).

Marriott, J A R. *The Makers of Modern Italy* (London; Macmillan, 1901).

Marsden, Arthur. 'Britain and her Conventional Rights in Tunis, 1888-1892' in *Revue de l'Occident musulman et de la Méditerranée*, Vol. 8, No. 1. (1970).

Martin, George. *The Red Shirt and the Cross of Savoy* (London; Eyre & Spottiswoode, 1969).

Mattei, Roberto De. *Pius IX* (Leominster; Gracewing, 2004).

Mattern, Johannes. *The Employment of the Plebiscite in the Determination of Sovereignty: A dissertation Submitted to the Board of University Studies of The Johns Hopkins University in conformity with the Requirements for the degree of Doctor of Philosophy* (Baltimore, MD; John Hopkins University. 1922).

Meini, Marco. *Il decimo corridoio* (Roma: Robin, 2005).

Midlarsky, Manus I. *The Killing Trap: Genocide in the Twentieth Century* (Cambridge; Cambridge University Press, 2005).

Milkias, Paulos and Metaferia, Getachew (Eds.). *The Battle of Adwa: Reflections on Ethiopia's Historic Victory Against European Colonialism* (New York; Algora, 2005).

Miller, William. *The Ottoman Empire 1801-1913* (Cambridge; Cambridge University Press, 1913).

Millman, Richard. 'The Bulgarian Massacres Reconsidered,' in *The Slavonic and East European Review*, Vol. 58, No. 2, (April, 1980).

[Ministry of Foreign Affairs], *The Bulgarian Question and the Balkan States* (Sofia; State printing Press, 1919).

Mirandoli, P. 'Le locomotive stradali' in *Rivista Militare Italiana*, January 1883, p. 73 and February 1883.

Mogherbi, Mohamed Zahi El. *Tribalism, Religion and the Challenge of Political Participation: The Case of Libya.* (A Paper presented to Conference on Democratic Challenges in the Arab World, Centre for Political and International Development Studies, Cairo, 22–27 September 1992).

Moltke, Helmuth von. *Briefe über Zustände und Begebenheiten in der Türkei aus den Jahren 1835-39* (Berlin; Mittler, 1841).

Montferrand, Bernard de. *Diplomatie: des volontés françaises* (Versailles; Alban, 2006).

Morris, A E J. *History of Urban Form: Before the Industrial Revolutions* (Harlow; Pearson, 1994).

Mugridge, Ian. *The View from Xanadu: William Randolph Hearst and United States Foreign Policy* (Montreal; McGill-Queen's University Press, 1995).

Muhammad, Shan (Ed.). *The Right Honourable Syed Ameer Ali: Political Writings* (New Delhi; Ashish, 1989).

Muldoon, James. *Empire and Order: The Concept of Empire, 800-1800* (Basingstoke; Palgrave Macmillan, 1999).

Mundy, [Rear-Admiral Sir] Rodney. *HMS Hannibal at Palermo and Naples During The Italian Revolution, 1859-1861, With Notices of Garibaldi, Francis II, and Victor Emanuel* (London; John Murray, 1863).

Munzi, Massimiliano. 'Italian Archaeology in Libya: From Colonial Romanita to Decolonization of the Past' in Michael L Galaty and Charles Watkinson, *Archaeology under Dictatorship* (New York, NY; Springer, 2004).

Mussolini, Benito. *Fascism: Doctrine and Institutions* (Rome; Ardita, 1935).

Naldi, Gino J. 'The Aouzou Strip Dispute-A Legal Analysis' in *Journal of African Law*, Vol. 33, No. 1 (Spring, 1989).

Neville, Peter. *Mussolini* (London; Routledge, 2004) p. 28. R N L Absalom, *Mussolini and the Rise of Italian Fascism* (London; Methuen, 1969).

Nicolle, David. *The Italian Army of World War I* (Oxford; Osprey, 2003).

Nitti, Francesco. *L'Europa senza pace* (Firenze; Bemporad & Figlio, 1921).

Obeidi, Amal. *Political Culture in Libya* (Richmond UK; Curzon, 2001).

Ocak, Murat, Celâl, Hasan, Güzel, O uz, Cem, and Karatay, Osman (Eds.). *The Turks,* 6 Volumes, Volume 4, *Ottomans* (Ankara; Yeni Turkiye, 2002).

Okey, Thomas. 'United Italy' in A W Ward, G W Prothero and Stanley Leathes (Eds.) *The Cambridge Modern History* (Cambridge; Cambridge University Press, 1910) Vol. XII.

Ohaegbulam, Festus Ugboaja. 'Towards an Understanding of the African Experience' from *Historical and Contemporary Perspectives* (Lanham, MD; University Press of America, 1990).

Olberg, Oda. 'Der italienische Generalstreik,' in *Die Neue Zeit*, 23:1 (1904-05).

Oliphant, Laurence. *Episodes in a Life of Adventure: Or, Moss from a Rolling Stone* (Edinburgh: William Blackwood, 1887).

Önsoy, Rifat. *Türk-Alman iktisadî münasebetleri (1871-1914)* (Istanbul; Ünal Matbaası, 1982).

Oppenheim, Lassa and Roxburgh, Ronald F (Eds.), *International Law: A Treatise, Vol. I. Peace* (London; Longmans, Green, 1920).

Ory, Pascal. *1889 La Mémoire des siècles: L'Expo universelle* (Paris; Editions Complexe, 1989).

Özcan, Azmi. *Pan-Islamism: Indian Muslims, the Ottomans and Britain (1877-1924)* (Leiden; Brill, 1997).

Pakenham, Thomas. *The Scramble for Africa 1876-1912* (London; Abacus, 1992).

Palamenghi-Crispi, Thomas (Ed.) (Trans. Mary Prichard-Agnetti). *The Memoirs Of Francesco Crispi: Compiled from Crispi's Diary and other Documents.* Vol. II. The Triple Alliance (London; Hodder and Stoughton, 1912).

Palmer, Alan. *The Decline and Fall of the Ottoman Empire* (London; Barnes and Noble, 1994).

Paoletti, Ciro. *A Military History of Italy* (Westport, CT; Praeger Security International, 2008).

Passerin d'Entreves, Ettore. *La giovinezza di Cesare Balbo* (Firenze; Felice Le Monnier, 1940).

Pataud, E and Pouget E. *Syndicalism and the Co-operative Commonwealth* (Oxford: New Internationalist Publications, 1913).

Pavan, Camillo. *Caporetto: storia, testimonianze, itinerari* (Treviso; Camillo Pavan, 1997).

Pavone, Claudio (Ed.). *Dalle carte di Giovanni Giolitti: Quarant'anni di politica italiana*, Volume III, *Dai prodromi della grande guerra al al fascismo* (Milano; Feltrinelli 1962).

Pedriali, Ferdinando. 'Aerei italiani in Libia (1911-1912)' in *Storia Militare* N° 170 - novembre 2007.

Pennell, C R. 'Women and Resistance to Colonialism in Morocco: the Rif 1916–1926' in *The Journal of African History*, Volume 28, 1987.

Pernicone, Nunzio. 'Luigi Galleani and Italian Anarchist Terrorism in the United States' in David C Rapoport (Ed.), *Terrorism: Critical Concepts in Political Science* (Abingdon; Routledge, 2006).

Perry, Amos. *Carthage and Tunis, Past and Present: In Two Parts* (Providence, RI; Providence Press, 1869).

Pierro, Antonio Di. *L'ultimo giorno del papa re: 20 settembre 1870, la breccia di Porta Pia* (Milan; Mondadori, 2007).

Pinney, Thomas (Ed.). *The Letters of Rudyard Kipling, Volume 4: 1911-19* (Iowa City, IA; University of Iowa Press, 1999).

Poggioli, Quinto. 'Aeroplanes at Tripoli' in *Flight* magazine, 11 November 1911.

Poincaré, Raymond and Arthur, Sir George (Trans.). *The Memoirs of Raymond Poincaré*, Volume I (London; Heinemann, 1926).

Pollard, John F. *Money and the Rise of the Modern Papacy: Financing the Vatican, 1850-1950* (Cambridge; Cambridge University Press, 2005).

Pollio, Maggior Generale Alberto. *Custoza 1866* (Torino; Roux e Viarengo, 1903).

Potter, E B (Ed.). *Sea Power: A Naval History* (Annapolis MD; Naval Institute Press, 1982).

Powell, E Alexander. *The New Frontiers Of Freedom: From The Alps To The Aegean* (New York; Charles Scribner's Sons, 1920).

Prasad, Rajendra. *India Divided* (Bombay; Hind Kitabs, 1947).

Questions diplomatiques et coloniales: revue de politique extérieure paraissant le 1ᵉʳ et le 16 de chaque mois quatorzieme. Année – 1919 tome XXX (Juillet-Décembre) (Paris; Rédaction at administration, 1910).

Quine, Maria Sophia. *Population Politics in Twentieth Century Europe* (London; Routledge, 1996).

Qureshi, M Naeem. *Pan-Islam in British Indian Politics: A Study of the Khilafat Movement, 1918-1924* (Leiden; Brill, 1999).

Rasheed, Haroon-ur. *Pakistan: The Successful Culmination* (Lahore; Publishers Emporium, 1996).

Rastelli, Achile. 'les operations navales durant la de guerre de 1911 entre l'Italie et la Turquie' in *revue Navires et Histoires*, No.s 22 and 23 fevrier and mars 2004.

Raswan, Carl R. *Drinkers of the Wind* (New York; Creative Age Press, 1942).

Re, Lucia. 'Italians and the Invention of Race: The Poetics and Politics of Difference in the Struggle over Libya, 1890-1913' in *California Italian Studies Journal* 1.1. (2010).

Reardon, Bernard. *Liberalism and Tradition: Aspects of Catholic Thought in Nineteenth-Century France* (Cambridge; Cambridge University Press, 1975).

Recchia, Stefano and Urbinati, Nadia (Eds.) (Trans. Stefano Recchia). *A Cosmopolitanism of Nations: Giuseppe Mazzini's Writings on Democracy* (Princeton NJ; Princeton University Press, 2009).

Rees, John. *The Algebra of Revolution: The Dialectic and the Classical Marxist Tradition* (London; Routledge, 1998).

Regan, Geoffrey. *The Brassey's Book of Naval Blunders* (Dulles, VA; Brassey's, 2000).

Regolo, Luciano. *Jelena: tutto il racconto della vita della regina Elena di Savoia* (Milano; Simonelli Editore, 2003).

Ress, Imre. 'The Value System of Serb Liberalism' in Iván Zoltán Dénes (Ed.), *Liberty and the Search for Identity: Liberal Nationalisms and the Legacy of Empires* (Budapest; Central European University Press, 2006)

Revel, Genova Thaon Di. *Il 1859 E L'Italia Centrale: Miei Ricordi* (Charleston, SC; BiblioLife, 2009).

Rhodes James, Robert (Ed.). *Winston S Churchill: His Complete Speeches, 1897-1963*, 8 Vols. (New York; Chelsea House Publishers, 1974) Vol. VII 1943-1949.

Riall, Lucy. *Sicily and the Unification of Italy: Liberal Policy and Local Power, 1859-1866* (Oxford; Oxford University Press, 2002).

Riall, Lucy. *Garibaldi: Invention of a Hero* (New Haven, CT; Yale University Press, 2007).

Rich, Norman and Fisher, M H (Eds). *The Holstein Papers: Volume 4: Correspondence 1897-1909* (London; Syndics of the Cambridge University Press, 1963).

Rinaldi, Carlo. 'I dirigibili italiani nella campagna di Libia' in *Storia Militare* N° 18 - marzo 1995.

Rochat, Giorgio and Massobrio, Giulio. *Breve storia dell'esercito italiano dal 1861 al 1943* (Turin; Einaudi, 1978).

Rodd, Francis Rennell. *General William Eaton: The Failure of an Idea* (New York: Minton, Balch, 1932).

Rodd, Sir James Rennell. *Social and Diplomatic Memories, Third Series* [Volume 3] *1902-1919* (London; Edward Arnold, 1925).

Rohlfs, Gerhard. *Kufra: Reise von Tripolis nach der Oase Kufra* (Leipzig; F A Brockhaus, 1881).

Romano, Sergio. *La quarta sponda: la guerra di Libia, 1911-1912* (Milano; Bompiani, 1977).

Romano, Sergio. *Giuseppe Volpi: Industrie e finanza fra Giolitti e Mussolini* (Milan: Bompiani, 1979).

Rooney, Chris B. 'The international significance of British naval missions to the Ottoman Empire, 1908-14' in *Middle Eastern Studies*, Volume 34, Issue 1 January 1998.

Ropp, Theodore. 'The Modern Italian Navy' in *Military Affairs*, Vol. 5, No. 2 (Summer, 1941).

Ropp, Theodore and Roberts, Stephen S (Ed.). *The Development of a Modern Navy: French Naval Policy 1871-1904* (Annapolis, MD; Naval Institute Press, 1987).

Rosa, Luigi De. *Storia del Banco di Roma* (Rome; Banco di Roma, 1982) Vol. I.

Rose, Arianna Sara De. *Marcello Piacentini: opere 1903-1926* (Modena; Panini, 1995).

Rossi, Gianluigi (Ed.). *Italia-Libia. Storia di un dialogo mai interrotto* (Roma; Apes, 2012

Rothenberg, Gunther E. *The Army of Francis Joseph* (West Lafayette, IN; Purdue University Press, 1998).

Roucek, Joseph S. 'The Legal Aspects of Sovereignty over the Dodecanese' in *The American Journal of International Law*, Vol. 38, No. 4 (Oct., 1944).

Rubinkowska, Hanna. Review of May Ydlibi and Bahru Zewde (Ed.), *With Ethiopian Rulers: a Biography of Hasib Ydlibi* (Addis Ababa; Addis Ababa University Press, 2006) in *Aethiopica: International Journal of Ethiopian and Eritrean Studies*, Volume 11, 2008.

Saladino, Salvatore. 'Italy' in Hans Rogger and Eugen Weber (Eds.), *The European Right: a Historical Profile* (Berkeley, CA; University of California Press, 1974).

Salem, Omar. 'Management of Shared Groundwater Basins in Libya' in *African Water Journal* Volume I, Number 1, March 2007.

Salis, Renzo Sertoli. *Le isole italiane dell'Egeo dall'occupazione alla sovranità* (Roma; Vittoriano, 1939).

Samo, Ritter zur Helle von. *Das Vilajet der Inseln des Weissen Meeres (Bahr i setid dschezairi), das privilegirte Beylik Samos (Syssam) und das Mutessariflik Cypern (Kybris). Statistische und militärische Notizen aus den Papieren des früheren Militär-Attaches der k.u.k. österreichisch-ungarischen Botschaft in Constantinopel* (Wien, C Gerold's sohn, 1877).

Samwer, Karl and Hoff, Jules (Eds). *Nouveau recueil général de traités, conventions et autres transactions remarquables, servant à la connaissance des relations étrangères des puissances et états dans leurs rapports mutuels.* 20 Vols. (Göttingen; J C Dietrich, 1843-75) Vol. V.

Schmitz, Leonhard. *A Manual of Ancient Geography* (Philadelphia, PA; Blanchard and Lea, 1857).

Scott, James Brown (Ed.). *Les travaux de la Cour permanente d'arbitrage de La Haye: recueil de ses sentences, accompagnees de resumes des differentes controverses, des compromis d'arbitrage et d'autres documents soumis a la cour et aux commissions internationales d'enquete en conformite des conventions de 1899 et de 1907 pour le reglement pacifique des conflits internationaux* (New York; Oxford University Press, 1921).

Selahaddin, Mehmed. *ttihad ve Terakki'nin Kurulu u ve Osmanlı Devleti'nin Yıkılı ı Hakkında Bildiklerim* (Istanbul; nkilab, 1989).

Sencourt, Robert. *Napoleon III: The Modern Emperor* (London; Ernest Benn, 1933).

Seton-Watson, Christopher. *Italy From Liberalism to Fascism, 1870-1925* (London; Methuen, 1967).

Severino, Baron Bernardo Quaranta di San 'The Peace Negotiations between Italy and Turkey' in *The New York Times*, 24 November 1912.

Scirocco, Alfonso (Trans. Allan Cameron). *Garibaldi: Citizen of the World* (Princeton, NJ; Princeton University Press, 2007).

Shorrock, William I. 'The Origin of the French Mandate in Syria and Lebanon: The Railroad Question, 1901–1914' in *International Journal of Middle East Studies* (1970), 1.

Shorrock, William I. 'The Tunisian Question in French Policy toward Italy, 1881-1940' in *The International Journal of African Historical Studies*, Vol. 16, No. 4 (1983).

Siemering, Carl Ludwig. 'Artikel Rundschau' in Alfred M Fried (Ed.), *Die Friedens-Warte: Zeitschrift für zwischenstaatliche Organisation* (Berlin; 1912).

Simon, Rachel. *Libya between Ottomanism and Nationalism: The Ottoman Involvement in Libya During the War with Italy, 1911-1919* (Berlin: K. Schwarz, 1987).

im ir, Bilâl N (Ed.). *Ege Sorunu: Belgeler Cilt-1 1912-1913* (Ankara : Türk Tarih Kurumu Yayınları, 1976).

Skene, James Henry. *The Three Eras of Ottoman History: A Political Essay on the Late Reform of Turkey, Considered Principally as Affecting her Position in the Event of a War Taking Place* (London; Chapman and Hall, 1851).

Smith, Denis Mack (Ed.). *Plombieres: Secret Diplomacy and the Rebirth of Italy* (New York; Oxford University Press, 1968).

Smith, Dennis Mack. *Italy: A Modern History.* (Ann Arbor, MI; University of Michigan Press, 1969).

Smith, Denis Mack. *Cavour and Garibaldi, 1860: A Study in Political Conflict* (Cambridge; Cambridge University Press, 1986).

Smith, Denis Mack. 'The Revolutions of 1848-1849 in Italy' in R J W Evans and Hartmut Pogge von Strandmann (Eds.) *The Revolutions in Europe, 1848-1849: From Reform to Reaction* (Oxford; Oxford University Press, 2000).

Smith RE, Captain R Murdoch, and Porcher RN, Commander E A. *History of the Recent Discoveries at Cyrene, made during an Expedition to the Cyrenaica in 1860-61, under the Auspices of Her Majesty's Government* (London; Day & Son, 1864).

Smyth, Rear-Admiral William Henry. *The Mediterranean: A Memoir Physical, Historical, and Nautical* (London; John Parker, 1854).

Sommerfeld, Adolf. *Der italienisch-türkische Krieg und seine Folgen* (Berlin; Continent, 1912).

Sondhaus, Lawrence. *The Naval Policy of Austria-Hungary, 1867 - 1918: Navalism, Industrial Development, and the Politics of Dualism* (West Lafayette, IN; Purdue University Press, 1994).

Sondhaus, Lawrence. *Na*val Warfare, 1815-1914 (London; Routledge, 2001).

Soresini, Franco. *90 anni di trasmissioni nell'esercito italiano: segnalazioni, telegrafia, telefonia e radio* (Maser; Mose, 1998).

Snyder, Louis Leo. *Historic Documents of World War I* (Westport, CT; Greenwood Press, 1977).

Spaulding, Jay and Kapteijns, Lidwien. *An Islamic Alliance: Ali Dinar and the Sanusiya, 1906-1916* (Evanston, IL; Northwestern University Press, 1994).

Spence, Ralph. 'Italy' in Ann Wall (Ed.), *Health Care Systems in Liberal Democracies* (London; Routledge, 1996).

Sperber, Jonathan. *The European Revolutions, 1848-1851* (Cambridge; Cambridge University Press, 2005).

Stavrianos, L S. *Balkan Federation: A History of the Movement Toward Balkan Unity in Modern Times* (Hamden, CT; Archon, 1964).

Staley, Eugene A. *War and the Private Investor: A Study in the Relations of International Politics and International Private Investment* (Garden City, NY; Doubleday Doran, 1935).

Stead, W T. *Tripoli and the Treaties or Britain's Duty in this War* (London; Stead's Publishing, 1911).

Stead, W T. 'Francis McCullagh of Tripoli' in W T Stead (Ed.) 'The Reviews Reviewed' in *The Review of Reviews for Australasia*, February 1912.

Stephenson, Charles. *The Fortifications of Malta, 1530-1945* (Oxford; Osprey, 2004).

Stephenson, Charles (Charles Blackwood Ed.). *'Servant to The King for His Fortifications:' Paul Ive and The Practise of Fortification* (Doncaster; DP&G, 2008).

Stephenson, Charles. *Germany's Asia-Pacific Empire: Colonialism and Naval Policy 1885-1914* (Woodbridge; Boydell Press, 2009).

Sternhell, Zeev with Sznaidr, Mario and Asheri, Maia (Trans. David Maisel), *The Birth of Fascist Ideology: From Cultural Rebellion to Political Revolution* (Princeton NJ; Princeton University press, 1994).

Stewart-Steinberg, Suzanne. *The Pinocchio Effect: On Making Italians, 1860-1920* (Chicago; University of Chicago Press, 2007).

Stoddard, Philip Hendrick (Trans. Tansel Demirel). *Te kilat-ı Mahsusa: Osmanlı Hükümeti ve Araplar 1911-1918 Te kilat-ı Mahsusa üzerine bir ön çalı ma* (Istanbul; Arba Yayinlari, 1994).

Strachan, Hew. *The First World War. Volume One: To Arms* (Oxford: Oxford University Press, 2003).

Sullivan, Brian R. 'The Strategy of the Decisive Weight: Italy, 1882-1922' in Williamson Murray, MacGregor Knox, and Alvin Bernstein (Eds.) *The Making of Strategy: Rulers, States, and War* (Cambridge; Cambridge University Press, 1994).

Sweet, D W. 'The Bosnian Crisis' in F H Hinsley (Ed.), *British Foreign Policy Under Sir Edward Grey* (Cambridge; Cambridge University Press, 1977).

Tanenbaum, Jan Karl. 'France and the Arab Middle East, 1914-1920' in *Transactions of the American Philosophical Society*, New Series, Vol. 68, No. 7 (1978).

Tardieu, Andre. *France and the Alliances: The Struggle for the Balance of Power* (New York; Macmillan, 1908).

Taylor, A J P. *The Habsburg Monarchy, 1809-1918: A History of the Austrian Empire and Austria-Hungary* (London; Hamish Hamilton, 1948).

Teitelbaum, Joshua. *The Rise and Fall of the Hashimite Kingdom of Arabia* (New York; New York University Press, 2001).

Tenderini, Mirella and Shandrick, Michael. *The Duke of the Abruzzi: An Explorer's Life* (Seattle, WA; The Mountaineers, 1997).

Thayer, William Roscoe. *The Life and Times of Cavour,* Two Volumes (Boston, MA; Houghton Mifflin, 1911).

Theodoli, Alberto. 'La preparazione dell'impresa di Tripoli. Ricordi di una missione in Turchia' in *Nuova Antologia,* 16 July 1934.

Tittoni, Renato. *The Italo-Turkish War (1911-12): Translated and Compiled from the Reports of the Italian General Staff* (Kansas City, MO; Franklin Hudson, 1914).

Tittoni, Tommaso (Trans. Bernardo Quaranta di San Severino). *Italy's Foreign and Colonial Policy: A Selection From the Speeches Delivered in the Italian Parliament by the Italian Foreign Affairs Minister Senator Tommaso Tittoni during his Six Years of Office (1903-1909),* (London; Smith, Elder, 1914).

Trevelyan, George Macaulay. *Garibaldi and the Thousand* (London; Longmans Green, 1912).

Tridon, André. *The New Unionism* (New York; B W Huebsch, 1913).

Tschudi, Clara (Trans. Ethel Harriet Hearn). *Maria Sophia, Queen of Naples: A Continuation of The Empress Elizabeth* (London; Swan Sonnenschein, 1905).

Tumiati, Domenico. 'Le fauci del Sahara' in *Tripolitania* (Milano; Fratelli Treves, 1911).

Turfan, N Naim. *Rise of the Young Turks: Politics, the Military and Ottoman Collapse* (New York; I B Tauris, 2000).

Tyler, Patrick E. 'Libya's Vast Pipe Dream Taps Into Desert's Ice Age Water' in *The New York Times,* 2 March 2004.

United Nations War Crimes Commission, The. *Law Reports of Trials of War Criminals* Volume IV. (London: HMSO, 1948).

Uyar, Mesut and Erickson, Edward J. *A Military History of the Ottomans: From Osman to Ataturk* (Westport, CT; Praeger, 2009).

Valera, Paolo. *I cannoni di Bava Beccaris* (Milano; Giordano, 1966).

Valeri, Nino. *La lotta politica in Italia dall'unità al 1925: Idee e documenti* (Firenze; Le Monnier, 1945).

Varvaro, Paolo. *L'orizzonte del Risorgimento: l'Italia vista dai prefetti* (Napoli; Dante & Descartes, 2001).

Vecchi, Paolo De. *Italy's Civilizing Mission in Africa* (New York, Brentano's, 1912).

Vickers, Miranda. *The Albanians: A Modern History* (London; I B Tauris, 2000).

Vikør, Knut S. *Sufi and Scholar on the Desert Edge: Muhammad b. Ali Al-Sanusi and His Brotherhood* (Evanston, Ill; Northwestern University Press, 1995).

Vischer, Adolf. 'Tripoli' in *The Geographical Journal,* Vol. 38, No. 5 (November 1911).

Vischer, Hanns. *Across the Sahara from Tripoli to Bornu* (London; Edward Arnold, 1910).

Volpe, Gioacchino. *Italia moderna: Volume III 1910-1914* (Firenze; Le lettere, 2002).

Walker, Mack (Ed.). *Plombières: Secret Diplomacy and the Rebirth of Italy* (New York; Oxford University Press USA, 1968).

Wawro, Geoffrey. *The Austro-Prussian War* (Cambridge; University Press, 1998).

Webster, Richard A. *The Cross and the Fasces: Christian Democracy and Fascism in Italy* (Stanford, CA; Stanford University Press, 1960).

Webster, Richard A (Trans. Mariangela Chiabrando). *L'imperialismo industriale italiano 1908-1915: Studio sul prefascismo* (Turin; Giulio Einaudi, 1974).

Weigall, Arthur E P Brome. *A History of Events in Egypt from 1798 to 1914* (London; William Blackwood, 1915).

Wheelan, Joseph. *Jefferson's War: America's First War on Terror 1801-1805* (New York; Carroll & Graf, 2003).

White, Arthur Silva. *The Development of Africa* (London; George Philip, 1890).

White, Arthur Silva. *The Expansion of Egypt under Anglo-Egyptian Condominium* (London; Methuen, 1899).

Whittam, John. *The Politics of the Italian Army 1861-1918* (London; Croon Helm, 1977).

Whittam, John. *Fascist Italy* (Manchester; Manchester University Press, 1995).

Whitley, M J. *Battleships of World War Two: An International Encyclopaedia* (Annapolis, MD; Naval Institute Press, 1998).

Whitridge, Arnold. *Men in Crisis: The Revolutions of 1848* (New York; Charles Scribner's Sons, 1949).

Whyte, Arthur James. *The Evolution of Modern Italy* (Oxford; Basil Blackwell & Mott, 1959).

Wilkinson-Latham, R. *From Our Special Correspondent: Victorian War Correspondents and their Campaigns* (London; Hodder & Stoughton, 1979).

Wilkinson, Richard. 'Lord Lansdowne and British Foreign Policy 1900-1917' in *History Today*, Issue 36, March 2000.

Willcox, Richard. *The Traction Engine Archive* (Stonehouse, UK; The Road Locomotive Society, 2004).

Williams, Claud H. *Report on the Military Geography of the North-Western Desert of Egypt* (London; HM Government, 1919).

Williamson, Samuel. R. *Austria-Hungary and the Origins of the First World War* (London; Macmillan, 1991).

Willmott, H P. *The Great Crusade: A New Complete History of the Second World War* (Dulles, VA; Potomac, 2008).

Willmott, H P. *The Last Century of Sea Power: Volume I, From Port Arthur to Chanak, 1894-1922* (Bloomington, IN; Indiana University Press, 2009).

Wittich, Alfred von (Trans. Oliver L Spaulding). *Marshal Conrad in the Preparation for War* (Washington, DC; Army War College, 1936).

Woolf, Leonard. *Empire & Commerce in Africa: A Study in Economic Imperialism* (London; Labour Research Department, 1920).

Wright, John L. *The Trans-Saharan Slave Trade* (London; Routledge, 2007).

Wyatt, Horace. *Motor Transports in War* (London; Hodder and Stoughton, 1914).

Yeats–Brown, Francis. *Bloody Years: A Decade of Plot and Counter-Plot by the Golden Horn* (New York; Viking Press, 1932).

Yilmazer, Bülent. 'Ottoman Aviation, Prelude to Military Use of Aircraft' Appendix A of Edward J Erickson, *Defeat in Detail: the Ottoman Army in the Balkans, 1912-1913* (Westport, CN; Praeger, 2003).

Yohannes, Okbazghi. *Eritrea, a Pawn in World Politics* (Gainesville, FL; University Press of Florida, 1991).

Zaccaria, Massimo. 'The Other Shots: Photography and the Turco-Italian War, 1911-1912 in Anna Baldinetti (Ed.) *Modern and Contemporary Libya: Sources and Historiographies* (Rome; Istituto Italiano Per L'Africa e L'Oriente, 2003).

Zamagni, Vera. *The Economic History of Italy, 1860-1990: Recovery After Decline* (Oxford; Clarendon Press, 1997).

Zariski, Raphael. *Italy: the Politics of Uneven Development* (Hinsdale, Ill; Dryden, 1972).

Zervos, Dr Skevos. *The Dodecanese: The History of the Dodecanese through the Ages - It's Services to Mankind and its Rights* (No Place; No Publisher, 1918-19).

Zervos, Dr Skevos. *Le Dodécanèse: l'histoire du Dodécanèse à travers les siècles - les services qu'il a rendus à l'humanité ses droits* (London; no publisher, no date -probably 1920).

Ziadeh, N A. *Sanusiya: A Study of a Revivalist Movement in Islam* (Leiden; Brill, 1958).

Zürcher, Erik Jan. *Turkey: A Modern History* (London; I B Tauris, 2004).

Internet

Boca, Daniela Del, and Venturini, Alessandra. *Italian Migration: Discussion Paper No. 938* (Bonn; Institut zur Zukunft der Arbeit, 2003). This work is available at: http://ftp.iza.org/dp938.pdf

Carabinieri http://www.carabinieri.it/Internet/Multilingua/EN/HistoricalReferences/01_EN.htm.

Chairman of the US Joint Chiefs of Staff, *Joint Publication 3-02; Amphibious Operations.* http://www.dtic.mil/doctrine/new_pubs/jp3_02.pdf

CIA World Factbook. https://www.cia.gov/library/publications/the-world-factbook/geos/ly.html

Dunnage, Jonathan. *The Policing Of Politics In Bologna, 1898-1914.* http://www.history.ac.uk/resources/e-seminars/dunnage-paper

Furlong, Charles Wellington. His papers are at the Rauner Special Collections Library, Dartmouth College, Hanover, NH. http://ead.dartmouth.edu/html/stem197.html

Hansard's Parliamentary Debates. https://market.android.com/details?id=book-baqYXsAKks8C

Henninger, Max. 'Italy, peasant movements, 19th–20th centuries,' in Immanuel Ness (Ed.) *The International Encyclopaedia of Revolution and Protest* available from: http://www.blackwellreference.com/public/tocnode?id=g9781405184649_chunk_g9781405184649807# citation

Kocatürk, Önder. *Hacı Ali (Wavell) Olayı*. Available from *stanbul Üniversitesi* website: http://www.istanbul.edu.tr/enstituler/ataturk/kisiler/docs/onderkocaturk-Wavell.pdf

Labriola, Antonio. A selection of his writings can be viewed at: http://www.marxists.org/archive/labriola/index.htm

Raafat, Samir. 'The Heliopolis Palace Hotel: A Desert Taj Mahal' in the *Cairo Times*, 19 March 1998. Available online at: www.egy.com/landmarks/98-03-19.php

Slight, John. *The British Empire and the hajj 1865-1939*. http://hdl.handle.net/10036/82014

Temperino, Dario. *Cavalleggeri di Lodi 1859-1995* www.bibliomil.com/pdf/cavalleggeri_lodi.pdf

INDEX